THE CONSTRUCTION
OF SPACE IN EARLY CHINA

SUNY series in
CHINESE PHILOSOPHY AND CULTURE

Roger T. Ames, *editor*

THE CONSTRUCTION

OF SPACE

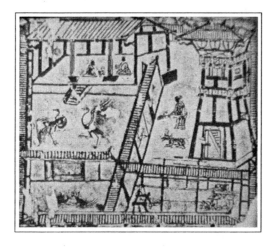

IN EARLY CHINA

MARK EDWARD LEWIS

STATE UNIVERSITY OF NEW YORK PRESS

Published by

STATE UNIVERSITY OF NEW YORK PRESS, ALBANY

For information, contact State University of New York Press, Albany, NY
www.sunypress.edu

Production, Laurie Searl
Marketing, Susan Petrie

Library of Congress Cataloging-in-Publication Data

Lewis, Mark Edward, 1954–
    The construction of space in early China / Mark Edward Lewis.
      p. cm.—(SUNY series in Chinese philosophy and culture)
    Includes bibliographical references and index.
    ISBN 0-7914-6607-8 (alk. paper)
    ISBN 0-7914-6608-6 (pbk.:alk.paper)
    1. Philosophy, Chinese–To 221 B.C.   2. Social groups–China.
I. Title. II. Series.

    B126.L38 2005
    181'.11—dc22

                                                        2004030455

10 9 8 7 6 5 4 3 2 1

CONTENTS

ACKNOWLEDGMENTS

My greatest debt is to all the scholars whose research has been incorporated into my own. Their names are listed in the notes and bibliography. I would also like to thank my wife, Kristin Ingrid Fryklund, for all of her work in the preparation of the manuscript.

INTRODUCTION

UNITS OF SPATIAL ORDER

This book is about the way in which the early Chinese constructed the space they inhabited. Both key terms in the title need explanation. The "space" in question is not the absolute, continuous, empty receptacle of material objects of Newtonian physics, nor Kant's "form of pure sensible intuition" which is the formal a priori condition for any perception of what is given to the senses as a whole.[1] The notion of "space" here follows Leibniz's assertion of its relational nature: "I hold space to be something merely relative, as time is. Time is an order of successions. Space denotes, in terms of possibility, an order to things which exist at the same time. . . . I do not say that matter and space are the same thing. I only say, there is no space where there is no matter, and that space in itself is not an absolute reality."[2] It is the relations between things, relations expressed by such oppositions as inside/outside, center/periphery, or superior/inferior, that defines space. This book examines how this "order of things" evolved in the process of creating a world empire. It studies in the Warring States and early imperial periods the significant units that made up the human world, how they were delimited, and what forms of relations existed between them.

As for "construction," this book examines the units of the human world and their relations as things produced and modified through effort. Cultivating bodies, organizing families, building cities, forming regional networks, and establishing a world empire were all *actions* in which the early Chinese imposed order and meaning on their world. Since space in this sense is produced through human actions, it is a useful topic for cross-cultural studies. The manner in which different peoples delimit the units of their world, arrange their locations, represent or rank them, and change them over time has become a major field of anthropological and historical studies.[3]

The early Chinese themselves had already developed discourses dealing with the historical construction of ordered human space. These began from the image of a primal state of undifferentiated chaos out of which all objects

1

and ultimately human society emerged. Perhaps the most influential was a cosmogonic discourse preserved as a complete narrative in four texts, as well as in scattered references.[4] These describe a formless, watery chaos at the beginning of time, and then depict the emergence of objects through a process of sequential division. This is sometimes described in mathematical terms as the division of an original unity into two parts, then three or four, ending in the formation of all things. While these divisions are not the work of men, the texts repeatedly insist that only the sage could understand the principles underlying this emergence of ordered space and use that understanding to regulate the world.

While the primal chaos had vanished, it survived as a permanent background condition to human existence. First, it formed a constant reservoir of infinite potentiality accessible to the sage who thereby obtained power to alter the spatially structured present. Second, it remained as a constant menace of universal dissolution and chaos should the principles that had forged order out of nondistinction ever be abandoned. This is the source of the specter of "chaos [luan 亂]" that has haunted the Chinese imagination for millennia. This parallel vision of a primal state of nondistinction that acts as both an inexhaustible source of vitality and a threat of all-consuming chaos has remained a feature of Chinese thought down to the present day.[5]

The creation of structured space out of chaos also figured in tales of a presocial age when men and animals had mixed freely. The tales described the technical, moral, and intellectual innovations that had separated a structured, human world from raw nature, attributing these changes to the work of the culture hero sages.[6] These stories, more clearly than the cosmogonies, present a model of the *construction* of human society through the progressive shaping and spatial distribution of objects and groups. Several Warring States accounts linked the cosmogonies and the separation from animals as either two steps in a larger process of structuring space, or as parallel recurrences of a single category of event.[7]

In addition to accounts of the construction of organized space, several texts insisted on the importance of continued action in their own day to protect this space from the threat of chaos. First, early discussions of ritual repeatedly asserted that it maintained order through imposing divisions.[8] It was through separating men from women, senior from junior, ruler from subject, or civilized from barbarian that ritual constituted social roles and groups. Without ritual's constant guidance to create and maintain these divisions, society would collapse back into undifferentiated chaos or animal savagery. Second, similar arguments were made for the role of the state and its legal codes. For its advocates, the new state order's maintenance of appropriate divisions preserved society.[9] Thus, virtually all major early Chinese theories of society and the physical world assumed an original undifferentiated chaos that remained in the background both as a source of potential power and as the threatening consequence of improper actions. The human world was a construct formed of delimited objects and their regulated distribution that was created and maintained only through constant effort.

To study this model, I have organized the exposition around the successive levels of constructed spatial objects and their relations. The first chapter deals with the human body, the second with the household, the third with the city, the fourth with the region, and the fifth with the world. This list derives from several early Chinese lists of spatial units. The most detailed such list comes from an account of the category of divinatory practices based on the examination of the external form of things (the "Models of Physical Forms [xing fa 形法]"):

> At its largest it presents the layout of the Nine Continents [the entire world], and thereby establishes proper forms for cities and houses. It studies the degrees and numbers of the physiognomies of men and beasts, as well as the forms and the capacities of vessels, in order to seek for the nobility or baseness, the good or bad fortune [indicated] in their endowment of vital energies and their tones. This is like the pitchpipes having different lengths, so that each verifies its own tone. This is not a question of ghosts or spirits; their numbers spontaneously make it so.[10]

Any object has a shape from which a skilled observer can deduce its character and its destiny. The objects that can be subjected to such analysis include vessels, animals, people, houses, cities, and ultimately the entire world. This coincides with my own list, except for my omission of vessels. Although this list deals with *observation* of forms rather than their construction, it shows that the units of study in this book already formed a category of analysis in early China.

Other early texts list four or five units. The best known of these appears near the beginning of the "Great Learning" essay in the *Li ji*:

> In ancient times those who desired to make clear through the whole world their brilliant virtuous power first put in order their state/capital. Those who desired to put in order their state/capital first arranged their household. Those who desired to arrange their household first cultivated their body/self. Those who desired to cultivate their body/self first corrected their mind. Those who desired to correct their minds first focused their thoughts. Those who desired to focus their thoughts first brought their knowledge to the fullest. Bringing knowledge to the fullest lies in confronting objects.[11]

Each level of space was ordered through regulating a lower level until one reached the center of centers in the human mind. A similar list of spatial units, with the addition of the village or neighborhood, appears in both the received *Dao de jing* and the proto-*Dao de jing* discovered at Guodian.[12] Other early texts contain reduced lists, most commonly referring to self, family, and state or world.[13] Still others assert or assume the relationship of the elements on this list, arguing that the body is a form of state or cosmos, the state a body, or the household a state. The chapter "Holding to the One" in the *Lü shi chun qiu* explains such lists:

> The king of Chu asked Master Zhan about governing a state. Master Zhan replied, "I have heard of governing the body/self [*shen* 身]; I have not heard about governing a state." How could it be that Master Zhan thought that a state could be left ungoverned? He thought that the root of governing a state lay in governing one's body/self. When the body/self was governed then the household was governed. When the household was governed then the state was governed. When the state was governed then the world was governed. There-fore it is said, "Use the body/self to govern the household, the house-hold to govern the state, and the state to govern the world." These four are different positions [*wei* 位] with a single root. So as for the affairs of the sage, if one extends them they will reach to the ends of the universe, every place shone upon by the sun and moon. However, treated in their essentials they do not go beyond the body.[14]

The title of the chapter and its opening passage show that it is about the necessity of maintaining unity through having a single controlling factor. All multiplicities must be held together by such a factor. Thus, all the objects in the world, while endlessly diverse in their attributes, are united as products of Heaven and Earth, or of yin and yang. All sights or sounds, while likewise infinite in their variety, are united through the sense that perceives them. Sim-ilarly any group of people—an army, a state, the world—is united in the one person who rules it.[15] The existence of ordered elements within the human world depended on the undivided rule of an undivided authority, and con-sequently all levels of spatial order shared a common "root" in the principle of avoiding division. Similarly, the "Great Learning" traced a cultivated self back to a corrected mind that in turn derived from the *undivided* integration of one's thoughts.

The preceding discussion indicates several features of early Chinese con-structions of space, beyond such ideas as the domination of center over periph-ery, of higher over lower, and of the importance of establishing a center as a prelude to any process of ordering. First, the units of spatial order were never naturally given. The bodies, households, villages, cities, states, and worlds in the lists were entities that had to be maintained by the conscious effort of some agent. This is indicated by the repeated use of verbs such as "controlled," "arranged," "governed," "fashioned," or "cultivated." The units themselves were never unitary; they were multiplicities that had to be *held* together. This is a direct consequence of the aforementioned model of the origins of the world and human society out of chaos. The undifferentiated origin contained no discrete, indivisible units or elements, so all objects had emerged from it through processes of division and confluence. Each of these temporary precipitates constantly moved and changed until it dissolved back into the boundless fluid out of which it emerged.

Not only were all spatial units temporary confluences of diverse substances, but they were also fragments of a larger whole. The primal chaos was without divisions, and all existing entities were produced through progressive separation and recombination. Ultimately, everything was a fragment of the primal chaos. As the Warring States Chinese developed the principle that the part found meaning only within an encompassing and hence superior whole, they came to think that all existing things had to be brought together in ever larger spatial wholes.[16] This is shown in the previously mentioned lists, in which the centripetal process of regulating ever smaller units as described in the "Great Learning" implies the reverse movement from self, to household, to capital, to state, to world that is described in "Holding to the One." To the extent that order and regulation were the ultimate aims of the process, and holding to unity a necessity, the end point had to be a unified world. The world, as the Lü shi chun qiu argued, had to have a Son of Heaven. Simple regulation of a body or a household, leaving the world full of other bodies or households not drawn together into a larger whole, resulted in neither order nor unity.

However, a final point was that absolute unity could not be attained, or rather that it could only be attained in a catastrophic return to primitive chaos. All objects existed through division, so the ultimate elimination of division as the culmination of the process of unification would have entailed universal dissolution. Thus, not only was the project of a universal state bounded by the presence of a celestial realm that in all but the most fervent imperial fantasies lay beyond the emperor's authority, but it also remained divided within and against itself. Universality was asserted as a privilege of the ruler and his agents, while ordinary people remained locked in the limited realms defined by their households, their village, or their region. This contrast justified the former's power and the latter's impotence. As will be discussed in the Conclusion, the tension between a "universal" empire constituted by a small percentage of the population and a private realm made up of the vast majority divided into households or villages remained fundamental to the spatial structure of the imperial state.

THE EMPIRE AND THE RECONSTRUCTION OF SPACE

As previously indicated, early Chinese discussions of the construction of space revolved around the theme of part and whole, a theme that justified the emergence of ever larger states and finally world empire. In this process of state formation, the body, family, city, and region were reinterpreted in light of their roles in the new order. In the discussions of families, cities, and regions this new analysis of spatial units facilitated the rejection and dismantling of the old Zhou order based on a hereditary nobility originally organized in city-states. The idea that these spatial units were all internally divided fragments of a greater whole also led to the celebration of ever larger political units as essential to peace, order, and even humanity. This reconstruction of space in search of ever larger units of order forms the subject of this book.

Chapter one examines the smallest spatial unit of the social order, the human body. In the middle of the Warring States period, in the context of the dissolution of the old order and increasing social mobility, the embodied individual became an important object of reflection. The earliest philosophical text, the *Lun yu*, emphasized the body in its discussions of ritual performances as central to the social order. Somewhat later, the Yangist philosophical tradition made the physical vitality of the body and its spontaneous responses the highest values of its program. It marked this idea through insisting on the folly of exchanging life or parts of the body for any other good. At about the same time, in the fourth century B.C., an intellectual tradition represented by the "Nei ye" chapter of the *Guanzi* developed a comprehensive program of self-cultivation that began with the proper placement and discipline of the body, and included the creation of supple muscles and radiant skin. This perfected body radiated its influence to the edges of the earth through the medium of an energetic substrate shared by the body and the world. Finally, at roughly the same time two major *ru* texts, the *Mencius* and the *Zuo zhuan*, also placed the body at the center of their theories of the world. The former articulated a moralized version of the world-encompassing bodily energies posited in the "Nei ye," but also insisted that the moral virtues that fed these energies were part of man's bodily endowment. The latter placed ritual at the center of its theory of society, and told elaborate stories of the relation between ritual, bodily health, and destiny.

The balance of the chapter examines major aspects of the discourse on bodies as linked to discussions of other spatial units. First, medical and philosophical texts developed elaborate models of the internal divisions of the body. One such model, the body as a replica of the state, dealt with the tension between the mind as the body's ruler and the sense organs as his officials. Carrying forward ideas articulated by the "Nei ye" and the Yangists, this model highlighted the limitations and partiality of the senses, each of which was prone to be captured by its own distinctive pleasures and thus to subject the body to domination by external objects. Only the authority of the encompassing mind over the rebellious senses preserved the body as an integrated and autonomous whole. Another model, that of the body as cosmos, also highlighted the divisions in the body between its more refined and dynamic celestial energies and its coarser and more substantial earthly ones. This model led to a range of therapies and self-cultivation practices based on the idea of strengthening life through augmenting one substance and reducing another, or by holding opposed substances together for as long as possible. The emphasis on the divisions within the body also figured in ideas about the common substances of patrilines, substances identified with the bones and flesh. These ideas developed into a range of funerary practices and procedures that involved the manipulation of the bones to guard against the return of ghosts.

Along with the idea of the body as composed of distinct and potentially rival substances, the early Chinese also developed theories of the body as a fragment of the cosmos with which it remained linked in substance. Thus, the theory of the body as formed from vital energies that were imagined as forms of breath became linked to ideas about the external "breaths" that were wind. Together these ideas formed a comprehensive model of the flow of energies into and out of the body. The character and timing of these flows induced either sickness or health. At the same time the skin, as the interface where these exchanges took place, became the primary site for diagnosis through visual examination or pulses, and therapy through moxibustion and needling. Closely linked to visual diagnosis was the early technique of physiognomy, in which the body's surface form was held to reveal its character and destiny. Further extensions of the body into the outer world were the shadow, which was read in many contexts as the visual form of the body's energies, and hair, which was also a physical manifestation of the body's internal energies that extended beyond the skin. Finally, both hair and clothing became sites for the transformation of the body as a means of assigning social roles and meanings.

Chapter two examines the spatial unit into which the body was absorbed, the household or family. It shows that the predominant form in this period was the small household, how this differed from the large, autarkic households formed by the Zhou nobility, and how the new household form was tied to the new type of state. It also examines how Chinese discussions of the family from this period insisted on the nature of the household as a fragment of a larger order on which it depended. In some cases this larger order was the state, made necessary by a division of labor that left every household dependent for its survival on the encompassing whole. Other texts described the individual household as a fragment of the larger kin group formed by the masculine patriline. The encompassment of the household within the patriline became a significant issue with the rise of powerful lineages formed from multiple households.

In addition to insisting on the small household as a fragment, early Chinese writers also treated it as divided against itself. The central division was based on gender. The division between men and women had both an economic aspect, with the conventional attribution of agriculture to men and cloth production to women, and a social aspect in terms of kin structures. For the individual household, the primary bond was that between husband and wife, while for the lineage it was that between father and son, or, more broadly, between successive generations of men. This tension between two alternative kin groups expressed itself in two distinct attitudes toward women and their place in the household. These tensions figure in stories reproduced in Han literature and art that deal with the questions of remarriage and evil stepmothers. Tension over the role of women also resulted in a contradiction between the actual power of women in households, best demonstrated in the authority of mothers over sons, and the refusal of the orthodox literature to sanction such power. This female power took many forms, from wills dictated by mothers to the power of dowager empresses at court, but these were treated as questionable, if not a positive scandal. Finally, this tension resulted in contradictions in the spatial logic of authority in China, where the interior of the household or palace was both the locus of the highest authority and the realm of women, even while women were denied any authority.

A last demonstration of the significance of this division of the household by gender is the evolution of funerary ritual. Throughout the Warring States and Han periods the grave was increasingly modeled on the household, and it also became a major site of offerings to the dead. The grave as a replica of the house was also routinely shared by husband and wife. Thus, as a cultic site the grave commemorated the individual household and gave a central role to women, while the temple was devoted to the masculine structure of the patriline with women appearing only as adjuncts. The importance granted to both these cultic sites in the Han was yet another demonstration of the enduring tensions between the household and the lineage.

Chapter three analyzes the shifting role and structure of the next level of spatial organization, the city. It begins with the early Eastern Zhou world composed of a multitude of largely autonomous city-states inhabited by nobles. With the emergence of macrostates, the city evolved in two major ways that once again highlighted the themes of internal division and encompassment in a larger order. The internal division of the city that emerged in the Warring States was the development of the classic model of the "double city." Such a city was divided by walls into two distinct parts, one devoted to public or political buildings and the other to residence, manufacture, and trade. In contrast to the earlier world, where the city had been a single unit formed of nobles and their adjuncts, the new city was divided between the agents of the state into which it was now incorporated, and the rest of the population who were excluded from political activity. This model of the city also elaborated the theme of the division of labor that was discussed in the preceding chapter. A spatial adjunct of this development was the increased emphasis on the vertical dimension in the towers and raised platforms of the public buildings, and the focus on a horizontal grid for purposes of control in the streets and the markets that made up the people's city.

The reduction of the city to an element within a larger political whole was marked by the reduction of all cities to secondary centers and the invention of a new urban form, the imperial capital.[17] Over a span of several centuries three separate cities—the Qin capital of Xianyang, the Western Han capital of Chang'an, and the Eastern Han capital of Luoyang—served as imperial capitals. Each one inherited certain features from its predecessor and modified others, until by the Eastern Han the classic lineaments of the Chinese imperial capital had emerged. This evolution was marked above all by the concentration of the major imperial rituals within the capital, for the capital was distinguished from lesser cities by its rituals. The most important such ritual was the cult of Heaven, which became the imperial cult par excellence for two primary reasons. First, as a cult observed in the southern suburbs of the capital it was tied strictly to the dynasty. Unlike cults to major mountains or rivers, the site of offerings to Heaven would shift whenever the dynasty did. Second, as a cult offered to the all-encompassing sky rather than to a feature of the earth, it expressed in cult the idea of a world empire with no local ties or loyalties. Closely correlated with the establishment of the imperial capital as a cultic center was its construction according to prescriptions found in the canonical ritual texts.

Chapter four moves from the cities to encompassing regions. As states came to control ever larger territories, they incorporated multiple regions marked by differences in language, costume, music, religion, and other cultural features. With the emergence of the empire, what had previously been states were themselves reduced to regions. For the advocates of the imperial state, all local ties became a threat to their vision of unit, so regions became an object of criticism. This critical discourse on regions, primarily associated with the idea of "custom [feng su 風俗]," began in the Warring States. In these early writings custom figured as the product of local environment, and was thus linked to the limited, parochial, and boorish. Custom also became closely tied to the perceived menace of external objects whose potential mastery over people is discussed in chapter one. The anti-custom rhetoric was employed by agents of the Qin state, as shown in a document discovered at Shuihudi, and in turn adopted by supporters of the Han to criticize Qin government and law as extensions of local custom and the influence of geography.

While supporters of the imperial state criticized locality and custom, and while the court fashioned an imperial culture based on an artificial written language detached from local pronunciations, the regions gradually reappeared as units of spatial order. The major agents of this development were the great families who came to dominate both Han local society and the access to high office. Building up power and influence in their localities on the basis of kinship ties, landholdings, conspicuous charity, and marriage alliances, such lineages came to dominate substantial areas. Toward the end of the Han, as relations with a court dominated by eunuchs and imperial affines broke down, many lineages concentrated attention on their own localities. This figures in the stone inscriptions from the period, as well as the emergence of new genres such as collective biographies based on places of origin. Moreover, many regions developed their own cults devoted to locally important mountains or to local figures thought to have become immortals. In the wake of the collapse of the Han, a range of new artistic practices and genres brought local cultural variations into the realms of literature and art.

Chapter five deals with the world as the unit in which all regions were to find their place. It examines the models or images in which Chinese of the period depicted the world, and the messages communicated therein. It is important to note that all the models of the earth from this period presented a world that outstripped the imperial state and even the actual explorations of the period. While the Qin and Han states had brought the whole Chinese world under a single ruler, at no point was this empire conflated with the actual limits of space.

One important early Chinese model for the world, manifested in the "Tribute of Yu" and the thought of Zou Yan, was the grid. This extended a pattern for spatial regulation at the local level to the entire world. One important version of the grid was the "Hall of Light," a ritual structure progressively imagined over the course of the late Warring States and the Han as a set of buildings or chambers through which the ruler moved or around which he gathered his court. In versions where the ruler moved, the Hall of Light served as a model for the annual cycle and hence the organization of time. In versions of the court assemblies it provided a model for all of space. During the Han, several rulers attempted to build such a complex, and archaeological excavations have revealed something of its structure.

Another set of geometric images that furnished models of the world was the decor patterns on diviner's boards, bronze mirrors, and *liu bo* game boards. These used circles, squares, grids, and hooks to indicate the key features of the structure of the cosmos as described in the protoscience of the period. Such objects reduced the world to an object that could be held in the hand or taken in at a glance. The manipulation of such objects—whether for divination, games to secure magical power from spirits, or funerary practices—allowed individuals to gain access to the realm of totality where people of the period believed that the highest authority resided.

A final set of world models was based on the spatial distribution of mountain chains or rivers. The aforementioned "Tribute of Yu" was such a model, but its greatest exemplar was the "Classic of the Mountains and Seas." In addition, a model of the world based on mountain chains also appears in several stone inscriptions associated with the local cults referred to earlier.

Ultimately, all these forms of ordering space were aspects of an encompassing vision of unity. The perfected body was fashioned on the image of the world state or the cosmos and culminated in an influence that reached to the edges of the earth. The household likewise was a microcosm of the state, and it became a unit for order within the larger structures of the empire or lineage. The divided city, or specifically its political half, became one element within a world empire formed by a network of such cities that culminated in an imperial capital constructed as a ritual center for the regulation of the cosmos. All regions were treated as fragments of a greater whole, drawn together through the centripetal flow of men and tribute goods to the encompassing culture of the capital and the court. And the world empire itself was only one element within a vaster cosmos formed through the progressive outward extension of the units that made up the Chinese world. However, as will be discussed in the Conclusion, each higher level still contained within itself as unabsorbed fragments the smaller units from which it was formed. This uneasy balance between a drive toward ever greater unity, together with the stubborn survival of incorporated subunits organized on principles at odds with the encompassing whole, reveals a fundamental truth about the Chinese empire. On the one hand, the court claimed to rule through a universalism embodied in its artificial, textual language freed from local attachments and through its cosmic cults that transcended all regional ties. On the other hand, its actual influence in local society depended on the support of powerful families that were based on principles of kinship and regional loyalties. Thus, the all-encompassing unity avoided collapse back into the original chaos of nondistinction only by preserving within itself the principles of division on the basis of family or region that it claimed to transcend.

CHAPTER ONE

THE HUMAN BODY

The smallest unit through which the early Chinese ordered their world was the body, including its physical and mental aspects. All peoples reveal much of themselves in methods of training their bodies, explanations of their workings, and applications of these to images of the world. Consequently, the body's transformations have become a major theme of modern historiography and social thought.[1] Moreover, in the twentieth century the body has become central in Western philosophy and the cognitive sciences as a focus for understanding human thought, often emphasizing how people's bodies structure and shape the spaces that they inhabit.[2] The history of the body in China, a field that remains relatively undeveloped, is essential to both these projects.[3]

This chapter will examine early Chinese ideas about the body as an aspect of their construction of orderly spaces. As described in the Introduction, early Chinese writers treated all entities as elements formed out of an initial unity/chaos through the process of division. These objects thus appeared as both compounds of diverse substances and as parts of a larger whole. As compounds of diverse substances, all spatial units were temporary and unstable conflations of disparate elements that tended to dissociate. As parts of larger wholes, they were dependent fragments that achieved stability and meaning only through incorporation into an encompassing structure. This recurring pattern already appeared at the level of the human body. In this chapter I will first examine how this pattern emerged in the fourth century B.C. in the earliest Chinese reflections on the nature and significance of the body. I will then show the consequences of depicting the body as a temporary compound of diverse elements. Finally, I will examine ways in which the body formed one element of a larger whole, with the skin figuring primarily not as a boundary but as an interface from which certain energies and substances were projected and through which others were absorbed.

13

DISCOVERY OF THE BODY IN THE
FOURTH CENTURY B.C.

The body became a central issue in Chinese thought in the fourth century B.C., when the school of Yang Zhu and the practice of self-cultivation described in the "Nei ye" theorized it as the natural and necessary center for organizing space, and the *Mencius* and *Zuo zhuan* presented it as the source of virtue and ritual order. Several of these ideas, however, were anticipated in the *Lun yu*. First, some passages describing ritual and the true gentleman focus on the correction of the body. Second, other passages use the body and its parts as measures of value. Third, two passages assert that correcting the body is the basis of social order. I will discuss each of these in turn.

Performing rituals in early China required considerable bodily control. Texts emphasize specified positions, kneeling, bowing, turning, and so on. Consequently, the establishment of "ritual" as a fundamental category by Confucius and his followers gave the body a central role in their social program. Several passages in the *Lun yu* are based on paronomastic glosses or word play that link the term "ritual (*li* *lier 禮)" to words referring to the body or its manipulation. Thus, there is a close phonetic and graphic link between "ritual" and "body (*ti* *t'lier 體)," a link noted in many texts. An essay in the *Li ji* places "bodiless ritual [*wu ti zhi li* 無體之禮]" in parallel with "soundless music" and "mourning without mourning garments," thus indicating that the body was the defining substance of ritual.[4] Though this gloss is not yet suggested in the *Lun yu*, some passages indicate a connection between *li* "ritual" and the verb "to stand (*li* *gliep 立)" as applied to taking up both a physical and a social position. One of these describes in the following terms the process by which a person employs the major Confucian educational disciplines to develop full humanity: "Inspired/initiated [*xing* 興] by the odes; established [*li* 立 "made to stand"] by ritual; completed in music."[5] The significance of correct placement of the body, without use of the character *li* 立, also figures in the account of Shun's ruling through simply "making himself reverent and correctly facing south."[6]

The link between ritual and body also figures in the passage on the "rectification of names": "If affairs are not completed, then ritual and music will not arise [*xing* 興]. If music and ritual do not arise, then punishments will not be correct. If punishments are not correct, then the people will have no place to set their hands and feet."[7] Again, the definition of true humanity as "taming the self and restoring the rituals" defines this injunction through an itemized list of the control of the body by ritual: "If it is not ritual do not look at it; if it is not ritual do not listen to it; if it is not ritual do not say it; if it is not ritual do not move."[8] This pattern of itemizing the body as a set of discrete units that had to be separately controlled became fundamental to Warring States accounts of both corporal and social order.

The clearest demonstrations that ritual was a bodily performance are the passages describing how Confucius, or, rarely, one of his disciples, held or

manipulated his body while performing rites. These detailed accounts of the
proper manner of standing, bowing, or walking occupy a prominent place in
several chapters. They show how early in China the belief in ritual as a
foundation of social order developed into a concern for the training of the
body. Some accounts of Confucius employ an elaborate series of descriptive
binomes, reminiscent of the poetry of the period, to suggest the sage's deportment. Other passages simply assert the central importance of physical bearing
and facial expression in ritual performances.[9] Literary passages describing Confucius's physical deportment also figured in several contemporary and later
works, along with accounts of his unusual bodily features.[10]

Some passages in the *Lun yu* also use the body as a measure of value. These
mark the supreme importance of certain values through asserting that the gentleman would sacrifice his body or his life rather than abandon them. Thus, one
passage argues: "The determined man of service and the humane man would
not seek life by harming their humanity. There are those who kill their own
bodies/selves in order to complete their humanity."[11] The syntactic parallel with
"life" and the description of it as something that could be killed suggest that
here the character *shen* 身 refers to the body. Similar parallels with "life" or
"lifespan," as well as a parallel between *shen* and *li* (力 "physical strength"), indicate that *shen* as a measure of worth in the *Lun yu* usually refers to the physical
or organic body.[12] This celebration of the willingness to sacrifice oneself in the
name of integrity is an extreme form of the anecdotes that demonstrate a
scholar's virtue through his failure to eat or enduring the most limited diet in
the pursuit of moral development.[13] Finally, two passages insist that correcting
the body is the first step to good government:

> The Master said, "If his self/body is correct, then his commands will
> be carried out without his even making them. If his self/body is not
> correct, even should he command others they will not obey.

> If someone could correct his own self/body, then what problem
> would there be to his devotion to governing? If he cannot correct
> his self/body, then what has he to do with correcting/governing
> other people?"[14]

The second of these passages is a direct parallel to the passage in the *Lun yu*
that asks: "If someone can govern the state through ritual and yielding, then
what problem is there? If he cannot, then what has he to do with ritual?"[15]
The parallel between these two passages once again demonstrates the focus of
ritual on correcting the body, since the two terms are treated as interchangeable. While these particular passages seem to employ *shen* in the broader sense
of person, with the organic body as only one aspect, they merit mention
because they closely link ritual with the body.

Although the *Lun yu* anticipated several major uses of the body in discussions of social order, it was only in the fourth century that this theme
became central. In A. C. Graham's *Disputers of the Tao* this period is treated

under a series of rubrics such as "retreat to private life," "idealisation of the small community," "the sharpening of rational debate," and "the discovery of subjectivity."[16] The thread running through these intellectual developments is the discovery of the individual: as the ultimate ground of social values in the Yangist tradition, as the source of authoritative argument that confounded conventional wisdom for the "sophists," as the autarkic producer of all his own needs in the tradition of Shen Nong, and as the basis of epistemology in Song Xing's doctrine of the situational limits of all knowledge. This new interest in the individual also entailed a key social role for the manipulation of the body.

This is clearest in the tradition associated with Yang Zhu, which took the individual person as the basis of its philosophical program. Like many Warring States philosophical traditions, Yangist ideas are known only from accounts by their enemies, or summaries in later philosophical compendia. The earliest references to these doctrines are the hostile caricatures in the *Mencius*, which paired the supposed selfishness of the Yangists with the "universal love" of the Mohists as two equally incorrect extremes of teaching about relations of the self to others: "Master Yang adopted 'being for oneself.' If plucking out one hair would benefit the entire world, he would not do it. Master Mo espoused 'concern for each and all.' If shaving his body from head to heel would benefit the world, he would do it."[17] While this cannot be accepted as an accurate presentation of Yangist teachings, it is significant that the contrast between Yang and Mo is framed in terms of their attitudes toward the body. Concern over the body, and the use of it as a marker of value, figure in all presentations of Yangist doctrines. Thus, a description of Yangist ideas in the Western Han *Huainanzi* states: "Keep one's life/nature intact [*quan xing* 全性], guard one's true self, and do not tie down one's body with external objects. These are the doctrines established by Master Yang."[18] These are elaborated in the *Zhuangzi* and the *Lü shi chun qiu*. Passages from the latter show that here 性 *xing* "nature" was still the same as 生 *sheng* "life" from which it derived. Thus, to "keep one's life/nature intact" meant to live out one's natural lifespan and preserve one's physical health.

Passages in the *Lü shi chun qiu* also elaborate the third dictum previously listed, which enjoins the individual against allowing him or herself to be tied down by objects.

> Man's nature is to live out his lifespan, but things disturb him, so that he is unable to live out this span. Things are the means to nourish life; one does not use one's life to nourish things. In the present age many of the deluded use their lives to nourish things. They do not recognize what is trivial and what is important, so the important is deemed trivial and the trivial important. . . .
>
> When a myriad of men pick up their bows and together shoot at a single target, certainly any such target would be struck. When the

myriad things in all their splendor are used to harm a single life, any life would be harmed. If used to benefit a single life, then any life would receive benefit. Thus the sage's regulating of all things is used to complete what he receives from Heaven [life]. When what is received from Heaven is completed then the spirit is harmonious, the eyes clear, the ears acute, the nose keen, the mouth perceptive, and the 360 joints all supple.[19]

These and related passages demonstrate that the core of Yangist teachings was the supreme value of life and the human body. "Preserving one's nature" entailed nourishing bodily energies and developing bodily powers. The dictum against being trapped by objects enjoined people to use objects to nourish the body, rather than dispersing bodily energies in pursuit of objects. The ruler and his officials existed in order to protect the lives of their subjects and the well-being of their bodies.[20] The sage was marked by the perfection of every element of his own body.

While the Yangist chapters of the *Lü shi chun qiu* do not refer to the dictum on preserving one's true self or what is "genuine [*zhen* 真]," this principle is elaborated with reference to the body in a chapter of the *Zhuangzi* derived from the Yangist tradition. Hearing that Confucius has devoted his life to benefiting the world through the cultivation of moral virtues and the social arts, even though he is neither a ruler nor an adviser to a ruler, an old fisherman observes:

"He may well be humane, but I fear he will be unable to extricate from disaster his body/self. Causing his mind to suffer, exhausting his physical form [*xing* 形], and thereby endangering what is genuine in him, he is indeed very far from the true Way.

. . .

If you diligently cultivate your body/self, carefully guard what is genuine in you, turn back and give objects to others, then nothing will tie you down. Now you do not cultivate your own body/self but seek it from others, is this not indeed wide of the mark?" Confucius pensively said, "May I ask what you mean by 'genuine'?" "The genuine is that which is most essential and refined [*jing* 精] and most sincere [*cheng* 誠]. What is not essential and sincere cannot move others. Forced tears however mournful will not cause grief; forced anger however severe will not inspire awe; forced amity, however much you smile, will not produce harmony. Genuine sorrow without emitting a sound induces grief; genuine anger with no outward manifestation inspires awe; genuine amity with no smiles induces harmony. The most refined energies [神] act outside oneself, which is why we value the genuine.[21]

In the first extract the fisherman challenges Confucius's conduct from the Yangist perspective by pointing out that he is exhausting his physical body and thereby endangering his embodied self. In the second he sketches the three principles by which the *Huainanzi* defines the teachings of Yang Zhu. Finally, in response to Confucius's question he defines the "genuine" as the complete and undivided focus [*cheng* 誠] of the refined energies that make possible higher human functions. These energies are manifest in the emotions that animate the body's actions, and marked in the highest state of refinement by being able to shape other's actions.

The clearest demonstrations of the central role of the body in Yangist thought are assertions of the absurdity of exchanging bodily parts for external objects. One example of this, or rather a parody of it, was the passage from the *Mencius* cited earlier in which the willingness to sacrifice bodily hairs distinguished rival philosophical traditions. A more elaborate version couched in terms favorable to the Yangist teachings appears in the fourth-century A.D. *Liezi*:

> Qin Guli asked Yang Zhu, "If you could save the whole world by giving up one hair, would you do it?" Master Yang replied, "The world could certainly not be saved by one hair." Master Qin said, "If it would be saved, would you do it?" Master Yang did not reply. Master Qin went out and spoke to Mengsun Yang. Mengsun Yang said, "You have not understood Master Yang's thoughts. Let me say them. If you could gain ten thousand in gold by having some of your skin peeled off, would you do it?" "I would." "If you could obtain a state by having one limb cut off at a joint, would you do it?" Master Qin remained silent for a while. Mengsun Yang said, "A hair is less than some skin, and some skin is less than a limb. This is plain. But if you accumulate individual hairs it forms a patch of skin, and if you accumulate skin it forms a limb. Even one hair is certainly a tiny part of the body, so how could you treat it lightly?"[22]

The relation between body and things is worked out in a set of hypothetical exchanges that mark the higher value of the former.

This demonstration of the supreme importance of the self through people's unwillingness to exchange their own life or body parts for other things also figures in anecdotes in the chapter "Rang wang" in the *Zhuangzi*. This begins with stories in which Yao or Shun offer world rulership to men who reject it because it could harm their health. One of these stories argues: "The world is extremely important, but he would not on account of it harm his life. How much less would he harm it for some other thing. Only one who would not take the world to govern it can be entrusted with it."[23] This insistence on bodily well-being as the highest good, and the consequent rejection of exterior things, follows the argument attributed to Yang Zhu. In the next story the man who rejects world rulership describes how he prefers wearing simple, natural clothing and obtaining exercise while feeding himself through agriculture. He contrasts the health and sufficiency of his body [xing 形 and shen 身] in his humble station with the false lure of the world and its objects.[24] Other stories repeat this passage's argument, which also figured in the Lü shi chun qiu Yangist passages previously cited, that only the man who values life and the body above all else can be a ruler.[25]

A related story in the Lü shi chun qiu is preceded by the following elaboration of the idea that the body is more valuable than the world:

> The body/self is that for which one acts; the world is the means by which one acts. Paying attention to your means, you will recognize what is important [the body] and what trivial [the world]. Now suppose there were a man who cut off his head to exchange it for a hat or killed his body [sha shen 殺身] to exchange it for some clothes. The world would certainly regard him as deluded. Why? Hats are the means of decorating the head, and clothes the means of decorating the body. To kill that which is decorated in order to secure the means of decorating it is not to understand the purpose of things. The present age's pursuit of profit often resembles this. They endanger their bodies/selves and harm their lives, slash their throats and cut off their heads. This likewise is not to understand the purpose of things.[26]

This passage anticipates the Liezi by ridiculing a hypothetical trade in body parts to demonstrate the supreme importance of the self. Similar passages pointing to the folly of exchanging parts of the body for external goods also figure in the Zhuangzi.[27] Thus, in the Yangist tradition, the insistence on preserving life, guarding one's nature, and avoiding the threat of external things was given its most dramatic expression in the repeated insistence that no sane man would exchange his life, or even a significant part of his body, for any external object, no matter how grand.

Rival intellectual traditions adopted this argument as a means of asserting their own programs. Thus, the Mozi appealed to a trade in body parts to demonstrate not the supreme value of the body itself, but rather the virtue of duty for which people would sacrifice their lives:

> Among all things nothing is more valuable than duty [yi 義]. Now if you say to someone, "I will give you a hat and shoes, and then cut off your hands and feet. Will you do it?" They certainly would not. Why? Because hat and shoes are less valuable than hands and feet. If you further said, "I will give you the whole world and then kill your body. Will you do it?" They certainly would not. Why? Because nothing in the world is more valuable than the body/self. But if people kill one another in a quarrel over a single

word, this means that duty/honor [*yi*] is more valuable than the body/self.[28]

This adoption of the body as a marker of supreme value also figures in the *Mencius*'s argument that just as one would give up good food for better, so one would give up life for moral virtue.[29] Thus, by the middle of the Warring States period the use of the body and of life as markers of supreme value had become conventional among all traditions.

When the body emerged in this manner as a theme in Chinese thought, it was defined in spatial terms, as a central self set against external objects. In the Western tradition the body usually figures in philosophy in terms of its dualistic opposition to the mind or the soul, as matter set against spirit. The Chinese, in contrast, accepted that the mind was part of the body, more refined and essentialized, but of the same substance.[30] Instead, the body became problematic as one spatial unit defined in opposition to others. Within the flux of ever-changing objects that emerged from chaos and ultimately returned to it, the body was a centered point whose well-being and efficacy depended on its relations to the objects and people surrounding it. Should it allow these objects to attain mastery through their powers of attraction, then the body/self would lose its genuine nature, become tied down by objects, and ultimately sacrifice itself for these external things. Should it defend its vital energies and genuine nature against the lure of objects, than it could generate a spirit-like power [*shen* 神] that commanded the feelings and actions of others without any visible manifestation. Thus, the dominant model of the body in early Chinese thinking portrayed it as a distinct center within a field of rival forces that could itself, if properly developed, radiate its own force outward. This model first appeared within the Yangist tradition, and was successively adopted by rivals to articulate their own positions.[31]

The earliest and most influential elaboration of the model of the embodied self as a center for the projection of cultivated energies was the program of self-cultivation elaborated in the fourth-century B.C. philosophical poem "Nei ye 內業 [Inward Training]."[32] The "Nei ye" describes a holistic transformation of the entire person. It begins with the physical body, works through the sense organs, and culminates in the perfection of the mind and spirit. Like the Yangist tradition, it places human vitality (*sheng* 生) at the center of its vision of the perfected self. It also resembles Yangist doctrines in its insistence on the pivotal importance of guiding the emotions and in stern warnings against the threat posed by external objects. The model developed in this text of the perfection of the mind and body through the regulation of emotions elicited by external objects became one of the dominant themes of Warring States thought.

Moreover, the "Nei ye" surpassed the Yangists by placing its program of self-cultivation within an overarching vision of a dynamic cosmos that, like the body, was constituted from a series of ever more refined vital energies—

qi 氣, *jing* 精, and *shen* 神. This model of energies or vital breaths shared by the body and the outer world permitted a more systematic exposition of the character of the body/self, the means of its perfection, and the consequences thereof. I will focus on the ways in which the text portrays the embodied self, and on the significant spatial aspects of this portrayal. The poem begins with a comprehensive vision of a world formed by vital energies.

> The vital essence [*jing* 精] of all things,
> In attainment it produces life.
> Below it produces the five grains,
> Above it forms the arrayed stars.
> Flowing between Heaven and Earth
> It is called ghosts and spirits.
> Stored in the human breast,
> It is called the sage.

This asserts the central importance of refined energy, and also lays out the vertical zones that form the cosmos. Each of these zones is distinguished by the most refined beings that appear within it. This structuring of space through the distribution of energies carries forward in the next lines, which describe the vital energy (*qi*) in the highest heavens, in the deepest abyss, in the seas that mark the ultimate edges of the world, and at the very center within the self.[33] Thus, the embodied self emerges as the central focus within an extended spatial field, a field linked together through the movement of a common energy.

Having begun with the self and its relation to the world, the text then devotes several passages to the manner in which the vital energies that fill the cosmos can be secured within the body. This is followed by the first reference to the heart/mind (*xin* 心) at the core of the person:

> All proper forms [*xing* 形] of the mind
> Spontaneously fill, spontaneously suffuse [with vital energies],
> Spontaneously give life [*sheng*], spontaneously complete [*cheng*].
> The means of losing it
> Must be sorrow, happiness, joy, anger, desire, and profit-seeking.
> If you can remove sorrow, happiness, anger, desire, and profit-seeking,
> Your mind will revert to completion [*ji* 濟].[34]

This introduces the emotions that threaten the mind's energies. Emotions, which in later texts will invariably be associated with the external things that elicit them, constitute the single greatest threat to self-perfection through the cultivation of mind and body. This theme recurs later in the text, and it became a commonplace in the Warring States and later China.[35]

After more descriptions of the mind, the text states that the Way "is that by which one fills the body [*xing* 形]" but that it is impossible to fix it in place. Having no fixed location, it can only be secured by the mind's remaining still to regulate its vital energies. This introduction of the physical body as a central theme is followed by enumerations of the levels of the cosmos—Heaven, Earth, and man—which leads to the statement:

Therefore the sage:

Changes with the seasons, but does not transform.

Shifts with things, but does not move.[36]

Here, as in the Yangist tradition, physical and mental mastery allows the sage to confront the world without being altered in his essence, to deal with external things but not be tied down by them. This theme reappears a few lines later, including the often quoted proposition that "the true gentleman commands things and is not commanded by things." A later passage states:

The numen [*shen* 神], none know its limits;

It illuminates all things.

Hold it at your center and do not alter.

Do not agitate your senses with external things,

Do not agitate your mind with your senses,

This is called "obtaining it at the center."[37]

This again shows the importance assigned to the contrast between the self and external objects, and the necessity of maintaining the proper separation between the two. It also defines this separation in terms of establishing the body as a secure center.

The distinction between self as center surrounded by external things takes on a more explicitly spatial form in a subsequent account of the perfection of the body:

Fix your heart at the center [*zhong* 中],

Your ears and eyes will be acute,

Your four limbs will be firm and fixed,

You can thereby be a dwelling for the vital essence [*jing*].

The insistence that the heart/mind must be established at the center so that the self can be perfected appears several times in the poem. In one passage this act of centering begins a process that radiates outward to culminate in ordering the entire world. Others describe how the sage's body is thereby protected from any menace whether human or natural, and how the freedom of properly centered mind manifests itself in the facial expression and the quality of the skin.[38]

The text thus insists that establishing the body as a center and a center within the body are pivotal to self-perfection and spatial organization. Since

Kant and Husserl, this role of the body in fixing the center around which people structure space has become a major theme of Western philosophy.[39] At each level of organizing space the establishment of a center—in the body, the household, the capital, the ruler in imperial ritual, or China itself as the "Middle Kingdom"—is an essential first step.[40] This constant return to the center culminates in an image of an ultimate center as the source of all well-being and power:

> That which regulates them [sense organs] is the heart/mind.
> That which pacifies them is the heart/mind.
> The heart serves to store a heart;
> At the center of the heart, there is yet another heart.
> This heart of the heart,
> Is an awareness that precedes all words.[41]

The inverse of this centripetal movement toward an ever-retreating center appears in depictions of the center's influence radiating through the entire universe. Such phrases as Heaven and Earth; Heaven, Earth, and man; the Nine Continents; the Four Limits; or the Four Frontier Zones are employed to describe the range of the perfected bodily center. These schematic ways of ordering space—up and down, the four directions, the nine-square grid, concentric circles or squares—all depend on the prior establishment of a center as a point of reference. The centering mind establishes itself as a fixed point in terms of which the order of space is laid out and from which the regulation of the cosmos proceeds.[42]

Between the mind and the cosmos, the key recurrent unit is the physical body. The body is the first step in the path to self-perfection. One must first "correct" or "align" [zheng 正] the body to attain the tranquillity that allows the mind to become fixed and clear:

> If your body [xing 形] is not correct,
> The inner power will not come.
> If at the center you are not tranquil,
> Your mind will not be well ordered.
> Correct [zheng] your body and gather in the power,
> Then it [the power] will pour in of its own accord.[43]

The link of a correct body with tranquility explains an earlier passage introducing the fixed or settled heart/mind: "If able to be correct and tranquil, Only then can you be settled." It also figures in another passage where the correction of the body leads to the perfection of the mind:

> When the four limbs are correct [zheng],
> And the blood and vital energy are tranquil [jing 靜],

Unify your thoughts, concentrate your mind.

Your eyes and ears will not be flooded,

And even what is distant will be like what is close.[44]

Thus, the correct positioning or disciplining of the body is the essential first step to the purification of the mind, the cultivation of the self, and, finally, the ordering of the cosmos.

However, the body is not only the *beginning* of the process of self-cultivation, but also its conclusion and fullest manifestation. The correct placement of the body ultimately results in a body that is completely correct.[45] This idea figured earlier in the description of the creation of acute senses and a firm body through the proper centering of the mind. It also appears in a passage quoted in note 33, in which the cultivation of refined energies results in the firmness of the four limbs and the openness of the nine apertures of the body. Moreover, passages in note 38 link a perfected or completed mind on the inside with a perfected body on the outside. Another passage proceeds directly from the correct placing of the body and consequent tranquillity of the mind to the perfection of every aspect of the physical body:

If people can be correct and tranquil [*zheng jing*],

Their skin will be ample and relaxed,

Their ears and eyes will be acute,

Their muscles supple and their bones strong.[46]

So central is the body to this vision of human perfection that the text ends with an account of a body that through its immersion in the Way has become invulnerable:

For people who attain the Way,

It permeates their skin and saturates their hair.

With the Way of restricting desires,

Nothing harms them.[47]

I have dwelt at length on the "Nei ye" because it announces many themes important to subsequent Chinese discourse on the body. Later texts often adopted the ideas that one first established the body at the center, drew in vital and refined energies, established a tranquil mind, avoided the disturbances produced by external objects and their associated emotions, and finally radiated influence out from the body through human society to the edges of the world.[48] Some texts adopted ideas about the body and its vital energies from the "Nei ye" while rejecting associated aspects of its philosophy. The clearest example of this is the discussion of the "flood-like [*hao ran* 浩然] *qi*" in the *Mencius*.

The links between the "Nei ye" and the *Mencius*'s discussion of the flood-like *qi* have been noted by several scholars, although they disagree over which text was the original model and which derivative.[49] My analysis will begin with the passage in the "Nei ye" that links "flood-like" to the vital energies, and also insists on their all-encompassing spatial range:

When the refined energies are concentrated they spontaneously give life.

His exterior is peaceful and glowing.

Storing it [the refined energies] inside,

We use it as the wellspring.

Flood-like [hao ran] it harmonizes and balances;

We use it as the fount of vital energy.

If the fount does not dry up,

The four limbs will be firm.

If the spring is not exhausted,

The nine apertures will be completely open [to the flow of energies].

You can then exhaust Heaven and Earth,

And cover the four seas.[50]

Here the refined energies within the body act as a reservoir of vitality that, if properly nourished and employed, result in the physical perfection of the body and the extension of its influence to the limits of the universe. These ideas reappear in the *Mencius*.

The *Mencius*'s discussion of vital energy opens with a consideration of the problem of courage and the means of preventing the heart/mind from being agitated. In response to a disciple's question whether his heart would be agitated by worries if he were put in charge of the government, Mencius replies that his heart has not been agitated since the age of forty. Mencius then modestly notes that his intellectual rival Master Gao attained this state at an even earlier age. When then asked whether there was a method to achieve such imperturbability, Mencius describes two heroic warriors who cultivated absolute fearlessness through refusal to tolerate any insult or to retreat before any foe. He then contrasts this courage with that of Master Zeng, who quoted Confucius to the effect that if one were in the wrong, then one was bound to be afraid, but that if one were upright and correct then one would be without fear. In conclusion he notes: "Mengshi She's [one of the warriors] holding his *qi* was no match for Master Zeng's holding to what was essential."[51] Here *qi* appears as the dynamic force that drives men to fight, in contrast with a heroic resolve based not on mere energy but rather on moral correctness.[52]

This contrast between energy and morality underpins Mencius's distinction of his own mastery of "flood-like *qi*" from that of Master Gao, and also from that of the "Nei ye."

"According to Master Gao, 'If you do not get it from the words, do not seek it in the heart/mind. If you do not get it from the heart/mind, do not seek it in the vital energy [*qi*].' If you do not get it from the heart/mind to not seek it in the vital energy is proper, but it is wrong to not seek it in the heart/mind if you do not get it from the words. The fixed intent [*zhi* 志, of the heart/mind] is the commander of the vital energy, while the vital energy fills the body. The fixed intent is supreme in this, while the vital energy is only secondary. Therefore I say, 'Keep hold of your fixed intent, but do no violence to your vital energy.'" "Having already said, 'The fixed intent is supreme in this, while the vital energy is only secondary,' why further say, 'Keep hold of your fixed intent, but do no violence to your vital energy'?"

"When the fixed intent is unified then it moves the vital energy, but when the vital energy is unified then it moves the fixed intent. Stumbling or hurrying are matters of energy/breath [*qi*], but contrary to what is proper they also affect the heart."

"May I venture to ask what are your strong points?" "I recognize the true sense of words, and I am good at cultivating my 'flood-like vital energy'." "May I venture to ask what is meant by 'flood-like vital energy'?" "That is difficult to speak of. Its character as vital energy is that it is supremely large and firm. If you nourish it with what is upright and do it no harm, then it will fill everything between Heaven and Earth. Its character as vital energy is that it is paired with rightness and the Way. Without these it will starve. It is produced by the accumulation of rightness; it cannot be seized through sudden raids in the name of rightness. Whenever your conduct has that with which the heart is ill at ease, then [the vital energy] starves. Hence I said that Master Gao never understood rightness, because he treated it as exterior."[53]

This passage overlaps with that in the "Nei ye" in the use of the epithet *hao ran*, in its insistence that this vital energy is internal, and in the assertion that when properly cultivated it fills the whole universe. It differs from the "Nei ye" on the same grounds as Mencius's contrast of himself from Master Gao. The precise meaning of the latter's proposition about words, heart/mind, and vital energy is unclear, but Mencius understands it to indicate that for Master Gao *qi* is primordial. Mencius, in contrast, assigns this role to the mind. Thus, he criticizes Master Gao for not attributing ultimate responsibility to the mind, and he argues that the mind is the primary factor. It is the mind's fixed intent that should control the movement of *qi*. This insistence on the primacy of the heart/mind is due to its role as the ground for the development of the sense of rightness and other virtues. Whereas *qi* in Master Gao's argument refers simply to vital energies, Mencius insists that *qi*, as something controlled by the mind, can only flourish when fed on the moral virtues. This distinction between a purely physical *qi* and a moral *qi* guided by the human mind also underlies the celebrated debate about human nature between Mencius and Master Gao.[54] The debate as presented in the *Mencius* is thus between a vision of *qi* as simple animal energies and one in which it is an expression of man's moral character.[55]

This argument suggests that it is the *Mencius* that is adapting an idea of *qi* borrowed from the "Nei ye." In the latter the forms of energy—*qi, jing,* and *shen*—were the ultimate grounds of explanation for the vitality and efficacy of the human body. In the *Mencius*, in contrast, *qi* is subordinated first to the mind and ultimately to the moral virtues that develop therein.[56] In insisting that the *qi* that permeates the universe and fills men's bodies is ultimately moral, and without morality would starve and die, the *Mencius* is clearly adapting rival contemporary ideas about the nature of the body and the cosmos to defend its own insistence that humanity is morally good by nature.

Identifying the vital energies that form the body with moral virtues, the *Mencius* argues that the virtues are consequently parts of the body:

> If one lacks a heart/mind of sympathy one is not a human. It is the same if one lacks a heart/mind of shame, yielding, or right and wrong. The heart/mind of sympathy is the sprout of humanity, that of shame is the sprout of rightness, that of yielding is the sprout of ritual, and that of right and wrong is the sprout of wisdom. People's having these four sprouts is like their having four limbs.[57]

The virtues that feed people's vital energies here become elements of their bodies like external limbs. The virtues also appear as parts of the body in passages that make them elements of the mind, which is an organ on a par with the eyes, ears, mouth, and nose.[58] The idea that the virtues are in the same class as attributes of other bodily parts also figures in the following passage:

> Now suppose one's fourth finger was bent and could not be straightened. Although this causes no pain and does not interfere with performing tasks, if there were someone who could straighten it one would think nothing of travelling all the way from Qin to Chu [to find him]. This is because the finger is not as good as those of others. One knows enough to loathe a finger which is not as good as those of others. However, when one's heart/mind is not as good as those of others one does not know enough to loathe it. This is called "not knowing categories."[59]

This assumes that the finger and the heart/mind belong to the same category so faults in the one are in the same category as faults in the other. Here again the virtues are elements of the body.

This idea finds its clearest expression in a passage, which, like the "Nei ye," insists that cultivation of the self culminates in the physical perfection of the body. In the *Mencius*, however, this physical perfection is a direct consequence of the perfection of the moral virtues: "That which a gentleman takes as his nature is the humanity, rightness, ritual, and wisdom which are rooted in his heart/mind. The complexion which these produce is visible in the shining radiance of his countenance. They also invigorate his back and extend to his four limbs. Without speaking he is understood."[60] Not only were the virtues in the same category as the limbs, but they were the ultimate source of the energies that perfected all parts of the body.

The location of virtues within the body also facilitated the *Mencius's* justification of hierarchy. The division of humans into higher and lower is justified by a parallel division within the body, where the mind represented the higher aspect and the muscles and limbs the lower.

> Some toil with their minds, and some toil with their muscles [*li* 力]. Those who toil with their minds rule, while those who toil with their muscles are ruled.[61]

> Bodies [*ti* 體] have what is noble and what is base, what is important and what trivial. Do not use the trivial to harm the important, nor the base to harm the noble. Those who nourish their trivial parts become petty men. Those who nourish their important parts become great men. . . . One who without realizing it nourished a single finger at the expense of his shoulders and back would be confused. If a man is devoted to eating and drinking then others despise him on account of his nourishing the trivial [stomach] and thereby losing the important.[62]

> The organs [*guan* 官] of hearing and sight do not think and thus are obscured by objects. As objects in contact with objects, they [the external objects] simply attract them [the organs]. The organ of the heart/mind thinks. If it thinks then it gets it, but if it does not think then it does not get it. This is what Heaven has given me. If one first becomes established on the greater [the heart/mind], then the lesser [the senses] cannot seize it. This cannot but become a great man.[63]

As in the Yangist passages and the "Nei ye," the attraction of external things poses the chief menace to self-cultivation and the bodily hierarchy. Through their immediate links to external objects the sense organs become objects themselves, and thus reduce the body to servitude. Only the mind with its powers of reflection can escape the attraction of things and hence preserve an integral self.[64] The senses are lesser because they are obscured by their own partiality and limitations, while the properly functioning mind transcends such limits and encompasses the entirety of bodily experience.[65] The *Mencius's* distinction between the greater and lesser parts of the body, and its call for rule by the former, are thus yet another version of the early Chinese insistence on the superiority of the whole to its parts. This model of the body as a state derived from the *Mencius*'s commitments to the bodily origins of the virtues and to the social domination of intellectuals, who were the social equivalents of the mind. While such ideas were not universal in the Warring States and early imperial periods, the vision of the body as a state and the state as a body became standard in Chinese thought.

Another fourth-century B.C. text that emphasized vital energy and the body was the *Zuo zhuan*. It shared several images with the *Mencius*, such as that of the body as a state in which the limbs or the senses played the role of ministers.[66] However, the *Zuo zhuan* also disagreed on key points. Whereas the *Mencius* had argued that the mind's fixed intent (*zhi*) had to control the body's vital energy to guarantee people's moral character, the *Zuo zhuan* reverses this relation: "Flavors put in motion the energies, the energies provide the substance of the intent, the intent fixes speech, and speech issues commands. I am in charge of flavors. That these should fail in their posts and the ruler not command their punishment is my crime."[67] This speech by a minister in charge of the kitchen asserts that the body's energies inform its intent, so that the ruler's failings result from inadequacies of diet. This insistence on the importance of cuisine and those in charge of it is closely related to the central role of sacrifice.[68] Here and in related passages it indicates a model of the body in which vital energy is fundamental to all mental operations, and hence decisive in moral and ritual issues.[69]

The idea that the body's energies guide its intent also appears in military contexts. One ruler argues that the ancient rules of chivalrous combat dictated that one should not strike an opponent twice, kill the aged, attack when the enemy is penned in a narrow defile, or launch an offensive when he has not yet formed his lines. A minister rebuts him in the following terms:

> You make clear what is shameful, instruct the people in warfare, and seek to kill the enemy. If you injure them but have not yet killed them, why should you not strike again? If you loathe to strike them twice, then you might as well not strike them at all. If you loathe to hurt the aged, then you might as well surrender. The army is employed for one's benefit. Gongs and drums use sound to stir up vital energies, and the sound at its fullest brings intent to its peak [*zhi zhi* 致志].[70]

Again the *Zuo zhuan* insists that bodily energies are prior to and control mental intent. The fact that the speaker here bases his argument on an appeal to "benefit" further highlights the dispute with the *Mencius*, which treats this term as an object of criticism.

Another passage that asserts the primacy of energy appears in a discussion of the nature of ritual attributed to Zi Chan, a celebrated intellectual hero of the *Zuo zhuan*:

Ritual is the guiding principle of Heaven, the true meaning of Earth, and the conduct [*xing* 行] of people. Since it is the guiding principle of Heaven and Earth, the people will pattern themselves on it. Patterning themselves on Heaven's brightness and following the nature of earth, they produce the "six energies [*liu qi* 六氣, glossed elsewhere in the *Zuo zhuan* as *yin* and *yang*, wind and rain, dark and light]" and use the Five Phases. The energies form the five flavors, emerge as the five colors, and find patterns as the five sounds. . . . The people have likes and dislikes, pleasure and anger, sorrow and joy. These are born from the six energies. Thus one examines patterns and accords with categories in order to control the "six intents [*liu zhi* 六志]." For sorrow there is formalized weeping, for joy there is music and dance, for pleasure there is bestowing gifts and rewards, for anger there is warfare and fighting. Pleasure is born from likes and anger from dislikes.[71]

Here the primary energies of the natural world manifest themselves within the body as emotions. These in turn provide the substance for all possible forms of intent that guide human action. Each of these forms of emotion/intent must in turn be guided by the appropriate form of ritual. Thus, whereas the *Mencius* derives intent from the sprouts of virtue in the human mind that must guide the body's energies to prevent them from withering, for Zi Chan intent is merely the mental expression of the energies, and both of these must be guided by rituals. This idea that rituals are the source of life and fundamental to human existence is a recurring theme in the *Zuo zhuan*, which routinely links ritual to the human body and its energies.[72]

The previous speech concludes that ritual is the means by which people are born, and that only one who can "bend and straighten" in accord with ritual is a "complete human [*cheng ren* 成人]." Other speeches state that ritual is the trunk of the body/self [*shen*], the means by which people stand, and the key to self-preservation.[73] These links between ritual, vital energies, and the body also figure in the use of ritual failings to predict death. Some ritual errors demonstrate the moral or political failings that will lead to death, but at least one passage articulates the links between ritual and physical existence:

I have heard that people are born through the harmonious joining of Heaven and Earth. This is called *ming* [命 "appointed lifespan"]. So there are patterns for actions, ritual, duty, and awesome deportment in order to fix this *ming*. The capable nourish it and thereby obtain blessings; the incompetent destroy it and thus obtain calamity. Therefore the gentleman is diligent in ritual, while the petty man uses up his physical strength.[74]

People's bodies are formed through the interaction of Heaven and Earth, but they can only be preserved by means of the patterns dictated in ritual. Hence, ritual failings become a direct cause of death. The passage also echoes the Mencian distinction between those who labor with their minds and those who labor with their bodies, but here it is between those who devote themselves to ritual and those who devote themselves to work. Thus, once again the *Zuo zhuan* places ritual and its regulation of bodily energies in the position that the *Mencius* assigns to the mind.

Prophecies of death due to failings in ritual also figure in explicitly medical contexts. Here again the vital energies, which constitute both exterior nature and the body, provide the link between ritual and death. The most elaborate medical prophecy is a pair of diagnoses of the lord of Jin. Diviners seeking the name of the spirit that had caused the ruler's illness obtained two names that none could recognize. Zi Chan identified the spirits as gods of a star and a river, but then asserted that such deities "do not affect the ruler's body." River gods cause droughts or epidemics, while astral gods produce untimely weather:

> As for the ruler's body [*shen*], it is a matter of his comings and goings, his diet, and his emotions. What have gods of mountains, rivers, or stars to do with this? I have heard that the ruler has four times: morning to attend court, daytime to pay visits, evening to write decrees, and night to give peace to his body. Therefore he is restrained in dispersing his energies [*qi*], and he does not allow anything to block their flow and thus weaken his body [*ti* 體]. Now is it not the case that the ruler of Jin puts all his energies into one thing, and thus produces sickness?
>
> I have also heard that the harem should not include those of the ruler's surname, for their children will not grow and multiply. When all beauties are consumed by one man, then this produces illness. So the true gentleman loathes such conduct, and the *Records* says, "If you purchase a concubine whose surname you do not know, then divine for it." The ancients were always careful not to violate these two principles. The separation of men's and women's surnames is the great principle of ritual. Now in your harem there are four women with your surname. Is not this the reason for your illness?[75]

Zi Chan's speech once again explains death as a product of ritual failure. He even extends the physical consequences of ritual failings to include sterility and perhaps even miscarriages. Moreover, Zi Chan here pairs the ritual explanation of ailment with an explanation based on the improper dispersion of bodily energies or the failure to maintain their circulation. This pairing of ritual with bodily energetics figures even more prominently in the second diagnosis.

After the Jin ruler praised and rewarded Zi Chan, he summoned a doctor from Qin for a second opinion. The doctor agreed that the disease was due to overly close relations with women, but he ignored the issue of sexual relations between those sharing a surname. Instead he reverted to Zi Chan's first point of the need for moderation or restraint in all things:

> The true gentleman approaches relations with women by means of the restraints of ceremony. He does not thereby cause any excess in his heart/mind. Heaven has the "six energies" which descend to form the five flavors, emerge to form the five colors, and gather to form the five musical tones. When in excess they produce six diseases. The six energies are *yin, yang,* wind, rain, dark, and light. When divided they form the four seasons [or the above mentioned "four times of the day"], and when properly ordered they form the five restraints. In excess they produce calamities. *Yin* in excess produces cold diseases, *yang* in excess hot diseases, wind in excess peripheral diseases, rain in excess diseases of the stomach, darkness in excess diseases of delusion, and brightness in excess diseases of the heart/mind. Women are creatures who go to the *yang* and whose time is the dark, so excess with them will produce a disease of internal heat and delusional *gu* [蠱, a category of disease derived from poisonous insects that was often associated with women]. Now the ruler is not restrained and does not observe the proper times. How could he not have arrived at this condition?[76]

Zi Chan's two themes, unrestrained expenditure of energies and improper relations with women, form a single explanation. More significantly, the body's energies are explicitly identified with those that fill the external world. External energies in the form of sound and color attract the senses through their shared nature, and excessive emotions excited by the senses produce disease. Whereas Zi Chan combined discussions of proper use of the body's energies with the question of ritual decorum, the doctor appeals entirely to control of the vital energies. Ritual appears only in the modified form of "ceremonial [*yi*]" as a means of restraining energetic expenditure.

This story is also notable for contrasting the literary generalist with the technical specialist.[77] The lord of Jin praises Zi Chan as a "true gentleman broadly versed in things" before doubling his parting gift. In contrast, a minister praises the doctor as a "fine doctor" before treating him generously and sending him back home. While the text treats both figures as worthy of respect, and even portrays the doctor doing graphic analysis and citing the *Yi jing*, it privileges the status of Zi Chan as marked by his appeal to a wider range of principles to explain disease.

Zi Chan explicitly paired the social and bodily consequences of ritual failings to predict death. In other anecdotes, medical diagnosis and the observation of ritual failings become indistinguishable, as errors are read as symptoms of physical collapse:

> Viscount Shan met with Viscount Xuan of Han at Qi. He gazed downward and his speech was slow. Shu Xiang said, "Viscount Shan will soon die. At court gatherings locations are fixed by screens and at interstate assemblies positions are marked by banners. Robes have prescribed collar-joins and belts prescribed knots. Words at these assemblies and courts must be heard in all the positions marked by screens and banners. This is the means of making clear the sequence of tasks. The gaze should be between the collar-join and the belt knot. This is the means of controlling the facial demeanour. Words are to give those at court commands, and demeanour to make them understand the significance of these commands. Any failing and there will be omissions. Now Viscount Shan is the chief minister of the king, but in giving commands at assemblies his gaze does not reach above the belt, and his words go no further than one pace. His facial expression is not a controlled demeanour and his words are not clear. If demeanour is not controlled, the others will not be respectful. If the words are not clear, they will not be obeyed. He lacks the protecting energies [shou qi 守氣]."[78]

Here the minister's imminent death is explained by his lack of energy, and this lack is demonstrated through his inability to carry out ritual protocol. Assemblies, like all rituals, are bodily acts, so failure to perform them can be evidence of bodily weakness and impending death.

The image of rituals as bodily performances is not merely a presupposition of a few anecdotes but a consciously articulated principle. Indeed, given the graphic and phonetic links noted earlier, the two characters could be interchanged.[79] The equivalence of "body" and "ritual" also figures in the passages previously mentioned that argued that ritual was the "trunk" of people's bodies. Other passages argued that ritual protected the body, or that it was the "carriage" of government, which in turn protected the body. This linkage of ritual to bodies through the medium of the government was elaborated in a speech on the loss of dynastic power in Lu:

> Ritual is the means of protecting the state, carrying out the government's decrees, and not losing the people. Now the decrees of the government are in the ministerial houses. . . .The lord's house is divided into four [by the ministers], so the people draw sustenance from others. None of their thoughts are on the lord, and he himself thinks nothing of how he will finish. As ruler of a state calamity reaches his body/self [shen], and he takes no heed of his position. How could a proper understanding of what is truly important in ritual lie in this?[80]

Here ritual's basis is the preservation of the state and thus of the person of the ruler. This makes explicit the assumptions underlying predictions of imminent death due to ritual errors.

This idea is developed in the opposite direction in passages that make a man's valuing of his body the basis of his care for the people: "Youshi will perish. A true gentleman values his body/self and only then can extend it to others. By means of this one has rituals. Now this noble holds his fellow hereditary officials in contempt and debases his ancestors. This is to devalue his own body/self. Could he have rituals? Without rituals he will certainly perish."[81] These ideas resemble the Yangist arguments that a man becomes qualified to rule by placing supreme value on his own person. However, the Yangist argument is modified by insisting that care for one's body is expressed through ritual.

The link between bodies and ritual also figures in accounts of alien customs. Zhou people are contrasted with southerners who cut their hair and tattoo their bodies, which demonstrates that they lie beyond the reach of ritual. Thus, in discussing ritual failure, Zi Gong draws an example from the history of the establishment of Zhou rule in the regions of Wu and Yue: "Tai Bo [when enfeoffed in Wu] wore the proper robes and cap in order to bring order through the rituals of Zhou. Zhongyong inherited his position. He cut off his hair and tattooed his body, using his naked body as his ornament. How could this be ritual?"[82] Here the founder attempted to employ Zhou ritual, as marked in his clothing, to bring order to this distant land. His successor, however, "went native" and adopted the practices of the people he ruled. Zi Gong describes this contrast, between covering the body with clothes and going naked while ornamenting the body with tattoos, as marking the presence or absence of ritual. The fullest discussion of ritual as a form of body is also written in the voice of Zi Gong:

> In the fifteenth year Lord Yin of Zhu came to Lu's court. He held his ceremonial jade high and turned his gaze upward. The lord of Lu received the jade low and turned his gaze down. Zi Gong said, "Viewed from the point of view of ritual, the two rulers will both perish. Ritual is the embodiment [ti] of life and death, survival or perishing. It is selected in moving left or right, circling, advancing and retreating, gazing up or down. It is observed in court assemblies, sacrifices, mourning, and military actions. Now in the court assembly of the first month both rulers lack proper measure. Their heart/minds have already lost all rituals. If auspicious affairs are not given proper bodily form, how can one last long? To hold the jade high and gaze up is arrogance. To receive the jade low and gaze down is deterioration. Arrogance is close to rebellion; deterioration is close to disease. Since our ruler is the host, he will perish first."[83]

Zi Gong describes ritual as the bodily form of human fate. It is defined by people's movements, and can be observed as a physical phenomenon whenever people gather. The specific actions of the rulers reveal their characters, which in turn show their destinies. As in the cases of the lord of Jin and Viscount Shan, the lord's ritual behavior manifests symptoms of the disease that will kill him. Just as the Zhou odes quoted in court ceremonial allowed a form of divination through listening to words, so court ritual allowed divination through observing the body.[84]

Thus, the *Zuo zhuan* assigned to the ritualized body the role that the *Mencius* attributed to the mind. The body, as guided by rituals, was the source of morality and order, while the intent was subordinated to the body and its energies. Although no passage in the *Zuo zhuan* explicitly argues that the ritualized body serves as the mind's guide, a text found at Guodian concludes with such a statement: "The gentleman in holding to his intent [*zhi*] must have a vast heart/mind, in speaking must have straightforward good faith, in guest ritual must have a respectful demeanour, in sacrificial ritual must have solemn reverence, and in observing mourning must have afflicted sorrows. The gentleman's body serves to control his heart/mind."[85] The idea that the ritualized body could guide the mind grows directly out of the aforementioned discussions of ritual bearing in the *Lun yu*. This led in turn to substantial, sometimes poetic, accounts in the *Xunzi* and ritual texts of how the gentleman or some historical exemplar guided his body while performing rituals. The *Rituals of Zhou*, for its part, describes officials who were responsible for teaching people the bodily deportment involved in rituals. In addition, a few passages in the *Li ji* insisted that the basis of ritual lay in the cultivation of bodily correctness: "That which makes people human is ritual decorum. The origins of ritual decorum lie in correcting the appearance and the body, arranging the facial expression, and putting in proper order one's words. Only when the appearance and the body are correct, the facial expression arranged, and the words in order are ritual and decorum completed."[86] The notion that bodily correctness could guide the mind derives from these repeated accounts of the training of the body as the foundation of ritual and thus the basis of the social order.

The historical significance of this identification of ritual with the body, both as the guide for proper bodily actions and the means of reading a body's condition and fate, is indicated in the previously mentioned diagnoses of the ruler of Jin. The explanations of the disease in terms of the wasting of bodily energies, and the closely related violation of ritual restraints, both offer alternatives to the traditional attribution of disease to hostile spirits. In the latter model, which appears in the Shang oracle inscriptions and still underlies the fourth-century B.C. divinations discovered at Baoshan, disease was cured through divining the identity of the hostile spirit and making offerings to it. In the former, which first appears in the fourth century B.C., disease is treated through identifying improper actions and correcting them. The contrast between an earlier medicine based on countering demonic attack and a new medicine based on the harmonization of bodily energies and their correspondences with cosmic energies has served as the organizing principle for accounts of the history of medicine in early China.[87] This anecdote gives a dramatic expression to this tension, and it highlights the manner in which the new theory was based on a reinterpretation of the human body.

However, within the *Zuo zhuan* this medical dispute is part of a larger critique of religious practices. Several *ru* texts argued that the perceptions or will of Heaven were those of the people, that to know human nature was to know Heaven, and that the will of the people was the mandate of Heaven. This idea appears in the *Zuo zhuan* in criticisms of the belief that one could discern the will of Heaven in omens and secure the support of spirits through sacrifices. Rather than seeking support from Heaven or celestial spirits, the *Zuo zhuan* argues that the ruler should base his power on the people. Instead of attributing prodigies of nature to spirits, he should recognize that they reflected disturbances in the human realm. One speaker even argues that people generated prodigies through their *qi*, the same vital energies invoked to explain diseases.[88] Just as the critique of omens and sacrifice took the form of replacing the spirits with physical and mental aspects of the human body, so the reinterpretation in the *Zuo zhuan* of divination took the form of replacing the will of the spirits as manifest in yarrow stalks with a future determined by human character and perspicacity.[89] Thus, the *Zuo zhuan* offers a systematic transformation of every aspect of the role of the spirits in ancient religious practice, reinterpreting each of them as a function of human character and conduct. Crucial to this new explanation of cosmic patterns was the vision of the mind and body as composites of the same energies that formed Heaven, Earth, and everything within them. Through the new vision of *qi* and the integrated cosmos articulated in the "Nei ye," the *Mencius*, and the *Zuo zhuan*, the human body came to occupy the center of Warring States visions of ordered space.

THE COMPOSITE BODY

These texts introduced many of the fundamental themes for discussions of the body in Warring States and early imperial China. Throughout this period, people wrote of the body as a measure of value, the smallest unit on which to base the social order, the potential center of the cosmos, the substance of ritual acts, the source and image of hierarchy, and an energetic compound exchanging substances with the surrounding environment. One image that became central to Chinese discussions of the body was the idea that it was a composite entity formed from materials of different character and quality. Much Chinese religious and medical practice adopted this image, along with the consequent idea that the body could be transformed through the augmentation of certain substances and the elimination of others. This is most notable in later Daoist alchemy, which aimed to fashion a new crystalline body through the incorporation of incorruptible substances and sloughing off of corruptible ones. Such controlled metamorphosis also figured in ancestor worship, which aimed to convert dead bodies into usable ancestors. Even Buddhism, which in its orthodox teachings developed to the highest degree the idea of the body as a temporary composite, elaborated visions of bodily metamorphosis. This was clearest in the tradition that the accumulated virtues of eminent monks turned their bodies into imperishable mummies.[90] In this section I discuss several ways in which the composite nature of the body and its progressive recombinations figured in early Chinese philosophic and medical discourses.

A common image of the composite body figures in discussions of the relation of the mind to the senses. As the senses were and still are called *guan* 官 "officials," this relation is often patterned on that of officials to their ruler. This turned the body into a reduced model of the polity. This image—anticipated in the fourth-century texts—was elaborated at the beginning of "Techniques of the Heart/Mind," a third-century B.C. commentarial elaboration of the "Nei ye":

> The heart/mind in the body has the position of the ruler. The roles of the nine openings are shared out as those of the officials. If the heart/mind holds to the Way, then the nine openings will follow their natural pattern. But if tastes and desires give way to excess, then the eyes will no longer see and the ears no longer hear. So it is said, "If the superior diverges from the Way, then the subordinates will fail in their tasks."[91]

Here again the functioning of the mind is threatened by desires for external objects. If such desires are indulged, then the mind in its obsessions will block the senses in their role of perceiving, and the possibility of accurate perception will disappear.

The image of the body as a state plays several roles. As Unschuld has pointed out, elements of the body in the *Huang Di nei jing*, in contrast to the earlier medical texts found at Mawangdui, were patterned on features of the imperial realm.[92] This indicates the increasing importance under the Han of the new form of polity as a model for structuring space through controlling the flows of substance.[93] Some passages elaborate the model of the body as state in parallel to the bureaucratic division of labor, where each bodily part is assigned a distinctive task. Others, however, present the mind and other organs as rivals for supremacy. In such a rivalry, the victory of the mind, which is the natural ruler, creates order, but the victory of other organs leads to chaos, ill health, and death. These two contrasting uses of state-body imagery lead to two different lists in which the heart/mind appears. In one list the heart/mind is one of the internal "viscera" or "depots [*zang* 藏]" along with the kidneys, liver, lungs, spleen, the heart-enclosing network, and sometimes the stomach and intestines. These lists emphasize the harmonious distribution of roles between the heart/mind and the other organs. The second type of list places the mind together with the sense organs. These usually emphasize the would-be independence of the senses, their challenge to the mind, and need to impose a proper hierarchy.[94]

Lists of the viscera are most common in the *Huang Di nei jing*. The most elaborate one, completely developing the analogy with the state, appears in the *Su wen*:

> The Yellow Emperor asked, "I would like to hear about mutual control of the twelve viscera. What manner of hierarchy have they?" Qi Bo replied, "What a question! Allow me to account for them in sequence. The heart/mind has the office of the ruler. The most refined spirit-intelligence comes from it. The lungs have the office of the chief minister. Rules and regulations come from it. The liver has the office of the general. Stratagems and plans come from it. The gall bladder has the office of the selector. Decisiveness comes from it. The heart-enclosing network has the office of carrying out commands. Joy and happiness come from it. The spleen and stomach have the office of controlling the granaries and warehouses. The five flavors come from them. The large intestine has the office of transmitting messages along the roads. Changes and transformations [digestion] come from it. The small intestine has the office of receiving and filling. The transformation of external objects comes from it. The kidneys have the office of exerting strength. Crafts and skills come from it. The triple-burner has the office of opening up the channels. The waterways come from it. The urine bladder has the office of controlling provincial capitals. The saliva is stored in it. When energy [*qi*] is transformed then it can emerge from it.
>
> None of these twelve offices can be set aside. So if the ruler is enlightened then the subordinates are at peace. Using this to nourish life one attains longevity. To the end of one's life there will be no peril. Using it to order the world means that there will be great flourishing. If the ruler is benighted then the twelve offices will be in danger. Causing roads to be closed up and not open, the body will be seriously damaged. Using this to nourish life creates disaster. Using it to administer the world means that one's lineage will be in great danger.[95]

This correlates organs with offices of government, and argues that fixing the proper division of labor within the body is the basis of government in the world. Here the heart/mind's command of the other organs is the key to universal order based on the distribution of administrative tasks.

This example is unusual among the *Huang di nei jing* organ lists in insist-ing that the heart/mind is the ruler. Although a few passages state that the heart/mind is the "master of the five depots and six storehouses," most lists of the internal organs treat them as roughly equal. Some lists correlate each organ with a direction, season, or one of the five phases; some make each of them the storehouse of a different substance; some assign to each of them a type of energy; and others state that each organ is the "master [*zhu*]" of some other part of the body, such as the sense organs.[96] None of these treats the body as a microcosm of the state with the mind as ruler.

In contrast with the *Huang Di nei jing*, where the heart/mind figures largely as one in a series of internal organs and a storehouse of substance, dis-cussions of the mind's relation to the senses in philosophical texts usually insist on hierarchical control. They describe the mind as a ruler while the senses are ministers who try to act on their own authority. This vision of the senses as rebellious elements within a larger unity figures in a passage from the *Lü shi chun qiu*: "Heaven, Earth, and the myriad things [the cosmos] or one person's body, these are called 'grand unities [*tai yi* 太一].' Grouped eyes, ears, nose, and mouth or the grouped 'five grains' and 'cold and hot,' these are called the 'grouping together of different things [*zhong yi* 眾異].'"[97] While the universe and the body treated as wholes are unities, they contain clusters of objects marked by their otherness [*yi* 異]. Within the body, for reasons discussed later, the clearest image of otherness is offered by the senses.

This threat of the senses is prominent in early Chinese philosophy. Unlike Western philosophy, which treats the senses as suspect because unreliable in their perceptions, early Chinese texts usually treat them as dangerous in their reckless desire for sensual stimulation: "There are innumerable sounds, colors, flavors, and precious and unusual things from distant lands which are suffi-cient to change the mind and alter the intent [*zhi*], to destabilise the refined spirit energies [*jing shen*], and disturb the blood and energy."[98] Sensual stim-ulation, associated with the exotic goods so prized in the Han dynasty, dis-turbs every dynamic aspect of the body: the mind, the mental energies, and the blood and vital energies.

Other texts attribute the threat to the sense organs. They portray these as agents with their own motives that they will recklessly pursue unless forced by the mind to serve the collective good. Examples of this appeared earlier in the "Nei ye" and the Yangist chapters of the *Lü shi chun qiu*. The latter is rich in discussions of the tensions between the mind and the senses:

> The ears, eyes, nose, and mouth are the servants of life. Even though the ears desire sounds, the eyes colors, the nose fragrances, and the mouth tastes, if these are harmful to life then you stop. Among those things desired by the four senses/officials [*guan*], those which are not beneficial to life will not be done. Seen from this point of view, the ears, eyes, nose, and mouth cannot act on their own authority. There

must be something controlling them. They are just like officials who
cannot act on their own authority, but must have someone controlling them.[99]

Here the political image of the body suggests that certain parts of the body
would, like certain officials, do as they pleased and create chaos if not rigorously controlled. The sense organs were, like officials, limited in their range.
Noting only the objects of the world, the senses were unable to perceive the
highest truths and actions, those of Heaven.[100] The *Zuo zhuan* presented this
idea in a passage that described the senses as potential traitors (see note 66).
Within the body, the control of the senses marked the proper functioning of
the mind, just as in society it revealed the presence of the sage:

> Heaven gives life to people and causes them to have desires. These
> desires have their essential nature, and this nature has its limits. The
> sage cultivates these limits in order to halt his desires. Therefore he
> only carries out his essential nature. The ears' desire for sounds, the
> eyes' for colors, the mouth's for taste, these are essential nature. The
> desires of noble and base, stupid and clever, worthy and unworthy
> are all identical; even Shen Nong and the Yellow Emperor are therein
> identical to Jie and Zhou. What distinguishes the sage is that he
> attains his essential nature. When actions are based on valuing life,
> then one attains one's nature. If not, then one loses one's nature.
> . . . The common rulers [*su zhu* 俗主, see chapter four] harm their
> essential nature, so all their actions result in loss and defeat. Their
> ears cannot be satiated, their eyes satisfied, or their mouths filled. So
> their bodies are all decaying and swelling, their sinews and bones stiff,
> their blood channels blocked up, and their nine openings void.[101]

Failure to control rebellious organs ruined the body, which here marks
absolute failure.[102]

Suspicion of the senses appeared in a late fourth-century text discovered
at Guodian, where it is part of a larger concern about the fate of the body
under the threat of stress and exertion:

> For agitation of the heart/mind, longing is the worst. For stress in
> planning, [worry about] calamities is the most serious. In the utmost
> use of emotions, joy and sorrow are the greatest. In disturbances of
> the body, that which pleases is the most extreme. In exhausting phys-
> ical strength, the pursuit of profit is worst. The eyes' love of colors
> and the ears' joy in sounds result in accumulated, repressed energies.
> These can easily cause a person's death.[103]

While worries over the senses and their desires do not appear in the proto-
Laozi discovered in the same tomb at Guodian, it does figure in the received
version.[104]

This tension between the senses and the mind also occurs in a discussion in the *Xunzi* of the relation of proper education to the body:

> The learning of the true gentleman enters through his ears, is stored in his mind, spreads through his four limbs, and is embodied [*xing* 形] in his movements and repose. . . . The learning of the petty man enters through his ears and comes out through his mouth. Since the distance between ear and mouth is only four inches, how could it be sufficient to make excellent the seven-[Chinese] foot body of a man?

Transforming the body is the ultimate goal of learning. Only by inserting the heart/mind between the gates to and from the outside world can learning transform the body. Otherwise it exits even as it enters, leaving the body unchanged. This chapter concludes with a reference to the *Lun yu*'s assertion that educated sense organs perceive nothing contrary to the dictates of what is right.[105]

The need to discipline the senses led to the elaboration of a theory of ritual and music as the bases of physical and social well-being. This topic forms the subject of a separate monograph that I am in the process of writing. Here it is only necessary to note that ritual and music provided a frame within which the desires of the senses could be given proper form. Colors, sounds, tastes, and smells that the senses desired all appeared within ritual and music, but were kept in the bounds of proper pattern. When ritual completely guided the body, then "his caution will not go against his body, nor his eyes and ears against his mind."[106] This theory developed ideas from the *Zuo zhuan*, in which ritual was the necessary form for the perfection of the body and the channeling of its energies.[107]

Texts in the Daoist tradition sometimes proposed the more radical alternative of renouncing the senses entirely:

> If he can be like this, then [the perfected man] forgets his internal organs and leaves his senses behind. His mind's intent [*zhi*] is completely focused within, attaining to a coupling with the One. Staying in place he does not know what he does; travelling he does not know where he goes. Muddled, he departs; abruptly he returns. His body is like dried out wood, his mind like dead ashes. He forgets his five depots and renounces his form and skeleton.[108]

Another passage in the *Huainanzi* states that blocking the senses allows one to enter into the Way and "return one's refined spirit energies to their ultimate genuine state." Senses can be renounced because ultimate things lie beyond vision or hearing.[109] While a program of abandoning the senses is radically at odds with the idea of perfecting them through ritual or music, the two share common ground in their suspicion of the sense organs.

In addition to its image as a state, the body was also depicted as a replica of the cosmos. This resemblance was hereditary, for the analogy of the body and the cosmos often figured in association with the idea that the union of Heaven and Earth produced all life, including the human body. This union, and the resultant bodies, were described in terms of the interaction of vital energy (*qi*). Like the body/state, which contained elements that would rebel unless curbed, so the body/cosmos was formed from disparate substances that were coarse or refined, noxious or beneficial. Just as the perfection of the body as a state required the discipline of ritual and music, so the perfection of the body as energetic world system required the expulsion of coarse or noxious substances and the incorporation of refined and beneficial ones.

The union of Heaven and Earth to produce life figured in accounts of both the origins of the cosmos and of the annual cycle that in spring reenacted the emergence of things. The latter appears in the "Monthly Ordinances" calendar's account of spring: "Heaven's energy descends, while Earth's energy leaps up. Heaven and Earth join together, and all the plants flourish and stir."[110] Here the descent of Heaven's energy to link up with the rising energy of Earth results in an act of mating that generates the return of life. The "Li yun" chapter of *Li ji* similarly states: "Humans come from the generative power of Heaven and Earth, the mating of yin and yang, the coming together of the spirits, and the finest energies of the Five Phases."[111] Imperial decrees consequently attributed prodigies to "*yin* and *yang* energies being separated."[112]

These abstract accounts become more graphic and explicitly sexual in two passages from the "Record on Music" that describe the generation of animal bodies and then human procreation:

When Heaven and Earth stimulate and join, while yin and yang attain one another, then they illumine, protectively cover, and nourish all things. Only then do plants flourish, buds emerge, wings begin to beat, horned animals procreate, and hibernating insects come into the light and return to life. Winged creatures cover and protect their eggs, while furry animals couple and then nurse their young. Neither animals born in wombs nor those born in eggs perish.

The energy of Earth rises up and that of Heaven descends. Yin and yang rub together. Heaven and Earth agitate one another. Drumming it with thunder and lightning, arousing it with wind and rain, setting it in motion with the four seasons, warming it with the sun and moon, all forms of fertilization [*hua* 化] arise. Thus music/joy is the harmony of Heaven and Earth. If the fertilization is not timely there will be no birth, and if men and women are not properly distinguished [through having different surnames] then chaos will arise. This is the nature of Heaven and Earth.[113]

The same essay provides another account of the fecundating process, although it invokes the work of powerful spirits who join together as intermediaries of Heaven and Earth: "Ritual and music rely on the nature of Heaven and Earth. They communicate with the generative power of the spirit intelligences. Causing the celestial spirits to descend and the earthly spirits to rise, they congeal [ning] in these refined and coarse bodies, and put in order the divisions between father and son, ruler and subject."[114] In the light of the other passages, the link between the rising and descending spirits and the formation of the bodies clearly echoes the mating of Heaven and Earth to generate life.

It remains uncertain whether the refined and coarse bodies are two categories of beings, as suggested by a syntactic parallel with the celestial and earthly spirits, or whether bodies are composed of both refined (celestial) and coarse (earthly). Both readings are supported by the "Jing shen" chapter of the *Huainanzi* that states that after the division into Heaven and Earth:

> It then divided into yin and yang and separated out into the eight extremities [of the Earth]. Hard and soft emerged together, and the myriad objects then took shape. Gross energies formed the creatures while refined energies formed people. Therefore the refined spirit energies belong to Heaven while the bones belong to the Earth. When the refined spirit energies enter their gate [of Heaven] and the bones return to their roots [the Earth], what will then remain of me?[115]

This posits both a hierarchy of creatures based on the refinement of their energies, and a human body formed from combining more and less refined substances derived from Heaven and Earth.

The idea of a body composed of refined and coarse substances was elaborated by Wang Chong in the late first century A.D. He also argued that life depended on the opposed substances remaining together, while death was a consequence of their separation:

> What people call spirits and ghosts are all made from the great yang energies. These are the energies of Heaven. Heaven can produce people's bodies, so it can also imitate their appearances. That from which people are born are yin and yang energies. The yin are responsible for making the bones and flesh; the yang are responsible for making the refined spirit energies [jing shen]. When people are alive, the yin and yang energies are both present. Therefore the bones and flesh are strong, and the refined spirit energies are full. The refined spirit energies form the intelligence; the bones and flesh form physical strength. Therefore the refined spirit energies speak, while the body holds firm. Bones, flesh, refined energy, and spirit energy mingle together and cling to one another. Therefore one can live a

long time without dying. When the great yang energies are isolated and without the yin, then they can only form images. They cannot form a body. They lack bone and flesh, while possessing refined spirit energies. Therefore they are only seen briefly flickering, and then return into nothingness.[116]

Life requires the union of complementary energies and is necessarily limited because such unions are brief. Bodies without refined energies are lifeless skeletons, while refined energies without a body are insubstantial, flickering ghosts. The text also posits a full hierarchy of substances rising from the most solid, the bones, to the most refined, the spirit energies. However, just as the fleshy, material substances lack all dynamism without the admixture of the more refined energies, so these energies lack any fixed substance without being joined to the bones and flesh.

Producing the human body from the union of Heaven and Earth also led to a point-by-point correspondence between the structure of the body and that of the cosmos. The refined and elevated parts of the body matched elements of Heaven and the less refined those of Earth.[117] Moreover, they shared a common energetic substance. Thus, one essay in the *Huainanzi* remarks: "Heaven, Earth, and the cosmos are one human body. Everything within the three dimensions is a single human frame. . . . The men of ancient times shared a common energy with Heaven and Earth."[118]

This parallel between the cosmos and the body is also indicated in the usages of the term "conjoining energy [*he qi* 合氣]." This term, which appears in both philosophical and medical texts from the late Warring States and Han periods, refers either to the union of the energies of Heaven and Earth that engendered all living things, or to the sexual union of a man and a woman that engendered offspring. Wang Chong explicitly put these two uses in parallel:

> When Heaven and Earth conjoin energies, people are born. It is like when husband and wife conjoin energies, offspring are spontaneously born. When husband and wife conjoin energies, it is not the case that at that moment they desire to obtain a child. Moved by emotional desires, they join, and thus generate children. Since husband and wife do not deliberately generate children, we know that Heaven and Earth do not deliberately generate people.[119]

This argument is based on the assumption that human mating is identical in form to the original union of Heaven and Earth, and that the former is fundamentally a direct extension of the latter. Ideas of bodies formed from congealing energies and the ranking of those energies in a hierarchy of refined and coarse lead directly to theories of the emergence of human hierarchies. Passages in the *Li ji* proceed from the generation of life by Heaven and Earth to the emergence of the household and the lineage as units of human reproduction, and then to the state.[120] Several passages assert that the life of the state depends on the union of the energies of Heaven and Earth, just as do the body and the household.

> Sacrificing to the ground at the altar of the soil, one guides the yin energy. . . . The sacrifice is made on a *jia* day, in order that one uses the origin of the days. The Son of Heaven's great altar of the soil must be open to frost, dew, wind, and rain in order to bring the energies of Heaven and Earth into contact. Therefore one builds a roof over the altar of the soil of a state that has perished, so it can no longer receive the yang energies of Heaven.[121]

The vitality of the state depends on the ruler's sacrifices joining the energies of Heaven and Earth. This is a ritual and to a certain extent sexual form of the idea that the ruler acted as a link between Heaven and Earth. Here that linkage appears as an organic process modeled on the primal conjoining of energies that first generated life.

The notion of maintaining life by preserving the energetic links between Heaven and Earth, and ending life by cutting those links, also figured in ideas about human immortality. In an anecdote preserved in the *Lü shi chun qiu* and later criticized by Wang Chong, the physician Wen Zhi deliberately offends the king of Qi in order to produce strong emotions that will cure his illness The outraged king orders that Wen Zhi be boiled alive. However, when the latter is tossed into the boiling liquid of a tripod, he remains there unaffected and totally composed for three days and three nights. Wen Zhi then remarks: "If you truly desire to kill me, then why not cover the tripod, in order to cut off the connection of the yin and yang energies? The king ordered them to cover it, and Wen Zhi thereupon died."[122] Wang Chong argues that the death resulted from suffocation, but the story explicitly states that covering the tripod "cut off the yin and yang energies," a fate identical to that of the altar of the soil. According to the text, it was the joining of those energies that allowed Wen Zhi to survive in the boiling liquid, just as masters of the Way become immune to harm from water or fire.[123]

Just as the ruler maintained his state through rituals that replicated the generation of the human body, he also helped in his rituals to produce the cosmos. Furthermore he surrounded himself with a corps of officials who formed a surrogate body for which he acted as mind:

> Sacrificing to god on high at the suburban altar is the means of fixing the position of Heaven. Sacrificing to the altar of the soil within the capital is the means of laying out the benefits of the Earth. The ancestral temple is the means of providing a root for true humanity. Sacrifices to the mountains and rivers are the means of guiding the spirits. The five domestic sacrifices are the means of providing a root for service. Therefore the invocators are in the ancestral temple, the

Three Lords in the court, and the Thrice Venerable in the schools. The king places the shamans in front, the astrologers behind, the diviners and blind musicians to his left and right, so that the king in the middle as the heart/mind will perform no actions.[124]

This maps the state's ritual sites onto the cosmos, so that their rituals help maintain the cosmic structure. At the same time, the masters of state ritual and religion form a four-sided mandala around the king, echoing the four directions of the earth, while he resides unmoving at the center as the heart/mind. This provides another version of the model in which a correct mind establishes a perfected body that propagates order to the edges of the earth.

Another passage depicts how the ruler draws on the powers of the cosmos to generate the state/body, and then helps reproduce the cosmos in his sacrifices. This again links the body of the ruler, the elements of the cosmos, and the key sites of the state's ritual program:

Government is the means of hiding the body/self of the ruler. So government must be rooted in Heaven. It imitates Heaven to send down commands. When commands are sent down from the altar of the soil, this is called imitating Earth. When sent down from the ancestral temple, this is called humanity and duty. When sent down from the altars of the mountains and rivers it is called summoning up [spirits]. When sent down from the five domestic sacrifices it is called the institutions. This is the means by which the sage can hide his body in complete security.[125]

Such accounts of the origins of the body, the household, and the state are linked in several texts to the origins of ritual. This again demonstrates the close ties between ideas about the body and those about rites. In lists of the "roots" from which ritual emerged, the *Xunzi* states twice that "Heaven and Earth are the root of life."[126] One list next names the ancestors as the root of "kind [*lei* 類]." This progression, which again traces a line from the initial generation of the human body by the cosmos to that of the household, recurs in a discussion of the suburban altar sacrifice: "The myriad things are rooted in Heaven, while humans are rooted in their ancestors. This is the reason for a human co-recipient to the High God. The suburban sacrifice is the great means of repaying one's roots and returning to one's beginnings."[127] The human co-recipient was the dynastic founder, so in this highest regular sacrifice the ruler made offerings to the two sources of his physical being, which were also the twin origins of human ritual. A related passage connects the cosmic origins of humanity and its rituals to the health of the body:

Ritual must be rooted in the Grand Unity [*tai yi* 太一]. Dividing, this forms Heaven and Earth. Revolving, it forms yin and yang. Changing, it forms the four seasons. Laid out, it forms the spirits.

Descending, it is called *ming* ["destiny," "allotted lifespan"]. Its organ/officers [*guan*] are in Heaven. Ritual must be rooted in Heaven. Moving, it reaches the Earth. Laid out, it reaches service. Changing, it follows the seasons. It accords with social roles and arts. Among humans it is called "nourishing." It is practiced in goods [gifts], toil, yielding, drinking, eating, capping, marriage, mourning, sacrifice, archery, charioteering, court assemblies, and visits. So the duties of ritual are the great beginnings of humanity. They are means of keeping faith and cultivating amity. They make firm the connections between skin and flesh, and the ties between tendons and bones. They are the means of nourishing the living and seeing off the dead.[128]

Here the perfection of ritual culminates in the perfection of the body and of the body politic.

Links of the perfected body to contact with the highest divinities figure in an account from the *Huainanzi* of the origin of omens in the energetic links between Heaven and the sage:

The sage is the one who contains the heart/mind of Heaven, who can thus thunderingly move and transform the whole world. When the total focus of his refined energies stimulates from within [his body], then the form-giving energies move in Heaven. Then brilliant stars appear, yellow dragons descend, the auspicious phoenixes arrive, sweet springs emerge, auspicious grains are born, the Yellow River does not flood, and no great waves well up in the oceans.[129]

This develops the idea in the *Zuo zhuan* that the energies of people produced anomalies, but it substitutes the sage for the collectivity. The passage also echoes accounts of the creation of all things through the interaction of the energies of Heaven and Earth, but the perfected energies of the sage join with those of Heaven to produce magical beings, rather than ordinary creatures.

These passages on the congealing of the energies of Heaven and Earth treat the human body as a composite of substances of contrasting degrees of refinement. A passage from the *Huainanzi* further suggests that such a fusion is inherently unstable and dangerous:

If Heaven has two types of energy then there will be a rainbow [an inauspicious sign]. If the Earth has two types of energy then it will let what it stores leak out. If men have two types of energy then this produces sickness. Yin and yang cannot be both winter [yin] and summer [yang]. The moon is not acquainted with the day, nor the sun with the night.[130]

Yin and yang are adversaries, as in the model of the annual cycle where the rise of one entails the decline of the other. Fusing the two produces illness.

Most texts do not argue for a program of purification by eliminating one or another substance. The energies of Heaven and Earth are correlates, both equally necessary to human health.[131] Nevertheless, a small number of passages identify the energies of Heaven with life and those of Earth with death, and argue that one should expel the latter. Thus, the "Death Signs of the Yin and Yang Vessels" discovered at Mawangdui begins with the statement:

> All three yang vessels are the energies of Heaven. Of their ailments, only those where bones break or the skin tears lead to death. All three yin vessels are the energies of Earth. These are the vessels of death. When yin diseases create disorder, then death occurs within ten days. The three yin [vessels] rot the depots and putrefy the intestines. They control death.[132]

Here the yin vessels and energies of Earth are not only specifically tied to death, but they are held responsible for the decay of the body's organs. While the energies of Heaven are not here linked with life, they lead to death only when parts of the body suffer serious physical damage.

The association of the yin vessels with death is described at length in the "Cauterization Canon of the Eleven Vessels of the Foot and Forearm." After listing the conditions that indicate death due to yin vessel diseases, the text adds: "When the ailments of the three yin vessels are mixed with ailments of the yang vessels, then they can be treated. . . . In yang vessel ailments where bones are broken and muscles severed, but there are no yin vessel ailments, one does not die."[133] Again the yin vessels are linked to death, while diseases of the yang vessels can even reduce the mortality of yin diseases. Other passages in which the term "yin" refers to the phallus note that it departs, (i.e., becomes impotent and therefore "dead") prior to the body itself. Impotence as death appears in a Mawangdui text that describes formulas for improving virility as the "way to raise the dead."[134]

Associating death with Earth and life with Heaven also appears in the Mawangdui text "Eliminating Grain and Consuming Energy." This is an early discussion of one of the most important techniques of immortality, replacing grain in the diet with herbs and breathing exercises.[135] Near the end of this heavily damaged text, it states: "One who eats grain eats what is square; one who eats energy eats what is round. The round is Heaven; the square is Earth."[136] This associates with Heaven the vital energies that secure life, and with Earth the grain whose consumption leads to death. To avoid grain and consume energies is to turn the body toward Heaven and life and away from the Earth and death.

A final link of yin with death and yang with life comes from a second-century B.C. lacquered human figurine discovered in Sichuan. This has what appear to be the body's main channels drawn as red lines.[137] However, the lines on the figurine do not correspond to any system of channels described in the received or discovered medical literature. One feature, pointed out by

Vivienne Lo, is the absence of the major yin channels, particularly those on the legs. Instead the channels largely converge on the sense organs. Lo has suggested that the figurine may depict a body perfected through breathing and gymnastic exercises described in the self-cultivation literature.[138] One aspect of this process is the elimination of corrupting yin elements. If this speculative reading proves to be correct, it would be another piece of evidence for a link between yin energies and death in early Han medical thought.

Although advocacy of accumulating aspects of Heaven and reducing those of Earth is rare, the idea that life could be extended through ingesting some energies and expelling others was widespread. Beginning in the late Warring States period, poetic, philosophical, and medical texts all mentioned breathing exercises that accumulated beneficial energies and eliminated harmful ones.[139] The rubrics for the beneficial and harmful energies that coexist in the body vary from text to text. Some contrast "true" or "correct" energies with "deviant" ones. Others contrast "new" with "old." However, they agree that the body contains both helpful and harmful energies and that one should augment the former and eliminate the latter.

In most cases these techniques consist of breathing exercises, often performed at specified times when beneficial energies in the environment were abundant and could be drawn into the body.[140] The aforementioned "Eliminating Grain and Consuming Energy" contains a breathing exercise coordinated to the time of day as a way of eating energy.[141] "Ten Questions," found in the same tomb, also discusses controlled breathing and repeated swallowing of saliva as means of expelling old substances, incorporating new energies, and circulating them through the body. Thus, one passage describes the "way of the Heavenly Teacher to eat spirit energies":

> The Yellow Emperor asked the Heavenly Teacher, "What do the myriad things get so they can move? What do the plants get so they can grow? What do the sun and moon get so they are bright?" The Heavenly Teacher replied, "If you examine the nature of Heaven and Earth, then yin and yang are the essential. If the myriad creatures lose them, then they have no progeny. If they gain them they thrive. Consume the yin to congeal [reading 擬 as *ning* 凝] the yang. Match it against the spirit illumination.
>
> The way of consuming yin: Empty your five depots and disperse your three malignancies, as though you could not eliminate them. This is what is most prized in consuming the simple/undivided [*pu* 樸, following an emendation suggested by Donald Harper]. Still your spirit wind, secure your ribcage, triply pound [an irregular pulse] but do not carry it to completion, then the spirit wind is born and the five tones respond. Suck it in not more than five times, bring it to your mouth, receive it into your heart/mind. This is prized by the

four limbs. The 'dark cup [saliva]' then arrives. Drink it not more than five times. The mouth invariably finds it sweet. Bring it into the five depots. The body will then be extremely relaxed. Spread it to your flesh and skin, so that it reaches the tips of your hairs. Then the hair vessels are permeated. The yin water than arrives, soaking into the yang blaze. Firm and sturdy, one will not die. Food and drink accord with the body."[142]

Many points here are obscure, and I have relied on Donald Harper's translation and commentary. What is clear is that once again the passage describes a process of emptying out certain parts of the body to remove destructive forces and then replacing them with new energies drawn in from the outside or from other parts of the body. In fact, as other passages in the same text show, the saliva that was swallowed was thought to be generated by inhaling exterior energies.[143] These energies ingested in the form of the saliva then had to be circulated through the body, reaching to its outermost tips.

Two other points are significant. First, yin energies must be consumed in order to strengthen the body. This seems to contradict the association of yin with death. However, all the Mawangdui macrobiotic texts and especially the "Ten Questions" repeatedly insist that the yin element of the body is the most subject to decay and death. Thus, one reply states, "If life suffers a calamity, it is invariably because the yin essence [jing 精] leaks out, so the hundred vessels grow clogged and abandoned."[144] It is precisely because yin, particularly in the male body, is prone to disease and death that it must be specially nourished. Second, yin and yang figure here under the emblematic elements water and fire. These two potentially warring elements must be brought together in the body as complementary powers to secure health and longevity. Yang "fire" seems to be preexisting, while yin "water" must be created through breathing and swallowing saliva. Apparently the cooling power of this newly generated liquid allows the yang energies to "congeal" and hence provide sustenance for the body.

Other discussions suggest similar models. A reply to a question about lifespans notes that Heaven is long-lived because its energies are exhausted and then recharged with the cycles of the moon. Earth similarly does not decay because it passes through seasonal cycles of hot and cold. The speaker then argues, "You must examine the true nature of Heaven and Earth, and practice this with your body." The program for bodily practicing the nature of Heaven and Earth consists of concentrating essential energies [jing] through breathing and swallowing exercises:

Those skilled at regulating their energies and concentrating essential energies accumulate the signless [energies of Heaven and Earth]. Essence and spirit well up like a spring. Breathe in the "sweet dew" [some kind of energy or vapor] and accumulate it. Drink the "blue-gem spring" and "numinous cup" [saliva] and make it circulate. Eliminate the foul and love proper habits. The spirit will then flow into the body.

The way to breath in energies: You must cause it to reach the extremities, then essence will be generated and not lacking. The upper and lower body will both be essence. Cold and warm will tranquilly generate [like Earth]. Breathing must be deep and long, so that new energies will be easily retained. Old energies create aging; new energies create longevity. Those skilled in regulating the energies cause old energies to disperse at night and new energies to gather in at dawn, so that the latter will penetrate the nine opening and fill the six storehouses.[145]

The text then gives rules for varying these procedures depending on the season and the time of day. These variations are necessary in order to guarantee that one draws in only the proper energies and expels all noxious influences, in accord with the ambient conditions.

A key development of the image of the body as a fusion of celestial and earthly energies appears in uses of the terms *hun* 魂 and *po* 魄 (or *hunpo* as a synonym compound), loosely translated as "souls." In the dominant interpretation of Western Sinology, these were twin components of a human being. One was an active yang element (*hun*) that at death returned to Heaven, and the second a passive yin element (*po*) that returned to Earth. The fate of these two souls was supposedly central to Han funerary cult.[146] Scholars who focused on evidence from tombs rather than scholastic texts have challenged this interpretation, and an article by Kenneth Brashier has effectively refuted it.[147] The materials collected and issues raised in this debate shed considerable light on early Chinese conceptions of the body and its constituent elements.

The clearest link between the cosmic image of the body and the discourse on *hun* and *po* appears in the "Zhu shu" chapter of the *Huainanzi*: "Heaven's energies become the *hun*, and Earth's energies become the *po*. Guide these back to their mysterious home, where each occupies its own dwelling. Guard them so they are not lost, and thus ascend to communicate with the Grand Unity."[148] Another passage indicates that the "mysterious home" referred to here is in the human body: "The *hun* and *po* occupy their dwellings, and the refined energies guard their root. Death and life will work no transformation within the self, so it is called the supreme spirit."[149] These passages employ the model of the body being produced through the union of Heaven and Earth, but they introduce the terms *hun* and *po* as equivalent to the energies referred to elsewhere.

As Brashier has pointed out, the central point here is the necessity of keeping the *hun* and the *po* within the body. The self is perfected by preserving these two entities that came, respectively, from Heaven and Earth in their bodily dwellings. The medical texts of the period evince the same attitude, associating the *hun* and *po* with other dynamic components of the body that are essential to health. Their chief worry is that the *hun* and the *po* will disperse and depart from the body.[150] Thus, the *Huang Di nei jing ling shu* argues: "When the blood and energies are in harmony, the constructive and defensive circulation completely open, the five depots completed, the spirit energies lodged in the heart/mind, and the *hun* and *po* both present, this forms a complete person."[151] Elsewhere in the medical literature *hun* and *po* appear in lists of rarefied entities that are stored within the five depots, or of the coarser dynamic substances of the human body.[152]

As Brashier has demonstrated, failing to concentrate the *hun* and *po* or losing them results in mental disturbancs such as bad dreams, confusion, loss of memory, or madness.[153] The most common cause for loss of the *hunpo* was some extreme emotion, usually fright.[154] Loss of the *hunpo* thus is related to the English phrase "frightened out of one's wits." This identification of the *hunpo* with mental faculties is already demonstrated in anecdotes from the *Zuo zhuan*, wherein loss of the *po* or the *hunpo* leads to disrespectful behavior in rituals or to inappropriate responses such as weeping at a joyful celebration.[155] In one anecdote an observer states: "I have heard, 'Mourning at the joyful and finding joy in the mournful are both cases of losing one's mind.' The mind's essential brightness [*jing shuang* 精爽] is called the *hunpo*. If their *hunpo* departs, how can they survive for long?"[156] This is another prophecy of death based on ritual failings, but it traces the inappropriate conduct to the loss of the essential mental powers here identified as the *hunpo*.

The retention of the *hunpo* is also central to the use of the term in Han funerary practice. In Han funerary inscriptions the *hun* or *hunpo* is said to linger in darkness in the tomb, while the more refined and ethereal spirit [*shen* 神] soars up to Heaven or moves freely through the world. References to the *hunpo* descending into the tomb, the earth, or the Yellow Springs appear in protective texts buried in tombs, in divinatory texts, and in the dynastic histories. Within the tomb, the *hunpo* is still linked with mental functions. Thus, the hymns that conclude inscriptions often pose the question of the consciousness or awareness of the *hun*.[157] Because the *hun* was the locus of the deceased's consciousness, efforts were made to try to keep it in the tomb. The late Eastern Han text *Feng su tong yi* reports that spirit masks could be placed on the corpse to keep the *hun* within.[158] Sealing its orifices with jade or covering it in a jade suit likewise kept its lingering energies from dispersing. This would prevent the corpse from disintegrating and returning into the earth from which it had emerged. The *Lun heng* states that people placed models of servants and stockpiles of food in the tomb in order to pacify the *hun*, here again identified as the element of consciousness.[159] The exposure of the skeleton in a tomb robbery could pollute the *hun*, indicating that the latter remained connected to the bones.[160] In short, the main goal of Han funerary rituals was to keep the lingering energies in the body to prevent its complete dissolution back into the elements whose union had led to its birth.

The aforementioned models of the body as a fusion of disparate energies advocated extending life through ingesting beneficial substances and removing harmful ones. However, in discussion of the *hunpo* both medical procedures and funerary rites tried to resist the natural tendency of disparate substances to separate and resolve back into their original condition. This theme of death as the separation of substances that had been temporarily joined figures in numerous texts. Thus, the frequently cited passage from the "Jiao te sheng" in the *Li ji* on the *hun* and *po* states: "The *hun* energies [or "*hun* and energies"] return to Heaven, and the bodily *po* [or "body and *po*"] return to Earth. Therefore one seeks the meaning of sacrifices in the principle of yin [Earth, body, and *po*] and yang [Heaven, the energies, and *hun*]."[161] Here death is the dispersal or separation of temporarily joined energies. It is significant that *hun* is not opposed to *po*. Instead *po*, linked with the body, is in syntactic opposition to the vital energies (*qi*). *Hun* is linked to the vital energies, and opposed to the body. The same linkages and oppositions, as well as the association of *hun* with refined spirit [*shen* 神], figure in other *Li ji* chapters that identify death with the return of the body's constituent elements to Heaven and Earth. The same idea also appears in other Han writings such as the *Yilin* and the *Lun heng*.[162]

However, most texts say that the *hun* remains with the body in the tomb, while the more refined *shen* separated at death and moved freely. Thus, in Han funerary practice the *shen* received offerings at the ancestral temple, rather than the grave.[163] The *Huainanzi* combines this idea with the aforementioned image of a battle for mastery between the mind and the senses:

> When the ruler of a great state dies, they bury his skeleton amid the vast fields, but sacrifice to his spirit in the Bright Hall [see chapter five]. This is because the spirit is nobler than the bodily form. Thus if the spirit rules then the bodily form will obey, but if the bodily form conquers then the spirit will be exhausted. Although acute hearing and vision are employed, one must lead them back into the spirit.[164]

Defining death through the separation of the body and the spirit also figures in the poem "Guo shang," which likewise invokes the theme of the *hunpo* existing in the realm of ghosts:

> Bodies having perished, spirits become numinously potent;
> Your *hunpo* become ghost heroes.[165]

The adjective *ling* applied to the *shen* in this passage functions elsewhere as a synonym for *shen*. Its possession distinguished powerful and efficacious spirits from harmless ghosts.[166] Moreover, Zi Chan in the *Zuo zhuan* defended the belief that spirits could return from the dead and kill people by explaining how an ordinary *hunpo* could achieve the status of *shen ming*.[167] According to Zi Chan, it was as a *shen* and not as a ghost that the dead could wreak havoc among the living. Death was also identified with the loss of the *shen* in the *Huang Di nei jing ling shu*:

> The one who loses his *shen* dies; the one who obtains his *shen* lives.
> . . . At fifty the energies of the liver begin to decline, so the "leaves"
> of the liver grow thin, fluids of the stomach reduce, and eyesight
> fades. At sixty the energies of the heart begin to decline, so one
> suffers, worries, and grieves. The energies of the blood grow lazy, so
> one loves to sleep. At seventy the energies of the spleen are void, so
> the skin dries out. At eighty the energies of the lungs decline, so the
> *po* departs, and therefore one is prone to garble one's words [associ-
> ating absence of *hunpo* with mental confusion]. At ninety the energy
> of the kidneys is scorched, and the channels of four of the depots
> are empty. At one hundred all five depots are empty, the spirit ener-
> gies [*shen qi*] all depart, and the physical body [*xing hai* 形骸 "form
> and skeleton"], left all alone, dies.[168]

The body's decline is a stripping away of ever higher substances: the physical energies, then the *hunpo*, and finally the spirit *shen*. The departure of the *shen* leaves only a dead, skeletal body.

The separation of spirit and body as the key moment in departing from the world figures also in the poem "Far Roaming," which tells of a Daoist adept's ascent to the realm of nondifferentiation and eternal existence. One couplet reads, "The spirit suddenly departs and does not return; The body dries out and all alone remains behind."[169] Although it shares images with the description of death in the *Huang Di nei jing ling shu*, this passage is not an account of death. Instead it tells how the adept escapes from the world of bodies formed from the mingled energies of Heaven and Earth. The process resembles dying in that it separates the temporarily conjoined substances and returns each to the cosmic realms from which they had emerged, but the cul-mination of the process is not the separation of the two kinds of energy. Instead it leads to an ultimate return to the " 'Grand Primordium', the realm of space and time prior to the differentiation of physical phenomena."[170] However, such an ultimate destination also figures in certain accounts of dying, particularly those described by critics of elaborate burials. In such argu-ments the goal is often the dissolution of bounded existences back into the unbounded. Thus, one Han speaker argued that the energies that made up the body returned not to Heaven and Earth, but to the primal realm of nondistinction that preceded all divisions: "As for those who die, their primal energies [*yuan qi* 元氣] depart the body, and their pure *hun* disperses. These go back to simplicity and return to their origins, going back to the limitless. Having already dissolved, [the body] rejoins the manure and soil."[171] Here, as in "Far Roaming," the result of the dissolution of the human body into its elements is a return to the primal, undivided simplicity prior to the separa-tion of Heaven and Earth.

Thus, during the late Warring States and Han, the terms *hun* and *po* did not generally refer to a pair of "souls" that divided at death, but rather to a refined bodily substance associated with mental faculties. The loss of this substance or substances led to mental disturbance or decline, rather than death. Moreover, they could continue to adhere to the body and function as mental powers even after death. They were in turn linked to other substances, the essential energies [*jing*] and spirit energies [*shen*], in a hierarchy of ascending refinement. The human body emerged from the fusion of all these energies, as well as the coarser energies that formed its physical structures.[172] The life cycle sketched in the *Huang Di nei jing ling shu* consisted of the sequential development of these substances followed by their progressive loss. The hierarchy could for rhetorical purposes be reduced to the simple polarity of Heaven and Earth, but in full versions it consisted of a series of substances and structures arranged on a scale from the most coarse and dense to the most ethereal and refined.

Within the body the most solid and coarse was the skeleton. In some accounts the key division in the body lay between the more refined and dynamic substances—*hunpo*, *qi*, *jing*, and *shen*—and the coarser flesh and bone. In this context, bones played two major roles. First, bone defined the body in images of the grave and the afterlife. Second, bones also defined the body as an element of the kin group. Kin were linked bodily as "bone and flesh [*gu rou* 骨肉]." These two closely related roles in burial and kinship suggest yet another aspect of the Chinese vision of the body as a temporary composite of opposed substances.

The skeleton endures in the ground longer than any other corporal substance. Consequently, the use of bones or the skeleton as a marker of death and funerary ritual occurs in many cultures. In the West the skeleton appears as the embodiment of death, the ultimate *memento mori*, and the image of the deceased in such works as the fifteenth-century "transi" tombs whose lower register depicted a rotting skeleton gnawed by vermin. In early Chinese texts the skeleton also marked death. Thus, the "Tan gong" and "Ji yi" chapters of the *Li ji* state:

> That the bone and flesh return to the Earth is destiny. As for the *hun* energies, there is nowhere that they do not go.

> All living things must die, and the dead must return [*gui* 歸] to the Earth. This is called a 'ghost [*gui* 鬼]'. The bones and flesh end down below. As yin they form the soil of the fields. The body's energies soar up on high to become shining light.[173]

The link also figured in denunciations of elaborate funerals: "[The wise] thought elaborate funerals beggared people and destroyed their livelihoods, while providing no benefit to the dried bones and rotting flesh. Therefore burials were sufficient to gather in and lay out the corpse, cover it, hide it, and that was all."[174] Only bones and flesh were buried, and these in turn rotted away and returned to the earth. Attempts to defer their decay with coffins and jade suits were doomed to failure.[175]

The association of the skeleton with death is even clearer in Wang Chong's critique of "liberation through the corpse." In this practice the devotee developed a new body in which he departed as an immortal, leaving behind his fleshly body like the castoff skin of a snake. The impossibility of such a practice, according to Wang Chong, was demonstrated by the lingering presence of the skeleton:

> What is this so-called "liberation through the corpse"? Does it mean that the body dies and the refined, spirit energies depart? Or does it mean that the body does not die but is able to escape from its skin? If it means that the body dies and the refined, spirit energies depart, this would be no different from death. All people are then immortals. Does it mean that the body does not die but escapes from the skin? All those who study this method and die leave their bones and flesh completely present. They are no different from ordinary corpses. When cicadas depart and are reborn, turtles shed their shells, deer shed their antlers, or any shelled thing sheds its shell, they all take their bones and flesh to depart. This could be called "liberation through the corpse." Now as for those who die through studying the Way, the corpse and that which is to be reborn are virtually identical. This cannot be called "liberation through the corpse."[176]

The presence of the skeleton demonstrated that what had taken place was an actual death and that what was left behind was a genuine corpse. Thus, the presence of a skeleton defined a corpse. Wang Chong likewise denied the possibility of altering the body's form to extend life. While hair and skin could undergo minor changes, such as the whitening and wrinkling that accompany an extended life, the bones are beyond change and hence mark the certainty of ultimate death.[177]

Since skeletons marked death, their presence in the world was a sign of social breakdown. In lesser cases a skeleton that had not been properly buried, or whose burial had been disturbed, appeared to a ruler in a dream to seek redress.[178] Mores serious were piles of "dried bones and rotting flesh" littering the countryside.[179] These demonstrated the horrors of war, the cruelty of rulers, or the barbaric nature of early times. Such was the importance of removing the bones of the dead that the *Zhou li* charged an official with the task of interring all skeletons left unburied. The "Monthly Ordinances" stipulated it as a duty of the first month to "cover bones and bury rotting flesh."[180] Moreover, these ideas were carried out. An Eastern Han commentator identifies an office that in his day performed the function of the *Zhou li* official. Furthermore, Han dynastic histories record many cases in which the government assumed the task of collecting and burying skeletons, or of providing subsidies so that impoverished families could inter the skeletons of their dead.[181] Finally, some wealthy families or individuals charitably organized burials for families that were too poor, or for whole families wiped out in floods and plagues.[182]

One writer justified this policy as a public health measure because corpses left unburied at the New Year caused plagues in the summer.[183] However, he also argued that one had to bury corpses in order "to give peace to the wandering *hun*," so there was clearly also a religious aspect. The *Zhou li* official gathered skeletons prior to major sacrifices, and elsewhere the burial of abandoned corpses preceded sacrifices to secure rain.[184] Moreover, stories show that the failure to bury corpses resulted in unhappy spirits who manifested themselves in strange phenomena:

> South of the city wall of Luoxian whenever it rained there was a wailing sound that was heard in the government offices. This had gone on for decades. [Chen] Chong, having heard of this, wondered about the reason for it. He sent some minor officials to investigate. They returned and said, "As the age has declined and the times grown chaotic, many people have died there without their skeletons being buried. Might the reason lie in this?" Chong mournfully gave a pitying sigh. He then ordered the district officials to collect and bury them. From this time the wailing sound ceased.

Wang Chong also mentions such wailing produced by unburied bodies, although he rejects the idea that these sounds are the mourning of unhappy spirits.[185]

Some stories state that corpses not buried could become "flying corpses" capable of killing people.[186] Stories in the post-Han *Sou shen ji* also show that improperly buried corpses could harm people, and that such corpses might appeal to officials to give them a proper burial.[187] The ideas underlying such government policies, ritual practices, and stories are clear. Bones and the flesh that clings to them were the parts of the body that belonged to the dead. Since the dead and the living should not mingle (see chapter two), the presence of skeletal bones in the world collapsed essential distinctions. The consequent pollution threatened the performance of rituals and even threatened life.

However, there was at least one context in which skeletons emerged in a licit manner: reburial. Han people usually buried husband and wife together, an act sometimes called "joining the bones."[188] Thus, most tombs were reopened and entered by the living, who would then witness the skeletal condition of human remains. Although the procedure was widespread, the propriety of resultant contact with corpses was sometimes still a matter of debate.[189]

Although the skeleton is paired with flesh in these passages, the bones were the ultimate foundation of the body and the locus of mortality. The dependence of flesh on bone is shown by early texts that describe returning the dead to life as "giving life to the dead and putting flesh on white bones."[190] Bones provided a frame on which the flesh could be restored. The reliance of flesh on bone is also indicated by medical texts' emphasis on maintaining the closeness of the former to the latter.[191] This same idea, with the valuations reversed, figures in the description of supple female dancers as "rich in flesh and minute (or 'lacking') in bone."[192]

While "bones and flesh" were both the image of death and the ground of mortality, they were also the substance of kin ties. They were the bodily element common to all kin who shared what in the West are called "blood ties." This use of the phrase "bones and flesh" is common in early literature, particularly figuring in such phrases as the "closeness [qin 親]" of kin, kin "ties [shu 屬]," or "separating [shu 疏]" kin.[193] The Lun heng opposes gu rou to ta zu 他族 "other lineages," using "bone and flesh" to describe members of a patriline.[194]

While most texts use "bone and flesh" as an idiom, the Lü shi chun qiu provides a gloss that offers insight into early Chinese ideas about the body. This follows a story in which a man long separated from his mother hears a beggar singing at the gate, is extraordinarily moved by the song, and discovers that it is his mother. This leads to the observation:

> Relations of parents to children or children to parents is like two parts of a single body or the same breath/energy being separately breathed. It is like plants having flowers and fruits, or trees having roots; even though they are in different places they remain linked. Hidden intents reach from one to the other, they rescue one another from pain or suffering, and they are moved by the other's worries or longings. In life they take joy in one another, and in death they mourn. This is called "the closeness of bone and flesh." Their spirit energies emerge from full devotion and find a response in the other's mind. Their refined energies attain one another, so what need is there of words?[195]

Here the "closeness of bone and flesh" denotes a shared substance that makes kin part of a single body. This substance provides a physical substrate joining kin together in the same manner that roots connect to plants or stems to flowers and fruits. Kin are further joined at every stage from the breath energy of qi to the refined energies jing and even the supreme spirit energies shen. But it is the bone that is the ultimate foundation and the locus of these shared energies.[196] The idea that kin share a common body is also expressed in the statement that the imperial heir "continued the body [ji ti 繼體]" of his predecessor.[197]

The idea of gu rou as a common body did not usually apply to relatives by marriage, who had no shared substance.[198] Although one imperial decree states that "husband and wife are a single body," this statement is used to justify a joint burial, which as previously noted could be called "conjoining the bones."[199] Thus, husband and wife, who shared no substance by birth, became a single body when their bones joined in the tomb. Once again it is in funerary rites, the central ritual for defining and preserving lineages, that bodies came to be defined through their core elements of "bone and flesh."

Another phrase identifying the skeleton with kinship is a formula that describes the request to retire from government as "begging for one's skeleton."[200] This formula reflects the idea that the early imperial world was divided into two spheres, the state and the family. Those who entered state service rose out of their households into a sphere defined by loyalty to the ruler who embodied universal order. Upon retirement they returned to a household realm defined by particularist kin ties. Biographies of officials were structured in terms of the movement between these two realms (see the Conclusion section).[201] In this context, possession of the skeleton that linked the body to a given kin group marked movement between the household and the state.

The skeleton as physical foundation of the body's energies also figures in early Chinese beliefs relating to the location of the *hunpo*.[202] Stories from the late Warring States and Han periods show that many Chinese believed that the *hunpo* resided in the skeleton, or, more precisely, the skull. The ritual expressions of this belief were noted earlier, in discussing the use of coffins, jade suits, and masks to keep the *hun* within the body while preventing the latter from rotting. However, the idea that the *hunpo* resided in the bones led to more unusual behavior.

The most dramatic case is that of Liu Qu, a grandson of Emperor Jing (r. B.C. 157–141) who became enamoured of his concubine Zhaoxin. Discovering that two earlier favorites were planning to eliminate this new rival, he and Zhaoxin murdered them and three of their maids. Zhaoxin subsequently fell ill and saw the murdered women in her dreams. To destroy the unhappy spirits, Liu Qu had their bodies dug up and burned them to ashes. After being promoted to official wife, Zhaoxin had all rivals murdered. One named Wangqing was tortured by Liu Qu, Zhaoxin, and the assembled concubines until she threw herself into a well and drowned:

> Zhaoxin fished her out, sealed her vagina with small wooden stakes, cut off her nose and lips, and cut out her tongue. She said to Liu Qu, "Previously when we killed Zhaoping, she came back to frighten me. I want to reduce Wangqing to a gruel to prevent her from becoming a powerful spirit [*shen*]." With Liu Qu she removed Wangqing's limbs, placed her body in a large pot, where she boiled it together with peach tree ash and poisons. She summoned all the concubines to observe it. It went on for several days and nights until the body was completely reduced to a gruel.[203]

In a later case the victim's corpse had its limbs cut off and was buried wrapped in brambles.

The apparition of the murdered women in dreams showed that their spirits were still conscious and active. To end this posthumous existence, their bones had to be pulverized. In the next case the process went further, boiling the corpse in poisons and demonifugic substances until the skeleton was reduced to the consistency of a gruel. This annihilation of the vestiges of the body, above all the skeleton, prevented the energies of the deceased from turning into a powerful spirit that could harm her killers. The rendering of the body into a gruel echoes the Yellow Emperor's disposal of the body of his rival Chi You, who also in certain versions of the myth returned after death. In some accounts the king of Yue boiled Wu Zixu's corpse to prevent his spirit from returning to wreak vengeance.[204] The boiling of the corpse in a pot for several days and nights also recalls the execution of Wen Zhi, perhaps explaining why the king of Qi chose such an unusual method in his attempt to eliminate a reputed master of esoteric techniques.

This treatment of the corpses of the murdered concubines was not unique. When Dong Zhong was executed for plotting a rebellion during the annual military training session, Wang Mang had his own personal guard chop up Dong Zhong's body in order to "suppress inauspicious events," and had the remains placed in a bamboo container: "He arrested all of Zhong's lineage and ground them into a meat sauce which was mixed with poisons. He placed the remains together in a pit lined with foot-long sword blades and ringed with bunches of brambles."[205] This combines the procedures employed by Liu Qu: first rendering them into a gruel mixed with poisons to neutralize any lingering energies, and then surrounding them with brambles to immobilize whatever remained. The aim was to destroy the powers of the deceased by pulverizing flesh and bone, and then confining in the tomb whatever energies survived.

Some believed that the skeleton with its *hun* could not only change into an evil creature, or allow the dead to haunt survivors, but also grow back flesh to return to life. This is discussed in Zhuang Zhou's address to a skull that subsequently appeared to him in a dream. In response to the skull's claim that death was the highest happiness Zhuang Zhou replied: "If I had the Master of Lifespans restore your body to life, to recreate your skeleton and flesh, and restore your parents, wife, children, and neighbors, would you desire this?"[206] The skull acted like the skeletons of the deceased concubines, using its *hun* to invade dreams. Zhuang Zhou's question also hints that the skeleton could through the intervention of a powerful spirit have its muscle and flesh restored and once again form a living body.

A text found at Fangmatan demonstrates that Zhuang Zhou's suggestion was not merely a literary conceit but an actual belief.[207] A man who had died and been buried for three years was brought back to life by the Master of Lifespans, and then dug up from the tomb. He remained on the tomb for three days, and only after four years was he able to hear and to eat the food of the living. Even then he still lacked hair, had black skin, and could not readily move his limbs. The long period before the dead man could return to the human world, even then lacking features of a living body, suggests that he had been reduced to a skeleton that only gradually grew back its exterior. Stories of skeletons at least temporarily reassuming a fleshly body also appear in later fiction.[208] Thus, not only could life be extended through methods of holding the body and spirit together, but even after death a form of existence continued so long as the *hun* and the skeleton remained united. In rare circumstances the continued union of the skeleton with the *hun* could even allow the resurrection of a living body.

INTERFACES OF THE BODY

The idea that the body emerged temporarily from diverse energies entailed not only that it was a composite, but also that the divisions between interior and exterior were not absolute. Early Chinese treated the limits of the body not as rigid boundaries but rather as permeable or extendable membranes. This already figured in the "Nei ye," which argued that self-cultivation could extend the body's influence from its own center to the edges of the world. Inversely, the desires of the senses for external objects could lead to the occupation of the human interior by the external world. Constant exchange through porous boundaries between the body and the outer world also figures prominently in early Chinese discussions of "wind" and "breath/energy (*qi* 氣)." These provided a medium for the transmission of influences between the bodily microcosm and the greater world.[209]

While the self endured by maintaining a separation between inner and outer, this division could never be absolute. Rather than denying the flow of energies between the person and the outer world, the dominant early Chinese model of the self demanded the regulation of such flows. It paid great attention to the interface of body and outside world, where dynamic exchanges took place. Like state frontiers, these were not fixed limits, but rather flexible zones that extended outward when the inner realm was well regulated, and collapsed inward when it was not.

This section deals with early Chinese accounts of the interfaces between the self and the outer world, and of the privileging of the body's surfaces as sites of meanings and zones of control. The topics are the skin as a means of diagnosis and a site of therapy, the physiognomy, shadows, and finally hair and clothing. Each of these has been the topic of essays or monographs in its own right. Here I will simply sketch those aspects that indicate how the body was understood as part of a larger whole within which the divisions between internal and external remained fluid and shifting.

Chinese medicine has always focused in diagnosis and therapy on the body's surface as a zone of exchange between internal and external forces. The organs, so central to the Western medical body, are ill-defined material substrata to what Manfred Porkert calls "orbs of functions" defined by energy flows.[210] As John Hay has argued, the system of acupuncture meridians posits that the patterns of energy within the body and including what we define as internal organs are palpable and manipulable at its surface. An energy identified with the wind circulated between the human body and the outer world, but also penetrated the body through the skin and its pores.[211] Finally, several of the major therapies, notably moxibustion and acupuncture, applied substances to the skin or pierced it with needles. The body's surface offered signs for reading its condition and provided a key therapeutic site. While important therapies involved ingesting medical recipes, the central concerns of Chinese medicine were more often then not focused on the boundaries of the body and the outer world.

Diagnosis through examining surfaces took several forms. In late imperial China these were hierarchically ranked in a series based on the senses employed in examining the patient. From lowest to highest these were touch, questioning, listening and smelling, and gazing. This sequence corresponds to a pattern found in many cultures in which the more immediate and physical senses, taste and touch, are inferior to those with a wider range that do not depend on contact, hearing, and sight.[212] However, for all senses with the exception of hearing, the object remained the body's surface.

The sense of touch read the body in a science of pulses.[213] One feature of the Chinese science of pulses that contrasts with that of the West is that each pulse point can provide information about different organs and conditions depending on the degree to which the doctor presses down.[214] This idea is part of a broader complex of notions that depict a "body structured by the logic of depth." In addition to diagnosis that proceeded from the outside inward, a common explanation of diseases described them as exterior energies, most often identified with the wind as the macrocosmic form of human breath, that progressively penetrated inward.[215] Both medical literature and literary anecdotes described diseases that moved from the outside inward, growing more difficult to cure as they penetrated more deeply. The skill of physicians depended on the stage of the disease's penetration at which they could recognize it.[216] Therapies also moved from the outside inward in the form of needles, and the texts emphasize the depth and frequency of needling in therapies for different diseases. Thus, while the skin divided self from world, it also constituted a zone of mutual influences that passed in both directions. Diagnosis, etiology, and therapy all moved inward and outward through this zone.

While the interior of the body was manifest at the surface in pulses that were read by touch, it was also *visible* to the expert gaze in its color and facial expressions.[217] Medical literature pairs the "colors (*se* 色)" of the complexion with the pulses as primary modes of diagnosis.[218] As Kuriyama Shigehisa has pointed out, there is considerable overlap between the vocabulary and practice of diagnosis through colors and certain divinatory procedures. Similarly, Warring States philosophers linked examining facial expressions (*se*) with listening to words to recognize true character or intent hidden behind overt declarations.[219] In some stories keen observers were able to detect secret plans in the expressions of those who had just made them.[220] More broadly, the people's facial colors could be used to diagnose the health of the body politic.[221] Thus, throughout the Warring States period, *se* figured in several contexts as the prognosticatory form of vision. Through the "colors" or "expressions" that moved across the surface one could detect the hidden or subtle aspects of a physical phenomenon.

Several passages pair *xing* 形 "physical form" with *se*.[222] Kuriyama posits a link between this pairing and phrases such as *xing shen* 形神 "form and spirit energies," *xing sheng* 形生 "form and vitality," or *xing qi* 形氣 "form and energy/breath." In each case the second element is lighter, more refined, more dynamic, and thus more liable to rapid change. A passage from the *Huang di nei jing ling shu* shows its medical significance:

> The Yellow Emperor asked, "When a pathogen strikes someone, what form does the illness take?" Qi Bo said, "When an empty pathogen strikes the body, there is trembling and moving. When a correct pathogen [seasonal wind] strikes someone, it remains minute. It is first perceived in the color/complexion, but not recognizable in the body. It seems to be present yet absent, existing yet vanishing, formed yet formless. No one can perceive its true nature."[223]

Unlike the physical form, which reveals ailments in visible trembling or movement, the complexion or expression provide fleeting hints noticed only by a skillful physician. Thus, the text argues that one who can perceive an ailment from complexion is "enlightened (*ming*)" while one who can do it from the pulse is "spirit-like (*shen*)." Recognition of disease from these fleeting signs at the body's surface marks a true physician, because only such percipience enables the identification of diseases while they are still incipient and hence susceptible to treatment.

Diagnosis from complexion or expression was closely related to physiognomy, the recognition of character and prediction of fate through examining the body, above all the face.[224] Physiognomy was extremely influential in early China, where it was applied not only to human beings but also to animals. The latter was best known in the received literature through references to Bole, a physiognomist of horses.[225] The practice has been confirmed by the discovery at Mawangdui of a manual on the art. The *Xunzi* also makes sneering references to men famous for physiognomizing chickens and dogs.[226]

However, the most important form of physiognomy was the reading of human character and fate. The best known discussion is the first section of the chapter "Contra Physiognomy" in the *Xunzi*. This denounces physiognomy's privileging of the body over the heart/mind in the determination of human destiny. To refute this belief, the *Xunzi* lists examples of the divergence of physical appearance and moral character. However, the fact that the authors devote so much effort to refuting physiognomy indicates its prestige, also shown by numerous references in Warring States and Han literature.[227] Physiognomists were employed by leading political figures to evaluate their sons, and they recognized the unique destinies of anonymous people who would later rise to greatness. The most notable example of this deals with the Han founder, but many others appear in the histories.[228] In the Age of Disunion, the literature accompanying the establishment of a new dynasty routinely noted the extraordinary physiognomy of the founder.[229] This proves that despite some scholars' scepticism, powerful political figures routinely employed physiognomy, which became an element of the state's institutions.

The most valuable discussions of physiognomy and related matters are those of the great fatalist Wang Chong. One chapter of his work is devoted to justifying the practice:

> People say that destiny is hard to know. In fact it is very easy to know. How do you know it? You know it from the structure of the bones. People receive their destiny from Heaven, and there are outward signs in the body. One examines these outward signs to know destiny. It is like examining units of volume to recognize capacity. The outward signs are the models for the bones.[230]

This chapter consists largely of pre-imperial examples of the extraordinary appearances of sages, and of Han examples demonstrating the accuracy of predictions based on physiognomy.[231]

This shows only that Wang Chong, like many people of his day, believed in a fate inscribed in the body.[232] However, an earlier chapter explains the reasoning that he believed underlay physiognomy. "There Is No Shaping" denies the possibility of changing one's form to alter one's destiny. It criticizes the belief that bodily cultivation would allow one to sprout wings and become an immortal. In the process of denouncing this belief, Wang Chong developed a theory of how destiny was fixed in external form. He also argued that only the ability to alter that form, an ability beyond human powers, could allow one to alter that destiny. The chapter begins:

> People receive their primal energies from Heaven. Each thus receives a predestined lifespan, which fixes the size of the body. It is like a potter using clay to make bowls or tiles, or a caster of metal using bronze to make drinking vessels. Once the vessel's form has been completed, it cannot be shrunk or enlarged. Likewise once the human body is fixed, it cannot be reduced or increased. Having used energy to form inborn nature, when the nature is complete then destiny is fixed. The body's energy and the skeleton cling to one another; life and death are fixed by the allotted lifespan. Bodily form

cannot be changed, and the allotted lifespan cannot be reduced or increased.[233]

It also discusses how some animals could change form and why men could not do likewise. Wang Chong then elaborates the link between endowment of energy and physical form:

> The body's containing blood and energy is like a sack's storing grain. The size of a sack with one *dan* exactly matches one *dan*. If one increased or reduced the grain, the sack would likewise increase or reduce. People's longevity is fixed by their primal energies. These energies are like grain, and the body is like the sack. If you increase or reduce the longevity, you also would increase or reduce the body. How could the form remain as it was before?[234]

The quantity of energy received at birth determined lifespans and other aspects of destiny. Since these energies filled and animated the body, a notion that goes back at least to the *Mencius*, they determined the person's size and shape. While the analogy with the sack cannot be pressed too far, for it implies that longevity is directly proportional to size, it provides a physical model for directly linking form to lifespan, and by extension to other aspects of an individual's fate.

In addition to justifying physiognomy in a model related to the medical traditions through its appeal to *qi*, this chapter also suggests how the extension of life was possible through the alteration of form. While denying that humans could metamorphose like certain animals, except in prodigies produced by poor government, one passage suggests limited possibilities for change:

> That which changes as a person grows old is the hair and the skin. When people are young their hair is black. When they grow old the hair grows white. When it has been white for a long time it turns yellow. The hair changes, but the body does not change. When people are young their skin is white. When they grow old it becomes black. When it has been black for a long time it becomes pitch black, as though covered with dirt. . . . Therefore people can grow old and die later [than they otherwise would]. But the bone and flesh cannot change, so when the limit of longevity is reached one dies.[235]

The substances forming the core of the person cannot alter, so radical extension of lifespan is not possible. However, limited changes occur in the skin and hair, and these changes permit people to defer death. Should one be unable to alter through the lightening of hair and darkening of skin, then one would die much younger. Here the physical aspects of aging manifest a limited capacity for metamorphosis that permits a modest extension of lifespan. The medical theories, as noted earlier, linked the reading of signs at the surface to the application there of therapies, and the therapies were directly linked to the signs. Similarly, in Wang Chong's theory of the inextricable linkage of form and longevity, the surface was both a visible sign of energetic endowment and, to a limited extent, a site of changes allowing a modest extension of lifespan.

Fluid boundaries between body and environment also appear in early Chinese ideas about the shadow.[236] Although the later Mohists had explained shadows as a result of blocking light, other texts treat the shadow as an extension of the body, sometimes associated with its refined energies.[237] The earliest examples of the latter approach are passages from the *Zhuangzi*:

> The penumbras asked the shadow, "A moment ago you looked down and now you look up. A moment ago your hair was bound and now it is untied. A moment ago you were sitting and now you are standing. A moment ago you were walking and now you have stopped. Why?" The shadow said, "Chatter, chatter, why bother to ask? I do these things but do not know why. I am the cicada's outer shell, the shed skin of the snake, something that resembles [the original] but is not. In fire or sunlight I come together, but in darkness or night I temporarily depart. But could they be that on which I depend? How much less could this be, when they are themselves dependent? When they come, then I come with them. When they depart then I depart with them."[238]

Scholars read this as a reflection on the idea of dependence or cause. The penumbra depends on the shadow, which depends on the body. Likewise the shadow depends on the penumbra, which defines its limits, and the body on the shadow. Nothing is an absolute and independent cause.

Less often noted are the references to the cicada's shell and the snake's skin. These are bodily coverings that in molting are left behind. They are empty forms of their former bodies, "something that resembles but is not." The shadow resembles them to the extent that it is the substanceless form of its body. However, the analogy implies that the shadow is part of the body, an outer limit like the skin. Also implicit is the possibility that the shadow could separate from the body if the latter mutated into something else. In fact, several Han stories indicate that the shadow *was* understood as an element of the body, and that the body might lose its shadow under certain circumstances. These suggest ideas about the nature of both the body and its shadow.

The clearest example of those who shed their shadows were immortals. The *Lie xian zhuan*, a work first compiled in the Han although later expanded, demonstrates this. One story tells of Xuan Su, who in the city market sold medicine that cured the king by expelling a dozen snakes that had formed a conglomeration in his stomach. The story continues: "An ancient retainer in the king's household said that in his father's time he had seen Su, and that

Su's body had no shadow. The king then called for Su and had him stand in the sunlight. Indeed he had no shadow."[239] Several post-Han texts record the idea that immortals had no shadows.[240]

As to why immortals lack shadows, Li Jianmin follows several modern scholars in arguing that since their bodies were purged of cruder substances, immortals were composed entirely of refined energies and hence were transparent. This is supported by the poem following the story of Xuan Su that states, "His substance emptied, this destroyed his shadow." Another possibility is suggested by a passage in the post-Han *Baopuzi*:

> Take the pill twice a day. After thirty days it cures all the diseases in your belly, and the Three Worms depart. Take it one hundred days, and your flesh and bones will become firm. After one thousand days, the Master of Lifespans will remove your name from the register of mortality. You will live as long as Heaven and Earth, see all that is illumined by the sun and moon, alter form and visage, and transform with no constant shape. In the sunlight you will have no shadow, for you will separately have a light.

"Separately having a light" refers to the fact that, as shown in the self-cultivation texts from Mawangdui, those who repelled old age glowed with their own radiance. Indeed, the "light" is regularly used in the Mawangdui texts to describe such people's skin.[241] Since immortals generated a light of their own, blockage of the sun's light would not produce a shadow.

Immortals' lack of a shadow suggests another aspect of the earlier reference to cicadas and snakes. The sloughing off of outer layers by these creatures was a standard image for "liberation through the corpse." (See the passage cited at note 176.) In this practice, the adept cultivated a new, inner body in which he or she ultimately departed, leaving the old body behind like the skin of the snake or the shell of the cicada. Thus, shadows, snakes, and cicadas all converge in ideas about the transformed bodies of immortals. It is also significant that a self-cultivation texts from Mawangdui that described the glowing skin of those who warded off old age also spoke of becoming a spirit [*shen*] and being able to achieve "liberation through the body." Although Donald Harper argues that these two practices were not identical, they were certainly close. The *Shi ji*, for example, treats "liberation through the body" specifically as an aspect of the "way of the immortals," and hence basically equivalent to "liberation through the corpse."[242]

Other transformed bodies that lacked a "shadow," or rather a reflection that in this period was also called a *ying* 影, were ancient animals who were able to adopt human form. Stories from the *Feng su tong yi* show that Han people already believed in such creatures.[243] The *Baopuzi* states that they menaced adepts who entered the mountains to cultivate their arts:

> Therefore Daoist masters who in ancient times entered the mountains all took with them a mirror of more than nine inches in diam-

eter. They hung it from their backs, so that ancient demons would not dare approach them. Sometimes a demon approaches people to test them, so you look in the mirror. If they are immortals or good spirits of the mountains, then in the mirror will be a human form just as it appears to you. If it is a perverse demon bird or beast, than its true appearance will be revealed in the mirror.[244]

Just as the immortals' altered body lacked the negative image that is the shadow, so the animals' altered state lacked the positive image of a reflection. In the case of demons, the reflection was the true body, which, unlike the physical body, could not be altered.

Immortals' lack of a shadow testifies to the heightened powers of their transformed bodies. However, in other contexts the absence of a shadow indicated that the body was diminished or lacked a key feature. Specifically, several texts suggest that the shadow either was a person's spirit (shen) or closely related to it. Wen Yiduo argued that the penumbra in the Zhuangzi stories was the person's spirit.[245] The link between spirits and shadows figures in the story of Shao Weng's conjuring up the spirit of a deceased concubine of Emperor Wu: "At night he set out lamps and candles, hung up curtains, laid out wine and meat, and had the emperor sit behind another curtain. Gazing from a distance the emperor saw a beautiful woman who resembled Lady Li walking back behind the curtain."[246] Several modern authors have argued that Emperor Wu saw only shadows cast on the fabrics, and that this was an early version of shadow puppet theater.[247] That the emperor believed that visions of a shadow were the spirit of the deceased shows that many people in Han times imagined the spirit in the image of the shadow, or understood the shadow as a visible form of the spirit.

This link between shadows and spirits also figures in the taboos associated with the height of summer on the fifth day of the fifth month.[248] Han texts indicate that a taboo on this date forbade going up on the roof for fear of encountering ghosts. A Tang work, the You yang za zu, explains this taboo through appeal to the themes of shadows and spirits: "Customs taboo going up on the roof in the fifth month. They say that in the fifth month 'People molt.' If they go up on the roof and see their shadow, their hun will depart."[249] The Zhuangzi already linked molting with shadows, and some modern scholars believe that the reference here to molting, the sight of the shadow, and the loss of the soul indicate that the shadow was also lost like the snakeskin or cicada shell with which it had been identified.[250] Calendrical literature from the Han also preceded accounts of the taboos with the statement that in the fifth month "yin and yang struggle, and life and death separate"; or "yin and yang struggle, and blood and energy disperse."[251] The fear that the shadow or the spirit might likewise separate or disperse fits closely with other ideas about the period of the solstice. Moreover, as Li Jianmin has pointed out, in early China, ascending the roof was an element in the ritual of calling back a departed soul.[252] Thus, this taboo clearly indicates that the shadow and the spirit are elements of the body that could possibly become detached, if not that the two are one and the same.

Another indication that a shadow, or, in this case a reflection, could act as a spirit or shape a body derives from a version of "fetal instruction" described in the Jin dynasty *Bo wu zhi*. Early Han versions of this theory argued that the character of the fetus could be shaped by controlling the environmental stimuli to which the mother was subjected. In the *Bo wu zhi* it was the body of the fetus that was thus shaped, and the shaping was done by gazing at a reflection: "When a woman has been pregnant for less than three months, if she puts on her husband's clothing and hat, and at dawn circles leftward three times around a well, casts her reflection/shadow in the well, looks at the reflection and departs, does not look back, and does not let her husband see this, she will invariably give birth to a son."[253] Before the sex of the fetus becomes fixed, the woman shapes it by dressing as a man whom she absorbs into herself by gazing at its reflection. Thus, the reflection of the mother shapes the body of the unborn child, which in turn possesses a shadow/spirit shaped by that reflection.

A final piece of Han evidence linking the body's energetic spirits and its shadow appears in the *Feng su tong yi*. A ninety-year-old man took a new wife, had sex with her once, and then died. When she subsequently gave birth to a son, the daughter of the deceased challenged the paternity of the child, arguing that such an old man could not have produced a son in one night of sex. After years of legal battles over the inheritance, the chief minister was called upon to settle the case. His decision stated:

> "The children of aged men have no shadows, and furthermore they fear the cold." At that time it was the eighth month (middle of autumn). They took [the disputed child] and a child of the same age, and stripped them naked. Only the old man's son cried out that it was cold. Again they had them walk side by side in the sunlight, and he had no shadow. Consequently they awarded the property to the son.[254]

Sons of old men lack a shadow because the father's lack of energy (*qi*) results in a son who is similarly bereft. Two facts show this. First, the father died because "after one act of intercourse his energy/breath was cut off [*qi jue* 氣絕]." Second, the unique susceptibility to cold of such children indicates that they lack the energy to keep their bodies warm. Thus, this story again indicates the belief that the shadow was a visible manifestation of the body's spirit or energy.[255]

Another extension of the skin that was closely linked to the body was hair. Hair is a key social marker and symbol in most cultures, indicating gender, class, age, character, social role, and degree of civilization.[256] Hair was just such a polyvalent marker in early China. First, like skin, it was a visible surface on which one could read the internal state of the body. Medical texts frequently describe conditions of hair and what these indicated about health.[257] Sometimes the hairs formed channels along which diseases or external energies moved into the body, or needles were manipulated.[258] Long hair indicated a vigorous old age, so later depictions of immortals often portrayed the length of their hair.

In these contexts, hair was largely an extension of the skin. It was distinctive largely in its mobility and capacity for growth. More important was the belief that great anger manifested itself in hair "standing on end," which in the modern West is read as a sign of fear. The *Huang Di nei jing ling shu* describes the physical state of the brave man thus:

> The brave man's eyes are deepset and fixed. The hairs of his long eyebrows rise up. His Triple Burner is ordered and horizontal. His heart/mind is straight and direct. His liver is big and sturdy. His gall bladder is full to overflowing. When angry then his energies [*qi*] overflow and his chest swells. His liver rises and his gall bladder moves horizontally. His eyes bulge from their sockets, his hair rises up, and his face flushes. This is the manner of the brave man.[259]

Bulging eyes with hair standing on end as an expression of rage appears also in a description of Fan Kuai during his confrontation with Xiang Yu at the Hongmen banquet.[260] Hair raised by heroic rage could knock the hat off the head, as when Lin Xiangru threatened to smash the jade coveted by the king of Qin.[261] Hair rising straight up also figures in collective scenes of heroic sentiment, as in the account of the witnesses to Jing Ke's departure on his attempt to assassinate Qin Shihuang.[262] This idea also was depicted in Han art, as in the representation at the Wu Liang shrine of Jing Ke's attempted assassination. Here the assassin's hair sticks straight up as he hurls his blade at Qin Shihuang.[263] In these scenes the overflowing energies of heroic warriors spilled out of their skin and through their hair out into the larger world. Hair was particularly suited to the expression of mental states because the *hun* resided in the skull. Consequently, the hairs on the head were virtually direct extensions of the body's spiritual energies.

Because movement of hair expressed dangerous emotions, its binding defined civilization and even humanity. Children wore their hair in fashions not employed by adults. Adulthood for men and women was marked by binding the hair, for men in the capping ceremony and for women in a parallel ritual involving the pinning of hair. Moreover, different genders and statuses among adults each had distinctive manners of wearing hair. Attention devoted to the binding of hair is particularly striking in the terra cotta army, whose soldiers and officers all feature elaborate hair styles. It is uncertain to what degree these complicated plaitings were utilitarian (to prevent the enemy from grasping hair), to what degree aesthetic, and to what degree a display of virility. In any case, it shows that styles of hair binding were of great interest, even among those engaged in the most masculine of activities.

Since the binding of hair marked adulthood and civilization, leaving hair unbound was characteristic of barbarians, madmen, and ghosts.[264] Not only was untied hair characteristic of ghosts, but the "Demonography" discovered at Shuihudi stipulates that, if the path is blocked by a ghost, one should undo one's hair, vigorously advance, and the trouble would cease.[265] Unbinding the hair might have unleashed some of the individual's spirit power, like the warriors' hair standing on end. Alternatively, unbinding the hair could have transformed the individual into a peer of the ghost who thus ceased to cause trouble. In any case, this apotropaic technique shows how binding and unbinding hair could alter one's status and/or generate power.

Clothing was closely related to shadows and hair as an interface between body and outside world. Attached to the fleshly body, it acted like hair style to define gender, status, age, or office. By putting on a particular costume, one adopted a social role and assumed its powers. Thus, it became a cliché that the sages had created clothing in order to distinguish people according to their rank and character.[266] The role of costume in delineating the self was particularly important in government service, where every official from the lowest local administrator to the emperor himself was distinguished by costumes and insignia. These became the topic of a considerable literature. The *Zuo zhuan, Xunzi*, and other early *ru* works contain numerous discussions of the significance of costume. The early ritual classics likewise frequently discuss what should be worn by whom. They even have specialized chapters on the significance of particular items of clothing, such as the "Meaning of Hats" chapter of the *Li ji*. Many of the later dynastic histories also included chapters on court costumes. Outside the court, all kin ties were defined by obligations of mourning measured in terms of types of garments worn and the periods of time for which they were worn. Thus, as Marcel Granet argued, it is significant that the term *fu* 服 meant on the one hand "clothing" or "to clothe," and on the other "to submit, to accept a role."[267] In correctly clothing themselves, people passed from the wild to the domestic and assumed appropriate social roles.

While clothing as an extension of the body plays a key role in all cultures, at least three features of the early Chinese understanding of clothes deserve note. First, as Roel Sterckx has noted, the "Xi ci" chapter of the *Yi jing* established the idea that all aspects of human civilization were derived from patterns observed in nature. The origins of human clothing were traced back to the bodies of animals that provided both material and inspiration. Thus, the *Hou Han shu* chapter on court clothing begins:

> In high antiquity people lived in caves or in the wilds. They wore clothing of fur and hats of hides, and did not yet have any institutions or measures. Sages of later generations changed this by the use of silk and hemp. They observed the patterns on the variegated pheasant and the colors of blossoming flowers, and then dyed their silk to imitate these. They first made the five colors, and then fin-

ished the process by making them into clothes. They saw that birds and beasts had a system of crests, horns, whiskers, and dewlaps, so they followed these in making hats, ceremonial caps, throat-bands, and fringes to make decorations for the head.[268]

This account, which recurred in other dynastic histories, traces an evolution from a primitive state where people clothed themselves with animal skins to a civilized state where they wore artificial fabrics patterned on the forms, colors, and functions of animal coverings. Clothing thus offered man-made bodies to make up for the vulnerable nudity of the original human condition.

In addition to providing artificial versions of the bodies of birds and beasts, clothing was also an extension of the body that served to express character. Thus, the *Guo yu* says: "Clothes are the outward patterning of one's heart/mind. It is like the tortoise [shell]. If you apply heat to its interior, a meaningful pattern will appear on the outside."[269] Here clothing is the human equivalent of the turtle's carapace, an outer covering whose meaningful patterns reveal hidden truths. This analogy is extended by reference to divination through cracking tortoise shells, suggesting that the energies of a person's character will produce outward visual signs like the heat applied to a shell to induce cracks. The expression of character in clothing took many forms. The wearing of animal hides by warriors or barbarians revealed their savage natures or their ferocity.[270] Similarly, the universality of the emperor's rule, both its lordship over all of nature and its complementary employment of civil power and punishing force, was indicated by the symbols woven into his robes.[271] In these and other cases clothing defined the person who wore it.

The interplay between body and costume is particularly notable in depictions of human figures in Chinese art. The general absence of the nude in Chinese art, in contrast with its centrality in the West, is a cliché, but nonetheless largely true. The body in Chinese art, as John Hay has argued, is unmistakably social.[272] Its meanings derive from its surroundings, from associated people, and above all from its clothing. The erotic attraction of images of the female body appears at its highest in the swirling lines of diaphanous robes, robes whose lightness and mobility express the Chinese ideal of the feminine. Similarly, the ferocity of warriors as depicted in art is expressed in the armor and skins that encase their bodies. In contrast to certain strains in Western thought, which seek truth in the act of stripping away coverings, the truth of the body in early Chinese literature and art had to be clothed in order to be expressed.

This idea also appears in Audrey Spiro's discussion of portraiture in early China.[273] As she argues, even portraits of specific individuals tended to be "ideal" portraits that communicated not a physical reality of face or form but a person's character, role, or conduct. This art aimed at defining people through placing them within the proper social context, clothing them with the appropriate garments, and demonstrating through gesture or pose the manner in which they related to others. As Nagahiro Toshio argued, the purpose of Han portraiture was to make the essence of the person's character and social role manifest in the "visible symbol of his person." The depiction of clothing was central to such a task.[274] When new ideals of human excellence developed in the Age of Disunion, as indicated in the collective portraits of the Seven Sages of the Bamboo Grove, their character and conduct were still formulaically expressed in the lineaments of their clothing and their manner of wearing it. Through all the changes in artistic practice, the self depicted was still largely through the second skin formed by clothing.

CONCLUSION

The body came to the fore in Chinese thought in the fourth century B.C. In that first emergence of Chinese philosophy, the body became a shared topic of discourse in which different traditions articulated their values. The theme was established as central by the Yangist tradition, which made the proper valuing of the self the premise of its arguments. Their central doctrines included protection of one's life as a chief value, respecting one's spontaneous inclinations, and avoiding the attractions of external objects that could damage life. Within these arguments the body and its various parts figured as markers of the supreme value placed on life and self.

In the same period the self-cultivation described in the "Nei ye" also made the body central to its concerns. Correct physical placement of the body was the first step in the mental disciplines demanded of its devotees. These mental disciplines included a rigorous focus on establishing the mind as the center of the body and the body in turn as the center of the world. The successful execution of the program of self-cultivation resulted in a perfected body marked by supple muscles and glowing skin. The influence of this body in turn was projected to the edges of the world. Like the Yangists, the authors of this text insisted on the necessity of avoiding the sensual spell cast by external objects; yielding to the desire for such objects granted them effective possession of the mind and body.

The *ru* tradition made the body central in its insistence on the importance of rites. In accounts of rituals, and the masters who exemplified their highest forms, the placement and movement of the body became a topic of central concern and careful attention. While attacking the philosophy of the Yangists, the *Mencius* also adopted its practice of making life and the body the measures of highest values, but the *Mencius* used these markers to assert the value of moral virtues. The text also adopted the "Nei ye'"s account of the body's vast energies that could potentially reach the edges of the earth, but as in its critique of the Yangists it moralized this idea by insisting that these energies derived from virtues. Strikingly, however, it insisted that these virtues were parts of the physical body in the same manner as limbs.

Another *ru* text, the *Zuo zhuan*, developed the idea that the perfection of the body is central to ritual. It includes stories in which ritual failings foretold imminent death as well as those in which bodily weaknesses explained ritual failings. One story linked new medical theories based on bodily energetics to an etiology of disease based on ritual failures and the social breakdowns that these engendered. The *Zuo zhuan* also challenged the *Mencius* by arguing that moral intent was ultimately derived from physical energies, so that correctly channeling these energies in ritual was prior to and determinative of the development of virtues. This same idea also figured in the concluding passage to one of the texts recently discovered at Guodian.

A discourse on the body in the late Warring States emerged from these foundational texts. It featured at least two major characteristics that recur at all levels of spatial organization. First, it insisted that the body was a composite of diverse and sometimes antagonistic substances. Some programs for the perfection of the body argued for the accumulation of some of these substances and the expulsion of others. Alternative programs insisted on holding the disparate elements together for as long as possible. Second, diverse intellectual traditions argued that the body was not itself an autonomous entity but rather an element of a larger whole. While it was necessary to maintain boundaries defining the body, these boundaries remained both mobile and permeable. Diverse substances, energies, and signs moved outward from the body, or inward from the larger world. Through this flow back and forth, the interface between body and world became an extended zone of progressively radiating influences. In this model the interface between the body and the world consequently became particularly important, and much attention was devoted to such features as skin, face, shadow, hair, and costume.

In the discourse on the divisions of the body, the most important models were the body as state and the body as cosmos. The former dealt primarily with relations between the heart/mind that played the role of ruler and the other organs. The most important of these were the sense organs, which were identified by a graph that also meant "officials." Most texts from the late Warring States and early imperial periods inherited ideas about the senses that had been developed in the fourth century B.C. Senses naturally desired to seize external objects that gratified them, and consequently they were prone to be trapped by the external world. The mind alone could restrain this tendency and thus preserve the integrity of the body. Consequently, the mind and the senses engaged in a constant struggle for mastery that determined the health of the individual and the ability to command the loyalty of others.

In the second model of internal division the body was a fusion of the energies of Heaven and Earth. The former were more refined, the latter coarser and more substantial. Some traditions of self-cultivation argued that one had to draw in new and more refined energies while expelling old and crude ones. Others developed the idea that death and decay derived from the yin energies of the earth. One either had to eliminate such energies by not eating grain, or to supplement them to counteract their tendency to rot away and perish. Other traditions, represented in the medical literature and accounts of funerary practice, argued that the body had been formed by the progressive accumulation of a gamut of energetic substances. Dying consisted of gradually stripping these away until nothing remained but the physical form. Writers in this tradition emphasized holding together the opposed substances for as long as possible, first to preserve life and then to keep the dead at peace in the tomb. Within this discourse the skeleton, or the "bone and flesh," was the coarsest and hence most enduring substance. As such, it came to define what endured in the tomb, and what was physically shared by kin.

The body as part of a larger whole figured in the discourse on "winds" and "breath/energy [qi]." In this model, outer world and human body shared dynamic energies that on the outside formed wind and on the inside breath or its vital energy. These two constituted a single system in which winds became a major source of disease if they were able to penetrate a body that was lacking in internal breath/energies. Such invasions took place at the skin, and the body was particularly susceptible to them when the pores were opened through exertion and sweating. While such diseases began at the surface, they progressively moved deeper into the body and, in the process of doing so, became ever more serious until they reached the bones and became mortal. At the same time the internal energies moved within the body, but their condition was known through manifestations at the surface in pulses and complexion. Major elements of therapy in turn were conducted at the surface in the form of moxibustion and acupuncture. The latter, however, like the winds operated within an extended transitional zone defined by progressive deepening, so the depth of needling was discussed at length in the medical traditions.

The focus on the body's interface with the outside world also manifested itself in physiognomy, the belief that a person's character and destiny were determined by the shape of the body, especially the face. This technique was widely practiced in Warring States and early imperial China, where it was applied to both animals and men. It was patronized by the political elite, and even incorporated into such state practices as the selection of heirs and the dynastic transitions of the Age of Disunion. As a correlate to the idea that destiny was determined by exterior form, exponents of the traditions of self-cultivation argued that destiny, above all longevity, could be altered through the transformation of the body. This idea was criticized in the first century A.D. by Wang Chong, but he still accepted that destiny was determined by exterior form, and that the limited changes of that form in the aging process extended life.

Another form of interface between body and world was the shadow. The Zhuangzi described this as the human version of the shell of cicadas or the skin of snakes, a substanceless copy of external form that had adhered to the body but could separate from it. One example of such separation was becoming an immortal, for Han and later texts state that immortals lost their shadows. Similarly, the shadow and the body's spirit with which it was associated could be lost through violation of the taboo against climbing on roofs at the peak of summer in the fifth month. This taboo derived from the belief that this period witnessed a struggle between the yin and yang energies that together formed the body, and perhaps by links with the practice of climbing on the roof to ceremonially call back a departed spirit. Finally, the shadow also figured as the visual manifestation of the body's energies in the belief that children sired by extremely old men would have no shadows.

The final aspects of the body's interface with the greater world were hair and clothing. Both were bodily extensions whose patterns distinguished people according to culture, gender, age, status, and rank. Hair was particularly important in this regard, because in growing from the head or skull it was a direct extension of the *hun* spirit energies. Energies generated by strong emotions, particularly rage, came out through the hair and caused it to stand on end. Because of the violence and passions marked by loose hair, its binding was crucial to rituals that marked the transition to adulthood of both men and women. As a correlate of this, unbound hair came to be a hallmark of barbarians, madmen, and ghosts.

Clothing similarly marked the transition between a state of savagery, when people had worn the skin of animals, and that of civilization, where they decked themselves in what several texts described as artificial versions of the coverings of birds and animals. More significantly, the body as depicted in Chinese art was almost invariably a clothed body. This, as several scholars have noted, reflects the fact that the body in early China, and indeed in all of Chinese history, was a social object. Its truth was not revealed in stripping away the costume to reveal the naked body beneath, for the naked body was not the true nature of man. Nudity demonstrated the unaccommodated condition in which men had lived as animals, and the return to which was a sign of social collapse in which people ceased to be human. As part of a society, a necessary condition of being human, one had to be clothed, for clothes generated or marked the diverse roles that made up the social order. Only in suitable attire marking social position, or status in the kin group distinguished by categories of mourning garments, did isolated people find their humanity within the broader order formed by the family and the state.

CHAPTER TWO

THE HOUSEHOLD

Bodies were in turn organized into "households" or "families" (*hu* 戶 or *jia* 家). The "family" as a cross-cultural unit has been the subject of much discussion in contemporary social thought, and most theories have focused on shared residence, kin ties, economic cooperation, and biological and social reproduction.[1] Despite variations in definition, most scholars agree that a "family" in different cultures remains a group of co-residential kin who work to accumulate cultural and material resources that they will transmit to the children they produce.

The themes of the evolving structure and role of the family in early China merit their own extended treatment but here only certain aspects will be discussed. This book deals with the levels of spatial organization, and thus the aspects of shared residence and the structure of the household take precedence. In fact, these were fundamental to early Chinese accounts of the family. However, other activities that defined the family—most notably its roles in reproduction and education, in the social division of labor, and in forming larger kin structures—will also be examined. As in the case of the body, we will see that early Chinese thought about the household emphasized its internal divisions and its character as a fragment of larger wholes. The former issue appears in the division between men and women. As for the latter, scholars and agents of the state described the household as an isolated unit that had to be incorporated within larger structures for the sake of its survival and to create a proper familial order. Apologists for the state order argued that families could obtain material subsistence and security only within a polity, while classicist scholars and members of the more powerful families saw the household as part of a larger kin order defined by the patriline.

Insistence on the household's dependence grew directly out of the history of the Warring States period. This era was defined by the destruction of the old nobility, whose power had been based in large, autarkic estates that included land and peasants, and the recreation of the state on the basis of service and labor provided by individual peasant households.[2] The destruction of the economic base of the large households that provided all their own needs, the division of the population into nuclear households, and the reincorporation of these households into the state defined the new political order. The household as a dependent fragment of a larger whole was thus a fundamental presupposition of the political and economic orders that emerged in the Warring States and culminated in the early empires.

However, the relation of the household to these encompassing units entailed basic contradictions. The state, formed by the ruler and his officials, and the patriline, formed by generations of fathers to sons, were male constructs. The household, in contrast, was built around the conjugal couple. The authority of women, particularly mothers, within the household was for advocates of state and lineage a scandalous fact that was denied or passed over in silence. Nevertheless, both stories and a few legal documents from the period prove the reality of female influence within the household. Moreover, the physical structure of the elite Chinese house, the spatial distribution of power within it, and the broader imagery of spatially defined power produced the curious phenomenon in which the place of women and the place of authority converged. Indeed, this hidden reality of female power defined the history of the ruling house and the imperial institution of the period, and played a fundamental role in the collapse of the dynasty. Thus, the tension between the structure of the household and the structure of the state and lineage that attempted to encompass it produced one of the fundamental fault lines of early Chinese society.

HOUSEHOLDS AS POLITICAL UNITS

While we have no statutes or records on family organization prior to the Qin and Han, scattered remarks in earlier sources provide evidence about the organization of households. The key reality of the earlier period is the division of households into those of nobles and commoners. Archaeological and textual evidence regarding commoners' dwellings will be discussed later. As to their makeup, there are only scattered references in the *Shi jing (Classic of Odes)*. One *topos* that provides evidence is the theme of parting from one's family. Several poems depict an individual leaving home, frequently a woman going off to be married, but also women eloping and men leaving on military duty. Some list the individuals whom the absentee will miss, usually the father, mother, and brothers; and in one case only the brothers.[3] While it is difficult to assign a social status to the characters, in one song of separation due to military service the speaker laments that since he will be away and cannot plant millet, his parents will have no one on whom to rely and thus nothing to eat.[4] This character is clearly from a modest household, certainly not a member of the high nobility who had fields worked by servile labor. The song "Seventh Month," which provides the earliest version of an agricultural calendar in China, also depicts peasant households composed only of parents and children.[5] Given these scattered remarks, the tiny size of the few excavated peasant homes from the period, and the structure of peasant households in subsequent centuries, it is likely that in the Zhou period commoner families consisted of a nuclear family of two parents and their children.

Evidence regarding elite households indicates that they were also based on a nuclear family, but that this formed the core of a larger whole. Two poems describing agricultural labor depict the lord bringing food to laborers in the field, and in both cases he is accompanied by his wife and children.[6] While exact repetition suggests that this was a fixed formula, its existence strengthens the assumption that the nuclear family was regarded as the typical unit. The fact that *all* the songs of separation cited also depict a nuclear family supports the theory that the nobility likewise lived with their parents or their wives. Several songs about feasts show that the brothers of the head of the household lived apart and had to be specially invited along with the uncles of the house.[7] The need to invite brothers to come from a distance, and the ritual distinction sometimes indicated between them and the chief couple, demonstrate that the nobility organized its households around a nuclear family, with brothers forming separate households when they reached maturity or married.

Although all levels of Zhou society were apparently organized around the nuclear unit of a couple and their children, there was a major difference between peasant households and their noble counterparts. For the former, the nuclear family defined the full extent of the household. For nobles, however, the core formed by the master, his wife, and children was surrounded by a network of other families that played a major role in the social and economic life of the household. First, there were the brothers and uncles with their own families. These men not only attended rituals and feasts, but, as described in a poem cited in the previous note, were the closest people in times of death and mourning, and would defend each other from any insult offered by the world at large.

Second, the noble household relied on the labor of dependent families. As described in several poems, men from these families were organized into pairs to collectively sow, weed, and harvest the fields under the direction of the lord or his officers. Part of these fields provided food for the tenant households, while others provisioned the lord. Songs also depict tenant women picking mulberry leaves, feeding silk worms, spinning thread, weaving and dying cloth, and finally producing robes for the lord's family. Others describe herdsmen tending the lord's flocks, as well as men taking fish from his marshes and streams. Finally, songs describe the great hunts conducted by the lord with his noble followers. They state that these hunts complemented the peasants' agricultural toil by producing meat for the lord's table to accompany the produce of his fields.[8] Poems also describe how the choicest produce of the land, the flawless animals from the flocks, and even booty from the hunts were sacrificed to the lord's ancestors to secure their blessings and thereby guarantee future prosperity.

This account of the workings of the lord's household reveals that while his nuclear family formed its core, and his brothers and uncles the most immediate allies, it was a complete community designed for economic autarky and de facto political autonomy. Producing its own foodstuffs and clothing, building its own houses, celebrating its own feasts, offering sacrifice to its own ancestors, hunting, and potentially even engaging in war, the noble household depicted in the *Shi jing* resembled the *oikos* of the Homeric poems. Based on the unfree labor of its tenants or serfs, as well as the "horizontal" division of labor by gender, this extended household secured both power and a degree of leisure for its masters, and established the noble house as a lesser replica of the Zhou ruler's court.[9]

The noble household's role as the center of an autonomous realm, as much a unit of politics as of kinship, distinguished it from both the small, nuclear families of its own workers and the similar peasant households of Warring States and early imperial China.[10] The state in these later periods had been built through destroying the nobility, and consequently both the institution and the conception of the later household aimed to prevent kin-based structures from forming an autonomous, political realm. Both laws and philosophical thought about the family during this period focused on the theme of the family as a dependent fragment of larger wholes in the spheres of economy and kinship.

The extended, autonomous households of the *Shi jing* still appear in the fourth-century B.C. *Zuo zhuan*. Although compiled in the Warring States period, it shows clear traces of a world organized around the warrior nobility, including the extended household as political unit. This figures in the use of the terms *jia* 家 and *shi* 室. Both originally referred to a dwelling, and during the Qin and Han periods they indicated the basic residential, kin unit. In the *Zuo zhuan*, however, they also refer to the extended households of the leading nobles, including their lands and dependent followers.

The idea that *jia* and *shi* referred to large, political units that were reduced versions of a city-state is articulated in the *Zuo zhuan's* account of the process of subinfeudation. "The Son of Heaven establishes city-states, the feudal lords establish 'households [*jia* 家]', and the hereditary officials establish 'subsidiary households [*ce shi* 側室]'."[11] *Jia* and *shi* were elements in the Zhou lineage system in which each level of political/kin unit (e.g., the king's realm or the nobles' states) passed from father to heir, while the other brothers were enfeoffed in subsidiary units that were reduced replicas of the higher ones. Just as the nobles' states were reduced replicas of the king's realm—each with their own cities, armies, and sacrifices—so the *jia* of hereditary officials were reduced replicas of the states, and the *shi* of "household minister/servants [*jia chen* 家臣]" reduced versions of the *jia*. The units in which noble kin resided each enjoyed the attributes of a small state, with lands worked by tenants and the ability to mobilize their own troops.

The fact that the noble "household" was a political organization is demonstrated in usages and anecdotes throughout the *Zuo zhuan*. Thus, the political realm is named "city-states and households [*guo jia* 國家]." This phrase, which came to mean "state" and then "nation-state," described the

polity as a combination of the realms of the feudal lords [*guo*] and those of
the hereditary ministers [*jia*]. Many passages treat *guo* and *jia* in parallel, either
as opponents in civil strife or as complementary units.[12] In some stories the
jia of leading ministerial houses engage in warfare or alliance with each other
and the states of the feudal lords. These *jia* also had their own ministers and
their "household masses [*jia zhong* 家眾]" who like the "inhabitants of the
capital [*guo ren* 國人]" were consulted in times of crisis and mobilized for
combat. Because the nobility's *jia* were political groupings, marriage was a
political decision whose stages were guided by an elaborate protocol involving household officials of specified ranks.[13] The *Mencius* shows the political
role of noble households in its opening argument that it would be the minister with a thousand chariots who destroyed a lord with ten thousand, or the
minister with one hundred who destroyed the lord with a thousand. Such
hereditary nobles, the text argued, would rebel against their ruler to benefit
their own households (*jia*).[14] Other texts worry that nobles' concern for their
households would lead them to ignore their duties towards the ruler.[15] Indeed
most of the major Warring States were formed around such ministerial houses.

While the *Zuo zhuan* applies the term *jia* most frequently to the hereditary officials' politicized households, it also referred to the individual household formed by the married couple, and to the nuclear households of the
peasants. Thus, the three commentaries to the *Spring and Autumn Annals* stipulated that within the *jia* a daughter should obey her father, or that all women
should have a *jia*, that is, a marriage.[16] Moreover, a few passages tell of peasant
households being granted to nobles for their meritorious achievements, or
being transferred from one state to another as tribute. One story tells of five
hundred households being presented in this way, and how the rulers planned
to physically resettle them in a new region.[17] These are important because
they show that the usage of the term *jia* in this period was not wholly distinct from earlier and later usages. A *jia* meant a household, but certain households consisted of nuclear families alone, while others were large political units
with dependent families who provided service, as well as officials to administer these families.

The character *shi* 室 which figured earlier as the lowest level of political
household also appears in many stories, but not in the sense suggested. It often
retains its original sense of a "house" or "room" that people construct, enter
into, and inhabit.[18] It also meant a "wife," probably because *shi* in the narrow
sense meant the inner chambers of a house.[19] However, in its political sense
it generally indicated the household of a ruling lineage, either the king or a
feudal lord, in opposition to the ministerial households identified by the word
jia. Thus, *shi* frequently follows the adjectives "royal [*wang* 王]," "Zhou [周],"
or "lord's [*gong* 公]," but never an adjective indicating a lower level of the
nobility.[20] Some texts speak of the *jia* or *zu* of hereditary officials bringing
either disorder or stability to the *shi* of the king or the feudal lords.[21] These
shi, like the *jia* of the hereditary officials, included large properties and many
people. They had officials to administer them.[22] Both property and people

could be divided up, in some cases by their master to reward his followers, but also when a noble lineage was destroyed. In one case, a man renounced noble status by giving up his *shi* and becoming a simple farmer.[23] The use of *shi* to indicate the lands and dependent followers of a noble also figures in the covenant inscriptions of Houma.[24] The character *shi*, like *jia*, also refers to nuclear, peasant households. This is demonstrated by passages that refer to "villages [*yi* 邑]" composed of ten or a hundred *shi*, or to rewarding nobles by giving them up to one thousand *shi*.[25] These show that *shi* and *jia* were recognized as residential units or households, but in the case of noble families such households included the attached territories and servile populations that provided their economic foundations.

With the decline of the nobility, large autarkic households ceased to characterize the elite. However, from the Warring States into the Han the great household did not vanish but only changed form. Throughout this period, leading officials received noble titles accompanied with incomes paid by the tax revenue from a specified number of households or villages, the so-called feeding towns [*shi yi* 食邑]. These sources of income differed from the earlier noble fiefs in at least two ways. First, the enfeoffed official did not command the towns' populations, but simply received income from them. Administration remained in the hands of state officials. Second, since the towns were only sources of income, enfeoffed officials often did not live on their fiefs and sometimes had no real ties. Thus, Shang Yang's fifteen *shi yi* were divided between two locations, and when he fell from favor he tried to flee elsewhere rather than return to his fief. Only after being rejected by all states did he go to his fief and try to lead followers there in rebellion. As shown in the cases of Shang Yang and Lü Buwei, officials resided in their fief only when stripped of office and forced to retire from the court.[26]

However, one practice *did* preserve the extended household as a form of political power. Political figures in the Warring States and early empires competed to gather large numbers of retainers who dwelt with them. These men were called either "guests [*ke* 客]" or "lodgers [*she ren* 舍人]," indicating that they were unrelated by blood or marriage but lived with their "host."[27] They exemplified the new form of interpersonal tie that defined the Warring States political order, in which the lord granted recognition and sustenance in exchange for service and devotion to the death. The insistence on their status as members of the leader's household shows that this new form of social tie had a strong spatial aspect, where the intimacy of the tie was marked by physical closeness and commensality.[28]

References in the historical sources provide evidence about the social role of the formal, long-term guest. First, the host provided his followers with lodging, food, clothing, chariots, and in some cases even support for their families. In one case the clothing was so rich that emissaries from a foreign state were ashamed of their own attire. Guests served their host as entertainers, spies, collectors of debts, emissaries, go-betweens, assassins, or in any manner that the master saw fit. Guests were formal members of the household, with their names listed on a register that dictated the schedule of their meetings with the host. Some stories indicate that there were multiple lodging places for the guests, with each building ranked according to its quality. Other stories suggest that guests dwelt in the same building as their host. It is likely that such arrangements varied from household to household.

At banquets, resident guests dined together with the master's blood kin. In two cases guests were even allowed to have regular contact with the ladies of the household. A story from the late Qin tells how guests arranged the marriage of the daughter of the house after her father's death. Guests not only often dwelt in the master's house and regularly interacted with members of his household, but also participated in family rituals. According to the *Li ji*, they could represent their master if he were absent when the ruler visited. Similarly parables of rivalry for the lord's favor between his guests and his women testify to the status of the former as members of the household.[29] The high status of guests is further shown by the use of the term *she* to describe both their lodgings and the dwellings of the master, or high-class buildings as opposed to the huts of peasants. Even in exceptional cases where *she* referred to a poor dwelling, it still indicated the house occupied by the master and his family.[30] The importance of the relationship, and the high status of the guests, is demonstrated by the fact that several texts tell of ritual rules dictating how a host should treat his resident guests.[31]

The number of guests displayed the wealth and status of the host. The most famous collectors of guests, the Four Princes, were each said to have had 3,000 followers. The number is formulaic, but it suggests an order of magnitude. Even lesser officials were said to have as a many as a thousand. One text states that a prince's retainers were so numerous that the income from his fief could not maintain them, so he resorted to moneylending. Another states that a master disbursed all his household's wealth to entertain his guests. The *Han Feizi*, *Guanzi*, and *Shi ji* indicate that guests acted as private armies and inspired fear of the "host" both in rival states and their own rulers.[32] As the *Han Feizi* argues, the practice of gathering guests led rulers and officials to compete to attract the same people.[33] Thus, this new form of great household, like the earlier type, could pose a critical challenge to the ruler.

Having numerous guests became a hallmark of status and power, as demonstrated by the competition of leading political figures to attract them. Lü Buwei exalted a Qin prince held hostage in Zhao by giving him money to "establish ties with guests," for only by having retainers could he be taken seriously by the political figures of his day. Later, when Lü Buwei became chief minister in Qin, he likewise felt it essential for his state's prestige to surpass the Four Princes in attracting guests.[34] The *Han Feizi* tells how a man argued that he could pass himself off as a "prince of one thousand chariots" if a particularly good-looking and well-mannered man pretended to be his high retainer.[35]

Attracting guests even became a law of nature. When Prince Mengchang fell from power, he was abandoned by all but one of his guests. Upon regaining authority, he vowed to spit in the faces of any former guest who showed himself. The sole loyal retainer remonstrated with him:

> "Things have that which inevitably arrives, and affairs that which is invariably so. Do you recognize this?" Prince Mengchang said, "I am stupid and do not know what you mean." "Everything living must die; this is what inevitably arrives. The rich and noble have many serve them, while the poor and humble have few friends; this is what is invariably so. Have you alone not seen men hurrying to the market? At dawn they bump shoulders fighting to get in the gate, but after dusk when they pass by the market they turn away and pay no heed. It is not that they love the morning and hate the evening, but that the things that they desire are no longer there. When you lost your position all your guests departed. This does not merit resenting these gentlemen and vainly cutting off guests' route of access. I request that you treat the guests as before."[36]

Guests gathering around men of influence is as inevitable as the coming of death.

The practice of gathering guests continued on a significant scale through the Qin and into the Western Han. The Han founder's chief followers surrounded themselves with retainers. Even wealthy merchants, such as Sima Xiangru's father-in-law, assembled many guests, and Sima Xiangru's own ability to attract guests was used to demonstrate his social importance. Leading political figures in the time of Emperor Wu still recruited guests, such as the emperor's uncle Liu An, who gathered large numbers of scholarly retainers. Powerful families and their guests became targets for the "cruel clerks" charged by Emperor Wu to destroy potential local challengers to his power. Likewise the criminal "swordsmen" or "bravoes [xia 俠]" gained status and power through gathering followers, and sometimes maintaining large numbers in their households.

Even high officials at court, and several of the cruel clerks themselves, sought status and power through assembling guests in their households. Indeed, writers specially note men who did *not* gather guests, suggesting that the practice was nearly universal. One such man without guests gathered more than a hundred followers who were described as "disciples." Thus, the pattern established in the Warring States, in which powerful families marked their status or extended their power by filling large households with retainers, continued through the Qin and well into the first centuries of Han rule.[37] This explains why the *Han Feizi*, begun under the First Emperor and finished during the early Han, still follows the fourth-century B.C. *Mencius* in arguing that the chief threat to the ruler comes from overly powerful families within his own state.[38]

Remarks about the size and makeup of peasant households in pre-imperial China are rare. Household registers are mentioned in surviving sources, but no examples have been found.[39] References in philosophical or divinatory texts of the period hint at the size of the typical peasant household, but these are often quite vague. Thus, the *Yi jing* states: "If the father acts as a father, a son as a son, an elder brother as an elder brother, a younger brother as a younger brother, a husband as a husband, and a wife as a wife, then the Way of the family is correct."[40] Here a family consists of father, mother, siblings, husband, and wife. Similar lists appear in other texts from the period.[41] In addition to not mentioning daughters, this passage also provides no information about the actual size of a typical family. All the roles listed would exist in a nuclear family of two parents and two sons, in a "stem family" where elderly parents lived with a married son and his children, or in a joint family with several married sons living with their parents. However, none of these lists, nor the *Lun yu*, mention the relation of grandfather to grandson or of nephew to uncle. Such relations would have been important in a stem or joint family. This suggests that the typical family imagined by Warring States scholars was a nuclear family.

The sole possible exception is the *Mencius*, which is the only surviving Warring States text that explicitly states the size of a typical peasant household. In one passage it says: "If you do not deprive the farm's hundred *mu* of labor in the agricultural seasons, then a family of eight mouths will not go hungry."[42] Another passage repeats the number "eight," while a passage that is otherwise identical to the one previously quoted refers to a "household of a few [*shu* 數] mouths." This second figure suggests a nuclear family.[43] Even the higher figure "eight" could refer to a nuclear family, since the *Han Feizi* states that five children in a family would not be considered exceptionally numerous.[44]

However, an earlier reference to people of seventy in the household suggests a stem family, in which elderly parents were living with a married son. Moreover, several passages refer to men supporting their parents, and one indicates that they did this while caring for their children: "[The enlightened ruler] must allow them to above have enough to serve their parents and below to have enough to feed their wives and children." Another passage depicts a family composed of the adult male's father and mother, some of his siblings, and his wife and children.[45] Thus, it seems that the authors of the *Mencius* regarded the stem family as the social ideal, if not always the reality, and a "family of eight mouths" probably refers to this.

The nuclear family and the stem family were not alternatives, however, but simply two points in a cycle. When parents reached an age at which they were less fit for labor but had adult sons, then they lived with one married son and perhaps his unmarried siblings. The death of the parents or quarrels between siblings resulted in a simple nuclear household. Given the relatively shorter lifespan of people and the frequency of sibling divisions (see later), the stem family would have existed in a limited number of cases for relatively brief periods of time. The predominant form would have remained the nuclear family. This fact is hinted at in yet another passage from the *Mencius*: "The true gentleman has three joys, and being king of the world is not one of them. For his parents to both be alive and his brothers to have no quarrels is the first joy."[46] To have living parents and brothers on good terms (i.e., a stem or joint family) was rare enough to count as the highest joy of the gentleman and more valuable than world kingship.

Not only were the nuclear and stem households simply two stages in the developmental cycle of a family, but they were also both tiny in comparison with those of the nobility. This is crucial, because the shift from the Zhou city-states to the macrostates and then to the empire was based on the progressive destruction of the nobility and their large, autarkic households. The latter, as sketched earlier, had been a basic unit of the political structure, a reduced form of the ruling lineage that served as a foundation of the Zhou order. This order was a version of Durkheim's "mechanical solidarity" based on likeness not of individuals but of the noble households.[47] Each city-state and fief of the Zhou replicated a common model, spread across the countryside to impose order on conquered territory. Thus, each noble household contained all the necessary elements of power within itself, including the land and servile labor that provided its economic foundations.

The ideal of autarky vanished as the nobility was incorporated into the state order and became dependent on tax revenue. Great households remained lesser replicas of the polity only by gathering retainers in a private version of the recruitment that created the new states. Like the staffs of the territorial states, their hundreds or thousands of followers were paid out of tax revenues collected by the emergent bureaucracies. However, their economic reliance on the taxation power of the state meant that the great families of the Warring States were increasingly creatures of the government. They would more accurately be described as the highest agents and beneficiaries of the central power than as semi-independent replicas of the central court.

In contrast with these great, political households, the nuclear or stem households of peasants under the Zhou were tiny units incorporated into a larger order by which they were controlled and on which they were dependent. They were dependent not only for security and public order, but even for agricultural production, which entailed substantial collective efforts. In the course of the Warring States, new tools and methods of water control increased productivity to the extent that individual households became the basic unit of economic production. However, as they detached from collective village labor, they were incorporated into new networks of exchange to obtain the tools that made possible their productivity. Consequently, both early philosophical writings and ritual texts on kin structure insisted that the residential household was a fragment of a larger whole. They were elements of economic networks of exchange, of the political order that gave them security in exchange for service, and of an encompassing kin structure formed by the patriline. But in all these arguments it was crucial that households could only be understood, and only survive, as parts of a greater whole.

HOUSEHOLDS AS RESIDENTIAL UNITS

These arguments that the household was a fragment of a larger whole presuppose knowledge of the scale and organization of the peasant family. The secondary literature on this subject employs the aforementioned categories of nuclear families, stem families, and multiple families or joint households (parents with several married sons, their spouses, and their children).[48] Only in the Qin and Han do we find evidence for detailed analysis of the structure of these families at the lower level of society. Important evidence derives from law. All scholars agree that typical forms of the Han household were directly inherited from the preceding Warring States period, and above all from the Qin pattern. In his reforms in the middle of the fourth century B.C., Shang Yang had levied double taxes on households in which sons lived with their fathers, and banned them from sharing a room. According to Jia Yi, this resulted in rich families regularly dividing their property and poor families sending out their sons as bond servants or hired labor. It had supposedly grown so bad that children treated their personal affects and tools as completely private property and regarded sharing them with their parents as an act of great kindness.[49] More valuable as evidence of actual practice is the following passage from the legal texts found at Shuihudi: "When someone's slave or slave woman robs their master's father or mother, is this 'robbing one's master', or is it not? If they [the parents] are household members [*tong ju zhe* 同居者, 'those who dwell together'], then it is 'robbing one's master'. If they are not household members, then it is not 'robbing one's master'."[50] This passage assumes that the division of households was common, although not universal. Whether fathers and sons dwelt together must be established in each case. The *Jin shu* states that the law penalizing children living with parents remained in force until the Wei dynasty—that is, throughout the entire period of the Han. It describes the law as a "Qin-Han" regulation.[51] Thus, throughout the Qin and Han dynasties the nuclear household was the legally proper form, but it was not universal.

Evidence for the predominance of the nuclear family goes beyond normative patterns indicated in terminology. First, the legal texts include examples either drawn from life or regarded as typical of the problems that an official would face. Thirty-two cases mention family members. In ninety percent of the cases the members mentioned would form a simple nuclear family, and in the rest a stem family. The average size of the families described was four people. Also significant is the fact that no cases deal with relations between brothers. One case involved the adoption of a younger brother's son who came to dwell with the family of his older brother, which indicates that the two brothers lived apart.[52] However, these examples are not exhaustive lists of households, for they cite only those involved in the cases. Only three cases list all household members, and these indicate total numbers of five, six, and ten. The family of five consists of the father, mother, and three children.

That of six includes the father, the mother, an unmarried adult daughter, a son who was still a minor, and two slaves. The family of ten included the parents and eight children.[53] While this is only anecdotal evidence, it is of interest that even the household of ten people consisted of nothing more than a nuclear family.

Another text from the same tomb, a chronicle of the life and career of the tomb's occupant along with major events of his day, indicates that he and his father each had three sons.[54] These families would thus have consisted of five people, a figure posited as typical in Qin and Han texts. However, the actual households would have been greater if they contained slaves or servants.

An almanac discovered in this tomb listed appropriate days for dividing property:

> This is what is called gen shan [艮 山]. [Gen is the name of the trigram whose image is "mountain" and of the hexagram formed by the duplication of this trigram.] It is the day of Yu's departure [to combat the flood]. . . . On this "departure day" it is not proper to marry out one's daughter or to bring in a wife, nor to bring slaves or domestic animals into the household. It is only beneficial for the division of the household.[55]

Thus, dividing property between brothers was a regular practice on a par with marriage or funerals. A Western Han text conventionally called the Yin yang shi ling zhan hou that was found at Yinqueshan also refers to appropriate days for dividing the household.[56] If division of property between brothers was routine, then the nuclear family would have been the most common.

Examples of dividing property between brothers, particularly after their marriages, are also common in the literary record. The early Han scholar Lu Jia divided his movable wealth among five sons, instructed them to each set up a household, and agreed that he would live with them in turn. Other stories treat the division of property as a ritual duty.[57] While only a few cases of brothers living together are recorded, there are more than thirty references in the literary sources and in stone inscriptions to division of the household while the father was still alive (sheng fen 生分). Such acts appear in all regions of the empire, and roughly in ratio to the distribution of the population.[58] Since such division during the father's life was less common than at his death, division of property and households between brothers was clearly the predominant practice in the period.

Cases where property was held in common for more than two generations (i.e., parents, adult children, and grandchildren living together) are cited as morally exemplary. This shows that they were unusual, and only a few examples are preserved in writings from the Eastern Han. In one case brothers do not divide their property in order to "improve local customs."[59] This indicates that division was conventional where they lived, and their own action was intended to introduce a pattern closer to that prescribed in ritual texts. In other cases families did not divide property simply because they were too poor to divide their land any further. This recalls the statement by Jia Yi that in Qin wealthy families divided property while poor ones sent out their sons as laborers. Writing in the late first century A.D, Wang Chong states as a self-evident maxim that it was the poor who did not divide property.[60] Thus, for brothers to stay together required either a heroic commitment to classicist morality or a degree of poverty such that the option of dividing land did not exist.[61]

The earliest known will in China, discovered in a Han tomb datable to A.D. 5, provides further evidence on the division of property among brothers.[62] First, it suggests that women had no right to inherit land. This will be discussed further in the next section. Second, because local officials were cited as witnesses to the will, it indicates that the state regularly participated in the generational transfer and division of property in order to guarantee that state registers were kept current. Third, it indicates that while division between brothers at the death of the father was conventional, the amount of land and the legal conditions under which it was held varied depending on the status of each child within the household, a status indicated by the Chinese term *jia ci* 家次 "familial sequence."

The principle of distributing property among family members according to a ranking had been established at least as early as the reforms of Shang Yang.[63] In the case of the Han will, the ranking was based on the age and status of the father. The second and third fathers in this household had been uxorilocal husbands, men who moved into their wife's household to preserve her property intact. Since Qin times such men had been of low status, and this apparently affected the position of their offspring.[64] Sons of the first father received property by right and, although the eldest son seems to have inherited a special position as household head, it is not clear that he received a larger share of land.[65] On the other hand, the single son in the will by a later, uxorilocal father had left the family at an early age, resumed the surname of his father's family, and had no right to a share of land. Moreover, he had been arrested for wounding someone and was performing penal labor when the will was written. Apparently out of a feeling of family responsibility, the will assigns two parcels of land to this "outsider" son, after being held in trust for one agricultural season by two of the daughters. However, he was not allowed to sell the land, which thus remained part of the holdings of the family proper.

Evidence from the late Warring States through the early Han indicates that the average size of the household was five or six people. A Western Han document from Yinqueshan divides families into three grades, with family size depending on grade. Those in the first grade contained seven people, those in the second six, and those in the third five.[66] While the text does not specify the criterion used to grade the households, the *Zhou li* offers an identical model based on the quality of land owned.

Then he equalizes the fields in order to examine the people and completely know their number. A household on top quality land will have seven people, of whom three could provide service. A household on middle quality land will have six people, of whom five people from every two households could provide service. A household on low quality land will have five people, of whom two could provide service.[67]

Here the quality of the land is assessed and then allocated to families depending on their size and their consequent need for food. While it is uncertain that the "Shou fa" document employed the same system, the exact correspondence of the grades and the numbers in the household is striking. At any rate, both texts suggest that the typical household was a nuclear family, with families on more productive land being able to support more children.

Several early texts refer to hypothetical families with as many as five offspring. However, such examples figure in arguments on the problem of rapid population growth and the difficulty that parents experienced in supervising all the children in such a large household.[68] This indicates that the authors considered five children to be a substantial, indeed an excessive, number. They clearly regarded two or three children as reasonable, which would give an average size of five or six people in a household.

Several Han texts indeed cite a family of five as typical. Ban Gu quotes a supposed fragment from Li Kui's middle Warring States work on the fiscal bases of the state. This posits the typical household as five people working one hundred *mu* of land. Chao Cuo's early Western Han account of the typical peasant family similarly describes a household of five people owning one hundred *mu* of land.[69] Some Han writers adopt the figure of five people as a normal household, but argue that this included an older father and mother, one son and his wife, and one grandson.[70] However, Chao Cuo explicitly cites the burden of caring for children but says nothing of caring for parents. Moreover, an early version of a "one-child policy" as posited here is virtually inconceivable, so this second model is a case of Han classicists attempting to accommodate the standard figure of five people per household with the ideal of dutiful sons caring for elderly parents. This indicates that the idea of the five-person family was so widely accepted that even those who would have desired an ideal family of eight, including aged parents as articulated in the *Mencius*, were obliged to accept the lower figure.

Evidence on the form and size of commoner households in the Western Han also comes from administrative documents discovered at the northwestern frontier post at Juyan. Sixteen strips in Lao Gan's early collection list family members. Nine of these included only two parents and unmarried children, five included unmarried siblings living with a married couple, and in three cases a son still lived with his parents. One family included a man, his mother, and two unmarried younger brothers. Another consisted of a married couple, their elder son and his wife, an unmarried younger son, and a daughter.[71] M. C. Lai collected strips on a further twenty-two families, which follow the pattern demonstrated by Lao Gan. Not a single family was more than two generations, and most included only three or four people. Although one family included six people and one ten, the average size is even lower than Chao Cuo's model. This smaller size may reflect the dangers and difficulties of life at the frontier, but the structure of the households follows the pattern found elsewhere.

The so-called Granary Record of Zhengli again indicates that even in the interior the standard household was a nuclear family of around five people. This document, found among the bamboo slips excavated at Fenghuangshan in Hubei, records seed loans from the government to farmers in the town of Zhengli. It lists the household head, the number of members in the household, and the amount of farmland that they owned.[72] There are twenty-five families listed on the strips. One was a single person, one had two members, six had three, five had four, two had five, seven had six, two had seven, and one had eight. Thus, the mean household size was 4.6, and the median was four. While ten of the households had more than the "typical" five members, virtually all of these had only six.

However, one point in this document suggests a different picture than the Han data discussed so far. It lists how many people in the household were capable of engaging in agricultural labor (*neng tian* 能田), and fifteen of the twenty-five households had three or four people in this category. It is unclear whether women were included in this category, but since one household of two people and one of three list all members as *neng tian* it is likely that they were. Nevertheless, the document shows that in this town the majority of households had at least one adult son working with the parents, and in many cases two or three. One explanation for this anomaly is that the average landholding is only twenty-five *mu*, and only a couple households have more than thirty. If one hundred *mu* was considered normal, and as described by Chao Cuo sufficient only for minimal subsistence for a family of five, then the families from Zhengli were quite poor, and the area was characterized by a high population density. Indeed it is probably because they were poor that they received seed loans from the state. As previously noted, Han authors stated that poor families could not divide property because their plots of land were already too small. This would explain the large number of extended households on this list.

These remarks by Han writers and evidence from administrative documents find support in the census data preserved in the *Han shu*. Since this provides figures for the number of households and the number of people, it allows calculation of average household size. For the two surviving empire-wide censuses from A.D. 2 and A.D. 140, the average household sizes are 4.87 and 5.07, respectively. Partial returns from ten other years between A.D. 57 and A.D. 157 show average size varying between a low of 4.91 and a high of 5.82. There is no long-term trend over the course of this century and a half, and the average always remains around the figure of five.[73] The slight upward shift in the Eastern Han could be accounted for by either the tendency of wealthy families to have more slaves and servants, or perhaps a greater prosperity that allowed for a modest increment in the average number of children per household. In any case, the change is too small to suggest any structural change in family organization or a significant modification of values and behavior. This confirms that throughout the four centuries of Han rule the most common form of household was a small nuclear family of only a handful of people, with a few extended families including elderly parents or unmarried siblings. The three-generation household, like those during the Tang who held collective property for five or six generations, was a normative ideal for many scholars, but an exceptional practice in reality.[74]

However, this conclusion must be modified. First, the previous discussion treats the household as a kinship group, but Chinese sources regularly defined *jia*, *hu*, or *shi* by common residence. Thus, the *Shuo wen jie zi* glosses *jia* as "to reside" or "to dwell [*chu* 處]." Writing around 100 A.D., Xu Shen identifies the *jia* as a *place* where people stay. He offers a similar gloss for *shi*, which is sometimes used interchangeably with *jia* or linked with it in compounds.[75] The fact that the characters have the "roof" signific emphasizes the dwelling, rather than the relation of the inhabitants. Duan Yucai and many modern scholars argue that since the graph is built from "roof" over "pig" it originally indicated a place to rear pigs, with its application to humans being a figurative extension. Xu Shen argues, more convincingly, that the seal form character for "pig (*shi* 豕)" was graphically close to that for "child (*hai* 亥)" and that the latter was originally depicted in the graph *jia*.[76] This would indicate that the term *jia* meant "to dwell" or "dwelling," and referred primarily to a residence including children.

The Qin legal documents from Shuihudi likewise emphasize the dwelling and the fact of co-residence. Thus, passages defining the legally relevant household state:

> Household [*hu*] means those who dwell together [*tong ju* 同居]. They implicate dependents [servants and slaves], but dependents do not implicate the household.

> What is meant by "people of the house [*shi ren* 室人]"? What is meant by "dwelling together"? "Dwelling together" means only those on the household register. "People of the house" means the entire household, all those who would be mutually implicated with a criminal.[77]

These show the existence of a household register that did not include all slaves and servants. While not on the register, the latter were still legally "people of the house" and were implicated in the crimes of their masters. Moreover, as shown in the passage on slaves robbing their master's parents, the legal relation of parents to children and thus the nature of the crime was determined by whether they dwelled together. Other passages that deal with "household/family crimes" indicate that acts in this category include only cases where the concerned parties shared residence. Crimes committed by a son against his father's property counted as crimes of the *jia* only if the two lived together.[78] The fact that the ascription of a crime to a *jia* hinged on residence rather than kinship shows that the Qin government viewed the former rather than the latter as definitive of the "family."

Similarly, a law stipulating that family members were not liable for payment of fines incurred by the household head while in office described these exempted people as "his wife and those who dwell with him [*tong ju*]."[79] *Tong ju* as both a legally significant group and a verb meaning "to dwell together" also figures in Han sources.[80] In a decree issued under Han Emperor Hui a group including the *tong ju* is semantically parallel with the *jia*. Thus, the two terms were regarded as synonymous.

This shows that in Qin-Han law shared residence defined the household, and that the key groups were those who dwelled together. The Tang commentator Yan Shigu argued that servants and slaves were not included under *tong ju*, and most subsequent scholars concur.[81] To the extent that *tong ju* was defined by the household register, in contrast to the more inclusive *shi ren*, this may be correct. However, extracts from Han household records have survived at Juyan, and these list slaves together with wives, children, and siblings.[82]

The identification of the family with shared residence is also suggested by the use of the character *shi* 室. This character in legal usage described all the people who lived in a household, and the same usage figured in ritual texts.[83] Conventionally, it meant a "house" as a physical structure, and could also refer to specific rooms within the house. In this sense it is often employed in compounds with the character *gong* 宮 to mean "palace" or *wu* 屋 to mean an ordinary "house."[84] The definition of the family as a residential unit is shown by the fact that this word was also used as a noun meaning "wife" or a verb meaning "to marry." This usage appeared as early as the *Zuo zhuan*. When Lord Huan of Lu was planning an illicit trip to Qi with the Lady Jiang, an official remonstrated: "A woman has a husband [*jia*] and a man a wife [*shi*]."[85] The *Zuo zhuan* also uses the word *shi* four times meaning "to marry" a man to a woman, and occasionally as a noun meaning "wife." The *Mencius* likewise pairs *jia* and *shi*, with the former meaning marriage for a woman and the latter for a man. The *Li ji* later used the term *shi* for marriage in indicating the proper age and procedure for a man to marry, and during the Han it continued to be used as a verb meaning for a man to marry.[86] This evidence again suggests that common residence was the key to defining a household, with kinship being important but not essential.

HOUSEHOLDS AS UNITS OF LARGER NETWORKS

The fact that in late Warring States and early imperial China the terms for "household" indicated shared residence or the residential building is signifi-

cant because it distinguishes households from kinship units. The latter were
extended networks defined by blood ties, marriage, and mourning obligations.
They formed larger groups of which the household was only a small unit.
Moreover, in terms of the kin structure articulated in lineage networks, the
household was a composite group consisting of full kin, partial kin, and non-
kin. The household was thus not only a fragmentary unit of a larger whole,
but also a unit composed of diverse elements that were divided against each
other.

The key terms for the larger networks of relatives by blood and marriage
are *zu* 族 and *zong* 宗. These indicated major social units as early as the Shang
dynasty. The Shang *zu* dwelt in towns and participated in military campaigns.
The fact that the oracle bone graph for *zu* included both arrows and a banner
suggests that their military function was paramount, but they also appear in
the inscriptions doing work such as clearing new agricultural fields. They seem
to have been linked by kinship, and scholars have argued that the Shang elite
was composed of several hundred *zu* lineages. In ritual contexts the *zu* were
organized as *zong*, a graph that depicts a roof with an altar or ancestral tablets.
In political contexts the groups were described as *shi* 氏, loosely translated as
"clan."[87]

For the Zhou nobles *zu* continued to be the major form of kin organization. The great noble households were called *zu* when referring to them
as kin units. Their destruction in the internecine warfare of the period was
called "partitioning the *zu*" or "destroying the *zu*."[88] In this usage *zu* was
interchangeable with *shi* 室. This common usage, and the senses of diverse
kin terms during this period, is best demonstrated in a discussion by Shu
Xiang of the imminent fall of the ruling house in Jin. After noting that actual
power now resided in the ministerial houses, he argued:

> Jin's ruling lineage [*gong zu* 公族] is finished. I have heard that when
> a ruling house [*gong shi* 公室] declines, the leaves and branches
> formed by kin with a common ancestor [*zong zu* 宗族] are the first
> to fall away. The ruling house follows them. There are eleven line-
> ages who share a common ancestor [*zong shi yi zu* 宗十一族] with
> me and the ruling house, and only the Yangshe clan [*shi* 氏] is
> present.[89]

In the senses of "lineage" or "household," both *zu* and *shi* indicated the total
social unit including land and dependent labor. *Zong* indicated ritual descent
from a common ancestor, as marked by naming the "ancestral temple" *zong
miao* 宗廟. The Zhou nobility was divided into greater and lesser *zong*
depending on the status of the common ancestor to whom they traced their
ancestry. Thus, the aristocratic warriors of Zhou China were organized into
kin associations known as *zu* or *shi*. They worshipped a common male ancestor, and those who traced themselves back to a common ancestor were called
a *zong*. Just as in the Shang, the characters *zu* and *zong* seem to have repre-

sented different aspects of the same groups, so that they appeared as the compound *zong zu* 宗族 in texts as early as the fourth century B.C. The synonym compound *zong shi* 宗氏 also appears, although less frequently.[90]

The macrostates that destroyed the nobility based themselves on service extracted from peasant households that consisted largely of nuclear families. *Zu* and *zong* continued to refer to large networks of kin who shared a common ancestor, but they no longer indicated groups living together on common property and coordinating actions for political ends. Instead they identified networks encompassing numerous individual households that might be separated by considerable distances and have no social contact. Such units were described in ritual texts, but their social reality remains unclear.

The *Er ya* and the *Bo hu tong* define *zong* and *zu* as used in the Han period. In the *Er ya* they form a synonym compound naming one of the four categories of kin terms. "The father's kin group [*dang* 黨] is called the *zong zu*."[91] Here *zong zu* is a compound indicating a specific kin group.[92] This echoes the earlier usage when *zong* and *zu* were two aspects of the same group. In addition to the father's group, here identified as the *zong zu* and defined by descent from a common male ancestor, the other three categories identified by the *Er ya* are the "mother's group," the "wife's group," and the "husband's group." The account of the *zong zu* is the most detailed, and it provides the structure for the other terms. *Zu* appears separately in a set of kin terms identifying all consanguineal kin from the fourth collateral line and beyond.[93] Thus, in this system it indicated a subset of the larger *zong zu*.

The *Bo hu tong* offers a more elaborate discussion of the two terms. It treats them as separate, although they are linked as the title of the section devoted to kin groups:

> What does *zong* [*tsuong] mean? It means "to honor [*zun* *tsuen 尊]." The one who is host [*zhu* 主] to the ancestors is honored by all members of the *zong*. The *Li* says, "When the head of the *zong* sacrifices, all his kin [*zu ren* 族人] wait upon him." . . . The great *zong* [ruler's line] directs the small ones [branch lines], and the small ones direct the collective younger brothers. They link together those who have with those who lack, and this is the means of giving proper order to all the kin [*zu ren*].[94]

Here the *zong* identifies all those with a common ancestor who are united in their service to the sacrificer. However, those united in ritual offerings to the founder are twice described as *zu ren*, indicating that in the Eastern Han *zong* continued to function as the ritual form of *zu*.[95] As for *zu*, the *Bo hu tong* defines it as follows.

> What is *zu* [*dz'uk]? *Zu* means *cou* [*ts'ug 湊] "to gather" or *ju* [*dz'iu 聚] "to assemble." It refers to those who in mutual kindness and love flow together [*liu cou* 流湊]. In life they are close and loving,

and in death mournful and in pain. They have the way of assembling together [*hui ju* 會聚], and so they are called *zu*. The *Shang shu* says, "[Yao] thereby was close with the nine *zu*." Why are there nine *zu*? "Nine [*jiu* 九]" means "to push to the end [*jiu* 究]." From closest to most distant, kindness and love are pushed to the very end. It is said that the father's kin [*zu*] are four categories, the mother's three, and the wife's two.[96]

Here *zu* is defined by the notion of gathering or assembling, so it applies to all those related by ties of ritual obligation and affection. This sense of *zu* as "gathering" or "binding together" is also posited by the *Shuo wen jie zi*, which uses the "arrow" element in the graph to assert that it originally indicated a bundle of arrows.[97] The *Bo hu tong* follows this gloss of *zu* in the broad sense by a more specific definition of the nine *zu*. These are said to include all those related to a given individual as divided into nine categories ranked according to degrees of closeness.

Throughout the late Warring States and the Han, *zong* indicated a group defined by ties to a common ancestor. It is thus a consistent term with a fixed meaning. *Zu*, on the other hand, had a broader range of meanings that could include virtually any kin grouping, from the entire surname group to the individual household. Only the context, or the addition of a modifying term such as the number "nine," indicated the specific sense in a given passage.

In its broadest sense *zu* indicated the social form of the ritual unit *zong*, or all those linked by a common surname. Thus, an anecdote in the *Xin xu* refers to "destroying the *zu* so that there was no longer a surname [*mie zu wu xing* 滅族無姓]." Similarly, Wang Chong stated: "If the eldest man of a shared-surname group [*tong xing zhi bo* 同姓之伯] is worthy, but one sets him aside and praises the elder of some other lineage [*ta zu zhi meng* 他族之孟], never yet has one who acted thus been successful."[98] Indeed, *xing zu* 姓族 figured as a synonym compound.[99]

However, *zu* usually indicated smaller groups. Even the great *zu* of the Zhou nobility were subsets of surnames. In several Han stories the *zu* are subunits of larger kin units called either *zong* or *shi* 氏.[100] That *zu* was a subset of a larger lineage is also supported by the use of *zu* and *zong* in the *Er ya*, as well as a passage in the *Li ji* where a term containing the graph *zu* applies only to distant kin.[101] Similarly, one passage in the *Lun heng* states that "the outer *zu*" mark the extreme limits reached by "what is linked through blood and vessels [*xue mai suo lian* 血脈所連]."[102] In these uses *zu* indicates kin groups broader than the household but smaller than the surname group or the *zong/shi* formed by all descendants of a founding ancestor. It also sometimes indicates more distant kin, as opposed to those who are closer.

This *zu* as a kin unit located between the common surname group or lineage, on the one hand, and the individual household, on the other, figures in many passages in the *Li ji*. The most important define the *zu* as equivalent to the "lesser *zong*," the collateral lines defined by an ancestry traced back to an impermanent, secondary ancestor. Thus, one passage states:

> All descendants of those who have one of the five altars in the ancestral temple and whose tablets have not yet been eliminated, even if they have descended to the rank of commoner, must formally notify the ruler in the event of a capping ceremony, marriage, death, or the making of the offerings that mark the second and third years of mourning. This is the way that kin [*zu*] act towards one another.[103]

This explicitly identifies the range of the *zu* with the lesser *zong* formed by descendants of ancestors who had temporary, shifting altars in the temple. Another passage states that the *zu* who gather for a banquet are descendants of those whose tablets are removed after five generations. The same idea is implied in another passage on *zu* banquets that states that people should be seated according to the alternating order of *zhao* 昭 and *mu* 穆 generations that fixed the arrangement of tablets in the ancestral temple.[104] Finally, a passage on nobles' powerful ancestral spirits operating outside the system of the ancestral temple describes those of the king as "great spirits [*tai li* 泰厲]," those of the feudal lords as "lordly spirits [*gong li* 公厲]," and those of the hereditary officials as "kin spirits [*zu li* 族厲]."[105] Again it is the hereditary officials, who formed lesser lineages in relation to the great lineages of the rulers, who are classed as *zu*.

A second feature of the *zu* described in the *Li ji* indicating that they were larger than a household but smaller than a lineage is that some passages pair the *zu* with the village community (*xiang li* 鄉里). The most important of these occurs in the "Record of Music":

> When there is music in the ancestral temple, so that ruler and minister, superior and subordinate, listen to it together, then all will be harmoniously reverent. When there is music among the heads of the kin [*zu zhang* 族長] and the village community, so that elder and younger listen to it together, then all will be harmoniously obedient. When there is music in the private quarters [*gui men* 閨門, also "women's chambers"], so that father, sons, and brothers listen to it together, then all will be harmoniously close.[106]

The *zu* appears between the descent group, identified with the ancestral temple and the state, and the household of a father and his male children. It is paired with the village, which is also larger than a household but smaller than the state. A second passage states that the lowest level of official is ranked by age rather than office in his home village, while an official of the second level is ranked by age rather than office in his *zu*. This again treats the *zu* as like a village, but one level closer to a household.

The distinction between *zu* and brothers contrasts the largest possible household with the next largest kin unit. Similarly, several passages list

brothers and *zu* sequentially to indicate widening circles of kinship, or place
them in parallel opposition.[107] The most explicit states:

> When an aunt who has been widowed dies, and there are no sur-
> viving brothers of her husband among his kin group [*dang* 黨], then
> have one of the husband's more distant kin [*zu ren* 族人] take charge
> of the funeral. Even though the wife's kin group would be closer
> [*qin* 親] they should not take charge. If the husband has no kin [*zu*],
> then entrust it to an immediate neighbor. If there are no neighbors
> then the village head will take charge of it.[108]

This shows that *zu* are kin beyond the range of the largest household formed
by all brothers with their parents, and it further treats the *zu* as a step between
the household and the village.

It also excludes relatives by marriage from the *zu*, which like the household in many ritual texts is a purely male unit. This point is also demonstrated by passages that contrast the men of the *zu* with those of "different
surnames [*yi xing* 異姓]": "When the lord holds a banquet with the members
of his *zu*, then people with a different surname play the role of the guests
and the head of the kitchen will play the role of host. The lord, fathers, and
elder brothers are ranked by age, and the other members of the *zu* in dining
will be reduced one degree for each generation [removed from the ruler]."[109]
This again shows that *zu* were kin beyond the immediate household. While
the identity of those of different surnames is not stipulated, it almost certainly
included relatives by marriage. This sense of the term *yi xing* is shown in
another passage, which contrasts it with *zu*: "For those of the same surname,
one follows their position in the lineage [*zong* 宗]. This links up the relatives
in the *zu* [*zu shu* 族屬]. For those of different surname [*yi xing*], it is
regulated by their title [*ming* 名]. This gives order to social gathering [*ji hui*
際會]. Titles being made clear, then men and women will be properly separated."[110] Thus, *yi xing* indicated people related by marriage. The explicit contrast with *zu* demonstrates that the latter term, as employed in this passage,
included only members of the patriline.

While *zu* could thus refer to any kin grouping ranging from the entire
surname group, through the lesser lineage, and occasionally to the household,
it also functioned in two technical usages marked by the numbers "three" and
"nine." The former figured in legal contexts, where particularly serious crimes
under Qin law were punished by the execution of the "three *zu*."[111] Although
supposedly abolished by Empress Lü in B.C. 187, the punishment was applied
sporadically throughout the Han dynasty to particularly serious crimes.[112] The
exact range included is uncertain. In general it was not broad, and in some
cases it was applied only to a single household (*jia*). This is noteworthy,
because while throughout the *Li ji* the *zu* denotes kin units larger than the
household, the one chapter that refers to the "three *zu*" suggests that the term
could be equivalent to the household.[113] However, "three *zu*" usually indi-

cated a larger group than this. Zhang Yan and Ru Shun, writing in the third century A.D., assert that the punishment of the "three *zu*" included the "father, mother, siblings, wife, and sons" or the "father's clan [*zu*], mother's clan, and wife's clan."[114] The former could have been confined in a single household, but usually included several. The latter would have been quite extensive.

Actual cases confirm that the range of punishments varied from case to case, with some limited to a single household while others implicated hundreds of people. Some cases involved several generations of a single family, including brothers and half-brothers who generally lived apart in this period. Others involved multiple households.[115] The treatise on punishments in the *Jin shu* relates that the Jin dynasty had revised the Han law so that grandparents and grandchildren were no longer implicated in cases of high treason.[116] This indicates that Han laws stipulated that five generations of a single family were implicated. In certain cases the executions reached not only to the clan of the criminal but to those of his wife as well. When Liang Ji was executed in 159 A.D. those put to death included his own clan, his wife's, distant relatives (*zhong wai zong qin* 中外宗親), and several dozen high officials at court who were allied with him. More than three hundred of his clients and retainers were also stripped of office, although not executed.[117] Thus, the *zu* punishment seems to have been as flexible as the term itself, ranging from single households to hundreds or even thousands of people.

Whereas the "three *zu*" was a regular term in legal contexts, the "nine *zu*" measured collective liability in only the most extreme cases. Usually it figured in discussions of the range of ritual obligations, where it marked the fullest extent of meaningful kin ties. As previously noted, in the *Bo hu tong* the character "nine (*jiu* *kiug 九)" was glossed with the near homophone *jiu* *kiog 究 "to push to the very end; ultimate(ly)." Consequently the number nine followed by a unit often indicated the totality of all such units, such as the "nine provinces" of China (see chapter five). Hence the term "nine *zu*" indicated all meaningful kin groups without specifying what these groups were.[118]

Han scholars developed two interpretations. One, associated with the "Old Text" tradition, argued that the nine *zu* were equivalent to the nine generations from the great-great grandfather to the great-great-grandson. This meant that kin consisted entirely of the patriline and excluded relatives by marriage. It became the dominant interpretation in the Chinese scholastic tradition from the Song dynasty on. The other, associated with the "New Text" tradition, defended the theory from the *Bo hu tong*: four groups linked to the father, three to the mother, and two to the wife.[119] This theory, in contrast to the first, included relatives by marriage, both through the ego's mother and his wife.

The term "nine *zu*" could have indicated all kin without referring to any specific nine categories, and the existence of a debate in the last century of Han rule suggests that there was no fixed definition in the period. However, since the two rival theories entail radically different versions of the larger kin units, some assessment of their relative merits is necessary.

It is likely that the "New Text" interpretation is closest to Han practice. First, if it is genuine, the *Bo hu tong* represents the consensus of a meeting of the leading intellectuals of the late first century A.D. Thus, it has more authority than later statements by individual scholars. Moreover, the model of kin ties in the *Er ya* also includes numerous groups of relatives by marriage. As the modern scholar Rui Yifu has shown, this model basically concurs with the "New Text" interpretation of kin structures.

Second, Han sources indicate that classicist models of the family and kin groups had little authority in the period. This point was made by Jack Dull; the data previously mentioned and in chapter four shows that the organization of households and larger kin units did not follow the ritual norms.[120] As Makino Tatsumi has argued, the exclusion by late Eastern Han scholars of relatives by marriage was probably a hostile response to the dominance of the court by imperial affines, and by eunuchs associated with imperial women through shared location in the inner quarters.[121]

Third, the "Old Text" exclusion of relatives by marriage implies a society in which patrilines had no interest in securing alliances with others.[122] As we will see in chapter four, this was not the case. Alliances formed through marriage were of central importance to leading families in the Eastern Han, and relatives through marriage formed an important part of their networks of significant kin.

Fourth, since only three or at most four generations would be alive at any time, a nine *zu* group formed by nine generations would be meaningless for collective punishments or the distribution of material resources. Nevertheless, there are rare cases in which nine *zu* were executed, and others in which an official distributed his income among his nine *zu*.[123] Such acts would have been impossible if the Old Text gloss were correct. The cumulative weight of this evidence indicates that affines played an important role in Han dynasty kin networks, and that the nine *zu* as conventionally understood included them. The alternative theory that excluded affines was developed only in the late Eastern Han in response to the social developments and political struggles that dominated the intellectual world of that period.

A final piece of evidence is the silk chart depicting kin relations from Mawangdui.[124] It consists of a red canopy over six vertical rows of red and black squares, of which seven of the former and twelve of the latter are still visible. These squares are connected to one another by thin black lines. That the chart depicts kin ties is shown by two accompanying passages of text. One states that the three-year mourning period means wearing the appropriate mourning attire for twenty-five months (i.e., across three years rather than for a full three years). The second lists the kinds of mourning attire for certain categories of kin: the father, grandfather, father's brothers,

brothers, brothers' sons, grandsons, father's sisters, sisters, daughters, and their offspring.

As Lai Guolong has argued in an unpublished paper, the kin relations depicted in this chart and described in the passages can best be explained by the "New Text" model of the nine *zu*.[125] If one places the ego at the center of the chart (a black square that is now missing), with his father and son in the black squares above and below, then the remaining categories—to whom ego owes nine months wearing even sackcloth—form a ring around them. Following the connecting black lines, one can fill in the outer squares with the kinship terms provided by the *Er ya* or the "Sangfu" section of the *Yi li*.[126] In such a reconstruction, the red squares would mark female kin and the black squares male.

The chart includes the children of the father's sisters, of ego's sisters, and of ego's daughters, all of whom would have had different surnames than ego. Not only are these figures included on the chart, but they are placed in the same degree of closeness to ego in terms of mourning relations as the father's brothers, brothers, and their offspring. This is important because all the "New Text" accounts of the "nine *zu*" include the offspring of females who had already married out. Thus, the kin group depicted on the chart corresponds to the four groups of "father's kin" as described in the "New Text" tradition, and roughly to the same category in the *Er ya*.[127] The inclusion of married female kin and their children in the system of mourning obligations indicates that, at least in the early decades of the Han, women's natal families continued to regard them as important members of the kin group. This evidence supports the previous points, and fits well with the evidence to be discussed in chapter four for the importance of marriage-based alliances in the organization of the great clans of the Eastern Han. The evidence gathered here thus shows that while individual households were the basic units of residence, economic production, and tax obligation, within the logic of the kin system defined by mourning obligations, they were constituent elements of larger networks.

Not only were households subunits of larger kin networks on which they relied for ritual order and political influence, they were also tied into networks of economic exchange on which they depended for material survival. This mutual reliance due to the social division of labor was significant because it served as a major justification for the state order. The division of labor and the consequent mutual interdependence of households was not simply a brute economic necessity, but a theoretically elaborated principle of state power and social hierarchy. Thus, mutual dependence of individual households, and the impossibility of the autarky that had marked the great noble's residences, became a fundamental axiom of the imperial order.

The most elaborate justification of the state through the necessity of the division of labor is Mencius's debate with Chen Xiang. The latter, converted

to the teachings of the school of Shen Nong by Xu Xing, argued that everyone including the king should grow his own grain:

> Mencius asked, "Does Master Xu eat only grain that he has grown
> himself?" "Yes." "Does Master Xu wear only clothing that he has
> woven himself?" "No, he wears a coarse laborer's loincloth." "Does
> Master Xu wear a cap?" "Yes." "What kind?" "Plain white silk." "Does
> he weave it himself?" "No, he exchanges grain for it." "Why doesn't
> Master Xu weave it himself?" "That would interfere with his farming
> work." "Does Master Xu use a pot and steamer to cook, and does
> he plow with an iron tool?" "Yes." "Does he make these himself?"
> "No, he exchanges grain for them." "To exchange grain for utensils
> and tools does not harm the potter or smith. The potter and smith
> also trade their products for grain; how could this be harming the
> farmer? Moreover, why doesn't Master Xu also be a potter and smith,
> so that without all this he could get these things for his use from his
> own house? Why all this prodigal trading with every sort of crafts-
> man? Why doesn't Master Xu resent all this nuisance?" "The work
> of all the different crafts naturally cannot be done together with
> farming."
>
> "Now is putting the whole world in order the only thing that
> can be done together with farming? There is the work of the great
> men and the work of the petty men. Moreover, each individual
> requires the products of all the crafts. If one had to make all these
> products oneself in order to use them, that would lead the whole
> world to exhaustion. Therefore it is said, 'There are those who toil
> with their minds and those who toil with their strength. Those who
> toil with their minds rule others; those who toil with their strength
> are ruled by others. Those who are ruled by others feed their rulers,
> while those who rule are fed by those they rule.' "

This argument for the necessity of dividing labor, and the origins therein of
rulership, is followed by an account of how Yao created an ordered human
society out of the chaos of the flood. This task was distributed among several
servants of Yao who respectively expelled the animals, drained off the flood-
waters to establish dry land, introduced agriculture, and instructed the people
in the duties that formed the family. In the course of such work, the *Mencius*
notes, they did not have time to engage in farming: "Being concerned about
the people to this extent, how could the sage have time for agriculture?
Yao was concerned about not finding someone like Shun, and Shun was
concerned about not finding people like Yu and Gao Yao. Someone who by
contrast is only concerned about the difficulties of his hundred *mu* of land
is a peasant."[128] This discussion of the works of Yao and his officials, and the
contrast of their broad concerns with the limited ones of the peasants, give

specific content to the distinction between mental and physical labor posited in the first passage. The man who works with his body is bound and limited by the object of his toil. In the case of the farmer this is his land, and by extension the craftsman would be constrained by his focus on the objects he fashions. Above these limited actors are rulers who, through encompassing mental toil, fashion a structured world and assign each person a place within it. Thus, the necessity of the division of labor creates a similar necessity of social hierarchy.

The *Xunzi* made a similar argument that derived government from the division of labor and consequent mental limitations of those engaged in production and exchange:

> Farmers are expert in using land, but they cannot be made supervisors of the land. Merchants are expert in markets, but they cannot be made supervisors of markets. Craftsmen are expert in vessels, but they cannot be made supervisors of vessel manufacture. However, there are people who do not have these three skills, but whom one can have take charge of these three offices. I say, "These are experts in the Way. They are not expert in objects. Those expert in objects treat an object as an object. Those expert in the Way take each and every object and make them into objects."[129]

Again people of specialized skills are constrained by their own expertise to a narrow focus that renders them incapable of the intellectual breadth that defines authority. By contrast, the rare individuals who focus on the universal Way attain an encompassing expertise that subjects all objects to their control. Social order requires that the latter category of individuals rule the former, so that the powers of each limited specialization can be combined in the service of the whole. Several other passages in the *Xunzi* similarly contrast the totalizing intellect of the sage with the technical skills of those involved in the production and circulation of goods.[130] Other philosophical traditions likewise argue that multiple specializations must be combined under the ruler to construct both a proper society and a bureaucratic government.[131]

This idea of a society divided by occupational specializations coordinated by the state became conventional in the Han, as exemplified in chapters on economics in the standard histories. The *Shi ji* chapter on the increasing of wealth (*huo zhi* 貨殖) begins by citing the *Dao de jing*'s ideal of autarkic communities that avoid communication with each other. It follows this immediately with a reference to Shen Nong, the target of the critique in the *Mencius* cited earlier. It dismisses these visions of societies without exchange as nostalgia for a vanished world. This leads to a recitation of the distinctive products of each region, and a listing of the economic specialties—farmers, foresters, craftsmen, and merchants—that produce, process, and exchange these products.[132] This image—a world of regions distinguished by diverse products but drawn together by exchange—transfers the model based on division of labor to the spatial level. This spatial model will be discussed in detail in chapter four. Here one need only note that the references in these economic writings to the division of labor follow the established pattern, except that Sima Qian insists that people's natures lead them to spontaneously link up through exchange so long as the state maintains order.[133]

The influence of the theory in which the state arises to counteract the division of labor among households is even clearer in the "Monograph on Food and Commodities" in the *Han shu*:

> Goods are the means by which rulers assemble people and preserve positions. . . . When the sage-kings set boundaries for people, they built walled cities to give them dwellings, instituted an agricultural grid with field huts to equally distribute them, opened rows of stalls in markets to link them together, and set up schools to educate them. Men of service, farmers, craftsmen, and merchants, each of these four categories of people had their inherited work. Those who studied to obtain positions were called "men of service"; those who opened up the earth and cultivated grain were called "farmers"; those who wielded their craft to complete utensils were called "craftsmen"; those who circulated goods and sold commodities were called "merchants." The sage-kings measured people's abilities and allotted them their tasks.[134]

Here the sages' creation of human society consisted of carving up the world into discrete units in which the people could dwell and work, and then establishing markets where they could gather and exchange the products of their labor. It also divided the people into economic specializations whose coordinated endeavors were possible only under the influence of the sages and their heirs in the imperial government. Thus, the small households of nuclear families, which had been an aim of government policy at least since the fourth century B.C., became not only the dominant social reality but also fundamental to the ideological justification of the state.

THE HOUSEHOLD DIVIDED

Like other spatial units in early China, the household was depicted as not only a limited, dependent part of a larger whole, but also as divided against itself. The primary division within the household was that between men and women.[135] Both forms of network previously discussed, that of kinship and that based on the division of labor, opposed women to men within the household. The division in the Chinese household is usually discussed in terms of kinship, and this will be examined, but the division based on economic roles also requires attention.

The classic economic specialization of women in China, as in many cultures, was weaving.[136] In the *Shi jing* many poems describe women as responsible for the process of cloth production, from the gathering of mulberry leaves for the silkworms to the weaving and dying of the cloth. These poems often pair women's task of weaving with men's work outside in the fields, and set both in turn against the noble's work of hunting.[137] While the rise of large-scale production of cloth in workshops owned by the state or by great families entailed some male labor, many workers were still women. Moreover, throughout the Warring States and early imperial period it remained a convention to pair women's work in the production of cloth with men's work in the cultivation of grain. Even empresses were, like the *Odyssey*'s Penelope, at least ceremonially involved in the production of cloth, as well as rituals to assist the process throughout the empire. Wives in wealthy households, as described in poems and depicted in Han tomb art, also engaged in cloth production. That weaving was women's work was even built into the pattern of the sky, where the "Weaver Girl" asterism played a prominent role.[138]

Thus, just as the state was composed of diverse economic roles that had to be integrated, so the household was divided into economic specializations whose joining provided for the needs of both the household itself and society at large. Indeed some passages link the social division of labor with the division between men and women in the household as parallel principles of order.[139] In contrast, some passages on the division of labor within the household are attributed to the tradition of Shen Nong, which argued against such a division in society as a whole. But whether the two levels of division of labor were regarded as correlates or substitutes, the principle of internal divisions being drawn together in a higher unity was common to both the individual household and the larger social order.

The division between men and women in the early Chinese household was also clearly marked in kin ties. The household in kin terms was an element in a patriline tracing descent from senior male to senior male back to the original male ancestor. As units of the patriline, the households in ritual texts are defined by the relations of father to son and brother to brother.[140] Women were outsiders introduced from other households for biological reproduction. In recognition of this fact, they retained their natal surnames, and enduring links with the household of their birth were crucial to their role as units of exchange used to secure alliances between lineages. Daughters usually moved out of the household upon marriage, and were thus not permanent members. As shown in the Han will, even daughters who stayed at home generally did not inherit a share of the family land. Within the structure of ancestral sacrifice, they also remained outsiders, although a mother could receive offerings in association with her husband.

This division between men and women within the household was part of a broader schema running through the philosophical and ritual texts, which insist that the role of ritual is to separate people into their respective social categories. This idea is most clearly articulated in remarks that pair the roles of ritual and music. These routinely assign to ritual the task of creating distinctions, while music then serves to forge a harmonious unity from the disparate units:

> Music creates identity while ritual creates difference. When there is identity, then there will be closeness [*qin* 親]. When there is difference, then there will be respect. If music conquers, then things flow together; if ritual conquers, then they fall apart. . . . When ritual duties are established, then noble and base will be ranked. When musical patterns are shared, then superiors and inferiors will be in harmony.[141]

These general remarks take on specific forms in dozens of passage which insist, as in the *Xunzi*, that the purpose of ritual is to maintain social divisions (*fen* 分). These divisions create human society and distinguish humans from beasts. Among these divisions, ritual texts place particular importance on maintaining the separation (*bie* 別) between men and women.[142]

While ritual texts insist on keeping women separate and subordinate, in order to protect the patriline, in practice women wielded considerable power in the house. The major basis of such power was the authority of a mother over her sons. In early imperial China the authority of age usually took precedence over that of gender, and filial obedience to both male and female parents was a son's highest obligation.[143] So while women were technically outsiders within the household, and according to doctrines such as the "three forms of obedience" should always be subject to men—first father, then husband, then son—in actual Han households they commanded sons who had to obey them in the name of filiality. This discrepancy between normative injunctions and actual practice informs the *Lie nü zhuan* story of Mencius's mother. It consists of episodes in which she instructs Mencius in how to behave as a scholar, a husband, and an official. At the end she quotes the *Li ji* maxim on women's obedience to men throughout their live's, but only to once again tell Mencius how to act.[144]

A further demonstration of the power of a mother over her sons is the aforementioned Han will. This document is written in the name of the mother, who calls on a group of local officials as witnesses in order that the will would be legally binding. It begins with her listing the members of the household and their relations. She then dictates how the fields are to be distributed and under what conditions they are to be held. The widowed mother's disposition of the family's land, within the limits imposed by an apparent rule against giving family land to daughters, is notable because the participation of officials shows that such a procedure was regarded as normal and proper. A similar case is recorded in a stone inscription erected in A.D. 178 that recounts how the distribution of family land was dictated by a widow surnamed Xu. Mothers also had the power to denounce their children to the government for capital crimes.[145] In these examples, as in the story of Mencius's mother, ritual strictures about widows obeying their sons seem to have had little impact on actual practice.

Literary texts also depict maternal power. The long poem "Kongque dongnan fei 孔雀東南飛" narrates from the point of view of an oppressed daughter-in-law the manner in which her husband's mother controls her son's life, even forcing him against his will to divorce his wife.[146] Another poem describes a woman as a model wife, the very sight of whom produces "a joy unique in all the world." The concluding line on this ideal woman states: "When such a stalwart woman controls the house, she even surpasses a man [*sheng yi zhangfu* 勝一丈夫]".[147] This last line could also be read "dominates a husband," although that is unlikely here.

A dramatic testament to the power of women in the household is the preface to the *Yan shi jia xun*. While this text dates from well after the Han, it testifies to a situation that probably existed throughout Chinese history. Yan Zhitui writes:

> The reason for which I am writing once again is not to provide a pattern for things nor a model for the age. My task [*ye* 業, also "inheritance" or "family tradition"] is to order my family and catch the ear of my descendants. Given the same words, one believes those who are closest. Given the same commands, one carries out those of the people who are most respected. In forbidding the violence of children, the injunctions of a teacher or friend are not as good as the commands of a nurse or maid. In stopping the quarrels of ordinary people, the teachings of Yao and Shun are not as good as the instructions of a widowed [mother] or wife. I hope that this book will be something you boys can trust more than a nurse, a maid, a widowed mother, or a wife.[148]

Following the platitude that people always believe and obey those whom they most love and respect, Yan Zhitui surprisingly assigns such authority exclusively to women. He takes it as a given that the people to whom men are bound by the strongest ties of emotion and respect, and whom they will spontaneously believe and obey, are the women in their households. This is true not only of mothers and wives but even of serving women. Here Yan Zhitui acknowledges a world that much of the literature up to his day had passed over in silence, a realm dominated by intimate ties of physical contact and emotional dependence. This realm, the family as experienced by most Chinese, was dominated by mothers, wives, and maidservants who served the physical needs of their husbands and children, rather than by the distant patriarchs and their ancestral cult. Against the immediate ties of sustenance and sentiment, Yan Zhitui presents his written text as the equivalent within the family of the way of Yao and Shun in the world at large. Acknowledging that women dominate the realm of lived experience and effective speech, he presents himself to his sons and grandsons in the form of a *written* text intended to negate the power of women. Like Plato, who attributed unreliable myths to mothers and nurses, or the early modern Frenchmen who collected fairy tales under the rubric of "Mother Goose," Yan Zhitui sets masculine writing against a dangerous, female realm of spoken words.[149] Thus, the genre of the family instruction is here justified as an attempt to reassert the text-based model of male domination against the fact of female power.

Another sign of women's power in the household is the Han concern over perpetuating the patriline when the death of one or both parents threatened the transmission of position or property. This worry over the fate of orphans figures in the Han "Song of the Orphan" that describes how the bereaved child was forced to toil as a peddlar by the brother and sister-in-law who took charge of his upbringing.[150] Sisters-in-law routinely figured as threats to the brotherly devotion that should have led to the proper treatment of a brother's son. The issue of caring for orphans also frequently appears in Eastern Han biographical materials (see chapter four).

More significant than the problem of orphans was that of stepmothers, or rather of the threat posed by remarriage. The Han will shows difficulties posed by a woman's remarriage, for the treatment of the sons depended on the relation of each of their fathers to the widow allocating the inheritance. However, the problematic nature of this case was mitigated by the fact that the woman remained in the household of her first husband. The later husbands were all uxorilocal. Thus, the well-being of the patriline, the first issue of concern for the normative texts, was not challenged.

A more serious problem was created by men's remarriage, for the second or third wife was mother only of her own biological children, but her position in the household depended on her role as mother. Thus, the worry found in so many cultures—that a stepmother would persecute the children of the first marriage to advance the cause of her own children—was virtually a structural feature of the Chinese household. The *Yan shi jia xun* devotes a chapter to remarriage that states, "A later wife will invariably be cruel to the son(s) of the previous wife."[151]

Anxiety about stepmothers and the care of children whose mother had died figured prominently in Han stories and art.[152] Some stories feature classic evil stepmothers who menace their young charges. In the story of Min Sun, the stepmother persecutes the son of the first marriage, until the father discovers how she is mistreating him. In that of Jiang Zhangxun, the stepmother attempts to kill the son after his father has died, until her repeated failures convince her that Heaven is protecting the child. Other stories celebrate exemplary women who protect the offspring of the first wife or of a male kinsman even at great personal cost. Thus, the story of the righteous stepmother of Qi in the *Lie nü zhuan* tells how her two sons were found next to the body of a murder victim. Each one confessed to protect the other. Since the officials could not decide who was guilty, they asked the mother to identify the guilty party to be executed:

Weeping, the mother replied, "Kill the younger." Having received her statement, the minister asked, "The youngest son is what people most love, yet now you desire to kill him. Why?" The mother replied, "The younger is my child; the elder is the son of the previous wife. When their father was ill and on the point of death he charged me, 'Raise him [the elder] well and look after him.' I said, 'I will.' Now having received a trust from him and agreed to it by saying, 'I will,' how could I forget that trust and be faithless to the promise? Moreover, to kill the elder and preserve the younger would be to abandon a public duty [*gong yi* 公義] for the sake of a private love [*si ai* 私愛]. To betray my words and forget good faith would be to cheat the dead man. If I disregard my words, forget my pledge, and having already accepted [an obligation] then not keep faith, how can I live among men?"[153]

While the king pardoned both sons out of respect for the woman's devotion, this tacked-on happy ending does not soften the harsh lesson of the story. Celebrating a woman for choosing to kill her own child in order to protect her husband's patriline offers a chilling demonstration of the moral convolutions entailed in the definition of kin ties exclusively through male transmission.

A similar story in the same work tells of the virtuous aunt of Lu. When fleeing an invading army, she abandons her own son in attempting to rescue that of her brother. When questioned, she once again justifies the action in terms of rejecting "private love" in the name of "public duty."[154] Another anecdote tells of a woman in Liang whose house caught fire. Trying to rescue her elder brother's son, she accidentally picked up her own, and by the time that she had discovered her mistake the flames were too advanced for her to return and rescue her nephew. When her companions tried to stop her from leaping back into the flames she exclaimed: "'Bearing the name of unrighteousness, what face can I have to meet my brothers and the men of the capital? I want to throw my son back into the fire, but this would disregard a mother's kindness. In this situation I can no longer live.' She then dashed into the flames and died."[155]

The correlate of the threat posed by the stepmother, or any woman whose loyalty to her own children took precedence over the patriline, was the danger that a widowed mother might remarry. The issue of remarriage was of considerable importance in the Han, for any patriline faced loss or extinction if a widow remarried and transferred her primary loyalties to the new family. As Wang Shuda has shown by collecting cases from the received literature, natal families of widows often encouraged them to remarry, in order to establish new alliances. Women themselves doubtless chose in some cases to wed again.[156] In such an event her new family would push her to favor her new husband's sons who would carry on the patriline. Thus, although it was not universally accepted, some ritual texts argued that a woman should not remarry:

> The marriage ritual is the origin of the myriad generations. One takes a wife from a different surname in order to bring close those who are distant and to emphasize the separation [of men and women]. The betrothal gifts must be correct and sincere, and not a single one of the formal words of the agreement can be improper. This instructs the woman in rectitude and good faith [*xin* 信]. With good faith she will serve others. Good faith is the virtue of a wife. Once having been united with her husband she will not change [*gai* 改] for her entire life. Thus if the husband dies she will not remarry.[157]

The role of the marriage rite is to produce "myriad" generations (i.e., a patri-line), while maintaining the separation of men and women. Significantly this passage immediately precedes the stipulation of the "Three Obediences."

The classic embodiment of avoiding remarriage was the widow Gao Xing ("Lofty Conduct") of Liang. Celebrated for her beauty and conduct, she was widowed at an early age and refused to remarry. When the King of Liang sent a minister with betrothal gifts the widow said:

> "I have heard that the duty of a wife is that once she has married she will not change [*gai* 改]. Thereby she preserves the integrity of chastity and good faith [*xin* 信]. To forget the dead and pursue the living is unfaithful. Perceiving honor to forget the humble [first husband] is unchaste. One who abandons duty and follows profit loses all means of being human." She took a mirror and knife in order to cut off her nose, saying, "I have already become a mutilated person. The reason I did not commit suicide is that I could not bear for the children to be orphaned again. The king's seeking me was for my beauty, but now as this mutilated remnant I can probably escape."[158]

Nor is this story a complete invention, for there are records of widows cutting off hair, ears, fingers, or noses to avoid remarriage, or even adopting the option of suicide rejected here.[159]

These stories tell us a great deal about the place of women within the early imperial household as understood by upholders of the ritual order. The true kin structure was the patriline. The nuclear family, the dominant form of household organization, was unsafe because it incorporated women from outside the line of masculine descent. The household consisted of ties between spouses, father and children, mother and children, and siblings, but in these stories the sole reliable tie was that between father and son. Linked to their natal families and potentially to second husbands, women were a menace both to their husband and his offspring. This was particularly true of stepmothers, but it was true of all women, even a mother whose remarriage might jeopardize her first husband's children. The structural basis of the perceived threat of women to the patriline is noted even by Yan Zhitui, who shared in the conventional suspicion:

> By nature later husbands will indulge the orphans of earlier ones, while later wives will invariably be cruel towards the sons of earlier ones. This is not just because women are jealous, while men tend towards indulgence. Force of circumstances [shi 勢] cause it to be thus. The orphan of a previous husband would not dare to dispute family property with the son of a later one, but will guide him by the hand, play with him, and nourish him, so that love gradually develops between them. Thus the father indulges him. The son of a previous wife, however, will always enjoy a higher ranking due to earlier birth. Whether in study for government service or marriage he will always block [the later wife's children]. Thus she is cruel to him.[160]

It is not women's character but their situation within the family that makes them a menace, but this does not alter the fact that they are treated as objects of suspicion.

The intensity of this suspicion is shown by the extraordinary actions enjoined on women to demonstrate loyalty to the husband's patriline. Suicide or physical mutilation were not only negations of the self, but for members of a patriline they were among the highest of crimes. That women were celebrated for such actions marks their position as outsiders. Even the most total violations of mother-child ties, abandonment or virtual murder of one's own child, were virtues when performed in the name of the bonds between father and son. This negation of the ties between a mother and her sons is justified through their identification as mere "private love" that must yield to the "public [gong] duty" of serving the patriline.

Using the contrast between private and public in such cases is unusual because the term si conventionally indicated the household and kin ties, while gong indicated the realm of the ruler and his servants. This contrast between family and state in terms of an opposition between "kindness/affection [en 恩]" (as in the story of the woman who mistakenly rescued her own child from the flames) and "duty [yi]" is articulated in the Li ji:

> Where kindness is greatest, mourning will be heaviest. Thus for a father one wears garments of unhemmed coarse hemp through three years. This is regulated by the debt of kindness. In the order within the gates of the household, debts of kindness [en] block off duties [yi]. In the order outside the gates of the household, duties cut off debts of kindness. Drawing upon the manner of serving a father in order to serve a prince, the reverence for them will be identical.[161]

The household is set in parallel opposition to the state, with the former ruled by obligations due to kindnesses given, and the latter by duty. Thus, the women in these stories are called on to betray the virtues of the household in order to serve the higher realm of the state. This equation of a woman's loyalty to the patriline with duty toward the state is noted by the aunt of Lu: "If I rejected public duty to opt for private love, abandoned my elder brother's son to preserve my own, then even if I were lucky enough to escape with my life, the ruler of Lu would not shelter me, his ministers would not nourish me, and the common people and inhabitants of the capital would not associate with me."[162] Preserving her own child rather than her brother's would have resulted in exclusion from the political order formed by the ruler, his ministers, and the men of the capital. This elaborates the stepmother of Qi's remark that she would be unable to live among men, but it makes clear that it is precisely a question of *men*. It is the purely masculine political order that would exclude her, just as it is the ruler who awards titles to those women who abandon their children, mutilate themselves, or commit suicide.

The duty for which women sacrificed themselves and their children was "public" because they negated themselves and their "private" households to serve the patriline. They denied the household—formed by ties of affection and obligation of married couples to each other and of both parents to their children—in the name of the encompassing orders of the lineage and the state. As Wu Hung noted, wives in these stories stood in the same relation to the masculine patriline as a household servant.[163] Outsiders tied to the household through the exchange of loyalty for employment or recognition, they related to the kin group in the same manner as assassins and ministers related to their lords in Warring States stories. Thus, it is no coincidence that the extreme acts through which the women in these stories prove themselves—abandonment of offspring, disfigurement, and suicide—are the same self-negating acts by which exemplary assassins and loyal ministers demonstrated devotion to the lords who employed them. Whereas the equation of ministers or assassins with women demonstrated the dependence and obedience of the former, it inserted the latter into the masculine realm of public duty.[164]

By contrast, fathers do not appear in these stories and their responsibility to orphans is never referred to as a "public duty." They required no exhortations to duty because within the patriline the private love (and material interest) of men coincided with public duty. For women, on the other hand, love and duty were antithetical, and the former had to be sacrificed to the latter.[165] These stories reflect a fundamental contradiction in the patriline, wherein women were both central (as producers and nurturers of offspring) and external (as excluded and hence threatening non-kin). The stories and images portray a cultural system that forced women into the position of outsider, condemned them as morally deficient for being in that position, and then offered them redemption through the renunciation of their emotions, the abandonment of their interests, the mutilation of their bodies, and ultimately the embracing of suicide.

While mothers threatened the patriline because multiple marriages produced divided loyalties, sisters-in-law were a menace because they encouraged the division of property. In the Han period the idea that women who married into a family would encourage their husbands to divide up the land so that each couple could form an independent household appears in only a few stories.[166] However, in the following centuries, in association with the dissemination of the ideal of larger households, it became conventional to blame wives for quarrels and property divisions between brothers. Thus, Yan Zhitui argued that brothers were "shared substance in separate bodies" (see chapter one) who together passed through all the experiences of childhood and thus "could not but love one another":

> But when they grow up, each takes his own wife and has his own sons. Even when there is deep and sincere affection, there will inevitably be a withering of their relations. Sisters-in-law, compared to brothers, are much more distant and shallow. Using people of such distant and shallow ties to regulate or measure the kindnesses of those with deep and sincere affection is like matching a square base with a round lid. They will certainly not fit. Only those of the deepest friendship and brotherly feelings will not be changed by these outsiders. . . . Sisters-in-law are the ground of most quarrels.[167]

As non-kin introduced into kin networks formed by shared physical substance, women were blamed for quarrels and divisions between members of the patriline.

The best evidence of the threat posed by female power comes from accounts of the political power of imperial affines and their associates. Just as mothers dominated private households, so dowager empresses regularly wielded great authority at court. The mother of the First Emperor was a power during his youth, the widow of the Han founder controlled the court and filled it with her kin, and the mother of Emperor Wu also controlled the court in the early years of his reign. After its first three emperors, the Eastern Han was ruled by a succession of boys whose courts were controlled by either their mothers and their kin, or by the eunuchs who shared the inner chambers with the imperial wives and concubines. In other cases the historical records assert that imperial women controlled their husbands. Thus, Emperor Cheng, whose reign was dominated by his inability to produce a male heir, supposedly killed two such heirs because they threatened the position of his favorite wife.[168]

The tension between the formal subservience of women and their actual power within the household thus manifested itself at every level of Chinese society. However, since the true state of affairs was at odds with the dictates of ritual texts and social theory, female power was treated as a scandal or an aberration. Nevertheless, the power of women was not merely a recurrent breakdown of norms, but a direct expression of basic principles of the organization of authority in early China. These principles and their contradictions can be demonstrated through examining the spatial organization of authority within the household, and within society in general.

Thus, the repeated domination by dowager empresses and emperor's wives was only one aspect of the shift of power from the official, outer bureaucracy to the inner court.[169] This resulted from the concentration of power in the person of the emperor. The actual conduct of government business was physically moved from the outer offices and court assemblies into the emperor's private quarters, so policy decisions and the dispatch of decrees came to be handled by those gathered around the emperor's person. First, this was his private secretaries. In time even greater influence was wielded by the eunuchs who acted as the emperor's body servants, or by the women who filled his harem and their kin. While none of these had formally sanctioned power, they came to control the conduct of political affairs through their immediate access to the person of the ruler. This same pattern was repeated in the centuries following the Han, when the secretariat became the officially recognized center of power only to be supplanted in turn by newly emergent offices that were closer to the emperor.

This shift of power from outer to inner had several reasons. First, Chinese political power from early times was articulated in terms of the authority of the inner over the outer. Second, during the Warring States and early imperial periods, political power was walled off from the outer world and rendered increasingly invisible, or visible only in the walls and towers that were its outer manifestation (see chapter three). This was true particularly of the rulers, who for reasons both of security and the cultivation of an aura of spiritual power, were increasingly hidden from the outside world. This contrasts with the spatial logic of power in the Roman empire, in India, or in early modern Europe, where rulers displayed themselves to the people. In the case of China's First Emperor, the tendency toward withdrawal and invisibility was treated as a function of his despotism and megalomania. However, the identification of imperial power as being hidden or "forbidden [jin 禁]" to ordinary people (as in the later "Forbidden City") became routine in the Western Han. In such a system, power was hidden behind a series of walls: those of the city, then the political city, the palace, the court, and finally the inner chambers. Passage through each of these walls was controlled, and each stage closer to the center was reserved for a smaller number of people. Thus, power and prestige were marked by the ability to move ever inward into the holy of holies that was the imperial presence. This focus on the person of the emperor was the third feature of the inward shift of power. For reasons that will be discussed in chapters three and four, the person of the emperor became the linchpin of the political structure, and as a consequence power came to those who had direct access to that person.

Consequently power lay within, and political authority increased as one moved physically closer to the ultimate, hidden center. At the same time, gender in China was also spatially structured by a logic of outer and inner.

However, it was the theoretically powerless female who occupied the inner spaces, while the male was assigned to the outer realm.[170] Some texts treat the inner realm of women as an autonomous zone that administered its own affairs in parallel to the masculine state, but within the overarching spatial structure of power in China the inner was routinely granted authority over the outer.[171] Thus, the Chinese world was marked by a conflicting set of equations in which power was located in the interior, women were also located in the interior, but women were to be excluded from power. The institutional expression of this contradiction was that power in imperial China perpetually flowed into the hands of women, their kin, and the eunuchs who shared their space, but that this ever-recurring phenomenon always appeared as a shock and a scandal. It also meant that there was always a radical disjunction between the formal institutions of power and its actual locations.

The paradoxical significance of being sealed inside, and the impact of this paradox on the position of women, can be further understood through examining the structure of Chinese public buildings and houses. As Andrew Boyd has pointed out, temples, palaces, and conventional houses in China were all constructed according to the same principles and followed related plans.[172] Such buildings were walled on the outside, and the inner space then structured through the alternation of courtyards and buildings. The first buildings after the entry gate were the more public areas in which men conducted their business. Such buildings were the place in which "insiders," that is, members of a family or the ruler and his household, would encounter people from the outside. As one moved toward the back, the buildings became more "inner" and private, and access to them became progressively more restricted. In a household these would be the private chambers of the men and women of the house. In an imperial palace they would be the emperor's living quarters, which in the Han became the locus of the inner court.

The links of this structure to the distribution of power can best be understood through examining its earliest known example, the Western Zhou temple/palace compound at Fengchu in Shaanxi.[173] The entry gate faced south and was shielded by an earthen screen wall. The gate itself led into a front courtyard across which lay the front hall. Behind this hall were two smaller courtyards divided by a corridor, and these in turn led to the back rooms or hall. Rows of side chambers lined the east and west walls. Thus, a single central axis led through the gate, across the courtyard, into the front hall, through a corridor between the two rear courtyards, and finally to the back hall. As Wu Hung has suggested, a ritual procession would have entered the walled town, then the walled palace/temple compound, and proceeded through the series of courtyards and buildings to end at the temple at the rear of the complex. The temple itself was arranged with the tablets of the most recent ancestors at the front, moving back through earlier generations as one moved inward, to culminate in the central rear shrine dedicated to the founding ancestor. This would thus have been an inward progression, with spirit power, secrecy, and authority (the "miracle, mystery, and authority" of Dostoevsky's Grand

Inquisitor) increasing steadily as one advanced toward the interior. This *inward* movement also marked a movement *backward* in time, from the present through the sequence of ancestors to the origins of the ruling house. Since the authority of the Zhou kings was based on their access to potent ancestors, this movement inward was a movement to the origins and center of power.[174]

This early Zhou temple provided the template for later Chinese palaces and elite dwellings. While no examples of Han houses survive, models of individual buildings have been found in tombs, and images of walled compounds composed of alternating courtyards and buildings appear on a few tomb walls.[175] Moreover, a handful of Warring States texts describe dwelling compounds formed through the alternation of courtyard and building, and also indicate how power was associated with different sites. Thus the *Lun yu* tells of Confucius's encounter with his son Bo Yu in the family home:

> Chen Kang asked Bo Yu, "Have you learned anything different [from what we have]?" Bo Yu replied, "Not yet. Once he was standing alone, and as I hastened respectfully past the courtyard he said, 'Have you studied the *Odes*?' I replied, 'Not yet.' He said, 'If you do not study the *Odes*, you will be unable to properly speak.' So I withdrew and studied the *Odes*. Another day when he was standing alone, I hastened respectfully past the courtyard and he said, 'Have you studied the *Rites*?' I replied, 'Not yet.' He said, 'If you do not study the *Rites*, you will be unable to properly stand.' So I withdrew and studied the *Rites*. I have learned these two things from him."
>
> Chen Kang withdrew and happily said, "Having asked one thing, I have learned three. I have learned about the *Odes* and the *Rites*, and I have also learned how the true gentleman keeps his son at a distance."[176]

Confucius as the ideal father stands in majesty overlooking the courtyard, like the ruler at a court assembly. His son respectfully scurries along the side corridors, speaking only when addressed. As Chen Kang remarks, the lesson about the relations of father and son is clear, and it is a lesson mapped out in the spatial placement and movement of people through the dwelling compound.

Passages in the *Zuo zhuan*, *Li ji*, and other texts also describe dwelling compounds formed along a horizontal axis from outer gate to private chambers [*shi* 室]. The exact sequence of courtyards and buildings varies, but the most common moves from the gate through the courtyard [*ting* 庭 or *xia* "beneath the hall"] to the outer hall [*tang* 堂] and then to the inner chamber [*shi*]. Some also refer to the doorway [*hu* 戶] from the inner chamber to the outer hall, and the steps [*jie* 階] between the outer hall and courtyard. One example indicates the ascent of authority as one moves toward the interior:

Sweet wine is placed in the inner chamber [with the impersonator of the deceased], the reddish wine in the outer hall [with the close kin], and the clarified wine in the courtyard [with the guests]. This [inverse hierarchy of honored station and potency of alcohol] shows that there should be no self-indulgence. The impersonator drinks three times, and guests only once. This shows that there are superiors and inferiors. . . . Those in the outer hall observe the inner chamber [as their model], and those in the courtyard observe the outer hall.[177]

The same terms also figure in descriptions of the disposition of the ancestral temple, thus showing that household and temple were spatially organized according to the same principles.[178]

The standard four elements of the horizontal axis—inner chamber, outer hall, courtyard, and gate—are also the first four members in the "seven dwellings of Punishment and Virtue (Xingde qi she 刑德七舍)" divinatory system.[179] This system, which is distinct from the Xingde divination system linked to the sexagenary cycle and the Jovian year count, uses the spatial series defining the compound—extended by the inclusion of the alley (xiang 巷), the main street (shu 術), and wilds (ye 野)—to designate the points along the eastern horizon that correlate with the shifting length of the noonday shadows cast by the gnomon between the two solstices:

Yin and yang, xing and de have seven dwellings. What is meant by "seven dwellings"? The inner chamber, the outer hall, the courtyard, the gate, the alley, the main street, and the wilds. In the eleventh month, Virtue dwells in the inner chamber thirty days, fifteen days before the solstice and fifteen days after. Where it dwells is in each case thirty days. When Virtue is in the inner chamber, then Punishment is in the wilds. When Virtue is in the outer hall, then Punishment is in the main street. When Virtue is in the courtyard, then Punishment is in the alley. When yin and yang share in potency, then Punishment and Virtue meet at the gate. In the eighth month and the second month the energy of yin and yang are in balance, so day and night are equally divided. Therefore it is said, "Punishment and Virtue meet at the gate." When Virtue is in the south then things are born; when Punishment is in the south then things die. Thus it is said, "When they meet in the second month, the myriad things are born. When they meet in the eighth month, the grasses and trees die."[180]

This system also appears in wooden strips from the Han frontier posts at Juyan in Gansu.[181]

This divination system also figures in Xu Shen's explanation of the origins of the "earth branch" graphs that correspond to the second and the eighth months. The second month corresponds to the branch "*mao* 卯" and the eighth month to "*you* 酉":

> The graph 卯 [*mlog] means "to burst forth [*mao* 冒, *mog]." In the second month the myriad things all come out, bursting forth from the ground. The graph imitates the form of an open gate. Thus the second month is called 'Heaven's gate [*tian men* 天門]'. The graph 酉 [*ziog] means "to reach [*jiu* 就, *dz'iog]." In the eighth month the millet is ripe and can be made into double-fermented wine. The graph imitates the old-style form of 酉 [which looked like the old style of 卯, except with a line across the top]. Every graph that has this signific follows from this old-style graph. The old form of 卯 depicts the gate of spring, when the myriad things have already come forth. The old form of 酉 depicts the gate of autumn, when the myriad objects have already gone back in. The line on top imitates a closed gate.[182]

This same idea figures in the "Monthly Ordinances" that stipulates that in the spring one sacrifices to the door (*hu*) and in the autumn to the gate (*men*), although the door and gate are sacrificed to in every month of their seasons, not just the second and the eighth.[183]

In this widespread theory the structure of the housing compound was built into the order of the universe in a divinatory system that explained the annual cycle of life and death in terms of a circular movement through the parts of the house and out into the world.[184] The beneficent, life-giving power starts in the innermost chamber of the house and progressively moves outward, while the killing power starts beyond the edges of human civilization and progressively moves in toward the house. At the ends the directions reverse. Twice a year, at the equinoxes, the two powers meet at the gateway of the compound. Thus, the stages of moving into the house was the spatial equivalent of the annual cycle, and the high point of beneficent, life-giving power was attained in the innermost chambers, the place of women and the married couple.

This spatial order established clear links between power, the interior, secrecy, and origins. Since women occupied the deepest interior and place of greatest secrecy, and since they were the ultimate physical origin, their place within the structure of the Chinese house was at one and the same time a form of restriction and a sign of power. However, it was a power that was hidden, rather than open, secret rather than acknowledged. The physical divisions within the household that excluded women from the patriline and from public service also marked them as wielders of power in an interior that was necessary to both lineage and state but from which both were excluded. These forms of hidden power conceded to women in the spatial arrangement of the house reappeared in the centripetal pattern of imperial power discussed earlier.

HOUSEHOLD AND TOMB

A final form of evidence about the household in the Warring States and early imperial China is changes in the structures of tombs and the role they played in rituals for the dead. As to the former, tombs came to be modeled on the dwellings of the period in both physical layout and social composition. Consequently, the tombs, and the images and objects they contain, provide the most detailed evidence at our disposal on the nature of the household. As to the latter, the shifting balance between the temple and the grave again demonstrates the tension between the household and the lineage. While the tomb cultically transferred the structures and membership of the household into the world of the dead, the temple remained the ultimate spatial articulation of the lineage. The cults to the dead at these two ritual sites depicted two competing models of the structure of kin ties.

From the fifth century B.C. certain tombs took on physical aspects of the household or the palace, and by the Eastern Han all tombs above the level of the very poorest were modeled on the houses of the period.[185] Earlier tombs had largely been versions of the "vertical pit tombs" in which multilayered coffin chambers were built into rectangular spaces at the bottom of large earthen pits. However, from the fifth century B.C., we have evidence of tombs that were horizontally spread out and divided into several chambers. Probably the earliest example of this attempt to recreate underground the surface dwelling of the deceased is the tomb of Marquis Yi of Zeng at Leigudun in Hubei, which dates to around 433 B.C.[186] It is divided into four chambers that correspond to functional elements of the ruler's palace compound: private quarters, ceremonial court, arsenal, and harem. Each chamber is filled with the objects, and in the case of private quarters and harem the human sacrifices, pertaining to its function. The idea of the tomb as a dwelling is further developed in the iconographic program on the inner coffin of the tomb's occupant, on which are painted windows, doors, and armed hybrid creatures as gatekeepers. The coffins of some sacrificial victims also have windows painted on them.

Several fourth-century B.C. tombs at Changtaiguan in Henan have multiple chambers and structural features copying palaces. One room even contained a lacquer-painted wooden bed. The most important example from this century of a tomb constructed as a dwelling is that of King Cuo of Zhongshan (d. 304 B.C.). The tomb itself contains evidence of chambers and structural features imitating a palace. Moreover, it contained a model for a necropolis, never actually constructed, consisting of five tomb mounds surrounded by two concentric walls and covered with architectural features. This necropolis would have formed a replica of the court or even the capital, and thus anticipated the "tomb palaces" of the Qin and Han emperors.[187]

The "catacomb" tombs in Qin provide the earliest evidence of an attempt to turn the tombs of humbler people into dwelling places.[188] These tombs were related to the vertical pit style, but instead of burying the corpse at the bottom of the shaft the builders opened up a lateral chamber in which the coffin was placed. More important, these tombs featured a wooden partition to separate the shaft from the lateral chamber, thus suggesting the imitation of surface architecture through the creation of multiple chambers separated by walls. Several scholars have noted the resemblance of these tombs to the loess-cave dwellings of Shaanxi, in which several rooms radiated out from a vertically excavated courtyard.[189]

By the late Warring States period the idea that the tomb was a replica of the house was articulated as a theoretical principle. Thus, the chapter on ritual in the *Xunzi* writes:

> In the funeral rites one adorns the dead with the trappings of the living. On a grand scale one imitates [*xiang* 象] what he had in life to send him off to the dead.

> They gather the utensils from his life in order to send them to the tomb. This provides the image [*xiang*] of his moving [to a new residence].

> Thus the form of the grave and grave mound imitates [*xiang*] the house. The form of the inner and outer coffins imitates the side, top, front, and back boards of a carriage. The cover over the coffin with its decorations imitates the screens, curtains, and hangings of a room. The wooden lining and frame of the tomb imitate the rafters and beams of a roof and a fence.[190]

Not only are the features and contents of the tomb described as an imitation or transfer of the structure and contents of a dwelling, but this practice of imitation is justified in terms of a general theory of funerary arrangements patterned on the existence of the living.

In the Han the patterning of the tomb on the household grew more detailed and widespread. By the middle of the Western Han the tombs of Prince Jing of Zhongshan at Mancheng in Hebei and Prince Lu of Qufu in Shandong were divided into compartments. In the former there was a front hall, a rear hall corresponding to the private quarters where the corpse was placed, and side chambers for storage of pottery on the north and horses with carriages on the south. In the front and side chambers there were buildings of timber with tile roofs, and in the rear hall a building of stone with stone doors.[191] In the same period middling or small landowners were buried in hollow-brick tombs that were usually shaped like a house with a gabled roof and a door-shaped front wall. The hollow bricks were often stamped with designs, and polychrome murals were painted in some tombs. These included images on the ceiling of the sun, the moon, and stars, as well as the animals of the four directions or stories from history and literature.[192] From the middle of the Western Han "brick-chamber tombs" with arches built of small bricks gradually supplanted all other tomb types throughout the empire. Tombs of nobles and high officials were built on a large scale with a layout patterned on the dwellings in which they had lived. Murals and frescoes often depicted scenes from the life of the tombs' denizens, or portrayed an idealized afterlife toward which the dead aspired.[193] Finally, in the Eastern Han there appeared in many regions a new type of tomb constructed from dressed stones with engraved designs and scenes. A few of these have now been excavated, and they once again demonstrate that the layout of the burial chamber imitated a house. Many of the designs on the stones also depicted household scenes, as well as incidents from the career of the tomb's occupant.[194] By the late first century A.D. the notion that a tomb was to be a replica of a house had become so conventional that Wang Chong could ask as a rhetorical question, "What difference is there between a house and a tomb?"[195]

The shift toward treating the tomb as a replica of the house was also marked in the grave goods. The grave goods of a Western Zhou noble tomb were basically ritual utensils, dominated by bronze vessels and accompanied by bronze weaponry and high-quality pottery. The assemblages of bronze vessels found in tombs were largely the same as those found in hoards, indicating that the types of vessels in tombs were the same as those employed during life in the ancestral temple. From the late Western Zhou the quantity and distribution of assemblages were increasingly determined by the status of the tomb's occupant. This suggests that Western Zhou grave goods were intended to transfer to the afterlife the ritual dimensions of a person's social existence. This was at first focused on the ties of the recently dead to earlier ancestors, but as the Zhou nobility divided into hierarchically ranked branches the issue of relative political ranking came increasingly to the fore.[196]

While Zhou grave goods indicate the early primacy of maintaining the ritual links of ancestors and descendants, certain features provided a ground for changes that took place in the Warring States period. The lower the rank of the occupant of a Zhou tomb, the more frequently bronze vessels were replaced by pottery. By the middle of the Eastern Zhou, substituting cheap imitations for costly originals had become common in all but the most elaborate aristocratic tombs. As Lothar von Falkenhausen has argued, this clear division between the ritual vessels of the living and those buried with the dead marks an early stage in the shift away from a Western Zhou world based on the shared existence of the living and the deceased. While early Zhou ritual had demonstrated the shared links between living and dead kin, who in the Zhou *Odes* are said to dine together in ceremonial banquets, by the late Warring States and early imperial period the *separation* of the living and the dead had become the ultimate aim of funerary ritual.

In place of the costly assemblages of ritual vessels that had defined Western Zhou funerary practice, the grave goods of the late Warring States and the Han were dominated by objects of daily use (clothing, lacquer bowls and plates, other pottery, food) or by models or images of such objects and other aspects of worldly life (houses, granaries, animals, and tools). Replicas and images also depicted human beings, both those buried in the tomb and all the servants, entertainers, cooks, agricultural laborers, and other people necessary to their leisured existence.[197] All this was intended to provide the dead with a happy existence in the tomb, but an existence based on objects that were only miniature replicas or images of the world of the living. Thus, the *Xunzi* argued that the objects buried with the dead, while imitating those of the living, had to be clearly distinct.

The significance of the idea that the tomb was a replica of the house and a locus of ritual for the dead has elicited some debate. Wu Hung has argued that the tomb gradually supplanted the temple as the center of ancestral sacrifice. This is marked by Warring States, Qin, and Han rulers' practice of building large tomb complexes with surface mounds, associated buildings, and elaborate subterranean dwellings. He states that each Han ruler built a temple in association with his grave, and these new grave/temple complexes supplanted the traditional temple in the capital. In A.D. 58 Emperor Ming supposedly abolished temple sacrifices.[198]

This argument has the virtue of situating the development of the new style of tomb in the context of the altering balance between the two sites of death ritual. It is particularly useful here because it allows us to focus on the tension between the lineage and the household. However, Wu Hung's argument is inadequate for at least three reasons. First, it ignores the fact that the rise of the new style of tomb/dwelling occurred at all levels of the Chinese elite, and instead discusses only the funerary customs of the rulers with their artificial mountain mausolea. Second, the argument provides no explanation for the changing role and structure of the tomb, but only suggests a motive for the increasing emphasis on tombs of rulers as sites of sacrifice. Third, the argument that temple sacrifices were abandoned is wrong. This is important because the use of temples and graves as two distinct sites for ancestor worship gave a ritual form to the tension between household and lineage which was central to kinship organization in the Han.

The narrow focus of Wu Hung's argument on royal tombs means that it cannot account for what took place. The shift in the nature and function of tombs had reached every level of society by the middle of the Western Han, so an appeal to rulers' changing status or ritual emphases explains nothing. As Lothar von Falkenhausen has argued, any useful discussion of this problem must consider the full range of evidence available from all levels of the elite and even middling landowners.[199] Rather than concentrating on the use of rulers' tombs as sites of sacrifice, an explanation of the new forms and contents of tombs must examine the changing conceptualization of the dead and their world. Only from the beginning of the fifth century B.C., as Alain Thote has noted, is there evidence of belief in a world of the dead that is patterned on that of the living. This is marked by the new practice of depositing in tombs objects of daily use that were devoid of any explicitly religious significance.[200] At the same time, as shown by the routine use of cheap copies in inferior materials, or of reduced replicas or images, it is clear that this realm of the dead was in some manner radically separate from the world of the living. This was the position articulated in the *Xunzi* and the related *Li ji*, both of which argued that while the treatment of the dead had to be patterned on that of the living, it also had to be distinct.[201]

Although these classicist texts on ritual do not usually discuss the reasons for separating the dead from the living, one passage in the *Li ji* makes the motive explicit: "When a ruler attended an official's funeral, he brought with him a shaman carrying a peach branch and reed broom [to expel evil spirits], as well as a soldier with a lance. This is because he dreads [spirits], so they distinguish them from the living."[202] The dead must be kept separate from the living because those who have died are a menace. Anna Seidel traced the emergence of the idea that the dead were potentially demonic figures who, if not sealed in the tomb, would return to wreak havoc on the living. The dead as depicted in texts in Eastern Han tombs are "terrifying revenants" who could inflict disease or misfortune, and who consequently "have to be securely locked away."[203] One "grave ordinance" inscribed on a jar in the year A.D. 175 uses rigorous parallelism to insist on the separation of the living and the dead:

High Heaven is blue [*cang cang*],
The underworld is limitless [*mang mang*].
The dead return to the shadows [*yin*],
The living return to the light [*yang*].
The living have their villages [*li*],
The dead have their hamlets [*xiang*].
The living are subordinate to the western Chang'an [*an*],
The dead are subordinate to the eastern Mt. Tai [*shan*].
In joy they do not remember one another,
In bitterness they do not long for one another.[204]

Other texts call for expelling the deceased by any means necessary:

The subject who died on the day *yi si* has the ghost name "Heavenly Brightness." This name has already been reported to the Spirit Master of the Heavenly Emperor. Instantly remove yourself three thousand leagues. If you do not immediately depart, the [. . .] of the Southern Mountain will be ordered to come and devour you. Act promptly, in accord with the ordinances and statutes.[205]

Even the lengthy "funeral narrative" found at Cangshan, which asks the deceased to grant prosperity and longevity to his descendants and describes all the pleasures depicted in the tomb's imagery, ends with a chilling insistence on the need for absolute separation:

Having entered the dark world,
You are completely separated from the living,

After the tomb is sealed,

It will never be opened again.[206]

This threat of the dead also figured in stories discussed in chapter one, in which skeletons of the deceased were pulverized and boiled in poisonous substances to prevent them from intruding into the dreams of the living. Burial was one method of removing the threat posed by the dead, but, if this failed, the more drastic measures depicted in these stories were also employed.

It remains uncertain why the early Chinese came to perceive the dead primarily as a threat. Under the Shang and the Western Zhou, the routine commensality of the living and the dead had ritually expressed a world in which the authority of the spirits followed the pattern set by living rulers—since ancestors were former rulers and their wives transposed into the spirit realm—and the authority of the living derived from the dead. With the spirit realm and the state established as mirror images, the progressive extension of the state to wider reaches of society during the Eastern Zhou entailed a similar extension of the spirit realm.[207] This new spirit world, however, was no longer structured around meals shared with deceased kin, but around the regulated impositions of oaths, registers, and legal codes. Like the emerging territorial states, this new underworld preserved order through maintaining clear divisions, a process sketched in the introduction to this book that recurs at every level of the ordering of space in early China. Along with the divisions between Heaven and Earth, higher and lower, elder and younger, or man and woman, the boundary between the living and the dead was a fundamental dividing line whose disappearance would lead to chaos. As Wu Hung has pointed out, death can be euphemistically referred to in Chinese as the "great boundary." Thus, it is significant that most of the tomb texts intended to separate the dead from the living invoked the bureaucratic powers of the spirit underworld to accomplish this task.[208]

While there is no direct testimony to support this model of the emergence of the belief in the dead as a menace to be controlled, much of the discussion of ghosts from the late Warring States and Han focuses on the theme of the avenging spirit who returns to kill. Already in the *Zuo zhuan* avenging ghosts such as Shen Sheng, Bo You, and other unhappy spirits came in dreams or visions to express their resentments or to take life. In the chapter of the *Mozi* on existence of ghosts, the cases of ghosts acting in the world of the living usually tell of avenging spirits who come back to punish those who wronged them in life.[209] The first of these cases, that of the ghost of Du Bo avenging himself on the king who unjustly executed him, is repeatedly cited by Wang Chong as metonym for the entire Mohist argument for the existence of ghosts.[210] Stories of avenging spirits also figure in the *Shi ji*, and they became a regular feature of Chinese history and fiction.[211] Apart from avenging ghosts, spirits appear in the world of men with demands for a proper burial, rescue from a coffin that has become flooded, or to seek assistance on some other matter. Finally, Wang Chong argues that ghosts appear to those who are sick and on the point of death, and that they will carry off the dying person.[212] In short, spirits in Warring States and early imperial China appear in the human world primarily when something has gone wrong, and they come to punish the living or to make demands on them. These stories offer specific form to the more general notion that in a properly functioning world the dead and the living would be rigorously separated, and that the dead return as figures of menace.

Given this vision of the dead as a threat, the construction of the tomb as a house can be understood as an attempt to provide all things necessary so that the deceased will remain in their own world and not return to trouble the living.[213] However, these tomb-households also reflect the idea discussed that the household could not form a complete, autarkic unit. This is shown by artistic elements that transform the tomb into a complete world. Trapped in a single household with its limited resources the dead would not be content, so an entire world was provided in which he or she could enjoy all possible pleasures.

This idea shaped the tomb of the First Emperor, which, according to Sima Qian, contained a replica of the heavens on its ceiling and the earth along its floors.[214] Similarly, tombs of the rich and powerful at the end of the Warring States are described as follows in the Lü shi chun qiu: "When making tumuli in the present age, they are as tall as mountains and their trees are thick as forests. Arranging tower-gates and courtyards, building halls and chambers with flights of steps for visitors, they make their mounds like towns and cities."[215] Thus, even as the tomb was fashioned in the shape of a household, both its external structure and internal contents suggest that it could be a mountain, a city, or a world.

One of the clearest examples of this multiplicity of roles is the early Western Han tomb no. 1 at Mawangdui near Changsha. As Wu Hung has demonstrated, the organization of this tomb and the images it contains suggest at least four realms for the dead: the underground household of the tomb, a larger underworld realm, an immortal paradise, and the entire universe.[216] Thus, the celebrated banner draped over the innermost coffin provides a model of the universe, with a watery underworld, a world of the living marked by an offering scene to the coffin found in the tomb, the deceased and her attendants in an intermediate zone, and a celestial plane marked by the sun and moon, along with their associated beings. Inside this banner the inner coffin becomes a complete universe where the soul could dwell.

This banner-draped inner coffin is surrounded in turn by outer coffins. The decor on the second coffin includes images of horned spirits who wield weapons and kill harmful creatures, as well as animal hybrids and magical creatures. These indicate a well-guarded underworld. The third coffin contains an image of a jagged mountain peak flanked by dragons, divine animals, and immortals. Sōfukawa Hiroshi has identified this mountain as Kunlun, the mountain at the western edge of the world that had become identified as the realm of the Queen Mother of the West and her court of immortals.[217] These suggest that the tomb or the coffin could also function as the paradise of the immortals. Given that immortals were aerial beings associated with the extreme west (Kunlun) or the extreme east (the floating mountains on the Eastern Sea), these images also once again suggest that this tomb could magically encompass the entire world.

Finally, the coffins were surrounded by a wooden frame built into the tomb. This equivalent of a house was divided into four chambers with the burial goods for a comfortable existence. The northern chamber imitated the inner chamber of an actual house, with curtains, floor mats, eating and drinking vessels, bedroom furniture, a painted screen, and clothed figurines representing musicians and attendants. The other three compartments contained stores of utensils and food, along with numerous figurines representing servants. This pattern in which the exterior layer provided the model of a house, while sets of images within the house indicated that the grave was a complete universe, became a recurrent feature in Han funerary art.

While this is one of the most elaborate and multifaceted of the tombs constructed as simultaneous households and worlds, related images appear in many Han tombs. Banners like that of Mawangdui no. 1, although simpler in contents, have been found in several tombs.[218] Moreover, in other tombs carvings on the coffin seem to play a similar role. Thus, the images on the coffin found at Guitoushan, which have the advantage of being labeled, include the "Gate of Heaven," the two cosmic deities Fu Xi and Nü Gua, the four directional animals, the sun and the moon, numerous immortals, and replicas of buildings such as a "Grand Granary."[219] The recurring figures on Sichuan coffins of Fu Xi and Nü Gua holding aloft the sun and the moon also figure as a reduced version of the Mawangdui banner, with the three realms of Heaven, man, and Earth linked together in the sweeping lines of the gods. The celestial realm is indicated by the sun and moon, the human world by the human upper halves of the deities, and the earth by their lower snake-form bodies.[220] Images indicating the cosmic expanse of the tomb were also applied to the ceilings and wall of the tombs. These included the sun, moon, constellations, animals of the four quarters, spirits of wind and rain, Queen Mother of the West and her paradise, and immortals. Images of the Queen Mother of the West and her immortal court also appear on objects buried in tombs, such as the bronze "money trees" found in Sichuan (see chapter three).[221] These recurring images suggest that a household was insufficient for the dead, who would only be satisfied in the plenitude of an entire world. Thus, even the household-tomb included within itself the critique of the household as a fragment of a larger whole.

The final weakness is Wu Hung's assertion that temple sacrifices were abolished. As Kenneth Brashier has shown, to the end of the dynasty, temple sacrifices continued to be central to imperial ancestral worship, and temple sacrifices also continued to be made by powerful lineages.[222] Both Han texts and Sima Biao's third-century A.D. record of Han ritual state that there were two imperial ancestral temples in Luoyang, one for which the apical ancestor was the Western Han founder and one that of the Eastern Han. The former contained five ancestral tablets, the latter seven, and both received seasonal offerings. Emperors were presented at these temples at the time of their accession, and officials debated the order of their tablets. There are records of the music and dances performed at the temples. Finally, temple prayers presented when the capital was moved back to Chang'an in A.D. 190 are preserved in the collected writings of their author, Cai Yong (A.D. 133–192).[223]

Limited evidence regarding the great families also shows that offerings at ancestral temples continued along with those at graves. A surviving fragment of Cui Shi's (A.D. ca. 110–170) *Si min yue ling*, a handbook for running an estate and a large household, states:

> The first day of the first month is called New Year's Day. [The patriarch] personally leads his wife and children to make pure offerings to his ancestors and parents. From three days prior to the appointed time, the household head and those playing roles in the ceremony will undergo purification. On the day of the offering, they present wine to cause the spirits to descend. Then all members of the household, both noble and base, without exception for young or old, are arrayed before the ancestors in order of age. Sons, their wives, grandchildren, and great grandchildren each present pepper blossom wine to the head of the household, happily offering toasts to wish him long life.[224]

This hierarchical array of the extended households in front of all the ancestors could only take place in an ancestral temple, where all the relevant tablets were present. Less detailed references to such ceremonies appear elsewhere in the text, and, like the imperial temple sacrifices, these were conducted at intervals through the year.[225] The text stipulates that offerings at the graves should take place the day *after* offerings in the temple, suggesting the ritual priority of the latter.[226] Unlike the temple offerings, these grave rituals also include offerings to non-kin.

Sima Biao's account of imperial sacrifices in the late Eastern Han also links temple sacrifices to grave sacrifices, with ritual priority given to the former: "In Emperor Ling's time, seasonal sacrifices in the capital were made to the five tablets in Gaozu's shrine, the seven tablets in Shizu's shrine, the three graves of the emperors who died young, and the three graves of the posthumously honored empresses."[227] This text, as well as Cai Yong's *Du duan*, notes that Emperor Ming, second emperor of the Eastern Han, established the precedent that the emperor should not erect a mausoleum at the site of his tomb, but simply place a tablet in the temple of the Eastern Han's founder. Grave sacrifices were offered only to selected women and to emperors who died before reaching adulthood and were thus not qualified to be placed in the lineage's ancestral temple. The *Du duan* stipulates: "Underage emperors who died before adulthood were all excluded from the temple. The three of them who thus used their graveside mausolea as their temples were Emperor Shang at Kangling, Emperor Chong at Huailing, and Emperor Zhi at Jingling." Sima Biao adds that their exclusion from the temple was because none of these emperors had actually reigned.[228]

The cumulative evidence shows that the temple remained the most important site, with the grave as an adjunct. This was because the temple remained the key ritual site for the lineage, while the grave was reserved for the individual or the household (in a joint burial). Thus, in the imperial sacrifices, graveside offerings were reserved for women and children, who were not full members of the lineage. Temple offerings indicated not only membership in the lineage, but also the fact of having wielded political authority. For the powerful local families, as indicated by Cui Shi's stipulations, temple offerings again took ritual precedence over those at the graveside. Temple offerings were the occasion for gathering the family, while graveside offerings in some cases were a ritual expression of more distant forms of sociability involving former political superiors, teachers, friends, village elders, or remote kin. This secondary character of the grave as a ritual site is suggested even in the organization of the clan cemeteries that began to appear in the Eastern Han, for these were only loose assemblages of graves without any overarching structure that expressed lineage organization.[229]

Several Eastern Han writers also privileged the temple over the grave. Because canonical texts elaborated the temple system, while records of graveside ritual did not antedate the Qin, these men attributed the former to the Zhou or high antiquity, but the latter to the late Warring States, or even the First Emperor. Thus, Cai Yong wrote: "In ancient times they did not sacrifice at graves. When it came to the time of the First Emperor of Qin, he removed the mausoleum from the capital and erected it at the side of his grave. The Han followed Qin without change."[230] In this model, graveside offerings are a deviant Qin innovation carried on by the Western Han, while the temple rites derive from the classics.

This same idea figures in the earlier writings of Wang Chong (A.D. 27–ca. 100). He remarks, "In ancient ritual [*li*] people sacrificed in the temple; in modern custom [*su* 俗] they sacrifice at graves."[231] This passage anticipates Cai Yong's condemnation of graveside sacrifices as a recent innovation. Moreover, describing temple sacrifice as a canonical ritual and graveside offerings as mere custom demonstrates his rejection of the latter as an inferior innovation (see chapter four). This also underlies his condemnation of such practices as the use of models to imitate the homes of the living.[232] In contrasting temples with recent innovations he writes:

> In ritual when one entered the ancestral temple, there was nothing
> to control [*zhu* 主] the thoughts. So they carved a piece of wood
> two *cun* long and called it a tablet [*zhu* 主]. This controlled the mind
> to serve [the ancestors]. They did not make human images. Now in
> the sacrifice to appease the earth they make a clay idol to imitate

the ghost's form. How could this appease? Spirits are vague and formless. They can exit or enter without a door, which is why they are called "spirits." Now to make an image of their form is contrary to ritual, and it completely misses the reality of the spirit.[233]

This contrast between the ritually correct use of tablets in the temple and the erroneous use of material images to deal with spirits clearly condemns the essential practices of grave worship.

A final aspect of constructing graves as replicas of houses is the pivotal role of women in the tomb. Although women had only a marginal role in the lineage's ancestral temple, the underworld household of the tomb was in many ways defined by the link of husband and wife. First, Han tombs were generally joint burials in which husband and wife were ultimately interred together. Husbands and wives not only resided in the tomb as a pair of corpses, but scenes of them sitting together, as well as scenes of intimacy and physical affection, were placed in many tombs. Sexual activities, perhaps as an aspect of some seasonal ritual, were also depicted.[234]

Women also figured in the tomb in various roles. Many scenes cited in the preceding note contain images of the female attendants of the wife. The aforementioned evidence for women's role in cloth production included depictions in tombs of the weaving and spinning of fabrics, as well as the collection of mulberry leaves. Women are also depicted in tomb art as entertainers—both dancers and musicians—and sometimes as workers in the kitchens where banquets are being prepared.[235] Thus, the tombs, like the great households themselves, were filled with women who played a major role in the existence of the deceased.

In addition to the major role of women in the household aspect of the tomb, they played important roles as deities who transformed the tomb into a cosmos. One female image that appears in several tombs is a woman in a half-open doorway, welcoming the deceased.[236] More important, the most frequently depicted deities in Han tomb art are the Queen Mother of the West and the pairing of Fu Xi and Nü Gua. The first is a powerful female divinity whose court was at the pinnacle of Kunlun. In Han art she was the patron goddess of immortality and the ruler of a blessed realm.[237] The importance of this goddess in tombs is noteworthy because in texts from the late Warring States and Han, she figures only briefly in the *Mu Tianzi zhuan* (see chapter five), in Sima Xiangru's "Da ren fu," and in an account of an ecstatic popular cult that burst into the historical records in 3 B.C. and then vanished. This disjunction between the pantheon of deities and sages depicted in the scholastic and literary traditions and that found in tomb art is remarkable. It marks among the deities the aforementioned split between the canonical, masculine tradition of the lineage and state, and the intimate world of the household where women's activity was important, and their authority sometimes decisive.

Fu Xi and Nü Gua are even more significant because they embody among the divinities the formation of couples, which was central to the household. Like the Queen Mother, they were minor figures in the written tradition, in which they were not identified as a married couple.[238] However, while texts separately emphasized the cultural innovations of Fu Xi and the physical fecundity of Nü Gua, the iconography of the period, in which they appear only in tombs, bound them closely together.[239] Indeed they can be identified with certainty only as a couple. The tomb art treats them as high divinities, and depicts their central role in maintaining the order of the cosmos. The art does this through the symbolism of the carpenter's square and compass that they hold, by treating them as reduced "charts" of the cosmos, and by using them as guardians for the inner doorways both of tombs and the houses in tomb art.

This contrast between the written tradition and tomb art is best demonstrated by the inscribed depiction of the divine couple from the ceiling of the Wu Liang shrine.[240] This image contains the classic elements of intertwined snake bodies, "offspring," and the carpenter's square and compass. The inscription, however, does not even mention Nü Gua. It refers only to Fu Xi, noting that he created kingship, devised the trigrams, and thereby governed the world. Thus, it follows the textual accounts of Fu Xi as an isolated figure, while the image depicts the paired deities as found in the tomb art. This hybrid creation reflects its role in a surface shrine that could be visited by living people, and which proclaimed the intellectual values of the Eastern Han elite. While the text speaks only of Fu Xi and the origins of kingship, the image depicts the generative powers of the married couple. In this way the surface shrine with its dual origins from orthodox literature and tomb art reflects the tension between the household and the lineage.

This opposition between tomb art and text reveals the diversity of Han beliefs and practices, and the tensions within them. While only a small minority could afford tombs with wall paintings, pictorial bricks, and carved stones, these still represent a much larger social group than the scholars who worked in the literary traditions. The couple Fu Xi and Nü Gua, and the Queen Mother of the West, secondary characters in the literary traditions, emerge as central figures whose dynamic images play a major role in the underworld universe. They control entry, maintain order on the wall or ceiling, transform the coffin into a microcosm, and establish paradise within the tomb.[241] The idealized world in Han tombs, where many people expressed their longings and aspirations, reveals to us aspects of a mental universe that had lain buried for millennia, where powerful women and the married couple played a fundamental role.

CONCLUSION

The major spatial form of kin organization in the early empires was the small household. Most of these consisted of nuclear families of four or five people, but at certain stages in their "life cycle" some turned into a "stem family" in which older parents lived with a married son and his children. Such households might have included nine or ten people. The legal household also included servants and in some cases large numbers of retainers, so wealthy families assembled large groups of non-kin. However, the vast majority of households remained relatively small.

The small size of households resulted from state policies to maximize the number of people liable for tax and service by dividing families into the largest number of units, and also from the destruction of the Zhou nobility. Nobles had lived in large, autarkic households, which included extensive lands and servile populations to meet all their needs. In contrast, the individual households that formed the basis of the Warring States polity performed specific economic roles, generally agriculture and cloth production but sometimes specialized craft manufacture, and then relied on exchange. This principle of the social division of labor was adopted by many Warring States philosophers as a justification for the existence of the state order, which they claimed was the sole means of linking an otherwise chaotic collection of isolated households. The consequent "universality" of the state, in contrast to the limited interests of the households, also justified the claims of the state's officers to a superior position in the social hierarchy. Thus, the individual households were depicted by advocates of state power as dependent fragments of a larger social and economic whole that relied on the political authorities for its survival.

Writers in Warring States and early imperial China described the household not only as a fragment of a political whole, but also of encompasing kin units. Ritual theories were dominated by the ideal of the male patriline that had constituted the central form of kinship for the great families of the Zhou era. While the lineage was probably not a central form of organization for the majority of the population, its textual prestige and its value for wealthier kin groups who desired to link together large numbers of households made it central to classicist scholars and members of the elite. The lineage as defined in the ancestral temple and the canonical texts was a male construct in which females participated only as adjuncts of their spouses. The household, on the other hand, was organized around the marriage bond between a man and a woman. Thus, these two levels of kin organization thus existed in a state of fundamental tension based on the differing roles that they gave to women.

For the lineage, women were outsiders, and the household formed a temporary union of disparate substances, a divided composite that threatened to split up the overarching unity of the patriline. This vision of the household as a realm of division was demonstrated in stories in Han texts and artistic images that portrayed the tendency of wives to turn brothers against one another, or the problems posed by remarriage. Such stories and images celebrated women who sacrificed themselves and their own children to preserve the lineage of their first husbands or their brothers. Several stories even lauded suicide and self-mutilation as the only means by which women could truly serve the lineage into which they had married. Such extreme prescriptions indicate just how problematic women, and the households they helped to form, could be from the point of view of the lineage.

While the ritual texts and hagiographic literature written in support of the lineage thus treated women as outsiders and objects of suspicion, scattered evidence of more widespread attitudes suggests a different picture. First, even the hagiographic literature celebrates the power of mothers over sons, despite a few often-quoted ritual texts that insisted that widowed mothers should obey their sons. This image of the power of mothers suggested by literature is confirmed by a Han will that shows how a mother dictated the distribution of her family's estate. The power of women in the household, a power based on the emotional and physical ties linking them to their husbands and sons, was also explicitly acknowledged in the later genre of "household instructions." There, however, it appears as a problem to be overcome. Finally, the power of women within the household is also demonstrated by the history of that highest of households, the imperial family. The central phenomenon in the history of Han political institutions was the transfer of power from the outer bureaucracy to the "inner court" in the emperor's private quarters. Within this realm, power concentrated into the hands of those who had immediate access to the person of the emperor, above all his wives and their kin, and the eunuchs who shared their existence.

The shift of power to imperial women, although treated as a scandal, reflected an underlying tension in the spatial distribution of authority in China. The basic spatial principle of political power in China from as early as the Zhou had been that authority was located at the center. The movement from outer to inner marked an ascent in power, whether in the ancestral temple or the palace complex, and fewer and fewer people were allowed access at each stage of movement toward the ultimate center. For this reason the imperial palace complex was called "forbidden," and emperors were sealed off behind layers of walls and courtyards. The structure of the Chinese house was based on the same principle. Behind more open and public outer rooms, the restricted rooms at the center were reserved for the actual family and their closest servants. However, just as power was spatially assigned to the center, to the most private and hidden part of any spatial structure, so were women. Whether in the imperial palace or in elite dwellings, women were assigned to the ultimate inner chambers. Thus, while women were to be formally excluded from power, they were forced to dwell in the places where authority was to be found. This helps to account for the fact that female power recurs constantly throughout Chinese history at every level of society, but that every occurrence is treated as a scandal by orthodox thinkers. Female power grew directly out of fundamental organizing principles of Chinese society without being explicitly articulated within those principles.

A final demonstration of the tension between the household and the lineage that supposedly encompassed it appears in the doubling of the sites of death ritual in the period. Classical Zhou death ritual had been located in the ancestral temple where the patriline was laid out in the order of the tablets of male ancestors. During the Warring States and early empires, however, the grave also emerged as a major ritual site. This is significant because over the same time period the grave came to be fashioned as a replica of the household of the living. Through using house architecture to build the tomb, and then filling it with replicas or images of all the goods that people had enjoyed in their homes or on their estates, the grave came to be a parallel home in which the dead would remain comfortably separated from their living descendants. This parallel between the house and the grave was also marked by the fact that husbands and wives were conventionally buried together, so that the marriage bond that formed the household was carried into the tomb. Thus, the two rival organizing principles, masculine descent constituting the lineage and marriage constituting the household, were in turn built into the structures of two rival sites of the death cult, the temple and the tomb.

The graves of Warring States and early imperial China as replicas of households again demonstrate the idea that the household was a fragment of a larger whole. While aspects of the grave were intended to provide a version of the house, other images and objects within it show that it was to form an entire world. Schematic depictions of the three levels of the cosmos were placed on banners to be draped on coffins or on the coffin lids themselves. Other images on coffins depicted the mountains and islands at the edges of the world or the immortal beings who dwelt in these places. Similarly asterisms and cosmic beings were depicted on the walls or ceilings of tombs. Such images, as indicated in later stories, took on actual reality in the shadowy, disembodied world of the dead. Apparently convinced that a simple house might prove too limiting, the makers of Chinese tombs thus invoked the power of images to provide an entire universe for the deceased. Interestingly, the most frequently depicted divinities in this universe of the dead were the Queen Mother of the West with her court of immortals, and the divine couple Fu Xi and Nü Gua, who structured the entire cosmos through the intertwining of their bodies and the magical instruments they wielded. Just as female power emerged unacknowledged in the realm of the household, so in the parallel household world of the tomb powerful female divinities who were marginal in the surviving literature of the period moved into central positions of authority.

CHAPTER THREE

CITIES AND CAPITALS

As a form of spatial order, the city is both one of the largest artificial structures and the realm of artifice par excellence, where a people are most free to construct a model of their visions of society and the cosmos. Separating people from their natural surroundings through its walls—both defensive walls ringing the town and those of buildings—the city forms a distinctively human space filled with all the products of craftsmanship that make up the constructed environment known as civilization.[1] Cities are also a primary form of political power, providing both the setting in which rulers and administrators gather and the stage on which they display their power. Finally, they are focal points of circulation and exchange, drawing in a steady stream of people and objects, and in turn producing new goods that flow outward to other cities or to secondary centers of human habitation.

This chapter examines the changing structure and role of cities in the Warring States and Han periods. The first section examines the earlier cities of the Shang and Zhou, focusing on the existence and nature of city-states. The second examines the major changes in the cities of the Warring States and early Han—increase in scale, physical division of the city into walled areas, new forms of public architecture—and links these to the political developments of the period. These developments highlight once again the theme of the spatial entity as an object divided against itself—in this case literally divided by walls. The final section examines the changing nature of the political capital in the emergent macrostates and ultimately a world empire. It traces first the emergence of a hierarchy of cities within a single administration, second the manner in which Qin's capital Xianyang reflected the nature of this first empire's triumph and its ultimate fall, and finally the progressive invention over the course of the Han of a new form of imperial capital. This new form of capital was defined by its ritual centrality, its text-based structure, and its detachment from all ties to region or locality. The capital, its cults, and the artificial language used in government became the purest expressions of the new political order defined by the transcendence of all local interests. The issue of the capital and its relation to other population

135

centers once again highlights the theme of the city as a fragment of larger wholes.

THE WORLD OF THE CITY-STATES

Urbanism in China has a long history. Neolithic villages of pit houses with thatched roofs were built on loess mounds along the Yellow River from at least 5000 B.C. In the second millennium B.C. people built large, defensive walls from tamped earth, and divided cities into ceremonial centers for temples and palaces, areas inhabited by lineages of artisans who produced ritual or luxury goods, and residential areas.[2] These settlements in turn were ultimately linked into a polity under the Shang (B.C. ca. 1600–ca. 1045) kings. However, the written evidence for the Shang state—the divination records found at the last Shang capital at Anyang—dates from several centuries after the establishment of the dynasty. Consequently, the origins of the state and its links to the rise of urbanism are not clear. The functioning of the state at its peak, however, can be reconstructed, and urban centers played a key role.

The late Shang state has been studied by David Keightley. By examining oracle records, he has determined whom the king commanded, what he demanded of them, where he proceeded without opposition, to whom and with whom he offered sacrifice, from whom he suffered attacks, and related questions.[3] The Shang state thus revealed was a web of walled settlements. The inhabitants of these towns formed one or more consanguineal kin groups (*zu* 族) that served as military units and performed sacrifice to their ancestors.[4] Scattered among the towns that obeyed the Shang were settlements, called *fang* 方, that were in a state of low-level conflict or open war with the Shang. A notable example are the pre-dynastic Zhou, who first appear in the Shang inscriptions as enemies to be fought, then become allies to be commanded, and finally disappear from the record in what appears to be a geographic contraction of Shang activities.[5] Thus, the Shang state was a network of pathways and encampments along which the king moved or sent commands, surrounded by regions that never saw the king or his messengers, and by peoples who figured as enemies in battle and sources of human sacrifice. It was not a continuous, territorial state, but a league of towns allied by kinship or shared religious practice, towns existing amid alien and hostile settlements.

Akatsuka Kiyoshi has developed a theory of the Shang state that would explain the emergence of such a structure. Given that men's names derived from their places of origins, he has shown that many chief diviners in the early records came from Shang allies, that several early kings in the royal genealogy originated in allied tribes or settlements, and that some gods sacrificed to by the Shang were originally the local gods of allied cities. The pre-dynastic Zhou similarly incorporated Shang ancestors into *their* pantheon.[6] From these observations, Akatsuka has argued that the Shang state originated from a world of tribes or clans, each having its own walled settlement, its own rulers, its own holy places, and its own spirits. The Shang court was created through a union of several such clans. As indicated by the placing of "alien" men or gods in the early generations of the Shang genealogy, the royal lineage itself may have been created through a fusion of leaders from several tribes. Groups who subsequently fell under Shang domination were drawn into the new state through the adoption of their leaders as diviners and the addition of their gods to the Shang pantheon. In this way kin ties, both real and ascriptive, and shared cult served to bind together a league of originally autonomous towns or cities.[7]

Keightley has also shown that the Shang king was always on the move. He displayed his power by traveling, hunting, and inspecting along the pathways of his realm. As he moved over the landscape, he sacrificed to local spirits, giving nourishment and receiving numinous power at each holy place, while renewing the religious and kin ties that linked him to the other settlements in the league. Apart from the performance of rituals that spiritually incorporated the diverse localities of his realm, the king also went on regular hunts. Divinations regarding these hunts constitute a significant percentage of the surviving inscriptions. The hunts served for military training, for showing the flag, and as a means of securing booty to reward his followers, but they also seem to have been essential to feed and clothe the court. This suggests that the king did not have a sophisticated administrative apparatus to extract taxes from a peasantry whose agricultural techniques had not changed since the Neolithic.

That the king spent so much time away from the capital—one military campaign kept him in the field for more than three hundred days—also suggests that he was not primarily an administrator. Indeed, such itinerant power indicates that the capital may have been a base of operation, a cult center, a necropolis, or an artisanal center rather than a fixed administrative and redistributive center. The lack of administration is demonstrated by the fact that the king rarely delegated his power, and then only to relatives and immediate followers. Armies were commanded by the king himself, his wives, or relatives from the Shang court. Moreover, the range of Shang divination was tightly circumscribed to the king and his kin, and included allies only where they were fighting together with Shang forces. Little delegation of authority and the narrow ambit of divinatory concerns both support the idea that even in its own capital the Shang state remained an extended clan or lineage structure. This patrimonial state lacked any substantial administrative apparatus, and in practice existed only where the king, his immediate relations, or the closest of his followers were present. Thus, only a thread held together the walled settlements that made up the Shang realm.

The Western Zhou (ca. 1045–771 B.C.) inherited and extended the model of the state as a league of cities bound together by the power of the ruling house. Having conquered the Yellow River valley, they enfeoffed relatives or allies in walled towns scattered across their realm. These cities occupied by the Zhou nobility served as armed garrisons to control conquered populations. They owed allegiance to the Zhou king, from whom they received titles and regalia, but they wielded religious and military authority within their own realms. Even the descendants of the Shang kings were established in the city of Song, in order to maintain the sacrifices to the potent shades of the deceased kings.[8]

Because the Zhou relied on walled towns occupied by relatives and allies to control their territory, their society was defined by an armed nobility based in the cities, surrounded by a countryside occupied by a servile peasantry. In light of this separation of nobility and citizens from the peasantry, the Zhou developed an elaborate vocabulary to hierarchize the cities' inhabitants, those dwelling in the villages immediately around the cities, and those who lived at great distances and played no role in the state.[9] Like the Shang cities, those of the Zhou were held together by the power and prestige of the king. As long as the king remained militarily supreme, and his conquests provided new territory to reward his followers, the Zhou dominated their feudatories. They could even shift them from one place to another. When expansion stopped after the death of King Zhao and the loss of his army in the south in 957 B.C., royal power declined. Kings increasingly secured allegiance and paid for offices through gifts of land that whittled away their resources.[10] With the seizure of the old capital by the Quan Rong and disaffected nobles in B.C. 771, and the transfer of the dynasty east to Luoyang under the domination of the rulers of Zheng and Jin, royal power vanished. All the fiefs, most of them individual towns and their hinterlands, were left as de facto independent states.

The Spring-and-Autumn period (B.C. 771–481) was the age of the city-state in China.[11] The city-states emerged from the collapse of the Zhou state, which had itself been a league of cities. Later overbuilding and lack of excavations have resulted in a paucity of information about Spring-and-Autumn cities, apart from the dimensions and shape of their tamped-earth walls. This indicates that larger cities were about 4 square miles, while some were a quarter of that size. While we have no evidence for populations, references to the size of armies and populations of much larger cities from the Warring States period suggest that a large population would have numbered in the tens of thousands, and that small ones would have had a few thousand people.[12]

Major public buildings were rectangular, constructed of wood, and had tamped-earth foundations. They seem to have been largely single-storied, and only toward the end of the period is there evidence of attempts to build higher foundations for the multistoried towers that became important later. Some large ceremonial buildings, sometimes associated with cemeteries, were located just outside the walls. The majority of the population, including some of the elite, lived in semisubterranean thatched rectangular or oval huts, much like those of the Neolithic.[13] Evidence for the scale of these city-states also derives from the number of them within a given area, the extent of their distribution, and the size of their territory. Again, there is no precise information on these questions, but some evidence can suggest orders of magnitude. Most of this evidence comes from the Warring States period, but since some smaller city-states still existed at that time, and some now-lost records may have been available, they can suggest the number, scale, and variety of city-states that existed in the Spring-and-Autumn period.

A text from the third century A.D. states that in the time of the mythic ruler Yu there were 10,000 states, at the beginning of the Shang 3,000, at the beginning of the Zhou 1,713, and at the beginning of the Spring-and-Autumn period 1,200.[14] While the later figures have no known textual basis, the initial figure of 10,000 (a notional figure meaning "myriad," "many thousands") states existing in the time of Yu appears in writings from the middle and late Warring States period.[15] One of these adds the remark that "none of their walls exceeded [a circumference of] 750 yards, and even the most populous of them did not exceed three thousand households."[16] Thus, as late as the middle Warring States period, scholars still applied the term "state" (*guo*) to walled settlements that could be quite small. They projected recent political history, in which large states absorbed numerous smaller ones, back into the distant past, consequently imagining that at the beginning of this history there were huge numbers of small city-states.

This Warring States model demonstrates the survival of city-states as an idea into later centuries, but it offers no insight into the actual number of states in the Spring-and-Autumn period. Serious study of this problem began with the nineteenth-century scholar Gu Donggao, who in the process of compiling a table of the events of the period produced a list of all named states. Supplements by twentieth-century scholars have resulted in a list of 209 names.[17] However, Chinese scholars in the sixth century A.D. identified with earlier "states" of the Spring-and-Autumn period many small towns that in the Han were ranked below district (*xian* 縣) level.[18] These towns were too small to figure in the political histories of the period, and many do not appear in the lists derived from Gu's work. This shows that the number of 200 city-states included only those of political significance. In addition to these larger city-states, there were many towns that functioned as states, which were not important enough to be cited in chronicles.

Further evidence derives from distribution. A few large states with several cities—Qi, Jin, Qin, and Chu—ringed the Chinese world and thus had room for expansion. Within this ring of larger states, hundreds of other states were restricted to the western part of the flood plain of the Yellow River. On the basis of the number of known states and the area in which they were distributed, Miyazaki has calculated that the average distance between two city-states was between 55 and 60 miles.[19] This is somewhat longer than the distance from Athens to Corinth. Many states, of course, were closer than this—for example, Lu and Teng were only 36 miles apart.

Warring States texts give further evidence on the size of city-states. The *Mencius* states that a major feudal lord should have a territory of a square of 100 *li* (about 30 miles) per side. The figure of 100 *li* is a round one, suggesting an order of magnitude. It appears elsewhere in the *Mencius* as the size of state from which the Shang and Zhou began their conquests, and is also cited in the *Shang jun shu* and the *Guanzi* as the size of a typical or average city-state. The *Mencius* also states that a state of less than 100 *li* per side would be unable to maintain the sacrifices of a proper ancestral temple. However, many city-states were clearly smaller than this figure, and the *Mencius* describes the state of Teng as having only 50 *li* per side.[20]

The figure of 100 *li* per side indicates a territory smaller than Miyazaki's average, but if one omitted from one's calculations land that was useless due to salt deposition, occupied by non-Chinese peoples, or left empty as a buffer between two states, the two figures become close.[21] Such a state would be less than one-third the size of Sparta and just smaller than Athens.[22] Assuming that the city lay at the center of the state, it would entail a 15-mile walk to the frontier, within the distance that an army of the period was able to march in one day. Granting that the figure of 100 *li* is simply an order of magnitude, it indicates that the majority of the states of Spring-and-Autumn China were sufficiently small that people could travel from the center to beyond the frontier in a day.

These small states consisted only of a single city and its hinterland. However, even in the Spring-and-Autumn period the leading powers, particularly those at the periphery, were no longer simple city-states. The most powerful states of the period were considerably larger and contained several cities. Thus, Mencius describes the state of Qi as consisting of a square with sides of 1,000 *li*, which he describes as proper to a Son of Heaven.[23] It may not be irrelevant that during Mencius's lifetime several of the leading states, including Qi, began to claim the title of king.

Nevertheless, even in larger states the individual city was often the unit of political control. This is demonstrated by the continued practice of subinfeudation through at least the first century of the Spring-and-Autumn period. Just as kin and allies of the Western Zhou king had been enfeoffed in cities, so in turn their collateral lines were established in secondary cities. In their own domains the collateral lines acted as reduced replicas of the state courts. Zhou power had thus been extended, and gaps filled in, through the multiplication of semiautonomous city-states that controlled their own affairs so long as they met minimal conditions of ritual obedience to their immediate superiors in the kin structure. This practice continued in several of the leading Spring-and-Autumn states.

When Jin took territory from the Di and Rong peoples, it established a secondary capital under a collateral line at Quwo in 746 B.C. In subsequent decades, other collateral lines, meritorious officials, and even refugee nobles from other states all received walled fiefs. This creation of a powerful nobility dispersed across the state in their own city-states was encouraged by the topology of Jin, which was divided by mountain ranges and narrow gorges that made communication difficult. In 678 the junior line at Quwo supplanted the original house of Jin. The new ruler destroyed most of the relatives of the former rulers, but replaced them with his own followers, who in subsequent decades emerged again as a rebellious nobility based in their own city-states. Struggles between the rulers and their nobility continued even in the period of Jin's greatest power, after the victory at Chengpu in 632. After the assassination of the ruler in 573 by two nobles, effective power passed into the hands of the nobility. These continued to fight sporadic civil wars from their local bases until Jin was partitioned in the late fifth century.[24] Thus, during the seventh and sixth centuries B.C., Jin, for most of the period the most powerful state in the Yellow River valley, was actually a congeries of semi-independent city-states that spent as much time fighting their ruler and each other as waging war against other states.

A similar case was the state of Lu. In 626 B.C., three sons of the ruler fighting over the succession were pacified by being granted their own walled city-states. From these bases they came to dominate the state, and an attempt to revive the ruler's power by destroying the walls of these collateral states ended in failure.[25] Thus, in the late fourth century the *Mencius* says that Lu was "five [units] of 100 *li* per side," that is, a state composed of five de facto city-states.[26]

Chu, the great power of the Yangzi valley, had a weak monarchy. It was probably the first state to introduce the institution of directly administered districts (*xian*) in newly conquered areas, the earliest record of which appears in 690 B.C. This institution was perhaps an attempt by the king to extend his own power and limit that of his nobles, so the governors were often the generals who had conquered them. However these early *xian* enjoyed considerable autonomy, and most seem to have reverted to the status of hereditary fiefs.[27] Thus, in seventh-century Chu, just as in Jin, attempts to expand the state's power simply produced more city-states serving as bases for ambitious men who claimed the status of the old nobility and challenged or supplanted the rulers.

Evidence of the tendency of larger and middle-sized Spring-and-Autumn states to split into multiple city-states also comes from the origin of surnames. In the Han dynasty Wang Fu (ca. A.D. 90–165) sought to trace the origins of the surnames that existed in his day. Many of these had appeared in the Spring-and-Autumn period, when aristocratic houses obtained new surnames in association with receiving a fief. Thus, each of the three collateral lines in Lu, and the six leading lineages that contested for power in fifth-century Jin, had established surnames. Seven surnames had originated from the state of Zheng, a middle-sized power located between the Yellow River and the Yangzi that had played a dominant role in the eastward shift of the Zhou capital, but soon sank to the level of a buffer state between Jin and Chu. Even more remarkable was the state of Song, another middle-sized buffer state, that produced no less than fifty-one named lineages.[28] It is unlikely that all of these held their own fiefs, but Song was in fact notorious for internal struggles between rival noble lines.

Thus, seventh-century B.C. China consisted of many small autonomous cities clustered in the flood plain of the Yellow River, and larger states on the periphery that were little more than leagues of semi-independent city-states loosely bound together through kinship or patronage. These larger states expanded by conquering non-Chinese peoples and smaller neighbors, but newly conquered areas were turned into city-states that soon threatened their nominal ruler's power as much as the "hostile" states they had replaced. During the next two centuries the larger states developed new institutions to administer larger territories and mobilize peasant populations for battle. However, the creation of these macrostates, the Warring States, was often a process of two steps forward and one back. Even Qin state—which from the middle of the fourth century B.C. had carried out the most thorough program of bureaucratically administering agricultural regions, registering peasants, and mobilizing them—still distributed newly conquered cities as fiefs to leading nobles who dominated the court. Only in the third century B.C., near the end of the Warring States period, did any political figure articulate the principle that all conquered territory should remain under the king's control.[29] Thus, the city-state as an idea, and a limited institutional reality, survived almost until the creation of the first empire.

Emerging from the collapse of the early monarchies that had held together leagues of cities through kinship, cult, and military power, the city-states of Spring-and-Autumn China continued to be members of leagues led by the most powerful states. However, in these new leagues, ties of kinship were nonexistent or ignored, while ritual suzerainty remained with the powerless Zhou dynasty. The leagues of Eastern Zhou city-states thus took the form of shifting alliances that recognized the leadership of whichever state could assert its military dominance. The ruler of the dominant state was given the title "senior" or "hegemon" (ba 霸) by the Zhou king, who charged him to defend what was still in name the Zhou realm. Formally these leagues were hierarchical groupings of independent states, bound together through treaties sanctified with blood oaths or "covenants" (meng 盟).

The political order formed by a league of city-states under a hegemon began to emerge shortly after the eastward shift of the Zhou capital. The state of Zheng, which had taken the lead in rescuing the king, soon overshadowed royal power. The defeat of the Zhou king and his allies in a war against Zheng ended all pretense of royal authority. The major states of north China recognized Zheng's leadership, until a civil war in 701 led to its ultimate eclipse.[30] With no effective monarchy or leading power, the Zhou city-states fell into turmoil. In the north the Rong and Di peoples destroyed several Zhou cities, while the state of Chu in the Yangzi valley—which had never recognized the Zhou—expanded northward. This crisis led to the state of Qi's establishment of the first formally recognized hegemony, which it attained through mobilizing the population of its capital and the immediate hinterland. In 667 an assembly of leading cities recognized Qi as leader, and the king bestowed the title of hegemon and charged the ruler of Qi to defend Zhou states in the name of the monarchy. In 659 Qi restored two city-states that had been destroyed by the Rong, and a few years later their coalition defeated Chu. Qi summoned the other states' rulers to an assembly that swore a blood covenant to recognize Qi's leadership.[31]

This demonstrates the role of the hegemonic league of city-states. Menaced by hostile forces on several sides, the Zhou cities could not defend themselves individually, but the monarchy was too weak to take the military lead. At the same time, no city-state was strong enough to claim the title of king for itself. The hegemony resolved this dilemma by preserving the Zhou monarch as a ritual figurehead who sanctioned the hegemon's military role while thwarting untoward ambitions. The hegemon, in turn, justified his pre-eminence by conspicuously restoring cities that had been destroyed by non-Zhou peoples, while absorbing smaller cities within his own region. The other city-states gained a power of collective action and the recognition of their independence. In the covenants that cemented the leagues, they pledged to respect each other's borders and not shelter rebels. This balance of ritual Zhou suzerainty, a de facto leading military power or powers, and a multitude of city-states joined in one or more leagues provided the political framework for the Spring-and-Autumn period. Although the identity of the leading state changed, and in some cases two states—each with a league of allies—battled for dominance, this structure preserved a world of city-states for two centuries. It continued into the sixth century, when civil wars between powerful ministerial houses created by subinfeudation tore apart the leading states. Only in the late sixth and the fifth centuries did practices and institutions introduced by the ministerial houses finally create a new political order that permanently transcended the city-state.

There are no accounts of the internal organization of the city-states, and the information from historical narratives is fragmentary. Nevertheless, the sources do reveal general patterns of the distribution of authority and the conduct of politics. These indicate the powers and limits of the rulers in the cities, the role of the citizenry and assemblies, the emergence of new forms of political actors, the political geography of the city, and the manner in which the devolution of power from the monarchical league to the individual cities was manifested in religious cult.

Spring-and-Autumn China was dominated by a nobility defined through participation in the "great services" of the state: sacrifice and warfare. This warrior elite was in turn ranked—king, feudal lord, hereditary minister, noble—according to their relation to the royal lineage. Ascent in this hierarchy was marked by the granting of additional forms or numbers of key ritual items—tripods in offerings, numbers of dancers, rows of bells, types of armor, layers of coffins—but all members of the elite shared a common nobility based on their participation in warfare and sacrifice. This idea of a common nobility led to a proximity of status and a sharing of authority within the city-states that were radically different from the later, imperial system.[32]

Under the Zhou monarchy, each city had been a lesser replica of the Zhou capital. Brothers and younger sons of the ruling house received offices at the courts of the Zhou king and the feudal lords along with fiefs to provide income and followers. Although in theory revocable at death, in practice both offices and the fiefs soon were transmitted from father to son as hereditary privileges.[33] Cities as domains of hereditary ministers in turn formed lesser replicas of the cities of the feudal lord. Thus, even when the monarchy was still powerful the Zhou state already contained a multitude of cities with their own rulers, courts, and temples. With the collapse of the monarchy, power shifted to the feudal lords, and in subsequent centuries it continued to devolve downward to the hereditary ministerial houses, or collateral lines established as city-states in the eighth and seventh centuries. Each of the city-states of the period had a hereditary ruler, but power was distributed among a group of noble families who had hereditary offices, their own ancestral temples, and servile followers.

The principle of shared nobility and the existence of hereditary offices led to a collegial mode of authority in which the ruler was first among equals, but decisions required a consensus. Power often depended on force of personality, and in many cases chief ministers or ministers of war wielded effective authority. Accounts of campaigns provide evidence of this pattern of authority. In some cases the ruler desired to launch a campaign, but was prevented from doing so by his minister of war. In other cases the minister of war was able to launch campaigns over the objection of the ruler. Sometimes the power to command the armies and decide on campaigns passed in rota among noble houses. The decision whether to fight could be taken by a collective decision of the leading nobles after an extended debate.[34]

Further evidence of collective authority comes from the makeup of armies. Each lineage provided a contingent of its own followers, and the state army was an amalgam of these lineage-based units. In the field these units remained under their own commanders, so major decisions were generally made by group consultation among the leaders. The units were so loosely bound that a commander might lead his own men to withdraw or attack without regard for the rest of the army. This form of organization also facilitated numerous armed feuds and civil wars.[35]

Commoners were defined by hereditary occupations. They were primarily artisans, merchants, and peasants, but also those who worked in orchards or gardens, stable hands, wood gatherers, herdsmen, menials, and female seamstresses. As individuals, urban commoners do not figure in the records, but they appear along with the lower levels of the nobility more than four hundred times in the major chronicles as the "people of the capital" or "citizens" (guo ren 國人). The nobles and some commoners served in the army. For important decisions the ruler or leading nobles summoned the "people of the capital" to make an appeal for support. While the assembly of the citizens was not a regular institution, they played a decisive political role in dozens of cases. Most frequently they were summoned in times of crisis, which required the mobilization of the populace for action, or at times of disputed successions, when their support secured the position of the victorious faction.[36]

Appeals for the support of the citizenry became so common that a chapter of the Shang shu written in the late Spring-and-Autumn or early

Warring States period depicts the Shang king Pan Geng assembling his people and delivering an elaborately crafted oration to persuade them of the necessity of moving the capital. An earlier chapter attributes a discussion of the importance of public opinion to the hero of the Zhou foundation, the Duke of Zhou. In the same manner the *Zhou li*, a late Warring States text, describes the existence of popular assemblies convoked in cases of crisis, succession, or moving the capital.[37] While describing these assemblies as a regular institution is wrong, it reflects the great frequency of their occurrence and the key role played by the citizens in times of crisis.

As struggles between nobles intensified, the citizens often played the decisive role in overthrowing one government and establishing another. The chronicles contain dozens of references to the citizens killing, expelling, or seizing a ruler, or of their blocking by force of arms the seizure of power by a noble faction.[38] It thus became a maxim that the anger of the populace was like a raging fire, or that their desires could not be blocked. Texts explain that a decision was undertaken to quiet or appease the citizens.[39] While the citizen body never took control of the government, their support was crucial to anyone who sought to do so.

The increasing power of the citizens led to the emergence of a new type of political actor, which in some ways resembles the tyrants in ancient Greece.[40] Some rulers extended their power through drawing members of the citizenry into their government and more completely mobilizing the populace. Lower nobles rose to power through skillfully playing off noble factions one against the other, while mobilizing the support of the populace. At the end of the Spring-and-Autumn period the citizens played a key role in establishing the power of several rising noble lines that took the lead in creating the Warring States forms of government.

The earliest example was Lord Huan of Qi's (r. 685–643) appointment of Guan Zhong and the reforms undertaken by the latter. Guan Zhong was supposedly of merchant origin, and his appointment to high office suggests that Lord Huan sought to secure his position by filling key posts with dependent commoners. It is thus perhaps not an accident that the practice of gathering refugees as dependent retainers is first recorded in the struggle for the succession to Lord Huan. Significantly, the reforms of Guan Zhong consisted in extending military service throughout the capital and its immediate hinterland, which probably allowed Qi to become the dominant power and establish the first hegemony.[41]

Another example is Zi Chan, who became virtual tyrant of Zheng in B.C. 543. A low noble, he first achieved prestige through his role in suppressing a rebellion of leading lineages. He then served as subordinate commander of an expedition, followed by several successful diplomatic missions. Proclaiming that the people's anger could not be confronted and that the ruler needed their support, Zi Chan persuaded the chief minister to burn covenant texts that aroused public opposition. He cultivated prestige through studying the arts and religious lore, so Confucius praised his literary skills while the celebrated connoisseur of music Wu Ji Zha saluted him as a kindred spirit. Fourth-century B.C. anecdotes cite him as an authority on the origins of states and their sacrifices, the nature of ghosts, the influence of the stars, and the interpretation of dreams. With the support of the citizenry he was selected to join the highest councils of government, and following another civil war in 543 he seized effective power. Shortly thereafter the chief minister of Zheng yielded the government to him.[42]

In Zi Chan's first year in power, a man reported that people were routinely gathering in the city's schools where they criticized government policy. He suggested that the schools be destroyed. Zi Chan refused, arguing that he would take public opinion as his guide. This was justified both because the people would know best the consequences of policies, and because the suppression of criticism would simply lead to rebellion.[43] Once established in power, Zi Chan initiated a series of reforms involving the building of irrigation channels to fix standardized units of land, the imposition of a land tax, the introduction of units of mutual responsibility for crimes, and the extension of military service. These reforms were at first criticized by the people, and although the populace soon came to support them, the balance of Zi Chan's career manifested less concern for the opinions of the populace. Instead he worked steadily to extend the authority of the government, announcing on his deathbed that severity was the only way to control the people.[44] His career thus followed the classic pattern of the tyrant who cultivated popular support to secure power, but then relied on increasing the state's wealth and military force to maintain it.

Other nobles in the sixth and fifth centuries sought the support of the citizenry through conspicuous displays of generosity. When the great sublineages of Lu defeated an attempted restoration of the ruler's power and drove him from the state, their victory was explained by the support gained through decades of philanthropy. Similarly the Tian clan came to dominate Qi through their generosity to the people.[45] Popular support proved crucial in their victory over the other great lineages of Qi, and their establishment as the new ruling house in 481.

The city-states of Spring-and-Autumn China still had relatively small populations, ranging from thousands to tens of thousands, so political activity was conducted on a face-to-face basis. There were several occasions for assembling the adult males of the city, and key sites at which the assemblies took place. The most common occasion was military campaigns. The army gathered at the ancestral temple, marched together, assembled in formation on the field of battle where prayers were given and oaths sworn, and held ceremonial assemblies and presentations at the ancestral temple after their return.

Much of the citizenry also sometimes assembled at the court, in major public squares, or in the market. Citizen assemblies called by rulers or nobles during crises or disputed successions were usually held in a courtyard facing the ancestral temple. When such assemblies lacked the sanction of the city's leaders, as in cases of attempted insurrection, they were held at major squares.

The market was also an important public gathering place. With crowds assembled to exchange goods and opinions, it sometimes served as a site for presenting arguments. The court and the market were also public spaces for exposing the corpses of major criminals or traitors who had been executed.[46] As shown in the anecdote about Zi Chan, schools were also places where citizens could assemble and discuss the issues or personalities of the day. Finally, much of the populace gathered at state altars for important rituals. The most important such assemblies were those convened at the altars of the grain and soil to seal blood covenants between the ruling lineage and the assembled heads of all households in the city. In all these sites both the day-to-day business of politics and major crises could be discussed and dealt with by either small groups of interested individuals or by the assembled citizenry.

A final aspect of the development of the city-states was the rise of new cults and rituals for the city as a unit, or the adoption of established rituals for the purpose of forging cities as self-conscious political units. The primary example of the former was the altars of the soil and grain, and the most important example of the latter was the extension of covenants to the entire city and hinterland in the process of mobilizing the population and forming new state structures.

The transformation of the Chinese state from a league of cities under a theocratic dynasty to a great territorial empire was marked by the shift of ritual primacy from the ancestral temple to cults devoted to Heaven and to major landscape features such as mountains.[47] In this process the age of the city-states witnessed the rising importance of the altars of the soil and grain. Since the Zhou state had been structured by kin links to the royal lineage, the most important cult was that for the ancestors. As the city-states became more independent units, and the political role of kinship declined, priority shifted to cults in which the entire city participated and that gave symbolic form to the city as a unit. Such were the cults to the altars of the soil and the grain.

The seeming incongruity that the central cult of the urban areas was devoted to agricultural deities can be explained. The altars of soil and grain had existed for centuries as the primary locus for offerings to the land, and each village had its own altars.[48] They were thus the standard cult for collections of human habitations that formed a territorial unit. For this reason they readily provided a cult for deities to be charged with the protection of the city as a territorial unit and to receive offerings from the populace. In texts of the late Spring-and-Autumn and Warring States periods, the "altars of the grain and soil" became the standard symbol of the state, and they were frequently employed as a metonym for the polity.[49]

Most cities had one pair of such altars, but an account of a covenant held to establish the tyranny of Yang Hu in Lu states that he performed the covenant with the ruler and nobles at the [Duke of] Zhou altar of the soil, and with the capital populace at the Bo altar of the soil. The subsequent ceremony of cursing those who violated the covenants was held at a major square in the capital.[50] The presence of two altars of the soil probably derived from the fact, shown in both bronzes and texts, that at Lu's foundation the Duke of Zhou received a large number of former Shang subjects organized in their lineages. Each group of his followers worshipped at its own altar. The Zhou colonists made sacrifices at an altar dedicated to the founder of their fief, while the Shang subjects employed an altar that came to serve as that of the non-noble citizenry.

The increasing centrality of the state's altars facilitated the articulation of a new theory of the relation between the people and the spirits. In a speech supposedly delivered at the end of the eighth century, a noble upbraided a ruler who thought that his sacrifices would assure victory with the observation that "the people are the masters of the spirits," so a ruler who failed to win the support of the people could not rely on help from the spirits. The "master" of a sacrifice was the person who sponsored it and on whose behalf it was made. Since the people provided the wealth for the sacrifices, and the altars of the state were their altars, they were the masters of the sacrifices and hence of the spirits.[51] By the Warring States this argument, which was discussed in chapter one, became a defense of the priority of good government over sacrifices, the insistence that Heaven shared the perceptions and desires of the people, and the Mencian theory of the propriety of rebellion against evil monarchs.

A second ritual innovation linked to the rise of the city-state was the swearing of blood covenants between rulers and citizens. This grew more frequent as citizens came to play a decisive role in civil wars between noble lineages. The covenants of Yang Hu cited earlier were classic examples, and it is significant that they were held at the altars of the soil. Since these altars had become the cultic embodiment of the city, it is natural that they served as the site for such ceremonies. New evidence on this form of covenant in the late Spring-and-Autumn has emerged in archaeological finds at Houma, Wenxian, and Qinyang. At Houma, archaeologists have excavated more than 300 pits containing fragments of covenant texts and the remains of sacrifices. All the texts refer to a political struggle that, according to the most likely theory, took place between 496 and 495 B.C. The participants were the members of the Zhao clan who had temporarily seized power, along with their followers. Most of the texts contain pledges of obedience, with the names of the gods who would enforce the pledge, or bans and collective death sentences placed on enemy lineages and households. These texts thus bound groups not related by kin ties together, and expelled other elements from the newly emerging body politic.[52]

These documents show the culmination of the use of covenants to establish new political units after the breakdown of the old state forms defined by kinship. In one of the civil wars that plagued Jin throughout the sixth century and led to its ultimate division, one party and its adherents gathered at the state altars where they sealed collective oaths that drew up itemized lists of the enemies who were to be driven from the state and killed if they returned.

Even as they tore apart the old state, they began to reconstitute it through binding its members with covenants and ostracizing all those who would not join. The inclusion of new elements in the public realm, the redefinition of the bonds between ruler and ruled, and the occasional focus on individual households show how the process of refashioning city-states also created the tools for forging the macrostates into which they would be absorbed.

Although the age of the city-state in China lasted for three centuries, it left little trace in later history. There are several reasons for this. First, unlike ancient Greece, where a long period separated bronze-age monarchies from the rise of the city-states, city-states in China emerged directly out of the collapse of royal power. They existed in a culture still defined by the heritage of the royal Zhou, in which the monarch continued to play a significant ritual role. The lingering presence of the Zhou monarchy as ritual reality and political idea checked the emergence of more collective forms of government. While the citizenry frequently played a decisive role in determining who would be ruler, at no point did they ever attempt to rule as a group.

Second, the expansion of states beyond the city through the extension of military service to some peasants had already begun in the middle of the seventh century. This and related practices such as population registration and land allocation gradually augmented the power of those lineage that seized control of the state machinery to mobilize the rural population. This spatial extension of the state also reduced the importance of the nobility and the urban population. Particularly in the wake of the partition of states or seizure of power by new lineages in the sixth and fifth centuries, this panoply of institutional reforms resulted in the concentration of power in the hands of the ruler even as the geographic extent of the states expanded. Squeezed between the lingering prestige of the old monarchy and the rising power of the emerging macrostates, the city-states of China created no radically new forms of authority.

Third, because early Chinese civilization was continental and had little access to water transport, large-scale trade in bulk commodities was impossible, and merchants played a relatively minor role. As merchants and merchant wealth have often provided the foundation for distinctive urban cultures and political forms, their relative weakness in early China inhibited the full-blown development of the city as a distinct and autonomous form of social organization.

Fourth, because the city-state was never able to establish itself as a political form distinct from the old theocracy or the emerging Warring States, Chinese thinkers developed no theory of the autonomous city or of general participation in government. This was exacerbated by the fact that philosophy did not begin to emerge until the late fifth century, and written works were not widely disseminated until the fourth. Thus, by the time of the Chinese equivalents of Plato and Aristotle, or even of the pre-Socratics, the city-state survived only in the form of a few dozen little polities clinging on in the gaps between the great powers. Moreover, since even these vestigial city-states were ruled by hereditary dynasties, they did not provide a model for alternative political forms. Instead, they simply inspired an imaginary antiquity in which the world had consisted of myriads of autonomous cities, or suggested the sorts of states from which the sage-kings of old might have achieved world domination through the power of virtue.

Thus, whereas the city-states of classical antiquity in the West left a written heritage that provided models for alternative forms of government, the intellectual legacy of the city-states of China was to serve in a discourse on the limitations of military power and the dangers of relying on conquest to create a state. Of all the Warring States philosophical texts it is the *Mencius* that speaks the most about small city-states, for this text more than any other rejected the panoply of new institutions that defined the Warring States polity, and proposed virtue as the basis of power rather than size or numbers. Although the city-state was the basic political unit in China for three centuries and provided the framework within which the institutional foundations of the Warring States and the later empire were created, the success of these new institutions swept away not only the city-states themselves but all memory of their historical reality.

CITIES OF THE WARRING STATES AND EARLY EMPIRES

The role and nature of the city in China were transformed by the absorption of the city-states into macrostates based on extracting taxes and services from the peasantry. The city ceased to be an autonomous entity in its own right, with a clear legal distinction between the inhabitants of the town and those of the fields. It became instead the capital of a rural region from which it was no longer administratively or legally separate.[53] According to Western scholarship, this meant that cities became nodes in an administrative network that "existed for the sake of the country and not vice versa." Asserting that the autonomous city with a distinctive bourgeois defined the Western urban experience, F. W. Mote posits China as the great other marked by the absence under the empire of a "self-identifying and self-perpetuating urban elite," so that "the rural component" rather than the cities "defined the Chinese way of life."[54]

While the creation of the empire, like the prior formation of macrostates, reduced the city's importance, at no time in Chinese history did cities exist for the sake of the countryside, nor was urban culture absorbed into an encompassing, rural world. The offices of the imperial government existed only in walled cities, so the cities alone were filled with the rich and mighty. Moreover, the early imperial cities were the center of a literary culture and refined fashion that spread to rural areas, and the most sophisticated pleasures and products were available only in cities. As throughout Chinese history, the cities contained everything that defined civilization, while the rural areas were associated with rusticity and boorishness.

Rather than inverting the relation between city and country, or absorbing cities into the rural world, making cities administrative centers had two consequences. First, all cities became subordinate elements of a larger whole. In the macrostates or empire, cities administered their own region but were absorbed in a hierarchy of administrative centers that culminated in the national or imperial capital. Second, the evolution of cities in the Warring States period created new social divisions that were expressed in the physical reconstruction of the urban landscape. Within the macrostates and empire the cities lost not only political autonomy but also the unity of shared membership in a largely self-sufficient enterprise. The Greek city-state as described by Aristotle was the smallest possible unit that could function as an autarkic totality in which a full human existence was possible.[55] Although this "totality" existed only by excluding merchants, foreigners, women, and slaves, the idea of a realm uniquely sufficient to make possible the realization of human potential—that is, to create "civilization"—was fundamental to the Greek *poleis* that serve as the archetypical model of Western urbanism, and this vision reappears in the city-states of renaissance Italy.[56] By contrast, early Chinese writers denied the possibility of completeness or autarky for the city, which was part of a larger whole. Moreover, the city was divided against itself, and each of its elements drawn into distinct spatial networks.

In the Warring States period many new cities were founded and older ones expanded.[57] This was made possible by economic development, such as improvements in crop yields due to better water control, the spread of iron tools, and the increased use of fertilizers. Commercial and craft activities also increased, as governments organized large workshops to produce clothing, weapons, vessels in bronze or lacquer, and other products for the court. Wealthy individuals pursued similar activities on a smaller scale. Consequently, whereas earlier cities had populations of a few thousand to a few tens of thousands, in the Warring States period cities of "ten thousand households" were common, and the largest cities apparently exceeded 200,000 in population.[58] Rising population led to the extension of walls and increase of the areas they enclosed. Archaeological excavations show that the walls of the Qi capital Linzi stretched over 15,000 yards, those at Xinzheng for 16,000 yards, and those at Wuyang over 27,000 yards.

More important than the increase in size was the structural transformation marked by the shift from the "concentric city" to the "double city."[59] The former was characterized by a single, outer wall that enclosed the entire urban space. The area within the walls had separate residential, craft, and temple/palace districts. The last (i.e., the district for nobles and political affairs) was built on rammed earth platforms and sometimes ringed by an inner wall. The "double city"—which describes such major Warring States foundations as Linzi in Qi, Wuyang in Yan, Xinzheng in Zheng, Handan in Zhao, and Anyi in Wei—consisted of two distinct walled enclosures, either sharing a single wall or completely detached from each other. One "citadel" served as the "palace-city" for rulers and administrators, while the other contained merchants, artisans, and peasants. Within these cities there were usually also distinct areas where craft production was concentrated, either near the palaces or the markets.

These cities clearly separate a "political" realm from a residual town devoted to residence and economic activity. This creation of a newly autonomous political space emerged in a wave of building or rebuilding capitals that swept through China from the middle of the Warring States period in association with the rise of the macrostates and the eclipse of the old nobility.[60] Whereas in the old, smaller cities of the Spring-and-Autumn period the entire male population participated at some level in politics, and in times of emergency were assembled to fight or swear loyalty, in the new cities those involved in politics and administration were physically separated from the rest of the population, which was treated purely as the object of registration and control.

This separation of the city marks the replacement of the nobility by agents of territorial lords, and the incorporation of cities into an administrative network. The transformation of political service from an inherited status into an occupational category shifted the meaning of the term *shi* 士 from the lowest category of noble to "man in government service."[61] The *shi* formed an occupational category who justified their right to govern by appeal to the division of labor in which they participated. As analyzed in chapter two, officials formed a superior occupational category because their encompassing vision created the totality within which other forms of labor found their limited places. Officials also claimed superiority to other occupations through their concern for principle and morality rather than material "things."[62] They thus embodied the authority of whole over part, and encompassing morality over specialized talent.[63]

Thus, the appearance of the double city marked a major shift in the structure of political power. In the world of the city-states those in authority had been the nobles who lived within the cities together with the "capital populace." Both were clearly distinguished from the "field people" who lived and toiled beyond the walls. With the rise of the territorial state the old separation between city and agricultural hinterlands was replaced by a new division between the administrative (and religious) "palace city" and the residual city devoted to manufacture, commerce, and trade. The clearest legal expression of this was laws that placed merchants on special registers, and banned people on these registers and their descendants from holding office, wearing silk, riding horses, or owning land.[64] Thus, the division between merchant and official, both of whom were necessarily inhabitants of the cities, replaced that between city dwellers and rural populace as the central legal divide. (In practice, only smaller traders were registered in the market, while truly wealthy merchants who engaged in the production of and long-distance trade in luxuries escaped the bans.) This new legal and physical division corresponded to the new social model propounded by the philosophers of the period, in which the rulers were an occupational category, but distinct from all other forms of work through their cultivation of their minds (and thus their close link with philosophers), their embodiment of totality, and the integrity that freed them from slavery to objects. Even as the line between town and country dissolved in the administrative models of the territorial state, new and sharper lines were imposed within the city itself. It is this physical and social division of the city between local and imperial, rather than any inversion of the relation with the countryside, that contrasts the imperial Chinese city from earlier Chinese city-states, as well as those of ancient Greece or Renaissance Italy.[65]

Clear evidence of the division of the city as a defining feature, and the preeminence of its political citadel, comes from the Eastern Han tomb of the Colonel Protecting the Wuhuan. Its wall paintings, which trace the career of the occupant, depict five cities in which he served. Each is portrayed as a "dual city" with two walled compounds, one for the general populace and the other for government buildings. While little is depicted of the outer cities—only city walls, gate towers, and in one case a schematic portrayal of the walls of the city market—the layout, buildings, inhabitants, and activities of the government cities are painted in considerable detail. Moreover, labels are added to many buildings to explain their identity or function. This portrayal confirms what is suggested in the texts of the period, that in the eyes of the political elite imperial cities were by their very nature divided into two parts, and that the essential, defining element was the palace city with its political functions.[66]

Another change in Warring States cities was the rise of architectural forms manifesting the ruler's power through insistence on verticality. The raised platform (*tai* 台), terrace pavilion (*ge* 閣), pillar gate (*que* 闕), and tower (*guan* 觀) all became major elements in the spatial construction of political power. As elaborated by Wu Hung, this emphasis on lofty structures displayed the rise to power of the territorial lords in the late Spring-and-Autumn and Warring States periods. The emphasis on height in the new palace complexes contrasted sharply with the spatialization of Zhou royal power described in chapter two. Zhou temples had a horizontal axis leading from an outer courtyard, where enfeoffments were staged, to an inner courtyard facing the ancestral temple, and through the arrayed ancestral tablets back to the ultimate founder.[67] The spatial arrangement had generated power by means of a physical and temporal movement horizontally back to powerful ancestral spirits, dramatizing authority based on noble birth. The new emphasis on towers and verticality demonstrated a power based on visibility and vision, with ties to the celestial spirits and natural powers supplanting those to ancestral ghosts.

This emphasis on height and range of vision figures in a passage by Wang Chong:

> To mount a high tower and glimpse as far as the four neighboring states is what people desire. To sit hidden in a closed room, turning into the darkness, boring into a grave and sleeping in a cave, reaching to the edge of the Yellow Springs [realm of the dead] is what

people hate. Someone with a closed mind and sealed-off thoughts who does not gaze from the heights is a companion of the dead.[68]

Here ascending a tower stands for everything that people desire, indeed the possibility of life itself. To fail to make such an ascent is equivalent to death.

The most prominent new architectural form was the raised platform or terrace (*tai*). Passages collected in the Song encyclopedia *Tai ping yu lan* contain references to terraces built in association with palaces in most states of the period, sometimes in clusters or rows. Anecdotes emphasize their great height, in one case saying that the tower was about 160 yards high and reached the clouds. This great height allowed a ruler to survey his own domain and even spy into neighboring states. Other stories show that the terraces were used to intimidate foreign visitors and gain their submission through demonstrating the wealth of the builder and the extent of his gaze. One passage states that the loftiness of the tower demonstrates the profundity of its builder's stratagems, so as to elicit a collective vow of loyalty from a group of visiting lords. The phenomenon even figures in the medical literature, for a passage from the *Huang Di nei jing* describes the dizzying effect of ascending a tower.[69]

Archaeological excavations have revealed the massive, packed-earth foundations of these terraces. Sometimes a single great mound led up to steps as in Linzi, and sometimes a series of ascending terraces was employed as at Houma. Architectural remains indicate that they were the most visible elements of large palace complexes. Late Eastern Zhou bronzes depict such mounds flanked by steps and topped with wooden platforms where ceremonies are being performed.[70] Terraces were also built for commoners whom a ruler wished to honor, as in the case of the First Emperor who built one for a wealthy woman merchant.[71]

Another elevated structure was the gate towers (*que*) flanking entries to city walls and palace complexes. Like the raised terraces behind them, these displayed the ruler's power. When Shang Yang in the middle of the fourth century B.C. began constructing a new Qin capital at Xianyang, the first items built were the paired Ji Gate Towers, and the same was true of the construction at the end of the third century B.C. of a new Han capital at Chang'an.[72] Han texts state that only the Son of Heaven was entitled to a gate flanked by two towers, that the height of the towers corresponded to the rank of a palace's occupant, or that towers flanking a gate "distinguished the superior from the inferior."[73] Passages in the *Zuo zhuan* suggest that towers figured at the entry to tombs, but this depends on the reading of a disputed term.[74] According to late Warring States texts, gate towers served also to display written decrees and newly promulgated laws.[75] The association between gates and the towers that flanked them became so close that the two terms were treated as mutual glosses in the earliest dictionaries.[76] Over the course of the Warring States and Han, the towered gateway became a more prominent symbol of authority than the wall of which it was a functional element. In the tomb art of the Eastern Han it is the gate towers to the city or a great family's compound that are most commonly depicted. So important were gates that the officials in charge of them could even be named for them.[77]

The final type of tall structure introduced in the Warring States period was the terrace pavilion. This was a series of rooms and corridors that was built around an earthen core so as to give the impression that it was a multistory building. As Wu Hung has pointed out, in an age that could still not construct true multistoried buildings, this allowed for the erection of far more visible and imposing structures. The most important such building was the palace of the Ji gate towers in the Qin capital.[78] This apparently originally consisted of two symmetrical wings. The foundation of the western wing still shows the structure of the pavilion, in which a row of columns on the first level gave the appearance of carrying the building's weight. Its raised earthen core was then ringed with bays, creating the impression of a three-story building. Patterned eave tiles found in excavations would have formed a series of rows that set off each level and accentuated the multistory effect.

Thus, the new palace cities became grandiose displays of the territorial lords' power through the towers flanking their entry gates, their rows of soaring terraces, and the palace buildings backing onto rising earthen cores that loomed above the flat, horizontal plane of the residential and business city.[79] However, in addition to displaying majesty and demonstrating powers of surveillance—the ruler showed his people that they were observed—these new structures served at least two other purposes.

First, the platforms, towers, and terrace pavilions that provided visible signs of the ruler's power were also tools of invisibility. They masked the ruler's person even while making his presence known, demonstrating his ability to scrutinize his people and his foes without himself being observed. The image of the ruler as an all-seeing eye that was itself invisible—anticipating by two millennia Foucault's celebrated meditations on Bentham's panopticon—expressed an idea that was central to Warring States and early imperial meditations on power. In the *Dao de jing* a handful of passages suggest that the ruler, the sage, and the Way are powerful because they are hidden from the knowledge of ordinary men.[80] The *Xunzi* similarly argues that one can only become eminent and successful through keeping secret one's intent (*zhi* 志) and one's work or affairs (*shi* 事).[81] This idea also developed in the military traditions, which make it a maxim and ultimately a cliché that the troops of the skillful commander are formless and invisible, and that the invisible conquers the visible because the former is invulnerable to attack.[82] The *Han Feizi* repeatedly argues that if the ruler shows himself or his desires, then his ministers can manipulate him. Thus, he must always remain quiet, unfathomable, and unknowable. The Way, which is the ultimate basis of the ruler's power is also without form and invisible.[83] By Eastern Han times the invisibility of the ruler had become so conventional that Wang Chong wrote: "Whenever sages anticipate calamity or good fortune, they calculate from the initial point to extrapolate by means of categories, trace back to the beginning to foresee the end. From the alleys of the wards they can judge the halls of the court; from the clear and bright they can perceive the dark and hidden."[84] The alleys of the capital make visible the condition of the court, which lies dark and hidden beyond the reach of direct perception. So common was the idea of the ruler's invisibility that Wang Chong simply took it for granted in the construction of his semantic parallel.

The ascription of power to invisibility, and invisibility to power, figured also in late Warring States attributions of potent texts to mysterious sages who remained unknown to the world. The crediting of the *Dao de jing* to Lao Dan, the compilation of books under the names of the "Pheasant-Cap Master (*Heguanzi*)" and "Master of Ghost Valley (*Guiguzi*)," and the ascription of a military text to a mysterious old man who was an incarnation of Laozi turned into a yellow stone are all examples of this.[85] Thus, by the early imperial period, the powers of invisibility—whether applied to the military commander, the ruler, or the sage—had become a common axiom.[86]

The links of building towers and terraces to this widespread theory of invisibility as a form of power are demonstrated in Sima Qian's narrative of the First Emperor. In his account of the rebuilding of Xianyang, the historian insists on the First Emperor's desire for concealment. Replicas of the palaces of states conquered by Qin were built along the northern bank of the Wei River linked by "elevated walks" and "fenced pavilions." A new palace built south of the Wei River to correspond to the Apex Star was linked to the Palace of the Sweet Springs at Mt. Li—site of the emperor's tomb—by a walled road. The front hall of the Epang Palace was ringed with walled walkways that led south to nearby mountains. Master Lu, a master of esoteric arts, argued that to achieve immortality the First Emperor had to move in secret to avoid evil spirits. He instructed the emperor to never let others know where he was, so the latter connected all 270 of his palaces and towers with elevated walks and walled roads. Anyone who revealed the emperor's presence at any time was to be put to death. He communicated orders only from his main palace in Xianyang, and at all other times was effectively in hiding. It is also significant that both of the men most instrumental in overthrowing the First Emperor—Xiang Yu and Liu Bang—caught glimpses of him when they were still commoners. The hiding of the emperor's corpse in a sealed carriage to return it to the capital, and the filling of the carriages with fish to mask the smell of decay, parody his withdrawal into hiding.[87]

The First Emperor's withdrawal, although presented as a consequence of paranoia and an obsession with immortality, demonstrated that one purpose of elevated towers and walkways was to render the person of the ruler invisible. Moreover, while this particular case was presented as irregular, raised walkways to mask the emperor's movements continued into the Han. Indeed, in imperial Chinese political practice, power was always marked by withdrawal from the gaze of the populace and even that of the court.[88] The emperor was sequestered behind a series of walls—a mythicizing version of this appears in a Kafka parable—in what was called in late imperial China the "forbidden city."[89] To be allowed to see him was a privilege even for his officials, and to actually come into his presence was the highest of honors. Thus, unlike ancient Rome, medieval Europe, or India—where the ruler showed himself to his people, received petitions, and publicly dispensed justice as a ritual of power— the ruler in China derived power from being hidden or invisible. Erecting towers and terraces displayed this hidden power.

The final purpose of the towers was religious, as indicated in the late Zhou bronzes depicting rituals on the terraces, and in the speech of Master Lu, where living in towers and moving on elevated walkways helped to achieve immortality. Many of the most powerful spirits in China, as in other cultures, were aerial or celestial beings to be approached through physical ascent. One form of this that figures prominently in the career of the First Emperor is the performance of rituals on the sides or the peaks of mountains.[90] Towers also allowed ascent toward divinities. Masters of esoteric arts argued that if a Han emperor built high towers, immortals would come to dwell in them, an idea depicted in Sima Xiangru's "Rhapsody on the Imperial Hunting Park." Decorating towers with images of Heaven, Earth, and the Grand Unity, as well as placing statues of immortals atop bronze pillars mounted on a terrace, likewise link high structures with powerful spirits.[91] This link figures in Han tomb art, where gate towers, multistoried houses, and granaries have auspicious birds on top of them. In fact, such depictions represented actual scenes, since bronze phoenixes, sometimes functioning as weather vanes, were placed on the top of many gate towers.[92] These birds were themselves potent spirits, messengers from divinities, and auspicious omens that signalled prosperity or good government. They were also linked to the immortals, who in Han art and literature were sometimes depicted as men who had sprouted feathers and grown wings.[93]

Another aspect of early Chinese religion that links vertical ascent to contact with immortals or spirits is the role of trees. Trees, like mountains or towers, were ascending spatial structures that linked men to the powers of Heaven or aerial spirits. This is shown in several ways. First, special express roads reserved for the emperor and his messengers were lined with trees planted at regular intervals. These echoed the pillars and walls that both called attention to the road and masked its users.[94]

Second, trees often covered mountains and extended them upward. Imperial tombs, themselves artificial mountains, were covered with trees. Under the Qin and Han, the number of trees planted on a tomb indicated the status of the occupant. Major altars of state, as well as local altars of grain and soil, also had trees to demonstrate the power and life-giving beneficence of the god who received sacrifices there.[95] This association of trees with graves and spirits was a convention in Han poetry, most notably the "Nineteen Ancient Songs."[96] So important were trees on graves that a man murdered the one who removed the tree from his mother's tomb.[97] Early Chinese mythology included many important trees, such as the Fusang tree from which the sun(s) rose in the east, the Ruo tree in which it set, and the Jian tree that formed "a canopy over the center of the world" and marked the grave of Hou Ji, creator of agriculture.[98]

Trees also figure in Han art. Some, such as the tree with the suns on the Mawangdui silk banner, seem to be linked to the written myths. Others, such as the tree with the horse tethered beneath it that appears frequently in Eastern Han tomb art, remain mysterious. One recurring motif, however, demonstrates the role of trees as vertical links between the world of men and that of aerial spirits. In several forms and media, Warring States and Han artists depicted trees with birds, monkeys, or immortals in the branches, while human beings and terrestrial animals clustered around the base. One of the earliest, an oil lamp in the shape of an abstracted tree, was found in the fourth-century B.C. tomb of the King of Zhongshan. Monkeys and birds move around the branches, and a large snake is coiled around the length of the central trunk, while men gaze up from the ground below.[99] A ceramic tree from a late Western Han tomb has a bird—perhaps the cockerel of the sun—perched on top, monkeys and birds on its branches, and human figures in relief around the base. A livelier ceramic version from a late Eastern Han tomb fills the branches of the tree with winged immortals, two-headed birds, and fabulous creatures, with magic fungi sprouting from the oil basins.[100] Closely related are the "money trees" found in late Han Sichuan and Yunnan. The bronze branches of these trees contain birds, monkeys, magic plants, coiling dragons, winged immortals, the Queen Mother of the West with her court, and human votaries of the Queen Mother. Their unique feature is the coins that fill the branches. These are not only cash but also cosmic symbols (round Heaven and square Earth) with projecting lines that indicate swirling rays of light. Some of the bases consist of mountains, individual animals, or humans riding animals, suggesting the mountains as a link between earth and sky. Twice, however, the base depicts the Queen Mother and her messenger bird.[101] Since the Queen Mother is depicted elsewhere perched on top of *que* gate pillars, the tree and the tower figure as two parallel modes of linking the world of men to that of immortal spirits.[102]

The ideas that towers were demonstrations of power, tools of invisibility, and links to the spirit world were all articulated in texts and depicted in art. Behind these positive—from the perspective of the rulers—messages lurked darker associations. Towers often are images of overweening ambition and the inevitability of collapse. The Tower of Babel is the great Western example of this theme. The Epang palace, whose towers, terraces, and network of elevated walks were never completed and soon fell into ruins, figures in the work of Sima Qian and later writers as an image of the evanescence of power. Similarly, a bronze immortal mounted on a pillar by Emperor Wu provided an image of the fall of the Han in Li He's classic "A Bronze Immortal Takes Leave of Han."[103] As we will see, capital cities with their lofty gate towers and terraces became standard poetic images of the fleeting nature of power and earthly achievements.

A second negative aspect of the tower is that the very breadth of view also revealed the tininess of the realm. When Confucius ascended the eastern peak, he found that Lu was small, and when he climbed Mt. Tai he discovered that the Zhou realm was small.[104] Centuries later, the view from the pinnacle of the Yongning Temple in Northern Wei Luoyang made the imperial palace seem "so small that it would fit in the palm of the hand."[105] Thus, the lofty vision offered by the tower makes the ruler, as well as his subjects, appear trivial. The themes of the revealing vision from on high and the tower's ultimate collapse come together in a moment of epiphany described by F. Scott Fitzgerald:

> I went to the roof of the last and most magnificent of towers. Then I understood—everything was explained: I had discovered the crowning error of the city, its Pandora's box. Full of vaunting pride the New Yorker had climbed here and seen with dismay what he had never suspected, that the city was not the endless succession of canyons that he had supposed but that it had limits—from the tallest structure he saw for the first time that it faded out into country on all sides, into the expanse of green and blue that alone was limitless. And with the awful realization that New York was a city after all and not a universe, the whole shining edifice that he had reared in his imagination came crashing to the ground.[106]

Texts and archaeological remains provide little evidence about the area of residence, commerce, and manufacture.[107] The residential areas of the Han capitals were structured by a grid of major thoroughfares, and then subdivided into walled wards supervised by a low-level government administrator and influential residents. Since dividing residential districts into a grid was a method for fixing and controlling the population, it is probable that the capitals and major cities of the Warring States and Han also had such a structure. However, the further one moved from the center and down the hierarchy of settlements, the less likely such rigor becomes.[108] In any case, the grid pattern—which is discussed in chapter five—indicates that in contrast to the emphasis on elevation and the vertical in the palace cities, the residential/economic cities were defined by their horizontal layout. This layout sought above all to prevent the easy assembling of crowds and the free movement of people under cover of darkness. It also marked the imposition of state power on the vagaries of natural landscape and local custom.[109]

Another pattern in the residential districts is that major thoroughfares were lined with the houses of the noble and wealthy, while the alleys radiating from them were occupied by poorer people.[110] Thus, the poverty of Zhuang Zhou is indicated by the fact that he "lived in a poverty-stricken alley of an impoverished neighborhood, impecunious and weaving sandals." Such alleys are often described as "impoverished" or "narrow." They could not

accommodate the large carriages that moved up and down the major boulevards, their houses were crumbling, and their inhabitants were impoverished
philosophers, low-class wastrels who indulged in song and cheap liquor, or
criminals.[111] By contrast, the boulevards were filled with the carriages of high
officials, and people wearing court hats and robes.

A key area of the residential/economic city was the market. Texts deal
largely with imperial capitals, but tomb art shows that similar features appeared
in the important provincial city markets, with local variations. As the center
of trade, the markets were in some ways the most important site for the activities of the merchants and craftsmen; they were also the center of government
power within the nongovernment city. Indeed, the market reduplicated within
itself the contrary spatial characteristics of the palace city and the residential
quarters, for it had both a multistory tower that served as symbol and locus
of authority, and a horizontal grid to facilitate control. Nevertheless, despite
these physical manifestations of authority and the presence of officials, the
market remained a site of public assembly featuring a range of activities that
challenged the authorities and their prescribed order.

The most visible manifestation of government control was a multistory
tower in the center of the market that served as the base of operations for
the officials in charge. The number of men assigned this task varied from place
to place and across time. We have details only for the markets in the Eastern
Han capital, Luoyang, where the market chief and his deputy had a staff of
thirty-six men.[112] These men assured that goods sold in the market were of
sufficient quality and all prices in line with standards imposed after a monthly
review of authorized agreements between buyers and sellers. They also collected a tax from all those on the market register, and sold government surplus
commodities or the products of government workshops. The tower had a flag
on top and a drum in the upper chamber that were used to signal the opening
and closing of the market. Its height apparently varied from city to city. The
towers in the markets of Chang'an are described in an Eastern Han poem as
five stories high, while a tomb tile depicting the market in Chengdu shows
a tower of only two stories.[113] However, they were the highest structure in
the market, both to manifest state power and to guarantee that signals were
clearly visible to people in the most distant corners.

The second spatial expression of government power in the markets was
the imposition of a grid. This is clearest in a depiction of the Chengdu market
on a Han tomb tile. It shows the market as a perfect square, with a gate on
each side and two major roads forming a cross between the gates. The two-
story tower is placed in the center. It thus resembles a reduced version of the
textually canonical ideal of a capital city as described in the Kao gong ji (see
next section), so that a leading scholar interpreted this tile as a depiction of
the city of Chengdu rather than its market.[114] Each of the four quarters is in
turn divided by rows of shops grouped according to the product being sold.
Human figures are shown engaging in activities on the four main streets. This
grid probably echoed the residential one in that the major shops lined the

central roads while lesser shops and stalls lined the alleyways. Such a pattern existed in the Tang capital markets, and it is likely to have been used in the Han.[115] This grid of shops figures in the texts of the period, which emphasize the clear separation of goods and the regularity of the lines of shops as evidence of imperial greatness and social order. Several tomb images also depict the arrayed stalls in lines or as a grid, and legal documents from the Qin insist on the regularity of stalls.[116]

As the chief spatial manifestations of authority in the markets, the grid and the tower displayed government power. Just as in city-states, the market was used for public punishments, both beatings and executions, and for exposing the heads or corpses of major criminals. There are dozens of references to executions and the exposure of corpses or heads in the market, so the *Li ji* and the *Sima fa* pair the market with the court as the respective sites of punishment and reward, the "two handles" of the ruler's power. Several passages note that the purpose of these displays was to instruct or persuade the masses.[117] Thus, the market became a place where the ruler's power was publicly displayed in the beating, mutilation, dismemberment, and decay of the bodies of those who defied him.

The market also served for less violent displays of authority or for political performances seeking an audience. Claiming that the *Lü shi chun qiu* contained all significant knowledge, Lü Buwei placed the text at the entrance to the Xianyang market, hung one thousand pieces of gold above the text, and offered these to whoever could delete or add a single character. Earlier, Shang Yang had shown that his rewards were trustworthy by announcing in the market that he would give cash to whoever performed a specified simple task, and in fact granting the reward.[118] Here the market became the privileged site for messages from the rulers to the masses of people, whether in the form of words, texts, money, or dismembered bodies.[119]

However, given their crowds and the confluence of merchant wealth, some market activities escaped government control. These unsanctioned activities involved at least three categories of the population: the merchants, the "wandering swordsmen" with their gangs of youthful idlers, and the masters of esoteric arts such as diviners and doctors. Each type challenged the state in their own manner, and sometimes they came together in threatening coalitions. First, while mercantile activity was the raison d'être of the market, merchant wealth provided status and influence that challenged the hierarchy instituted by the government, a hierarchy supposed to be based on agriculture and military service.[120] Although merchants posed no political challenge to the ruler and his agents, their accumulated wealth allowed a life of luxury that surpassed that of their political superiors, who thus became susceptible to corruption, and tempted away from a life of toil the poor peasants whose taxes and service were the basis of the state order. This split between the merchant order defined by wealth and that of the state defined by rank was built into the structure of the dual cities and the legal ban on registered merchants and their descendants holding office. It was this denial of the state's sump-

tuary order, and the ability of merchant wealth to purchase the land and services of the free peasants, that figure prominently in the writings of the
period.[121]

Thus, Jia Yi and later rhapsodies on Chang'an noted that in the markets
leisured gentlemen matched nobles, and shopgirls dressed more lavishly than
women of the ruling house.[122] The *Guanzi* describes the market as the place
where merchants were allowed to "wander freely and at ease (*you* 游)."[123] Wang
Fu (c. A.D. 78–163) reviled the brocades, tortoiseshell ornaments, pearls, jade,
deerskin slippers, and lace worn by arrogant merchants and landlords whose
wealth surpassed that of the emperor. Like Jia Yi and the poets, Wang Fu com-
plains that even the servant girls of wealthy merchants are more finely attired
than empresses. In a version of the debate over lavish funerals or simple ones,
he laments that for the wealthy merchants of Luoyang coffins had to be made
of fine catalpa trees from distant Jiangnan.[124]

In addition to violating the sumptuary order, merchant wealth also challenged the efficacy of the laws. While it was a principle that no one should
be exempt from punishments, a common saying stated that the sons of rich
families would never die in the marketplace (i.e., be executed).[125] As some
writers argued that high officials should be exempt from degrading punishments to preserve the prestige of the emperor, this unsanctioned legal privilege of wealthy families was all the more annoying to defenders of the state
order.[126] Moreover, officials in charge of coinage attached to the market sometimes collaborated with merchants in forging cash or manipulating currency.[127]
Thus, throughout the Warring States and Han, supporters of the state feared
the market as a site where men gained power and status not awarded by the
state, displayed this power and wealth to the detriment of sumptuary regulations, and manipulated wealth to the detriment of criminal law and government administration.

The issue of display also figures in accounts of the market as a place
where crowds gathered for spectacles and amusements, or where men of
political ambition might find an audience.[128] In this it was a distilled version
of city life, for as several Han texts point out, urban crowds always gathered
to watch something interesting. The most common spectacle was the daily
round of departures and arrivals of eminent people in their fine carriages and
elaborate costumes. Less frequent were performances by political pretenders
who displayed unusual costumes and paraphernalia to urban crowds to gain
attention or support.[129] The costumes of the urban elite, as in so many societies, became the standards for others to emulate.

> In the city, if they love to have their hair dressed up high,
> Then everywhere else they dress their hair an inch higher.
> In the city, if they love to enlarge their eyebrows,
> Then everywhere else they will make their eyebrows cover
>   half their foreheads.

In the city, if they love large sleeves,

Then everywhere else they will use up whole bolts of silk.[130]

This authority in fashion challenged the state, for in theory it was the tastes of the ruler, such as Lord Huan of Qi's infectious passion for the color purple, that were to set the model for others.[131]

The most common spectacles in the market were the punishments and executions. Judging from cases observed in late imperial China and other cultures, these acts were probably more entertainments and a break from routine than the salutary lesson that the state intended. Although not usually mentioned, crowd participation figures prominently in the story of the exposure of the corpse of the assassin Nie Zheng and the self-sacrifice of his sister, who died in the market to assure fame for her brother.[132] Similarly the *History of the Later Han* relates that at the release of a virtuous official imprisoned through the maneuvers of imperial affines "the entire market quarter of the capital shouted, 'Long life!'"[133] Here again the crowd in the market figures as a political actor.

The markets were also the scene for events that occur whenever many people gather in a relatively small space. Most would have been too trivial for notice, but a few stories describe the reaction of the market crowd to unusual events. Some of these had political overtones, as when in 609 B.C. the mother of a slain heir-apparent in Lu publicly mourned for him in the market, and was joined in weeping by the crowd of onlookers.[134] Although it had no immediate political consequences, this collective mourning of a man slain by the ruler shows how in the market individuals could collectively mobilize potentially subversive ideas or emotions.

Another story tells how Prince Xinling honored the recluse Hou Ying by accompanying him to the market and standing quietly by while the latter chatted with the butcher Zhu Hai, so that the entire market marveled at the spectacle. As Hou Ying explained, this elevated Prince Xinling's reputation among the populace who witnessed the scene.[135] Although cultivating the crowd through performances in the market did not challenge the ruler, it provided a form of power that was closer to that cultivated by leagues of bravoes than to state authority.[136] The butcher Zhu Hai, with whom a social bond was formed in this event, later helped Prince Xinling to disobey the king's commands, steal a royal tiger tally to call out the army, and lead this usurped force to victory in battle.

A final example of spectacle in the market deals with Han Xin, a major ally of the Han founder. In his youth Han Xin often strode through the market carrying a sword, despite a Qin ban on weapons. One of the wastrel youths among the butchers, both groups that were stock figures for violence and criminality in the period, called Han Xin a coward and ordered him to crawl between the youth's legs unless he desired to die. Han Xin complied, to the mocking laughter of the entire market that watched the scene.[137] This story of illegal weapons, violent butchers, and threats of murder suggests the sorts of incidents that broke out in the market, and the sorts of people who were likely to provoke them.

The theme of the markets as scenes of violence and criminality runs throughout the written record, generally associated with the related figures of the "wandering swordsmen" or gangsters (*you xia*), the butchers, and the "wicked youths."[138] The most important of these were the gangsters who lived by an ethic of vengeance, faithfulness to oaths, and mutual devotion to the death. The rhapsodies on Han capitals locate these gangs in the markets, where they were linked to the great merchants. The histories similarly situate them in the "alleys" and "wards" of the major cities, and like other denizens of the market they are said to act for profit.[139] Texts portray them as bandits, kidnappers, and grave robbers, but their most important activity was to serve as assassins for wealthy families or officials. They even formed associations of professional killers who intimidated or bribed officials.[140] The *Han Feizi* treated these groups of criminals as violent versions of scholarly associations, both of which it described as challenges to public order. Memorials written in the Eastern Han called them the creators of a "private law" based on vengeance that threatened to supplant the state's legal codes.[141]

The butchers, for their part, were accustomed to hacking flesh and shedding blood. Men of violence who went into hiding often took up work as butchers, and stories tell of men who sought among the butchers to obtain an assassin.[142] Like other trades they were gathered together in their rows in the market. As indicated in the anecdotes, this area was distinguished from that of other trades by the routine violence of those who worked there, and occasionally by the prestige and wealth of clients who came in search of men willing to cut more than fresh meat.

The "wicked youths" are a broader category closely tied to the other two through the presumed proclivity of youth for reckless violence.[143] Many leading criminals described in *Shi ji* are admired by gangs of youths who emulate them or assist in their illegal activities.[144] Another passage states that the "youths of the wards and alleys" often became gangsters to earn money.[145] A band of youths acted as accomplices for an imperial prince who engaged in robbery and murder for sport.[146] "Cruel clerks" employed by the state to destroy powerful families were recruited from among these "youths" or assisted by them.[147] Anticipating the use of criminals in frontier garrisons in the Eastern Han, "wicked youths" were sent on expeditions to Central Asia.[148] Similarly, the butcher who bullied Han Xin was a violent "youth." More broadly, youths are portrayed as gangs of wastrels who had no occupations but instead passed their time in the marketplace engaging in gambling, cock fighting, and coursing hounds. These violent activities were so common that they were depicted on tomb tiles.[149]

The "wicked youths" routinely formed a crowd of idle delinquents who gathered in the markets. They engaged in regular, low-level violence or criminality, occasionally joining with professional gangsters to perpetrate more serious crimes. However, in times of disorder these youths provided a reservoir of recruits for those engaged in large-scale vendetta or rebellion. The biographies of many of the leaders of the revolt against Qin indicate that when they first rebelled their followers were recruited from among the "youths."[150] The Han founder himself appears as a classic wastrel youth, refusing to work on his family's property and passing his time in bars. His father consequently regarded him as "worthless and unreliable." His earliest followers—Xiao He, Cao Can, and Fan Kuai—are described as "youths and bold clerks," that is, wild youths or aspirant swordsmen who had obtained low-level government posts. The same pattern of relying on idle youths to initiate a rebellion figures in the history of the fall of Wang Mang. The men who started the rebellion of the Red Eyebrows are described as wild "youths" who called themselves "fierce tigers." They first gathered around a woman named Lü Mu who provided them with liquor in hopes that they would avenge her son who had been slain by an official.[151] Thus, the histories suggest that the gangsters and youths who gathered in the markets were simple criminals in times of social order, but played an important role in the toppling and founding of dynasties in times of chaos.[152]

The last category found in the market that challenged the state was the masters of esoteric techniques, particularly the diviners and "shaman doctors (wu yi 巫醫)." The clearest expression of the tension between such figures and the state is the "Diviners of Lucky Days" chapter, in the Shi ji.[153] In the story that forms this chapter, two eminent scholar-officials note that when the ancient sages did not hold positions at court, they were found among the diviners and doctors in the market. Proceeding to the market, they find a diviner who discourses brilliantly on the structure of the universe. When they ask him why such a talented man remains in such a humble position, he retorts by pointing out the dangers of office and the superiority of a career as a diviner in the markets. This story thus posits a rivalry between two possible socioeconomic roles—diviner in the market versus official at court—and insists that wise and virtuous people choose the former. Consequently, the market figures as a space antagonistic to the court.

What appears in the Shi ji as a parable about rival occupations becomes in Wang Chong a contrast between kinds of prediction. In two chapters he refutes the idea that sages had powers of prophecy, and particularly the idea that Confucius predicted the Han. Sages foresee events through the ability to recognize trends at their inception and to fit facts into correct categories. He contrasts this with a foreknowledge based on "arts and calculations (shu shu 術數)," a compound linked to "recipes and techniques (fang ji 方技)" as generic terms for the methods of natural experts and occultists such as astrologers, diviners, physicians, and hemerologists.[154] "Those who use arts and calculations,'" Wang Chong explains, are "those in the present day skilled in the crafts of divination and prophetic riddles." Both sagely and divinatory predictions were in turn distinct from uncanny types of foreknowledge classed as demonic (yao 妖), such as prophetic children's ditties or spirit possession.

The first category of foreknowledge is "sagely," the last is "daemonic (*shen* 神)" or "uncanny (*guai* 怪)," while the middle category, diviners and techni-cal traditions, straddles the two. However, "combining arts and calculations with [knowledge of] human affairs is no different than the daemonic." As Wang Chong stresses, "The daemonic and uncanny are completely different Ways from the sagely and worthy," so shamans "are a completely different cat-egory from the sage."[155] Thus, this argument translates into modes of knowl-edge the sociological division in the *Shi ji* parable between scholarly traditions, state employees, and the technical or mantic traditions.[156] It is also significant that Wang Chong links the arts of the technical traditions to those of the shaman.

There is scattered evidence on the social reality behind these parables and philosophical arguments. First, several biographies show that many people worked as diviners and physicians in the markets, and that some did this to avoid political appointments. Alternatively, some individuals who had begun as diviners or physicians and then obtained appointments sought to keep their earlier careers secret.[157] Moreover, a decree of Wang Mang states: "Carpenters, shaman/doctors, diviners, other masters of techniques, merchants, and ped-dlers, whether in their market stalls, at home, or in travellers' lodgings must all report their wealth to the district officials of wherever they are. They must declare their capital, calculate their profit, take one tenth of it and pay it as tribute."[158] This lumps together doctors, diviners, the other technical traditions, and merchants/peddlers, as market-based occupations that were not paying sufficient tax to the state and thus subjected to a revived version of Emperor Wu's special levy on merchants. Equally important is the link of doctors and shamans as a single category; the two terms often form a compound in the literature of the period. Moreover, many doctors commanded spirits, divined about illnesses, and performed other mantic arts as part of their practice.[159] According to the *Lü shi chun qiu*, both divination and medicine were invented by shamans. Even a chapter of this book that condemns shaman/doctors in the name of newer practices based on "energy" or "vapor (*qi* 氣)" suggests that the shamanic medical practices were more highly honored in the period.[160] Thus, while devotees of natural philosophy and new medical prac-tices in the period were at pains to distinguish themselves from shamans, the government and intellectuals in other traditions lumped them together, and many actual practitioners combined elements of newer theories and tech-niques with the older, religious methods. Shamans and doctors also overlapped as rivals who worked in the same places and competed for the same clientele.

Polemics attacked these shamans, diviners, and shaman/doctors as threats to the social order for two reasons. First, they falsely claimed supernatural powers in order to swindle peasants. Second, shamans, diviners, and doctors were accused of luring idle young people away from proper occupations into their own disreputable, but potentially profitable, pursuits:

Following the customs of the age, hypocrites practice deceit and become shamans and invocators [zhu 祝] for the common people in order to extract payments from them. With brazen-faced effrontery and powerful tongues, some establish enterprises and attain wealth. So those who dread work [dan shi 憚事] abandon agriculture to study with them. Consequently in the alleys there are shamans and in the wards invocators.[161]

The Qian fu lun makes similar accusations, but it focuses on women as both followers of shamans and their victims, and it states that curing disease through appeals to spirits is the method by which shamans swindle people and attract disciples. The fourth-century A.D. Baopuzi tells of shaman/doctors who practiced false healing methods to dupe commoners, and were thus able to gather as many as a thousand followers who hoped to "avoid corvee."[162]

These passages note how the numerous followers of the shaman/doctors "dreaded work," abandoned licit activities—agriculture or sericulture—and avoided labor service.[163] Such dreading or avoiding work was also a defining attribute of the "wicked youths" who stood in the same relation to the gangsters as did these disciples to the shamans. Thus, the Xunzi states: "The thieving pedants dread work [dan shi 憚事]. Lacking honesty and shame, they love to eat and drink. One can call them "wicked youths." If one adds a wild, ferocious disobedience and a dangerous, criminal disorderliness, then one could call them "ill-omened youths." It would be proper to execute and expose them [in the market]."[164] This describes the "wicked youths" in terms later applied by the Yan tie lun to disciples of shamans. These people, actually deviant scholars, are fleshed out in terms that could describe the "wandering swordsmen." This characterization of "wicked youths" by their refusal to work in regular occupations also figures in other texts.[165] Thus, gangsters, idle youths, shamans, diviners, doctors, their disciples, the great merchants, and those seduced by their example formed—out of loathing for conventional labor—a countersociety in the market that negated the state-imposed model of a world of peasants and peddlers held in their places by the ruler's agents.

While noncanonical groups in the markets were less a threat to the state than an alternative to it, they could come together in coalitions that challenged or corrupted state power. When a newly appointed magistrate decided to stamp out the league of professional assassins who were bribing and murdering officials in Chang'an, he gathered hundreds of government employees and arrested all the "insolent youths and wicked sons, merchants and other occupations who were not on the market register, and those wearing unusual clothing and armor and carrying weapons." He accused them of being accessories to banditry, and most of them were sealed in a tiger cave where they died.[166] While the text does not specify the other occupations of those not registered in the markets, from the list that Wang Mang included under his expanded tax on capital, it is likely that most of them were diviners and shaman/doctors. Thus, the story indicates the development of a large, armed association of gangsters, merchants, butchers, diviners, shaman/doctors, and idle youths who murdered and intimidated the agents of the state. This association was eliminated only by a general, state-organized massacre of all the nonregistered population of the market, which numbered several hundred people.

Stories also depict leagues of shamans with merchants or powerful local families to organize large-scale cults not sanctioned by the state (see chapter four).[167] Another account of leagues of shamans with gangsters and "wastrels" is in the *Baopuzi*. This fourth-century A.D. work lists late Han religious practitioners who used what Ge Hong dismisses as minor magical arts to dazzle the masses. The deceivers assembled bands of wicked followers and accumulated fabulous wealth that "surpassed that of princes and nobles." After describing their luxurious mode of living, Ge Hong tells how they gathered assassins and refugees. These people formed private armies that inspired fear that could "topple the state's ruler" and attained power that could "humiliate the officials." Many officials, suspecting that they actually had spiritual powers, feared to suppress them. Others felt that it was not an urgent matter, or met resistance from believers among their wives, children, and minor local officials. Surrounded by voices urging him to take no action, the isolated magistrate often had little choice but to tolerate these coalitions of shamans and gangsters.[168] While the *Baopuzi* is relatively late, Han historical sources refer to such coalitions of religious practitioners with armed gangs, and to newly arrived officials being surrounded by defenders of local cults and practitioners.[169] Finally, the Yellow Turban rebellion in Shandong that triggered the fall of the Han was just such a coalition of practitioners of religious healing with a large military organization.

The market was also a site for other illicit activities. First, it was often the scene of pushing and shoving that could become a mob or a riot.[170] Second, it and nearby drinking establishments were frequented by prostitutes.[171] Finally, it was a favorite site for beggars. While ordinary beggars were at worst a nuisance, would-be avengers sometimes took refuge as beggars in the market. Thus, the celebrated Wu Zixu and Yu Rang kept both themselves and their violent schemes alive by begging for food in the market.[172]

In summation, the physical division of the city in the Warring States led to a permanent legal and social division that left the imperial Chinese city forever divided against itself. In the early imperial period, the state was spatially formed by a hierarchical network of "palace cities" with their surrounding agricultural lands. The outer cities formed of residences, workshops, and markets played a necessary role in the production and exchange of goods, but in both ideology and fiscal practice they were marginal and potentially threatening to the state. Despite attempts to impose order in these commoner cities through grids in streets and markets, as well as the market tower, their populations remained alien to the government's ideal patterns of service and hierarchy. Even the licit population of craftsmen and merchants threatened the state through creating alternative hierarchies based on wealth that lured rural people to abandon their sanctioned work and seek fortunes in the city. The markets became an assembly point for these marginal people who gathered in the cities to seek a living outside their sanctioned occupations. Condemned as "lazy" or "wicked" by writers, such people made a living through non-registered businesses, criminality, religious forms of the mantic arts, and pros-titution. Sharing a common space in the market and a common status as unsanctioned or unregistered enterprises, they created a distinctive urban culture that lay beyond the reach of the state. They also interacted across the empire in networks of trade and criminality that paralleled the network of official cities, but remained permanently apart from it.

INVENTION OF THE IMPERIAL CAPITAL

Premodern states have always had difficulty imposing authority over vast dis-tances. As Lord Acton observed, the word of the king of Persia was law, but this law went no further than the presence of his officials. This applies equally to early China. As a result, the capital, marked by the presence of the ruler and the highest concentration of his officials, was uniquely important to the state, of which it was both center and embodiment. As the center it was the ultimate destination of the inward flow of people and goods that spatially defined the empire. It functioned as a capital only so long as it could draw to itself people and objects from the outside. As the embodiment of the state, it was an architectural and ritual microcosm where the political whole was depicted and created through potent performance. Consequently the capital provides a model in which the structure or organizing principles of the entire state can be grasped. It is both *the* exemplary city and yet distinct from all other cities. What made it both exemplary and distinct was its adherence to a textually sanctioned ritual program. Thus, the invention of the Chinese imperial capital is ultimately the process of gathering the central rituals of the state into the city and its vicinity, the building of the city through adherence to a canonical body of texts, and the development of the city and its rites as a literary topos.

The unique nature of the capital requires emphasis. Many studies of urbanism in China have produced generalizations about *the* Chinese city by examining imperial capitals and treating other cities as imperfect reproduc-tions of the imperial center.[173] This *was* true of the Zhou state, where noble cities were reduced versions of the royal capital, but the imperial government insisted on a radical difference in kind between its capital and all other cities. This difference, as noted by Xu Yinong, reflected the chasm separating the emperor, whose presence defined the imperial capital, from his agents, who served in the capitals of districts or prefectures.[174] The emperor was a quasidivine figure, the regent of Heaven on earth and the source of political authority and order, while all of his officials only held power from him. Consequently, the imperial capital was built as the spatial representation of the ordering power of Heaven, while local cities were—in their political aspect— only administrative centers. The structure and rituals of the imperial capital dramatized a political authority that encompassed the world, while all other cities were merely local fragments of the imperial whole. In the early impe- rial centuries many of these local cities had once been capitals, and in later periods cities copied aspects of the capital as expressions of loyalty, but to have copied those aspects that defined the imperial capital would have been not loyalty but treason. The contrast between the two types of city was not simply one of degree (e.g., the size of the area administered), but of their symbolism and nature.

The defining feature of the new capital was its denial of ties to its local- ity. Earlier cities were the centers of regions to which they were bound by shared population, cult, and custom. To serve as capital of an empire that united the regions that had formerly been independent states—each with its own language, character, and customs—the emperor's city had to be free from traits that bound it to any particular region and its interests. As a consequence, regional character and customs, discussed in chapter four, became targets of criticism. Although real and inevitable, they were marks of fragmentation and inferiority that had to be eliminated at the imperial level. This was achieved in several ways: by a text-based urban plan that marked the artificiality of the city, by a cult of Heaven that demonstrated power descending from on high and thus not rooted in the regions of the earth, by resettling major families from across the empire in the capital region to serve as an imperial service class, by developing an artificial, text-based language distinct from regional, spoken dialects, and by creating the role of emperor and the identification of the capital with his person and family.

This section analyzes the invention of the imperial capital through exam- ining three cases in historical sequence: the Qin capital Xianyang, the Western Han capital Chang'an, and the Eastern Han capital Luoyang. To summarize the process, Xianyang was a state capital that suddenly became the center of an empire. It was in part recreated as a model of the world, but it remained a state capital that embodied a perpetual victory in a war that would never end. Chang'an was an imperial city created by its rulers, men of commoner origins from a different region. Not only the ruling house but most leading officials were drawn from elsewhere, and the city region was gradually filled with forced immigrant populations settled around the imperial tombs. However, it remained ritually void, like Xianyang before it, and was only in part textually canonical. Eastern Han Luoyang completed the process, being the first imperial capital that realized a textual program from the state canon, and the first in which the highest rituals of the state were concentrated in the capital and its suburbs. The emergence of this new model of the true imperial capital was the subject of the Han rhapsodies on capitals. The chapter concludes with a reflection on the characteristics of the imperial capital pro- duced by this process: the insistence on the capital as a city created by the ruling house, the consequent artificiality of the capital, and the idea of the capital's necessary impermanence. This last was a buried theme that could not be applied to the present capital, but served as a topos in poems and essays meditating on the vanished capitals of fallen dynasties.[175]

Construction of the Qin capital Xianyang was begun in the middle of the fourth century B.C. by Shang Yang.[176] He centered the city on a two-winged palatial complex that consisted of simulated three-story structures built on earthen cores. These cores served as artificial hills around which the structures rose, and their verticality was heightened by the use of patterned eave tiles. Xianyang was expanded beyond its walls in a large palace district built by subsequent rulers. This reached a peak under the First Emperor, who launched a program to create a new type of capital corresponding to the creation of the first state ruling all of China. In 220 B.C. he built the Xin Palace south of the Wei River (the capital proper was to the north), and then renamed the palace the Apex Temple, as the earthly image of the Heavenly Apex star. This star was the center of Heaven and the palace of the High God or Grand Unity, the star with which Sima Qian began his account of the Han sky.[177]

The First Emperor patterned elements of his capital on the sky in order to mark his own role as the earthly version of celestial power. This was carried forward in 212 B.C. when he began construction of a great palace in the Shanglin park. According to the *Shi ji*, two mountain peaks were used as gates to this palace, which was to boast an upper hall that could contain 10,000 people. From this hall he planned to build a covered walk to South Mountain, on whose summit he placed a plaque declaring the mountain the gate-tower of the palace. An elevated walk for secret movement was to connect this new palace to the old one north of the river "in imitation of the way in which in the heavens a corridor leads from the Heavenly Apex Star across the Milky Way to the Royal Chamber Star."[178] The First Emperor built numerous other palaces and villas in the Qin capital region, so that there were "300 palaces within the passes."[179] He also constructed elevated walks or walled roads linking his other palaces and towers so that he could move from one to another without being observed.

The First Emperor not only began to rebuild Xianyang as an earthly replica of the Heavens and a maze of towers and raised walkways in which he could move about like a spirit—both programs that were carried forward in the first Han capital—but also sought to transform the vicinity of the capital into a microcosm of the empire.[180] The *Shi ji* records that each time Qin conquered a state, a replica of its palace was built on the northern bank of the Wei River. These replica palaces were connected by covered walkways with walled-in towers, and filled with musical instruments and singing girls from the vanquished states. This shows that the towered palace had become the embodiment of the polity, so that one could symbolically annex a state by destroying its original palace and rebuilding a "captive" replica in one's own capital. Although the subsequent Han empire did not emphasize the fact of conquest, it still copied patterns of palaces from the different parts of the empire.[181]

Thus, Qin's new capital inherited the emphasis on verticality and display that characterized political architecture in the Warring States, and added to it an elaborate symbolism of empire based on replication through images.[182] This imperial symbolism combined an astral dimension based on patterning the capital on the Heavens with an earthly dimension based on reproducing the palaces of conquered states. The First Emperor's capital depicted the new reality of an empire that included the known world and aspired to cosmic mastery. The First Emperor also collected weapons from across the empire, melted them down, and cast them into twelve bronze statues. According to Han sources, these represented twelve giants, wearing non-Chinese clothing, who had been seen at Lintao.[183] Judging from cases in the "Monograph on the *Feng* and *Shan* Sacrifices" of the *Shi ji*, these figures probably represented immortals who signaled approval of the First Emperor's achievements, and perhaps his future attainment of immortality.

Giving literal form to the symbolic recreation of the conquered states within the capital, the First Emperor also forcibly resettled 120,000 of their most powerful families in Xianyang.[184] Later he resettled populations to the site of his tomb, to his summer palace at Sweet Springs, and even to tend one of the stone inscriptions that he placed on the major mountains in the east to mark his suzerainty over newly conquered territories.[185] Drawing the human resources of the empire into the center reduced the possibility of resistance in what had become provinces, placed dangerous elements within the purview of the emperor and his court, and made the inhabitants of the capital as well as its buildings demonstrations that Xianyang was an epitome of empire. It also realized the formula in Chinese political philosophy in which a ruler demonstrated his power by causing people from far away to come to his court and submit.

This replication of the newly conquered world also figured in the First Emperor's construction of his tomb mound. As a passage in the *Lü shi chun qiu* had noted, in the late Warring States period rulers built tomb complexes that resembled their palace cities. This observation, as discussed in chapter two, is confirmed by the model of the tomb complex of the King of Zhongshan.[186] The greatest of these Warring States tomb mounds was the artificial mountain erected by the First Emperor at Lishan, the tomb now best known for the terra cotta army. This tomb followed the Qin tradition of raising an earthen tumulus and then building wood-framed architectural complexes beside them. It also adopted the eastern tradition of ringing this complex with a double wall, thus assimilating it to the status of a palace city. The First Emperor's innovation was to also make it a replica of the world. His central tomb, according to the *Shi ji*, was filled with models of palaces and towers, his officials, and numerous rare objects. All those concubines who had not given birth to children were also to be buried in this replica of the court. This was then surrounded by a model of the earth, with seas and rivers made from liquid mercury, and representations of the Heavens on the ceiling.[187] The excavation, which has only examined the outskirts of the tomb, shows that the area between the inner and outer walls was filled with sculptures of more officials, as well as the terra cotta army. These in turn were ringed by tombs of high officials, members of the royal family, and an underground stable. Thus, the tomb complex formed a replica of the capital, the state, and the world.[188]

While both capital and tomb were rebuilt as replicas of the cosmos to demonstrate Qin's world mastery, several features of Xianyang suggest the limits of Qin's transition from a state organized for conquest into a universal empire. First, although it was a political capital, Xianyang was ritually empty. The major altars of state were elsewhere. The most important were located at the Fu Altar and the Four Altars of Mt. Wu in the hills near the old capital Yong. These included the altars to the four directional deities—the highest Qin gods—the altar for the "Treasures of Chen," and altars to most celestial and meteorological phenomena. The earlier capital in Longxi also had several dozen shrines.[189] Apart from these there were numerous shrines to minor gods and spirits scattered across Qin.

When the First Emperor conquered the other states, he paraded through the east where he ascended major mountains and left inscriptions celebrating his achievements. In some cases he made sacrifices to important regional gods, most notably the Eight Spirits in Qi. However, the principle was that when the emperor passed a place he would make offerings, while at other times regional cults were left to the local people.[190] He also performed the *feng* and *shan* sacrifices on Mt. Tai and Mt. Liangfu, once again attributing the highest spiritual potency to sacrifices far from the Qin capital. Finally, he standardized the cults to major mountains and rivers, deciding which natural features throughout the empire would receive sacrifice. However, Mt. Hua was the sole feature of sacred landscape that was even close to the capital. The only ritual privilege of the capital was that seven lesser rivers near Xianyang were accorded the same ritual status as the major rivers. However, in practice they did not receive all the offerings granted to the great rivers.[191] Thus, the religious and ritual policy of the new empire was to recognize and rationalize existing cults. This reflected not the present distribution of power, but the features of natural geography and the cultic practices that had evolved in past centuries. Whether this indicates a lack of interest in ritual or a devotion to received practice, it is completely different from the idea of a capital that emerged in imperial China.

The second limitation included the very features by which the First Emperor created a new style of political center: the replica palaces, metal men, and forcibly resettled population. While intended to create an empire-wide capital by metonymically absorbing the other states, it instead erected a monument to Qin's victory. The replica palaces and the metal men were permanent physical reminders of the Qin conquest, testimony to an eternal victory in a war that thus never truly ended. Even as the stone inscriptions of the

First Emperor proclaimed his creation of a new world, they also froze in stone the supposed villainy of Qin's rivals and the fact of Qin's military triumph. Thus, the new capital spatially expressed the fundamental dilemma of Qin sketched by Jia Yi, that the ability to seize and keep what one has seized were not the same, that one could not rule people with the same methods by which one conquered them.[192] Having ended the Warring States period and become ruler of the world, Qin continued to act as a state organized for war that was devoted to collecting taxes and mobilizing troops for the sake of expansion. This failure to make the transition from world conqueror to world ruler, a failure expressed in the physical features of the capital, led to Qin's downfall.

Before discussing the Han capitals, one further aspect of the First Emperor's building program merits discussion. From the beginning, writers described the First Emperor's restructuring of the world as an attempt to impose his will on Heaven and Earth, a veritable war with nature.[193] Jia Yi describes how the First Emperor "cracked his long whip to drive the universe before him," "flogged the entire world," and "shook the four seas":

> He toppled the celebrated [interstate] walls, killed the local leaders, gathered the weapons of the world into Xianyang where he melted them down into bells and to cast twelve statues of men, in order to weaken the common people. Then he trod upon Mt. Hua as his city wall and used the Yellow River as his moat. Based on this towering wall he gazed down into the fathomless depths and thought that he was secure.[194]

The First Emperor whips the world as his chariot, and turns mountains and rivers into his personal defenses, just as he used hills and mountain peaks as gates and bases for his palaces.

Sima Qian elaborated this theme of the First Emperor commanding or punishing natural powers. He describes the ruler enfeoffing a tree for providing shelter—a standard practice in imperial China. Later the emperor denuded Mt. Xiang of trees because a storm caused by the goddess of a local shrine blocked his passage. He cut through mountains and filled up valleys to run a road straight from Jiuyuan in the northwest to Yunyang.[195] When seeking for the isles of the immortals, he dreamt that he was wrestling with the sea god, who tried to block him. He armed himself and the boats he dispatched with repeating crossbows to kill the whales that threatened his search, and shot and killed one. His practice of ascending peaks and placing on them stone inscriptions recounting his achievements is yet another form of attempting to impose, or rather to inscribe, his will on the natural world.

Several inscriptions refer to commanding nature. The Langya text states that the First Emperor's laws extend "wherever sun and moon shine," and that "his blessings reach the oxen and horses." The Eastern Tower inscription describes how his power "shakes the four extremities of the earth" and "regulates the universe." The Jieshi inscription narrates how he destroyed walls, cut through embankments to open up the courses of rivers, and leveled steep defiles to eliminate obstructions. This is described as "fixing the shape of the land."[196] The idea that the First Emperor in his hubris sought to command natural objects and the heavenly bodies became a topos in later Chinese literature.[197]

These stories treat the First Emperor as a megalomaniac, and later poems depict him as an Ozymandias figure, ending with reflections on his death and the collapse of all his works. Nevertheless, they highlight aspects of the idea of emperorship. First, the emperor's rule of the natural world, reaching down to the plants and animals, and the related practice of enfeoffing trees or rocks, were generally accepted in imperial China.[198] Second, the emperor's commanding powerful spirits and making war on deities is not restricted to the First Emperor. Sima Xiangru's "Great Man Rhapsody" depicts Emperor Wu commanding a retinue of gods and storming the gates of Heaven to carry off a jade maiden, and similar themes figure in other poems on imperial hunts or journeys.[199] Finally, imperial authors state that building a canonical imperial capital—with rectangular walls, grids, and towers—entails the imposition of imperial will on the landscape. The First Emperor's innovations in capital design, such as building palaces on celestial patterns and incorporating replica palaces or their stylistic elements from around the empire, were carried forward in Han and later imperial practice. While the First Emperor's actions became a topic for later censure, they also provided an unacknowledged pattern for imperial power, an ideal type at the origin that later rulers emulated in disguised versions.

A substantial literature on the Han capitals describes their structures, narrates their construction, and provides maps.[200] Due to the brevity of Qin's existence, its ambitious building program was not completed, and most of the capital was destroyed by Xiang Yu's army in 206 B.C. Thus, when the first Han emperor decided to make his capital in the old Qin heartland, he had to rebuild largely from scratch. One surviving palace was a summer retreat, the Xingle Palace, which was located south of the Wei River. Renamed Changle, it was adapted to act as the Han founder's primary palace, and consequently the Han capital, Chang'an, was shifted to the south of the river. Here Shusun Tong, a Confucian scholar who had served the Qin, staged the first great Han imperial ritual in which the entire court prostrated themselves before Gaozu (the Han founder) and congratulated him for his triumph.[201] This was the first step in the creation of an imperial capital through ritual performance.

The decision to locate the capital in Guanzhong marked a significant development for imperial capitals. While this had been the Qin capital region, the Han founder was a man of Chu state in the south, so his decision detached the dynasty from its place of origin. This decision to break the ties that bound the dynastic house to its place of origin and its local culture—despite the importation of elements of Chu culture such as the wearing of short Chu tunics, the playing of Chu music, and the use of Chu verse forms such as the epideictic rhapsody—was a first step in creating an artificial, imperial culture with no local attachments.[202] This imperial culture found its clearest spatial expression in the perfected structure of the imperial capital.

The theme of detachment from local culture is highlighted in the *Shi ji* account of Gaozu. He regularly appears as lacking loyalty to family and home, and the history makes this lack a major element in his triumph. This facet of Gaozu's character is portrayed in many ways. First, in the myth of his birth his true father was a dragon with whom his mother had sexual intercourse by the side of a swamp. This divine paternity was not only a standard element in the mythology of sages and dynastic founders, but it also explained and justified the absence of loyalty to his father and his home.[203] Second, as a youth, Gaozu refused to work in his family's business, and instead—in the manner of a "wicked youth"—spent his time drinking with friends. In his rise to power he demonstrated lack of concern for his family by such actions as throwing his children out of a carriage to assist his own escape. When his father was threatened with being boiled and eaten, he asked to share the soup. After becoming ruler, he richly rewarded a follower who persuaded his father to serve him as a subject, since there could be only one sun in the sky.[204]

Gaozu's lack of devotion to his place of origin is contrasted with that of his chief rival, Xiang Yu. The latter was advised that having occupied the Qin capital, he should make his own capital there. He instead chose to return to Chu and enfeoff allies across the north of China: "To become rich and famous and then not go back to your old home is like putting on an embroidered coat and going out walking in the night. Who would know about it?"[205] Xiang Yu would not leave his home for the sake of an empire, while Gaozu would and thus triumphed. This parable makes clear the importance that Sima Qian attached to the renunciation of localist ties in founding an empire.

Although Gaozu spent most of his time elsewhere, work was done to establish Chang'an as a ceremonial center and a capital. In addition to the Changle palace, the Han government constructed an armory, a granary, and an official market, but no ancestral temple. This is probably because Gaozu's commoner genealogy went back no further than his grandfather. More important, the chief minister Xiao He supervised the construction of a larger palace, the Weiyang, on the Dragon Head Hills just to the southwest of the Changle Palace. Using these hills permitted the construction of buildings that towered over the city, and had the further advantage that the dragon was symbolic of the emperor. Built on a rising series of terraces, these structures symbolized the nature of imperial power, as Xiao He explained when criticized by Gaozu for wasting money when the empire was not yet secure: "It is precisely because the fate of the empire is still uncertain that we must build such palaces and halls. A true Son of Heaven takes the whole world within the four seas as his family. If he does not dwell in magnificence and beauty, he will have no way to manifest his authority, nor will he leave anything for his heirs to build upon."[206] Raising a palace above his capital displayed Gaozu's authority, and the survival of the building signified the dynasty's endurance. The palace was the "foundation" of the empire and the guarantor of its security. It also demonstrated the pivotal role of the emperor as the center of the new political structure. Whereas the *Zuo zhuan* had defined a capital as a "city with an ancestral temple," the Han dynasty dictionary *Shi ming* said that the "capital is the seat of the emperor."[207]

Subsequent emperors developed the capital further. The second ruler, Emperor Hui, a child who was guided by his tutor Shusun Tong, began to shape the city according to the precepts for the capital described in the "Kao gong ji." This text, an independent work probably compiled in the Warring States that was attached to the *Zhou li* in place of the missing section on "winter" officials, achieved prominence within the Confucian textual canon. In the account of the "chief carpenter (*jiangren* 匠人)" it gave what was to become the classical model for a capital: "The chief carpenter constructs the capital as a square of nine *li* per side. Each side has three gates. In the capital there are nine north-south boulevards and nine east-west. The north-south ones are nine carriage tracks wide. On the left is the ancestral temple, on the right the altar of the soil, to the front the court, and to the rear the market."[208] Emperor Hui followed elements of this program. First, he built a Temple for Gaozu, to the east of the Weiyang Palace. Second, he built a new market, the West Market, directly to the north of his palace. Finally, he built an outer wall to contain the palaces, temples, and markets within a single boundary. While walls had ringed the imperial palaces under Gaozu, no outer walls had defined the city proper. Because the wall that was built availed itself of the outer walls of existing structures, it was irregular in shape rather than the square proposed by the "Kao gong ji." However, it clearly followed the text in its decision to place twelve gates in the outer walls, for four of these gates were effectively blocked by the Weiyang and Changle Palaces and thus existed only to show that the city was textually orthodox.

This orthodoxy, however, was not obsessive. Due to the scale and locations of the palace complexes, the major streets did not form a grid in the manner suggested by the *Zhou li*. Moreover, each major street had a special lane reserved for imperial use, a feature that had no textual foundation. The procession carrying Gaozu's crown and robes from his mausoleum to his temple passed *under* an elevated walkway used by Emperor Hui to visit his mother, an act that was judged to be unfilial. As a result, the ancestral temple was moved from the city to the mausoleum north of the river, a reform that affected the later practice of the Han ancestral cult.[209]

The last great builder in Chang'an was the fifth ruler, Emperor Wu. He rebuilt the two existing palaces, and also filled out the empty spaces within the walls by building three new palaces. He further built a massive new sacrificial center, the Sweet Springs Palace, to the northwest of the capital, where a Qin summer palace had been located. However, his most ambitious work was the restoration of the Shanglin hunting park to the southwest of

Chang'an. This had been the site of Qin palaces and pavilions, but it had largely fallen into disuse. Emperor Wu filled the park with dozens of pavilions and palaces. He also carved out an artificial lake, and erected statues representing the Weaving Maid and Cowherd stars to make it a replica of the Milky Way. He likewise placed a statue of a whale in the middle of the lake to make it a microcosm of the ocean, the earthly equivalent of the Milky Way. All three statues have been found in recent excavations. In the park he built the massive Jianzhang Palace complex, whose main gate was named Changhe, the gate of Heaven, and whose primary building was the Jade Hall, the Heavenly emperor's palace. This building was surrounded by a labyrinth of corridors, and topped with a gilded phoenix weather vane. It was said to have risen above even the Weiyang Palace. Thus, the hunting park in many ways supplanted the capital itself as the primary imperial residence and ritual center.

In addition to his building program, Emperor Wu also filled the park with rare plants, animals, and rocks received as tribute from distant nations, brought back as booty by expeditions to Central Asia, or confiscated from private collectors. The emperor's collection of exotica included a black rhinoceros, a white elephant, talking birds, and forests of tropical vegetation. They not only proved his charismatic power to bring tribute from distant places, but also made the park an equivalent of the Isles of the Immortals, which were depicted in Han art as covered with strange animals and birds. Thus, in building up this great park next to the capital, Emperor Wu demonstrated his own vision of cosmic lordship and his dream of personal immortality.

The dream, however, was in vain, and like his predecessors Emperor Wu was buried beneath an artificial mountain north of the Wei River. These imperial tumuli, beginning with that of Gaozu at Changling and continuing for each of the subsequent Western Han emperors, modified the landscape of the capital by forming a line of artificial "mountains" rising above the capital to the north. Each tumulus had accompanying wooden buildings for the performance of rituals, and these were maintained by the populations of towns created solely for their upkeep. Gaozu populated the town attached to the tomb of his father by forcibly resettling leading families of the empire, as under the Qin. This policy was followed in turn by his successors.[210] These towns grew to have populations of 200,000–300,000 and according to a census of 2 A.D. more people lived in the tomb towns of Emperors Wu and Xuan than within the walls of Chang'an. Many leading officials and scholars of the Han dynasty came from these towns or lived there while serving at the court. Thus, maintaining the ancestral cult drew population and wealth into the capital, just as the parks drew in rare beasts.

In a study of the Qin and Han empires, Yoshinami Takeshi shows the importance of these towns.[211] Two centuries of resettlement greatly increased the population of the Guanzhong region, which came to rely on imported grain. These newcomers, like the imperial family, were alien to the customs and folkways of Guanzhong. As Yoshinami has shown, the population of the mausoleum towns formed the greatest pool for the recruitment of imperial officials. Thus, even as the policy of resettlement weakened the ability of localities throughout the empire to challenge the center, it also created a distinctive capital culture based on service to the Han house. While such policies did not recur in most later imperial capitals, it established a pattern in which the capital became the unique physical embodiment of the empire, and its population the highest exponents of an imperial culture.

However, there were limits to Chang'an's stature as imperial capital. For the first century, power was partially dispersed among feudatory states. The courts of Huainan, Hejian, and Liang all were major rival centers of patronage of intellectual and religious activities. Leading scholars and writers chose to move to the feudatory courts rather than the capital. Only with the eclipse of the feudatories in the second century of Han rule did this problem fade. A more important limitation, signaled by the importance of the mausoleum towns, was that the first Han capital, like its Qin predecessor, remained largely a ritual void. There was an ancestral temple within the walls, but this played a lesser role both in ritual and politics than the tombside temples attached to the mausolea. More important, temples to Gaozu and subsequently to later emperors were established in every prefecture in the empire. Thus, the primary cults in the capital region were duplicated throughout the empire, reducing the importance of the capital as a ritual center.

At the same time, the major cults to cosmic and natural deities followed the Qin pattern of being scattered across the countryside. Sacrifices to mountains and rivers were carried on in their traditional sites. The sacrifices to the directional *di* deities, the highest gods of the Qin and still among the highest in Han, were located in the temples around Yong. The addition of a fifth *di* by Gaozu simply increased the importance of the Yong site. He also set up sacrifices to Hou Ji in every prefecture, feudal kingdom, and district. Gaozu further established an altar to the war god Chi You in Chang'an, but this did not last. Finally, he imported shamans from throughout the empire to perform cults in the palace.[212]

Under Emperor Wen the cult of the five *di* was briefly shifted to north of the capital, but the *jiao* "suburban" sacrifice continued to be staged at Yong, as was the cult to the *di*. He introduced numerous cults, some near Chang'an and some more distant. The cult of the Grand Unity, a major Chu god, was first installed to the southeast of the capital. The altar to the Empress Earth was set up at Fenyin, a considerable distance from the capital. Emperor Wu also turned the old Qin summer palace at Sweet Springs into a major ritual center, where he shifted the chief altar to the Grand Unity. The greatest sacrifices of the Western Han, the *feng* and *shan*, were performed near Mt. Tai in Shandong. The "Hall of Light," which many scholars argued should be built in the capital, was erected instead near Mt. Tai. Thus, when Confucians began to rise to authority at the court in the last decades of the Western Han, they complained about the massive expense of the ancestral temples dispersed throughout the empire, about how prefectural sacrifices entailed offerings from non-kin, and about the fact that the emperor had to travel to Yong, Sweet Springs, and Fenyin for all the major state sacrifices. The concentration of temples and palaces in the Shanglin Park also undercut the ritual status of the capital proper.[213]

After Emperor Wu's death there was little further construction in Chang'an. The Jianzhang Palace and many buildings in the Shanglin Park were torn down by Wang Mang to provide building materials to construct a "Hall of Light" and related ritual structures prescribed in the Confucian ritual classics. These, however, were largely destroyed in the civil war that toppled Wang Mang and led to the transfer of the capital to Luoyang.

The Eastern Han capital was smaller in area than Chang'an, but more densely populated. Its wall was nearly a perfect rectangle with proper directional orientation, and it had the requisite twelve gates, although not placed at regular intervals. It had two palace compounds, like Chang'an, but they were aligned on a north–south axis. Palaces and government buildings occupied a much smaller proportion of its surface area, which allowed for the creation of a more regular grid of major boulevards as prescribed in the "Kao gong ji." It was also more austere in its architecture. This austerity and regularity were apparently a deliberate policy to demonstrate a change in the nature of imperial power. Specifically, Luoyang in its severity and new range of ritual buildings demonstrated in architecture and spatial arrangements the establishment of the Confucian canon as the state orthodoxy.[214]

This is the central theme of Ban Gu's "Rhapsody on the Two Capitals." Presented to the Han court in 65 A.D., it offers rival encomia on Chang'an and Luoyang. The work follows Sima Xiangru's model of a series of rhetorical set pieces in which fictive speakers celebrate in turn the glories of their respective courts. At the end, the earlier speakers submit, stammering apologies for their ignorance. Sima Xiangru had used the form to celebrate the imperial hunting park and thereby glorify the triumph of imperial power over the feudatories. His decision to focus on the hunting park rather than the capital confirms that the Western Han capital was a ritual void and not truly the center of the empire. Ban Gu adapted the genre of the rhapsody to glorify the Eastern Han court through a poetic triumph over the Western, as well as a personal triumph over Sima Xiangru. Thus, in his poem he argued for both the superiority of morally serious, Confucian literature to the baroque fancies of Sima Xiangru, and that of the ritually proper Luoyang to the corrupt ornamentations of Chang'an. He presented a textual victory to celebrate the triumph of the canonical texts within the structure of the Han capital, a triumph marked by the creation of a ritually correct space and the performance within it of proper rituals.

Official architecture in late imperial China was placed under the Board of Rites, as palaces, halls, and other buildings were ritual objects. This was already true in the Han, so the rhapsodies on capitals dealt with imperial rites. Just as the design of the capitals constructed and enacted the centrality of the emperor, so the arguments of the rhapsodies aimed to delineate the nature of the supreme ruler as a master of rites and the father of his people. These poem's debates, both internal and external, trace the connections of texts, rituals, and power as these evolved over the course of four centuries. At the same time, the conventions of the rhapsodic genre evolved in association with changing ideas of the nature of an empire and its capital. Thus, the textually correct capital served as the basis for the "rectification" of a genre originally devoted to the depiction and celebration of empire.

Ban Gu begins by announcing his intent to produce a "Confucian" rhapsody based on the *Odes* that will correct the failings of Sima Xiangru, and a celebration of Luoyang that will make clear the corruption of the earlier Han capital.[215] The first half of the poem is placed in the mouth of a celebrant of Chang'an, but his praises are crafted to reveal the failings of the early Han court. This is a use of the indirection and polyvocality that were held to characterize the genre; Ban Gu criticizes the earlier regime through self-cancelling praises that redound to the glory of the later.

The Western Guest begins with praise for the strategic location of Chang'an, ringed by rivers and mountains that made attack impossible. These praises evoke the proposition attributed to Wu Qi in several texts that security lies not in the advantages of terrain, but in the support of the people.[216] The description of the city proper celebrates its wealth and luxury, but the praise is undercut by such remarks as "Men of pleasure were comparable to dukes and marquises; shopgirls were dressed more lavishly than ladies of the Ji and Jiang [Zhou royal family and ruling house of Qi and Qin]." The threat of merchant wealth to the social hierarchy figured prominently in Han writings.[217] The corruption of the Western Han capital is also indicated by the presence of "knights-errant." Memorials from Ban Gu's time show that these figures served as metonyms for the amoral bellicosity of the Western Han.[218]

Early in the poem the Western Guest states that the Han founder, gazing westward from his temporary capital in Luoyang, created the capital by fiat. He later notes that each emperor, from the founder to the last, added ornament to the capital.[219] This passage, like a later poem by Zhang Heng, announces the idea that the capital was created virtually ex nihilo by the will of the founder. It comes into existence together with the dynasty, and its fate is inexorably tied to that of the ruling house responsible for its creation and expansion.

The poem shifts to the imperial domain proper, describing the huge size and rich contents of the Shanglin Park. Here the author invokes Sima Xiangru, but also criticisms of the scale of this park. Next comes an account of the fabulous palaces and halls, which dwells on the subtlety of workmanship and intricacy of design. However, such craft was an object of censure for the intended audience, who espoused an aesthetic of simplicity and restraint. A passage on the official sponsorship of scholarship sounds like praise, but several lines come from Ban Gu's attack on the pedantic scholasticism of his day.[220] The account of the Jianzhang Palace notes how it leaves the "vision blurred," the "mind perplexed," and the "soul confused." It concludes, "It is truly a lodging for immortals, not a place where humans are at ease."[221] Finally, Ban Gu describes the imperial hunt, which in the light of the earlier implied criticism appears as the ultimate expression of the moral failings of the Chang'an regime. The first half concludes with a veiled criticism of Emperor Wu's sacrifices, which were held in the Shanglin Park, at Sweet Springs Palace, at Yong, and at Mount Tai, while the capital itself was left a ritual void.[222]

To celebrate the Eastern capital, Ban Gu invokes a new set of topoi. The hymn to Chang'an employed a logic of spatial ascent, praising the geographic setting, the fertility of the soil, the scale and wealth of the city, the splendor of the parks and palaces, and finally the grandeur of the hunts. The poem on Luoyang by contrast omits landscape and city scenes, and instead devotes its first third to the virtues of the Eastern Han emperors. It describes the fall of Wang Mang as an apocalypse that left nothing but fields of rotting flesh and rivers of blood, and then traces the recreation of civilization by the Eastern Han rulers, who reestablished the divisions between husband and wife, father and son, and ruler and subject. It identifies them with the ancient sages who created civilization and with Gaozu. It culminates in the building of the capital at Luoyang and its hunting park in accord with the ancient Zhou model.[223] This section ends in the building of the textually sanctioned capital ritual complex of the Hall of Light, Circular Moat, and Numinous Tower and their ceremonial initiation.

Thus, the dimension of space in the first poem—terrain, local produce, and custom—is replaced by that of time: the achievements of the dynastic founders, their equivalence to the sages who created civilization, and their restoration of ritual. Luoyang is justified as a capital not by its location and physical characteristics but by its textual pedigree and ritual contents. This negation of locality and custom, which are denounced at the beginning of the second rhapsody, by a text-based program of revived sagehood and restored ritual articulates the issues at stake in creating a true capital.[224]

The speaker then describes three rituals. First, he depicts an imperial hunt, but one following rules from the canonical "Royal Regulations" that induce moderation in slaughter and sparing eggs and young. The second ceremony offers sacrifices at three canonical ritual sites. The last consists of entertaining tribute missions from surrounding peoples. This celebrates the success of the Luoyang regime in subduing the Xiongnu with diplomacy and barbarian allies, in contrast to the futile and ruinously expensive expeditions of Emperor Wu. Finally, the emperor decrees a new regime of frugality and restraint, abandons ornament in palace decoration, restricts the numbers of imperial garments and carriages, and curbs all excesses of craftsmen.[225]

As in earlier rhapsodies, the final verses lead to a prose epilogue in which the first speaker admits his error. Ban Gu, however, follows this with five lyrics written in the four-character meter of the *Shi jing*. These celebrate the Hall of Light, the Circular Moat Hall, the Numinous Tower, the Precious Tripods, and the White Pheasants.[226] The first three were textually canonical ritual sites that had been absent from Western Han Chang'an, but were built in Luoyang. The tripods were the symbols of Zhou sovereignty and marked the Eastern Han's claim to be the heirs of the Zhou, ruling from the Zhou capital, while the Western Han had been based in the Qin capital region. They also symbolized a spiritual sovereignty that could not be seized by force.[227] The final poem depicts divine omens that proved Heaven's support of the Eastern Han. Thus, these lyrics celebrate the *text-based* rituals and *spiritual* power that distinguished the Eastern Han from the violence of its predecessor. It was this triumph of Confucian orthodoxy that the austere Luoyang with its new set of ritual buildings embodied.

The concluding lyrics are significant as part of Ban Gu's attempt to create a canonically based poetic form. Like the rest of the rhapsody, they "correct" Sima Xiangru. The latter had concluded his rhapsody on the imperial park with a rhetorical conceit in which the emperor hunted no longer in the park but instead made expeditions through the classical writings and brought back as booty not wild animals but poetry. In this *jeu d'esprit* the poet not only offered the moral suasion that validated his work as serious, but also figuratively revealed the magic of his own poem, which had given the emperor the rare objects of his park and the magnificence of his hunt entirely in the realm of language.[228] Ban Gu insisted that the rhapsody derived from the odes and sought to write verse that met the moral and political criteria imposed by the Confucian understanding of these songs. This culminates in his concluding lyrics, where the rhapsody turns into a suite of odes that present the ritual, spiritual essence of Eastern Han superiority. Thus, the evolving prosody of the poem parallels the historic process that is its subject matter, moving from the elaborate, intoxicating rhetoric of objects and ornament in the style of Sima Xiangru, to a restrained, discursive verse narration of sagely precedent and ritual performance, and climaxing in the reappearance of the canonical meter in an apotheosis of ritual renaissance and celestial approval.

The poetic theme of a ritually correct capital announced the actual transformation of the capital into the imperial ritual center in the last decades of the Han and under Wang Mang. One aspect of this was the creation in the capital of the text-based ritual complex, first by Wang Mang and then the Eastern Han rulers. The abolition of the prefectural ancestral temples in the 30s B.C., at the same time that the cult of Heaven first received Han imperial sponsorship, was dictated not by simple questions of economy, as is often asserted, but by the rising influence of the belief that only descendants could make sacrifices to ancestors and that therefore these sacrifices by local officials to Han ancestors were illicit. This led to a new concentration of imperial ancestral cult in the environs of the capital. It also marked the removal of ancestor worship as the central official cult and the increased emphasis on more public or cosmic cults.

The greatest cosmic cult that emerged under Wang Mang and the Eastern Han was, of course, the altar sacrifice to Heaven. While this is often presented

as a self-conscious harking back to the Zhou, it in fact marked a ritual realization of the new nature of the imperial state. First, being placed in the
southern suburbs of the capital, unlike the Qin and Western Han *jiao* that
were offered at Yong, it asserted the ritual centrality of the capital. As the altar
would be established wherever the capital was moved, it detached the highest
state cult from any fixed locality, and marked the unbreakable linkage of this
cult to the dynasty in its cosmic aspect.

This movability of the cult shows its second crucial feature. As a cult to
Heaven, it was offered up to an omnipresent sky rather than to any feature
of the earth. It gave cultic and ritual form to the detachment from locality,
custom, and particularism that was essential to the imperial state and a true
imperial capital. Far from being an archaic revival, the Han cult of Heaven
was a ritual innovation that gave a novel formulation to one of the central
social alterations entailed in creating a pan-regional, overarching imperial
structure in place of multiple states.[229]

A second pair of rhapsodies on capitals, Zhang Heng's (A.D. 78–139)
"Rhapsody on the Western Metropolis" and "Rhapsody on the Eastern
Metropolis," point toward the ultimate fate of this Eastern Han style of imperial capital. They were written a few decades after the rhapsodies of Ban Gu
and superficially follow a similar pattern at much greater length. In the first
rhapsody, "Sir Based-on-Nothing" praises the terrain, palaces, hunting parks,
markets, and buildings of Chang'an, and then gives an elaborate account of
an imperial hunt. Here Zhang Heng also enumerates the feats of strength and
sorcery in the competitive games (*jue di*) staged for the emperor. The poem
then narrates how the emperor, not satiated by his harem, travels through the
capital incognito to find new pleasures with prostitutes and singing girls, and
concludes with references to the imperial favorites who dominated the court
in the late Western Han.[230] The rebuttal in the second rhapsody likewise
devotes itself to singing the praises of the Han rulers, narrating their
ritual performances, and praising the measure, restraint, and simplicity that
characterize the court. Nevertheless, these rhapsodies differ significantly from
those of Ban Gu, in ways that reflect the changing political and intellectual
world.

Ban Gu witnessed the peak of the Eastern Han, which he attributed to
the triumph of Confucian doctrines as the guiding principles of state ritual
and imperial action. Consequently, his poems celebrate the Eastern Han court.
Zhang Heng, by contrast, lived through the reigns of the Emperors Ho, Shang,
An, and Shun, when power at the court fell into the hands of imperial
affines and eunuchs; the great families grew more wealthy and lavish; and
famine, flood, and barbarian incursions reduced many to misery. Thus, while
the earlier rhapsodies had *celebrated* their rulers, the great opus of Zhang Heng
warned against excess and prophesied impending calamity. While formally
still comparing capitals to present a triumphalist model of history, the text
actually prescribes revived imperial ritual as an antidote to contemporary
corruption.

The critical intent of Zhang Heng is revealed by reading him against his immediate model and target, Ban Gu. The true changes in the "Rhapsody on the Western Metropolis" appear at the end, with the lengthy account of the diverse "competitive games," the emperor's insatiable pursuit of sexual pleasures, and the references to the power of imperial favorites in the late Western Han court. From Eastern Han records, as well as the tomb art of the period, we know that lavish banquet entertainments like those described in the rhapsody were prevalent throughout the Eastern Han elite.[231] Moreover, the problems of sexual excess, domination by women, and overpowerful favorites marked the Eastern Han court in Zhang Heng's maturity. Thus, the new features in his critique of the Western Han capital target the problems of his own day.

The second rhapsody also downgrades the contrast between the two capitals, thereby making the denunciation of luxury and call for ritual correctness matters of present concern rather than historical achievement. First, where Ban Gu began the second part of his rhapsody with an apotheosis of the first two Eastern Han rulers, Zhang Heng recapitulates the history of the Western Han down to Emperor Xuan. He praises the achievements of these rulers, presents the historical conditions that guided their actions, and denies that the prodigality celebrated by the first speaker was their defining characteristic. Second, whereas Ban Gu had omitted a physical account of the palaces and parks of the Eastern Capital, Zhang Heng gives a detailed description of its geographic situation and its splendors.[232] In this way, he obliterates the contrast of physical magnificence with ritual excellence that informed Ban Gu's work. Where Ban Gu spoke only of the imperial hunt and the later feasting of the tribute bearers to mark the contrast of martial West versus civil East, Zhang Heng's poem goes through the entire ritual calendar: New Year's court assembly and tribute; suburban sacrifice to Heaven, Grand Unity, and directional gods; offerings to ancestors; plowing the sacred field; the annual archery rite; feasting the Thrice Venerable; the hunt; and the Great Exorcism.[233] From the historical records we know that most of these rites were scarcely observed in Zhang Heng's adulthood, so this calendar marks the corruption of his own day rather than the inadequacies of the Western court. Finally, toward the end of the poem there is a meditation on the fall of earlier states and the difficulty of maintaining power. Zhang Heng points to the achievements of the first two Eastern Han rulers, their endless toils, and their fears for the future. His silence about the later rulers is deafening. At the very end, where Sima Xiangru offered his hunt in the realms of language and Ban Gu his triumphant resurgence of lyrics on rites, Zhang Heng speaks of the failures of his predecessors, the impotence of verse, and people's inability to distinguish true music from the croaking of frogs.[234]

This vision of ritual and literary bankruptcy was Zhang Heng's response to the increasing female domination of the court. Apart from the concentration of power in the inner quarters, which alienated members of the bureaucracy and the powerful families, the collapse of the Eastern Han court also resulted from certain features of the new capital previously discussed. As the capital and its rituals became more closely tied to a textual program preserved in archaizing texts, as these rituals increasingly focused on the celestial nature of the dynasty, and as the policy of resettlement was abandoned, the ties between the imperial center and local society grew ever more tenuous. With a ritual program that highlighted the negation of local or regional ties, and the shift of power away from the outer court staffed by the representatives of local society, the Eastern Han capital progressively detached from the outer world and imploded. In becoming a truly imperial capital, it had lost the ties to its empire.

CONCLUSION

The earliest Chinese states were networks of settlements linked by royal power. When this power faded in the late Western Zhou, local centers that had been reduced replicas of the royal capital emerged as independent city-states. The core of the Zhou state was filled with dozens of such city-states, many no bigger than a day's walk. The larger states at the periphery consisted of multiple cities, but as under the earlier Zhou these cities were generally distributed as fiefs to followers, and hence formed de facto city-states in their own right. This subinfeudation provided bases for the rising lineages that destroyed the older states and introduced the institutional reforms that established macrostates in their place.

Within the macrostates and the unitary empire, cities played a new role. First, the conventional city was the so-called double city in which there were separate walled compounds for the government/ritual center and for residential/business wards. This division of the city between an administrative center and residential or business districts became an enduring feature of Chinese urbanism, a feature that divided the city against itself. This was theorized by writers of the period in terms of a social division of labor, in which government officials were an occupational category separated from the general populace through the encompassing vision that allowed them to hold together all the economic specializations.

Second, new modes of using space emerged. The vertical dimension became crucial in the form of platforms, towers, and elevated roads that raised political buildings and their activities above the populace. As demonstrations of power, places for observation, and means of moving in secret, elevated structures became essential to political power. The horizontal dimension, for its part, took the form of grids, both in the layout of streets and stalls in the market. The symbolism and role of such grids are discussed at length in chapter five.

The marketplace became a key site in Warring States and early imperial cities, a site marked both by a tower and a grid. It provided the interface between politics and commerce. Walled, laid out in a grid, dominated by a multistory tower from which officials observed and signaled, it was a scene of state authority. This included not only regulation of prices and the quality of goods, but also the proclamation of decrees, the carrying out of punishments, and the display of corpses. Despite these attempts at control, the market was also a site for activities outside the state sphere. First, it contained crowds and their often unpredictable behavior. Second, it was a site for the activities of many people operating outside, or even against, the state order. Apart from the merchants themselves, whose wealth menaced both the sumptuary order imposed by the state and the integrity of its officials, the market and environs were a crucial locus for the activities of organized criminals, gangs of wastrel youths, diviners and other practitioners of the occult arts, and prostitutes. Even such legitimate trades as butchery provided a pool of potential assassins for hire and a hiding place for people seeking private vengeance.

In addition to the changing nature of ordinary cities, the Warring States and early imperial periods witnessed the emergence of a new urban form, the imperial capital. This can be traced through examining the evolving nature of capitals from the Qin capital Xianyang through Chang'an in the Western Han to the first full-blown imperial capital at Luoyang in the Eastern Han. This development was defined above all by the concentration of key rituals within the capital, which was thus distinguished from lesser cities, and the performance of these rituals according to a textual program that removed them from the realm of custom. The supreme expression of this was the emergence of the cult of Heaven as the highest imperial ritual. In offering sacrifices to a celestial god from whom they claimed power, and in locating these at an altar whose location was defined by the presence of the dynasty, the Han emperors ritually marked their transcendence of all local or particularist ties, and asserted their character as a universal polity whose authority covered everything beneath the sky.

This new style of capital had several distinctive features. First, it was the creation of the dynasty or its founder. This creation or recreation ex nihilo separates the capital from preexisting cities that were natural products of trade or limited, regional powers. Instead, the creation of the capital appeared as yet another element in the institutional establishment of a dynasty—the legal code, standard measures and weights, proper graphic forms, court costumes, and especially the ritual program to which the capital was tied and of which it was an expression. In the era of an imperial canon, all these aspects were associated with the authority of the sanctioned textual heritage. Second, this emphasis on the capital as a political creation led to insistence on its artificiality. The walls, the gates, and the grid of streets all mark the imposition of human design on the natural world and its chaotic elements. They served as spatial images of the control and hierarchy that defined imperial rule, and provided a physical structure for the control and policing of a potentially unruly populace. This artifice is also expressed in fashion and taste, for which the ruler and his court served as ultimate sources and exemplars.

A final aspect, derived from the first two, is the theme of transience. While no one could speak of the death of an emperor or the fall of a dynasty, such events were inevitable. The capital, as an artificial creation of the dynasty, would collapse with the ruling house that created it.[235] Created out of nothing by dictate or decree, it would return to nothing when those decrees lost their hold. Even in the time of their glory, the capitals were the scenes of fleeting glories and pleasures, as sung in the "Nineteen Old Poems" of the Han. This evanescence of Chinese capitals was intensified by the reliance on wood for building. Whereas the stone ruins of ancient Rome and Greece remained as sources for meditation and revival in the West, the ancient capitals of China were swept away in an apocalyptic fall. Thus, Xianyang was burned to the ground by Xiang Yu, the *Han shu* ends with an account of Chang'an as a devastated waste, and Luoyang was destroyed and depopulated by Dong Zhuo.[236] Han Luoyang left no remains, as is shown in the meditation on the glory and disappearance of a later version of the same city, the *Luoyang qielan ji*. Just as the capital was defined primarily not through physical structures but ritual performances, the capital as historical memory relied on literary meditations rather than the vision of stone ruins. Thus, Eastern Han Luoyang survived as a topic of writing, as in the poem by Cao Zhi (A.D. 192–232), son of Cao Cao and brother of the first emperor of the Wei Dynasty, who knew the Han capitals only as a wasteland:

> Climbing to the ridge of Beimang Mountain
> From afar I look down on Luoyang.
> Luoyang, how lonesome and still!
> Palaces and houses all burnt to ashes.
> Walls and fences all broken and gaping,
> Thorns and brambles rising to the sky.
> I do not see the old men;
> I only see the new youths.
> I turn aside, no straight road to walk.
> Waste fields, no longer ploughed.
> I have been away so long
> That I do not recognize the paths.
> Amidst the fields, how sad and desolate.
> A thousand miles without chimney smoke.
> Thinking of the house I lived in all those years.
> My emotions twisted, I cannot speak.[237]

CHAPTER FOUR

REGIONS AND CUSTOMS

The region is a key form of spatial organization in which urban centers extend across the countryside along routes for moving goods and people. Within a roughly delimited area around one or more cities, people form regular networks of exchange and communication. While by no means watertight, regions are significant because the people within them interact with each other far more than with those in adjacent areas. Each region thus develops diverse forms of historical association or traditions that distinguish them from others. The size of regions varies with the technology of transport and the scale of economic activities, ranging from the hinterland of a single city to the drainage basin of a large river system, and in some circumstances matching the boundaries of a political state.[1]

The study of regions in China has largely been confined to the late imperial period. G. William Skinner's schema of eight macroregions formed from a hierarchy of local marketing systems and their central places has become a major model in terms of or against which scholars define their understanding of the late imperial social order.[2] Whatever the value and limits of Skinner's model, there is no doubt that Chinese history has been a history of regions. All its long-term developments and major catastrophes have had a regional character, taking place in certain areas and leaving others untouched. This regional character was, if anything, greater in the early period, when both economic and cultural integration were much less developed than they became in China after the Song.

However, while the history of early China was a history of regions marked by great diversity, the *writing* of that history in the early imperial centuries paid little attention to these divergences. This is not simply due to a textual focus on the pan-imperial elite and its culture, or the organization of the major histories around the court.[3] In this period the region was a target of suspicion that was deliberately excluded from the historical record. In the emergent empire the major regions were largely identical with the former Warring States. Their conquest had been necessary to attain unity and their court-based chronicles had been destroyed by Qin in a literary version of its

189

military victories. Thus, any suggestion of the cultural or political autonomy of regions was anathema to advocates of the imperial order, and many policies—most notably the forced resettlement of leading families in the capital region—were instituted to eliminate bearers of distinctive regional cultures. This criticism of local culture took the form of attacks on the inevitable limits, and frequent evils, of "custom (su 俗)." This term thus became one of the keys for discussing the spatial character of the empire.

In Warring States and Han thought "custom" became a negative category indicating what was local, partial, and tied to the characteristics of a specific place or region. It was positive only as a medium—usually identified with "wind"—through which the transforming power of a sage ruler altered the people. The relation of these two terms is essential to any spatial analysis of the early empire. "Custom" indicated local practices or attributes that distinguished the inhabitants of one region from another, while "wind" referred to the influence of terrain and climate on a region's inhabitants. By extension wind also referred to the influence of the ruler or government.[4] As regional variations of human conduct, customs could be treated almost from an anthropological perspective. They also stood, however, in opposition to the universal, normative, or ideal; they thus were usually treated in a negative manner. In his discussion of wind, Ban Gu noted that all people shared a constant nature, but that the influence of "wind/environment" led to variations in firmness of character, speed of action, and characteristic sounds (i.e., language and music).[5] An explicit discussion of the potentially negative character of customs appears in Ying Shao's *Comprehensive Meanings of Wind-Customs*:

> "Wind" means the cold or warmth of Heavenly energies, the difficulty or ease of Earthly terrain, the excellence or vileness of water and springs, and the firmness or softness of grasses and trees. "Custom" means the way in which creatures with blood live through imitation of these features. Therefore the different sounds of languages and songs or the distinct forms of drummed dances and movements are sometimes straight and sometimes crooked, sometimes excellent and sometimes perverse. When the sage arises he balances and equalizes them, so they all return to what is correct [*zheng*]. When the sage is abandoned they return to their original customs.[6]

Here custom explicitly opposes the work of the sages and that which is "correct" or properly governed. It is the genius of place versus universal norms, the practices of the people versus the reforming influence of the sage, the spoken or sung versus the written—as indicated by Ban Gu's and Ying Shao's references to "sound"—and the periphery versus the capital or center.

These points are important because the Han defined itself as a universal empire that transcended loyalties to the individual Warring States. Han critiques of Qin emphasized its failure to shift from a regional power, limited to

Guanzhong and Sichuan, to a universal state. The Han state, in contrast, transformed itself into a true imperial structure through detachment from local ties, first from the dynasts' place of origin in Chu and then from their capital in Guanzhong. They initiated policies to incorporate the power and loyalties of leading figures from the regions that had previously been independent states. These included the resettlement of major families to the capital region, the collection of exotics and tribute in the imperial park, the suppression of provincial temples and transfer of cultic sites to the capital in association with the rise of the cult of Heaven, and the creation of a new capital at Luoyang defined through its conformity to canonical texts. In these ways the Han transferred people's devotion away from their places of origin to the empire. The empire, in turn, was increasingly defined by an artificial language detached from local, spoken dialects, and a ritual system that suppressed contemporary practices in the name of performances derived from ancient texts.[7] Consequently, all earlier states, including imperial Qin, were reinterpreted as manifestations of localism, which was relegated to a position of inferiority under the rubric of "custom."

This chapter examines the Warring States origins of the critique of custom, its development as a vision of empire under the Han, and the major forms of regional organization that emerged in opposition to the imperial center. The first section traces the origins of the discourse on regions to ideas in the Warring States philosophical traditions. In this period the idea of custom referred not to regions, but to the beliefs and practices of the unlettered masses and unenlightened elites. The philosophical traditions, particularly the *ru*, defined themselves against such "conventional wisdom." The second section discusses how the critique of custom shifted to the geographic sphere as an element of the creation of a unitary state. This shift was most clear in discussions of the limits of the Qin state, which, according to Han critics, had remained one regional power ruling others rather than creating a truly imperial, pan-Chinese polity. Han criticisms explained the Qin legal system as a function of local custom, thus assimilating law to the status of custom rather than contrasting them as in the modern, Western discourse.[8] The discourse on custom also incorporated discussions from Warring States military treatises of the strengths and weaknesses of different states as explained by their geography and local practices. Finally, writings about regions and regionalism figured in accounts of distinctive local products in trade and tribute. These discussions of tribute, like those on Qin, used non-Chinese peoples as the extreme case of diverse customs.

The balance of the chapter examines the social reality of regionalism, and the limits to the rule of the center. The third and fourth sections examine the issue of regions in Han policies toward locally powerful families, these families' economic and political power, and their role in local religious cults. This reveals a fundamental contradiction in the project of imperial unification, for while the court attempted to prevent the rise of regional powers, it depended on the support of such powers to impose its writ in local society.[9]

While the great families' regional power defied the imperial center's author-ity, it was also essential to that authority. Without the link between great clans and court provided by regular recruitment into major offices, the court lost its ties to the countryside and imploded. The final section of the chapter looks at shifting attitudes toward regions at the end of the Han, when the center was beginning to crumble. This shift will be demonstrated through an exam-ination of the new character of rhapsodies on the capital as written by Zuo Si. These works brought to the fore the themes of region and custom in the wake of the collapse of imperial institutions.

THE WARRING STATES PHILOSOPHICAL CRITIQUE OF CUSTOM

The discourse in which custom and region figured as images of limitation and error originated in the Warring States philosophical traditions. Pushed by economic, social, and intellectual conditions to define themselves through rejection of current practice, they used the rubric "custom" to describe the unexamined errors to which they claimed to offer a corrective. To the extent that the philosophical traditions produced status and income through work as educators, one of their major social roles, they also had to show that their program of education was superior to the conventional instruction that people received in their households or places of work.[10] Thus, all the philosophical traditions used "custom" as a negative rubric for the targets of their attacks. However, conventional education and the ideas that it transmitted were above all a target for the classicist *ru* tradition that placed the greatest emphasis on education and was linked to a broad social category including those involved in low-level teaching.[11]

The texts later grouped under the rubric Daoism (i.e., the *Dao de jing* and the *Zhuangzi*) inverted conventional values. They insisted that what ordi-nary people regarded as truth or beauty were in fact error and misprision, the arbitrary adoption of one position among a myriad of possibilities. All posi-tions except their own resulted from taking limited and subjective visions to be eternal standards. Thus, conventional wisdom and custom were by defini-tion one of their major targets. Invariably in these texts the beliefs of the "masses of people" or the "whole world" form targets of criticism against which the truths of the sage or perfected man are established: "The vulgar people [*su ren* 俗人] are sunny and bright, while I alone am glum. The vulgar people are clear and discerning, while I alone am repressed and withdrawn."[12] Other lines in the same passage refer to the "crowd" or "masses" (*zhong ren* 眾人) in a term used interchangeably with the "vulgar people" who are con-trolled by custom.

The *Zhuangzi* develops this usage at greater length. The conventional wisdom that makes groundless distinctions between the "gentleman" and the "petty man" or mistakenly identifies wisdom with the judgments of the world is regularly labeled "custom" or "custom of the age (*shi su* 世俗)," which confuses limited perception with totalizing truth.[13] Custom in education perverts people's inborn nature, as described in the chapter "Mending Nature": "Those who mend their nature through custom, using customary learning to try to return to their origins, and who muddle their desires through custom, hoping thereby to attain illumination, these are called the benighted people. . . . Those who lose themselves in objects or lose their nature in customs are called the upside-down people."[14] "Custom" also refers to rival philosophical traditions, as though their ideas were identical to the unexamined prejudices of ordinary people, and their crowds of disciples nothing but a mob.[15]

The *Zhuangzi* does, however, present two cases in which custom can function as a positive term. First, "custom" can be a term of praise when it refers to the virtuous character of people under the influence of a sage. In the *Zhuangzi* this occurs particularly in accounts of the virtuous customs of the primitive people who lived before the appearance of the historical sages.[16] Second, the *Zhuangzi* frequently advises the aspirant sage or perfected man to blend into the world of custom so as not to be noted and to be able to move freely. This, however, is not praise for actual immersion in custom, but only for a pretense of being ordinary as a means of achieving freedom and self-preservation.[17]

Even as the *Zhuangzi* was developing, the major texts of the classicist *ru* tradition were also discussing custom in relation to education. These texts shared major core beliefs about education: a sagehood accessible to all men as the ultimate goal and standard, the essential role of the heart/mind as an active arbiter between competing courses of action, and above all the decisive impact of education on an almost infinitely malleable nature.[18] The power of education was so great that its results came to be conventionally described as a "second nature." The *ru* texts also shared the assumption that the ritual and textual education they offered was vastly superior to a conventional social upbringing. The education that led to the fully moral nature identified with sagehood was possible only for those committed to the program defined by the classical heritage as adapted by the Warring States *ru*. The teachings that ordinary people derived from their immediate social environment were criticized under the rubric of "custom," which either perverted innate moral tendencies as argued in the *Mencius*, or reinforced an anarchic nature according to the *Xunzi*. Custom thus became a recurrent issue in early *ru* discussions of nature and education, where it figured as a path to bestiality.

The *Xunzi* develops these criticisms at greatest length when arguing that not only man's inborn nature but his conventional upbringing produced moral deviance or social collapse. Several of these ideas had been anticipated in the *Mencius*, but they are best understood in light of the more elaborate arguments in the *Xunzi*. By the end of the Warring States, these ideas about custom had become so pervasive that they functioned as clichés or fixed idioms in the syncretic philosophical compendium *Lü shi chun qiu*. Finally, this discourse was carried into the Han classical traditions by Jia Yi in his detailed discussion of the education of the heir apparent and the need for "fetal instruction."

The *Xunzi* argued that people's innate desire for pleasures inevitably produced struggles to obtain the scarce goods necessary to those pleasures. These struggles resulted in social disorder that could be curbed only by restraining innate desires through imposing the ritual regime created by the sages. However, as the *Xunzi* and other *ru* texts acknowledge, this ritual regime does not ordinarily exist within the villages and families that controlled people's early experiences and education. It had to be instilled by the government of a sage ruler and the teachings of great *ru* scholars. As outlined in the chapter "Efficacy of the *Ru*," proper teachers were essential because they alone could transmit the "model" of the sages and thus prevent people from becoming thieves and murderers.[19] However, the target of instruction is not simply people's asocial nature, but also the disorderly conduct and deviant morality embedded in the customs that they absorbed from their childhood surroundings:

> People's natures are inevitably those of the petty man. Without teachers and laws/models they see nothing but profit. . . . Moreover, when they encounter a chaotic age (*shi*) with chaotic customs (*su*) this redoubles their pettiness and the chaos. If a true gentleman does not gain a position of authority to supervise them, then there is no means to open their minds.[20]

Here the second nature acquired in learning intensifies people's original nature, the small-minded materialism with which they are born. Only the imposition of a classicist authority embodied in the true gentleman can bring genuine education to those still trapped in the realm of custom.

Not all customs, however, are "chaotic."[21] Rectified by law, ritual, or music, they can guide the conventional behavior of ordinary people. However, in the *Xunzi* such reliance on custom marks a mediocre person who cannot rise above the constraints of a limited experience: "Making his conventional speech trustworthy and his conventional behavior cautious, fearing the laws, following the customs, and not daring on his own authority to assert anything to be correct—this can be called a 'diligent' scholar."[22] Conduct in accord with custom characterizes the lowest form of scholar who is dutiful and obedient but incapable of real achievements. Thus, even where it remains a potentially neutral term, "custom" in the *Xunzi* figures as a negative category. The major reasons for this hostility to conventional social practice are summarized:

> The man on the street who completely accumulates goodness is called a sage. One obtains it [goodness] only by seeking, perfects it only by performance, elevates it only through accumulation, and becomes a sage only through its completion. Being a sage is that which a man accumulates. If a man accumulates hoeing and plowing,

then he becomes a farmer. If he accumulates carving and scraping, then he becomes a craftsman or carpenter. If he accumulates the peddling of goods, then he becomes a merchant. If he accumulates the principles of ritual then he becomes a gentleman.

The sons of craftsmen and carpenters all carry on their fathers' work, and the people of cities and countries are all comfortable in and used to their own customs. Dwelling in Chu one becomes a person of Chu; dwelling in Yue one becomes a person of Yue; dwelling in Xia [the central Chinese states] one becomes a person of Xia. This is not inborn nature, but caused by accumulation and polishing. Thus if a man is able to carefully focus on his actions, to be cautious against growing habituated to customs, and to greatly accumulate and polish, then he will become a gentleman.[23]

The first paragraph defines the sage by completeness and the gentleman by ritual. These two serve the state through comprehensive intellect and mastery of principles. Each of the three lower occupational categories masters only a single, limited skill that is useful only under the comprehensive guidance of the state and its servants. Thus, custom is the realm of the partial and limited. It defines the inferior social roles of those devoted to a specific trade or skill, and contrasts with the encompassing intelligence of the scholars who are distinguished by their ritual expertise and textual mastery.

The second paragraph reiterates the contrast of partiality and totality, but here in the context of spatial rather than social divisions. Just as people are limited by the occupations into which they develop through the accumulated imitation of their fathers, so they are restricted by the customs and conventions of the region where they grow up. Each region knows only its own customs and consequently confuses its limited repertoire of tastes and activities for the totality of the human condition. In contrast with this is the culture that is identified by "Xia," the earliest Chinese dynasty and the name for Chinese civilization as opposed to barbarian. In the parallel passage translated in note 23 the sage is the man of "ya," a character originally homophonous and interchangeable with "Xia" and descriptive of classical pronunciation, the literary language, Zhou court music, and high refinement or elegance. By the Eastern Han, the contrast between the language of the sage and that of "current custom (shi su 世俗)" had become a standard theme: "The prophetic texts were not created by the sage [Confucius]. Within them are many variant graphs which border on the vulgar, and they closely resemble the language of contemporary custom [shi su]. I suspect that they originated later through some error."[24] This refined culture, which characterizes the gentleman, is distinct from the other cultures because it defines not just another region, like Chu or Yue, but an idealized, encompassing ancient realm that survived in the form of archaic music, refined language, and correct ritual. Whereas conventional men were trapped in the custom of their time and place, the classicist escaped it through his access to a superior realm preserved in the cultural heritage of his rituals and texts. Thus, the argument for the necessity of a ritual or textual education to overcome the influence of custom had already begun to develop into a critique of the limits and cultural deficiencies of regionalism.

The *Mencius* contrasted the "refined" (*ya*) music of the ancient Zhou court with music produced by "contemporary customs (*shi su*)." This last phrase is a recurring term of opprobrium that appears also in the *Zhuangzi* and the *Xunzi*, meaning something like "the conventional wisdom." It continued to be used as a negative, critical term throughout the Han and in later Chinese history.[25] Pairing "custom" with "the present age" marks human partiality in both spatial and temporal dimensions. As shown earlier, "custom" indicated the guiding rules or practices of those constrained by the limited social group or region to which they belonged. Consequently, texts often refer to the customs of a delimited spatial unit such as a clan, village, or state.[26] In the same way *shi* 世 indicates a practice or idea adopted at the present time, but not manifest throughout history. In the philosophical usage of the period, it was a term of opprobrium.[27] Thus, in the *Xunzi* most of the erroneous doctrines criticized in the chapter "Correcting Judgments" are described as being articulated by "conventional ['custom-bound'] practitioners of persuasions of the present age."[28]

In contrast with the creatures of custom, who were spatially limited and bound by the practices of the region and occupation in which they grew up, the sage transcended spatial bonds. He did this by either drawing all regions together in a unitary political whole, or suppressing the rule of custom by creating a realm whose values or forms of conduct were valid across time and space. In the *Xunzi* the former model is adopted in "Dispelling Blindness": "The distant regions all sent in their treasures. Consequently his [the sage's] eyes saw all colors, his ears heard all sounds, his mouth ate all tastes, his body dwelt in all forms of palace, and as names he bestowed universally correct appellations."[29] Here the treasures of the distant regions of the earth, each characteristic of its own region and thus serving as the material equivalent of custom, converge in the center as tribute to the sage. This allows the sage to combine all physical or sensual experiences in a regime whose completeness is the physical equivalent of his all-encompassing virtue. Closely related is the idea that the sage should correct the diverse localities so that all people share in his universal practices. However, the sage is able to combine or correct customs only because he rises above the limits of his own experience through identification with the Way and thus "brings peace to those with different customs."[30]

This model of regional divergences overcome by establishing a unifying center is part of a larger discourse on the relation of topography, fauna, and local customs. As Roel Sterckx demonstrated in his recent monograph *The Animal and the Daemon in Early China*, many early Chinese texts argued that both animals and people were the distinctive products of their regions. Each region had its own characteristics determined by its soil, waters, and wind. The plants, animals, and people that developed in such regions had a physical and moral concordance with the environment that had produced them. Some texts argued that animals could not live outside their native regions, or that people could only eat the sorts of animals produced by a common environment. Similarly, local sacrifices should use animals characteristic of the region, and armies should use horses who were native to the land where they would fight. In this model political power was generated by the movement of animals from their regions of origin into the imperial hunting park that at times defined the center of the realm (see chapter three). Similarly, animals with powers of mobility and mutation, such as the dragon and the phoenix, were the natural correlates of the sages, who could transcend the limitations of locality and place.[31] In this way the discourse on custom merged with the discourse on animals. People and animals tied to their places of origin formed a common image of limitation and inferiority, while movement to the center transformed them through incorporation into the realm of the sage.

The second model, that of suppression or correction, figures most prominently in the *Mencius*. This text opposes the sages, particularly the Duke of Zhou, to the barbarians from the distant regions of the earth. With their strange languages and deviant customs, barbarians figure in Warring States and early imperial texts as the ultimate exemplars of deviance due to the dominance of custom. Under the spell of local customs barbarians abandoned their aged parents, ate their children, married their mothers, lived on horseback, tattooed their bodies, and wore their hair loose in the manner of madmen or ghosts. The *Mencius* describes how the Duke of Zhou converted such people by moral example, launched military expeditions against them, or "subjugated the northern and southern barbarians and drove away the wild animals to bring security to the people."[32] Another passage states that the sage Shun was an eastern barbarian and Zhou King Wen a western barbarian, but despite the vast spatial separation of their origins, their actions as sages in the middle kingdoms "matched like the two halves of a tally."[33] Here sagehood rises above the partiality of regional cultures, marked by the opposite points of the compass, and finds its place in the center where all regions converge. This schematic use of the directions of the compass to signal the triumph of the sagely center over the rule of custom at the periphery also figures in Mencian accounts of the Zhou royal processions.[34]

"Custom" was also negative because it was linked with the lower strata of society. This was shown in earlier passages where farmers, craftsmen, and merchants were bound by their respective customs, and the scholar guided by custom was invariably "mediocre" or "common" (*yong* 庸). This word has strong overtones of low social status, for it is homophonous and interchangeable with the character "hired labor (*yong* 傭)." *Yong* and *su* form a synonym compound describing the "rustic fellow" or "yokel" who values only substance (*shi* 實) and pays no heed to ornament or culture (*wen* 文).[35] Elsewhere "custom" defines the actions of the "masses of commoners," in contrast to officials whose actions are defined as "tasks" or "service."[36] Other passages link custom to commoners and the uneducated even more explicitly. Thus, "Efficacy of the *Ru*" states:

> To regard following custom as excellent, view material goods as precious, and take "nourishing life" to be the highest way for one's self, this is the virtue of the common people. Carrying out laws with supreme steadfastness and not muddling what he learns with selfish desires, this can be called a "sturdy scholar." Carrying out laws with supreme steadfastness, liking to correct what he has learned in order to rectify and improve his nature . . . this can be called an "earnest and generous gentleman". Cultivating the ways of the ancient kings as easily as distinguishing black from white, responding to the changes of the times as easily as counting from "one" to "two" . . . this may be called a "sage."[37]

Here obedience to custom defines the commoner, acceptance of law and received learning marks the lowly scholar, obedience to law with the ability to make minor adjustments in learning defines the superior scholar, and mastery of all laws and the ability to change them mark the sage. Blind servitude to custom and a consequent inability to change with the times are also what distinguish the "vulgar classicists [literally the 'classicists of custom' (*su ru* 俗儒)]" who are denounced in the *Xunzi*.[38]

That the common man is dominated by custom is also indicated by the link between custom and the farming village. In the *Xunzi* the "disorderly people of current custom" are mentioned in parallel to the "frivolous sons of the farming villages," indicating that the two groups were closely related.[39] Thus, the villages were regarded as sites particularly prone to the tyranny of custom. The same idea figures in the *Mencius*'s discussion of the "village honest men." It describes these figures, whom the *Lun yu* had called the "destroyers of virtue," as those who insist that one must act in accord with the practices of the present age. This is described as "servile flattery addressed to the present age," and those who practice it are "identical with current custom and at one with the sordid age."[40]

The idea that custom dominates the common people and makes them limited or partial, in contrast with the sage who is complete or universal, also guides the use of certain adjectives. The most important is *lou* 陋, which means "limited," "rustic," or "provincial" and is thus linked to custom as that which marks regions, commoners, or villagers. One passage argues that the reason people abandon the way of the sages and emulate such villains as Jie and the Robber Zhi is because they are *lou*. Another states that *lou* people fail to mourn their kin and in this way are "lower than beasts" and incapable of living in society.[41]

A final negative aspect of the creature of custom is an obsession with material objects. This exclusive interest in what is substantial or physical, treating physical objects as though they, rather than moral virtues, were the highest treasures, or "not studying, having no sense of duty, and regarding wealth and profit as glory" are hallmarks of people whose world is defined by the teachings of custom.[42] These criticisms are aspects of the idea that men under the sway of custom are the lower classes, who remain trapped in the greed that defines "the petty man." The lack of interest in study, due to a belief in the correctness of customary practices that require no additional study, is also linked to the inability to change. The *Xunzi* argues repeatedly that study is the key to the transformation of oneself and one's position in the world. The person who does not study is incapable of changing either self or world, and thus remains trapped forever by the customs acquired in childhood.[43]

The idea that those dominated by custom value only material objects is linked to the argument, which figured in chapter one as one aspect of the divided body, that what separates the true ruler from ordinary men is his freedom from the tyranny of external things. People's senses tend to be captured by the objects that provide agreeable experiences. They are thus reduced to objects by the things that they desire. The true ruler, in contrast, has cultivated a mind that can control his sense organs. As a result, he does not value or cling to objects, so he can manipulate them for his own purposes, or like a mirror automatically and correctly respond to objects and then let them go.[44] In contrast, those in lesser occupations such as farmer, merchant, or craftsmen are "skilled in individual things," but unable to deal comprehensively with all things. The *Xunzi* concludes, in a formula that appears in several middle and late Warring States texts, "The gentleman makes things serve him (*yi wu* 役物); the petty man is reduced to the service of things (*yi yu wu* 役於物)."[45] Thus, the *Lü shi chun qiu* argues: "One who is prince and desires to cause the lands beyond the seas to submit must restrain to a high degree his use of things and place no value on petty profit. Freeing his senses from the sway of custom, he can participate in the settling of the age."[46] The true ruler is marked by a lack of interest in material objects that in turn entails the liberation of his senses from the domination of custom. In contrast, the obsession with objects of those controlled by their senses and custom marks their low status and servitude. The partiality of their position in the world is echoed in the partiality in their own bodies.

By the end of the Warring States period these ideas about the tyranny of custom had become a regular topos verging on cliché, as seen most clearly in the *Lü shi chun qiu*. The idea that men under the influence of custom become the slaves of objects appears repeatedly in this text, most notably in the "Yangist" chapters discussed in chapter one that criticize people who foolishly squander in the pursuit of objects the time and energy that constitute their lives.[47] More important, the term *su* serves as an adjective meaning "limited," "benighted," or "stupid," most notably in the recurring phrase "*su zhu*, ruler controlled by custom."[48] The same epithet was used in the Han period to describe negligent or incompetent local officials. It applied to those who were too immersed in human affairs to understand the great principles of Heaven (i.e., calendrics as a guide to government) or who only followed the fashions of the times.[49] In contrast, the actions of those who follow the Way and do not pursue material wealth are described as "distinct from [or 'far separated from'] custom." Those who have attained the Way "treat custom with contempt" and instead take Heaven as their model. Through departing from the customs that guide the masses, the sage is able to transform those customs.[50]

Thus, the *Xunzi's* arguments are in the *Lü shi chun qiu* taken for granted in usages that attribute the moral and intellectual failings of the world to the tyranny of custom. Due to its links with objects and local environment, custom appears tied to the deficiencies of a prehuman nature, so the creature of custom is no better than a beast. Education must redeem men not only from the potential savagery of their nature, but from their immersion in the sensual desires and material objects that form the realm of custom. This is the work of the sage or scholar, who rises above the partiality and blindness of custom and is thus able to transform the common people.

This equation of "custom" and "nature" in the context of regionally determined practices figures in the *Wuzi*. In the chapter "Evaluating the Enemy," Wu Qi discusses the "customs" of the six Warring States that threaten Wei. He describes the "nature (*xing* 性)" of the people in each of the states, along with the character of the terrain and institutions of government. In this passage, which is discussed next, the nature or character of people is equated with the customs that shape them.[51]

These ideas on nature and custom underlay the theories of education developed at the beginning of the Han in relation to the heir apparent. These include the earliest known discussions in China of the use of "fetal instruction" and the rearing of infants.[52] This argument that education must begin in the womb and be carried on throughout infancy appears in the writings of Jia Yi (200–168 B.C.).[53] He develops ideas about the dangers of custom and its links to human nature in at least three ways.

First, Jia Yi argues that human nature is identical across time and space, and that it is the same in the sages and the evil kings. What separates the former from the latter, and successful dynasties from fallen ones, is education. The key to education lies in controlling the child's environment in the womb and in infancy. This is because the child's early formative experiences form a "second nature":

> When the heir apparent is born he sees correct actions, hears correct language, and on all sides there are correct people. Becoming habituated to living with correct people, he cannot but be correct in all things. It is just as if one grew up in Chu, one could not but speak the Chu tongue. Confucius said, "What takes shape early is like one's inborn nature [*tian xing* 天性]. That to which one becomes habituated is like that which is spontaneously so [*zi ran* 自然]."[54]

The second nature formed by early experience is compared to the acquisition of a language, a standard image for the formative power of custom in its sense of regional culture.

Second, the education advocated by Jia Yi entails removing the child from its surroundings (i.e., from the world of custom) and creating an artificial environment defined by a literary and ritual program. In the previous passage this is marked by the insistence on the "correctness" of everything the child sees or hears, and every person with whom he comes in contact. Elsewhere Jia Yi prescribes the separation of the pregnant mother from her ordinary life, so that everything she sees, hears, touches, or eats can be controlled by officials. Once the child is born, this program is continued by surrounding him with tutors, protectors, and companions who assure the propriety of everything he comes in contact with. This creation of an artificial environment by officials who guarantee the ritual correctness of the heir's experience is continued throughout his maturation.[55] Moreover, the educational process was to be written down on jade tablets that were stored in a metal box placed in the ancestral temple.[56] In this way it replaced the dominance of contemporary custom with the authority of classicist texts and rituals, just as advocated in the writings of the Warring States *ru* philosophers.

Third, custom explains the failure of Qin. After describing how the Zhou surrounded the infant ruler with officials to create a ritually correct environment, Jia Yi proceeds:

> When it came down to Qin then it was not so. Their customs did not honor polite yielding; what they elevated were legal accusations. Their customs did not honor ritual and duty; what they elevated were punishments. They had Zhao Gao instruct Hu Hai [the heir] in legal judgments, so if what he grew accustomed to was not cutting off people's limbs and noses, then it was executing three generations of their families. Consequently the day after becoming ruler he shot a man. Loyal remonstrance was called slander; profound reckoning was called groundless assertion. How could it be that Hu Hai's nature was bad? That with which he grew familiar led him to be thus.

Jia Yi then compares the shaping of Hu Hai by his environment with the way in which the northern and southern barbarians, though identical at birth, develop mutually unintelligible languages and irreconcilable conduct through "the formation of custom."[57] Within the classicist tradition the imagined Zhou state had become an exemplary realm in which scholars could transcend the bonds of local custom. Here this structure was repeated as an explicit historical model. Correct ritual education had separated the Zhou king from the rule of custom, while the subsequent Qin had trained its heir apparent in local customs and thus submerged both ruler and state in a savagery that led to their destruction.

CUSTOM AND REGION

Jia Yi's model of a Qin dominated by custom emerged from the definition of custom as the local characteristics that trapped each state or region in its own partiality. While the philosophical traditions used the term "custom" to stigmatize conventional ideas, it also cast a negative light on the ideas or practices that characterized a village, state, or other spatial unit. First, in passages cited earlier, it figured as an image of limitations imposed by childhood experience. Second, it figured in several discussions of military affairs in the context of assessing the respective strengths and weaknesses of states. Third, theoreticians of statecraft employed it to distinguish received administrative practices from the legal reforms advocated by leading political thinkers. In this context it was applied particularly to discussions of Qin. In the Han this developed into a trope in which Qin law, and aspects of law in general, were criticized as products of custom. Finally, the spatial use of "custom" developed in association with schematic models of tribute and trade, wherein distinctive regional products functioned as a material equivalent to characteristic regional practices.

The key text in military discourse on regional customs is "Evaluating the Enemy," in the *Wuzi*. In response to a question from Marquis Wu of Wei about coping with the six hostile states that surrounded him, Wu Qi replied that he would assess their "customs." He discusses them under a fixed series of rubrics: their people's nature or character (*xing* 性), their land or territory, their government policies, the typical conduct of their armies, and the way to defeat them:

> Qin's nature is strong. Its land is difficult. Its government is severe.
> Its rewards and punishments are reliable. Its people do not yield; they
> are all belligerent. Therefore they scatter and fight as individuals. To
> attack them, one must first entice them with profit and lead them
> away. Their officers are greedy for gain and will separate from their
> generals. Take advantage of their separation to attack them when scat-
> tered, set traps and seize the key moment, then their generals can be
> captured.
>
> Chu's nature is weak. Its territory is broad. Its government is
> disorderly. Its people are weary. Therefore when placed in formations
> they cannot maintain them long. To attack them, strike and cause
> disorder in their camp. First ruin their morale by nimbly advancing
> and then rapidly withdrawing. Cause them fatigue and toil. Do not
> join in actual combat, and their army can be destroyed.[58]

This anticipates the Han discourse on the power of custom as exemplified by Qin. Under the rubric of "custom" it describes links between terrain, char-acter, and government. The difficulty of Qin's terrain fostered the unyielding character of its people, which in turn led to the severity of its government.

This severity manifested itself in the fixity of rewards and punishments, a reference to the laws of Shang Yang and the philosophy of Han Fei. Chu's terrain, in contrast, was broad, open, and, although it is not mentioned, watery. This resulted in a weak character and disorderly government that left the people without energy. Consequently, its army could not hold together for long. Each of the other states is subjected to a similar analysis.

Here a body of custom shaped by landscape determines the character of the inhabitants of each region. This regional character further shapes the nature of the government and the capacities of the army. Custom thus limits the actions of the people of each region to habitual patterns that make them vulnerable to manipulation and defeat. Just as "custom" in the writing of the philosophers confined commoners within the narrow bounds of their experience and thus subjected them to the encompassing wisdom of the sage, so in the *Wuzi* "custom" constrains each state to act within the limits of its own character, and thus allows them to be manipulated by the stratagems of a skillful commander.

A variant argument appears in the *Xunzi*. Rather than discuss all the states, it speaks only of the leading military powers Qi, Wei, and Qin. Moreover, it links the states' patterns of combat to their government institutions, without always appealing to customs and terrain. However, in its discussion of Qin it *does* proceed from topography to character and institutions, with an emphasis on law:

> As for the people of Qin, [the land] which provisions them is narrow and cut off, so the control of the people is stern and harsh. They are coerced by circumstances and hidden away in their isolation. They are accustomed [to service] by rewards and manipulated by punishments. The lowly people have no means of obtaining benefit from their superiors except through combat. Only after deprivation are they employed, and only after obtaining some success are they recognized for merit. Merit and rewards increase in tandem.[59]

Like the *Wuzi*, this argues that the difficulty of Qin's terrain produced a hardy people who were controllable only through a rigorous system of rewards and punishments. These ideas became central to Han discussions of Qin as the definitive case of the negative power of custom.

The second innovation in the *Xunzi* is that after comparing the troops of Qi, Wei, and Qin, it insists that the soldiers of Qi were no match for those of Wei, and those of Wei no match for those of Qin. After rating these armies in order of ascending efficacy, it asserts that the armies of Qin were no match for those of the Spring-and-Autumn period hegemons, and these in turn could not withstand the sage founders of the Shang and Zhou. These bizarre assertions, for the earlier armies would have been tiny by comparison with those under discussion and equipped with primitive weapons, derive directly from the chapter's argument that Warring States military technology and generalship could not overcome the true king's ability to win the devotion of his people. Thus armies from states who fought under the sway of their local customs are explicitly contrasted with an idealized and all-conquering authority based on ritual and moral perfection. This authority transcends custom because it is derived from the textual and ritual program of the *ru* tradition.[60] The *Xunzi* follows the pattern of the *Wuzi*, except that it is the moral power of the sage ruler rather than the mental skills of the commander that conquer soldiers bound by local custom.

A final development in Warring States texts' use of "custom" as a negative category came in the texts of the philosophers of statecraft, the *Shang Jun shu* and the *Han Feizi*. The former largely uses the term "custom" in the same manner as the other philosophical traditions—that is, to indicate the conventional wisdom denounced by the authors. Thus, Shang Yang states: "Those who discuss supreme power/virtue (*zhi de* 至德) will not be in harmony with custom; those who achieve great merit will not make plans with the masses." He dismisses his opponent's speech as the "words of contemporary custom" and states that ordinary people remain at ease in old customs, just as scholars "drown in what they have learned."[61] People who reject reliance on law and punishments, or states that do not devote themselves to agriculture and warfare are denounced as acting under the influence of "custom."[62] "Custom" also describes the unsatisfactory social order that is transformed through the imposition of law by the sage ruler.[63]

The exceptions to this pattern are arguments that the sage must observe custom as a preliminary to creating laws.[64] These express the idea that laws must accord with the times. In one of them, moreover, "customs" are linked to the simplicity of peasants in contrast with the sophistication of philosophers. This seems to be based on the idea, discussed earlier, that agricultural villages are the realm of custom par excellence.

While the use of "custom" as a negative term in the *Shang Jun shu* is closely linked to that in the other traditions, it is distinct in one way. The text advocates rule through rigorous legal codes and stern punishments, which will transform custom. Later Han discussions of Qin custom as shaped by Shang Yang focused on the links between law and custom. Thus, the establishment of this linkage within the legalist tradition proved important to the later history of the topos.

The *Han Feizi* articulated the links between law and custom in its discussions of Qin and of Chu. It speaks of Wu Qi and Shang Yang, both executed for reforming their state's institutions: "Wu Qi instructed King Dao in the customs of Chu. 'The great ministers are too powerful, and the enfeoffed princes too numerous. Above they encroach on the ruler and below they oppress the people. This is the way of impoverishing the state and weakening the army'."[65] Here "customs" refers to political institutions and policies. This passage leads to a description of the reforms of Shang Yang, and how the resistance of ministers and nobles resulted in the execution and dismemberment of the two reformers. It concludes that the current political situation is even worse than the "customs" of Chu and Qin. Thus, in this discussion "custom" indicates conventional political practices that follow established precedent, as opposed to the reforms put in place by "scholars of law and method" who create new institutions in order to strengthen the state. The same model informs a passage that also deals with the reforms of Shang Yang:

> In Qin's ancient customs ministers set aside the law and served private interests. Therefore, with the state in disorder and the army weak, the ruler was humbled. Lord Shang made clear the ruler's way, persuaded Lord Xiao to change the laws and alter the customs, rewarded those who denounced treachery, and restricted commerce to encourage agriculture. At this time the people of Qin were accustomed to the ancient customs' allowing criminals to go free and honoring those who had no achievements, so they lightly violated the new laws.[66]

Here "custom" again refers to political practice uninformed by the new policies advocated by the *Han Feizi* under the rubric of "law." However, "law" and "custom" also function as near synonyms, as in the parallel phrase "change the laws and alter the customs." That they could be synonyms is shown by the fact that when a story from the *Han Feizi* was incorporated some decades later into the *Huainanzi*, the sentence "in Chu law the fiefs of salaried ministers reverted to the state at the accession of their sons" was changed to "Chu custom."[67] Thus, although the *Han Feizi* tended to regard law as a positive policy that overcame the dangers of custom, it still treated the two terms as potentially equivalent.

The contrast between proper law and deficient custom figured not only in the philosophical traditions associated with Qin, but also in Qin government documents. A text found at Shuihudi that describes the proper conduct of local officials begins by denouncing custom in the name of law:

> In ancient times the people each had their local custom, so what they regarded as profitable, liked, or hated were different. This was sometimes not beneficial to the people, and it was harmful to the state. Therefore the sage kings made laws and measures in order to correct and rectify the people, to eliminate their deviant boorishness, and to purge their wicked customs. . . . Now the legal codes and decrees are all complete, but the people do not use them. Dissipated people controlled by local custom do not cease, which means abandoning the ruler's enlightened laws. . . . Now the legal codes and decrees have already been promulgated, but I hear that the minor officials and people who violate the laws do not cease. Their hearts, controlled by private likings and local custom, do not change.[68]

This contrast between the enlightened laws of the ruler and the benighted rule of custom virtually quotes the philosophers of statecraft. It indicates the difficulties of Qin's central government in imposing its will both on powerful nobles and conquered territories.[69] In the same manner, Jun Zhong described the Han occupation of Nanyue under Emperor Wu as a case of using Han law to correct the "customs" of the conquered Yue people.[70] Thus, from the Warring States through the Han, tensions between centralizing courts and the regions that they absorbed were articulated in terms of the suppression of local custom by the ruler's laws.

While denunciations of the tyranny of local custom continued under the Han, the Han discourse came to focus largely on the state of Qin that had earlier made extensive use of this theme. Whereas the Qin had treated their own laws as a universal standard and denounced local practices as custom, the Han treated Qin law itself as a manifestation of local prejudices created by geography and social practice. This criticism of Qin as a creature of custom, and of its law as a manifestation of local practices, began with Jia Yi. His most celebrated discussion of Qin, the "Discursive Judgment Censuring Qin," traced the limitations of Qin's rulers and their downfall to the interlinked character of Qin's terrain and customs. Its account of Qin history begins, "Qin's territory was enveloped by mountains and belted by the Yellow River, so that it was secure. It was a state cut off on all sides."[71] Thus, Qin's excellent strategic location was at the same time the cause of its supposed isolation. This image of isolation reappears in Jia Yi's description of the situation of Qin's imperial rulers:

> [The First Emperor] thought he was sufficient to himself and never asked others, so he committed errors without being corrected. The Second Emperor inherited this, following his father without changing. Through violence and cruelty he redoubled the calamity. Ziying [the third ruler] was completely alone without intimates, imperiled and young he had no assistance.

Jia Yi explains the rulers' isolation by noting that "customs of Qin" tabooed all criticism so that when the rulers committed errors no loyal officials remonstrated with them. In contrast with the Zhou, whose feudal lords preserved it even after it lost real power, Qin relied entirely on "numerous laws and stern punishments." Consequently, it had no supporters at the end.[72] The geographic isolation of Qin shaped its customs, which in turn isolated the rulers and led to their exclusive reliance on punishments.

Other writings by Jia Yi linked custom, law, and the fate of Qin even more explicitly. His *Xin shu* argues that the Han had inherited without change the reliance on violence and emphasis on luxury that characterized the Qin state. He describes this as a matter of inherited "custom" and then explains the decline of Qin customs thus:

> Lord Shang turned against ritual and duty, abandoned proper human relations, and put his whole heart and mind into expansion. After

practicing this for two years, Qin's customs grew worse by the day. Whenever Qin people's sons grew to adulthood, if the family was rich they sent them out as separate households, and if they were poor they sent them out as indentured laborers. If someone lent his father a rake, hoe, staff, or broom, then he put on airs of great generosity. If a mother took a gourd dipper, bowl, dust pan, or broom, then her offspring would immediately upbraid her. Women suckled their infants in the presence of their fathers-in-law, and if the wife and mother-in-law were not on good terms then they snarled and glared at one another. Loving their young children and material gain while holding their parents in contempt and having no proper relations, they were scarcely different from animals.[73]

This treats Shang Yang's reforms as the cause of certain features of local Qin custom, specifically the tendency to break up families into nuclear households and the consequent devaluation of kin ties. This policy of encouraging the division of households to maximize taxes and military service was frequently cited in Han references to the links of law and custom in Qin.

A final discussion by Jia Yi of the links between custom and law in Qin appears in his essays on the education of the heir apparent and "fetal instruction." As previously described, these advocated the separation of the pregnant mother and then the child from the outside world so that they could be shaped by a textually prescribed world of ritual and music rather than customs. By contrast, Qin's reliance on law and punishments was a direct outgrowth of its customs, which were transmitted to the ruler through an education that dealt exclusively with punishments.

Jia Yi's derivation of Qin's legalist penchant from its customs, which in turn were shaped by its topography, became a standard topos in Han writing. Thus, the *Huainanzi*'s account of the sequential emergence of textual types in response to historical conditions states:

> The customs of Qin consisted of wolflike greed and violence. The people lacked a sense of duty and pursued profit. They could be awed through punishments, but not transformed through goodness. They could be encouraged with rewards, but not urged on with reputation. Enveloped in difficult terrain and belted by the Yellow River, they were cut off on all sides and thus secure. The land was profitable and the topography beneficial, so they accumulated great wealth. Lord Xiao wanted to use his wolflike or tigerlike power to swallow up the feudal lords. The laws of Lord Shang were produced from this situation.[74]

This quotes almost verbatim Jia Yi's account of Qin's topography, repeats his assertion that its people lacked a sense of duty, and concludes by deriving Shang Yang's legal reforms directly from the constraints imposed by the nature of Qin's people and their customs. Rule through elaborate legal codes, and the political theory that justified this, both derived from the local conditions in Qin.

Similar arguments appear a few decades later in Sima Qian's preface to his table on the chronology of the Warring States: "Qin mixed in the customs of the Rong and Di barbarians, so it placed violence and cruelty first and treated humanity and duty as secondary. Its position was that of frontier vassal, but it offered suburban sacrifices [of the Son of Heaven]. The true gentleman was terrified by this."[75] Here the cruelty of Qin laws and the martial tendencies of its people are once again explained in terms of its customs, but these are attributed to Qin's being a frontier state located in a region inhabited by non-Chinese people. The use of "custom" to explain Qin is pushed further by identifying its customs with those of alien peoples, and greater emphasis is placed on its geographic separation from the civilized central states. The violence of customs in the Qin region is also mentioned in Sima Qian's account of the local allies of one of the "cruel clerks" who attacked the great families.[76] Sima Qian places the same themes in the mouth of Lord Shang in the latter's biography: "Lord Shang said, 'At first Qin had the teachings of the Rong and Di. They did not distinguish fathers and sons, who dwelt in the same room. Now I have reformed their teachings, and established for them the division between men and women. I have built the great Jique Palace, and set up a capital like those of Lu or Wey.'"[77] Shang Yang's claims about building a palace and a capital like those of Lu or Wey (discussed in chapter three) indicate Qin's status as a barbaric state that sought to imitate its betters. Interestingly, Qin's lack of proper relations between kin that was attributed by Jia Yi to Shang Yang's reforms here reappears as evidence of barbarian influence, while the penchant for dividing households is claimed by Shang Yang as a consequence of his efforts to impose proper ritual divisions within the family.

At roughly the same time as the writing of the *Huainanzi* and shortly before the composition of the *Shi ji*, Dong Zhongshu also wrote about Qin's customs in response to Emperor Wu's questions:

> King Wu [of Zhou] carried out his duties by pacifying the destructive and criminal. The Duke of Zhou set up rites and music to give them a pattern, so when it reached the flourishing age of Kings Cheng and Kang the prisons were empty for more than forty years. . . . When it came to Qin then it was not like this. They took the laws of Shen Buhai and Shang Yang as their teachers, and practiced the theories of Han Fei. They hated the way of the true ruler, and took wolflike greed as their custom. They had no cultivated potency to instruct their inferiors. They executed people based on reports but did not examine the facts. Those who did good did not inevitably escape punishment, and those who violated laws were not inevitably punished. . . . Therefore those punished were numerous, people died

in rapid succession, but treachery did not cease. Custom caused it to be thus.[78]

Again the argument is based on the contrast between Zhou and Qin. Qin was violent and cruel because of its customs as expressed in the laws of Shang Yang and the theories of Han Fei.

Thus, by the end of the first century of Han rule, the idea that the severity of Qin's law both expressed and in turn corrupted its customs had become a cliché. Some writers also linked these customs to the character of Qin's neighbors or the shape of its terrain.[79] Even in the Eastern Han, Diwu Lun spoke of officials prone to cruel punishments as "clerks dominated by custom (su li 俗吏)," men who were still under the lingering influence of the supposedly violent government of Wang Mang. He explicitly linked such men to the earlier example of Qin.[80]

One final example of the Han use of the theme of Qin customs and laws comes from the debate over the abolition of mutilating punishments. Ban Gu discusses this in his monograph on punishments and law, where he describes how Emperor Wen of the Han had sought to eliminate the policies of Qin through abolishing mutilating punishments. As a result, "moral transformation spread through the world, and the custom of making legal accusations was changed." This reference to a "custom of making legal accusations" indicates the Qin litigiousness that had been inherited by the early Han. At the end of the monograph, however, Ban Gu approvingly cites the *Xunzi's* argument for the necessity of preserving mutilating punishments, and then continues:

> Yu [of Xia] followed after Yao and Shun, and thinking that his own virtuous power had waned, he instituted mutilating punishments. That Tang [of Shang] and Wu [of Zhou] followed his lead in this practice was because the customs of their own day were inferior to those of Yao and Shun. Now Han follows in the wake of the waning Zhou and violent Qin, so its customs are inferior even to those of the Xia, Shang, and Zhou. To practice the punishments of Yao and Shun would be like trying to control a wild horse with nothing but a rope in its mouth. It is completely contrary to what would be suitable for rescuing the age.[81]

Here the idea that Qin's law expressed its customs is widened into a general historical model in which the deterioration of customs across the centuries led to increasingly brutal punishments. In this model Qin is no longer a uniquely violent regime, but rather a precedent for Han whose own customs are insufficiently refined to allow the abandonment of mutilation. The Zhou dynasty, which in the Han served frequently as a counter-Qin, is here grouped with the rest of the Three Dynasties as a time of decay marked by the use of mutilating punishments. However, even this more inclusive model assumes the existence of a golden age, identified with Yao and Shun, set against the period of the dominance of custom. Custom once again is a negative category linked to inferior forms of law.

Thus, the Han discourse on Qin insisted that it was prey to savage customs that both informed and were reinforced by its laws.[82] The violence of Qin custom, in turn, was due to the influence of harsh landscape or neighboring barbarians, and Qin's location at the frontier. However, this theme of the link between law and regional custom did not originate in the Han, nor did it exclusively deal with Qin. It had already appeared in the Warring States, particularly in the context of military institutions that were closely related to law in Chinese thought. Only when Qin emerged as the dominant power did it increasingly focus on that state.

While the *Xunzi* passages sketched several of the themes that developed into the Han discourse on custom and law, they did not link the two terms, nor did they define custom through regional variations.[83] However, one idea in the *Xunzi* does anticipate Han discussions of custom in relation to law and authority. Specifically, the *Xunzi* discusses the products that distinguish each region, and then asserts that these converge in the central states or the person of the ruler:

> The north sea has running horses and barking dogs, but the central states obtain, raise, and command them. The south sea has feathers, plumes, elephant tusks, rhinoceros hides, copper, and cinnabar, but the central states obtain them and turn them into wealth. The eastern sea has purple-dye plants, white silks, fish, and salt, but the central states obtain them and wear or eat them. The western sea has skins, hides, and patterned yak tails, but the central states obtain and employ them. . . . Thus all things covered by Heaven or carried by the earth are brought to their highest beauty and utility. The distant regions all sent in their treasures. Consequently his [the sage's] eyes saw all colors, his ears heard all sounds, his mouth ate all tastes, his body dwelt in all forms of palace, and as names he bestowed universally correct appellations.[84]

These are the geographic version of the Warring States philosophical insistence on the inferiority of anything limited or partial to the encompassing whole. The regions form parts that converge in the perfect totality of the ruler or the culture of the central states. This geographic schema was carried forward into the Han, but these later versions identified regional cultures explicitly as the carriers of divergent custom, which in turn were linked to criminality or law.

The clearest development of this is a large section of Sima Qian's chapter on leading merchants and manufacturers. He begins by noting that the Han had united the world, opened up trade and communication between the regions, and moved the former ruling houses and powerful local families to the capital. He then divides China into regions that are delineated by their geographic boundaries and identified with states of the Warring States period. Each region is described in terms of its distinctive products and the characteristic temperaments or patterns of behavior that mark its people:

> Handan [former capital of Zhao] is also a major city located between the Zhang and Yellow Rivers. To the north it is in communication with Yan and Zhuo, while to the south there are Zheng and Wei. The customs of Zheng and Wei are similar to those of Zhao, but as they are near to Liang and Lu they are somewhat more solemn and take pride in self-control. The inhabitants of Yewang were moved there from their city on the Pu River. The people of Yewang are prone to violence and act as bravoes/gangsters. This is the influence of Wey.

> Zou and Lu border on the Zhu and Si rivers. They still have the lingering influence of the Duke of Zhou, so by custom they are fond of the classicists and do everything by ritual. Consequently their people are fussy and punctilious. They have a considerable industry in sericulture and hemp, but no wealth from forests or wetlands. The territory is small and people numerous, so the people are very frugal. They have an aversion to crimes and avoid heterodoxy. In their decline, however, they have grown fond of trade and pursue profit, in this regard being worse than the men of Zhou.[85]

This elaborates the *Xunzi*'s model, in which a unified polity unites regions that are marked by distinctive products and, in Sima Qian's case, customs. There are, however, several innovations.

First, local customs and temperament are central to Sima Qian. Goods and their exchange are mentioned, but characteristic emotions and behavior are the focus of attention. Second, the regions defined by their diverse customs are identified with the Warring States, and the role in the *Xunzi* of the sage ruler is played by the Han. Thus, custom is here identified with the Warring States and the fact of political or cultural division. The regular identification of Qin with custom thus suggests that, as Jia Yi had argued, the first imperial polity had remained institutionally within the world of the Warring States.[86] This identification of "custom" with division into states or regions was so strong that Jia Yi referred to the states allied against Qin as "the diverse customs" and when Sima Qian divided Chu into three distinct regions he referred to them as "three customs."[87] Indeed linking the division into states with the divergence of customs became a standard formula in the Han: "In ancient times the states of the feudal lords were separate and their customs were divided. Every hundred *li* they diverged."[88] The *Shi ji* usually explains regions that are prone to violence by the admixture of barbarian customs, as in accounts of Qin, or on the lingering influence of an evil king. However, in two cases, including that of Handan, violence is explained through the earlier resettlement of criminal populations or of people under the lingering influence of ancient evil rulers.[89]

These suggest key features in linking the law of Qin with custom. First, these laws were objects of criticism not only because of their specific features (e.g., cruelty), but because they were the products of an age of competing states and reflect the limited and partial character of all policies determined by the temperament and interests of one region. The case of Qin was the most prominent, but not unique. Second, the limits of custom and local interest were overcome within the encompassing order of the Han state. The model for the world empire that transcended custom was provided by Heaven itself, which as an all-encompassing entity was explicitly contrasted with local practice: "Customs know how to follow men, but they know nothing about following Heaven".[90] Even within the limits of local custom the good behavior of peoples from regions under the lingering influence of sages could correct or suppress the volatile or violent tendencies of others. Great scholars and rulers past or present, who themselves escaped the limitations of local custom through the mastery of texts and rituals, drew ordinary people away from the dominance of topography and folkways into the higher sphere of the state. Thus, the way of the sages was explicitly contrasted with the "barbarian customs" that had been mixed into those of Qin and other states.[91] The clearest expression of the Han transcendence of local custom was the aforementioned transfer of local families to the capital where they gradually formed an imperial elite steeped in the mores of the capital and traditions of service. In the Eastern Han, this procedure was replaced by the practice of drawing people away from their localities into state service through the imperial academy and recommendation for office.

The critique of custom adapted from Warring States philosophers by Qin officials to defend their centralized administration and uniform law code was thus in turn used by Han writers to formulate a spatial theory of empire that dismissed the governments of Qin and the Warring States as products of local custom. What had been celebrated as proper law against local custom was itself dismissed as a product of local customs that were particularly destructive because of the supposed admixture of barbarian influence and the separation of Qin from the Chinese heartland. In place of the Qin legal code and to some extent its Han successor, which were now linked to limited local customs, the highest standard was located in the evolving and flexible ritual practices of the sages that transcended ties to locality through linguistic archaism and ties to the imaginary model of a unitary Zhou state.

REGIONS AND THE GREAT FAMILIES

The philosophical negation of regionalism not only celebrated unification, but also supported the claims of the imperial center against locally powerful fam-

ilies. This link between the discourse against law and custom discussed above
and the problem of the great families as regional powers during the Han
figures in the following narrative:

> In Yingchuan there were many powerful families [*hao qiang* 豪強], so
> it was difficult to govern. The state regularly selected the highest offi-
> cials to govern this area. Earlier, when Zhao Guanghan had been
> Grand Administrator, he had worried that due to custom the fami-
> lies formed numerous political cliques. Therefore he had assembled
> the lower officials and common people, and urged them to make
> legal accusations against one another. Everyone regarded this as
> clever, so consequently the region of Yingchuan adopted [legal accu-
> sations] as a custom and the people harbored mutual resentment and
> enmity. [Han] Yanshou wanted to change this, and to instruct them
> in ritual and yielding. Fearing that the peasants would not comply,
> he sequentially summoned several dozen of the elders who were
> trusted and admired in the villages of the commandery. He set out
> wine and food and personally conversed with them, receiving them
> with ritual and consideration. He asked everyone about their songs
> and customs, and that which caused suffering among the people.[92]

The prevalence of legal accusations is linked to local custom, which is contrasted with the superiority of ritual. The people of Yingchuan's custom-based
love of litigation recalls Jia Yi's account of the breakdown of family ties in
Qin produced by customary recourse to law. What is new is that this legal-
istic local culture is closely tied to the predominance of powerful local families in Yingchuan. This close link between the threat of regionalism and the
existence of powerful families is central to the spatial reordering of China
during the Han.

The evolving role of powerful local families figures in all accounts of the
first empires.[93] Here I will focus on the geographic aspect of the great
families who challenged the imperial spatial order through forming political
units at the level of the district, commandery, and region. To understand the
significance of this requires a brief consideration of the administrative ideal
that had emerged in the Warring States and characterized the early empires.

The political order that emerged in the Warring States and continued
into the empire was based on the progressive destruction of all independent
political powers that lay between the ruler and the peasant household. It
resulted in a state based on the direct administration by the ruler's servants of
the individual households that provided taxes and services.[94] This fragmentation of the society into its smallest elements for purposes of control demonstrated the basic principle of imperial administration that unity could be
maintained only by preventing the formation of any unit large enough to
threaten the center. This strategy of division into the smallest possible units

to render them dependent on the encompassing political and economic orders was discussed in chapter two.

In the first century of Han rule, the primary threat was the resurgence of the old Warring States. With distinctive languages, scripts, and customs, as well as families that had been rulers or hereditary officials, these states were distinct units defined by geography and shared culture. Their survival as political entities negated any possibility of a unified empire.[95] One policy to eliminate such regional political structures was the aforementioned resettlement by the Qin and early Han rulers of leading local families to the capital region. In addition, the Qin imposed a two-tier administration in which most large, walled settlements functioned as the capitals of districts (*xian* 縣) which were in turn grouped into commanderies (*jun* 郡). Whereas the late Warring States world had consisted of seven major states, the Qin empire was divided into thirty-six commanderies. This number was probably selected as the square of the number six, which according to Sima Qian had been adopted by the Qin court as key to its ritual numerology. However, the adoption of this number also meant that the average commandery would have been one-sixth the size of an earlier state. This reduced the possibility that any unit of local administration could command sufficient resources to challenge the center.

The Han dynasty extended this policy of administrative division by increasing the number of commanderies and feudatory states to over one hundred.[96] Consequently, each local administrative unit could mobilize only small amounts of wealth and manpower. In the wake of the rebellion of the feudatories in B.C. 154, the Han court ended their power not by eliminating them outright but instead through a process of steady division among heirs. This resulted in their political neutralization through a rapid reduction in their average size. This policy was justified through the principle articulated by Jia Yi that where the nobles' states were small, they would be easy to control and not rebel.[97]

Related to the principle of fragmenting local administration was the policy of making sure that administrative units did not coincide with those defined by geography and custom. Furthermore, the state sought to guarantee that local officials were not from the locality.[98] Just as regions were divided into numerous commanderies and these into myriad districts, so villages were grouped together into artificial clusters called *xiang* (鄉) under the control of officials dispatched from the central court. These in turn were grouped into districts and commanderies under the control of outsiders. Reversing the transfer of leading local families to the capital region, senior officials were sent out from the court to administer alien regions. Even their major subordinates were outsiders appointed by the court. This was clearest at the district level, where the head and his major subordinates were not only never from the district being administered, but never from the same commandery. This principle was demonstrated by Yan Gengwang from an examination of the transmitted Han literary sources and stone inscriptions, and it has been confirmed by the lists of subordinate officials in Donghai Commandery recently discovered in a Han tomb.[99] Only at the village level were leading local people permitted to play a role in administration, as Village Chiefs (*li dian* 里典) or Elders (*fu lao* 父老) under the Qin or as the Thrice Venerable (*san lao* 三老) under the Han. Even these local leaders, however, participated in government only under the supervision of such centrally appointed officials as the Overseers (*sefu* 嗇夫) who were responsible for such matters as agriculture, granaries, stables, and animals.[100] Through the division of regions into the smallest possible units and the separation of local administration from locally based powers, the Qin and Han courts sought to prevent the formation of any powerful associations outside the state apparatus.

As discussed in chapter two, the typical Han household consisted of a nuclear family of four to six people, which near the end of parents' lives became a stem household of around eight. Some scholars have argued that locally powerful families, given their greater resources, would as in later imperial China have kept more generations living in a single compound. As noted earlier, however, the limited surviving evidence shows few families of three generations or more, and there is nothing to suggest that wealthy families were committed to the classicist vision of larger households where brothers lived together. To the extent that the households of great families were larger, it was through the inclusion of servants or retainers. Indeed remarks and anecdotes indicate that division of property among kinsmen characterized wealthier families who could afford it, while brothers in poorer families could not divide farms that were the minimum amount on which a family could survive. "One with a position in a state can entrust it to another and depart. If you had no position what could you entrust? To divide up property and yield a share to those below is the same as this. If you had no property what could be divided? If you are starving, what can you yield?"[101]

There is substantial evidence that locally powerful lineages divided themselves into many—in some cases hundreds—of nuclear households. They dominated their districts, commanderies, or regions through reliance on these households or marriage with other great surnames. Great families thus based their power not primarily on increasing the size and wealth of their own household, but through the formation of large networks or leagues that were denounced by their critics as "cliques." This pattern was noted in the account of Yingchuan. I will now present the evidence for this phenomenon, discuss the reasons for it and its impact on Han society, and relate it to the broader issue of imperial hostility to nonstate organizations that transcended the individual household.

One key type of evidence that powerful lineages or surnames were defined by their extensive networks is the terminology used to describe weaker families. Texts from the Eastern Han and immediate post-Han period describe weak or lowly families with terms that insist on their isolation or lack of ties. Among these are "lone family (*dan jia* 單家)," "lone gate (*dan men* 單門)," "orphan gate (*gu men* 孤門)," "lone and cold (*dan han* 單寒)," "lone and obscure (*dan wei* 單微)," "orphaned and obscure (*gu wei* 孤微)," or "orphaned and provincial (*gu bi* 孤鄙)."[102] These terms were even applied to wealthy families who lacked high status or influence. The *Discourse on Salt and Iron* goes so far as to argue that to be cut off from human relations is the highest form of punishment: "In the *Spring and Autumn Annals* criminals have no names, and when it refers to them it just says, 'Bandits'. By this means it humbles criminals and cuts them off from human relations. Therefore a ruler will not take them as minister, a scholar will not take them as a friend, and they will not be allowed in the wards and villages."[103] There is a more positively valued form of isolation that is marked by such terms as *jie* 介 "scrupulous, uncompromising," *jie te* 介特 "isolated," or *jie ran te li* 介然特立 "uncompromisingly standing alone." These identify the self-chosen solitude of the pure hermit. However, even this form of withdrawal is criticized as a masked form of selfishness, a hypocritical affectation reflecting the decline of the age, or a failure to attain excellence in the world by insisting on absolute rectitude.[104]

This definition of lower status or criminality through isolation suggests that higher status and influence were defined by social ties with kin and influential neighbors. Such an emphasis on networks and social ties is indeed revealed in the literary sources' obsession with the theme of forming links. This is marked by the recurrence of such terms as "to connect (*jie* 結)," "to contact (*jiao* 交)," or "to communicate (*tong* 通)." These terms often appear as compounds and have a large range of meanings. They can indicate a formal relation of friendship entered into by people through an explicit compact. Thus, in the biography of Wang Dan, two individuals in succession ask to enter into a relation with him of friendship or alliance (*jie jiao* 結交), but both are rejected because Wang Dan disapproves of them. In the same biography the companions assembled for a trip are also said "to connect fellowship (*jie lü* 結侶)."[105] Almost any association to work toward a common purpose, such as forming an army in times of civil war or conspiring to rebel, would use these graphs.[106] The links between patron and retainer are routinely described in these terms, as are the associations of gangsters and violent youths.[107] These graphs are also linked closely to such terms as "kindred spirit" (*zhi ji* 知己), for virtuous men established links with those who shared their values, and shunned ties with those who were not of their kind.[108] The cunning and ambitious likewise gravitated to their own kind.[109] Such links were not only crucial to power and prestige, but also fundamental to defining oneself and one's place in the world. Consequently, Liu Bosheng "expended himself totally and bankrupted his family to establish ties with the empire's heros," and later the imperial affine Ma Liao "expended himself totally in establishing ties" so that those in office "competed in hastening to attach themselves to him."[110]

So fundamental was the question of forming personal ties and social networks that it became a topic for essays and discussions in the Eastern Han. Apparently in response to a remark in the *Biographies of Literary Scholars* that "in no age did people cut off their connections," Zhu Mu wrote an "Essay on Cutting Connections." He argued that in antiquity men had not formed private networks, but assembled only in the court or at ritually dictated public gatherings. By contrast, in the present age men devoted themselves to forming connections for their private benefit, which destroyed public order. He also wrote a poem on the theme. This presented the parable of the owl and the phoenix, who were destined to live totally separate lives due to the devotion to purity of the latter and the taste of the former for rotting flesh and filth. He thus contrasted public service, for which associating was proper, with private interest, for which it was destructive.[111] In the corrupt present day, Zhu Mu indicated, the only proper action was to withdraw from the world and cultivate oneself in isolation.

In response to Zhu Mu, whom he described as "unsullied but consequently isolated," Cai Yong wrote an essay "Correcting Connections." He argued that the profusion of cliques reflected the decline of government, and that associations based on shared moral worth, rather than on wealth or power, remained acceptable. While agreeing with Zhu Mu's rejection of cliques based on private interest and the pursuit of power, he maintained that it was still possible for like-minded scholars to join in study and the cultivation of virtue. As evidence, he cited the example of Confucius and his disciples, and their statements about the conditional propriety of social links.[112]

The *Hidden Tally of Duke Tai* goes beyond simply distinguishing the proper from the improper. It lists ten faults that will destroy a state, including patrilines being too strong and bullying the peasants, private wealth being greater than the state's, and imbalances or improprieties in the relations between the people and officials. One of the items is also "reputations that reach one hundred *li*, or social connections that reach one thousand." This emphasizes the danger of social connections that cover great distances, and thus unite whole regions under the sway of private alliances.[113] The *Hidden Tally* thus treats networks not as a moral problem but a political one, in which a key distinction is the geographic range of influence. The danger of networks is thus an extension of the related dangers of powerful lineages, excessive private wealth, and people's being either superior to the officials or too generous toward them.

While these forms of association were largely political, lineages also extended their social contacts and geographic range through marriage. Marriage as a means of elevating a family is found in virtually all civilizations, and it had a classic pedigree in the Han. The founder Liu Bang's father-in-law gave his daughter in marriage only because Liu Bang's physiognomy revealed a glorious future that would raise his relatives to eminence.[114] Han sources describe intermarriage between the leading lineages in certain regions as a conventional procedure or custom by means of which each lineage enhanced its own power. Forces rebelling against Wang Mang were sometimes assembled through combining one man's lineage members with his relatives by marriage. There are also accounts of Han lineages attempting to marry a daughter to someone because his family background or eminent talent and reputation made him valuable as a kinsman. In at least one case such a marriage is described as a means of "linking support and establishing a party." Sometimes the proposed son-in-law demonstrated his character by refusing to establish ties with questionable lineages.[115] However, even these parables of virtue presuppose the conventional practice of arranging marriages with outstanding individuals or lineages to strengthen the patriline.

More important, scholars of late imperial and contemporary China have noted that the practice of dividing households characterizes those who emphasize affinal ties. Dividing households when the sons marry protects the wife from persecution by her mother-in-law and places greater emphasis on the conjugal tie. Such a practice thus strengthens ties with the wife's relatives.[116] Quarrels between mothers-in-law and daughters-in-law were sufficiently common in Han China that a book of "recipes (*fang* 方)" discovered at Mawangdui contains a spell to prevent them.[117] Thus, the predilection of wealthy Han families to divide their households and the emphasis placed on establishing networks through marriage were two aspects of the same phenomenon. Moreover, the relative institutional weakness of Han patrilines—the absence of such later practices as an annual festival for grave offerings, collective cemeteries for lineages, and collective property—facilitated the establishment of extended networks through emphasis on ties by marriage.[118] By weakening the patriline, they increased the strength of marital bonds and thereby furthered their own ability to extend social networks.

A classic example of a powerful surname and how it secured power is the Fan clan of Nantang. They are described as an eminent surname in their home villages who "for generations were skilled at farming and at accumulating wealth (*huo zhi* 貨殖, i.e., manufacture and trade)." Under Fan Zhong, they became particularly attentive to ritual so three generations shared common property. With labor provided by dependent households, they built up an estate of about 1,200 hectares with fish ponds and some animal husbandry. Like all estates mentioned in the Han, this is not large by European standards, and the total number of kinsmen in the household was probably no more than a couple dozen. In terms of the number of people and amount of land it could command, this family was more powerful than its neighbors, but of little consequence above the village level. However, with its accumulated wealth, the Fan family "relieved and supported financially lineage and kin, and bestowed charity on the villages where they lived." When the rebellion against Wang Mang broke out, Fan Hong's wife—who was a relative of leading Liu rebels—was seized as a hostage. However, ultimately the state did not dare to execute her because the conspicuous charity of the Fan clan had won devoted local support. After her release the Fan clan led families of their patriline and kin to build a fort in which more than one thousand families took shelter from the Red Eyebrows.[119]

What made the Fan clan important in their region and an influence at the imperial level was not their own estate or household. Instead they became powerful by employing their wealth to form ties of obligation or loyalty first with more distant kin households that shared their surname, and then with their neighbors. The establishment of alliances with households sharing ancestry or local residence allowed them to call upon the services of thousands of people, and thus to dominate non-kin.

Before proceeding, it is useful to situate this phenomenon within a broader historical perspective. As Masubuchi Tatsuo first pointed out, and as I have elaborated in earlier works, the new forms of power that emerged in the Warring States and culminated in the empire were based on the replacement of political power rooted in the kin structures of the nobility by groups formed through artificial, hierarchical ties created between individuals. Appearing first in certain rulers' recruitment of "free-floating" agents produced by the destruction of states and lineages, such personalist ties—consecrated by oaths and based on an ethic of exchanging total devotion for recognition— formed the basis of the states' bureaucracies, the leagues of avengers or gangsters, and the philosophical and technical traditions that reshaped the intellectual world. Just as new forms of polity, intellectual association, and organized criminality were created through establishing and maintaining networks of personal ties, so certain lineages transformed themselves into important political actors by using their material and intellectual capital to place others in their debt and then command their services.

However, unlike the ties of obligation that formed the state apparatus, leagues of gangsters, and scholarly traditions, the networks that constituted the power of the great families were not created from individual bonds. They instead emerged from a hierarchically graded series of links beginning with the household, extended to other households that shared a common ancestor (zong zu 宗族 or zong jia 宗家), then to retainers (ke), then to neighbors from the same or nearby villages, and finally to people from across the region linked by shared study or political service. Due to this ever-wider extension, sometimes in the Eastern Han the range of collective legal responsibility went beyond the conventional three generations that defined the largest household. Thus, the "Great Proscription" extended the ban on office holding to kin who shared a common ancestor five generations earlier, and even to those linked only by patron-client ties (men sheng 門生 and gu li 故吏). Other major crimes also entailed collective punishments reaching beyond three generations of kin, and even into the broader social networks that defined political power.[120] So large was the scale of such collective action and punishments that politically important cases resulted in the execution of more than 10,000 people.[121]

The nature of these leagues is also indicated in lists of the groups brought together under the leading lineages. These appear most frequently in descriptions of the private armies mobilized in the rebellion against Wang Mang or in the breakdown at the end of the Han. Others appear in accounts of the groups who were included in the collective punishments inflicted by the state. Lists of the beneficiaries of a lineage's power also often move from kin to more distant retainers, as do accounts of large-scale charity by eminent local lineages in times of famine.[122] Such lists of widening circles could also appear in more peaceful circumstances, as Cui Shi's account of those to whom people pay greetings at the New Year.[123] The same pattern figures in the accounts of the Fan clan's charity, which moved from distant kin of the same surname to neighbors in general, and in the account of the groups who took refuge in their fort. When the Yin lineage rebelled against Wang Mang, they led a force of two thousand men composed of "sons and younger brothers, other lineages of the patriline, and retainers." When Li Tong rebelled, Wang Mang executed all his relations in the capital and in Nanyang. The latter group totalled sixty-four people, divided into "brothers and households of the patriline" whose corpses were publicly burned in the marketplace.[124] The presence of kin in Chang'an, as well as the number and description of the people executed in Nanyang, show that the politically relevant group for a major family went well beyond their own household and its estate.

This extension of leading households' authority through forming networks based on gifts or services meant that a major lineage's power could cover whole districts, commanderies, and regions. Thus, the actual target of the imperial state's hostility to regions and regionalism was the powerful lineages or, more precisely, the leagues of households and villages formed around them. The earliest examples were the old ruling houses, noble families, and hereditary lines of ministers and generals who had formed the elite of the Warring States. Such families served as foci for many of the rebellions against Qin. They likewise were the target of the forced resettlements to the capital region.[125] However, the last of these families were eliminated under Emperor Wu. For Han social history, the important lineages were those who gained wealth through office holding, trade, and the accumulation of land during the Han itself, and used this wealth to establish networks of prestige and influence across ever-wider geographical areas.

The links between the great lineages and the problem of regionalism figure prominently in the geographical monograph of the *Han shu*. Ban Gu concludes this chapter with a section echoing Sima Qian's account of the regions and their customs or character. He cites each of the regions occupied by the old Warring States, gives their astronomical equivalents (*fen ye* 分野), lists their major cities, and traces their history and character through the quotation of passages from canonical texts. He then discusses contemporary customs and forms of economic activity, often directly quoting the *Shi ji*.

However, unlike the *Shi ji*, Ban Gu's discussion of regional customs and character frequently mentions the tendency to establish powerful lineages that buy up land, form political cliques, and develop alliances, having recourse to violence to further their ends. Thus, Ban Gu states that due to constant resettlement of lineages, the capital region had not only families with traditions of scholarship and state service, and many wealthy merchants, but also powerful lineages that formed violent leagues in the manner of gangsters. In Sichuan, people honored and respected only those who were locally powerful. There was also a tradition deriving from Sima Xiangru of delighting in ornamental language and skillful criticism. In Henei, "the customs encourage an inflexible strength, so there are many powerful families who encroach and seize land. They treat kindness and ritual as unimportant, and are fond of dividing property while the father is still living." The men of Zhou pursued material profit, honoring wealth and property while treating duty with contempt and humbling those who were poor. The people of Yingchuan by custom were extravagant and violent. They loved trade, as well as hunting and fishing. Because they hid their wealth from the government, they were difficult to administer. Moreover, due to their greed they constantly engaged in lawsuits and divided property while the father was still living. Powerful families in Taiyuan and Shangdang, some of them descended from the Jin nobility, battled one another through cunning and force. They frequently resorted to vengeance and vendetta against the family members and more distant kin of their enemies. They also relied on force to make themselves feared, and were difficult to control. The people of Qi were extravagant and formed political cliques. Finally, in many regions, the rich families were prone to excess and waste in their wedding ceremonies and funerals.[126]

This section also states that powerful families tended to divide property when the father was alive, while the families where brothers lived together were largely poor. The link between local eminence and the tendency to divide into many households figures in other accounts: "The Xian branch surname (shi 氏) of Ji'nan had more than three hundred households (jia 家) who were members of the patriline (zong ren 宗人). They were powerful and treacherous, and none of the high officials could control them." A similar case from the time of Emperor Wu is described in the Shi ji's chapter on cruel clerks.[127]

Thus, in the first century of the Han, several single surname groups were divided into three hundred or more households linked by a common ancestor. Such a situation almost certainly resulted from generation after generation dividing property among brothers, while remaining in the same area. Although the families were divided in terms of property, they lived close together and could act in unison to oppose the central government's attempts to control them. Consequently, according to one author, Emperor Wu not only forcibly moved powerful families to the capital region, but also forbade their living closely together as a patriline.[128] By the end of the Han, a single patriline could consist of more than one thousand families, as in the case of Han Rong, who gathered members of his patriline and more distant kin with a common surname in a fortified compound.[129] Texts also tell of rich families dividing property to form separate households. The most celebrated case is that of Zhuo Wangsun, who ultimately gave a huge amount of cash and property, as well as numerous servants, to his daughter Wenjun so that she could establish a proper household with Sima Xiangru.[130]

Further evidence indicating that the powerful and wealthy lineages based their power on the formation of associations above the level of the household is the practice in the collective chapters on merchants in both the Shi *ji* and the *Han shu* of referring to such wealthy people not as individuals but as branch surnames (*shi* 氏). Thus, the *Shi ji* refers in succession to the Zhuo branch surname, the Shi, the Kong, the Bing, the Ren, the Tian, the Li, and the Du. We saw how the Zhuo divided into separate households. The Tian also consisted of multiple households, and the Du existed in several geographically distinct branches.[131] Similarly, the great lineages moved to the capital region are often identified as branch surnames, as are the locally powerful lineages attacked by the "cruel clerks," the leading lineages involved in the underworld, those who dominate commanderies, and imperial affines.[132] This terminology indicates that the wealthy and powerful lineages were recognized as consisting of multiple households linked together by a common ancestor.

Testimony to dividing powerful patrilines into multiple households appears in the stone inscriptions left behind by Eastern Han local elite. As Patricia Ebrey has noted, eleven inscriptions preserved in late imperial collections contain lists of those who contributed to the erection of the stelae. Because these are inscriptions written to commemorate significant achievements in the district or commandery (e.g., to mark the construction of a temple or a bridge), those who sponsored them would be an important segment of local society. Most were retired regular officials, retired provincial or commandery officials, district officers, retired gentlemen, or students. In nine of the eleven inscriptions with lists of sponsors, at least one surname recurred frequently. In four of them, the predominant surname accounted for over twenty percent of those listed. The three lists that have more than one hundred names show officials, subordinates, and nonofficials of the same surname. Among the 157 sponsors of one stele, there were twenty-four men named Li, fourteen named Su, and thirteen named Yin.[133] While we cannot prove kin ties between these men, nor analyze their household arrangements, it is unlikely that many influential individuals with the same surname living within a single district were unrelated. It is equally unlikely that dozens of adult men were living in the same household. The most probable model suggested by these inscriptions is a local society in which many related households belonging to a major patriline lived in close physical proximity to engage in collective activities of importance to their families and community.

This shift between the *Shi ji* and the *Han shu* in their accounts of the dangers of regionalism is significant. In the former the problems posed by regions are linked to the character of the people and derive from history and local terrain. In the latter the failings of local people and what makes them difficult to govern often derive from the conduct of powerful families and wealthy merchants. Thus, by the middle of the Eastern Han, the problem of regionalism had become inseparable from the existence of major lineages who used wealth and influence to dominate localities. Through their ability to command the support or obedience of large numbers of villagers, they formed organizations at the village, district, commandery, and regional level that challenged government authority.[134]

Evidence of this at the level of the district and the commandery is the practice of describing lineages with such phrases as "a major surname of the district [or 'commandery']," "a powerful lineage of the commandery," "a surname that formed a lineage in the commandery," or a "major surname" of some named administrative area.[135] Such phrases show that many powerful lineages were extended spatial entities that exerted influence at least across one of the state's administrative units. The records indicate that in such units they often matched or exceeded the authority of the officials.

There is more evidence for this at the village level. Texts refer to a typical village of one hundred households, and villages granted as fiefs routinely have a few hundred. If regular division of property meant that powerful lineages were composed of hundreds of households living in proximity, then a significant percentage of a village could consist of a single surname. Any family not belonging to that patriline would become an ally or client. That the village could form an extension of the kin structure was recognized by the state, which appointed locally powerful people as "fathers and elders (fu lao 父老)" to handle local affairs and serve as intermediaries.[136] Similarly, the elder women of the village were referred to as the "village mothers (li mu 里母)" or the "various mothers (zhu mu)."[137] That the patriline and village could closely overlap was recognized by Wang Chong in a discussion of the tradition that the First Emperor had executed the entire village of his attempted assassin Jing Ke:

> What crime against Qin had Jing Ke's village committed that they should all be killed? If someone had stabbed the King of Qin in the village and they did not know who, then it would have been acceptable to kill them all. But Jing Ke had already died, so they had the assassin. How could one implicate an entire village? . . . [Texts] say nothing about executing his village. Perhaps they executed Ke's entire patriline [jiu zu 九族]. An entire patriline would be extremely numerous and would live in the same village. If one killed the entire patriline, then virtually the entire village would be eliminated.[138]

Thus, someone living in the middle of the Eastern Han accepted it as an obvious fact that a large patriline could constitute virtually an entire village.

This close association of patriline with village, which also featured in passages from the Li ji cited in chapter two, is also suggested by the way in which the two terms are placed together or in parallel. Thus, the account of the Fan clan's charity proceeded in grammatical parallelism from patriline to village. Similarly, the lists of the categories that made up the major lineages' social networks, expanding in concentric circles from immediate kin through patriline, retainers, and client/disciples, often included fellow villagers. Thus, a list of those invited to share in the feasts and banquets sponsored with a parting gift of gold from the emperor by the retired official Shu Guang includes his "patriline, old acquaintances, and retainers." When his immediate family began to worry that he was spending all the household's wealth, they asked "brothers and village elders" whom he trusted to persuade him to purchase land as a foundation for the family's future. Shu Guang replied:

> How could I be so old and muddleheaded as to not think of my descendants? I have my old fields and shacks, and if my descendants work diligently they are sufficient to provide food and clothing as good as those of ordinary people. If I should increase them in order to have a surplus, I would just cause my descendants to be lazy. For the worthy man, having much wealth diminishes his ambition. For the stupid man, having much wealth augments his faults. Moreover, wealth is what is hated and resented by the masses. Since I am unable to morally transform my descendants, I do not desire to augment their faults and produce resentment against them. Moreover, the money that I am spending is that which was granted by the sage ruler to nourish his old servant. Therefore I am happy to enjoy what he has given me together with my fellow villagers and members of my patriline, and thus live out my remaining days.[139]

Both lists of those who participated in the feasts joined villagers with members of the patriline, and the argument justified dispersing wealth for the benefit of these people rather than reserving it for the use of the immediate family. Here once again we see that for powerful and ambitious lineages, as Okazaki Fumio has argued, the patriline and the village were not opposed concepts, but rather that the extended kin group could determine the structure of village society.[140]

This also indicates, as did the account of the Fan lineage, the importance of conspicuous generosity and charity in the conduct of eminent local families. Such a practice was noted by Sima Qian, who asserted that conspicuous generosity was the key to enduring local power.[141] Shu Guang further justifies the regular dispersal of wealth throughout the village with an argument that expresses the "moral economy" of the peasant village described in modern studies.[142] In this model, village society is constituted in reciprocal ties of obligation created by the regular exchange of gifts or services. The richer members of the community are under moral pressure to distribute their wealth among their poorer neighbors, in exchange for which they receive status and customary forms of service. This method of reducing inequalities, as well as establishing moral and emotional links, was still visible in late imperial and republican China, where wealthier families in a village sponsored feasts, operas, and religious festivals that secured their own position and gained the support of their neighbors. As Shu Guang argued, wealth was of value only when circulated. If hoarded, it poisoned both household and village, but, when dispersed, it turned potential enemies into allies and dependants.

It is also significant that in the process of sharing this gift from the emperor Shu Guang was both imitating the ruler as a distributer of gifts and extending the emperor's work to the village level. Like the practice of dividing property among siblings, the dispersal of money in banquets or charity multiplied the number of households attached to the lineage through ties of obligation. It thereby maximized the number of people whose services it could command. Since the agriculture of the period relied on intensive labor inputs in an almost horticultural style of farming, there was little advantage to converting smallholdings into unitary large estates. This was why great families left tenants to work their own plots and collected income through sharecropping.[143] Similarly, the state did not have most of the large quantities of land that it obtained through confiscations worked by teams of slaves, but instead distributed it to peasant households from whom it collected taxes. To maximize its wealth and power, the goal of the lineage was to accumulate people rather than land or cash.[144] For this reason, even when the power of the central state collapsed at the end of the Han, locally powerful families did not shift toward primogeniture to preserve their estates intact. Instead they continued to divide property among sons and to seek marriage alliances to increase the number of their followers and the geographic range of their influence.

There are many examples of conspicuous generosity or charity such as those of Shu Guang. Wang Dan, eschewing political service under Wang Mang, regularly used his wealth to rescue fellow villagers in need, and distributed food and wine as rewards to those who worked hard in the fields. He arranged funerals and provided gifts for the bereaved. His biography notes that he detested the powerful families. Consequently, he rejected an offer to establish ties of friendship (*jie jiao* 結交) with Chen Zun, who came from the same commandery and served as a Grand Administrator but was described as a "bravo." Nevertheless, it is interesting that Chen Zun also arranged for the funerals of his friends, and made lavish presents.[145] The scholarly recluse and the political gangster operated in the same universe of securing influence through generosity. There are many similar accounts of families bestowing charity on members of their own patriline or village.[146] This emphasis on charity, once again radiating out from patriline to villagers, also figures in Cui Shi's prescriptions for an influential local family in his *Monthly Ordinances*.[147] The histories also tell of officials engaging in charity, sometimes making use of the village elders to carry it out.[148] Other stories describe the criticism heaped on those who were miserly or unwilling to share their fortune.[149] The charity of landlords also appears in Han tomb art, suggesting its importance to their self-image.[150] This charitable activity, like many aspects of Eastern Han local elite conduct, imitated the emperor, who also granted charity to the poor, the orphaned, and the widowed, as well as distributing gifts to his officials.[151]

Such accounts of local charity occur not only in the literary sources, but also in stone inscriptions. Thus, Wu Zhongshan is described as giving loans to those in need and never demanding repayment. He also secretly used the leftovers from his banquets to feed orphans. Other inscriptions mention the distribution of wealth among kin, or the charitable acts and welfare activities of local officials.[152] Similar charitable actions are credited to a general who dispersed among his men all the gifts he received from the emperor.[153] The chapter in the *History of the Later Han* devoted to men who refused office and cultivated virtue in retirement contains several stories of exemplary generosity. Some of these deal with wealthy families who gave material aid to neighbors or rescued hundreds from death in times of famine or civil war. Others focus on kindnesses done to individuals.[154] Still other stories note how individuals or lineages expended all their wealth rescuing those in need. As a result, the generous families were left with no surplus, while "the orphaned and widowed, both within the patriline and from the outside, took refuge with them."[155]

This reference to orphans highlights another aspect of the moral economy of charity. Many biographies note that the subject was orphaned, and that a related family adopted him and raised him as a son. Thus, when Zhu Hui was orphaned at an early age, he was taken in by his maternal grandfather's line. When Hui was thirteen, this line and other kin fled to Wan during the rebellion against Wang Mang. On the road they were attacked by bandits who began to strip the women at knife point. The other men prostrated themselves in terror. Only Hui challenged the bandits in order to rescue the women whom he described as the "various mothers (*zhu mu*)."[156] This story indicates the possibility among multiple households linked by common ancestry or mutual obligations for collective action or communal responsibility, including the protection of talented younger kin. This meant that property or scholastic traditions could pass not only from father to son, but also to a younger relative of a collateral line.[157] In addition to the numerous stories, the theme of servants or kin protecting orphaned children also appears in Han tomb and shrine art.[158]

Charity and gift giving were sufficiently important in generating authority that they were mythicized in tales in which the wealth and power of certain clans originated in earlier generosity. This entailed either "secret kindness" to strangers who turned out to be spirits, or exceptional devotion to sacrifices. Thus, He Bigan's sheltering more than eighty white-haired old men from a heavy rain led to their granting him nine hundred and ninety-nine inch-long counting rods. His descendants who would attain office would be as numerous as the rods. A member of the Zhang clan living alone in a single-roomed dwelling was visited by a magic bird that he sheltered in his breast. It turned into a belt buckle, and so long as the lineage kept this buckle its wealth flourished. The Yin clan made annual sacrifices to Guan Zhong, whom they claimed as an ancestor. One New Year's morning, the Stove God appeared to them, paid his greetings, and received the sacrifice of a yellow sheep. They grew fabulously wealthy, and the sacrifice of a yellow sheep to the Stove God at New Year became a family tradition. Several of these stories became the stuff of popular sayings in the capital region.[159] These tales in which piety and charity led to great wealth present in the form of parables the social reality of lineages that employed public generosity to secure prestige and power.

While great clans used public displays of charity to secure support from their neighbors, attract allies among scholars and officials, and expand their networks, their wealth was also poured into less reputable channels—that is, gifts or bribes to those in power. However, these gifts or bribes were also a form of generosity that extended the lineage's networks. One scholar defended in the name of ritual and proper sentiment the practice of villagers presenting gifts to a worthy local official, so long as he did not demand them.[160] High officials also showered gifts on guests and potential clients to build up large networks of supporters.[161] A merchant family gave gifts to leading nobles to establish links to people with political power. The merchants then used the fear inspired by these links to guarantee repayment of loans they made.[162] Ma Rong, the famous scholar, was reputed to be greedy and of low moral character. In some stories both he and his son awarded offices for cash payments. In another story a low official in the late Han used all his wealth to present gifts to the servants of the official who dominated the court and thereby "established links of intimacy and generosity with them." On the basis of the debt established, once again presented in terms of creating ties, he passed by the crowds of petitioners and was escorted directly into the presence of the official, from whom he received a post.[163] This last story is particularly revealing of the thin line between charity and bribes. It focuses on the establishment of social bonds through giving gifts over a period of time, with reciprocation delayed for a decent interval. Moreover, the recipients were themselves of technically humble status, being merely servants rather than the official himself.

While using gifts to gain patronage or attract retainers shares some vocabulary with charity toward members of the patriline or villagers, it differs in its geographic character. Aid to kin and villagers flowed primarily within the face-to-face world of the local community, and at most would expand to cover a district or commandery. Ties to officials and retainers, on the other hand, often entailed crossing great distances and established networks across the empire. The clearest evidence of this geographic range comes from stone inscriptions, where the obligations of clients to patrons often included contributing to the erection of a memorial stele. The lists of contributors on these stelae indicate the geographic range of the networks established in official circles. The stele for Liu Kuan lists the names of over three hundred clients from across north-central China, while that for Kong Zhou was erected by forty-three clients from ten different commanderies. Other examples reveal the same pattern of social links based on patronage spanning large regions.[164]

Transregional networks were also established through education. Many clients listed on the funerary inscriptions of political figures are described as students, and in some cases their relations may have involved instruction. More important, sources describe many figures as shunning political office to devote themselves to teaching. Their students numbered in the hundreds or the thousands. In the case of Fa Zhen, his "disciples came from great distances," and some students joined together to erect a laudatory stone inscription even before his death.[165] Other passages note the vast territories covered by scholars in search of the best teachers, and the social ties created in the process.[166] Because his own region, Shandong, had no major scholars, Zheng Xuan went to Guanzhong to study with Ma Rong, who already had more than 400 disciples. Zheng Xuan spent more than a decade studying in various parts of the empire before returning home to likewise gather hundreds of disciples.[167] So important were the ties between teacher and disciple that not only was mourning often observed, but a teacher might give his daughter in marriage to a prize disciple.[168] Since the state and scholarly associations, along with gangster leagues, were the major social groups created through cultivating personal links, it is not surprising that politics and education provided the means by which major lineages extended their influence beyond their home region.

A final form of association that was crucial to the great lineages in their regional bases was the local cult. The right to make sacrifices to specified deities had been a hallmark of power and status in China at least since the Shang dynasty, and continued to be so under the Han: "The Son of Heaven sacrifices to Heaven and Earth. The feudal lords sacrifice to the altars of soil and grain. The hereditary officials make the household sacrifices. The Son of Heaven sacrifices to the world's famous peaks and great rivers. . . . The feudal lords sacrifice to the famous mountains and great rivers within their own territories."[169] This passage, still cited as authoritative by officials at the end of the Han, stipulates that the right to make sacrifices had pertained solely to the Zhou nobility. The recipient of the sacrifice, moreover, determined the status of the proper sacrificer. Thus, only those in power could sacrifice to territorial spirits, and the loftier the spirit or the greater its "catchment area," the higher the rank of the sacrificer. Thus, one form of the power of great families in their regions was offering sacrifice to the major natural spirits of the area, or to individuals whose careers or lives qualified them to receive offerings.

Sacrifices to human spirits were divided into two categories. First, people could sacrifice to their own ancestors. Second, officials alone could offer sacrifices to unrelated individuals. Such offerings could be made only to those on the sacrificial registers of the state who met criteria stipulated in the ritual codes.[170] In short, in order to prevent the formation of unsanctioned organizations above the level of the household, the state sought to reserve for itself a monopoly of sacrifices other than those to ancestors. The great lineages, however, in constructing social networks to extend their power at the local level organized sacrificial cults to individuals and to spirits of nature who were important to their regions. In this way they usurped the prerogatives of the state.[171]

REGIONAL AND LOCAL CULTS

One form of arrogating imperial rights was the establishment of cults to meritorious local officials. The Han state itself established such cults, or the emperor offered a single sacrifice to a successful general or meritorious official.[172] However, in many cases local initiative established cults to individuals who had not been recognized by the state. Thus, in the Warring States period the people of Wu supposedly initiated an unsanctioned cult to Wu Zixu. The people or scholars of Lu similarly began to make regular sacrifices to Confucius that were only later adopted by the Han founder. A chief minister of Qi in the reign of the Emperor Wu became the recipient of sacrifice even while still alive, as did a legal official in Donghai Commandery around 50 B.C. The texts stipulate that the people of the commandery initiated these cults. Similarly, the clerks and people of one commandery established a cult to a deceased Grand Commandant. In at least one case the cult established by the people involved appealing to a deceased meritorious official to cure diseases.[173]

The most long-lived and politically influential local cult to a deceased individual was that in the Shandong region to Liu Zhang, the Marquis of Zhuxu and later King Jing of Chengyang. This grandson of the Han founder was enfeoffed in Chengyang in Shandong for playing a decisive role in the defeat of the clan of Empress Lü and the establishment of Emperor Wen. After his death, the Han established a cult to him in the town of his fief. For reasons that are not clear, the cult became widespread throughout the Shandong region. When the Red Eyebrows rose up in Shandong against Wang Mang, they adopted the cult to King Jing of Chengyang, the official version of which had been based in the town where their rebellion began, as their central political sacrifice. They thus combined regional loyalties with devotion to the Liu house against the power of imperial affines that had distinguished King Jing's career. In their armies, shamans drummed and danced as offerings were made to King Jing to gain them blessings. When a shaman announced that King Jing was unhappy over their disloyalty to the Han, they adopted Liu Penzi, a teenager from the imperial house, to become their figurehead chief and make sacrifices to King Jing.[174] After the defeat of the Red Eyebrows and the reestablishment of the Han, the cult to King Jing resumed its status as an official Han cult with numerous unofficial branches scattered throughout Shandong.

This cult continued without notice during the Eastern Han, until Ying Shao became a magistrate in the area in the last decades of the dynasty. He described the cult as follows:

> From Langya and the six commanderies of Qingzhou down to Bohai, every city, town, village, and settlement had established a

shrine to him. They had fashioned and ornamented five chariots in the style of the highest officials. Merchants in turn took charge of it, putting up [statues in] official costumes with seals at their belts to establish a full retinue of subordinate officials. They boiled sacrifices with accompanying songs. The hubbub went on for days, and wild stories were transmitted that there was a spirit present whose responses to questions immediately proved true. This continued for years, and no one could rectify it. Only the Grand Tutor of Le'an, Chen Fan, and the chief minister of Ji'nan, Cao Cao, were able to completely suppress it, so that the government solemnly was purified. After Chen and Cao departed, it returned to a certain extent to its former condition.[175]

This is the most detailed account of any Han local cult. It suggests the scale and organization that these attained, as well as the fervor they inspired. With its pan-regional spread, merchant sponsorship, lavish expenditure on the simulated props of imperial government, and role as a local oracle, such a cult exerted great influence. It also demonstrates the role that cults played in creating autonomous local organizations across commanderies and regions. The account notes the existence of numerous village shrines to the cult, along with the great organized festivals sponsored by wealthy merchants and powerful lineages. The inability of local officials to control it and its resurgence following periods of forceful suppression are both characteristic of local cults throughout the history of imperial China.

Local cults also sprang up around celebrated recluses or men who were proclaimed as immortals. The cults to recluses were in many ways like those to virtuous officials, except that the men were thought to have blessed their region, or gained the power to do so, through a purity cultivated in isolation from the world. One of the most interesting stories of such a cult describes a supposed friend and correspondent of Sima Qian who retired to a mountain near Chang'an. Sima Qian wrote a letter urging him to return to a life of service. The letter argued that only Laozi was able to purify his body and his resolve by cutting himself off from the world of men, and that even he could not "fully trace back the origins of the Most High." The hermit modestly replied that he lacked the abilities to serve the world, and desired only to wander free and easy for the rest of his days. The story concludes with the moral that Sima Qian was castrated and thus degraded, while his friend remained loftily free. When the hermit died, the people near the mountain established an altar for him where sacrifices were unceasingly offered. This parable echoes the story cited in the previous chapter of Jia Yi's meeting the diviner who hid from the dangers of the court as a fortune teller in the market. A second, less elaborate, story also features a hermit praised by a leading literary official, in this case Yang Xiong, and ends with an identical formula about the permanence of the cult. It is noteworthy in that it speaks of a stone inscription to the memory of the hermit.[176]

Stone inscriptions also figure in the cults that emerged in the last century of Han rule around those who had supposedly attained immortality. The most notable of these inscriptions describes the career of the immortal Tang Gongfang in the Hanzhong region of Shaanxi. A transcription of this stele was recorded in the Song dynasty *Li shi*, and Ouyang Xiu judged it on the basis of its calligraphic style to be a genuine Eastern Han stele. This conclusion is supported by numerous references to the cult of Tang Gongfang in local placenames, and to his story and his cult in works from the Age of Disunion.[177] The detail provided in the stele and the frequent citations in later sources offer valuable insights into the nature of cults that were confined to a single locality and its immediate environs.

The stele itself is primarily devoted to Tang Gongfang's career. It narrates how he became an immortal, used his powers to assist the government of his locality, was recommended to a governor for whom he trapped and killed a rat that had damaged the governor's chariot canopy, refused to divulge his arts to the governor, and fled the latter's wrath with a magic potion that allowed him and his entire household to rise into the sky.[178] After comparing him favorably to the famous immortals of antiquity, the inscription states that due to his lingering influence neither insects in the summer nor frosts in the winter harmed the people. Epidemics and evil influences did not linger, all pests were eradicated, and harvests were more abundant than in other places. The head of the commandery, in association with a group of local patrons, states that he had repaired the temple to Tang Gongfang and had the inscription carved in order to pray for blessings and to preserve the memory of the immortal.

This story insists on the local nature of the cult. Tang benefited his own town, but was menaced and forced to flee by a provincial governor. After departing, he continued to bless his own locality, granting it good fortune not found elsewhere. The list of donors on the back of the stele names fifteen people, two of whom are from Tang Gongfang's hometown, and the rest from a neighboring district. These appear to be local notables, many who had served as local magistrates or minor officials, and the rest described as "retired scholars." None of them appears in any literary source, which indicates that they did not make a career in the higher levels of the imperial government. From later sources, cited in the preceding note, we know that several temples to the cult were built in nearby towns.

A more recently discovered inscription tells of an otherwise unknown immortal named Fei Zhi. In addition to relating his eccentric behavior and his relations with the imperial court, the inscription tells how he gathered disciples, especially members of the Xu family. Xu You is said to have encountered the Queen Mother of the West, and his son Xu Jian initiated sacrifices to Fei Zhi in A.D. 169. Five disciples of Xu You are said to have consumed a drug called "stone marrow" and thus become immortals. In addition to these two stelae, historical documents also mention a cult to the immortal Wangzi Qiao established in A.D. 165 near Mount Song.[179]

There are also many references to local cults dedicated to immortals in the *Biographies of Arrayed Immortals*. This work was almost certainly begun under the Han, although the current edition includes later additions.[180] It is an anthology of the lives of celebrated immortals, but many biographies describe the popular cults that grew up around their subjects. Thus, Xiaofu, a man who repaired sandals in the market of his town, never grew old and ultimately rose into the sky. Many people in his town offered sacrifice to him.[181] Ma Dan, a man of Jin in the Spring-and-Autumn period, departed in a whirlwind and "the men of the north honored and made sacrifices to him." Ge You ascended Mt. Sui as an immortal, followed by many of the nobles of Shu. Several dozen shrines to him were erected at the base of the mountain. Master Guan was put to death by a ruler to whom he refused to reveal his arts, much like Tang Gongfang. He reappeared several decades later, only to fly off after a few weeks. As a result, "every household in Song made offerings to him." Many other stories in the collection follow this pattern in which an immortal departs from the human world and then becomes the object of a cult. They are notable in that all the cults, even those to figures such as Wangzi Qiao who were known throughout the empire, are described as being confined to a single site or region, often in the place where he or she was last seen.[182] Other figures are associated with particular families, such as You Bozi who reappears several times over the course of the decade to assist the Su family, with whom he had been a retainer under the Zhou.[183] This echoes the stories of wealthy Eastern Han lineages who were reputed to be beneficiaries of spiritual assistance due to the generosity of their ancestors.

While the historicity of the cults in the *Lie xian zhuan* is uncertain, the stone inscriptions to Tang Gongfang and Fei Zhi, as well as stories in literary works, show that such cults existed. Moreover, several Han inscriptions to mountain cults show links between mountain worship and the celebration of the immortals who dwelt on mountains or used them to depart the world.[184] This is also demonstrated in the tradition of the so-called Isles of the Immortals, which in early texts are described as floating mountains and are thus depicted in the numerous mountain-shaped incense burners produced during the Han. Another mountain cult dedicated to the legendary Bo Yi and Shu Qi is demonstrated by a partially preserved inscription and later records.[185] Finally, details in the *Lie xian zhuan* about motives for founding and methods of maintaining cults fit with what we know of the religious practices in the period. It is not surprising that immortals and hermits, both associated with the mountains and wild areas just beyond the city and clearly distinguished from the state-sponsored exemplars on the sacrificial registers, became local benefactors and the deities of cults devoted exclusively to the well-being of a specific town or small region. The recurring theme in the stories of tensions with kings and high officials likewise expresses the particularist, local nature of many of these cults.

In addition to local cults devoted to individuals, many were also dedicated to natural powers. Some of these are described in accounts of officials who attempted to stamp them out.[186] Such accounts emphasize the regional character of the cults, treating them as extensions of local custom. They ascribe their administration to "shamans," who seek to dupe the people for profit. One of the cults involved the illicit sacrifice of oxen, who were not to be killed because of their importance for agriculture. Another was a mountain cult involving the regular dedication of young men and women from the locality to the god of the mountain, to whom they were permanently linked and thus forbidden to marry. As noted earlier, several of the cults to immortals were also linked to mountains.

This recurrence of mountain cults in the localities is not an isolated phenomenon, for these were a major element of Han religion. While the imperial *feng* and *shan* sacrifices at Mt. Tai were very rare, local officials or kings gave regular offerings to major mountains in their areas. Moreover, a recently discovered inscription has shown how sacrifices to Mt. Hua were offered in an attempt to treat the ailment of a Qin noble.[187] Just as the state determined those individuals who could legally receive public sacrifices, so only mountain cults recorded on official sacrificial registers were licit. Accounts of such sacrifices and their sanction by the state appear in numerous Han stone inscriptions devoted to mountain cults. Kenneth Brashier has collected eighteen examples of such inscriptions, although a couple are little more than fragments. These provide evidence about the prevalence of mountain cults, the role of local people, and the question of registration with the central government.[188]

The most important inscriptions on the role of local people in mountain cults deal with the Yuanshi district: Mt. Baishi, Mt. Fenglong, Mt. Sangong, and Mt. Wuji. These inscriptions focus on the local nature of the cults in several ways. First, they emphasize that prayers and offerings to the mountain began well before recognition by the court. It is because such offerings proved to be efficacious that the court, after sending out inspectors to check the local people's claims, added the mountain to the register. They also insist that even after imperial sanction was obtained, the expenses for paraphernalia and sacrifices were paid by the district. Second, several inscriptions emphasize that the blessings were specific to the region, being limited to the "state region" or within the "state's frontiers." One inscription mentions the two commanderies that contributed to the sacrifice.[189] Third, each inscription describes the rain and abundant crops that result from the sacrifice, leading to a low price for grain. Since grain prices varied from one area to another, this demonstrates the regional character of the cult.

This regional character of the cults in Yuanshi contrasts with the imperial cults to the Five Marchmounts, the most sacred peaks of China that formed a cosmic mandala of the four directions and the center. We have inscriptions for two of these peaks. These inscriptions to Mt. Hua and Mt. Song, unlike those from Yuanshi, focus on the links of the mountains to the imperial house and world rulership. The one to Mt. Hua proper begins like several inscriptions by linking the major mountains to the origins of the world. It proceeds from canonical accounts of the ritual role of mountains to the cultic activities of the sage kings of antiquity, through the succession of dynasties, and finally gives almost a ruler-by-ruler account of the Han emperors' relations to mountain cults. The inscription to the hall and gateposts on Mount Hua includes similar elements. However, it also discusses how mountains generate the omens of dynastic transition, and recounts royal progressions through the mandala formed by the mountains as a ritual of power. There are no references to local beliefs, offerings or prayers by local people prior to official recognition, or such regional features as the price of grain.[190]

These inscriptions and the literary sources indicate a wide range of cults dedicated to or located on mountains. At one end of the spectrum were the august imperial cults to the most sacred mountains that had a long, if sometimes imaginary, history of cult and a grounding in the canonical texts. At the other end were illicit cults grounded entirely in local custom or practice. These were organized by "shamans" or powerful families and dedicated to mountain spirits or to hermits or immortals known only in the locality. They involved a range of unorthodox ritual practices. In between these were cults to regionally important mountains that were initiated by local people but employed conventional prayers and sacrifices, primarily appeals for rain, and that sought imperial sanction. This diversity of cults rooted in topography and their shifting ties to the imperial center indicate the variable relations of regions and powerful clans to the state.

RHAPSODIES ON REGIONS

As previously noted, due to its size and physical diversity the history of "China" has always been one of regions. However, the fact of regional variations did not necessarily produce discourses or practices in which regionalism could be legitimately articulated. During the Han, regional cultures were associated with "custom" as a negative category, the power of lineages, and unorthodox cults. They were problematic for a court that insisted on the unity of a Chinese world defined by imperial culture. The literate, high culture of Han China was based on ancient texts in an archaic tongue, and largely focused on the court. Regions at best were lesser, peripheral derivatives of an exemplary center and at worst zones of savagery. In the last century of the Han, however, members of the literate elite began to detach themselves from the court-based model of society. They and their followers developed new literary genres, social practices, methods of textual transmission, and religious cults that celebrated the "genius" of place at the expense of the center.

As will be discussed in the next chapter, Han literati elaborated several comprehensive world models: the "Tribute of Yu," the theories of Zou Yan, Chapter Four of the *Huainanzi*, geographic accounts in the "apocryphal" literature, and the *Classic of Mountains and Seas* or associated definitions of China through a number of mountain ranges. These models either negated regional cultures or reduced them to appendages of the capital. These took the form of mathematizing schemata based on the "magic square-nine regions-nine heavens" model or the "five zones of submission." Around a capital/axis mundi, the world was structured as a geometric grid, or a series of zones in which civilization declined as one moved away from the center. In this second approach, regional characteristics were embodied as exotica that moved to the center as "tribute." Regional cultural variations figured solely as markers of inferiority that delimited and defined the civilized center. As noted in Roel Sterckx's discussion of the early Chinese discourse on animals, local custom and animal character formed a single complex tied to their places of origin. The extreme form of this discourse was accounts of barbarians in distant lands who took on the attributes of the animals with whom they lived. Thus, northern nomads had no cities but lived on horseback and moved with their herds, while southern peoples wore their hair loose and tattooed their bodies in imitation of dragons or fish, and peoples of the southwest slept with their mothers and ate their eldest sons. These accounts blended into the mythic geography of the *Classic of the Mountains and Seas* where peripheral lands were populated by man-animal hybrids or monsters.

The negation of regional cultures in these models extended into administrative geography. The aforementioned mathematizing schemata underlay early theories of administration in Warring States texts, wherein a fixed number of households constituted a first-level unit, a specified number of first-level units constituted a second level unit, and so on up to the level of the state. While Han administrative units lacked the recurring numerical character of these models, they were still by policy detached from the units of local society. In the administrative geography of the *Han shu*, the state consisted of a hierarchized network of cities containing government offices, but the majority of the population lived in villages below this level. This population remained hidden in an administrative territory that was not differentiated in nomenclature from the local capital.[191] Like the "natural" villages, the "natural" regions corresponding to the old Warring States had no place in Han administrative geography after the suppression of the feudatory states.

Han literature was likewise a product of the court, both sociologically and thematically. The most prestigious literary genre was the epideictic rhapsody, which developed in Warring States court debates and was used to seek service either with the feudal lords or ultimately the emperor. Its topics were, if critical, the failure of the ruler to employ the poet or, if celebratory, the glories of the imperial hunts, capitals, and rituals. Rhapsodies treated imperial hunting parks and capitals as replicas of the cosmos or definitions of civilization, and the "Shanglin Rhapsody" reduced regions to deficient versions of the center. The histories of the period also centered on the ruler and his court.[192] They were structured according to "Fundamental Chronicles" narrating the actions of the ruler, while individuals, peoples, and social practices were incorporated only to the extent that they played a role in the fate of the dynasty.

The court-based writing of the period culminated in the official canon and the Grand Academy. At least since the time of Emperor Wu, the Han court had claimed authority to fix a canon. Its texts were exemplary for all writing and provided models for the literary genres of the period.[193] In fixing this canon, the Han court specifically rejected the claims of such regional rivals as the courts of Huainan and Hejian. The imperial court also claimed authority to resolve differences between regional versions of texts—for example, choosing readings derived from the Qi-based school of the *Spring and Autumn Annals* over those from Lu. Thus, the establishment of the canon likewise served to exalt the center and strip regional variations of significance. Recruitment of poets and scholars into the court or the Grand Academy also served to draw all literary and scholastic talents from the regions into the court.

The hegemonic claims of the center and the denial of regional cultures weakened with literati alienation from the court due to the domination of eunuchs and imperial affines, along with the increasing prestige of the non-canonical Old School texts. Groups based on kinship and teacher–student or patron–client ties articulated local interests at the expense of the center. As Patricia Ebrey has shown, stone inscriptions, shrine art, and collective biographies of worthies show locally influential people's development of a new sense of themselves as a distinct group with a unique form of life. Notably, such collective biographies were organized on a regional basis. They told of important figures from a specific region, or compared those of one region with those of another. Since biographies had previously been a hallmark of the court-based histories, collecting them on the basis of region placed the locality in the role of the imperial center.[194] Thus, the emerging self-consciousness of the late Han elite also marked an increasing regional assertiveness. This later led to the writing of regional histories, of which the earliest example to have survived substantially intact is the *Huayang guo zhi*, a fourth-century-history of Sichuan.[195] The breakup of the empire into the Three Kingdoms further stimulated the development of regional consciousness in Sichuan and Jiangnan, but these developments depended on new literary and social practices.

The major literary revolution at the fall of the Han was the emergence of the literati lyric. From the Jian'an reign period and the rise of the Cao clan date the earliest verifiable lyric verses by named authors, in contrast to the "folk songs" and liturgical chants composed by professional musicians, or the handful of brief verses in the Han histories intoned by members of the ruling house. The rise of the lyric entailed changes in both the themes of poetry and the social practices which underlay it. In contrast to the court-based rhapsody used as a means of critique or suasion addressed to the ruler, the lyric was to be the veridical presentation of the experience and emotional response of the poet. Thus, Zhi Yu's third-century A.D. "Essay on the Different Genres [Currents] of Literary Writing" argued: "One who voices himself in verse should sing his true feelings. One who climbs to a height and composes should celebrate what he has seen. One who praises an object considers first and foremost its true nature, and one who honors a deed should base himself on the facts."[196] The insistence on the veracity of a poem to emotion and experience had its classical foundations in the "Mao Preface," and it defined the ideal of the lyric that emerged in the Cao-Wei dynasty. Abandoning the totalizing vision of the rhapsodies, the lyric was devoted to the limited impressions of the individual mind as rooted in a sense of place. Its topics were no longer imperial parks, capitals, and rituals, but banquets of peers, moments of parting, or the sight of mountains at dusk.

These themes suggest another aspect of the transformation of poetry at the end of the Han—the development of new social settings for verse composition. The Jian'an reign period at the end of the Han saw the emergence of poetry as the social discourse of a small group of like-minded friends, whose life of banquets, excursions, meetings, and partings was accompanied by a stream of lyrics and shorter rhapsodies. This new world, in which poetry ceased to be a courtly language for addressing the ruler and became instead the highest expression of sociability, was announced in Cao Pi's letter to Wu Zhi: "In the past we drove our carriages side by side, and when we halted we placed our mats together. When were we ever apart? Every time the wine was passed round, accompanied by the music of pipes and strings, our ears reddening in intoxication, we would lift up our eyes and chant lyrics, not even aware of our own happiness."[197] This lists the major elements that defined the social life of poetry during the Age of Disunion and beyond: excursions, banquets, wine, music, and verse. The life described here was repeated and elaborated by a series of salons that in the following centuries accompanied their gatherings with verse. However, the Jian'an circle was supplanted as the prototype for such groups by the Seven Sages of the Bamboo Grove. As Audrey Spiro has shown, by the sixth century these figures had become recurring images in imperial tomb art, where members of the ruling dynasty surrounded themselves in death with the greatest of the poetic circles that defined the cultural ideal of the period.[198] Morino Shigeo consequently organized his study of Six Dynasties poetry around the "collective literature" practiced in the salons of the Jiangnan region formed during the Jin, Song, Qi, and Liang dynasties.[199]

Even as the performance of lyric poetry, pure conversation, calligraphy, and painting redefined structures of prestige and authority in southern China, charging rural and mountain landscapes with a new significance, the rhapsody was also adapted to celebrate regional and local interests at the expense of the imperial center. The clearest example of this is the contrast between the Han rhapsodies on the imperial capitals and those composed by Zuo Si between 280 and 300 on the capitals of the Three Kingdoms. However, one should first note features in the earlier rhapsodies on capitals by Zhang Heng that anticipated shifting attitudes toward regional specificity and local cultures.

Throughout his poems, Zhang, the leading scientist of his age, seeks an ultimate ground for the imperial capital in the study of nature. The first speaker argues that the rival characters of the Western and Eastern courts resulted from the fact that the former arose in a time of cosmic ascent (*yang*) and a region of natural wealth, while the latter arose in a time of decline (*yin*) in a more barren region. The character of the courts emerged from their physical environments, which thus made them expressions of regional traits.[200] The second speaker rejects this appeal to the influence of soil and terrain, but defends the superiority of the Eastern capital through the science of astronomy, supported by *fengshui*. Measurements with the gnomon, according to this speaker, proved Luoyang to be the center of the earth. Meteorological studies likewise showed it to be the place where winds and rain found their harmony. Finally, the lay of the land revealed an array of auspicious influences.[201] The reference to the gnomon has a canonical basis in the account of founding a capital in the *Rituals of Zhou*, but linking the gnomon with meteorology and environment appears for the first time in chapter 3 of the *Huainanzi* in the early Western Han.[202] The same appeal to natural principle also figures in the ritual calendar that occupies most of Zhang Heng's rhapsody on the Eastern capital. This is based on the theory that the emperor performs rituals and policies in accord with the shifting of the seasons. These passages, although grounded in the ritual calendar of the "Monthly Ordinances" and related texts, mark Zhang Heng as a precursor of the tendency at the end of the Han to underpin ritual and government with cosmic principles. After the fall of the Han, such principles were often derived from Taoist texts, as in the works of Wang Bi and his contemporaries.

This shift toward nature and the genius of place in the rhapsodic invocation of capitals culminates in the last great series on the subject by Zuo Si. The author's preface to this work describes it as a derivative of those of Ban Gu and Zhang Heng, but in fact it differs in several ways.[203] First, by abandoning the chronological dimension and dealing with three simultaneous capitals, it suppresses the themes of historical evolution and the perfection of rites that had structured its predecessors. Second, by omitting the capital of his own day, Zuo withholds the idealized portrait of an imperial capital or rather imperial rituals that hitherto had been the inevitable culmination of the capital rhapsody. In effect, he presented a rhapsody without a capital and its rites. Finally, these rhapsodies create a dramatic sense of place through elaborate depictions of local landscape, society, and folkways; they more closely resemble a proto-ethnography than the old poetics of empire. These collective changes reflect the end of the Han order embodied in the ritually perfect capital, and point toward the great changes in Chinese society and poetics that took place during the centuries of imperial collapse.

Zuo Si announces in the preface his intent to celebrate personal experience and affirm regional culture. The poet cities the "Mao Preface" and Ban Gu to the effect that the rhapsody derived from the classical odes. However, he reverses the stance of the earlier authors by citing the putative use of Zhou songs as evidence gathered for the king to "observe local customs." He thus announces that his rhapsodies will give accounts of locality and custom. He cites lines from the Zhou odes to show how they can be used as evidence for the vegetation of one region and the house-building practices of another. The primary failing of the Han rhapsodies, he argues, was to ignore such clearly observable facts. In their fascination with obscure language and dramatic effect, the Han poets had filled their accounts of parks and capitals with creatures, plants, geologic formations, and supernatural beings that could not be found in the places where they appeared. Thus, their poems lacked substance and could not serve as a guide for the reader. Zuo Si, in contrast, argued for accuracy as the foundation of poetry. He then presented his credentials as an author by noting that he had consulted maps and local gazetteers to guarantee the accuracy of all his accounts of landscape, flora, and fauna.[204]

While Sima Xiangru had presented a totalizing vision of empire and a celebration of the powers of language, and Ban Gu had written both to articulate and reenact the ritual triumph of the Eastern Han over its predecessor, Zuo Si justified his rhapsodies as an accurate account of the diverse regional cultures that emerged at the end of the Han. His insistence on the veracity of a poem to emotion and experience is yet another attempt to apply the lyric aesthetic to the rhapsody. However, here it is no longer the moral purpose of the canonical lyric that is invoked, as in Ban Gu, but the veridical and experiential ideal of the lyric that had emerged in the final decades of the Han as articulated by Cao Zhi.

The briefer rhapsodies that began to be written in this period often took the form of "singing of objects" in which the poet described such diverse phenomena as the ocean, a river, wind, clouds, trees, vessels, and so on or "excursion rhapsodies" in which the poet ascended a high place or took a journey and recounted what he saw. From these new forms of rhapsodies on objects and excursions, Zuo Si drew the rhetoric and standards of his poem on capitals. Its intended audience was the cultivated elite who lived in the new world of verse exchanges and pure conversation with like-minded men of elegance. This elite from its beginnings in the Eastern Han had cultivated a strong sense of attachment to specific places and the importance of regional variations in customs and character. This new audience and aesthetic explains Zuo Si's decision to make rhapsodies on what were in effect local capitals, and to claim superiority through the accurate rendition of local landscapes and custom.

His "Shu Capital Rhapsody" thus begins with a reference to the "Nine Provinces" of Yu, the canonical division of China into regions distinguished by the local products that formed their tribute to the center. This leads to a description of the geography of Sichuan devoted largely to its mountains, including not only generic descriptions of their twisting forms but also accurate names and locations. The same rigor is subsequently applied to other features such as minerals, flora, and fauna. These passages also include references to local tribes and their distinctive songs and, most strikingly, to some of the immortals whose local cults figured in the *Lie xian zhuan* as described in the preceding section.[205]

The description of the capital Chengdu similarly recounts distinctive local features culled from books. After an elaborate portrayal of palaces and gate towers, the poem describes its markets with a list of local products derived from the "Tribute of Yu," the *Shi ji* chapter on "producers of wealth," and similar works. The rhapsody then describes historically eminent local families. It notes their devotion to "linking with allies and bringing together cliques," as well as describing their large armed escorts. Thus, it depicts the great families of Sichuan in terms that derive directly from Han accounts of the power and menace of regionally powerful clans. Their banquet, with entertainment provided by women in distinctive local attire, is described as "custom." As in the Han, this term identifies local culture, but here it is no longer negative.[206]

In place of the imperial hunts in earlier rhapsodies, Zuo Si narrates a hunt of the local grandees of Chengdu, although the structure of the hunt follows its more illustrious predecessors. The course of the hunt leads through an inventory of actual Sichuan sites, and the animals and tribal peoples slain are derived from geographic accounts of the region. After lists of the uncanny wonders that occurred in Sichuan and the great writers who were born there, the section concludes with a celebration of the awesome topography of mountains and defiles that ringed the region and made it impregnable. This echoes the earlier descriptions of the topography of Qin, but again it is no longer a negative feature.[207]

The rhapsody on Wu is similar, although grander. The speaker mocks the praise of Shu as provincial and limited, and for dealing with things that do not appear in ancient canonical or ritual texts. He dismisses the knowledge of the first speaker as simple "familiarity" or "habituation" with the customs of a "lowly town."[208] His own recitation moves from a brief mention of mountains through an elaborate account of the watery elements that characterized the southeast—rivers, water creatures, the Isles of the Immortals, plants—and finishes with lists of trees, animals, fruit, and gems. It then describes the capital, including the surrounding areas, the markets, and the great clans of the region. These last are once again identified by their large armed retinues and by their devotion to "forming alliances."[209] The rhapsody likewise contains a hunt, this time royal and on a much grander scale. It concludes with an account of a musical performance and an assertion of the superiority of Wu to Shu.

However, while the speaker depicts the scale and power of Wu, many phrases still insist on its regional character. The plants and animals are things noted in "local gazetteers," rather than in the *Shi jing*. Although these objects are "coveted by the central provinces," Wu itself is not a central state but a frontier zone that normally pays rather than collects tribute. The description of the area around the capital also mentions Wu as a payer of tribute. Moreover, the same passage says that the view of the capital reveals it as "the base of a hegemon king," rather than the capital of a true king or emperor.[210] That the king of Wu was a hegemon who ruled a limited area through force is also indicated by references to Kings Helü and Fuchai, who in the Eastern Zhou had sought to dominate China by force from their base in the southeast.[211] The account of the markets also emphasizes the presence of barbarian peoples and the exotic character of local products, marking its nature as a frontier region rather than part of the traditional heartland. The same emphasis on the alien or barbarian character of the people also figures in the list of the chieftains who participate in the royal hunt, and the warriors tattooed to appear like dragons who take the lead in the fishing.[212] The musical performance that concludes the hunt is said to be "entirely in accord with local folk songs and customs."[213]

The final section, while asserting the superiority of Wu to Shu, covertly points to the peripheral character of Wu state. The first line distinguishes it from the "central, Chinese (*zhong xia* 中夏)" states. Though Shun and Yu wandered through the region, it was not their home. The next lines assert that there are myriad states, each with their own customs, which are distinguished only in their wealth, scale, and topography. Pairing Shu in the west with Wu in the east, the poet points out that the latter is larger and richer in contents. He concludes that Wu has:

Hidden and remote, solitary and deep, vast and empty, still and secluded, what the eye has not seen and the ear not heard, where the feet of people have never trod, the most extraordinary of unconventional things, the most diverse of uncanny affairs, with its truths hidden away since high antiquity, so that it was not recognized even by prescient former sages.[214]

The final seeming panegyric describes Wu as remote, hidden, and strange. It lay at the edges of the world, beyond the range of the sages, and thus outside true Chinese civilization.

The final rhapsody makes explicit the critique suggested in the preceding poems. It points out that differences between regions result from local environmental influence and customs formed through habit. A recapitulation of the creation of the world by successive divisions of primal chaos culminates with the separation of the barbarians at the edges of the earth from the ruler at the center. In the central lands, the ruler does not rely, like Wu and Shu, on difficult terrain to protect himself, but rather commands through virtue and a mastery of canonical texts and calendars. The first two speakers are dismissed as those who willingly follow "bandits (*fei ren* 匪人, also 'wicked people' or 'subhumans')." They willingly live in "distant, cut-off regions," glorifying barbarians with tattooed bodies and savage temperaments. To correct their errors, he announces that he will speak of the "limits of the Spirit Continent, the royal domain of the Red District," that is, he will tell them about the true China.[215]

In contrast with the earlier poems—devoted to terrain, flora, fauna, and custom—the Wei capital rhapsody follows its introduction with an account of the fall of the Han and Cao Cao's restoration of political order in the Yellow River valley. Cao Cao's kingdom was a land in which the lingering influence of the sages still existed. It lay at the center of the empire, bordering on the central states, where climatic phenomena were in perfect balance.[216] It describes every aspect of the capital: its construction patterned on the earlier capitals of the sages, its extraordinary workmanship, its government buildings, its roads, its streets and towers, its parks, its markets, and the surrounding countryside. If this set of rhapsodies had followed the model of Ban Gu and Zhang Heng, it would have described Wei's capital as a true imperial city marked by correct rituals. It does not, however, fulfill this expectation. Whereas for the Eastern Han court poets proper imperial ritual had been the culmination of the dynasty, as well as the necessary climax of a capital rhapsody, such an epiphany does not figure here. The sole section devoted to rituals describes a feast for surrendered barbarians. This extends the earlier criticism of "barbarian" Wu and Shu by describing people from the four quarters of the earth in their outlandish attire bearing tribute to the center. However, it is followed by a simple enumeration of the other major rites, a few lines on Wei's supplanting of the Han, and then a panegyric to the Wei's modesty in yielding the throne to the Jin.[217] The rituals of Wei are treated as significant only to the extent that they included the submission of distant peoples, marking once again the inferiority of regions such as Wu and Shu, and that they pointed to the ultimate triumph of Jin. This dynasty that reunified China remains hidden as the unspoken climax of the three rhapsodies.

Once the empire is yielded to Jin, the rhapsody shifts to an account of local features in Wei. It describes its mountains, rivers, plants, animals, features of local society, and local immortals, some of whom are described in the *Biographies of Arrayed Immortals* as the recipients of cult.[218] Once Wei has ceased to be the imperial center, the features of local environment and custom that had defined Wu and Shu surge to the fore. No longer home to a capital, the state of Wei becomes simply a third region. The speaker concludes with encomia for eminent historical individuals from the Wei region, and a dismissal of Shu and Wu as distant regions cut off behind difficult topography where barbarism flourishes under the name of local custom. The two earlier speakers stammeringly concur in this condemnation and, acknowledging that they have never seen the tracks of an imperial carriage, they conclude with a reassertion of the necessary unity of the world under a single ruler.[219]

In the absence of a true imperial capital, marked by the non-account of the rituals of Wei, the region comes to the fore. The first two speakers had celebrated their respective regional capitals in terms of topography, custom, and local history. They thereby undercut their own claims to greatness, even as they demonstrated the possibilities of a new discourse on the region and the genius of place. The final speaker sings the praises of a capital in a form more conventional for the genre, but the last capital, no longer imperial, emerges as yet another regional center. Thus, while affirming the *ultimate* superiority of the imperial center to all regions, Zuo Si's rhapsody portrays regions through themes and images that had emerged in the new lyric tradition. The imperial capital that had been the inevitable climax of earlier rhapsodies was relegated to a vanished unity, whose resurgence would prove as brief in life as in the poem. In its place appears a literary culture steeped in the lore of regional variations.[220]

CONCLUSION

Early Chinese reflections on regions were articulated primarily in terms of a discourse on "custom." Reflections on this term originated within the philosophical traditions, which applied it to all that was limited, conventional, and bound up with material interests. This category became a target for criticism as the contrary or negation of the universal truths that each of the philosophical traditions claimed to present. At the same time, some passages in the military and philosophical traditions gave "custom" a specifically spatial form. They described the manner in which people were constrained by the characteristics of the restricted environments in which they were born. Qin official documents likewise used the term "custom" to define local deviations from state imposed legal and administrative systems.

With the creation of a unified empire, the Warring States were reduced to the status of regions. Even the failings of imperial Qin were explained as a result of the limitations and weaknesses imposed by its regional culture. In this context, "custom" remained a negative category defined by limitation, partiality, and constraint. Regional cultures, for which the extreme figures were the barbarians at the frontiers of China, were set against the "refined" culture of the imperial center defined by the literary language and its textual heritage. This artificial culture, which escaped the spatial limitations of regionalism through its temporal distance and its association with the Zhou court, became the core of an imperial civilization that asserted its superiority as a transcendant whole encompassing the limited regions with their distinctive practices and products. The institutional expressions of this model were repeated resettlements of local elites to the capital region, the practice of making government office dependent on mastery of a literary language detached from local or spoken forms, and the regular dispatching of distinctive regional products to the court in the form of tribute.

However, the attempt to impose unity through the suppression of regional variations was limited by the imperial state's dependence on locally powerful families to impose its will. Unable to achieve order solely through the efforts of bureaucrats who were sent to administer non-native regions, the Eastern

Han imperial center finally reached a modus vivendi with powerful local families who constituted unofficial regional powers. These families extended their authority through their regions by means of accumulating wealth, dividing property among hundreds of families who were members of their lineage, making marriage alliances with other great families, and providing charity to their poorer neighbors. They emphasized not the building up of large estates, which offered few economic advantages given the agricultural technologies of the day, but rather the creating of networks of dependents and allies who provided diverse services. These families also increasingly took the lead in organizing unofficial cults to meritorious local officials or heros, recluses and immortals, or local geographic features such as mountains.

In the first century A.D., these families remained committed to the imperial order, seeking offices for their members or state recognition for many of their cults. However, the increasing dominance of the inner court led to the decline of the great families' position in the capital and the gradual shifting of their interests to the localities. As imperial power imploded, regionally powerful lineages increasingly began to take on themselves many of the prerogatives of the imperial center. These included such institutional arrogations as the assembling of private armies, and such localist cultural claims as the compilation of collective biographies of regional worthies and the assertion of regional characteristics as describing of literary treatment. At the very end of the Han and the early Age of Disunion, this cultural revaluation of the region found expression in the increasing emphasis on landscape and sociability in the emergent literati lyric. It also led to Zuo Si's composition of a set of rhapsodies on the imperial capital in which the ritualized imperial center that had hitherto been the ultimate topic of this subgenre disappeared, to be replaced by the poetic depiction of distinctive regional landscape, folkways, and history.

CHAPTER FIVE

WORLD AND COSMOS

Encompassing the cities and their regions, the world is yet another form of constructed spatial order. It is "constructed" because people's images of the world have always served to elaborate fundamental images of themselves, their community, and the principles of its organization. Having never seen the entire earth on a detailed map or globe, nor satellite photographs, the vast majority of the human race have gone beyond the narrow limits of personal experience and oral report to construct images of the world based on theory, myth, and fantasy. Even those who in recent times have been able to map the world in detail still insert elaborate political and social theories into their depictions.[1]

Such constructs work in several ways. Some, such as medieval maps of a cruciform world centered on Jerusalem, combined geographic information with basic ideas or images of the culture. Others, such as Herodotus writing about the Persians, Ethiopians, Scythians and other peoples at the edges of the earth, used schematizing observations or mythic tales of alien cultures to define their own civilization by exclusion or negation. Exhaustive lists of peoples or nations have been used to claim authority for histories or geographic works by demonstrating their encyclopedic nature. Accounts of the world have also taken the form of travelogues cobbled together from earlier writings. The author describes moving from point to point, noting the time required for each stage and then recounting miscellaneous tales and wonders about each site. In each of these forms, writers elaborated their own categories and interests through accounts of the broader world or distant peoples. Even accounts of the structure of the heavens borrowed ideas and images from people's understanding of their own society. Consequently such accounts provide valuable evidence for the study of the people who created them.

The "world" is also as a mode of thinking that distinguishes humans from lesser creatures, or superior men from lower ones. Classical Western thinkers argued that man could escape the confines of his physical condition through powers of thought that traversed vast distances in an instant, rose up from the corrupt earth to the immutable heavens, or made the entire cosmos the object of cognition. The ability to achieve such feats, however, depended on powers of cognition obtainable only through training in philosophy or, later, religion. Mastering totality as a condition of full humanity has also been a fundamental theme of modern philosophy, from Kant who described totality as a necessary condition of transcendental ideas, through Heidegger who distinguished humans from animals on the basis of the former's ability to constitute a total world as dwelling. Such a total world was not achieved by the exhaustive enumeration of things, but by a mode of experience or thought that forged unity out of disparate experience. Thus, insistence on mastering a complete world implied a model of human excellence, and the claim that one's own program fulfilled that model.[2]

Chinese of the late Warring States and early imperial period developed models of the world that extrapolated the principles they observed in their own society. These models sought mastery through claims of totality, and they were associated with the encompassing mode of knowing that defined the sage. Since all the units of spatial organization discussed earlier were fragments of larger wholes, it was at the level of the world that unity and thus ultimate power were to be found. These theories of the world, and the mode of knowing it, were thus ultimately theories of a world ruler.

First, writers employed the grid to organize the human world and all of space. The grid was not limited to cities but was basic to all spatial administration of the period, and it provided models of the greater world. Another geometric model was that of concentric squares radiating in ever-weakening stages from the ruler, who thus became the center and defining point of the world. The dynamic form of this model was the centripetal flow of regionally distinctive goods that was discussed in chapter four. Versions have likewise appeared previously in the bands of influence radiating from the perfected body, and in the concentric rings of the social networks of the great families. In addition, Warring States and early imperial accounts structured the world according to geographic features such as the correlate pair of mountains and waters. These models grew out of the cultic importance of these geographic features, and were closely linked to movement across the landscape in royal processions to offer sacrifice at major sites. The great world model based on mountains and seas, the *Shan hai jing*, also demonstrated how rulers spatially structured the world. All these models could also incorporate accounts of alien peoples or nonhuman creatures from the distant reaches of the earth. These peoples marked out the structure of human space, defined Chinese civilization by negation, and through movement into the center once again gave a spatial definition of the ruler's power. The divinatory charts and related objects from the period, which manipulated schematic models of the universe as a means of guiding action, also offered ordinary people success through assuming aspects of the totalizing vision of the world ruler.

However, while world models of the period sought to escape the problem of partiality in the figure of the ruler, they also preserved the principle of structuring through internal divisions. Thus, the grid fashioned space and society through carving it up into smaller units, while the model of concentric squares structured the world by dividing it into zones. The attainment of an orderly world through dividing it into smaller units also figured in ritual enactments of cosmic order, such as the ruler's Bright Hall, or symbolic depictions of it in the patterns on diviner's boards, *liu bo* game boards, and some bronze mirrors. This reappearance of division and partiality as necessary elements of the world empire, yet another version of the resurfacing of the repressed, will be discussed in the Conclusion.

GRIDS AND MAGIC SQUARES

The earliest Chinese world models for which we have evidence were based on the ritual structure of the four directions. Excavations have revealed concern for directional alignment in the neolithic. A tomb from Puyang in the Yangshao cultural area contained depictions of a tiger and a dragon, later animal emblems of the West and East, that were aligned in their appropriate directions on either side of the corpse. A tomb in Anhui contained a piece of jade carved with four directional arrows in an outer circle and eight in an inner one.[3] Shang divinatory inscriptions reveal a strong concern with the center and the four directions, particularly in association with a sacrificial cult to the four winds.[4] Moreover, evidence suggests that the Shang world was divided into four directional quadrants, which along with a central square would form the character *ya* 亞. There were also divinations about four states distributed according to the four directions.[5] Since the word "quadrant (*fang* 方)" also indicated non-Shang states, it is possible that the directions were originally associated with alien peoples who surrounded the Shang, and that the model of five quadrants was a stylization of a Shang center surrounded by potentially hostile forces. References to the four quadrants to designate the world also appear frequently on Zhou bronzes and in such early texts as the *Shi jing* and *Shang shu*.[6] This use of directional symbolism also appears on a lacquerware chest from the tomb of Marquis Yi of Zeng (second half of the fifth century B.C.), where the dragon of the East and tiger of the West flank the Big Dipper and the twenty-eight lunar lodgings.[7] Defining the world through fixing the four directions around a center continued as a standard model throughout the imperial period, and significant debates in political cosmology were articulated in terms of evolving forms of the model.[8]

Although the four quadrants remained conventional, early writers also developed new models of the world. An important example was the grid, which played several roles. First, it provided an image of creating multiplicity from unity. One line divides a plane into two parts, another creates four, and each additional line increases the number of bounded spaces.[9] Thus, the grid depicted the standard cosmogony, described in the introduction, of a structured multiplicity created out of an undifferentiated whole by repeated division. Second, the grid divided space into bounded units for the regulation of human activities.[10] This was sketched in chapter three's account of the grid structure of major streets in the city and stalls in the markets. Third, in the divinatory charts unearthed in early Han tombs and in later magic squares, the grid provided an image of the manner in which mathematical structures underlay a spatial order. In this way the grid became one of the most powerful tools for applying to space the numerological mode of thought that became so important by the end of the Warring States. In the "nine fields" theory it also constituted the most important mechanism for correlating earthly events to astral phenomena.[11] Finally, the grid provided an image of cyclical movement through a controlled space, thus forming a frame for linking cosmological models and ritual actions. The classic example of this was the "Bright Hall (*ming tang* 明堂)."

The most common form of grid was nine squares formed by the intersection at right angles of two horizontal lines and two vertical ones. Its earliest literary occurrence was in the *Mencius's* model of the "well-field" system. This system, a pattern of land use attributed to the Zhou, consisted of a nine-square grid in the shape of the Chinese graph "well (*jing* 井)". The idea of such a system was probably inspired by references to an ancient pattern of land use that was no longer understood. Having only the name *jing*, the authors of the *Mencius* imagined a nine-square grid. The eight outer squares were owned by individual households who worked them for their own subsistence, while the last belonged to the lord and was worked collectively. Since income from the central field provided for the public purse, the people paid tax only in the form of their labor. This pattern is justified in several ways:

> Benevolent government must begin with demarcating boundaries (*jing jie* 經界). If the demarcation of boundaries is not correct, then the well-field will not be even and the salaries in grain not equitable. Therefore violent rulers and corrupt officials are always sloppy in the demarcation of boundaries. Once boundaries are correctly demarcated, then the division of fields and the regulation of salaries can be fixed without exertion.[12]

Thus, the "well-field" system derives from the idea that division is the basis of social order and good government. The character *jing* (經) is used in early texts to indicate the division of the city by a grid of streets and the market by stalls. It had the broader meaning of "to put in order" or "rule," and came to be applied to the canonical texts that provided order in the world.[13] Thus, the imposition of a grid first appears as the spatial form of the making of distinctions that was the basis of all order.

Second, the grid assured equity by creating standard units. Demarcating equal plots of land in a grid, and using these plots as units for taxation and reward, already figured in administration by the middle of the fourth century B.C., when the *Mencius* was being composed. The practice is associated with the Qin reformer Shang Yang, who divided fields into a grid of equal plots by constructing a network of paths called *qian* and *mo*. This grid in theory produced equal units of land so that each household had identical holdings to provide their taxes and service, and they also fixed a standard unit for the allocation of rewards to those who earned merit in military service.[14] The Mencian model simply projected contemporary practices into antiquity.

While the *Mencius* insists on the rural character of the "well-field" and posits a separate mode of taxation for cities, other grids defined urban space, as discussed in chapter three.[15] Authors regularly linked grids in the country-side and those in the city.[16] A striking demonstration of this is the phrase "market-well (*shi jing*)." This identifies the market's structure with that of the Zhou field system in the *Mencius*. The phrase appears in the *Mencius* itself, and continues down through the Han.[17]

Thus, grids were a feature of life, both in cities and the countryside. Since the square of the four directions had long been basic to world structure, the application of grid-squares to world models was an easy step. There are references in late songs from the *Shi jing* to a division of the Shang world into nine sections, and the *Mencius* divides the area within the seas into "nine areas of ten thousand *li* square."[18] However, the first systematic development of this idea is the "Yu gong" chapter of the *Shang shu*. This chapter, which was almost certainly written in the Warring States period, traces the travels of Yu through the realm as he restores the rivers to their channels and thus rescues or, more accurately, recreates, China from the flood.[19] It will be discussed in detail in a companion volume on the flood mythology of China, so here I will only note that the "Yu gong" divided China into nine provinces, but did not organize the world as a mathematical grid. The provinces that Yu created were not fixed along geometric lines aligned with the cardinal directions and had no fixed, recurring dimensions. Instead the narrative is structured entirely according to the movements of Yu and the associated tribute, both of which took place along the rivers. Moreover, its nine provinces appear to be actual regions defined by geographic features and distinctive products. Although not all the mountains and rivers can be identified, it would at first seem to present a naturalistic account of the China of its day rather than a geometric model. Rather than being a grid, it was primarily a world model structured around the hierarchical movement of goods that converged on the ruler.

Converting the nine provinces of China into a grid, and inserting these in a series of numerically generated grids, was attributed to Zou Yan (c. 250 B.C.). He is known primarily from an account of his career in the *Shi ji*, which describes his methods as follows:

> He insisted that you first verified small things and then extended these through extrapolation, reaching to the infinite. He first ordered the chronological sequence back from the present day to the Yellow Emperor, things that were narrated by all scholars, and combined this with accounts of successive flourishing and decline. Following this he recorded their omens and [changes in] their institutions, pushed this ever further back through extrapolation, and traced them to their

source prior to the birth of Heaven and Earth, in the dark and fathomless that could not be examined.

This process of temporal extrapolation from the present day to the world's origins in undivided unity was followed by a parallel spatial operation:

> He first laid out the central kingdoms' famous mountains, great rivers, all-penetrating valleys, birds, beasts, what grew in the soil and water of each region, and what was precious among the different varieties. Following this he extrapolated, reaching beyond the seas to what people could not observe. He proclaimed that since Heaven and Earth had split apart, the Five Powers had moved in a cycle, that each period of order had the Power appropriate to it, and that [omens] responded like a tally to this. He thought that what the classicists called China occupied only one out of eighty-one parts of all under Heaven. China was called "the Divine Continent of the Red District." Within the Divine Continent of the Red District there were nine provinces, and these were the nine provinces put in order by Yu. They could not be counted as true continents [zhou 州]. Outside of China there were nine [actually eight] units like the Divine Continent of the Red District, and these were what should be called the nine continents. Then there were lesser seas circling them, so that no people, birds, or beasts could get from one to the other. Each region like this was one continent. There were nine of these, and then a great ocean circling outside all of them. This was where Heaven and Earth meet.[20]

Here the world is a full-blown grid. The nine provinces of Yu make up one zhou. Nine of these zhou in turn make up a single unit of a grid, which forms a single unit in a larger grid. This larger grid is ringed by the ocean, which is the true edge of the world, the point at which Heaven and Earth meet.

This also shows reasons for adopting the grid as a model of the world. The earlier reference to backward temporal extrapolation posits sequential divisions from a primal unity as fundamental to the emergence of the world. As noted earlier, the grid is a spatial image for such a process. What is novel here is the explicit appeal to the grid as *the* visual image of a potentially limitless extension based on a fundamental unit that retained a fixed and simple structure. Alexis de Toqueville observed that the grid was a clear and simple structure that could be reproduced endlessly to generate a city at whatever scale was desired without losing its internal order. This is the role assigned to the grid in Zou Yan's world. Yu's nine provinces are a first grid that forms one unit of a second grid of nine, which in turn forms a unit of a third. He stops the process at that point, but there is no inherent reason he could not have repeated it a fourth or fifth time. For a process of finding small units and then extrapolating them to infinity, the grid offered an ideal spatial mechanism.

The grid was not only useful for Zou Yan's purposes, but also a genuine result of extrapolating empirical observations. Both the fields and the cities of Zou Yan's world were structured in grids, and even the houses discussed in chapter two were based on the multiplication of recurring square units. With the idea that China consisted of nine units, and the tendency to visualize such an arrangement as a grid, the process of arguing from lesser to greater was already developed.[21] Fields and cities formed grids at the local level, and each of these formed a unit in the larger grid of China. To create a model of the entire world it was only necessary to repeat the process.

The appeal of the grid, as John Major has argued, also derived from the development of the magic square. Two cosmograms, the Luo Writing and the River Chart, lay out the two major orders of the Five Phases as a 3×3 grid. While the earliest reproductions of these date only from the Song, references to them and charts with similar organizations date back to the late Warring States or early Han.[22] More important, grid structures are a recurring feature of Han divinatory charts that were used to assign proper positions in time and space. Such charts included the *Xing-de* divinatory charts, the "Nine Palace" chart, the chart attributed to Yu for the disposal of the placenta, and the Tai Yi diviner's board discovered at Fuyang.[23] Thus, it is likely that at the end of the Warring States grids in the form of magic squares or related structures were used in the visual demonstration of the Five Phases cycles, which, according to Sima Qian, were crucial to Zou Yan's model of history.

While Sima Qian provides the longest account of Zou Yan's work, elements of it, and later Han developments, also appear in chapter four of the *Huainanzi*, the *Yan tie lun*, Wang Chong's *Lun heng*, and in the later apocryphal literature.[24] The *Huainanzi* chapter, which gives an account of the world, has been translated and analyzed by John Major. Here I will simply examine the significance of Zou Yan's model within the text.[25]

What most clearly affiliates the *Huainanzi* chapter with the writings of Zou Yan, rather than the "Yu gong," is that little of it deals with the topography of China. Instead it focuses on the model and attributes of the larger world. It includes both the great grid of Zou Yan and mythic realms filled with strange creature, as well as information on the mythic origins of animals, their relations to deities and the directional winds, and the processes that shape minerals in the bowels of the earth. Apart from two brief sections from the "Yu gong" dealing with the distinctive products of each region and with the rivers of China, the rest of the chapter derives from the writings of Zou Yan, traditions associated with the *Shan hai jing*, and the technical traditions transmitted by the masters of esoteric lore.[26]

The best example of the relation of this chapter to Zou Yan are as follows: Between Heaven and Earth there are nine continents and

eight extreme points. The land has nine mountains and the mountains have nine passes. As for wastes, there are nine marshes. There
are eight winds and six rivers. What is meant by "the nine continents"? In the southeast there is the Divine Continent, which is
called the land of agriculture.[27]

Since "Divine Continent" is the name given to China, the world described
here is Zou Yan's "Red District," that is, one of his nine large continents. This
is supported by the fact that, as Major has pointed out, the dimensions of the
area "within the four seas" would have been about nine times the area of the
China known in the early Han.[28] Thus, for unknown reasons the second stage
that produced eighty-one continents had been abandoned. It is worth noting
that even to provide accounts of the areas outside China proper, the authors
of the *Huainanzi* had been forced to appeal to traditions about strange creatures at the edges of the world, or myths of the axis mundi, Mt. Kunlun.
Filling in seventy-two more continents of the same scale with descriptions of
their inhabitants would have required extraordinary powers of invention, and
served no purpose. While a grid was easily multiplied for numerological purposes or to create a sense of a vast space, like the grids actually experienced
in life it remained devoid of content. Thus, the decision not to posit too many
continents made sense for someone trying to give a comprehensive account
of the world.

Another important feature is locating China in the southeast corner. It
is unclear whether this idea figured in the writings of Zou Yan, or whether
it was a later development, but it became the standard Han version.[29] There
are at least two reasons for this. First, the Qin and Han empires had largely
filled out the historical limits of China. They had reached the boundaries
formed by the ocean to the east and the south, and had come into increasing contact with the peoples of the grasslands to the north and those of
Central Asia to the northwest. Hence, it seemed that China was at the southeast corner of a great land mass, an idea that proved correct. Second, the
mythological prominence of Mt. Kunlun as an *axis mundi* to the northwest
of China made it persuasive to place that mountain at the center with China
thus shifted to the southeast corner.[30]

These two features, making China a small part of a greater whole and
placing it off center, deny the centrality of Chinese civilization. This feature
of Zou Yan's model became a major theme of debate in the Han. The model
was espoused by the *Huainanzi* and the apocryphal literature, but denounced
in the *Shi ji*, the *Yan tie lun*, and the *Lun heng*. Since those who espoused the
model largely took it for granted, we can best see the significance of the
debate in the writings that adopted the hostile position.

While not entirely negative, Sima Qian condemns Zou Yan's theories for
being "vast and absurd." The historian describes at length the honors heaped
on Zou Yan by ambitious rulers of his day, and contrasts this with the suffer-
ings of Confucius and Mencius. Unlike the latter two "square pegs put in

round holes," who refused to trim arguments to fit popular ideas, Zou Yan "toadied to contemporary custom and expediently went along with things."[31] Sima Qian thus attributed to Warring States times the same pattern that he found in the Han, where scholars and commanders of integrity—such as Ji An, Dong Zhongshu, Li Guang, and himself—found their careers blocked, while servile flatterers were honored and promoted.[32] At the end of his account, Sima Qian conceded that Zou Yan's complaisance may have been a tactic by which he could gain the sympathies of the rulers in order to then lead them to the true Way, but he never suggested that it actually achieved such a result.

While Sima Qian denounced Zou Yan for currying favor with his doctrines, he did not indicate why ambitious rulers of the late Warring States found this talk of vast historical cycles and huge continents so appealing. The answer to this is suggested in the brief chapter on Zou Yan in the *Yan tie lun*. This work, written some decades after Sima Qian's history, dramatizes a debate between those around Emperor Wu's minister, Sang Hongyang, and a group of classicist scholars. The former espouses an expansionist state funded by monopolies, while the scholars cite the classics to defend a quietist vision of a state aiming only to enhance the welfare of the peasantry. At one point the positions of the two sides are articulated through reference to Zou Yan. The spokesman for the court states:

> Master Zou detested the inability of the classicists and Mohists of the late Warring States to recognize the vastness of Heaven and Earth, and the far-ranging illumination achieved by the Way. They wanted to use one bend to expound the other nine twists, to cling to one corner and thereby understand the myriad aspects. This is like wanting to learn height and weight without straight edges and balances, or to recognize the round and square without compasses and carpenter's squares.

After a summary of Zou Yan's teachings that closely follows Sima Qian, the official concludes:

> The "Yu gong" also wrote of mountains and rivers, high and low places, plains and swamps, but it did not recognize the true dimensions of the great Way. Therefore Qin desired to reach to the nine continents and approach the great, outer sea, to shepherd the barbarians and bring the myriad states to its court. You scholars all cling to the petty worries of the agricultural fields and the obstinacy of the alleys, so you have not yet understood the truth about the world.

In response the scholars argued:

> Yao made Yu his master of works to level the water and soil, chop down trees as he followed the mountains, and bring order to the

nine provinces through establishing high and low. Zou Yan was not a sage. He created bizarre errors to delude the rulers and thereby get his theories accepted. This is what the *Spring and Autumn Annals* calls "a commoner dazzling the feudal lords." Confucius said, "Not yet being able to serve men, how can one serve spirits?" Not having understood what is near, how can one know about the great sea at the edge of the world? Therefore the gentleman does nothing that is not directly useful and follows no path that does not benefit public order. The Three Kings believed in the canonical Way and their virtue illumined all within the seas. Warring States rulers believed in pleasing words and their destruction befouled the mountains. Formerly the First Emperor had already swallowed up the known world, but in desiring to conquer the myriad states he lost his own thirty-six commanderies, and in wanting to reach the outer sea, he lost his own provinces and districts. To know such great "truths" is not as good as holding to one's own petty calculations.[33]

The dispute contains at least three issues. First, the government spokesman adopts the doctrine of the superiority of whole to part, and of an encompassing intellect to the partial, biased mind of the commoner. The world of classical antiquity, as epitomized by the "Yu gong," is the limited horizon of a superseded age. What had been wisdom for the Shang or Zhou was revealed by Zou Yan to be identical with the error of the frog in the well. Scholars who still defended such antiquated wisdom are dismissed for the conservatism and limited vision that characterizes a peasant or a pauper. Second, since the wisdom of antiquity was inferior to that attained in the Warring States, the most authoritative texts would be the more recent ones that reflected expanding knowledge of the world. Third, more recent ages were not only more knowledgeable than antiquity, and their writings thus superior, but their power and glory surpassed that of earlier ages because of their greater geographic range. Thus, Zou Yan's theory, with its revelation that what the classics had treated as the whole was only one part out of eighty-one, implied the intellectual, textual, and political superiority of the Warring States and the early empires to the world of antiquity and its classics.

The scholars' rebuttal attacks these very points. It asserts the exemplary nature of the earlier rulers as sages, and cites the authority of the classics and their putative editor/author, Confucius. It dismisses Zou Yan by classifying him under a negative rubric from the *Spring and Autumn Annals*, and refutes him with a quotation from the supposed author of that text. In the same way, Sima Qian had attacked Zou Yan precisely for being "uncanonical (*bu jing*)" and contrasted him with Confucius. The rebuttal ends by proving the superiority of earlier dynasties to Qin through contrasting the longevity of the former to the rapid and total destruction of the latter. Encoded within the acceptance or rejection of Zou Yan, as depicted in the *Yan tie lun*, were two rival theories of history, models of intellectual authority, and ideas about the nature of the state. To accept Zou Yan was to adopt an evolutionary model of history, recognize the superiority of recent writings, and display a positive attitude toward the expansionist model of the state that emerged in the Warring States. While not all these positions will be found in every supporter or critic of Zou Yan's grids, the debate in the *Yan tie lun* lays out the fullest range of meanings attributed to his model in the Han. Some of these themes are developed in the writings of Wang Chong:

Zou Yan's writings say that under Heaven there are nine continents. The nine provinces in the "Yu gong" are what he would call a single continent. Above those in the "Yu gong" there are nine of them. The nine provinces in the "Yu gong" are the nine provinces of the currently known world. They are in the southeast corner and are called "Divine Continent of the Red District." There are a further eight continents, each of which is surrounded by four seas. These are called the "lesser seas." Beyond the nine continents there is a further "great sea."

These words are bizarre. Those who hear them are startled and frightened, but they cannot ascertain whether or not they are accurate. So they pass them around, reading them and repeating them as a topic of conversation. Thus error and truth are transmitted together, and the true and false are not separated. Men of the present age are deluded by them, so I will assess and criticize them.

I say that Master Zou's knowledge was less than that of Yu. When Yu mastered the flood, he was assisted by Yi. Yu was in charge of controlling the waters, and Yi was in charge of recording all things. They reached to the full width of Heaven and exhausted the length of the earth. They distinguished what lay beyond the Four Seas, and reached the limits of the outer edges of the Four Mountains. Of the territory of the thirty-five states [the sorts of materials in the *Shan hai jing*], the birds, beasts, grasses, trees, metals, stones, waters, and soils, there was nothing they did not record. But they say nothing about there being a further nine continents. The king of Huainan, Liu An, gathered masters of technical traditions such as Wu Bei and Zuo Wu, so they filled his palaces and halls. They wrote a text on the techniques of the Way, and assessed the affairs of all under Heaven. The chapter "Shape of the Earth" told of unusual species of objects and the uncanny things from foreign lands. It listed the marvels of the thirty-five states, but it said nothing about there being a further nine continents.

The travels of Master Zou did not match those of Yu and Yi. His experience did not surpass that of [Wu] Bei and [Zuo] Wu. He did not have the talents of a sage. Facts are not revealed by Heaven, so how did he obtain such knowledge? Using Yu's *Canon of the Mountains* and the *Huainanzi*'s "Shape of the Earth" chapter to examine Master Zou's writings, we know that these last are false and reckless.[34]

Again it argues for the superiority of the ancient sages and canonical texts over recent scholars. This is followed with a reference to the *Huainanzi*, but, as discussed in note 28, Wang Chong misunderstood this text, which accepts Zou Yan's nine continents while omitting the second stage that generated eighty-one.[35] The issue is thus presented as a choice between the "Yu gong" and the writings of Zou Yan. Wang Chong defends the former on two grounds. First, its author is a sage, while Zou Yan is not. Second, for Wang Chong the "Yu gong" is a true record of actual observations made through extensive journeys. Here the debate between the two models becomes an element in Wang Chong's limited use of empirical evidence to criticize many of the beliefs of his day.

This reference to current beliefs raises another issue that is not explicitly mentioned by Wang Chong, but may be part of his argument. As several modern scholars have shown, the most direct Han heirs of Zou Yan's theories are the "apocryphal (*chen wei* 讖緯)" texts that emerged in the late Western Han and flourished in the Eastern Han. When Wang Chong states that Zou Yan's theories were widely transmitted in the world, this probably referred to the Han apocrypha. These writings were denounced by several writers whom Wang Chong admired, and he subjects them to fierce criticism, using the same adjectives as he applies to Zou Yan. In his denunciations Wang Chong associates the apocryphal literature with the technical traditions (marked by the graphs *gong* 工 and *ji* 伎 or 技) and with those who use numerology. These traditions are placed in opposition to the "classicists (*ru ya* 儒雅)."[36] Thus, the attack on Zou Yan, which was framed as a defense of the classicists and the ancient sages, also served in attacks on the technical traditions clustered around the mantic and divinatory arts.

Despite Wang Chong's dismissal of Zou Yan and his successors, he was not averse to using their ideas. While he defended the smaller model of the earth depicted in the "Yu gong" over the multicontinent theory of Zou Yan, he accepted the proposition that a larger geographic range was testimony to both greater power as well as cultural superiority. Specifically, he argued that the Han was greater than the Zhou because it had obtained tribute and submission from northern barbarians and states in Central Asia that were not even known to the Zhou. What had been alien territory had become China, and what had been the edges of the earth had become tributaries.[37] Thus, he applied the principles of Zou Yan's argument to his own argument for the superiority of the Han to earlier dynasties.[38]

Since Zou Yan's critics were defenders of the ancient textual heritage, it is not surprising that arguments supporting him appear in the works of rival traditions. While the *Huainanzi* was a synthesizing text, its intellectual foundations lay in the texts that were combined in the Han to form the Daoist tradition. Not only did the text itself begin with a chapter "Tracing the Way to Its Source" but individual chapters opened with accounts of cosmic origins, or descriptions of the all-encompassing nature of the Way. This literary topos was a distinguishing feature of texts in the Daoist tradition that either rejected the classical sages, or encompassed them in a vaster historical span.[39] The *Huainanzi* uses this strategy in its final chapter, where the texts of the *ru* canon and others are explained as the products of specific historical situations, whereas the *Huainanzi* includes all of space and time:

> The writings of Master Liu observe the images of Heaven and Earth, and comprehensively penetrate affairs from ancient times to the present. They assess affairs to establish institutions, and measure forms to apply what is suitable. They trace the heart of the Way back to its origins and unite the moral influences of the Three Dynasties in order to assemble all that is most vast. . . . Thereby they unite all under Heaven, bring order to all things, respond to changes, and comprehensively penetrate the classes and categories. They do not follow one established path, cling to the meaning of one corner, nor become trapped by entangling objects so they do not change with the times. Therefore applied to the ordinary they will not fill it up, but applied to all under Heaven they will leave no gap.[40]

This claim to the universality of the text, in contrast to all earlier ones, led to the decision to incorporate the more expansive cosmology of Zou Yan along with myths of Kunlun and the edges of the world. The rival world model of the "Yu gong" is incorporated as one element within a vaster picture.

The apocryphal literature is too diverse and fragmentary to allow any simple explanation for its adoption of the eighty-one continent grid. However, several features of these texts help to explain their choice of Zou Yan's version. First, like the *Huainanzi*, the apocrypha claim to include all time and space. Fragments of the *He tu kuo di xiang*, the apocryphal text from which survive the fullest versions of Zou Yan's grid, also include accounts of the primal energy, as well as the origin of Heaven and Earth. The fragments also echo the *Huainanzi* by incorporating elaborate descriptions of Mt. Kunlun and mountains at the edges of the world, and by dismissing the part of the world that had been regulated by Yu as a small fragment of the whole.[41] Thus, the authors of the apocryphal literature probably used Zou Yan's model for much the same reasons as did the writers of the *Huainanzi*.

Second, links between Zou Yan and the apocryphal texts are not limited to the world model. He was also credited with pioneering the Five Phases historical model.[42] While such ideas were not restricted to the apocryphal literature, they were highly developed therein. Chen Pan argued that the apocryphal literature ultimately derived from the writings of Zou Yan, as transmitted and distorted by the masters of esoteric techniques (*fang shi*) from the northeast of China where Zou Yan had originated. While this argument asserts undemonstrable links on the basis of vague categories, the hypothesis of some transmission of texts or ideas between the tradition of Zou Yan and that of the apocrypha is not implausible.[43] The links of the *fang shi*, often pursuers of immortality, with the *Huainanzi* and Liu An are reinforced by the existence of a set of "inner chapters" of the *Huainanzi* dealing with the attainment of immortality. The techniques transmitted in these chapters are identified as deriving from Zou Yan.[44]

In summary, the dispute over Zou Yan's model derived from two visions of the world. Those committed to the *ru* tradition treated the textual legacy of Zhou as the highest wisdom. Consequently their model of the world stayed within the limits set by the "Yu gong," that is, the world known when the canonical texts were being compiled. Similarly, their model of history stayed within the bonds defined by the presence of the sages. Those who rejected this tradition espoused a vaster world in which the China defined by Yu occupied only a small corner, and in which time extended back beyond the human sages to the beginnings of the cosmos. Zou Yan's work thus became a banner for those who treated the classical inheritance as the product of a limited time and space, which could be rejected as an ultimate authority through insistence on the vaster horizons provided by later models of the world and of history.

The theme of a larger world that eclipsed Yu's work was anticipated in the *Mu Tianzi zhuan*, probably composed in the fourth century B.C. and thus close in time to the "Yu gong." The first four chapters, which form the authentic core of the text, recount a fictional journey by King Mu of the Zhou (r. 956–918 B.C.) to the distant west and the tribute that he received from the peoples whom he met. As noted by Rémi Mathieu, this account of a journey to the ends of the earth "reflects a Chinese attempt to take possession of the whole earth, and raises the question of the control that a sovereign and his court may exercise over all people under the skies."[45] As a narrative of taking possession of the earth through making a journey, this text has clear thematic links with the account in the "Yu gong."

However, the relation of the tale of King Mu to accounts of Yu is closer than linked themes of voyage, tribute, and world domination. As several scholars, notably Deborah Porter, have pointed out, there are numerous echoes between the two texts.[46] Most prominent are their geographic overlap. Not only are numerous placenames mentioned in both texts, but the two kings visit several of the same places. Moreover, King Mu witnesses the physical traces of figures in the Yu story, and some of these appear in his dreams. As both Porter and Mathieu have suggested, the story of King Mu was formed through the transposition of mythological themes and traditions into a fictional romance set within a mock historical framework. The most important of the myths that formed the tale of King Mu and his journey were those devoted to Yu and his taming of the flood.[47]

While the account of King Mu draws on tales of Yu, it does so in order to surpass them. Just as the eighty-one continents of Zou Yan dwarfed the nine-continent world of Yu, so the realms visited by King Mu went far beyond the confines set by his predecessor. This is clearest in the use of the mythology of Kunlun. In the "Yu gong," Kunlun is one of three ranges of mountains in the far west whose tribesmen sent in tribute of felt and skins.[48] In the tale of King Mu, however, it becomes a promised land at the edge of the world that is announced to the king by the god of the Yellow River as the culmination of an elaborate sacrificial ritual. When King Mu arrives at Kunlun, he rests at its foot for three days, the period of purification before performing a major ritual, and begins his ascent on an auspicious day. He views the palace of the Yellow Emperor and erects a mound on the tomb of Fenglong, usually described as a god of thunder. He ascends Mt. Zhong, which he declares to be the highest in the world, and views the wildernesses at the four edges of the world. King Mu then finds a land of pure water, mild climate, and no winds that the former kings called the "Suspended Garden." In other texts from the late Warring States and early Han this is linked with Kunlun as a site at the western edge of the world where the sun sets, the earth meets the sky, or one ascends to immortality.[49]

He then journeys westward to the country of the Queen Mother of the West (xiwangmu). The significance of this figure in the Mu Tianzi zhuan has been the topic of much debate. By the late Warring States she is an immortal who lived at the western edge of the world, usually on Mt. Kunlun. Scholars have noted that in the Bamboo Annals a "Xiwangmu" offered tribute both to Shun and King Mu, who lived thousands of years apart. They conclude that it was originally the name of a state or people, probably transcribing a non-Chinese word. The mythical "Queen Mother" would then have been invented by later readers who attributed a sense to a purely phonetic transcription. These scholars have concluded that the "Xiwangmu" in the story of King Mu is simply another tribal chieftain.[50]

However, in the Mu Tianzi zhuan Xiwangmu is already the immortal woman living on Mt. Kunlun. Links between accounts of the Queen Mother and the figure in the story of King Mu are discussed by Deborah Porter, who has shown how terms applied to her and her role in the story tie her to the solar mythology of Kunlun, as well as with the myths of Yu.[51] I will add a few points. First, the Queen Mother is linked to Kunlun. Not only is she geographically close, but the narratives of the ascent of the mountain and the banquet with the Queen Mother follow an identical pattern. Each begins on an auspicious day and concludes with the erection of an inscription on a mountain peak. Moreover, the day for receiving the Queen Mother is a jia zi day, that is, the beginning of a cycle.[52] This shows her pivotal role in the narrative, distinguishes her from mere tribal chieftains, and through the association with Kunlun identifies her as the deity described in other late Warring States and Han texts.

More important, the Queen Mother is distinguished from other chieftains by her exchange of verses with King Mu. Moreover, their content derives from the myths of the Queen Mother of the West. In her first poem the Queen Mother offers King Mu immortality, one of her classic functions in Han myth. Furthermore, the name of the place where the poems are exchanged is closely related to a name for the store of saliva under the tongue that vitalized the body in breathing exercises.[53] Finally, in the exchange of poems the Queen Mother calls on King Mu to return, the latter indicates his resolve to return to China to govern his people, and the Queen Mother declares her sorrow while chiding him for granting more importance to mere commoners than a daughter of God-on-High.[54] This shows that the Queen Mother is a divine woman, links the story with later narratives of encounters between the goddess and rulers such as Emperor Wu of the Han, and indicates a romantic element to the story that links it with an account in a later chapter of King Mu's love for a concubine who died young.[55]

Introducing Kunlun as an *axis mundi* and the Queen Mother of the West as a divine spirit draws the *Mu Tianzi zhuan*, otherwise closely linked to the "Yu gong," into a greater spatial range. Like the cosmography of Zou Yan, the romance of King Mu with his voyage to Kunlun to encounter the goddess went beyond the limits of China in the canonical model, portraying a vast world of which reports had been heard in the late Warring States. These two versions of transcending the "Yu gong" came together in the *Huainanzi*'s model that combined Zou Yan's grid with accounts of Kunlun and its environs to depict a world within which the petty nine continents of Yu were completely absorbed.

These models of a vast world lost influence after the Han and were eclipsed by the infinite universes of Buddhism. Thus, the resurgence of Confucianism after the Tang was marked by what Wolfgang Bauer described as "the shrinkage of the world."[56] The works of Zou Yan, which had been so influential in the Han, were largely forgotten. Only the name "Divine Continent of the Red District" survived as a literary name for China.[57] However, even at the end of imperial China the name still contained traces of the challenge that it had once presented to the vision of a China spatially defined by the Zhou classics. When early in the twentieth century Liang Qichao in exile wrote an account of the first three decades of his life, he began by locating his natal village in the extreme southeast corner of "the Divine Continent of the Red District." In doing this he displayed his knowledge of the *Shi ji*, of which he claimed to be able to recite eighty or ninety percent from memory. However, he also signaled his modern recognition that China indeed occupied only the southeast corner of a great land mass that was itself only one continent among many.[58]

THE BRIGHT HALL AND RULER-CENTERED MODELS

Another world model that sometimes was a grid, but one so important as to require separate treatment, was the "Bright Hall (*ming tang* 明堂)."[59] According to Han texts, the Bright Hall was a ritual building or palace that imitated the structure of the cosmos, and through which the ruler enacted the cycle of the seasons. Although accounts varied, they generally agreed that the building was a grid in which the rooms corresponded to the months of the year. It was thus related to the "monthly ordinances" in which the emperor changed his dwelling, costume, and every aspect of his life and government in association with the passage of the seasons. Here I focus on the spatial aspects of the Bright Hall as a cosmic chart, but the temporal aspect will also require discussion.

Before examining texts about the Bright Hall, it is useful to consider early images and charts that are related to the idea of a directionally oriented ritual building complex that served as both a chart of the cosmos and a theater for enacting the cycle of the seasons.[60] The earliest image, which has no accompanying text or contemporary references to explain it, is on the lid of a lacquerware vessel found in a fifth-century B.C. tomb.[61] Although the lid is damaged, enough survives to show that it depicted a circle, marked as water by an intertwining braid pattern, ringing a set of four rectangular buildings that in turn surrounded a circular shape enclosing three animals that form a ring by swallowing each other's tails. This inner complex of buildings forms a *ya* shape (亞). Each of the buildings has three chambers, some with window frames and some with paired human figures. Each space between the buildings is occupied by a tree. With its alternation of circles and squares to symbolize Heaven and Earth, its four buildings and twelve rooms to symbolize the seasons and months, and its round central structure, this fits closely with textual accounts of the Bright Hall. Since none of these are as early as the illustration, this is valuable evidence indicating the existence of ritual structures related to the Bright Hall as early as the fifth century B.C., that is, the early Warring States period. This also indicates that the model of the cosmos depicted in the Bright Hall had been established by this period.

A second Warring States object with links to the Bright Hall and monthly ordinances is the famous Chu silk manuscript.[62] Although this text was stolen from a tomb, the tomb was later systematically excavated and dated to the middle of the Warring States period.[63] Around the edge of the square silk there are twelve strange figures, largely human-animal hybrids, distributed three on each side. To the side of each figure there is a three-character label of its name. Since the first character of each name is one of the twelve months recorded in the *Er ya*, Li Xueqin argued that they represent the gods of the months.[64] Each god is accompanied by a brief passage describing what one should and should not do in that month. As the instructions are addressed exclusively to the ruler, the document clearly anticipates the "monthly ordinances" texts.[65] At each corner there is a tree of a different color, reminiscent of the four trees that separated the buildings on the lacquerware lid.

In the center there are two passages of text that read in opposite directions. One tells the story of the creation of the world out of primal chaos by Fu Xi, his wife, and their four sons. They first fixed the proper order of the mountains and the waters, and then the celestial lights. Following this, the directional spirits or the sons paced out the four seasons. At this time there was no sun or moon, and the seasons remain fixed only by the pacing of footsteps. When Heaven fell off balance it obscured the five trees that corresponded to the Five Phases. These are presumably the trees depicted on the manuscript's edges. Then the Fiery Emperor commanded Zhurong, another fire deity and divine ancestor of the Chu ruling house, to lead the spirits of the four seasons to restore the Heavens. At this point the seasons fixed by the movement of the sun, moon, and stars came into existence.[66] This account forms a cosmogony in which the establishment of space with its four directions precedes and makes possible the introduction of time with its four seasons and Five Phases. This cosmogony figures in the illustration, with its four sides corresponding to the four directions and seasons, and its trees indicating the Five Phases (assuming that a central tree mentioned in the narrative should be found in the place where the two passages are located). The final establishment of order in the world is credited to the ancestor of Chu, where the manuscript was presumably created.

The second passage reads in the opposite direction, probably to indicate that the passages form a cycle like the months and seasons in the outer illustrations and in the narrative. This text is longer than the other and deals with astral phenomena in a seasonal context. Although the relation of the two is disputed, this seems to follow the other passage, for it deals with the situation established in the earlier cosmogony. The first section discusses how the moon, which appeared only near the end of the cosmogony, must follow a fixed pace. If it is too quick or too slow then the normal attributes of the seasons would be lost. Moreover, all the asterisms would lose their order, and calamities—such as the fall of comets, the collapse of mountains, the death of vegetation, the descent of untimely frost and snow, and the outbreak of wars—would take place. The second section speaks of the Sui cycle and the need of people to match their actions with the cycle to avoid Heaven's punishment. The passage concludes that people must make regular seasonal offerings to Heaven, Earth, the mountains, and the rivers. Failure to offer sacrifices, like the failure to observe the taboos, will result in disaster.[67]

While clearly not a Bright Hall, as it represents no building, it anticipates the square distribution of the months—in the form of the gods—around a central structure formed by textual passages that are cyclical if not circular. A closely related textual structure was the "Dark Palace Chart" that probably took the form of four textual passages corresponding to the directions and seasons around a block of text in the center to form a ya 亞 shape. As a chart and a calendar, it stipulated a set of seasonal taboos and ritual observances to be held within the Dark Palace. While the chart was lost, the title of the chapter in the *Guanzi* "You guan 幼官" is probably a corruption due to graphic resemblance of "Xuan gong 玄宮" that is discussed at length in the chapter. An accompanying notation assigns each section of the text to a specific location, and on the basis of these Wang Tingfang and Guo Moruo produced a hypothetical reconstruction of the original chart.[68] Other scholars have proposed alternative reconstructions that vary in important details, but all agree on the overall structure in five blocks aligned with the four directions and the center.[69]

Thus, both the structure and the function of this complex were closely related to the Bright Hall as described in late Warring States and Han textual accounts. Moreover, the names "Dark Palace" and "Bright Hall" were clearly coined in relation to one another. The name "Dark Palace" figures in several late Warring States texts, but we do not know if the building mentioned was identical with the one sketched in the *Guanzi*. Only in the *Lü shi chun qiu*, where the emperor dwells in the "Bright Hall" in the summer and the "Dark Hall" in the winter can we see a clear link between the two terms as parts of a cosmic chart that laid out the calendar in space.[70] As for the "Xuan gong" chapter of the *Guanzi* and its associated chart, Rickett argues that the calendar portion of the chapter was composed sometime between the middle of the third century B.C. and middle of the second century B.C. He believes that it was reorganized as a chart only in the middle or later years of the Western Han, when the construction of "River Charts" based on magic squares became popular.[71] In conclusion, it appears that the "Dark Palace" and the "Bright Hall" emerged at roughly the same time as closely related models of the world linked to calendrical systems. The Bright Hall was probably somewhat earlier.[72]

From the late Warring States through the Han dynasty several accounts, most quite brief, described the structure and uses of the Bright Hall. Occasional references also invoked features of this structure to support an argument. One of the most widespread early accounts describes a great assembly of peoples held at the Bright Hall under the Duke of Zhou following the building of the new Zhou capital at Luoyang. These accounts demonstrate certain key points of the Bright Hall as a spatial model. One cluster of misplaced slips now found in the "Kang gao" chapter of the *Shang shu* describes the time and place of the assembly, and lists its participants, but it does not refer to the Bright Hall.[73] Three texts recount the assembly: the chapter "Ming tang wei" in the *Li ji*, and the chapters "Ming tang" and "Wang hui" in the *Yi Zhou shu*. The second of these is almost certainly a later forgery that incorporates the earlier *Li ji* chapter or some common source.[74] It consequently merits no separate discussion, but can be used to suggest alternative readings or as a supplement to the "Ming tang wei."

The title "Ming tang wei" means "Positions at the Bright Hall," and the opening section describes the positions assumed by the participants in the assembly staged by the Duke of Zhou:

> Long ago the Duke of Zhou brought the feudal lords to court in their positions at the Bright Hall. The Son of Heaven stood facing south with his back to an axe-embroidered screen. The Three Dukes stood facing north in front of the central steps. [Among them] east was the superior position. The positions of the marquises was to stand

facing west at the east of the eastern steps. North was the superior position. As for the states of the earls, they stood facing east at the west of the western steps. North was the superior position. As for the states of the counts, they stood facing north to the east of the gate. East was the superior position. As for the states of the barons, they stood facing north to the west of the gate. East was the superior position. As for the states of the nine eastern barbarians, they stood facing west outside the eastern gate. North was the superior position. As for the states of the eight southern barbarians, they stood facing north outside the southern gate. East was the superior position. As for the states of six western barbarians, they stood facing east outside the western gate. South was the superior position. As for the states of the five northern barbarians, they stood facing south outside the northern gate. East was the superior position. As for the states of the nine *cai* [采] and the four *sai* [塞, literally "passes," i.e., those from the edges of the world], who came to report only once in a lifetime, they stood facing north outside the Ying Gate. East was the superior position. These are the positions of the Duke of Zhou's Bright Hall. The Bright Hall illumines [*ming* 明] the relative status of all the nobility. He instituted ritual and created music, promulgated degrees and measures, and so all under Heaven completely submitted. The myriad states each sent in the characteristic offerings of their region.[75]

This tells us nothing of the building, except for references to at least two levels of platforms and a set of gates.[76] Instead it arranges people around the hall to map out the relations that formed the Zhou realm. The king is the center of the realm, and the rest are grouped in concentric squares around him with the extent of physical separation marking their closeness. The barbarian peoples are outside the gates, indicating that the walls of the compound symbolized the limits of the Zhou realm.

The structure here has no relation to more influential accounts in which the Bright Hall was a cosmic chart where the ruler enacted the "monthly ordinances." Instead it more closely resembles the temple-palace compounds found at Shang-Zhou archaeological sites and recorded in early texts.[77] Indeed the chapter later explicitly identifies the structure with the Zhou ancestral temple.[78] Moreover, several passages in the *Li ji* state that one held sacrifices in the Bright Hall to instruct the people or the feudal lords in filial piety. This would make sense only if the sacrifices in question were offered to ancestors.[79] The *Huainanzi* states that the Duke of Zhou sacrificed to King Wu in the Bright Hall, and the *Han shu* says that he sacrificed there to King Wen.[80] This identification of the Bright Hall with ancestral spirits is strengthened by the fact that funerary implements were known as *ming qi*, literally "bright implements." Moreover spirits were sometimes called "spirit brightnesses (*shen ming*)," particularly the spirits to whom one sacrificed.[81] Classicist scholars of the Warring States reinterpreted this Zhou temple, like the Zhou state itself, as an ideal, a potent structure that had existed once and could be constructed again by a ruler who restored the way of the sages.[82] The Bright Hall as an ancestral temple figured also in synthetic Han accounts that emphasized its all-encompassing nature.

The Bright Hall also appears as the Zhou ancestral temple in the "Art of Rulership" chapter of the *Huainanzi*, but here it is the site not only of ancestral rites but of a comprehensive model of history that underpins sage rule. Early in the chapter an account of the primitive paradise under Shen Nong relates that the assessment of the year's accomplishments culminated with seasonal sacrifices in the Bright Hall. This building is described as a simple structure that had no walls but that remained impervious to the elements due to the ruler's virtue and justice. Near the end of the chapter the building reappears in a celebration of the virtues of the Zhou conquerors and their beneficent rule:

> King Wen comprehensively examined the successes and failures [of rulers] and completely inspected their rights and wrongs. The reasons that Yao and Shun prospered while Jie and Zhou perished were all recorded in the Bright Hall. Thereby they simplified their wisdom while broadening their learning, so that they could respond to that which had no fixed category [i.e., the new and unprecedented]. Viewed in this way, the wisdom of the sages is round [i.e., complete yet always moving].
>
> Kings Cheng and Kang carried on the inheritance of Wen and Wu, and preserved the institution of the Bright Hall. They observed the historical traces of preservation or destruction, and looked at the alternation between success and failure. They said nothing that was not according to the Way and did nothing not according to duty. Their words were never carelessly spoken nor their actions carelessly done. They selected what was good and then devoted themselves to it. Viewed in this way, the actions of the sages are square [i.e., moral].[83]

Here the Bright Hall is the site of both an ancestral genealogy and a comprehensive history. The entire political past is preserved in the temple and provides the basis of Zhou wisdom. This temple in turn becomes the dynastic inheritance of those who extend the history through their own record of events. Moreover, the pairing of round and square structures here becomes a chart of the attributes of kingship.

Other texts treat the Bright Hall not as a temple but as a microcosm in which the ruler acts in accord with seasonal alternations. Most important in this category are the "monthly ordinances" in the first twelve chapters of the *Lü shi chun qiu*, the "Yue ling" chapter of *Li ji*, and the fifth chapter of the *Huainanzi*. In these texts, the Bright Hall consists of four buildings associated with the directions and a Grand Temple in the center. "Bright Hall" in the narrow sense also names the southern building that corresponds to summer, in contrast to the "Dark Hall" in the north that corresponds to winter. The ruler moves through the rooms following the sequence of the months, changing his clothes, regalia, diet, and policies in accord with the seasons. The spatial depiction of the state in a grand assembly plays no role. Instead the sole actor is the ruler, and space becomes a means of enacting the passage of time through the annual cycle in order to provide a natural sanction for the ruler's powers and policies.

By the early Han, traditions of the Bright Hall as ancient temple and as microcosm in which the year was ritually enacted had combined. The clearest evidence of this is a passage from the *Huainanzi*:

> In the past the policies and teachings of the Five Emperors and Three Kings invariably used "three" and "five." What is meant by "three" and "five"? They looked up to adopt images from Heaven and looked down to adopt measures from Earth. In the middle they took their models from men. They then established their courts in the Bright Hall and practiced the ordinances of the Bright Hall in order to balance the energies of *yin* and *yang* and to harmonize the rhythms of the four seasons . . . To investigate the sequence of the four seasons and their months in order to establish the rituals of senior and junior and complete the government offices is called "three." To institute the duties of prince and minister, the kinship of father and son, the distinction of husband and wife, the order of senior and junior, and the meetings of friends is called "five."[84]

The "courts" of the Bright Hall refer to ceremonies like those of the Duke of Zhou, while the "ordinances" denoted patterning government on the cycle of the seasons. The first of these is "five" because that was the number of the basic human relations, and the court assembly created a complete social order. The second was "three" because it patterned government on the triad of Heaven, Earth, and man. Thus the synthesis of the diverse traditions of the Bright Hall period availed itself of the numerological systems that had emerged to prominence by the late Warring States.

Several texts also described the physical appearance of the buildings. Probably the earliest and most important surviving text on the subject is a passage from the "Kao gong ji."[85] This gives the dimensions of the Bright Hall as part of constructing a capital. After specifying dimensions of the four walls based on the number nine, the three gates in each wall, the grid formed by nine streets running north–south and nine running east–west, and the dimensions for the streets, the text then describes the major ritual buildings. It names and gives dimensions for the ritual buildings of the Xia, Shang, and Zhou, and it is this last building that was called "Bright Hall." The units of measure appear archaic, and the only clear element of the structure is that it had "five rooms." Although scholars since the Han have attempted to construct models based on this account, these are largely speculation.[86]

In addition to this numerological model, several texts described features of the Bright Hall to justify philosophical positions. The Lü shi chun qiu states that in the Bright Hall metal objects were placed at the back, to show that virtuous power preceded military action; that the outer gate was never locked in order to teach people not to conceal things; and that the building had a thatched roof, pillars of artemisia, and three earthen steps, to demonstrate frugality. Versions of this last point appear in many Han texts.[87] These passages, which still treat the hall as a Zhou temple, adopted the idea that it was a microcosm that gave material form to principles of government or human virtues.

An important early Han description of the Bright Hall is the chapter "Ming tang" in the Da Dai li ji.[88] Having little coherence, it is probably a collection of all the bamboo strips on the topic obtained by Dai De in the first century B.C. Several of its ideas were well established: that the Bright Hall had a thatched roof, that it fixed hierarchy by positioning people around it, that barbarians were arrayed outside it, and that it was the Zhou ancestral temple. However, the Da Dai li ji also recorded several important new ideas. First, it is the earliest known text to state that the Bright Hall had nine rooms, forming a grid, rather than twelve rooms matching the months. The nine rooms form the basis of a numerological elaboration, for each room had four doors and eight windows to yield the magic numbers thirty-six and seventy-two.[89] There follow numbers that link the Bright Hall to the magic square of the "River Chart," but this passage may have been added only in the Age of Disunion.[90] Second, this is the earliest known text to state that the building had a square foundation to symbolize Earth and a round roof to symbolize Heaven. Third, for the first time it surrounds the Bright Hall with a body of water called the Piyong, which represented the ocean encircling the world. This water was depicted on the laquer lid, and it became a fundamental element of Han constructions of the Bright Hall.[91]

Another essay of probable Western Han origin is the "Li ji mingtang yin yang lu," preserved in fragments in the Taiping yu lan and the Sui shu. It maps the Bright Hall onto the sky as defined in the "five palaces" model.[92] Each building in the complex corresponds to a constellation, which in turn is identified as the palace of a god of the seasons or directions:

> The yin and yang of the Bright Hall is the means by which the king responds to Heaven. In creating a Bright Hall one encircles it with water that flows counter-clockwise as an image of Heaven. In the center was the Great Chamber as image of the Purple Palace. Projecting to the south was the Bright Hall as image of Taiwei. Projecting

to the west was the Comprehensive Pattern as image of Wuhuang. Projecting to the north was the Dark Hall as image of Yingshi. Projecting to the east was the Green Yang as image of Tianshi [Heavenly Market]. God-on-High and the Four Seasons each govern their own palace. The king receives [the pattern of] Heaven and controls all things.[93]

In moving through the Bright Hall the ruler assimilates the patterns of Heaven that he in turn imposes on Earth through directional and seasonal correlations. Similar models of a celestial palace system figure in other Han works, where it was used to establish a foundation in the structure of the Heavens for the newly created empire.[94] Thus, in this essay the Bright Hall provides an earthly chart of a celestial structure that in turn sanctioned the imperial state.

There were also several Han attempts to build a Bright Hall. The first was undertaken by Emperor Wu, who built a Bright Hall near Mt. Tai in association with performing the *feng* and *shan* sacrifices. The structure was built according to a chart that claimed to depict the Bright Hall as it had been constructed in the time of the Yellow Emperor:

> In the center of the "Bright Hall Chart" was a hall that had no walls on its four sides. It was covered with thatch and water flowed beside the wall encircling the compound. They made a raised, covered road with towers that entered from the southwest, and called it Kunlun. The Son of Heaven would enter from the southwest to bow and offer sacrifice to God-on-High. Thereupon Emperor Wu ordered the people of Fenggao to erect a Bright Hall next to the Fen River patterned on Dai's chart.
>
> When in the fifth year [of *yuan feng*, 106 B.C.] the *feng* sacrifice was renewed, then altars to the Grand Unity and the Five Directional Gods in the Bright Hall and the altar to Han Gaozu were placed facing them. They offered twenty *tai lao* sacrifices to the Empress Earth at a lower room. The Son of Heaven entered from the Kunlun road, and first made offerings at the Bright Hall in the manner of the suburban sacrifice. When the ceremony was completed the sacrifices were burned at the foot of the hall.[95]

Here the Bright Hall is a model of space. As the scene of sacrifices to the Directional Gods, the Grand Unity who ruled them (as depicted in the "Spirit Chart" from Mawangdui), and the Earth as correlate to the Grand Unity, it encompassed the world. This is also shown by the ring of water representing the ocean. This horizontal scheme gained a vertical dimension through sacrifices to the celestial God-on-High and through entry by means of a raised road that was named Kunlun. In the *Mu Tianzi zhuan* and the *Huainanzi* the Kunlun massif formed the avenue of ascent to Heaven. To ascend Kunlun and sacrifice at the Bright Hall was a preliminary to the ultimate climb to the summit of Mt. Tai to perform the supreme offerings to the highest god.[96] This model, with its attribution to the Yellow Emperor and its incorporation of the mythology of Kunlun, diverged from canonical models in a manner characteristic of Emperor Wu, but it had little impact on the later history of the Bright Hall.

A more important model for later periods was the Bright Hall constructed by Wang Mang. Some first-century B.C. texts—the "Mingtang yin yang lu" and the chapter in the Da Dai li ji—discussed constructing a Bright Hall as a means of ending natural calamities and restoring world order. These ideas were adopted by Wang Mang in his campaign to establish a dynasty.[97] Because he rose to power as regent of a child emperor, he adopted the model of the Duke of Zhou. The Bright Hall in its political role was identified with the Duke of Zhou, so Wang Mang staged a "spontaneous" reconstruction of the hall outside Chang'an in 4 A.D. Memorials calling for granting him titles and establishing a new dynasty cited construction of the Bright Hall to prove his sagehood.[98] Wang Mang also constructed a historical genealogy of earlier sages linked through the succession of Heaven's Mandate as guided by the Five Phases cycle. All previous rulers were mapped onto the movements of the ruler through the Bright Hall as specified in the monthly ordinances, each assigned to the quadrant of the phase under which he had governed.[99] This system synthesized all earlier readings of the Bright Hall. The building was a site of rituals to regulate society, an ancestral temple, and a theater of performances to enact both the sequence of the seasons and that of rulers through history. These two sequences were in turn linked by a common origin in the Five Phases. This grand synthesis of the Bright Hall is summarized in the Eastern Han doctrinal compilation, the Bo hu tong: "The Son of Heaven establishes the Bright Hall in order to communicate with the spirits, move Heaven and Earth, correct the four seasons, produce instruction and transformation, give a foundation to those of virtuous power, honor those who have the Way, make eminent those who are capable, and reward those of good conduct."[100]

Wang Mang's hall has been excavated, and reconstructions have been made.[101] While these vary considerably, and reflect much guesswork, some features are clear. First, the complex was constructed through alternating squares and circles that symbolized Heaven with Earth. It was surrounded by a circular moat, and a square wall with a gate at the center of each wall enclosed the main complex. This complex consisted of a circular platform on which was constructed a square, or more accurately a ya-shaped 亞 building. The building may have surrounded a circular structure, although this proposition is based largely on textual evidence from Cai Yong rather than the excavation itself. This pattern marks Wang Mang's Bright Hall as a model of the cosmos in which the ruler could enact the cycles of the seasons and of history, and where assemblies formed microcosms of the empire.

Based on the size of the stone foundations, it appears that the outside of the structure was only a single story high. There is no evidence of external or partition walls, which suggests that the areas were verandahs rather than rooms. This would conform to the argument previously noted that the Bright Hall had no walls on its four sides. On each side of a square-shaped central stamped earth foundation is a rectangle divided into three rooms. Since the stone foundations of these areas are larger than the other, it appears that this area was covered by two or more stories. These twelve rooms would have corresponded to the twelve months, as described in the textual accounts of the monthly ordinances. The southern side is distinctive in that its central room is much larger than the two side chambers. This indicates a southern orientation for the central building, which would accord with its function as a ceremonial hall for the emperor. Indeed the final passages in the *Da Dai li ji* chapter insist that the ruler holds his court at the south building and makes his entrance through the south door. Thus, the structure of Wang Mang's complex, which was intended as a synthesis of all earlier traditions about the Bright Hall, largely complied with the principles articulated in the textual accounts.

While the Bright Hall built in 4 A.D. brought together the ideas from earlier writings, the grand textual synthesis was Cai Yong's (A.D. 133–192) "Mingtang yue ling lun."[102] This includes discussions of history, terminology, function, and structure. It begins with the assertion that the Bright Hall is the temple where the Son of Heaven makes sacrifices to his ancestors in association with Heaven. After citing the canonical passage on the titles of the structure under earlier dynasties, it names the five buildings in the complex. "Bright Hall," it points out, is in the narrow sense only the name of the southern building, but, given the priority of the south, the whole complex is named for this component. After noting that in the temple the ruler follows the monthly ordinances to accord with Heaven, Cai Yong lists all the elements of social hierarchy that are established there. The teachings of the academies, he asserts, are all established in the Bright Hall, and officialdom is completed within it:

> It is like the North Star which occupies its own place while the masses of stars bow to it and the myriad celestial images [*xiang*] assist it. All government and teachings are produced from it, and all changes come from it. It makes clear (*ming*) the unification of the world, so it is called the Bright Hall. It is the greatest of human affairs and the most profound of all meanings. Named for the character of its ancestral sacrifices, it is called the "Pure Temple." Named for its central chamber it is called the "Great Temple." Named for its eminence, it is called "Great Chamber." Named for its facing towards the light [i.e., the south], it is called "Bright Hall." Named for the teachings at its four gates, it is called "Grand Academy." Named for being ringed on all sides by water that is round like a ritual jade *bi*, it is

named "Piyong." These are different names but the same affair, and in reality they are all one.[103]

The Bright Hall is a microcosm in which both cosmos and state are completely realized. It is a ritual complex that combines rites to ancestors and cosmic deities; an administrative center where all officials are gathered and all policies enacted; and an educational institution in which all true teachings are presented. It is also the summation of the ritual structures of earlier dynasties. As a chart of the cosmos, the source of order, and a summation of history, it becomes the perfect image of power.

The rest of the essay elaborates these themes, assembling quotes from the classics to demonstrate or reiterate the attributes of the Bright Hall.[104] It also cites many earlier discussions, noting its thatched roof, round top, and square bottom. At the end, Cai Yong discusses the dimensions of the buildings and the numbers of their doors and windows. Every number has a meaning that is explained by the author in terms of the symbolism of yin and yang, the hexagrams, the pitchpipes, the major constellations, the divisions of the year, and the structure of the world. Thus, the numbers that define the complex, like its structure and organization, mark it as the schematic embodiment of the cosmos, natural processes, and the social order.

The distinctive feature of the Bright Hall as a world model was placing the ruler at the center. In the monthly ordinances the ruler's movement paced out the cycle of the seasons, just as they had been paced out by the sons of Fu Xi in the Chu silk manuscript, while the ruler's conduct and policies linked natural phenomena to the human world. In accounts of the Bright Hall as the Grand Academy it was the ruler who was the source of teaching and his own family that was its first recipients. As a temple, the Bright Hall was the ruler's ancestral temple, so offerings to Heaven or other high gods were paired with those to the imperial ancestors. Finally, in the texts dealing with the "positions" in the Bright Hall, every element of human society was mapped out in terms of their closeness to the ruler.

This model where the ruler was the central point of a hierarchized spatial structure also figured in five-zone or nine-zone models of the world.[105] This model, which appeared first in the final section of the "Yu gong," divided the world into a series of zones of declining order and civility. These begin with the area under the ruler, that is, the capital region, then move through regions controlled by feudal lords, those occupied or pacified by the current dynasty, and finally those under barbarians. The magic numbers "five" and "nine," selected for their numerological value, were applied to more realistic accounts articulated by late Warring States political actors in which the world had been divided into the royal domain, the states of the feudal lords, and the territories of the barbarians.[106] The underlying principle of this model was thus the same as that of the "positions" of the Bright Hall, but the zones included the entire world rather than a microcosm created in the court assemblies.

Links between the two models were even closer. "Royal Assembly" in the *Yi zhou shu*, one of the earliest accounts of the assembly staged by the Duke of Zhou, incorporates the multizone model of the world into its account of the positions of the participants. After describing the positions and attire of the Duke of Zhou and the highest Zhou lords, it proceeds:

> On the inner platform facing west, with north as the most presti-gious position, were the Marquis of Ying [the king's younger brother], Cao Shu [the king's paternal uncle], the king's elder mater-nal uncle, and his middle maternal uncle. After that came the adja-cent [*bi* 比] zone, the controlled [*yao* 要] zone, and the wild [*huang* 荒] zone. On the west, facing east, with north as the most presti-gious position, were the rulers of the Ji-surnamed states [the surname of the Zhou house] and their sons. Beyond a square of one thou-sand *li* was the adjacent zone, beyond two thousand *li* was the con-trolled zone, beyond three thousand *li* was the wild zone.[107]

The assembly proceeds outward from the kin of the ruling house through zones of declining authority. This list of those who attended the court on the inside ends with those guarding the wall, followed by an account of the bar-barian tribes arrayed outside the walls in the directions from which they came, and of their exotic tribute.[108] The chapter concludes with a text attributed to Yi Yin of the Shang, which lists the sorts of items that were suitable for tribute by the people of each of the four directions.[109]

These accounts of tribute in the *Yi Zhou shu* highlight another feature of the multizone models of the world, in which the frequency of paying tribute and attending court is inversely proportional to the distance from the capital. As discussed in chapter four, some Warring States and Han texts listed the characteristic products of each region, and then stated that these diverse items all converged in the capital. The partiality of each region was thus marked by its production of a limited range of distinctive products, and the flow of tribute to the center transcended the limits of regional cultures by gathering all goods around the person of the ruler. This schema, in which all parts of the empire were equal in their partiality, underlay the accounts of the concentric zones. In these latter, however, the emphasis was not on the con-fluence of goods to form an all-encompassing whole, but rather the spatial hierarchy of the incorporated parts as marked by the frequency of their offerings.

The complementary roles of partiality and hierarchy is shown by the prac-tice of pairing the multizone model with the nine provinces of Yu. The nine provinces were distinguished by their distinctive regional products, but not ranked in terms of differential relations to the capital. The five-zone or nine-zone model introduced the ruler and his capital into this schema, marking their centrality through establishing a graded hierarchy moving from core to periphery. Thus, these multizone models combined the ruler-centered cosmos of the Bright Hall with the replicating grids of the "Yu gong" or of Zou Yan. The model of concentric zones of declining influence around the ruler also provided an implicit model for the schema noted in chapter four, in which the networks of the great families were described through graded lists that moved from close kin out to more distant allies and clients.

A final feature of the multizone models, one that they share with accounts of the positions at the Bright Hall, is the doubling of geography with social relations. This feature is best demonstrated by the two presentations of multizone models in the *Zhou li*. The first appears under the office of the "Master Administering the Quadrants." He controls the charts or maps (*tu*) of the world and uses them to divide up the territories, enumerate their contents, and thereby know their strong and weak points. The account of this office describes each of the "nine continents" with material drawn largely from the "Yu gong," and then lists the nine zones in order of increasing distance from the royal domain. The second list of zones appears under the office of the "Great Emissary," who is in charge of ceremonies for guests and periodic court assemblies. Whereas the list under the "Master Administering the Quadrants" noted only distances, this second list also notes the frequency of attendance at court imposed on each of the zones, and the type of objects that they had to present as tribute.[110] Thus, the ruler-centered, multizone schema is both a model of the physical divisions of the world, and also a dynamic chart of hierarchical social relations as marked in the content and frequency of the flow of tribute to the center. In the first version it is closely linked to the model of the Nine Continents, while in the second it is a variant of theories of the Bright Hall and the assemblies staged there.

MIRRORS, DIVINER'S BOARDS, AND OTHER COSMIC CHARTS

Another form of world model that was regularly employed in late Warring States and early imperial China was the decor patterns on TLV mirrors, diviner's boards, the *liu bo* game boards, and related objects. A "TLV mirror" is a loose term applied to several styles of mirror produced during the Han, although the classical examples date roughly from the time of Wang Mang through the middle of the Eastern Han. The name given them by Western scholars derives from their distinctive pattern formed from marks resembling the letters T, L, and V from the Latin alphabet.[111] The significance of this pattern and the relations of the various objects on which versions of it appear have been debated in many books and articles. Here I will discuss only evidence for its use as a world model.

The earliest accounts of the decoration of TLV mirrors argued that these objects were in some manner depictions of the cosmos. Thus, the first description in English by W. P. Yetts stated that the central boss signified the dome of Heaven's vault around the celestial pole and noted that the four symbolic animals clearly marked the square around the boss as a symbol of the earth.

He also pointed out the relation of the decor to the *liu bo* game board and gnomon chronometers of the period.[112] Schuyler Cammann argued that the pattern represented the universe as seen looking down from the palace of God-on-High. The central boss was again the center of the universe. The twelve lesser bosses formed a grid that divided the surface into nine squares modeled on the nine continents of Yu. They would also have corresponded to the months. The eight outer bosses represented the Eight Pillars of Heaven mentioned in several early texts. The central square represented the Middle Kingdom with the four Ts as its gates. The Vs and Ls represented, respectively, the boundaries of the four quarters of the world and barriers marking off the swamps or wastes at the edges of the world in the four cardinal directions. He also suggested a link between this cosmic schema and the Bright Hall, which had many of the same features. A. G. Bulling likewise suggested that the decor depicted the scheme of the universe, but that this scheme was patterned in part on buildings. According to her, the Ts, Ls, and Vs represented struts, brackets, and other architectural features. The Vs, however, also represented the cosmic mountains at the four corners of the universe, and the ring of chevrons around the outer edge was also read as mountains. The center represented the pole star, the palace of the ruler, or Kunlun.[113]

Hayashi Minao concurred that the pattern was clearly intended as a model of Heaven and Earth. However, he rejected almost all derivations from building techniques and canopies. Instead he argued that the four Ts that stood at the center of each side of the square earth were the four cardinal points, and that together they traced the lines of the two cosmic ropes that defined the structure of the earth in some early texts. The four Vs facing the corners of the square marked the corners of Heaven as described in the *Huainanzi*. As several scholars have since pointed out, these latter correspond to the "four hooks" also mentioned in the *Huainanzi*, and with the cords they form a "cord-hook" design that figures prominently in many Warring States and Han divinatory charts, cosmic models, and decorative patterns.[114] For the Ls, Hayashi strangely abandoned the cosmic program and identified them as representations of a device used by carpenters to trace straight lines.[115]

Michael Loewe, following an idea of Sidney Kaplan, argued that the pattern of the TLV mirror was derived from the Han diviner's board.[116] This object was composed of two pieces, one circular and the other square. The circular part fit into the square or was attached to it by a pivot. Two straight lines, one horizontal and one vertical, linked the center to the four sides of the square disk. Similarly, two diagonal lines linked the corners of the square. Both parts were bounded by written graphs, whose content varies from board to board. In one case the rim of both pieces was graduated with degree markings. In several examples, the seven stars of the Dipper were inscribed in the center. Thus, as Loewe and other scholars have pointed out, the diviner's board is also clearly an image of the cosmos. Indeed, a speaker in one Han text states that in using the board the diviner had to: "take Heaven and Earth as his models [*fa*] and the four seasons as his images [*xiang*], accord with benev-

olence and duty, divide the sticks to fix the hexagrams, and revolve the divining board on a correctly placed square base."[117] Several anecdotes on people
using the diviner's board also show that they had to examine current astral
phenomena to set the board properly and adjust their own position in relation to it.[118] In short, the diviner's board was a replica of Heaven and Earth
that allowed men to situate their place in relation to the dynamic trends of
the cosmos and thus obtain success in their affairs. Loewe argued that the
TLV mirror was a replica of the board that was permanently fixed in the most
auspicious position in order to secure the position of the owner in relation
to the cosmos. It was particularly important in funerary ritual, where it would
have secured the deceased a safe passage to an ideal existence in the hereafter.
This theory has found widespread acceptance and been cited as an established
fact by some scholars.[119]

However, others have pointed out problems with this argument. The most
extended critique appeared in a paper by K. E. Brashier. While the main
purpose of the paper was to point out the great importance attributed in
mirror inscriptions and other writings to the *metallic substance* of the mirrors,
he also devotes some pages to a discussion of previous scholars who had
focused entirely on questions of decor. In response to Loewe's hypothesis, he
follows other scholars in pointing out that the *liu bo* game board also has many
similarities to the TLV mirror. However, *liu bo* boards are mentioned in late
Warring States texts and have been found in the middle fourth-century B.C.
tomb from Yutaishan, the late fourth-century B.C. grave of the king of Zhongshan, two third-century B.C. Qin tombs at Shuihudi, and in several early Han
tombs.[120] The earliest known diviner's board, in contrast, was found in a tomb
dated 165 B.C. at Fuyang in Anhui.[121] Although other Han examples have
been found, and textual references hint at similar instruments in the third
century B.C., it would still be difficult to treat the later appearing diviner's
board as the source of all TLV-like patterns.[122] This is supported by the fact
that both the *liu bo* board and the TLV mirror have incorporated the signs
that resemble the Latin letters in similar formats, while the diviner's board has
no such marks.[123]

Brashier further challenges the emphasis of earlier scholars on decor. He
points out that mirrors given valued positions in burials, usually in the coffin
near the corpse's head, are not invariably TLV mirrors. A set of five mirrors
placed in a ring around the toad in the moon in a stone relief found in Ji'ning
county feature the joined-arc pattern rather than the TLV decor.[124] He also
points out that while earlier scholars have interpreted the mirror's roundness
as a demonstration of its cosmological character, in fact these mirrors had to
be round in order to maintain a convex surface that permitted the largest possible reflection to be captured in a small surface area. In addition, he notes,
the roundness of mirrors long predates the TLV pattern and any presumptive
cosmological referent.

While the last argument is weak, since it is the alternation of round and
square in the decor rather than the roundness of the mirror that is at issue,

to caution against exclusive focus on the TLV pattern to explain the significance of mirrors and insist on the importance of their metal substance are both important. The argument against privileging the diviner's board as the exemplary or original pattern from which all the others derive is also convincing. While the TLV mirrors, diviner's boards, *liu bo* boards, and various cosmic charts all share a common set of images and numerological tools, it is unlikely that any one of these objects was the source from which all the others derived.[125] Instead they are probably all products of a common mental universe or store of images that could be recombined in different manners to perform different intellectual or aesthetic functions.

So the essential tasks are to establish their common attributes, ascertain how these attributes relate to their use, and thus explain their popularity.[126] As to the first point, the crucial attributes of these objects could be summarized under the rubrics of totality, abstraction, enumeration, and dynamism. As to the second and third, they are primarily forms of securing power that work through transferring the attributes of the semidivine ruler or of the gods to the individual who used them.

The role of these objects in Warring States and Han society was similar to that of the numerological systems that rose to prominence in the same period: they allowed the representation and manipulation of potentially infinite phenomena with finite means.[127] As argued earlier, the superiority of whole to part and the equation of mastery with totality operated in Chinese conceptions of space just as in the intellectual realm. The body, the household, the city, and the region were ultimately inadequate because they were both limited and composite, fragments of a larger whole that were in turn divided against themselves. Even intellectual models of the world, such as the aforementioned grids and zones, achieved order only through maintaining divisions. The search for meaning, order, and power consisted of a constant attempt to move beyond the limits of these lesser units to an encompassing whole within which all the lesser units and their conflicting elements found a place.

However, any whole could dissolve into myriad particulars. Such a collapse found philosophic form in proto-Daoist cosmogonic accounts where creation through division led ultimately to corruption. It figured in the political world in the specter of the collapse of the imperial whole into warring bandit gangs. To forge a whole required a ruthless abstraction that stripped away distracting details to reveal structures, analyzed those structures into basic elements, and traced the patterns by which those elements operated. This was the key role of Warring States and Han numerology, which grouped all phenomena under numeric headings and explained their interactions through correspondences revealed by the mapping of one numbered group onto another that shared a common number. It also underlay astrology, in which patterns buried by the clutter of worldly objects became visible in the disembodied images of astral movements whose very distance allowed for abstraction and clarity.[128]

Clarity achieved by replacing concrete particulars with abstracted shapes and numbers was also the function of the world models constructed from circles, squares, cords, and hooks. Their geometric simplicity with clearly enumerable dots and lines brought the entirety of existence within a space that could fit comfortably in a human hand and be taken in at a single glance. Consequently it could be manipulated for the benefit of the user, who could situate himself within the schema generated in the chart. Thus an account of the use of a divining board at the end of the reign of Wang Mang states: "The astrologer placed the diviner's board in front and added in the positions of the sun and the season. Wang Mang then revolved his mat to sit in the position indicated by the handle of the Dipper [on the circular disk]. He stated, 'Since Heaven has produced virtuous power in me, what can the Han troops do to me?'"[129] Here the admittedly misguided ruler assumes that the guidance of the diviner's board allows him to place himself appropriately in the world so as to guarantee the continued support of Heaven.

To transform the world into charts, the early Chinese used numerological categories—the four directions, five positions (with the center), eight positions (with the intermediate directions), nine palaces (a grid), and twelve degrees—that could be mapped onto corresponding elements. Thus, the four directions were routinely associated with the seasons and the winds, and the eight positions were likewise associated with winds. The twelve degrees corresponded to the months and their gods, such as the figures on the Chu silk manuscript. In this way the charts brought their user into a proper relationship with virtually any phenomenon and directed his actions in all fields. Most commonly, they were used to select auspicious days, as in the *Xingde* texts and related astro-calendrical systems, but they were also applied in activities such as selecting the lucky direction in which to bury the afterbirth during a given month.[130] The links between abstraction and enumeration were particularly clear in early Chinese models that assigned numbers to the five positions or the nine-square grid, resulting in the hook-and-cord grids, magic squares, and the charts known as "River Chart" and "Luo Writing."[131]

This last point brings up the final feature of the charts, dynamism. Movement was central to the function of the objects, as in the circular disk which was rotated on the diviner's board, the pieces that moved across the *liu bo* board, or the TLV mirror, which, through the rings formed by the Twelve Branches in the inner square or the inscriptions in the outer ring, marked the surface as a visual expression of temporal process. This insistence on movement and process figures in related visual charts, such as the so-called *Xingde* charts from Mawangdui that map out astro-calendrical systems.[132] Usually the actual or implied mobility of these charts mapped temporal processes onto the structure of space, thereby achieving a complete cosmos.[133] The night sky was exemplary as a moving spatial structure that fixed temporal order. On earth the same role was played by the monsoon patterns that linked directions with seasons through the regular alternation of the winds.

The purpose of these charts and their manipulation, as stated earlier, was to secure power for their user, a power comparable to that of a ruler or a deity. The ruler was the image of a power that derived from mastering totality. This was demonstrated in all major forms of writing in which the ruler became the model of the philosopher, the subject and ordering principle of history, and the hermeneutic key to the origins and arrangement of poetic anthologies.[134] Similarly, Donald Harper has pointed out how the almanacs and astro-calendrical literature found in so many tombs show how the Warring States and Han elites applied in their own lives injunctions to act or avoid action that were a reduced version of the instructions and taboos prescribed for the ruler in the monthly ordinances.[135] In the same manner, the ruler was the model of the man who through situating himself within the order of the cosmos as revealed in charts could assure order in the world and generate his own power.

The classic example of the ruler's use of cosmic charts is the aforementioned Bright Hall. The Bright Hall, as noted in the case of Emperor Wu, was constructed according to charts, and the hall was itself a chart of the cosmos within which the ruler placed himself and guided his actions to accord with Heaven. Thus, the ruler's use of the Bright Hall paralleled the use of a diviner's board and, as we saw in the case of Wang Mang, the same figure could be linked to both charts. Indeed the Bright Hall with its alternation of round and square elements, its numerologically guided number of squares, its ring of water that is echoed in the cloud or wave pattern that forms the outer edge of most mirrors, and in some cases its sacred four trees at the corners, could be a pattern for or a three-dimensional realization of the decor of a TLV mirror. Some modern scholars, notably Schuyler Cammann and Hwang Ming-chorng, have argued that the Bright Hall was the model for the design on the *liu bo* boards and TLV mirrors.[136] While this argument is no more persuasive than the assertion that the pattern derived from the diviner's board, the close analogies and historical links between the Bright Hall and the cosmic charts show their derivation from a shared fund of ideas and images. This indicates that the charts were at least in part a mode of applying the royal model of power to the lives of other people.

In addition to the parallel between mirror decor and the structure of the Bright Hall previously sketched, uses of the ritual complex and the charts were similar. Just as the user of the charts aligned with the forces of the cosmos, so the ruler used the Bright Hall to bring his actions into accord with the processes of nature as dictated by the season. Each season in turn was linked to celestial processes through ties to a specific star. Not only was the Bright Hall the three-dimensional realization of the structures traced in the charts, boards, and mirrors, but the ruler's movements through the ritual complex was a temporal and spatial extension of the more limited movements that the user of a diviner's board or chart employed to adjust his own position to the patterns of Heaven and Earth.

Another link between the Bright Hall and cosmic charts was their shared prominence in the career of Wang Mang. Several scholars have pointed out

that this ruler's reign was the most likely period both for the emergence of
the classic TLV mirror decor and for the production of some of the finest
examples of the diviner's board.[137] Since Wang Mang built a Bright Hall as
part of the campaign to secure his rule, it is possible that the sudden prominence of the TLV mirror pattern, which was a schematic reproduction of the
major features of the ritual complex, was a means of dispersing the image or
idea of the Bright Hall throughout the elite.

Several mirror inscriptions praise the building of the Bright Hall:

> In the second year of the Shijianguo reign period the Xin Dynasty
> was honored. Decrees sent down great and numerous favors. Mer-
> chants devoted themselves to the marketplace and did not treat agri-
> cultural land as wealth. [Wang Mang] reconstructed the Piyong and
> put in order the schools with their officials [a reference to the impe-
> rial academy attached to the Bright Hall].[138]

Another inscription translated variously by Karlgren and Hwang Ming-chorng
appears on several mirrors in longer and shorter forms. The passage pertaining to the Bright Hall states: "The Xin Dynasty has erected the Piyong and
built the Bright Hall, where it arrayed the promoted scholars, the marquises,
and princes; along with the lines of generals, ministers, and common people.
The myriad dwellings of the students were to its north. Joy without end."[139]
Thus, the building of the Bright Hall by Wang Mang figured as a topic and
a justification for the casting of TLV mirrors during the decades of the Xin
dynasty.

Moreover, several concepts related to the Bright Hall also figure in
inscriptions from the Xin period. One inscription appeals to the animals of
the four directions to keep order throughout the four quadrants, that is, to
regulate space, and to cause yin and yang to flow in proper order, that is, to
regulate time and the order of the seasons.[140] These sacred animals of the four
directions appear regularly on the classic TLV mirrors, but the mastery of space
and harmonization of time by means of controlling the four directions and
their associated seasons was also central to the use of the Bright Hall.

Another inscription links the mirror to the barbarians from the four
directions:

> Master Wang [Mang] illumined the mirror and the barbarians of
> the four quadrants submitted. Greatly felicitate the Xin dynasty; its
> people are at peace. The barbarian captives are destroyed, and the
> world restored to order. Wind and rain come in time with the
> seasons, and the five grains ripen.[141]

As noted, texts related to the "Positions in the Bright Hall" all describe the
submission of the barbarians from the four edges of the earth and their
assumption of positions outside the four gates of the Bright Hall. Since the
building of a Bright Hall brings the barbarians from the four directions to

submit, this linking of the casting of the mirror with the same submission clearly associates the making of the mirror with the making of the Bright Hall.[142]

A rhyme in the *Huainanzi* also links mirrors with the Bright Hall, and surrounds both of these with the standard geometric images of the universe that define the cosmic charts: "He who wears the great circle of Heaven as his hat will take the great square of Earth as his shoes. He who mirrors the Great Purity perceives the Great Illumination. He who establishes the Great Peace [*tai ping*] stands in the Great Hall. He who is able to wander freely through pitch darkness will shine brilliant as the sun and moon."[143] The Eastern Han writer Gao You explains that this "Great Hall" is the Bright Hall. Thus, the combination of round and square that forms the cosmos combines with the radiant illumination of a mirror to culminate in the universal peace that is created and enacted in the Bright Hall.

This remark on the illumination of mirrors is significant, for it signals that mirrors in general, and not just those with TLV decor, are potent objects and potential cosmic charts. This is also shown by the fact that the mirrors placed within the coffin or at the head of the deceased in burials in the Eastern Han are not exclusively decorated with the TLV patterns. One pattern connected with the theme of illumination, both in decor and in inscriptions, is the so-called solar-brilliance mirror. This pattern has many attributes of the cosmic chart, with a circle in the center surrounded by two squares. It takes its name from an outer circle in the pattern of a starburst. In several cases the inscription also refers to the sun and its power to illumine, much like the passage in the *Huainanzi*. Thus, one inscription states, "Perceiving the light of the sun, the whole world is greatly illumined."[144]

These mirrors also often have stylized trees at the four corners, echoing the trees on the lacquer lid and the Chu silk manuscript. Other pre-Han mirrors also feature four trees regularly spaced to divide up the decor around the inner circle. As discussed in chapter three, trees linked the worlds of gods and men. Hwang Ming-chorng has collected material to demonstrate that sets of four sacred trees were used at early religious sites that evolved into the Bright Hall of the late Warring States and the Han. The trees in these decor patterns may well be playing such a cosmic role.[145]

If links between the chart patterns and the Bright Hall demonstrate how the former take on the powers of the ruler, accounts and depictions of the *liu bo* game show the links of the charts with the gods. This is clearest in early anecdotes collected by Yang Lien-sheng.[146] In these stories, ambitious mortals seek to play *liu bo* with spirits or celestial powers to obtain superhuman powers from them. In one *Shi ji* story, a Shang king had a statue made to represent a Heavenly spirit, and then played *liu bo* against it with one of the king's subjects making moves for the god. When the spirit was defeated, the king insulted it. In the *Han Feizi*, King Zhao of Qin ordered artisans to climb Mt. Hua and there make giant *bo* throwing sticks from the cores of trees. Afterward he wrote an inscription stating, "King Zhao once played *bo* against a

Heavenly spirit here." Finally a speaker in the *Zhanguo ce* tells of a "bold youth" who challenged the deity of an earth-god shrine to a game of *bo*. The stakes stipulated that if he should win he would borrow the god's power for three days, while if he lost the god could make him suffer. He made throws for the god with his left hand, throws for himself with his right, and won the match. He accordingly borrowed the god's power but did not return it. After three days the god went to seek him, and consequently the grove around the shrine withered and died.[147]

In a story from the *Feng su tong yi* that Yang Lien-sheng omitted, Han Emperor Wu played *bo* with an immortal at Mt. Tai, but the sticks that he cast were swallowed up in the rock. While the stakes of the game are not stated, Ying Shao linked this story directly to a tale in which at the top of Mt. Tai there was a metal box with jade strips that foretold people's lifespans. Emperor Wu, apparently while making his *feng* sacrifice in pursuit of immortality, drew out tallies indicating eighteen, but reversed them to read eighty-one and thus was able to live until he was eighty years old.[148] Since the issue discussed in this section of the *Feng su tong yi* is the folly of the emperor's pursuit of immortality, and the first story deals with the extension of lifespan through the manipulation of magic strips, it is likely that Ying Shao thought that the game of *liu bo* with the immortal was also about gaining immortality.

The last two stories show that the stake was magical power for the winner, but this is also suggested by other accounts. The king in the first story shot arrows into a leather sack filled with blood and said that he was "shooting Heaven." He was struck by lightning while hunting, so the *bo* game was clearly part of a struggle with celestial powers that the king lost. Similarly, climbing a mountain, a standard mode of communicating with spirits, and placing an inscription atop it was a means of claiming mastery over a state or the world. This is exemplified in the mountain inscriptions of the First Emperor, and in the *feng* and *shan* sacrifices of Emperor Wu that likewise became conflated in myth with *bo* games against spirits. Thus, in every case playing *bo* with a spirit was an attempt to gain its power to secure mastery in the world. This theme of playing *bo* with spirits also figures in Han tomb art and in later mirrors, although the examples that involve supernatural beings depict two immortals playing against one another, rather than against a mortal. Nevertheless the links in art of *liu bo* and immortals is significant in light of the story about Emperor Wu. It is also significant that many of these matches in art between immortals are depicted on mountain tops, as in the stories of Emperor Wu and King Zhao.[149] The relation between *liu bo* and immortality is also probably linked to the rise of immortals as the major motif in mirror decor in the last century of the Han.[150]

Since we have only vague ideas of how *liu bo* was played, it is unclear how it could secure power. In some texts *liu bo* is a method of divination, that is, a method of manipulating spirits to secure knowledge and power to be used for the benefit of the diviner or a client.[151] The casting of six rods in the games likewise echoed the divinatory use of the *Yi jing*, and in some depictions in Han art of immortals playing the game the rods form the visual equivalent of the hexagram *qian*. The discovery of dice at a tomb in Wangjiatai apparently for use in the generation of hexagrams shows that the casting of dice to move the pieces in *liu bo* also echoed elements of some forms of *Yi* divination.[152]

However, the clearest demonstration of the links of *liu bo* to divination comes from the Han tomb at Yinwan. Excavators there found a wooden document, the upper register of which was a replica of the roads of the *liu bo* board, while the bottom register contained five blocks of text. Each block consisted of nine lines of divinatory formulae dealing with different categories of concern: marriage, travel, illness, and so on. The top of the chart is inscribed "south," which shows a directional orientation linked to the structure of the world. The center of the chart is marked by the character *fang* 方, and the sixty pairs formed by the "Heavenly Stems" and "Earthly Branches" are distributed along the roads. At the top of the nine columns of formulae are nine characters that are virtually identical with those in a formula dealing with *liu bo* that is preserved in the post-Han *Xi jing za ji*. According to this anecdote, the formula was coined by a certain Xu Bochang (博昌, "propagator of [*liu*] *bo*") who lived in the middle of the second century B.C. The formula was "recited by all the children in the capital region."[153] This shows that the words of the formula were widely known, which would facilitate their use in divination by ordinary people as suggested by the Yinwan chart.

A series of articles by Chinese scholars has worked out the method of linking the *liu bo* chart to the formulae for divinatory purposes.[154] The method, as thus far established, is based on the use of the sexagenary cycle that is inscribed on the chart to identify specific days. By reciting the gambling formula while moving through the sixty-day cycle along the paths of the *liu bo* diagram as marked on the board, each day would be associated with one of the nine terms that headed the columns. The questioner would then select the topic of interest, which would establish which horizontal block of the text was to be consulted, and indicate a day, which would establish the vertical column. By consulting the formula where the two lines intersected, the questioner could find whether the given day was auspicious for the desired activity. Alternatively, he or she could establish all days within the next two-month period that would be propitious for a given activity. While the exact relation of this form of divination to the game remains unclear, it is certain that the chart and the terms used to obtain formulae derive from *liu bo*. It is also likely that the order of the sexagenary signs on the chart followed the same sequence along the paths as did the *liu bo* pieces. Thus, it seems that the movement of the *liu bo* pieces within the game, as dictated by casting rods or dice, followed a sequence either patterned on, or providing a pattern for, a system of divination.

Like other charts, *liu bo* depicted the structure of the cosmos as a means to attain power. Writing in the Wei dynasty immediately after the Han, Xue Xiaotong observed:

Wu Cao invented *bo*. Its origins are ancient! The two casting sticks
are an image of the illumination given by the sun and moon, and
twelve pieces an image of the movements of the twelve asterisms.
Next it takes as a pattern the movements of Heaven and Earth, and
imitates the waxing and waning of *yin* and *yang*. It manifests a total
mastery of all human affairs, and exhausts the subtle starting points
of all changes.[155]

This maps the game's elements onto the physical world, and treats it as an
image of natural processes. The playing of *liu bo* was thus like the diviner's
manipulation of his cosmic board, or the ruler's movements through the Bright
Hall. In every case, the actor created a microcosm of the universe, and then
acted so as to bring his actions in accord with that model.

Hwang Ming-chorng has suggested another aspect of *liu bo* that is linked
to the stories of games against heavenly spirits or immortals. On the T-shaped
banner from tomb no. 1 at Mawangdui two upside-down Ts mark the
entrance to the upper section with the sun(s), moon, cranes, and flying
dragons. The passage between the Ts is flanked by two leopards who seem to
guard it, as well as two seated figures. Another T at the bottom of the middle
section is also flanked by a pair of leopards. On this T stands a figure in an
ornate robe leaning on a staff, faced by two kneeling figures and followed by
three smaller figures in plain robes.[156] Scholars concur that the upper pair of
Ts represents the gateway to Heaven. Similarly, the figures standing on top
of the lower T are clearly the deceased and her servants, separated by the T
from the world of the living in which is depicted the funeral. In short, the
Ts on the banner mark the key transitions in the ascent of the soul, first from
the world of the living to that of the dead and then the entry into Heaven.[157]
This supports Schuyler Cammann, who in discussing the TLV pattern and the
Bright Hall had suggested that the four Ts ringing the central square represented the gates which figured so prominently in accounts of the great
assemblies.

This argument finds support in texts that describe tigers or leopards
guarding the gates of Heaven. Thus, the summoning of the spirit of the
deceased in the poem "Zhao hun" calls out: "O soul, come back! Do not
ascend to Heaven! Tigers and leopards at its nine gates will devour
people from below."[158] Moreover, the *Shan hai jing* states that the eight
gates to Kunlun, the link between Earth and Heaven, are guarded either by
the Kaiming beast or the god Lu Wu.[159] The former has a tiger's body with
nine human heads, and the latter a tiger's body with nine tails. In short, there
was a widespread tradition that the paths to Heaven were guarded by fierce
beasts.

Leopards also figure on the two earliest *liu bo* boards thus far discovered,
those from the tomb of the King of Zhongshan.[160] On one board a leopard
is enclosed in each of the Vs at the four corners. On the other a leopard
flanks every V and L. The remaining marks are framed by snakes. The eight
Ls and Vs that ring the edges in the TLV mirror and *liu bo* boards could well

stand for the eight *terrae ultimae* (*ba ji* 八極) that mark the edges of the earth in the *Huainanzi's* account of the world. According to this, each of these ultimate end points had a mountain that rose toward the sky, and also a gate through which clouds, rain, and wind entered the world to regulate the cycle of the seasons.[161]

The evidence suggests that the TLV marks on the mirrors and boards indicate the points of transition from one realm to the next. Consequently, the religious point of the game *liu bo* could well have been to secure passage from one state of existence to a higher one, like Emperor Wu trying to become an immortal, or the "bold youth" seeking to gain a god's powers. Similarly, the placement of mirrors directly above the head of the deceased, in the same position as the Mawangdui banner, could indicate that both objects sought to secure the passage of the dead person to a new existence within the tomb.[162] The chart patterns used in life for divination may in death have served to move the dead to a different state. The primarily horizontal layout of these charts would thus change into a vertical movement, indicated on the mirrors only in the raised bosses that stood for Heaven and the eight mountains that marked the endpoints of the earth. The mountains and Heaven that thus played a key role in these charts were also a major element of Warring States and Han models of the world.

MOUNTAINS AND WORLD MODELS

Thus far the discussion of mountains in early Chinese world models has been restricted to Kunlun. However, the chief world model built around mountains is the *Shan hai jing*, the "Classic of Mountains and Seas." More accurately, it is the first five chapters of this work that form the "Classic of Mountains (*shan jing*)." Most scholars agree that these five chapters form the original core of a work that evolved over several centuries during the Warring States and the Han.[163] The later sections, which present a vision of the world quite different from the core, consist of the "Classic of the Seas (*hai jing*)" and the "Classic of the Great Waste (or 'Wilderness' *da huang jing* 大荒經)." These are treated by some scholars as a single work and by others as two distinct strata. In addition to the *Shan jing*, some stone inscriptions devoted to mountain cults also suggest a world structured by mountain ranges.

The *Shan hai jing* has had a difficult classificatory history. It consists of 837 passages that are usually quite short, around forty characters on average.[164] Each entry describes one location, and these are grouped together on the basis of spatial proximity so that each chapter deals with a geographic area. The chapters together form a comprehensive account of the world. However, the sites discussed are never places where ordinary people dwell, but rather mountains and distant regions inhabited by strange races. Moreover, it deals only with the unusual or the monstrous. This includes strange creatures or plants—often hybrids of conventional ones—monstrous races, or divine beings. Thus, the world of the *Shan hai jing* is that of the interfaces between the animal, the human, and the divine.

As a result, such writers as Sima Qian and Ban Gu dismissed the work as nonsense. In the earliest catalogue of Chinese texts it was classified under the section "Calculations and [Mantic] Arts," under the subcategory of "Methods of Forms (*xing fa* 形法)." This category contains books on the physiognomy of men and animals, as well as early examples of what would evolve into the science of environmental influence known as *feng shui*. The classification thus indicates that the *Shan hai jing* was viewed as a manual for divination based on the physical shape of the world.[165] It may also reflect the fact that the text contains numerous accounts of natural prodigies and what they foretold.

In the twentieth century, the work was treated as a geography, a compendium of myths, an early ethnohistory, and a set of labels for lost illustrations. A large literature has also attempted to gloss the places mentioned with modern or historical names.[166] While all of these classifications are relevant to the work, none captures its basic nature, and none of the reconstructions of locations fit with observed topography. Indeed, they cannot fit, for as Dorofeeva-Lichtmann has argued, the authors of the *Shan hai jing* and modern geographers are attempting two contradictory tasks. The *Shan hai jing*, despite the impression given by the exact distances between sites, does not depict the world's physical form. Instead it is a "conceptual organization of space" conveying fundamental ideas about the world through its overarching schema. These include the ideas that the world is square, oriented in the cardinal directions, balanced if not symmetrical between the directions, and clearly distinguished between center and periphery. It offers a variant of the "Five Zones" model, in which there is a progressive decline as one moves away from the center through a series of concentric squares.[167]

In this geometric schema of the earth, however, the *Shan hai jing*'s contents offer a model of the entire cosmos. It is in fact the earliest cosmography in China. It was compiled during what I have described as the "encyclopedic era" when Chinese working in every category of text aimed to produce comprehensive compendia that distilled everything worth knowing into a single work.[168] It forged diverse myths and local lore into a systematic account by assigning every creature, divine being, or ancient story to a place. These places were then compiled to form a world picture that was marked as complete through employing the structural model provided by the Bright Hall and related charts. By distributing the hybrid creatures, divinities, and monstrous races across a schematic model based on the four quadrates and the center, it formed a complete sacred geography of the world.

It dealt with mountains in the *Shan jing*, treating them as the zone that linked men to gods. Then in the *Hai jing* it shifted attention to distant places at the edge of the earth where one found both strange races of men and tales from a distant past when gods and men had mingled freely. The great distance from the center made possible uncanny things that were separated from the conventional world in both space and time.[169] This model of the world thus incorporated not only the human realm but also the celestial, and not only the present day but also the ancient events that had created the world of its authors. In this way it formed a complete model incorporating the entirety of space and time.

The *Shan jing* is divided into twenty-six subsections formed from lists of mountains, describing a total of 447 mountains found in the central land. These mountains are linked as a journey or a procession. It thus uses the same method as Renaissance cosmographies and *insulaires* that organized lists of marvels and curiosities under the place where they were found, and structured the presentation by moving from place to place while locating each site only in terms of the direction and distance from the preceding one.[170] Each entry consists of the name of the mountain and information about its flora, fauna, and minerals. Some also note prodigies, miraculous or divine beings that dwell on the mountain, and mythological events. Rivers are mentioned only in assocation with the mountains from which they emerge. Twenty-four of the twenty-six sections end with an account of the characteristics of the divinities of the region and the offerings that should be made to them. Many entries also discuss the medicinal uses of plants and the events presaged by the appearance of some divine being or prodigy. I will here discuss the significance of organizing the text as a procession, the import of focusing on mountains, and the principles underlying the selection and categorization of contents.

As to organizing the text as a journey, Dorofeeva-Lichtmann has pointed out that the *Shan jing* provides not just a model of the world, but "a process-oriented scheme." By specifying a series of movements as its ground, the text indicates the possibility of its repetition and thus provides both a prescription and a model for the performance of actions that organize space.[171] Like the Bright Hall and the charts, the text of the *Shan hai jing* provides a world model within which the reader can situate him or her self and actions in order to secure power or efficacy.

In the text, and the memorial presented by its first editor, Liu Xin, this organization of space is attributed to Yu. The work is a by-product of his labors to tame the flood. These labors, as shown in the "Yu gong," took the form of a journey across the length and breadth of the subcelestial realm to trace out the courses of the rivers, examine the character of each region and rate its soil, and assign the forms of tribute to be offered. According to Liu Xin this same journey produced the *Shan hai jing*:

> The *Shan hai jing* appeared in the time of Yao and Shun. Long ago the great flood raged and swept through the Middle Kingdoms. The people lacked any foundation, perilously perched on hilltops or in nests in trees. Gun having failed, Emperor Yao had Yu carry on the work. Yu traveled for four years, following the mountains to cut down their trees and thereby fixing the high mountains and the great rivers. Yi and Bo Yi were in charge of driving away the animals [who

lived mixed with the people], naming the mountains and rivers, classifying the plants, and distinguishing the quality of water and soil.
The gods of the four sacred mountains assisted them to make a complete tour of the four quadrates, reaching to places where the tracks
of men were rare, and where boats and chariots seldom came. On
the inside they distinguished the mountains of the four quadrates and
the center, and on the outside they separated the seas of the eight
directions. They recorded the treasures and strange objects; the products of different regions; the places where waters, soils, plants, animals,
insects, scaly creatures, and birds were found; where auspicious por-
tents were concealed; and, beyond the four seas in isolated states, the
unusual kinds of people. Yu divided the Nine Provinces and created
tribute in accord with the quality of their soil, while Yi rated the
quality of the different categories of things and thus wrote the *Shan
hai jing*.[172]

Many themes discussed here are treated in the companion volume on myths
of the flood, so only a few points need be noted. First, remarks about following mountains to cut down trees, rating soils to establish tribute, and dividing the Nine Provinces refer to the "Yu gong." However, these are mixed with
matters that figure only in the *Shan hai jing*. Thus, like other accounts of the
world—the model of Zou Yan, that of the *Huainanzi*, the *Mu Tianzi zhuan*—
the *Shan hai jing* begins with the canonical "Yu gong" and then extends it,
insisting that the classic is too restricted in its geography and interests to
account for the world. The *Shan hai jing* geographically extended the "Yu
gong" by going beyond the realm of men to include materials from "beyond
the four seas." It extended its contents by incorporating new materials on
plants, animals, treasures, prodigies, spirits, and omens. In this way Liu Xin
defended the importance of the *Shan hai jing* by asserting its encyclopedic
character.

Second, Liu Xin cites numerology and the aforementioned schematic
models. He emphasizes movement through the four quadrates and the center,
so that the world-ordering travels of Yu appear as an enlarged version of the
annual procession of the ruler through the Bright Hall. References to the
"four sacred mountains" and the "eight directions" highlight the importance
of the numerical schemata that underlay the profusion of prodigies and strange
objects. This emphasis on numbers also pervades the account of the biblio-
graphic category to which the text was assigned in the imperial catalogue that
derived from the works of none other than Liu Xin (see note 165). Like the
emphasis on geographic range and richness of contents, the invocation of
numerology marks the claim to totality.

Third, the account calls attention to the creation of the text. It stipulates
that it is Yu who tames the flood and divides the provinces, but that it is Bo
Yi and Yi who name, classify, rate, and ultimately write. This pattern, in which

the actions of the ruler or sage become the topic for writing by others so that political *authority* and *authorship* are separated and the latter subordinated to the former, was a major theme in Warring States writing.[173] Thus, Liu Xin's remarks link the production of this text to major Warring States and Han ideas about the politics of composition, and the interplay between ruler and writer. Liu Xin also distinguishes the contents of the two major sections of the book, which indicates that it had largely attained something like its present form by the end of the Western Han.

All these points show that the text is above all a means to authority. The idea that the king organized his realm by moving through it was established in the Shang. In this earliest dynasty, the ruler had regularly moved through the landscape of his realm, securing the loyalty of followers who presented offerings and the aid of local gods with whom he renewed ties through sacrifice.[174] While royal processions became less frequent in later dynasties, they survived in myths of the journeys of earlier rulers and in ceremonial processions patterned on those myths. Such tours figured in the careers of the First Emperor and Han rulers such as Emperor Wu.[175] Moreover, rituals related to travel were elements of major religious festivals, such as the new year rites, and were performed when the ruler moved from place to place.[176] Thus, treating the journeys of Yu as a precondition to the creation of the *Shan hai jing* and the "Yu gong," as well as his own kingship, links these totalizing accounts of the world to theories and rituals of rulership that were prominent in the time of their compositions.

Mountains were also closely tied to the ruler's travels as a source of power. While the earliest accounts of travels as the form of the ruler's authority had no relation to mountains, the processions of the First Emperor and Emperor Wu highlighted the ascent of mountains and the making of offerings there. Stone inscriptions also show that some localities developed cults to their own mountains, and that mountain cults devoted to immortals became a major form of local religiosity. The *Shan jing* as a catalogue of mountains, their treasures, their prodigies, and their cults offers an encyclopedic treatment of this central element of cult and politics in the period.

Mountains figure in the text as a space that is separate from ordinary human experience. They form an intermediate zone between the human world and that of Heaven, where people or spirits could move into the other's world.[177] However, the *Shan hai jing* differs from other accounts of mountain cults in early China in that it never discusses the status of sacrificers. This forms the central theme of the ritual texts, and it figures even in mountain inscriptions. Matsuda Minoru argues that the absence of any concern for the political rank of those who worship the mountains or their spirits indicates that the *Shan hai jing* was aimed at a general audience of literate people. It thus had the same relation to ritual texts on state sponsored cults as the charts and diagrams had to the texts on the Bright Hall.[178]

That mountains could be an object of reverence for anyone with access to the text is also marked by its emphasis on mountains as a source of medicinal plants or minerals, and of the use of these materials in magical spells.[179] Moreover, the *Shan hai jing* extends its reverence to all mountains as a distinct zone, while the official cults and those in the stone inscriptions were devoted to designated peaks. This sacred zone of mountains is distinguished by its contents. These can be roughly divided into creatures, plants, and minerals; spirits; and God-on-High with his offspring and agents.[180]

Creatures are one of the more important categories, with 193 recorded in the five chapters of the *Shan jing*.[181] They are routinely identified by type, that is, animals, birds, fish, snakes, and so on. Animals and birds are the most common, as the rest are associated with the bodies of water that play a secondary role. The emphasis is on unusual creatures, most of which are hybrids of two or more species of animals or humans, like the chimera or sphinx of Greek mythology. Others are formed through multiplying bodily parts, or placing parts in unusual locations on the body. These hybrids are produced by variations on a few simple patterns.[182] Some provide resources for humans, particularly medicines or the material basis for spells.[183] Typical examples are:

> 370 *li* further east is Mt. Niuyang. Its south side has much copper and the north much silver. There is an animal there whose form is like a horse with a white head. It has stripes like a tiger and a red tail. Its sound is like the prophetic songs of humans, and it is called a *lushu*. One who wears its hairs at the waist will have many descendants. 300 *li* further east is Mt. Ji. On its south side there is much jade. On its north side there are many strange trees. There is a beast which has a form like a goat with nine tails and four ears. Its eyes are on its back. It is called *boshi*. One who wears its hairs at the belt will have no fear. There is a bird there, which in form is like a chicken with 306 eyes, six legs, and three wings. It is called *changfu*. One who eats it will no longer sleep.[184]

Other hybrid animals function as signs. Most of these are negative, indicating imminent wars, floods, or droughts. Typical examples of these are:

> Four hundred *li* further west is a mountain named Mt. Xiaoci. On top of it there is much white jade. Below it there is much copper. There is a beast there that resembles an ape but has a white head and red feet. It is called *zhuyan*. When it appears then there is a great war.

> Two hundred *li* further northeast is a mountain called Mt. Yan. It has much metal and jade. There is a beast there whose shape is like a pig but with a human face. It has a yellow body and a red tail. Its name is the *heyu*. It has the sound of a human infant. This beast eats people, and it also eats insects and snakes. When it appears then there will be great floods in the world.[185]

Only a handful are auspicious. This suggests that the mountains are an appropriate place for hybrids, but such violations of normal boundaries in the world of men constitute a danger.

While many passages relate to plants and minerals, these are different from accounts of creatures. Most plants are simply named, and only a handful are identified as hybrids of different plants. Both for plants and animals there are far more examples of their only being named in the chapter dealing with the central region. This suggests that the authors assumed that this region, identifiable with the central regions of China, was both more ordinary and more familiar to the readers. The few hybrid plants that appear function as medicines or poisons, but they do not manifest themselves in the world of men as omens.[186]

Similarly the metals are precious and useful, but entirely conventional: gold, silver, copper, and iron. Many jades are listed, but only one passage mentions the magical attributes of jade and the eating of jade to secure power.[187] One story tells of an edible stone used to poison rats, a function linked to the alchemical pursuit of immortality in the tale of the immortal Lord Tang.[188] Interest in immortality also figures in the numerous substances that seem to be variants of cinnabar, but, like the other minerals in the *Shan jing*, there is no real discussion of the attributes or uses of these compounds.

Thus, apart from the hybrid creatures, the only beings that are the subject of extended discussion are the spirits. These are identified with the character *shen* 神, and they appear in relatively few places. As Suh Kyung Ho has noted, accounts of spirits are concentrated in chapters two and five, that is, in the western and central regions. The former reflected the influence of the mythology of Kunlun with its idea that the links between Earth and Heaven lay in the mountains of the distant west. The latter acknowledged the presence of a certain number of mountain cults within the Chinese realm.

In fact the structural similarities between accounts of creatures and those of spirits are striking. Like the former, the latter sometimes consist of nothing more than a name, which includes the character 神 or *gui* 鬼. Many entries also describe the spirits' unusual or hybrid forms, and a few mention the sounds that they produce.[189] This theme of hybridization is crucial to the significance of the mountains as a sacred zone, for it is the physical embodiment of the liminal status that is the key to the mountain's power. Mountains were spiritually potent as a zone of transition between the world of men and Heaven. The condition of lying between two worlds is marked in the hybrid character of the mountains' inhabitants, both creatures and spirits. As beings who blur the boundaries between that which is distinct in the ordinary world, the hybrids who inhabit the mountains demonstrate on a reduced scale the transition between states that was desired by those who climbed into the mountain realm.

Although both creatures and spirits were hybrids, they were clearly distinguished. First, with one exception, all the spirits introduced outside accounts of sacrifice are described as "resembling people" or possessing a significant human attribute. While some creatures also possessed aspects of humanity, the regularity of such attributions to spirits clearly indicates their closeness to the human realm. Second, eight entries describe a spirit control- ling an aspect of the universe, an attribute only once attributed to a creature in the sacred realm of Kunlun. In one case the actions attributed to a group of spirits even resemble that assigned to the ruler in the context of the Bright Hall: "One hundred and fifty *li* further east is Bear Mountain. There is a cave there, a bear cave that regularly sends forth and brings back spirit men. It is open in the summer and closed in the winter. If this cave is open in the winter, then there will be war."[190] Here the boundaries between spirits and men blur, particularly the "one man" who acted as the link between Heaven and Earth and the "spirit men" of the celestial government.

Third, in contrast with the accounts of creatures, only one entry describes the manifestation of spirits to men as an omen. Moreover, in no case can spirits be consumed or manipulated to work magic.[191] Thus, while spirits visu- ally differ little from the hybrid creatures, the two categories are clearly sep- arated in the roles that they play and the manner in which people relate to them. Spirits are divine administrators and the recipients of sacrifice, beings with whom men deal on the model of their earthly superiors. Creatures offer material resources or natural signs, and men deal with them on the model of the animals, both domesticated and wild, with whom they shared the terres- trial world.

This distinction of the categories in their relation to men is clearest in the passages that describe the spirits who control the mountain ranges, and the types and timing of offerings that should be made to them.[192] As recipi- ents of regular offerings from men, the mountain spirits contrast with the hybrid creatures and plants who are often listed as items of consumption. This contrast between the feeding of spirits and the consumption of beasts or plants resembles Greek myths on the origins of sacrifice in which patterns of consumption distinguish and rank gods, men, and beasts.[193] Moreover, like the spirits who appear outside the context of sacrifice, those to whom offerings are made almost always resemble people or possess major human traits.[194] While only eight deities are given specific administrative functions, the insis- tence on regular sacrifices to the gods of the mountains indicates that they also guard or control their mountains. Such control would allow them to regulate the links between men and spirits, as well as the environmental influ- ences associated with mountains. It is because of their power over features of the world crucial to human life that they had to receive offerings.

Such offerings for divine support was the basis of earthly power over defined spaces. As Dorofeeva-Lichtmann has pointed out, in the *Shan hai jing* the earth's surface is divided into distinct blocks that are distinguished by assignment to their respective spirit powers. Each section of the earth has its own tutelary deities, who form a "spiritual landscape, or a geography of divine influences." Consequently the control of space requires "a specific kind of landscape knowledge, that is, an ability to distinguish properly the local spirits and to communicate with them through the performance of correct sacrifices."[195] The generation of power by the ruler through his journeys and accompanying sacrifices likewise depended on his ability to recognize local spirits and the offerings that suited them. The *Shan hai jing* offered this same form of power to those who knew how to use it.

The final category of beings on the mountains is what could be described as traces of God-on-High or of the spirits known as *di*. While these most potent gods do not themselves appear, evidence of their presence and activities is scattered throughout the text. First, many geographic features are described as belonging to one or another of the gods. One mountain is called "the mountain of the Heavenly *di*," while other features assigned to a *di* that is probably God-on-High include shallows, a suspended garden, a lower capital, a secret capital, and a tower.[196]

In addition to these natural features assigned to God-on-High there are beings encountered on the mountains who are linked to the *di*. They fall into two categories. First are agents of the high god who carry out his work on earth. Examples are those mentioned earlier who perform a cosmic task. Second is a small number of beings whose location and physical appearance are explained by a story of how God-on-High transformed them and brought them to their present place. Unlike the other divine beings who are embodiments of mountains, or the creatures indigenous to their mountains, these are not local genii of the place, but rather the creatures of mythic narrative. They thus demonstrate not the character or powers of terrain, but the activities in the world of God-on-High, as in the following story:

> One hundred and twenty *li* further west is Mt. Zhong. The mountain god's son was named Gu [Drum]. He had the body of a dragon with a face that resembled a person's. He and Qinpi killed Baojiang on the northern side of Kunlun. God-on-High executed them on the eastern side of Mt. Zhong. . . . Qinpi was transformed into a large osprey. It resembles a hawk, but with black markings, a white head, a red beak, and tiger claws. Its sound is like that of a morning crane. When it appears, then there will be a great war. Gu was also transformed into a bird called *jun*. It resembles an owl, but with red claws, a straight beak, yellow markings, and a white head. It sounds like a crane. When it appears, then there will be a great drought in the district.[197]

This example, unique in the *Shan jing*, depicts a conflict between the high celestial god and a mountain deity. This recapitulates the relation between the imperially sanctioned cults and those dedicated to lesser mountains by the cities and towns in their locality. The son of the mountain god commits a capital crime on the very slopes of God-on-High's earthly palace, and, as a punishment, he and his accomplice are executed on the side of his father's mountain. But they do not stay fully dead. Instead, they reappear as malevolent, hybrid birds of prey whose entry into the world signals war and drought. As we will see, stories of this kind appear much more frequently in the *Hai jing*.

In most cases, the beings in the *Shan jing* linked to the high gods are daughters who were transformed into strange plants or animals, sometimes associated with silk production. There are four such stories that yield few generalizations.[198] Two cases involve daughters linked to sericulture of spirits of fire and drought who are mythic transforms of a common figure.[199] One case deals with Nü Gua, the mythic consort of Fu Xi who in some accounts tames the great flood (see the companion volume). Here she appears as a pathetic figure who applies the discredited techniques of damming and diking to the impossible task of controlling the Eastern Sea. Two cases involve metamorphoses into hybrids. One daughter appears not in a physical transformation, but rather as an object that she left behind when, in later versions, she ascended to immortality. In a final case the daughters live in their original state, playing the classic role of rain maidens who bring storms in their wake.[200] These are important because they show the highest gods manifesting themselves in the world not only through their agents and the natural features that form their gardens and palaces, but also as progenitors of lesser spirits. The role of the *di* as fathers and ancestors figures more prominently in the *Hai jing*.

Other texts also structured the world by a set of mountain ranges. Several Eastern Han mountain inscriptions describe a world structured by three mountain chains. An inscription from A.D. 183 to the god of Mt. Baishi states: "The spirit lord of Mt. Baishi is numbered among the Nine Mountains and is part of one of the Three Ranges. . . . His body [*ti* 體] links with Mt. Fenglong and his vital energy [*qi*] connects with the northern marchmount [Mt. Heng], giving hidden assistance to Heaven and Earth, and long nourishing the myriad things." The mountain demonstrates its power by securing within its own region the arrival of rain, the absence of fires, the circulation of water, and the ripening of grain. Similarly, the inscription to Mt. Fenglong from A.D. 164 identifies the mountain as a "collateral spirit [*bie shen* 別神]" of the Three Ranges, that "separated off its body to a distinct place [*fen ti yi chu* 分體異處] within the state." Finally, the inscription to Mt. Sangong (Three Lords) from A.D. 117 also describes this mountain as a "collateral spirit of the Three Ranges, far removed to the west of the central range."[201]

The exact sense of these references to the Three Ranges and their "collateral spirits" is not clear, but the parallel with the Nine Mountains in the Mt. Baishi inscription indicates that these three ranges were a way of numerologically organizing the earth. The phrase "Nine Mountains" figures as a metonym for all mountains as an element of the earth's structure in such early world models as the "Yu gong," the *Lü shi chun qiu*'s numerological account of the world, and the *Huainanzi* chapter.[202] Although the phrase "Three Ranges" does not appear in these early texts, the repeated references to them in the mountain inscriptions shows that the term was well known among the Han elite.

Moreover, Yuan Weichun has collected later discussions, from Ma Rong in the Eastern Han and Wang Su in the Three Kingdoms period down to Qian Daxin in the Qing, who argued that this idea was widespread in the Han and present in versions of the "Yu gong" then in use. The monograph on geography in the *Han shu* cites two mountains named "Mt. Jing." It identifies one as the "Mt. Jing of the northern range in the 'Yu gong'" and the other as the "Mt. Jing of the southern range in the 'Yu gong'."[203] In the "Yu gong" the twenty-seven mountains visited by Yu are divided into a northern range north of the Wei and Yellow Rivers, a middle range south of the Wei and Yellow Rivers, and a southern range corresponding roughly to the Daba and Dabie ranges. This theory that the "Yu gong" organized its mountains into three ranges was still cited by the Tang scholars who compiled its *zheng yi* commentary.[204] In short, there is clear evidence that, throughout the Han, scholars dealing with the division of the world into mountain ranges routinely grouped these under the numerologically potent number "three." This model was applied both to reading the "Yu gong" and to panegyrics to mountains in inscriptions on mountain cults, and knowledge of it survived at least into the Tang.

Equally significant are the internal structure of the mountain ranges. Thus, the inscription on Mt. Baishi states that the god of the mountain is linked to other peaks both by the material substance of his "body" and through the movement of his "energy." These linkages that move through the earth are "hidden," but they allow the mountain spirit to assist the twin powers of Heaven and Earth, which it links together. In contrast with this mountain that connects directly to the other major peaks, the gods of Mt. Fenglong and of Mt. Sangong are described as "collateral spirits," that is, gods who do not belong to the central line. In early kinship terminology, collateral indicated those who were not in the direct line of descent, either the heir's younger brothers or those born of a secondary wife.[205] The status of the mountains as "collateral" thus indicates that they are "separate" but linked to the chain. This assimilates the connections of mountains that structure the earth to the principles of kinship. Their links are formed through the sharing of bodily substance and energy, but these vary in degrees of closeness. This identification of the links that bind mountains together with those of kinship is in turn made possible by the identification of the mountains with the gods who control them.[206]

While mountains and their vertical ascents form the organizing principle of the first five chapters, the balance of the work is organized on the horizontal plane. The *Hai jing* and *Da huang jing* are structured according to a logic of distance from the center. They focus on the exotics at the edges of the earth, and their exposition is structured on the principle of dividing inner from outer. In recent decades, Western scholars have produced diagrams depicting the geographic relations of the successive zones in the text. They do not agree on the details, and even individual authors present multiple diagrams to indicate different aspects of the text.[207] Thus, it is unlikely that the authors of the *Shan hai jing* had a precise image in mind, or that one could compose a single diagram that would depict its contents. However, it is clear that each successive section extended the physical horizon, and that each was laid out beginning with the outer edges and then circling in toward the center.

Moreover, those who have most carefully examined the question agree that the successive zones do not constitute a set of concentric rectangles in which each area begins where the preceding one ends. Instead there is considerable overlap. Thus, "Outside the Seas" and "Vast Wilds" discuss many of the same topographic features or mythological figures. Indeed Gu Jiegang and Hou Renzhi argued that the second is a revised version of the first.[208] However, as Dorofeeva-Lichtmann has noted, there is more important structural evidence of the overlap between sections. Both the "Mountains" and "Inside the Seas" include five sections traced onto the four cardinal directions and center. "Outside the Seas" and the "Vast Wilds," however, consist of four sections oriented to the directions with no center. Thus, there is a clear overlap between the "Mountains" and "Inside the Seas," with the second being either identical to the first or an extension that includes it. Similarly, "Outside the Seas" and "Vast Wilds" are either identical regions, or the latter includes the former but extends further outward. If the areas covered are the same or heavily overlapping, then the differences between the accounts represent a shift of perspective.[209] The key to understanding the work is thus to establish the significance of the shift from the emphasis on the vertical dimension in the first section, originally an integral work, to the horizontal dimension in the later ones.

To summarize my argument, the shift toward the horizontal dimension played two major roles. First, it focused on the distinction between inner and outer by structuring the earth according to the diverse peoples on its surface rather than the mountain chains that linked it to the sky. This shift away from the vertical is also marked by the abandonment as a structuring principle of the hierarchy from beasts through men to spirits marked by the relations of consumption and feeding. Instead it emphasized the different varieties of men, a horizontal relation in which beings sharing a common nature varied across space through the influence of custom. In this new structure, attention shifted from the median zone that defined exchanges between Earth and Heaven to a world structured by three horizontal zones: the central region, the inner periphery, and the outer edges of the world.

The later sections of the book did not abandon *all* interest in the celestial, but rather linked Heaven and Earth not in vertical ascents but by moving to the edges of the world. The celestial realm had figured in the "Mountains" section through accounts of giving omens and receiving sacrifice. In contrast, the celestial world figures in the later sections in tales of the ancient sages. These beings play two major roles in the later sections, where they are identified by the title "gods" *di* 帝 and work magic. First, they imposed order on the world by defeating or punishing rebels and criminals. Second, they are the progenitors of virtually all the peoples who dwelt on the earth, a fact marked by numerous genealogies and the assignment of surnames. In this model, the unity of the celestial and earthly realms, and the possibility of order in the latter, reside in the punitive actions of the sagely *di* who are the ultimate parents of humanity. Thus, the later sections, which define the world's structure through the distribution of states and insist on the centrality of the sages, mark the absorption of the text into the ruler-centered vision of the universe that emerged in the late Warring States period and early empires.[210]

The opening out of the world in the "Seas" section with its emphasis on celestial links and the sage rulers is signaled in its first passage:

> As for all that is carried by the earth, which exists within the three dimensions, and is located within the seas, illumine it with the sun and moon, guide it with the constellations, fix its calendar with the four seasons, and control it with the Great Year-star. As for that which is produced by the spirit powers, the things and their diverse physical forms are sometimes shortlived and sometimes longlived. Only the sage can completely understand their Way.[211]

This presents the seas as the major boundary; the sun, moon, and other celestial bodies as the chief guiding principles; and the sages as the only beings who can truly understand the world and give it order. In this way it epitomizes the structure and themes of the balance of the text.

The switch to the horizontal dimension is further demonstrated in two ways. First, each section of "Beyond the Seas" concludes with a description of the god who ruled the direction in question.[212] This shows that the text reaches the edges of the world in each direction. There are also references to mountains from which the sun and moon rose or at which they set, once again showing that the account of the world reached its edges. Passages on gods who control the movements of these celestial bodies, care for them, or "supervise the night" also stress the cosmic inclusiveness of the later sections.[213]

The major difference between the "Mountains" section and the later chapters on the "Seas" and "Waste" is the switch of structuring unit from chains of mountains to states.[214] While mountains and other topographic features figure in later chapters, they are features of the states in which they are found. Moreover, the hybrid creatures, plants, minerals, and spirits who fill the first five chapters are almost never mentioned in the last thirteen. Instead of moving from mountain to mountain, with exact distances given, the text moves from state to state, giving only approximate directions.

The states are generally characterized by brief accounts of their inhabitants. In the "Seas" section these accounts focus on their bizarre physical appearances:

> The Linked-Chest Country is to its southwest. Their defining characteristic is that their chests are linked together.

The Feather-People Country is to its southeast. Their defining characteristics are that they have long heads and their bodies sprout feathers. Some say that they are to the southeast of the jointly flying birds,
and that their defining characteristic is that they have long
cheekbones.[215]

The text never explains the significance of listing monstrous peoples, who
at first seem to be variants of the hybrids in the "Mountain" chapters.
However, their role is completely different, for they are never omens or
material for making medicine or magic. An answer is suggested by a list of
such peoples in the *Huainanzi*'s account of the world.[216] These appear after
descriptions of how topography affects physique and character, soil and diet
shape bodies, kinds of animals diverge, different types of water contain different minerals and plants, and directional orientation determines physical traits.
Thus, the bizarre features of the peoples at the edges of the world mark the
manner in which the influence of terrain and the five-phases correspondences
of the directions shape the inhabitants of different regions. Even within China,
different types of terrain produce physically different peoples, and the monstrous peoples at the edges of the earth are the extreme version of this phenomenon. Their monstrosity is the physical expression of their remoteness and
of the alien character of their land. This is demonstrated in the *Shan hai jing*
by the fact that the chapters "Within the Seas" contain far fewer accounts of
monstrous peoples than do those "Beyond the Seas." The earlier chapters
instead devote most of their space to lists of state names, accounts of topography or animal life, and the work of the sages.[217]

The idea that the bizarre features of distant peoples in the *Shan hai jing*
and the *Huainanzi* indicate distance and otherness is reinforced by the fact
that Liu Xin insists that it could be used to "examine portentous, bizarre creatures and observe the folk songs and customs of distant states and alien
peoples."[218] The first phrase refers to the "Mountains" chapters and the second
to the later ones. Thus, Liu Xin asserts that accounts of distant peoples are a
form of ethnography. Although these sections in fact provide little information on customs or folkways, modern scholars both in China and the West
have endorsed Liu Xin's statement by seeking to identify odd physical appearances described in the text with curious practices of self-decoration employed
among the contemporary peoples of Tibet, Southeast Asia, and other neighboring lands. Others have treated it as a proto-ethnology representing more
or less distorted empirical knowledge of early, tribal societies.[219]

While data in the *Shan hai jing* about distant peoples is minimal, and
efforts to read it as ethnography are misplaced, the text *is* part of a trend in
which early Chinese writers used accounts of alien peoples as a form of self-
definition. The ancient Greeks had defined themselves and their city-state
culture through contrasts with Persia, the Egyptians, more distant peoples such
as the Scythians and Ethiopians, and even the mythical Hyperboreans.[220]
Similarly, Warring States Chinese increasingly established what was distinctive
about themselves by describing alien peoples. Such descriptions defined the

truly Chinese by showing what those in the "middle kingdoms" were not. Whereas the Chinese in the *Zuo zhuan* still intermarried or made alliances with the Di and other peoples who were later identified as barbarians, late Warring States philosophical texts told of alien peoples who expelled widows, devoured their eldest sons, or in other ways provided a counterimage to China. Others used non-Chinese peoples as rhetorical markers to identify that which was the opposite of the Way of the sages and the refined (*ya*) culture of China, or to indicate the negation of human society.[221]

However, with the creation of a unified empire, the division of the world into a civilized center defined by China and a periphery marked by the strange customs and attire of the "barbarians" came to the fore. In his memorials on dealing with the Xiongnu, the early Western Han writer Chao Cuo bases his arguments on a vision of the diametrically opposed cultures of the two peoples:

> The land of the northern barbarians is a place of accumulated dark-
> ness [*ji yin* 積陰]. The tree bark grows three inches thick, and the
> ice pack is six feet deep. They eat meat and drink milk products.
> The people are compact and solid, while the birds and beasts have
> down and dense hair, so by nature they can endure the cold. The
> lands of the southern barbarians have little shade and much sunshine
> [*shao yin duo yang* 少陰多陽]. The people are flaccid, while the birds
> and beasts have thin feathers or hair, so by nature they can endure
> heat. Qin's garrison soldiers could not cope with these environments.
> . . . To provide clothing and food the northern barbarians are not
> attached to the ground, so their circumstances are conducive to
> causing disorder at the frontier. How can I prove this? The north-
> ern barbarians eat meat and drink fermented milk. They wear leather
> and skins. They have no settled abode inside city walls or in dwellings
> in the fields, so they are like flying birds or running beasts in the
> vast wilds. When there is excellent grass and fresh water they stop,
> but when the grass is all eaten and the water used up then they move
> on. Seen in this way, going round and round in a circuit, now arriv-
> ing and now departing, is the way of life of the northern barbarians,
> but it would separate the Chinese from agriculture.[222]

This schema echoes both the discourse on regions and the *Shan hai jing* with its orientation to the cardinal directions, its use of *yin* and *yang* as a mode of explanation, its treatment of different peoples as distinct physical types linked to local fauna, and the clear distinction between the Chinese at the center from those at the periphery whose culture makes their condition close to that of beasts.

Writing some decades before Chao Cuo, Jia Yi sketched a world in which the barbarians, linked with animals both in livelihood and character, stood at one end of a spectrum and the Han emperor at the other. Whereas a true ruler encompassed the earth, Emperor Wen controlled the "Nine Provinces," but not the Xiongnu or other non-Chinese peoples. Instead it was the Xiongnu who extracted tribute from the Chinese, a situation of "the world turned upside down." He also described the southern Yue people as being on a level with animals because they lacked ritual and violated covenants. As noted in other Han texts, these peoples cut off their hair and tattooed their bodies to take on the appearance and abilities of scaly, water creatures.[223] Strikingly, Jia Yi depicted Yao's transforming power spreading outward from the central states, through nearby non-Chinese states such as Shu and Yue, to the realm of the Queen Mother of the West, and in the north passing through the mythical "Dark Capital" out through a "dog country," a land of pygmies, and finally a land of creatures with human bodies but the heads of birds. In short, he treated the distant lands of monstrous humans described in the *Huainanzi* and the *Shan hai jing* as the logical extension of the progressive blurring of the boundary between humans and animals observed at China's frontiers.[224]

The treatment of the distant, monstrous peoples undergoes a marked shift in the transition from the "Seas" chapters to the "Vast Waste." These give no accounts of bizarre forms, but instead trace their genealogical descent from ancient sages, and describe their diets and animal husbandry. Only this last feature is marked as bizarre through the assertion that these peoples raised and controlled wild creatures rather than domestic animals:

> There is a Zhongrong State. The god [*di*] Jun sired Zhongrong. The people of Zhongrong eat four-legged creatures and fruit from trees. They command the four types of birds, tiger, leopards, black bears, and brown bears.

> There is the state of the Zhi people. The god Shun sired Wuyin, who descended to the land of the Zhi. They are called the Shaman Zhi people. The Shaman Zhi people are surnamed Fen. They eat grain. They wear clothes that are not woven or sewn, and eat food that they do not plant or harvest. Here there are birds which sing and dance; simurghs that spontaneously sing and phoenixes that spontaneously dance. All varieties of four-legged creature assemble here, and all types of grain can be gathered.[225]

Some peoples whose bizarre appearances figure in earlier chapters reappear in the "Waste," but are described solely in terms of their genealogies and cultures.[226] The interest in customs accords with many early Chinese texts that state that all people shared a common nature and differed only in their customs.[227] The emphasis on the role of the early sages, however, requires explanation.

The sages play two key roles in the later sections of the *Shan hai jing*. First, they are the mythic forebears of virtually all the peoples listed in the

"Vast Waste" chapters. Their role as ancestors is suggested by the fact that throughout the text there are references to their tombs.[228] More important is that the chapters of the final section of the book insist on the sagely or divine origins of the vast majority of the peoples mentioned, and they name the sages in question.[229] Most of the genealogies trace the peoples' origins back to the god Jun, the Yellow God, Zhuan Xu, and Yu. Such figures as Fu Xi, the god Ku, the Fiery God, and several little known deities are also represented.

The text marks these figures as spirits by placing them in the celestial realm. In the passage on the Zhi state, their ancestor "descended (*jiang* 降)" into the world after being sired by Shun. This is a standard term for a spirit entering the human world, often when it possesses a medium. It applies to divine birth in other works, such as the opening of "Li sao."[230] Moreover, the actions of the sages are often identified with the verb *xia* 下 "to come [or send] down," showing that they dwelled in Heaven, above the world of men. Finally, virtually all of the sages listed in the text have towers associated with their world-ordering work. As discussed in chapter three, such towers were the means by which spirits descended into the world of men or mortals ascended to Heaven.[231]

The second function of the sages in the last section of the *Shan hai jing* is to impose order on the world, primarily through executing and mutilating criminals or rebels. Some accounts are brief and lack all context, such as the statement that the archer Yi killed Zuochi.[232] More detailed are several accounts of rebels who challenged the gods and were defeated in battle: "Xingtian [形天 'taking the form of Heaven'] battled for spirit power with the god. The god cut off his head and buried him at Mt. Changyang. Then Xingtian made his nipples into eyes, his navel into a mouth, and took up his axe and shield to dance."[233] This posthumous defiance is not unique, for the text is full of transformed corpses. Some are mutilated remains of criminals who changed into sources of malevolent power that still wielded their weapons. Another is not itself a rebel but a victim of the simultaneous appearance of ten suns in the sky, who became a physical trace of cosmic rebellion.[234] Thus, outer sections are filled with mutated corpses that are the bloody inverse of the sages' tombs, the still potent traces of their work.

The two most important sets of tales deal with the Yellow God's battle with Chi You and with Yu's battles to control the flood. The former are part of a larger set of narratives using stories about the battle between drought and storm to develop a mythology of the introduction of combat into the human world as a form of political control.[235] In one story the Yellow God kills Kui and the Thunder Beast to produce a drum, the chief means of giving signals in battle, with which he intimidates the world. In another the Yellow God sent down the Responding Dragon and the woman Ba who both halted the rain and allowed the god to kill Chi You. Both these agents, however, remained in the world as producers of drought who figured in drought prevention rituals in the period.[236] These divine agents who linger in the world as figures of drought and famine resemble the rebels' corpses in being powerful and dangerous traces of the ancient work of the sages left in the world.

The largest body of references to sagely combat in the later sections deal with Yu, who was the mythic progenitor of its first part. As these tales will be discussed in the companion volume on myths of the flood, I will simply note here that they provide further examples of the early sages creating order through killing rebels, and leaving visible traces of their work at the edges of the earth.

A final problem is to explain why the ancient sages, their tombs, and their battles figure in accounts of monstrous peoples and landscapes at the edges of the earth, or in an area "Within the Seas" that thematically extends the distant lands. Why are the founding heroes of Chinese civilization progenitors of alien peoples, and actors at the periphery? There are at least four reasons. First, distant realms can be equivalent to the ancient times when the sages lived. The equivalence of distance in space and in time, the vision of remote realms as a present antiquity, is familiar to the modern West. Some early accounts of the New World suggested that its inhabitants still lived in the Golden Age, or even had escaped the Fall. Hostile versions placed them at the bottom of a scale of societies, corresponding to the early stages of men in the old world.[237] Later tales of noble savages linked them with the warrior peoples of antiquity. Modern anthropology provided a complete discourse based on the assumption that tribal peoples in distant lands were "primitive" or "stone age" men, versions of our own remote ancestors still living in our world but not in our time. The conflation of remoteness in time and space thus became part of an ideology of power in which the "other" was assigned to the developmental status of infancy from which we had long escaped.[238]

The authors of the *Shan hai jing* discovering antiquity in distant places is not dissimilar to Western ethnology. Some early Chinese classified non-Chinese as more primitive and thus closer to the original human condition. As one moved away from the familiar world into distant lands and ancient times, the constraints of direct knowledge fell away and familiar creatures were replaced by beings that were ever more bizarre and monstrous, or ever closer to the perfect and the divine. Just as the ancient Greeks invented Ethiopians or Hyperboreans, and improvised freely on Scythians, as images of alterity, so they imagined people in antiquity who were radically different from themselves. The heroes of the Homeric epic were stronger than any modern man, and the people of the Golden and Silver Ages even more alien. High antiquity and the earth's peripheries were alike as lands of fantasy and myth, so the creatures of one could slip easily into the other.

The second reason for finding sages amid the monstrous peoples at the edges of the earth is that the former were often man–animal hybrids or marked by bizarre physical features. Early texts tell how the Yellow Emperor had four faces or four eyes, others give him the features or body of a dragon, and still other call him a bear.[239] Fu Xi, the first of the sages in several accounts, and his consort Nü Gua were depicted in Han art with the lower bodies of snakes and the upper bodies of humans. Scattered passages in early texts also refer to physical deformities of sages, such as Shun's having four pupils in his eyes.[240] Finally, and most important, the idea of sages as hybrids and monsters had become sufficiently common that the *Xunzi* and other texts presented lists of virtually all the sages and their respective deformities, arguing that physical abnormality was a condition of sagehood.[241] These ideas were closely linked to the practice of physiognomy discussed in chapter one. There are several reasons for this belief: the nonhuman paternity of sages, their superhuman status, or their close links to the natural world. Whatever the reasons, there is no doubt that in the late Warring States and the early empires any discussion of hybrids or monstrosities could include reflections on sages.

Third, the work of the sages in early Chinese accounts had been to separate humans from the animal domain. Nearly all philosophical traditions spoke of a primitive age when humans had lived both physically and morally unseparated from animals. The sages had created the tools and introduced the moral and ritual practices that rescued people from their animal condition and created distinctions where none had existed before.[242] Given this model as a background, it was to be expected that one would find the sages at work in distant realms where both the cultural and physical separation of men from animals was blurred. This is particularly true in a text like the *Shan hai jing*, which takes as its ultimate theme the order underlying the cosmos and the manner in which that order came into being. The thematic importance of the sages' inventions is demonstrated by the fact that the final chapter concludes with a series of entries enumerating many of them, from the invention of boats and chariots (related to the text's interest in travel), through that of bows, to the creation of musical instruments and dancing, and on to the introduction of crafts, agriculture, and the political state. Yu's fixing the Nine Provinces concludes the last of these lists, marking the final step in the work of the sages.[243]

The final reason for finding the sages at the periphery is the idea that the ultimate demonstration of a ruler's power was the submission of distant peoples. This became a commonplace in the texts of the period, which note the range of a ruler's pacifying power as the highest mark of his success.[244] This idea also manifested itself in the Han fascination with rare goods from distant places, whose arrival showed that the ruler's power reached all corners of the earth. The clearest demonstrations of this idea are in the writings of Sima Xiangru, but it also figures in hymns for the Han ancestral temple from the reign of Emperor Wu.[245] Thus, placing the early sages amid the monstrous peoples at the edges of the earth was related to emerging representations of power within the imperial state.

In conclusion, in writing of the edges of the earth, the authors of the later sections of the *Shan hai jing* once again claimed greater authority by widening the range of their spatial model. Moreover, they moved away from the earlier chapters by making the ruler the key to their account of space.

Tales of the battles of the sages, their overcoming the forces of disorder, and their ultimate invention of civilization depicted the historical process by which the regulated sacred geography of the "Mountains" section was created. In interspersing accounts of the sage kings' deeds and the material traces of their victories, the "Seas" and "Waste" chapters present a physical world defined by the transforming powers of the ruler: his destruction of the forces of chaos, his incorporation of the most distant and monstrous peoples within the human order, and his pivotal role in linking Heaven and Earth. Ending with a reference to Yu's taming the flood echoes ending the "Mountain" section with Yu's measurement of the world and definition of its structure, but like the entirety of the later section it deals with what came before the world of the "Mountains" and made it possible.

CONCLUSION

In the late Warring States and early imperial periods, claims to authority were claims to totality. To be limited meant to be subjected to an encompassing whole. Writers projected the totalist claims of the supreme ruler into the structure of the world in several forms. First, the grid that structured the Qin field system, organized city streets and markets, and defined the *Mencius's* "well-field" system served to order all space. Projecting a grid to the level of the world was anticipated in the "nine continents" of the "Yu gong." It achieved full expression in the grids of the eighty-one continent model of Zou Yan, which eclipsed the restricted model of the "Yu gong," and thereby offered a vaster sweep to ambitious rulers of the late Warring States. A similar attempt to outstrip the "Yu gong" in visions of expanding royal power was the account of Zhou King Mu's journey to the edge of the world.

The grid also appeared in models of the Bright Hall, a ritual complex that during the Han was widely discussed and was constructed by several rulers. Images and ideas that later emerged in this structure already appeared in lacquer decor and texts from the fourth-century B.C. By the late Warring States, it was cited as a Zhou ancestral temple that figured both as a microcosm and as the site for great assemblies that epitomized the structure of the world. In the former role, the Bright Hall was composed of alternating circles and squares that symbolized the cosmos, and provided a square of a dozen rooms through which the ruler moved to enact the passage of the months. In this microcosm, the ruler performed the annual cycle, and also sequentially proclaimed the calendrical ordinances that assimilated his rule to that of Heaven. In other versions, the hall was a grid of five or nine rooms, magical numbers which once again assimilated the ruler to the cosmos.

As a site of assemblies, the Bright Hall presented a hierarchical display of how peoples were distributed on the face of the earth. Most important are texts describing how the Duke of Zhou assembled the court and representatives of people from the furthest reaches of the earth. This assembly was laid out around the Bright Hall to recapitulate the world's spatial order and social hierarchy. Those closest to the ruler gathered in his presence at the center. More distant figures such as the feudal lords stood on the steps around the building, each in the direction corresponding to his state. Finally, the barbarians from the edges of the world were each placed at the outer gates of the compound in the direction from which they came. This model thus defined a world by placing the ruler at the center and then laying out successive bands, moving from the most controlled and civilized near the center to the wildest and most barbaric at the edges. This same model was also articulated in the "Five Zones of Submission" model appended to the end of the "Yu gong" and related texts.

Related to the Bright Hall, but on a smaller scale and hence with a greater diffusion, were the geometrical figures employed in bronze mirror decor, diviner's boards, and the *liu bo* game board. Like the Bright Hall, these employed circles, squares, and other geometric figures to indicate Heaven, Earth, the Eight Pillars at the edges of the world, and other features that defined the cosmos. By providing a model of the world that could be perceived at a glance and manipulated by hand, these objects allowed users to situate themselves in relation to current trends in the cosmos and thereby guide their actions. Whether used for divination, in games played between men or spirits, or to secure the position of the deceased in the tomb, all these geometrizing charts of the world offered ordinary people the chance to imitate the power-generating activities of the ruler within the Bright Hall.

A final set of world models was structured around mountains and water. These were the most important sacred sites in early China and the right of offering sacrifices to them defined authority over a delimited region, or the entire world. The earliest surviving textual world model, the "Yu gong," was structured according to the movements of Yu and tribute along the rivers. It also depicted the distribution of mountains and Yu's activities in bringing them into the human realm. World models based on numerologically significant numbers of mountain chains are also preserved in a few Han texts, most notably several of the stone inscriptions devoted to mountain cults.

However, the most elaborate model of a world structured by the disposition of mountains and waters was the "Classic of Mountains and Seas." It consists of several sections, the earliest of which probably dates to the late Warring States. This "Classic of Mountains" is, like the "Yu gong," structured as a journey, but in this case from one mountain to the next. These are portrayed as links between the human and the divine, thus emphasizing the vertical dimension. Each is characterized by the magical flora and fauna found on it, the precious substances within it, and the gods of the place to whom sacrifices are due. Plants serve primarily as the basis for medicines, while the animals are hybrids that are eaten to attain a desired state, or whose manifestations provide omens. Whereas the ritual texts of the period reserve mountain sacrifices for the rulers of a region or the world, the *Shan jing* indicates no restrictions on the status of the sacrificer.

In contrast to the *Shan jing*, the later sections on "seas" and "wastelands" order the world horizontally according to a schema of center and periphery. They also differ from the earlier section in emphasizing the pivotal role of rulers in shaping the world. Whereas the first section uses mountains as its basic unit, the later sections employ the state. Each passage introduces a state and describes its strange inhabitants. Thus, they are variants of such ruler-based models as the "Five Zones of Submission" or the assemblies at the Bright Hall, which placed the ruler at the center and then traced a progressive decline in civilization and a blurring of the boundaries between men and animals as one moved outward. In this manner the monstrous peoples in the later sections of the *Shan hai jing* are the ultimate markers of barbarism. The role of the ruler is also emphasized by describing the peripheral peoples as descendants of the early sages who served as mythic prototypes for the rulers of the day. Finally, the ruler appears in the later sections in tales of wars between the early sages and evil rebels. The victory of the sages created or preserved the spatial order of the world, and the text shows how physical traces of these victories define the landscape. The greatest of these victories, which marks the end of the *Shan hai jing*, was Yu's conquest of the flood which made possible ordered human space.

CONCLUSION

The preceding chapters have shown how the early Chinese articulated every level of spatial order in terms of the relation of part to whole. Whether discussing cosmology, society, or politics, they presupposed an original, undivided totality that in the human world appeared as chaos. All objects or groups emerged from this original state of nondifferentiation through sequential division and recombination. The classic form of this model was the division of the whole into Heaven and Earth, which then rejoined to produce all life. Apart from the primal chaos itself, there was no absolute, eternal foundation or element that existed outside the realm of flux and change. Everything that existed was a temporary confluence of the diverse energies and substances that had emerged from nondifferentiation; without constant effort, they would return to that state. The specifically human forms of space—bodies, families, cities, regions, states, and world—were the products of conscious and continuous human endeavor. They likewise tended to lapse back into chaos or nondifferentiation.

In addition to being unstable confluences of diverse energies, all things human were fragments of a primal unity. As ever larger macrostates were created through absorbing city-states, the authority of whole over part became a standard theme of intellectual and social analysis. In intellectual polemics it took the form of rival traditions, each claiming an all-encompassing wisdom of which their rivals possessed only a limited part. In political analysis it took the form of seeking an end to the constant warfare of the period through the construction of a single, unitary state. In social thought it took the form of a vision of the state as an encompassing order within which the division of labor and the segmentation into households could be transcended in networks of exchange. Warring States Chinese found a world divided against itself in intellectual polemics, wars, and economic specializations. All hope for truth, peace, and order hinged on achieving unity, and all intellectual and political authority were assigned to those who could fashion such a unity and bring all others within its bounds.

307

The categories of spatial analysis discussed in this book emerged within this overarching vision. To avoid disintegration, each level of space needed a defining center around which the rest could be organized. Within the body, the authority of the mind over the senses maintained an autonomous self, while the unity of the spirit energies and the skeleton/skull perpetuated the self beyond death. In the household, the authority of the father provided the orthodox center, and behind him lay a patriline defined in ancestral cult. However, the authority of the mother provided a countercenter in which the household was defined by the husband-wife tie and the authority of both parents over children, rather than the purely masculine line of descent. The tension between these two models of organization resulted in two visions of the household that in turn produced such phenomena as the perpetual scandal of female authority at court and the pairing of the ancestral temple and joint husband-wife tomb as parallel loci of the death cult. In the city, the political district became the center through its unique vertical dimension, and then extended order outward through the grids of the market and the streets. At the same time, the imperial capital developed as a new ritual center and model of a text-based city under which all other urban centers were subsumed as partial replicas. Finally, all the former states were reduced to the status of regions, which found order only through participation in the political realm embodied by the capital and the urban political districts. The high culture of the epoch was defined in the language and art of the court, and the regional centers were drawn in through the centripetal flow of men and tribute goods to the capital.

However, in a world in which truth and order were identified with unification, these units remained fragments that could never in themselves achieve harmony. The perfected body in the "Nei ye" and related traditions found fulfillment only when its influence radiated to the ends of the earth. A household achieved full order only when, as in Han readings of the "lesser prosperity" in the "Li yun" chapter of the Li ji, "the whole world was a household." This itself was a decline from true unity when the "whole world was public."[1] Each city functioned only as part of a network that converged in the capital, which itself played its role only to the extent that it drew together both Heaven and Earth in its ritual program. Regions, as noted, were fragments which contributed to order only through sending men and objects to the imperial center where they provisioned the unifying empire.

Thus, every level of spatial order pointed to a world empire in which lost unity was finally regained. The body, family, city, and region all found completion and meaning only within the new empire that ideally absorbed the entire world. However, although world empire was the logical culmination of the vision of unification, it remained distinct from the primal unity. First, the Chinese knew of peoples beyond their reach: earlier, the mythic states where strange creatures lived at the ends of the earth and, later, in lands such as Central Asia and Korea. More important, however, was the fact that even a universal state remained distinct from the absolute unity of nondifferentiation.

The latter appeared in an ordered society only as chaos: the vanishing of frontiers, the overturning of hierarchy, the end of the distinction between men and women, and the disappearance of the separation of humans and beasts. The closest approximations to this in Chinese history were the cataclysmic civil wars that marked the collapse of major dynasties. Thus, the world empire needed within itself all the fragments that underlay its establishment: regulated bodies, ordered households, policed cities, and structured regions. This was the truth indicated in the lists of ordered spatial units with which this book began. Like all the other forms of ordered space, the empire was a whole that remained divided against itself.

This is demonstrated in the relation between the family and the state in the empire, as elaborated in a monograph by Ogata Isamu.[2] Despite classicist models that saw the state as an extension of the household, in practice the imperial state and the family were built on different principles, and the political order incorporated those differences. The state was constructed on the basis of relations between the ruler and his ministers/servants. The latter term originally indicated a slave or a dependent servant, and as in early modern Europe the early bureaucracy was formed by "the king's servants." Early Chinese officials, and people in general, could never refer to themselves by their family name in communications with the emperor. Instead they used the formula "your servant + personal name." The right to name one's family in the presence of the emperor was given only occasionally as a political privilege to the chief of the Xiongnu. This is important because slaves likewise had no surname and no legal family. In becoming the emperor's servants, people left their own family, lost their surname, and became the emperor's slaves.

The idea that one ceased to be a member of a family when in imperial service was marked not only in self-reference, but also in formulae pertaining to career patterns. To begin an official career was to "remove [from the household] one's body/self [*chu shen* 出身]" or to "rise up out of the household [*qi jia* 起家]." A request to retire was indicated by the formula "to beg for one's skeleton," where the skeleton was the part of the body that belonged to one's "bone and flesh" kin. Furthermore, biographical sketches of officials often specified whether they died "in office" or "in the household." All these usages indicate the assumption that the state and the family constituted two distinct and even antithetical realms, and that participation in one meant withdrawal from the other.

Ogata also examines the terms in which these two realms were understood. He shows that the state was identified as the realm of *gong* 公 "the lord, public, universal," while the household or family was the realm of *si* 私 "the private, partial, limited." Thus, he explains the tension between the two in terms of the dichotomy of part and whole around which this book has been structured. Families were by nature partial and limited in their interests, as demonstrated in the disputes between the Mohists and the *ru* classicists over whether the notion of a "concern for each and every individual" was reconcilable with the differential affections owed to kin. Arguments in the *Lun yu*, the *Mencius*, and the *Han Feizi* on whether fathers and sons should testify in court against one another indicate the same tension. The state was intended to be an encompassing structure in which all were equally subject to laws, rewards, and punishments. The household, in contrast, was a limited or partial realm which privileged members over outsiders, and rated even outsiders in terms of kin ties.

While the state and household were thus diametrically opposed, the state could not do without the household realm. Although certain utopian classicists imagined a high antiquity in which "the whole world was public," and radical statist philosophers like Han Fei advocated a world in which political loyalties superseded devotion to kin, in practice households remained indispensable elements of the state order. First, the Warring States polity depended on the service and taxes provided by peasant households, and the imperial state was built on the same foundation. Second, the Chinese empire remained a dynastic state, so the family unit remained embedded at the pinnacle of the imperial order. Third, and most important, given the limited number of personnel that the early Chinese state could recruit and pay, the government relied on powerful families to impose order at the local level.[3] The state order was thus not limited to those in state service, but necessarily included within itself large numbers of kin groups with particularist, local interests. These groups were drawn into the state order through the wealth and prestige gained in service, but they also assisted in preserving order through their pursuit of local power in forms condemned by statist visionaries such as Han Fei.

Thus, while the empire was itself the culmination of the drive toward total unity, it was a unity that harbored within itself, and depended on, many limited groups pursuing their own partial interests. The official public realm consisted of the imperial house and the few tens of thousands in state service, and secondarily those engaged in the study of the artificial, text-based language propagated by the court and its servants. Only these would, in the categories of the day, have been involved in "public service [*gong shi* 公事]." The vast majority of the population spent their entire lives within the partial realm of private interests defined by the household and economic enterprises. The link between the two, and the key to the ability of the Chinese empire to establish some degree of local order, lay in the fact that members of the great families moved back and forth between the two realms, thus establishing a single realm consisting of both state and families (*guo jia* 國家). In the combination of these two, the addition of the single "universal" to the huge number of "partials," the Chinese empire came as close as it possibly could to the vision of total unity. Since this approximation of unity was achieved only in the shifting of members of the great families between public service and private interest, the dream of constructing a universal space was achieved only within the dimension of time. But that is another book.

NOTES

INTRODUCTION

1. G. Nerlich, *The Shape of Space* (Cambridge: Cambridge University, 1976); H. Reichenbach, *The Philosophy of Space and Time* (New York: Dover, 1957); Christopher Ray, *Time, Space and Philosophy* (London: Routledge, 1991); Murad D. Akhundov, *Conceptions of Space and Time*, tr. Charles Rougle (Cambridge: MIT, 1986); Edward S. Casey, *The Fate of Place: A Philosophical History* (Berkeley: University of California, 1997), Parts 2–3. On the classical background to these theories, see Richard Sorabji, *Matter, Space and Motion: Theories in Antiquity and Their Sequel* (London: Duckworth, 1988).

2. *The Leibniz-Clarke Correspondence*, ed. H. G. Alexander (Manchester: Manchester University, 1956), pp. 25–26, 77. For discussions of the philosophical import of Leibniz's theory of space, see Casey, *The Fate of Place*, pp. 167–179; Michel Serres, *Le système de Leibniz et ses modèles mathématiques* (Paris: Presses Universitaires de France, 1968), pp. 172–192, 251–255, 657–664, 705–712, 756–796.

3. Henri Lefebvre, *La production de l'espace* (Paris: Editions anthropos, 1974); Pierre Bourdieu, *La distinction: critique social du jugement* (Paris: Minuit, 1979), ch. 2–3; Bourdieu, *Méditations pascaliennes* (Paris: Seuil, 1997), ch. 4. For urban design, see Bill Hillier and Julienne Hanson, *The Social Logic of Space* (Cambridge: Cambridge University, 1984); Bill Hillier, *Space Is the Machine* (Cambridge: Cambridge University, 1996); Eric Hirsch and Michael O'Hanlon, eds., *The Anthropology of Landscape: Perspectives on Place and Space* (Cambridge: Cambridge University, 1995).

4. Mark Edward Lewis, *Writing and Authority in Early China* (Albany: State University of New York, 1999), pp. 124–127, 198–202, 280–281; Marc Kalinowski, "Mythe, cosmogénèse et théogonie dans la Chine ancienne," *L'Homme* 137 (Jan.-March 1996), pp. 41–60.

5. On this parallel vision applied to a primal wilderness in Lu Ling's twentieth-century novel *Caizhu de ernümen* 財主底兒女們 (*Children of the Rich*), see Kirk A. Denton, *The Problematic of Self in Modern Chinese Literature: Hu Feng and Lu Ling* (Stanford: Stanford University, 1998), pp. 222–243.

6. Mark Edward Lewis, *Sanctioned Violence in Early China* (Albany: State University of New York, 1990), pp. 165–174; Lewis, *Writing and Authority*, pp. 127–129.

7. For a discussion of some early Western accounts of the generation of political states and a human world through processes of division out of a world that was orig-

311

inally without limits or distinctions, see Michel Serres, *Les origines de la géométrie* (Paris: Flammarion, 1993).

8. See chapter two, note 142, for examples of this argument.

9. Robin D. S. Yates, "Body, Space, Time and Bureaucracy: Boundary Creation and Control Mechanisms in Early China," in *Boundaries in China*, ed. John Hay (London: Reaktion Books, 1994), pp. 56–80; Yates, "Cosmos, Central Authority, and Communities in the Early Chinese Empire," in *Empires*, ed. Susan E. Alcock et al. (Cambridge: Cambridge University, 2000), pp. 360–368; Yates, "Purity and Pollution in Early China," in *Integrated Studies of Chinese Archaeology and Historiography*, Symposium Series of the Institute of History and Philology, Academia Sinica 4 (July 1997), pp. 479–536.

10. *Han shu* 漢書 (Beijing: Zhonghua, 1962) 30, p. 1775.

11. *Li ji zhu shu* 禮記注疏, in *Shisan jing zhu shu* 十三經注疏, vol. 5 (Taipei: Yiwen, 1976), ch. 60, "Da xue," pp. 1a–b. The relation of total self-mastery and the confrontation with objects will be discussed at length in chapter one and again in chapter four. A related discussion figures in the introduction to the chapter "Li yun 禮運," see *Li ji zhu shu*, ch. 21, "Li yun," pp. 3a–6b.

12. *Laozi dao de jing zhu* 老子道德經注, in *Xin bian zhu zi ji cheng* 新編諸子集成, vol. 3 (Taipei: Shijie, 1974), #54, p. 33; *Guodian Chu mu zhu jian* 郭店楚墓竹簡 (Beijing: Wenwu, 1998), p. 118 (2). The *Han Feizi* also includes the list in a commentary on this passage. See *Han Feizi ji shi* 韓非子集釋, annotated by Chen Qiyou 陳奇猷 (Shanghai: Renmin, 1974), ch. 6, "Jie Lao 解老," p. 384. Reduced versions of the list appear in the same chapter on pp. 357, 377.

13. *Mengzi zheng yi* 孟子正義, in *Xin bian zhu zi ji cheng*, vol. 1, IA, "Liang Hui Wang shang 粱惠王上," p. 22: "If Your Majesty says, 'How can I profit my state?' then your ministers will say, 'How can I profit my family?' and your men in service and commoners will say, 'How can I profit myself [*shen* 身]?'" p. 52; IVA, "Li Lou shang 離婁," p. 290: "People have a common saying, 'The world, the state, the family.' The world is rooted in the state, the state in the family, and the family in the body/self"; p. 295. See also *Huainanzi* 淮南子, in *Xin bian zhu zi ji cheng*, vol. 7, ch. 20, "Tai zu 泰族," p. 351.

14. *Lü shi chun qiu jiao shi* 呂氏春秋校釋, annotated by Chen Qiyou (Shanghai: Xuelin, 1984), ch. 17, "Zhi yi," pp. 1132–1133.

15. The chapter begins as follows: "Heaven and Earth, and yin and yang, do not change, but the myriad things formed from them are not the same. The eye does not become blind in seeing such differences as white and black. The ear does not become deaf in hearing such differences as clear or turbid sounds. The king holds to the one, and thereby is the standard for all things. The army must have a commander, who is the means of uniting it. The state must have a ruler, who is the means of uniting it. The world must have a Son of Heaven, who is the means of uniting it. The Son of Heaven must hold to the one, which is his means of drawing it [the world] together."

16. On the partial being ruled by the whole see Lewis, *Writing and Authority*, pp. 79–83, 287–336, 351.

17. On the mechanisms and significance of a shift from multiple independent cities to a single imperial center, see Michel Serres, *Rome: le livre des fondations* (Paris: Bernard Grasset, 1983), esp. pp. 11–16.

CHAPTER ONE

1. Modern accounts of the history or anthropology of the human body began with Marcel Mauss, "Les techniques du corps," in *Sociologie et anthropologie* (Paris: Presses Universitaires de France, 1950), pp. 365–386. A useful introduction to the massive literature is Michael Feher, Ramona Naddaff, and Nadia Tazi, eds., *Fragments for a History of the Human Body*, 3 vols. (New York: Zone, 1989). The third volume contains an annotated, eighty-page bibliography, admittedly more than a decade out of date.

2. Donn Welton, ed., *The Body: Classic and Contemporary Readings* (Oxford: Blackwell, 1999); Edward J. Casey, *Getting Back into Place: Toward a Renewed Understanding of the Place-World* (Bloomington: Indiana University, 1993), ch. 3–4; Casey, *The Fate of Place*, ch. 10–12; Rémi Brague, *Aristote et la question du monde* (Paris: PUF, 1988), ch. 6. On the body in human thought from the perspective of cognitive science, see George Lakoff and Mark Johnson, *The Metaphors We Live By* (Chicago: University of Chicago, 1980); Lakoff, *Women, Fire, and Dangerous Things: What Categories Reveal about the Mind* (Chicago: University of Chicago, 1987); Lakoff and Johnson, *Philosophy in the Flesh: The Embodied Mind and its Challenge to Western Thought* (New York: Basic Books, 1999). On the central role of the body in Chinese thought see Kuang-ming Wu, *On Chinese Body Thinking: A Cultural Hermeneutic* (Leiden: E. J. Brill, 1997).

3. Catherine Despeux, *Taoisme et corps humain* (Paris: Guy Tredaniel, 1994); Despeux, "Le corps, champ spatio-temporel, souche d'identité," *L'Homme* 137 (January–March 1996), pp. 87–118; Thomas P. Kasulis, Roger T. Ames, and Wimal Dissanayake, eds. *Self as Body in Asian Theory and Practice* (Albany: State University of New York, 1993), pp. 149–291; Angela Zito and Tani E. Barlow, eds., *Body, Subject and Power in China* (Chicago: University of Chicago, 1994); Zito, *Of Body and Brush: Grand Sacrifice as Text/Performance in Eighteenth-Century China* (Chicago: University of Chicago, 1997); Shigehisa Kuriyama, *The Expressiveness of the Body and the Divergence of Greek and Chinese Medicine* (New York: Zone, 1999); Gail Hershatter, Emily Honig, Jonathan N. Lipman, and Randall Strauss, eds., *Remapping China: Fissures in Historical Terrain* (Stanford: Stanford University, 1996), part II, "Bodies"; James L. Watson, "Of Flesh and Bones: The Management of Death Pollution in Cantonese Society," in *Death and the Regeneration of Life*, ed. Maurice Bloch and Jonathan Parry (Cambridge: Cambridge University, 1982), pp. 155–186; Frederic Wakeman, Jr., "Mao's Remains," in *Death Ritual in Late Imperial and Modern China*, ed. James L. Watson and Evelyn S. Rawski (Berkeley: University of California, 1988), pp. 254–288; Martin K. Whyte, "Death in the People's Republic of China," in *Death Ritual in Late Imperial and Modern China*, pp. 289–316; Anne Behnke Kinney, *Representations of Childhood & Youth in Early China* (Stanford: Stanford University, 2004), ch. 6; Susan Brownell, *Training the Body for China: Sport in the Moral Order of the People's Republic* (Chicago: University of Chicago, 1995); Yamaguchi Ichiro, *Ki als leibhaftige Vernunft: Beitrag zur interkulturellen Phänomenologie der Leiblichkeit* (Munich: Wilhelm Fink, 1997); Li Jianmin 李建民, *Sisheng zhi yu: Zhou Qin Han maixue zhi yuanliu* 死生之域：周秦漢脈學之源流 (Taipei: Zhongyang Yanjiuyuan, 2000); Li Jianmin, *Fangshu, yixue, lishi* 方術，醫學，歷史 (Taipei: Nantian, 2000), pp. 1–146; Du Zhengsheng 杜正勝 "Xingti, jingqi yu hunpo—Zhongguo chuantong dui 'ren' renshi de xingcheng 形體，精氣與魂魄—人·認識的形成," *Xin shixue* 2:3 (1991), pp. 1–65; Cai Biming 蔡璧名, *Shenti yu ziran—yi "Huangdi nei jing suwen" wei zhongxin lun gudai sixiang chuantong zhong de shenti guan* 身體與自然—以黃帝內經素問為中心論古代思想傳統中的身體觀 (Taipei: Guoli Taiwan Daxue,

1997); *Xin shixue* 10:4 (December 1999), special issue on "The History of the Body."

4. *Li ji zhu shu*, ch. 51, "Kongzi xian ju 孔子閒居," p. 2b. Another passage in which an argument is built on the homophony of the words for "ritual" and "body" is *Huainanzi* 淮南子, in *Xin bian zhu zi ji cheng*, vol. 7, ch. 11, "Qi su 齊俗," p. 176.

5. *Lun yu zheng yi* 論語正義, in *Xin bian zhu zi ji cheng*, vol. 1, ch. 9, "Tai Bo 泰伯," p. 160. See also ch. 23, "Yao yue 堯曰," p. 419: "If one does not understand fate [*ming* 命] one cannot be a gentleman; if one does not understand ritual, one cannot stand; if one does not understand words, one cannot appreciate people." Ch. 10, "Zi han 子罕," p. 193: "The people with whom one can study are not necessarily appropriate for travelling on the same Way. Those appropriate for travelling on the same Way are not necessarily appropriate to stand [*li*] together."

6. *Lun yu zheng yi*, ch. 18, "Wei Ling Gong 衛靈公," p. 334.

7. *Lun yu zheng yi*, ch. 16, "Zi Lu 子路," p. 283.

8. *Lun yu zheng yi*, ch. 15, "Yan Yuan 顏淵," p. 262. An even longer list of aspects of the body that the gentleman must constantly keep in mind appears in ch. 19, "Ji Shi 季氏," p. 361.

9. *Lun yu zheng yi*, ch. 9, "Tai Bo," p. 157; ch. 10, "Zi han," p. 180; ch. 11, "Xiang dang 鄉黨," pp. 199–206; ch. 12–13, "Xiang dang," pp. 207–233; ch. 17, "Xian wen 憲問," pp. 329, 330.

10. *Li ji zhu shu*, ch. 47, "Ji yi 祭義," pp. 5b–6a; *Mengzi zheng yi* 孟子正義, in *Xin bian zhuzi ji cheng*, vol. 1, IIIB, "Teng Wen Gong xia 滕文公下," p. 247; VIIB, "Jin xin xia 盡心下," pp. 575, 605 (this describes the gait of the hypocritical "village honest men"); *Zhuangzi ji shi* 莊子集釋, in *Xin bian zhu zi ji cheng*, vol. 3, ch. 29, "Dao Zhi 盜跖," pp. 428, 432; *Yanzi chun qiu ji shi* 晏子春秋集釋, annotated by Wu Zeyu 吳則虞 (Beijing: Zhonghua, 1962), p. 491; Han Ying 韓嬰, *Han shi wai zhuan ji shi* 韓氏外傳集釋, annotated by Xu Weiyu 許維遹 (Beijing: Zhonghua, 1980), pp. 323–324, 333; *Shi ji* 史記 (Beijing: Zhonghua, 1959) 47, pp. 1921–1922; *Shuo yuan* 說苑, in *Han Wei cong shu*, vol. 1 (Taipei: Xin xing, 1977), ch. 14, "Zhi gong 至公," p. 11b. On accounts of Confucius's bodily performances, see David Schaberg, "Confucius as Body and Text: On the Generation of Knowledge in Warring States and Han Anecdotal Literature," presented at "Text and Ritual in Early China," Princeton University, October 20–22, 2000. On Confucius's unusual bodily features, see also Lionel M. Jensen, "Wise Man of the Wilds: Fatherlessness, Fertility, and the Mythic Exemplar, Kongzi," *Early China* 20 (1995), pp. 418–419. For accounts of these features in Han apocryphal literature see examples in Jiang Yihua 姜義華 et al., *Kongzi—Zhou Qin Han Jin wenxian ji* 孔子—周秦漢晉文獻集 (Shanghai: Fudan Daxue, 1990), pp. 561, 581.

11. *Lun yu zheng yi*, ch. 18, "Wei Ling Gong," p. 337.

12. *Lun yu zheng yi*, ch. 1, "Xue er 學而," p. 11: "In serving his parents he is capable of using up his physical strength [*jie li* 竭力]; in serving his prince he is capable of bringing an end to his body [*zhi qi shen* 致其身, i.e., 'sacrificing his life']." The link between *shen* and physical strength, showing that the former refers to the organic body, also figures in ch. 5, "Li ren 里仁," p. 77: "One who hated inhumanity would practice humanity in such a way that inhumanity could gain no purchase on his *shen*. Is anyone capable of devoting his physical strength to humanity for a single day?" Two

passages use the phrase *zhong shen* 終身, literally "to the end of one's body," in the sense of the later more common *zhong sheng* 終生 "to the end of one's life." Again the equation of *shen* with "life" in reference to a span of time or quantity of vital energy indicates that it refers to the organic body. See ch. 10, "Zi han," p. 192; ch. 18, "Wei Ling Gong," p. 343. On the use of "*zhong* + unit of time" to specify duration, see ch. 2, "Wei zheng 為政," p. 28; ch. 5, "Li ren," p. 76; ch. 18, "Wei Ling Gong," pp. 341, 346 (2); ch. 20, "Yang Huo 陽貨," p. 383. Further evidence for the use of *shen* in the *Lun yu* to mean "body" is the phrase "personally in his *shen* 親於其身", where the translation of *shen* as "person" or "self" would be redundant. See ch. 20, "Yang Huo," p. 371. Finally, one passage uses *shen* to define the length of a garment, showing that the term again refers to the body and not the broader notion of "self." See ch. 12, "Xiang dang," p. 214. For a brief discussion of the range of meanings of *shen* as a term for the body, see Roger Ames, "The Meaning of Body in Classical Chinese Philosophy," in *Self as Body in Asian Theory and Practice*, p. 165.

13. *Lun yu zheng yi*, ch. 1, "Xue er," p. 18; ch. 2, "Wei zheng," pp. 26–27; ch. 7, "Yong ye 雍也," p. 121; ch. 8, "Shu er 述而," pp. 139, 141 (2), 143, 145; ch. 9, "Tai Bo," p. 169; ch. 17, "Xian wen," p. 305; ch. 18, "Wei Ling Gong," p. 346; ch. 20, "Yang Huo," p. 383. On the role played by these tales of suffering hunger or a humble diet in later accounts of Confucius, see Lewis, *Writing and Authority*, pp. 230–233.

14. *Lun yu zheng yi*, ch. 16, "Zi Lu," pp. 286, 289.

15. *Lun yu zheng yi*, ch. 5, "Li ren," p. 80.

16. Graham, *Disputers of the Tao*, pp. 53–111.

17. *Mengzi zheng yi*, VIIA, "Jin xin shang 盡心上," pp. 539–540. See also IIIB, "Teng Wen Gong xia 滕文公下," p. 269: "Yang's 'being for oneself' means to have no ruler. Mo's 'concern for each and all' means to have no father. To have no father and no ruler is to be an animal."

18. *Huainanzi*, ch. 13, "Fan lun 氾論." p. 218.

19. *Lü shi chun qiu jiao shi*, ch. 1, "Ben sheng 本生," pp. 20–21. On the same pages: "Now if there were sounds that would invariably please the ear, but which having heard would cause people to go deaf, certainly they would not listen to them. If there were sights that would invariably please the eye, but which having looked at would cause people to go blind, certainly they would not look at them. If there were flavors that were invariably agreeable to the mouth, but which having eaten would cause people to become mute, certainly they would not eat them. Therefore the sage's attitude to sounds, sights, and tastes is that he selects those which benefit his nature/life and rejects those which harm his nature/life. This is the way of keeping one's nature/life intact [*quan xing*]."

20. *Lü shi chun qiu jiao shi*, ch. 1, "Ben sheng," pp. 20–21: "That which initiates life is Heaven, and that which nourishes it to completion is man. The one who can nourish that which is given life by Heaven and not disturb it becomes the Son of Heaven. The actions of the Son of Heaven are intended to complete [*quan* 全] Heaven. It is for this reason that he establishes officials. The establishment of officials is to keep life intact [*quan sheng* 全生 = 全性]."

21. *Zhuangzi ji shi*, ch. 32, "Yu fu 漁父," pp. 443, 446–447. Linking *zhen* to the body and rejection of external things also figures in ch. 28, "Rang wang 讓王," pp. 417–418: "The most genuine [*zhen*] aspect of the Way regulates the body/self. Its

residue is used to rule a state. Its dirt and weeds are used to regulate the world. Seen from this point of view, the achievements of rulers are the residue of the work of the true sage. These are not the Way of keeping the body intact and nourishing life. Now the conventional gentlemen of the present age endanger their bodies and abandon their lives in pursuit of things." This story appears also in *Lü shi chun qiu jiao shi*, ch. 2, "Gui sheng 貴生," p. 75

22. *Liezi ji shi* 列子集釋, annotated by Yang Bojun 楊伯峻 (Beijing: Zhonghua, 1979), pp. 230–231. The body as measure of value also figures in the proto-*Laozi*, *Guodian Chu mu zhu jian*, p. 113: "Fame or your body, which is more dear? Your body or possessions, which is more important?" Life and the body are also the highest values in the "Ten Questions" found at Mawangdui. See Ma Jixing 馬繼興, *Mawangdui gu yi shu kaoshi* 馬王堆古醫書考釋 (Changsha: Hunan kexue jishu, 1992), p. 917; Donald Harper, *Early Chinese Medical Literature* (London: Kegan Paul, 1998), p. 399.

23. *Zhuangzi ji shi*, ch. 28, "Rang wang," pp. 414–415. A second story on p. 415 insists that one would not alter one's nature/life for the world. The first story also appears in *Lü shi chun qiu jiao shi*, ch. 2.2, "Gui sheng," p. 74. This story also appears earlier in *Zhuangzi ji shi*, ch. 1, "Xiao yao you 逍遙遊," pp. 12–13.

24. Tales demonstrating the rejection of things by depicting men who prefer humble life to high office appear in "Rang wang," pp. 418–419, 419, 419–420, 420–421, 421, 421–422, 422–423, 423–424.

25. *Zhuangzi ji shi*, ch. 28, "Rang wang," p. 416: "Great King Danfu can be said to have been able to reverence life. Those able to reverence life, even if they are noble and rich will not use that which nourishes life [the world] to harm their body/self. Even if they are poor and humble they will not use what benefits life to trammel their bodies." The idea that only one who rejects rulership for the sake of survival can be a ruler also figures in ch. 28, "Rang wang," p. 416. This argument also appears in *Laozi dao de jing* 老子道德經, in *Xin bian zhu zi ji cheng*, vol. 3, *zhang* 13, p. 7: "Thus one who honors his self/body as the whole world can be entrusted with the world. One who loves his self/body as the whole world can be entrusted with the world." A version of this passage figures in the fourth-century proto-*Dao de jing* found at Guodian. See *Guodian Chu mu zhu jian*, p. 118. See also *Huainanzi*, ch. 14, "Quan yan 詮言," p. 249: "Therefore it is proper to discuss the Way with one who, not worrying about the world being in chaos, takes pleasure in his own body being well-ordered."

26. *Lü shi chun qiu jiao shi*, ch. 21, "Shen wei 審為," p. 1453. This contrast of body parts with the clothing that covers them also appears in *Huainanzi*, ch. 20, "Tai zu 泰族," p. 364.

27. *Zhuangzi ji shi*, ch. 28, "Rang wang," p. 417: Zihuazi said, "Suppose we had 'world document' inscribed in front of you. This document would say, 'If you grasp this with your left hand, then your right hand will be removed. If you grasp it with your right hand, then your left hand will be removed. But the one who grasps it will certainly possess the world.' Would you be able to grasp it?" Marquis Zhaoxi said, "I would not." Zihuazi said, "Very good. Viewed from this point, the two hands are more important than the world. The body is likewise more important than the two hands. The state of Han is likewise far less important than the world, and what you are fighting for today is far less important than Han."

28. *Mozi jian gu* 墨子閒詁, annotated by Sun Yirang 孫詒讓, in *Xin bian zhu zi ji cheng*, vol. 6, ch. 12, "Gui yi 貴義," p. 265.

29. *Mengzi zheng yi*, VIA, "Gaozi shang 告子上," pp. 461–462: "Fish are what I desire. Bears' paws are also what I desire. If I could not get both, then I would give up fish to get bears' paws. Life is what I desire. Virtue is also what I desire. If I could not get both, then I would give up life in order to obtain virtue. Life is indeed what I desire, but there are things that I desire more than life."

30. The absence of a mind/body problem in China, and the tendency to view the mind and thought as aspects of the body have been noted by several scholars. See Roger Ames, "The Meaning of Body in Classical Chinese Philosophy," pp. 157–177; Kuang-ming Wu, *On Chinese Body Thinking*.

31. Hall and Ames, *Thinking Through Confucius* (Albany: State University of New York, 1987), pp. 237–244, 247, 263; Ames, "The Focus-Field Self in Classical Confucianism," in *Self as Person in Asian Theory and Practice*, ed. Roger T. Ames with Wimal Dissanayake and Thomas P. Kasulis (Albany: State University of New York, 1994), pp. 187–212; Hall and Ames, *Thinking from the Han: Self, Truth, and Transcendence in Chinese and Western Culture* (Albany: State University of New York, 1998), pp. 23–77; Ames, "The Local and Focal in Realizing a Daoist World," in *Daoism and Ecology: Ways within a Cosmic Landscape*, ed. N. J. Girardot, James Miller, and Liu Xiaogan (Cambridge: Harvard University, 2001), pp. 265–282; Tu Wei-ming, "Embodying the Universe," in *Self as Body in Asian Theory and Practice*, pp. 177–186.

32. The "Nei ye" has become the object of considerable attention in recent years. In China and Japan it is linked closely with the chapters "Xin shu shang," "Xin shu xia," and "Bai xin." Western scholars tend to focus on the "Nei ye," which is treated as the earliest and most original. On the chapters and their dating, see W. Allyn Rickett, *Guanzi: Political, Economic, and Philosophical Essays from Early China, A Study and Translation*, vol. 2 (Princeton: Princeton University, 1998), pp. 15–39, 56–58, 65–70, 82–85. Rickett provides a good coverage of the significant studies in Western languages and Chinese, and some of the major ones in Japanese. The "Nei ye" and to a lesser extent the other chapters have been the subject of a long-term study by Harold Roth, culminating in *Original Tao: Inward Training and the Foundations of Taoist Mysticism* (New York: Columbia University, 1999). Another useful study is Romain Graziani, "De la régence du monde à la souveraineté intérieure: Une étude des quatre chapitres de 'L'art de l'esprit' du *Guanzi*" (Ph. D. dissertation, Université Paris VII, 2001), 2 vols. Graziani has published in *T'oung Pao* 87 (2001) a review of Roth's book that indicates some of the differences in their approaches to the text. The brief presentation of the "Nei ye" in Graham, *Disputers of the Tao*, pp. 100–105 is also of value.

33. *Guanzi jiao zheng* 管子校正, annotated by Dai Wang 戴望, in *Xin bian zhu zi ji cheng*, vol. 5, ch. 16, "Nei ye 內業," pp. 268–269. Roth emends the text to refer to mountains rather than the self in the name of "preserving the meaning of the line and the parallel with line 4." In fact, the emendation loses the parallel that forms a complete spatial mandala. The epithet that Roth emends to apply to mountains appears a few lines later descriptive of "being within the heart," that is, within the core of the self. See *Original Tao*, pp. 48–49, 52–53. Moreover, another passage in the text is organized around the spatial coordinates of Heaven, Earth, four seas, and self, with the heart/mind at the center: "Storing [the refined energy] inside, We use it as the well spring. Flood-like it harmonizes and balances; We use it as the fount of vital energy. If the fount does not dry up, The four limbs will be firm. If the spring is not exhausted, The nine apertures will be completely open [to the flow of energies]. You can then exhaust Heaven and Earth, And cover the four seas." The idea of placing oneself at the

center and radiating influence to the edges of the world also appears in *Mengzi zheng yi*, VIIA, "Jin xin shang," p. 534: "The gentleman desires vast lands and numerous people, but he does not delight in them. He delights in placing himself at the center of the world and thereby fixing in place all the people within the seas, but his nature does not lie in this."

34. *Guanzi jiao zheng*, p. 269. Roth follows the emendation of *ji* 濟 to *qi* 齊, hence "equanimity." However, since before and after the text insists on the "completion" *cheng* of the heart/mind and worries about its "loss," it is reasonable to keep the character *ji* that can be a synonym of *cheng*.

35. *Guanzi jiao zheng*, ch. 16, "Nei ye," p. 272 (3): (1) "All vitality, Always comes through balance and correctness. The reason for its loss, Always is pleasure, anger, worry, and anxiety." (2) "All vitality, Always comes from satisfaction. When worried then you lose the guiding thread; When angry you lose the point of departure. When worried, sad, pleased, or angry, The Way then has no place within you. Love and desire, still them." (3) "The efficacious energy within the heart/mind; Now it comes, now it departs; So fine that there is nothing inside it; So vast that there is nothing outside it. The cause of losing it, Is the harm caused by agitation. If the heart/mind can maintain tranquillity, The Way will settle of itself."

36. *Guanzi jiao zheng*, ch. 16, "Nei ye," pp. 269–270.

37. *Guanzi jiao zheng*, ch. 16, "Nei ye," p. 270 (3). The second discussion of "things" states: "Those who can transform a thing are called 'spirits [*shen* 神]'; Those who can change an event are called 'wise'. But to transform [a thing] without expending vital energy, To change an event without expending wisdom, Only a true gentleman who holds fast to the One can do this." See also *Huainanzi*, ch. 21, "Yao lüe," p. 373: "On the outside to have contact with things and not be dazzled, on the inside to have the means to situate one's spirit [*shen*] and nourish one's energies, at peace and totally harmonious, finding joy in oneself, these are what one receives from Heaven and Earth."

38. *Guanzi jiao zheng*, ch. 16, "Nei ye," p. 270: "With an ordered heart/mind at the center, Ordered words come from your mouth, Ordered tasks are imposed upon others, and then the whole world is ordered." "Grasp [the refined energies] and do not let them go; Then the ears and eyes will not be flooded, And the mind will have no other designs. Correct the heart/mind at the center, The myriad things will obtain their proper degree;" p. 271: "The heart/mind is complete in the center; The body is complete on the outside; They encounter no heavenly [natural] disasters; Nor meet with harm from other people." "With a complete heart/mind, You cannot be blocked or hidden. It will be known from your facial expression; And seen in your skin color." A body perfected through holding in all its powers, with this perfection marked by immunity to injuries, also appears in the proto-*Laozi*. See *Guodian Chu mu zhu jian*, p. 113: "One who holds within [the body] the fullness of his or her power is like a new-born baby. Vipers, scorpions, poisonous insects, and snakes will not bite. Birds of prey and fierce beasts will not strike. Bones soft, muscles pliant, but the grasp is firm."

39. Immanuel Kant, "Concerning the Ultimate Ground of the Differentiation of Regions in Space," in *Theoretical Philosophy, 1755–1770*, tr. D. Walford and R. Meerbote (Cambridge: Cambridge University, 1992), pp. 361–372; Edmund Husserl, "Material Things in Their Relation to the Body" and "The Constitution of Psychic Reality

Through the Body," in *The Body*, ed, Donn Welton, pp. 11–37; Elmar Holenstein, "The Zero-Point of Orientation: The Placement of the I in Perceived Space," in *The Body*, pp. 57–94; Casey, *The Fate of Place*, ch. 10; Bernhard Waldenfels, *Das leibliche Selbst: Vorlesungen zur Phänomenologies des Leibes* (Frankfurt am Main: Suhrkamp Verlag, 2000), ch. 3.

40. The theme of the center and centering in early China, based on the passages in the "Nei ye," is discussed in Graziani, "De la régence du monde," pp. 59–66. His discussion derives in part from the discussion of "centering" as an element of Chinese imperial ritual in Zito, *Of Body and Brush*, ch. 5–6.

41. *Guanzi jiao zheng*, ch. 16, "Nei ye," p. 270.

42. *Guanzi jiao zheng*, ch. 16, "Nei ye," p. 270: "Released by a single word, Above you will discern Heaven, Below you reach to the limits of the Earth, You pervade the Nine Continents. How can you release it? It lies in the calmness of the mind"; p. 271: "If reverent and cautious, without alteration, You daily renew your inner power, You will completely know all under Heaven, Exhaust all within the Four Limits. Reverently bringing forth that which fills your body [the Way], This is called 'obtaining it within'."

43. *Guanzi jiao zheng*, ch. 16, "Nei ye," p. 270. The terms "correct" and "tranquil" are linked elsewhere in the poem: "Heaven's ruling principle is to be correct; Earth's ruling principle is to be level; Man's ruling principle is to be tranquil." See p. 269.

44. *Guanzi jiao zheng*, ch. 16, "Nei ye," p. 271. See also p. 272: "When your body is at peace and does not shift, You can hold to the One and discard all disturbances."

45. This is indicated in a passage stating that the Way is "the means by which we cultivate the heart/mind and correct the body."

46. *Guanzi jiao zheng*, ch. 16, "Nei ye," p. 271. These lines are followed by yet another passage that ties perfection of the self to the ordering of the cosmos: "They are then able to wear the Great Circle [Heaven] as their hat, and the Great Square [Earth] as their shoes. They will be mirrored in the Great Purity, And see in the Great Brightness."

47. *Guanzi jiao zheng*, ch. 16, "Nei ye," pp. 272–273.

48. *Zhou yi zheng yi* 周易正義, in *Shi san jing zhu shu* 十三經注疏, vol. 1 (Taipei: Yiwen, 1976), ch. 1, p. 27b: "The gentleman with yellow at the center comprehends all patterns. In the correct position he places his body. With excellence at his center, it flows through his limbs and emerges in his deeds."

49. Guo Moruo argues that the "Nei ye" influenced the *Mencius*. See Guo 郭沫若, *Shi pipan shu* 十批判書 (Beijing: Kexue chubanshe, 1956), pp. 161–162. Akatsuka Kiyoshi argues that the "Nei ye" is derivative. See Akatsuka 赤塚忠, "Dōka shisō no gensho no keitai 道家思想の原初の形態," *Tōkyō Daigaku Bungakubu kenkyū hōkoku: Tetsugaku ronbunshū* (1968). Yoshinaga Shinjirō follows Akatsuka. See Yoshinaga 吉永慎二郎, "Mō Ka no fudōshin no shisōshi teki yimi 孟軻の不動心の思想史的意味," *Nippon Chūgoku Gakkai hō* 37 (1985), p. 36.

50. *Guanzi jiao zheng*, ch. 16, "Nei ye," pp. 270–271.

51. *Mengzi zheng yi*, IIA, "Gongsun Chou shang 公孫丑上," pp. 210–214.

52. On the relations of *qi* to bellicosity see Lewis, *Sanctioned Violence*, pp. 222–226.

53. *Mengzi zheng yi*, IIA, "Gongsun Chou shang," pp. 214–219. The link between environment and body through *qi* is also in VIIA, "Jin xin shang," p. 550: "Dwelling's altering the *qi* and nourishment's altering the body are indeed great!" The *Mencius*'s discussion of *qi* also overlaps with the "Nei ye" in the story of the man who tries to help his sprouts to grow by pulling them up. This assertion that men's vital energy should not be pulled in order to develop it echoes the "Nei ye" that "one must not pull or push" human vitality or the "numinous *qi*." See *Guanzi jiao zheng*, ch. 16, "Nei ye," p. 272.

The image of personal energy filling up all between Heaven and Earth appears in an essay in the *Li ji*, where it is called the "energy of intent [*zhi qi* 志氣]." See *Li ji zhu shu*, ch. 51, "Kongzi xian ju," p. 2a. This apparently derives from the Mencian notion of an energy directed by the person's intent. Another passage praising a person's vast "energy of intent" whose "essential energies fill up Heaven and Earth, and are never exhausted" is *Lü shi chun qiu jiao shi*, ch. 15, "Xia xian 下賢," pp. 878–879.

For a different reading of Mencius's discussion of "flood-like *qi*," see Alan K. L. Chan, "A Matter of Taste: *Qi* (Vital Energy) and the Tending of the Heart (*Xin*) in *Mencius* 2A2," in *Mencius: Contexts and Interpretations*, ed. Alan K. L. Chan (Honolulu: University of Hawai'i, 2002), pp. 42–71.

54. See *Mengzi zheng yi*, VIA, "Gaozi shang 告子上," pp. 431–435. Master Gao compares human nature/life to plants, then to water, and finally asserts the identity of "nature" and "physical vitality" or "longevity." Mencius challenges him by arguing that people's nature includes an innate tendency to moral development, and that consequently human "nature" must be distinguished from mere animal vitality. Master Gao sees nature/life as mere energy, that is, *qi*, while Mencius insists that there is a human nature/life distinguished by its moral tendencies. Similarly Master Gao equates nature/life with the desire for food and sex, that is, the physical needs that people share with animals, and insists that all sense of moral rightness is exterior. See p. 437. This is precisely the argument that Mencius cites at the conclusion of his discussion of the moral nature of the "flood-like *qi*" to epitomize Master Gao's error. The parable of Ox Mountain also associates men's moral nature with their proper *qi*. See p. 457.

55. *Mengzi zheng yi*, VIA, "Gaozi shang," pp. 461–462. This is also the contrast exemplified by the comparison of the courage of the two warriors and that of Master Zeng.

56. On the heart/mind as the locus of the moral virtues see *Mengzi zheng yi*, IA, "Liang Hui Wang shang," p. 49; IIA, "Gongsun Chou shang," pp. 120, 138: "Every person has a heart/mind that cannot bear the suffering of others"; p. 144: "the heart/mind which hates evil"; IIIA, "Teng Wen Gong shang," p. 238; IVA, "Li Lou shang 離婁," p. 284; IVB, "Li Lou xia," pp. 327, 350: "A gentleman differs from others because he preserves his heart/mind. He preserves it with humanity and ritual"; VA, "Wan Zhang shang 萬章," p. 360; VB, "Wang Zhang xia," p. 411; VIA, "Gaozi shang," p. 446: "The heart/mind of sympathy, people all possess it; likewise the heart/mind of shame, respect, and right and wrong. The heart/mind of sympathy leads to humanity; that of shame to rightness, that of respect to ritual, and that of right and wrong to wisdom;" p. 451: "What is common to all heart/minds? Reason and rightness;" pp. 457, 458, 463, 464: "Humanity is the human heart/mind;" VIIA, "Jin xin shang," pp. 517, 534–535: "Humanity, rightness, ritual, and wisdom are all rooted in the heart/mind."

57. *Mengzi zheng yi*, IIA, "Gongsun Chou shang," pp. 238–239.

58. *Mengzi zheng yi*, VIA, "Gaozi shang," pp. 450–451.

59. *Mengzi zheng yi*, VIA, "Gaozi shang," p. 464. A version of this argument appears in *Huainanzi*, ch. 20, "Tai zu," p. 363.

60. *Mengzi zheng yi*, VIIA, "Jin xin shang, pp. 534–535. The links of moral and physical perfection are also suggested in two other passages. See p. 544: "Yao and Shun took it as their nature [*xing zhi* 性之]. Kings Tang and Wu embodied it [*shen zhi* 身之]. The Five Hegemons borrowed it"; p. 552: "The body and the complexion are our Heaven-given nature. Only the sage can put into practice the full capacities of his body." On the link of human nature and the heart/mind with the body see also p. 517: "One who fully realizes his heart/mind will know his nature. If one knows one's nature then one knows Heaven. Preserving one's heart/mind and nourishing one's nature are the way to serve Heaven. Whether dying young or living out a full lifespan he will not betray this, but cultivate his body/self to await Heaven."

61. *Mengzi zheng yi*, IIIA, "Teng Wen Gong shang," p. 219.

62. *Mengzi zheng yi*, VIA, "Gaozi shang," pp. 466–467. Deriving social hierarchy from bodily hierarchy is questioned in one of the early chapters of the *Zhuangzi*. See *Zhuangzi ji shi*, ch. 2, "Qi wu lun 齊物論," pp. 27–28: "The hundred joints, nine orifices, and six viscera are all present, so which one should I treat as more kin to me? Are you equally pleased with them all? No, you are partial to one among them. It being so, does it have the rest as servants and concubines? Are these servants and concubines not up to regulating one another? Or do they take turns being ruler and servant?"

63. *Mengzi zheng yi*, VIA, "Gaozi shang," p. 467.

64. On this theme see also VIIB, "Jin xin xia," p. 583: "The mouth's relation to tastes, the eyes' to colors, the ears' to sounds, the nose's to smells, and the four limbs to leisure are all nature. However, there is also a mandate [*ming* 命, i.e., something imposed from the outside] in this, so the gentleman does not call it nature. True humanity's relation to the ties of father and son, duty's to the ties of ruler and minister, ritual's to the ties of host and guest, knowledge's to the worthy man, and the sage's to the Way of Heaven are all mandated. However, there is also human nature within them, so the gentleman does not call them a mandate." Here the senses and their links to things are contrasted with the virtues, and by extension with the mind. IVB, "Li Lou xia," pp. 352–353: "There are five things that ordinary people call unfilial. The first is to allow one's limbs to be lazy and fail to nourish one's parents. The second is to play *liu bo* and chess and be fond of eating and drinking and fail to nourish one's parents. The third is to be fond of material wealth, be partial to one's wife, and thereby fail to nourish one's parents. The fourth is to indulge in the desires of the ear and eye, so that one's parents are humiliated. The fifth is to be fond of courage and fighting, so that one's parents are endangered." Each of the five forms of unfiliality expresses an improper relation between the mind and the lesser parts of the body, with the tendency to fight being an expression of vital energy. On filiality as a feature of the heart/mind see VA, "Wan Zhang shang," p. 360.

65. Jane Geaney points out passages in *Xunzi*, *Zhuangzi*, and *Mencius* where the mind supplants the sense organs' functions. See *On the Epistemology of the Senses in Early Chinese Thought* (Honolulu: University of Hawai'i, 2002), pp. 99–100. However,

she argues incorrectly that this shows that the mind is treated as another sense organ, rather than that it encompasses and hence rules the other organs.

66. [*Chun qiu*] *Zuo zhuan zhu* 春秋左傳注, annotated by Yang Bojun 楊伯峻 (Beijing: Zhonghua, 1981), Xi 24, p. 425: here the senses and the heart/mind are described as "traitors" if they do not perform their functions; Xiang 30, pp. 1178–1179; Zhao 9, pp. 1311, 1311–1312; Ai 6, pp. 1635–1636.

67. *Zuo zhuan zhu*, Zhao 9, p. 1312.

68. Roel Sterckx, "Le Pouvoir du Sens: Sagesse et Perception Sensorielle en Chine Ancienne," in *Cahiers d'Institut Marcel Granet* 1 (Paris: Presses Universitaires de France, 2003).

69. *Zuo zhuan shu*, Zhao 20, pp. 1419–1420: "Harmony is like a stew with water, fire, vinegar, meat sauce, salt, and plum sauce used to cook meat or fish. Cooking them over a fire, the chief cook harmonizes them. He adds what is lacking to reduce what is excessive. The gentleman eats this in order to balance his heart/mind. Rulers and ministers are also like this. . . . The former kings' adding of the five flavors and harmonizing of the five tones was in order to balance their heart/minds and perfect their government. See also Zhao 25, pp. 1457–1458.

70. *Zuo zhuan zhu*, Xi 22, p. 398. On drums to manipulate the army's *qi* see also Zhuang 10, p. 183. For other passages linking *qi* to combat see Xi 15, pp. 354–355; Zhao 10, p. 1317. On these and related passages, see Lewis, *Sanctioned Violence*, pp. 36–43, 227–228. On the links of sound, music, and energy as forms of control see also Xiang 31, p. 1195.

71. *Zuo zhuan zhu*, Zhao 25, pp. 1458–1459. For the gloss of the "six energies" see Zhao 1, p. 1222. The linkage of energy and intent also appears in an account of the body and senses found at Guodian. See *Guodian Chu mu zhu jian*, "Yu cong yi 語叢一, p. 195. See also *Xunzi ji jie* 荀子集解, in *Xin bian zhu zi ji cheng*, vol. 2, ch. 8, "Jun dao 君道," p. 154: "[The sage's] blood and energy are harmoniously balanced, and his intent and thoughts are vast. His performance of duty fills all between Heaven and Earth"; ch. 18, "Fu 賦," p. 314: "[Wisdom] is the essence of blood and energy, the florescence of intent and thought." The debate over the relation of energy and intent also appears in the medical literature. The "Shi wen" advocates using the intent to guide the energy. See Ma, *Mawangdui gu yi shu kaoshi*, p. 945; Harper, *Early Chinese Medical Literature*, p. 405 (2). In the *Huang Di nei jing su wen* "intent" appears as a substance in the body, mentioned in parallel with energy. See *Huang Di nei jing su wen ji zhu* 黃帝內徑素問集注, annotated by Zhang Yin'an 張隱菴 (Shanghai: Shanghai kexue jishu, 1959) 61, pp. 223–224: "[Diseases] are all produced from the five depots. The heart/mind stores spirit; the lungs store energy/breath [*qi*]; the liver stores blood; the spleen stores flesh; the kidneys store intent [*zhi*]. These form the body. When the intent is completely open, on the inside it links up with bone marrow, completing the body and giving proper form to the five depots."

72. Lewis, *Writing and Authority*, pp. 133–140.

73. *Zuo zhuan zhu*, Wen 15, pp. 612, 614; Cheng 13, p. 860; Cheng 15, p. 873; Zhao 7, p. 1295.

74. *Zuo zhuan zhu*, Cheng 13, pp. 860–861. An earlier passage on p. 860 makes the same links between ritual, *ming*, and a prophecy of death, but it uses *ming* in the sense of a ruler's charge.

75. *Zuo zhuan zhu*, Zhao 1, pp. 1219, 1220–1221.

76. *Zuo zhuan zhu*, Zhao 1, pp. 1221–1222. On *gu* diseases see Paul Unschuld, *Medicine in China: A History of Ideas* (Berkeley: University of California, 1985), pp. 46–50; Harper, *Early Chinese Medical Literature*, pp. 74–75, 158–159; 300–302. The doctor in the *Zuo zhuan* anecdote glosses it as follows: "It is produced by excess and disorderly conduct. As for the graph, the characters 'blood [*xue* 血]' and 'insect [*chong* 蟲]' form '*gu* 蠱'. Flying insects in grain are also *gu*. In the *Zhou yi* women deluding men or wind bringing down a mountain are called *gu*. These things are all in the same category."

77. On this issue see Lewis, *Writing and Authority*, pp. 79–82, 243–251.

78. *Zuo zhuan zhu*, Zhao 11, pp. 1325–1326.

79. The interchange of the two characters in different editions of the "Xi ci zhuan" in the *Yi jing* is noted in *Harvard-Yenching Institute Sinological Index Series*, supplement no. 10, *A Concordance to Yi Ching* (rep. ed., Taipei: Ch'eng-wen, 1973), p. 41.

80. *Zuo zhuan zhu*, Cheng 15, p. 873. The epithet "protector of the body [*shen zhi suo bi* 身之所庇]" is also applied to offices in Xiang 31, pp. 1192–1193; Xiang 21, p. 1063; Zhao 5, p. 1266.

81. *Zuo zhuan zhu*, Zhao 25, p. 1455.

82. *Zuo zhuan zhu*, Ai 7, p. 1641.

83. *Zuo zhuan zhu*, Ding 15, pp. 1600–1601.

84. On the practice in the *Zuo zhuan* of predicting fate through listening to the odes quoted in court ceremonial, see Lewis, *Writing and Authority*, pp. 155–163, as well as the numerous works cited therein.

85. *Guodian Chu mu zhu jian*, p. 181. On this passage see Liu Xingang 劉昕崗, "Guodian Chu jian 'Xing zi ming chu' pian jianshi 郭店楚簡 '性自命出' 篇箋釋," in *Guodian Chu jian Guoji Xueshu Yantaohui: lunwen ji* 郭店楚簡國際學術研討會： 論文集 (Wuhan: Hubei renmin, 2000), pp. 352–353.

86. *Li ji zhu shu*, ch. 61, "Guan yi 冠義," p. 1b. See also ch. 30, "Yu zao 玉藻," pp. 23a–b, 23b; ch. 48, "Ji yi 祭義," pp. 15b–16a; ch. 54, "Biao ji 表記," pp. 9a–b; ch. 55, "Zi yi 緇衣," p. 13b; *Zuo zhuan zhu*, Xiang 31, pp. 1194–1195; *Xunzi ji jie*, ch. 3, "Fei shier zi 非十二子," pp. 64–66—this contrasts the physical deportment of the true scholar with that of debased contemporary students; ch. 13, "Li lun 禮論," pp. 238, 242; ch. 15, "Jie bi 解蔽," p. 265—this includes a brief "rhapsody" on the physical appearance of the "Great Man"; *Zhou li zhu shu* 周禮注疏, in *Shisan jing zhu shu*, vol. 3, ch. 14, "Bao shi 保氏," p. 6b—this official instructs the people in the six forms of bodily decorum; ch. 38, "Si yi 司儀," p. 1a ff.

87. Unschuld, *Medicine in China: A History of Ideas*, ch. 2–3. For Chinese medicine based on the harmonization of energies see also Manfred Porkert, *The Theoretical Foundations of Chinese Medicine* (Cambridge: MIT Press, 1974); Porkert, *Die chinesische Medizin* (Dusseldorf, 1982).

88. *Shang shu zheng yi* 尚書正義, in *Shisan jing zhu shu*, vol. 1, "Gao Yao mo 皋陶 謨," ch. 4, p. 23b; "Tai shi 泰誓," ch. 11, p. 10a; *Mengzi zheng yi*, IB, "Liang Hui Wang xia," p. 89; IIA, "Gongsun Chou shang," p. 133; IVA, "Li Lou shang," p. 295; VA, "Wan Zhang shang," pp. 379–380, 381; *Li ji zhu shu*, ch. 52, "Zhong yong 中庸," p. 1a; *Zuo zhuan zhu*, Huan 6, pp. 111–112; Zhuang 10, pp. 182–183; Zhuang 14,

pp. 196–197; Zhuang 32, pp. 251–252; Xi 5, pp. 309–310; Xi 15, p. 365; Xi 16, p. 369; Xi 19, pp. 381–382; Xi 21, p. 390; Xi 28, pp. 467–468; Xuan 15, pp. 762–763. The idea that the people's *qi* produced natural prodigies also appears in *Chun qiu fan lu yi zheng* 春秋繁露義證, annotated by Su Yu 蘇輿 (Beijing: Zhonghua, 1992), ch. 81, "Tian di yin yang 天地陰陽," p. 466. See Lewis, *Sanctioned Violence*, pp. 236–237. The idea was even incorporated into imperial decrees. See, for example, *Hou Han shu* 後漢書 (Beijing: Zhonghua, 1965) 1a, p. 39; 6, p. 280.

89. On this argument see Lewis, *Writing and Authority*, pp. 243–251.

90. Bernard Faure, *The Rhetoric of Immediacy: A Cultural Critique of Chan/Zen Buddhism* (Princeton: Princeton University, 1991), ch. 8.

91. *Guanzi jiao zheng*, ch. 13, "Xin shu shang," pp. 219, 220. See also *Li ji zhu shu*, ch. 55, "Zi yi," p. 13b: "The people take the ruler as their heart/mind, and the ruler takes the people as his body. When the heart/mind is strong, then the body is relaxed. When the heart/mind is solemn then the body's appearance is respectful. If the heart/mind loves it, then the body will be at peace with it. If the ruler loves it, then the people will certainly desire it. The heart/mind is completed by the body, and it is also harmed by the body. The ruler is preserved by the people, but he also perishes by the people."

92. Unschuld, *Medicine in China: A History of Ideas*, pp. 79–83.

93. Li Jianmin argues that the image of the body formed by the flow of vital energies through *mai* channels was based on the observation of circulation in the Heavens, and the extension of this model to other realms in the numerological cosmology based on *qi*, *yin/yang*, and the Five Phases. See *Si sheng zhi yu: Zhou Qin Han maixue zhi yuanliu*, esp. pp. 107–140.

94. Three exceptions are listed in Geaney, *On the Epistemology of the Senses in Early China*, pp. 97–98. One example from the *Laozi* lists the mind with the senses as organs that can be perverted by sensual pleasure. Two from the *Xunzi* list the mind with the senses, and in one case the body, as things that have natural tendencies. See *Laozi dao de jing zhu*, #12, p. 6; *Xunzi ji jie*, ch. 7, "Wang ba 王霸," pp. 137, 141.

95. *Huang Di nei jing su wen ji zhu* 8, pp. 35–36. Another model in which the heart/mind is the ruler in the castle/inner wall of the chest appears in *Huang Di nei jing ling shu jiao zhu yu yi* 黃帝內徑靈樞校注語譯, annotated by Guo Aichun 郭靄春 (Tianjin: Tianjin kexue jishu, 1989) 35, p. 277. Yet another version linked to a system of correspondences between the human body and the cosmos is in *Huainanzi*, ch. 7, "Jing shen 精神," p. 100: "The roundness of the head imitates Heaven; the squareness of the feet imitates Earth. Heaven has the four seasons, the five phases, the nine sections, and 366 days. People also have the four limbs, five depots, nine openings, and 366 bodily segments. Heaven has wind, rain, cold, and heat. People also have taking, giving, happiness, and anger. Therefore the stomach is the clouds, the lungs are the breath/energy [*qi*], the liver is the wind, the kidneys are the rain, and the spleen is the thunder. In this way the body can be a third with Heaven and Earth, and the heart/mind is its master." For a briefer version, see *Huainanzi*, ch. 1, "Yuan dao 原道," p. 14.

96. For passages that describe the heart/mind as the master, or in one case the "concentrated essence [*zhuan jing* 專精]," of the other internal organs, see *Huang Di nei jing su wen ji zhu* 81, p. 378; *Huang Di nei jing ling shu jiao zhu yu yi* 28, p. 250; 71, p. 457. See also *Huainanzi*, ch. 1, "Yuan dao 原道," pp. 14–15: "The heart/mind

is the master of the five depots. It is the means of commanding the four limbs, and of causing blood and energy to flow"; ch. 9, "Zhu shu," p. 148: "The heart/mind cannot do even one of the tasks of the nine openings and the four limbs. However, in moving, remaining still, listening, or seeing, they completely take the mind as their master, because it never forgets its desire to benefit them." For lists of the organs with no insistence on the authority of the heart/mind, see *Huang Di nei jing su wen ji zhu* 4, pp. 14, 16, 16–17; 5, pp. 22–24, 27; 9, pp. 41–42; 10, p. 43; 17, pp. 67–68; 22, pp. 94–98; 23, p. 100 (2); 44, p. 169; 62, p. 224; *Huang Di nei jing ling shu jiao zhu yu yi* 1, p. 11; 23, pp. 212–214; 42, pp. 307–310; 43, p. 314; 49, p. 356; 56, p. 381; 77, p. 511; *Huainanzi*, ch. 7, "Jing shen," p. 100.

97. *Lü shi chun qiu jiao shi*, ch. 13, "You shi 有始," p. 659. Treating the cosmos and the body as parallel unities also figures in passages such as *Huainanzi* 8, "Ben jing," p. 115: "Seen from this point of view, Heaven, Earth, and the entire cosmos are one person's body; everything within the three dimensions is one person's frame."

98. *Huainanzi*, ch. 8, p. 123.

99. *Lü shi chun qiu jiao shi*, ch. 2, "Gui shen," p. 74. See also ch. 5, "Shi yin 適音," p. 272: "The ears' nature is to desire sounds, but if the heart/mind does not delight in them, then they will not listen to the five tones. The eyes' nature is to desire colors, but if the heart/mind does not delight in them, then they will not look at the five colors. The nose's nature is to desire fragrances, but if the heart/mind does not delight in them then it will not smell them. The mouth's nature is to desire tastes, but if the heart/mind does not delight in them then it will not taste them. What desires them is the ears, eyes, nose, and mouth, but what delights or does not delight is the mind. . . . The mind must be delighted before the senses possess what they desire"; *Huainanzi*, ch. 9, "Zhu shu," p. 127: "If the eye recklessly sees, then there is excess. If the ear recklessly hears, then there is delusion. If the mouth recklessly speaks, then there is chaos. These three gates must be scrupulously guarded"; ch. 20, "Tai zu," p. 361: "Now the eyes delight in the five colors, the mouth tastes the five flavors, and the ears go to excess in the five sounds. The seven openings [including the nose] fight one another and thereby harm their life." The "Wu xing 五行" text discovered at Mawangdui and Guodian also states, "The ears, eyes, nose, mouth, hands, and feet are the servants of the mind." However, it argues that these organs are all obedient to the mind so that the body will be "harmonious" and "excellent." See *Guodian Chu mu zhu jian*, p. 151; Ikeda Tomohisa 池田知久, *Maōtai Kan bo hakusho gogyōhen kenkyū* 馬王堆漢墓帛書五行篇研究 (Tokyo: Kyūko Shoin, 1993), p. 476.

100. See *Li ji zhu shu*, ch. 53, "Zhong yong," pp. 14b, 18a.

101. *Lü shi chun qiu jiao shi*, ch. 2, "Qing yu 情慾," pp. 84–85.

102. An account of rebellious senses destroying the body also appears in *Huainanzi*, ch. 7, "Jing shen," p. 101: "When the ears and eyes enjoy excess in the pleasures of sound and color, then the five depots will be shaken and unsettled. When the five depots are shaken and unsettled then the blood and energy will overflow without ceasing. When blood and energy overflow without ceasing, then the spirit energy runs out wildly and is not retained." See also ch. 2 "Chu zhen 俶真," p. 28: "When desires are tied to objects and the senses seduced by the outside world, then one loses one's nature and allotted life span;" ch. 9, "Zhu shu," pp. 127, 138, 139, 144; ch. 10, "Miu cheng 繆稱," p. 165; ch. 11, "Qi su," pp. 173, 186; ch. 14, "Quan yan 詮言," p. 242: "The sage is ruled by the mind; the masses by their desires. The gentleman guides

correct energy; the petty man guides deviant energy. That which on the inside accords with one's nature, on the outside accords with duties, moves in accord with proper pattern, and is not bound by objects is correct energy. That which is moved by taste, given up to excesses in sounds and colors, emerges from the emotions, and pays no heed to future disasters is deviant energy. . . . The eyes delight in color, the ears in sound, the mouth in tastes. When they come in contact with these they are delighted. That which does not recognize what is beneficial or harmful is the desires. To eat it does not agree with your body. To hear it does not accord with the Way. To see it is not good for your nature. These three gateways [senses] are in combat one with another, and that which controls them with the demands of duty is the mind. . . . These four, the ears, eyes, nose, and mouth, do not know what to take or to reject. The mind makes regulations for them, so that each gets its proper place"; p. 248; ch. 15, "Bing lüe 兵略," p. 256.

103. *Guodian Chu mu zhu jian*, "Xing zi ming chu," p. 180.

104. *Laozi dao de jing*, # 12, p. 6: "The five colors cause people's eyes to go blind. The five tones cause their ears to go deaf. The five tastes cause their mouths to lose all relish. Racing and hunting cause their heart/minds to go insane. Rare goods cause their actions to go astray. So the sage works for the belly and not the eye."

105. *Xunzi ji jie*, ch. 1, "Quan xue 勸學," pp. 7, 11.

106. *Li ji zhu shu*, ch. 48, "Ji yi," pp. 15b–16a.

107. See, for example, *Lü shi chun qiu jiao shi*, ch. 4, "Zun shi 尊師," p. 205; ch. 5, "Shi yin," p. 273; ch. 12, "Xu yi 序意," p. 648; ch. 14, "Xiao xing 孝行," p. 732; ch. 17, "Ren shu 任術," p. 1065. Two chapters in the *Xunzi* elaborate the thesis that ritual and music form sense experience to curb desires: "Li lun," and "Yue lun 樂論." The chapter "Xing e 性惡" also argues that the desires of the sense organs lead men to wanton conduct that destroys social order, and that only ritual can curb these desires. The essay "Li lun" begins, "From what does ritual arise? People have desires at birth. If they cannot satisfy these desires then they must seek for things. If in seeking there are no degrees, measures, divisions, or limits, then there must be fights. If there are fights there will be chaos, and if there is chaos there will be poverty. The former kings detested this chaos, so they instituted rituals in order to divide things, to satisfy people's desires, and to provide for people's needs. They made it so that desires would not lack the things to satisfy them, and things not be completely used up by the desires." See *Xunzi ji jie*, ch. 13, p. 231. References to this idea, linking the mind with the senses and identifying ritual as the key to self-control and order, appear throughout the text. See ch. 1, "Xiu shen 修身," pp. 13–14, 15–16, 21; ch. 2, "Rong ru 榮辱," pp. 40–41, 42–44; ch. 3, "Fei xiang 非相," p. 50; ch. 4, "Ru xiao 儒效," p. 92; ch. 5, "Wang zhi 王制," pp. 96, 101; ch. 6, "Fu guo 富國," pp. 113, 115, 116, 116–117, 121; ch. 7, "Wang ba," pp. 137, 141, 148; ch. 8, "Jun dao," pp. 157, 163; ch. 10, "Yi bing 議兵," p. 184; ch. 15, "Jie bi," p. 267; ch. 16, "Zheng ming 正名," pp. 283–284, 284–285. The "Yue ji" chapter of the *Li ji* also espouses this model. See also ch. 50, "Zhong Ni yan ju 仲尼燕居," p. 18a: "If there is no ritual, then the hands and feet cannot be placed, and the eyes and ears cannot be applied. Advancing, retreating, and yielding will have nothing to control them. If one dwells in this manner, then senior and junior will cease to be separated, and the women's quarters and wider kin will lose all harmony. The court's offices and titles will lose all order." Here bodily collapse induced by the absence of ritual spreads outward to destroy order in the household and the state.

108. *Huainanzi*, ch. 7, "Jing shen," pp. 103–104. See also ch. 7, p. 109; ch. 12, "Dao ying 道應," p. 203. The reference to "dead ashes" is in *Zhuangzi ji shi*, ch. 2, "Qi wu lun," p. 22.

109. *Huainanzi*, ch. 8, "Ben jing," pp. 120–121; ch. 16, "Shuo shan 説山," p. 271; ch. 20, "Tai zu," p. 347.

110. *Lü shi chun qiu jiao shi*, ch. 1, "Meng chun ji," p. 3. See also *Li ji zhu shu*, ch. 14, "Yue ling 月令," p. 21b. The season of death, winter, is marked by the reversal of the process. "The Heavenly energy leaps up, while Earth's energy descends. Heaven and Earth do not link up. They are sealed off and form winter." See *Lü shi chun qiu jiao shi*, ch. 10, "Meng dong," p. 516; *Li ji zhu shu*, ch. 17, "Yue ling," p. 11b. See also *Guanzi jiao zheng*, ch. 18, "Duo di 度地," p. 305; *Huang Di nei jing su wen ji zhu* 2, p. 5; 5, p. 20; 25, p. 102; 68, p. 267; 71, p. 309; 74, p. 335; *Lun heng ji jie* 論衡集解, written by Wang Chong 王充, annotated by Liu Pansui 劉盼遂 (Beijing: Gu ji, 1957), ch. 3, "Gu xiang 骨相," p. 57: "One receives the energies from Heaven and establishes the physical form from the Earth."

111. *Li ji zhu shu*, ch. 22, "Li yun," p. 5a. See also ch. 50, "Ai Gong wen 哀公問," p. 10a: "If Heaven and Earth do not join, the myriad objects will not generate"; *Huang Di nei jing su wen ji zhu* 25, pp. 102–103: "Heaven covers and Earth supports, so the myriad things are all complete. None of them is nobler than humanity. Humanity is born from the energies of Heaven and Earth, and completed on the model of the four seasons"; *Huang Di nei jing ling shu jiao zhu yu yi* 8, p. 81: "Heaven within me is the generative power; Earth within me is the energy. When the power flows and the energy grapples with it life is produced"; *Huainanzi*, ch. 8, "Ben jing," p. 115: "When Heaven and Earth join in harmony, and yin and yang fashion and fertilize, then the myriad objects all avail themselves of this single energy"; p. 119: "The Grand Unity encompasses Heaven and Earth, presses down the mountains and rivers, swallows in and spits out yin and yang. . . . Yin and yang inherit the harmonious joining of Heaven and Earth, form the bodies of the myriad diverse things, swallow in the energies and generate the things, and thereby complete the category of formed things"; ch. 13, "Fan lun 氾論," p. 216: "When [Heaven and Earth] harmonize then yin and yang coordinate, day and night divide, and they give birth to things. At the division of spring they are born, and at the division of autumn they are complete"; ch. 20, "Tai zu," p. 348.

112. *Hou Han shu* 6, pp. 255, 259.

113. *Li ji zhu shu*, ch. 37, "Yue ji," p. 21a; ch. 38, "Yue ji," pp. 16b–17a. On "hua" in association with "wind" as fertilization, see *Zhuangzi ji shi*, ch 14, "Tian yun 天運," pp. 217–218; *Huainanzi*, ch. 20, "Tai zu," p. 349. *Huang Di nei jing su wen ji zhu* 66, p. 246 states, "When things are born we call it 'hua'." See also *Li ji zhu shu*, ch. 53, "Zhong yong," p. 3a: "If one can totally follow the nature of things, then one can assist the generation and nourishing done by Heaven and Earth." Similar accounts of the rise of Heavenly energies, the descent of Earthly energies, the joining of yin and yang, and the generation of objects also appear in *Huainanzi*, ch. 2, "Chu zhen," p. 19; ch. 3, "Tian wen 天文," pp. 35 (2), 51. See also *Lü shi chun qiu jiao shi*, ch. 13, "You shi," p. 657: "Heaven rarefied in order to be completed, and Earth filled in order to take shape. Heaven and Earth's joining in harmony is the great principle of procreation."

114. *Li ji zhu shu*, ch. 38, "Yue ji," p. 16a. The formation of objects through the congealing of energies also appears in *Lü shi chun qiu jiao shi*, ch. 5, "Da yüe 大樂,"

p. 255. *Huainanzi*, ch. 21, "Yao lüe," p. 373, also proceeds from the "congealing of Heaven and Earth" to the fashioning of the myriad things and the generation of all life. The congealing of energy, indicated by the character *ling* 凌, is also invoked as a key to physical health in the text "Ten Questions" found at Mawangdui. See Ma, *Mawangdui gu yi shu*, p. 972; Harper, *Early Chinese Medical Literature*, p. 411.

115. *Huainanzi*, ch. 7, "Jing shen," p. 99. This same page says, "The refined spirit energies are what is received from Heaven; the body is what is received from Earth." On dividing the body into essential energies that return to Heaven and bones that go back to the Earth, see also *Hou Han shu* 52, p. 1724.

116. *Lun heng ji jie*, ch. 22, "Ding gui 訂鬼," pp. 455–456.

117. *Huainanzi*, ch. 3, "Tian wen," p. 51; ch. 7, "Jing shen," p. 100; ch. 8, "Ben jing" p. 120; *Huang Di nei jing su wen ji zhu* 5, pp. 21, 26–27; 9, pp. 38–39; 25, p. 103; 27, p. 109; 66, p. 245; *Huang Di nei jing ling shu jiao zhu yu yi* 12, p. 144; 71, p. 454. See also *Chun qiu fan lu yi zheng*, ch. 13, "Ren fu tian shu 人副天數," pp. 354–355.

118. *Huainanzi*, ch. 8, "Ben jing," p. 115.

119. *Lun heng ji jie*, ch. 3, "Wu shi 物勢," p. 68. The use of *he qi* to refer to the cosmos's generation of life also appears in *Huang Di nei jing su wen ji zhu* 9, p. 41. The use of *he qi* in relation to human sexual activity figures in *Guanzi jiao zheng*, ch. 14, "Shui di 水地," p. 236. See also "Recipes for Nurturing Life" found at Mawangdui: "Yu said, 'I wish to conjoin energies, so that men and women propagate. How can this be done?'" Ma, *Mawangdui gu yi shu*, p. 744; Harper, *Early Chinese Medical Literature*, p. 358. *Huang Di nei jing ling shu jiao zhu yu yi* 12, p. 142: "The five depots conjoin the spirit energies, the *hun*, and the *po*, and store them"; 44, p. 316: "When the energies conjoin there will be a body." This last phrase also appears in *Huang Di nei jing su wen ji zhu* 9, p. 41.

120. *Li ji zhu shu*, ch. 23, "Li qi 禮器," p. 4a: "The joining of Heaven and Earth, the service of the ancestral temples, the way of father and son, the duty of ruler and subject, these are all sequences." Ch. 26, "Jiao te sheng," p. 18b: "Only after Heaven and Earth join do the myriad things arise. Marriage ritual is the origin of the myriad generations. Selecting brides from different surnames is the means of attaching oneself to those who are distant and placing emphasis on divisions [*bie* 別]."

121. *Li ji zhu shu*, ch. 25, "Jiao te sheng," pp. 20a–b. The passage continues: "One takes material substance from the Earth and the model from Heaven. Therefore one reveres Heaven and treats the Earth as kin." Covering the Altar of the Soil of a state that has perished "to demonstrate that it has been cut off from Heaven and Earth" also appears in *Lun heng ji jie*, ch. 13, "Bie tong 別通," p. 273.

122. *Lü shi chun qiu jiao shi*, ch. 11, "Zhi zhong 至忠," p. 578; *Lun heng ji jie*, ch. 7, "Dao xu," p. 152. See Harper, *Early Chinese Medical Literature*, pp. 42, 48, 65, 98, 102, 112–113, 142, 406–410.

123. See *Zhuangzi ji shi*, ch. 6, "Da zong shi 大宗師," p. 103; ch. 17, "Qiu shui 秋水," p. 259; ch. 19, "Da sheng 達生," p. 279; *Huainanzi*, ch. 1, "Yuan dao," p. 16; ch. 2 "Chu zhen," pp. 29, 31.

124. *Li ji zhu shu*, ch. 22, "Li yun," p. 17a.

125. *Li ji zhu shu*, ch. 21, "Li yun," p. 22b.

126. *Xunzi ji jie*, ch. 5, "Wang zhi," p. 103; ch. 13, "Li lun," p. 233. See also *Li ji zhu shu*, ch. 22, "Li yun," pp. 10b–11a: "Humans are the heart/mind of Heaven and

Earth, and the starting point of the Five Phases. Through eating the flavors, distinguishing the sounds, and wearing the colors they live. So when the sage arises, then he takes Heaven and Earth as his root, yin and yang as his origin, the four seasons as his handles, the sun and stars as his guiding cord, the moon as his measure, the spirits as his followers, the Five Phases as his substance, ritual and duty as his implements, human emotions as his field, and the magical beasts of the four directions as his livestock."

127. *Li ji zhu shu*, ch. 26, "Jiao te sheng," p. 7a.

128. *Li ji zhu shu*, ch. 22, "Li yun," pp. 18a–19b. See also ch. 21, "Li yun," p. 6b: "Ritual must be rooted in Heaven, patterned on Earth, and laid out among the spirits"; ch. 23, "Li qi," p. 2a: "Ritual is that which accords with the seasons of Heaven, bases itself on the resources of Earth, follows the spirits, accords with the human heart, and regulates the myriad things." The passage on "hiding" the ruler's body also makes this point. The links of body, ritual, and Heaven and Earth again appear in *Li ji zhu shu*, ch. 63, "Sang fu si zhi 喪服四制," p. 11b: "The great form [*ti* 體] of all rituals is that they embody [*ti*] Heaven and Earth, imitate the four seasons, pattern themselves on *yin* and *yang*, and accord with human emotions. Consequently they are called rituals." This argument is based on the homophony of "ritual" and "body."

129. *Huainanzi*, ch. 20, "Tai zu," p. 347. The preceding lines describe how the sage "is like the spring rain watering the myriad things. Formlessly flowing, vastly bestowing, there is no land that is not moistened and no creature that is not born." A subsequent passage elaborates how the sage "contains the energies of Heaven, and embraces the heart/mind of Heaven." See p. 348.

130. *Huainanzi*, ch. 16, "Shuo shan," p. 275.

131. See, for example, *Huang Di nei jing su wen ji zhu* 73, p. 332.

132. Ma, *Mawangdui gu yi shu*, pp. 304–306; Harper, *Early Chinese Medical Literature*, p. 219.

133. Ma, *Mawangdui gu yi shu*, pp. 203–207; Harper, *Early Chinese Medical Literature*, pp. 199–200.

134. Ma, *Mawangdui gu yi shu*, p. 917; Harper, *Early Chinese Medical Literature*, p. 399. See also "Discussion of the Supreme Way in the World." See Ma, *Mawangdui gu yi shu*, p. 1012 (here placed at the end of the preceding text); Harper, *Early Chinese Medical Literature*, p. 425. On impotence as death, see Ma, *Mawangdui gu yi shu*, pp. 883–885; Harper, *Early Chinese Medical Literature*, p. 389.

135. Early Han avoidance of grain to prolong life is also cited in the *Shi ji* 史記 (Beijing: Zhonghua, 1959) 55, p. 2048: here Zhang Liang avoids grains, practices physical exercises, and "lightens his body"; *Xin yu* 新語, attributed to Lu Jia 陸賈, in *Xin bian zhu zi ji cheng*, vol. 2, ch. 6, p. 10.

136. Ma, *Mawangdui gu yi shu*, p. 846; Harper, *Early Chinese Medical Literature*, p. 309.

137. He Zhiguo 何志國, "Woguo zuizao de renti jingmai qidiao 我國最早的人體經脈漆雕," *Zhongguo wenwu bao* 15 (1994), p. 4; He, "Xi Han renti jingmai qidiao kao 西漢人體經脈漆雕考," *Daziran tansuo* (1995:3), pp. 16–20; He and Vivienne Lo, "The Channels: A Preliminary Examination of a Lacquered Figurine from the Western Han Period," *Early China* 21 (1996), pp. 81–123.

138. Vivienne Lo, "Imagining Practice: Sense and Sensuality in Early Chinese Medical Illustration," to be published in an as yet unnamed volume being edited by Georges Métailié.

139. For a discussion of these ideas, with emphasis on the Mawangdui literature, see Ma, *Mawangdui gu yi shu*, pp. 151–158. For references in various genres, see "Yuan you 遠遊, in *Chu ci bu zhu* 楚辭補注, annotated by Hong Xingzu 洪興祖, Si bu cong kan edition (Taipei: Yiwen, 1974), ch. 5, p. 3b; *Han Feizi ji shi* 韓非子集釋, annotated by Chen Qiyou 陳奇猷 (Shanghai: Renmin, 1974), ch. 6, "Jie Lao 解老," p. 351; *Zhuangzi ji shi*, ch. 6, "Da zong shi 大宗師," p. 103; *Huainanzi*, ch. 20, "Tai zu," pp. 353–354; *Huang Di nei jing su wen ji zhu* 1, p. 4; *Huang Di nei jing ling shu jiao zhu yu yi* 75, p. 497: here the "true energy" that one draws in from Heaven combines with the "energy from grain" to permeate the body.

140. Ma, *Mawangdui gu yi shu*, pp. 890, 903–905, 925, 952, 960, 966–967, 969–972, 983, 1004, 1020, 1038, 1049; Harper, *Early Chinese Medical Literature*, pp. 390, 395–396, 401, 407, 409–410, 410–411, 416, 420, 426–427, 430, 433; Gao Dalun 高大倫, *Zhangjiashan Han jian "Yin shu" yanjiu* 張家山漢簡 "引書" 研究 (Chengdu: Ba Shu, 1995), pp. 90–97, 129, 148, 158, 167, 172. Timing could also be essential for acupuncture, as in *Huang Di nei jing su wen ji zhu* 67, p. 105: "In the rules for all needling, one must await the correct energies of the sun, moon, asterisms, four seasons, and eight winds. When these energies are settled then one needles."

141. Ma, *Mawangdui gu yi shu*, p. 829; Harper, *Early Chinese Medical Literature*, pp. 306–307.

142. Ma, *Mawangdui gu yi shu*, pp. 867–876; Harper, *Early Chinese Medical Literature*, pp. 385–387.

143. Ma, *Mawangdui gu yi shu*, pp. 903–905; Harper, *Early Chinese Medical Literature*, p. 394.

144. Ma, *Mawangdui gu yi shu*, p. 927; Harper, *Early Chinese Medical Literature*, p. 397. There is a debate over where the relevant strips should be inserted, but the precise location is not essential to the point being made here. Other references in the "Ten Questions" to the need to replenish yin and the methods for doing so also appear in Ma, *Mawangdui gu yi shu*, pp. 882, 934, 969, 972, 1044; Harper, *Early Chinese Medical Literature*, pp. 388, 402, 410, 411, 432; Gao, *Zhangjiashan Han jian "Yin shu" yanjiu*, p. 170. The focus on improving the yin is also shown in the physical exercises called "pulling yin." See Ma, *Mawangdui gu yi shu*, pp. 746, 947, Harper, *Early Chinese Medical Literature*, pp. 359, 405; Gao, *Zhangjiashan Han jian "Yin shu" yanjiu*, pp. 102, 112, 134, 145.

145. Ma, *Mawangdui gu yi shu*, pp. 897–905; Harper, *Early Chinese Medical Literature*, pp. 393–396.

146. Michael Loewe, *Ways to Paradise: The Chinese Quest for Immortality* (London: Allen & Unwin, 1979), pp. 9–13; Loewe, *Chinese Ideas of Life and Death: Faith, Myth and Reason in the Han Period* (London: George Allen & Unwin, 1982), ch. 11; Yü Yingshih, " 'O Soul, Come Back!': A Study in the Changing Conceptions of the Soul and Afterlife in Pre-Buddhist China," *Harvard Journal of Asiatic Studies* 47:2 (1987), pp. 363–395.

147. Anna Seidel, "Tokens of Immortality in Han Graves," *Numen* 29 (1982), p. 107; Seidel, "Traces of Han Religion in Funeral Texts Found in Tombs," in *Dōkyō to*

shūkyō bunka 道教と宗教文化, ed. Akizuki Kan'ei 秋月觀暎 (Tokyo: Hirakawa, 1987), pp. 21–57; Seidel, "*Post-Mortem* Immortality, or The Taoist Resurrection of the Body," in *Gilgul: Essays on Transformation, Revolution and Permanence in the History of Religions*, ed. Sh. Shaked, et al. (Leiden: E. J. Brill, 1987), p. 227; Pu Muzhou (Mu-chou Poo) 蒲慕州, *Muzang yu shengsi: Zhongguo gudai zongjiao zhi xingsi* 墓葬與生死: 中國古代宗教之省思 (Taipei: Lianjing, 1993), p. 216; K. E. Brashier, "Han Thanatology and the Division of 'Souls'," *Early China* 21 (1996), pp. 125–158.

148. *Huainanzi*, ch. 9, "Zhu shu," p. 127.

149. *Huainanzi*, ch. 7, "Jing shen," p. 103.

150. Brashier, "Han Thanatology," pp. 138–146. In addition to the passages cited by Brashier, see also *Huang Di nei jing ling shu jiao zhu yu yi* 9, p. 98: "Dwelling deeply in a quiet place, moving with the spirit, closing the doors and sealing the windows, so the *hunpo* will not scatter. Concentrate your thoughts and unite your spirit, so the essential energies will not separate"; 47, p. 330: "If the intent and ideas are harmonized, then the essential spirit energies will be concentrated and straight, the *hunpo* will not scatter, resentment and anger will not arise, and the five depots will receive no pernicious energies."

151. *Huang Di nei jing ling shu jiao zhu yu yi* 54, p. 375. On the constructive (*ying* 營) and defensive (*wei* 衛) circulation see Nathan Sivin, *Traditional Medicine in Contemporary China* (Ann Arbor: Center for Chinese Studies, University of Michigan, 1987), pp. 46–53.

152. *Huang Di nei jing su wen ji zhu* 9, pp. 41–42; 23, p. 100; *Huang Di nei jing ling shu jiao zhu yu yi* 8, p. 85; 12, p. 142.

153. In addition to Brashier's citations on disturbances of the *hun* producing bad dreams, see *Lun heng ji jie*, ch. 22, "Ji yao 紀妖," p. 440: "As for people's dreams, diviners say that they are the movement of the *hun*. To dream that one sees god-on-high means that the *hun* has ascended to Heaven." On damage of the *hun* and madness, see *Lun heng ji jie*, ch. 13, "Xiao li 效力," p. 267: "Exerting oneself for tens or hundreds [lines of text], one spits blood into the pot. Losing the *hun* one becomes crazy and disordered, going so far as to cut off the vital energies [= dying]." Also linking *hun* to thinking is the idea that the *hun* of the deceased possesses the shaman and speaks through him. See *Lun heng ji jie*, ch. 20, "Lun si 論死," p. 417.

154. Brashier, "Han Thanatology," pp. 142–145. In addition to the passages cited by Brashier, see also *Huang Di nei jing ling shu jiao zhu yu yi* 8, p. 80: "When [the contents] overflow and leave the depots, then essence [*jing*] is lost, the *hunpo* flies off, the intent and ideas become confused and disordered, and cunning and forethought depart from the body"; p. 83: "When grief or sorrow strikes the liver, this harms the *hun*. When the *hun* is harmed then one becomes crazy, forgets, and cannot concentrate [?]."

155. *Zuo zhuan zhu*, Xuan 15, p. 765; Zhao 25, p. 1456.

156. *Zuo zhuan zhu*, Zhao 25, p. 1456. This gloss of the *hunpo* as the "essential brightness" of the mind helps explain a well-known passage in the *Zuo zhuan*. See Zhao 7, pp. 1292–1293: "When human life is first fertilized it is called *po*. Having given life to the *po*, its yang aspect is called *hun*. [or "When it emerges into the light of day, it is called *hun*."] If by means of much material its essence grows abundant, then the *hunpo* grows strong, and thereby its essential brightness [*jing shuang*] attains to 'spirit illumination [*shen ming* 神明]'." "Spirit illumination" refers both to powerful

spirits and to the highest state of human mental powers which matches those of the spirits. Given the linked definitions of *hunpo* and *jingshuang* as the essence of mental powers, the progression from *po* through *hun* to *shen ming* is consistent. The *hunpo* as the essence of mental powers appears also in *Huang Di nei jing ling shu jiao zhu yu yi* 47, p. 330: "Intent [*zhi*] and ideas are the means of directing the essential spirit and of concentrating the *hunpo*."

157. Brashier, "Han Thanatology," pp. 134–138. On the consciousness of the *hun* within the grave, see pp. 149–151. In addition to the eight examples from stone inscriptions, see *Lun heng ji jie*, ch. 18, "Gan lei 感類," p. 377; ch. 21, "Si wei 死偽," pp. 426, 427, 428; ch. 23, "Bo zang 薄葬," p. 463.

158. *Feng su tong yi jiaoshi* 風俗通義校釋, annotated by Wu Shuping 吳樹平 (Tianjin: Tianjin renmin, 1980), p. 428.

159. *Lun heng ji jie*, ch. 23, "Bo zang," p. 461.

160. Robert L. Thorp, "Mountain Tombs and Jade Burial Suits: Preparations for Eternity in the Western Han," in *Ancient Mortuary Traditions of China: Papers on the Chinese Ceramic Funerary Sculptures*, ed. George Kuwayama (Los Angeles: Los Angeles County Museum of Art, 1991), p. 34. On the defilement of the *hun* through the exposure of the skeleton, see *Hou Han shu* 56, p. 1832. Covering the corpse and placing jade in its orifices to prevent decay was criticized thus by a Han speaker: "The essential spirits belong to Heaven, the form and skeleton to earth. When the essential spirits depart the body, then each returns [*gui* 歸] to its true nature. Therefore we call them 'ghosts [*gui* 鬼]'. 'Ghosts [*gui*]' means 'to return [*gui*]'. Its corpse lies all alone as a lump of earth. How could it have consciousness? You wrap it in silks and cloth, separate it from the soil with inner and outer coffins, bind its limbs, fill its mouth with jade, so even though it wishes to transform it cannot. Pent up and depressed it becomes dried meat. Only after a thousand years when the coffins rot away is it able to return to the earth and thus go to its true home." See *Han shu* 67, p. 2908. Advocacy of allowing the body to rot also appears in *Guanzi jiao zheng*, ch. 17, "Jin zang," p. 290. On the *hun* and the Yellow Springs see *Hou Han shu* 32, p. 1121; *San guo zhi* 三國志 (Beijing: Zhonghua, 1975) 28, p. 783. The link of the well-being of the *hun* to the integrity of the grave is also suggested in Wang Chong's argument denying the possibility that a river changed course to avoid harming Confucius's tomb. This unique posthumous miracle would indicate that "Confucius's *hun* was sagely, while the essential energies [*jing*] of the Five Thearchs [who had no posthumous miracles] could not become spiritually powerful [*shen* 神]." See *Lun heng ji jie*, ch. 4, "Shu xu 書虛," p. 86. Wang Chong also states that his contemporaries believed that the *hun* could join with the corpse to make it perceive or act. See *Lun heng ji jie*, ch. 21, "Si wei," p. 426. He also makes a parallel between the *hun*'s action in death and the muscles' action in life. See ch. 4, "Shu xu," p. 84.

161. *Li ji zhu shu*, ch. 26, "Jiao te sheng," p. 31b.

162. Brashier, "Han Thanatology," pp. 128–129. He cites *Li ji zhu shu*, ch. 10, "Tan gong xia 檀弓下," p. 19: "The bones and flesh return to the Earth. This is allotted lifespan [*ming*]. As for the *hun* and vital energies, they can go everywhere"; ch. 21, "Li yun," p. 9b: "Thus [the mourners] looked up to Heaven but buried the body in the Earth. The body [*ti*] and *po* descended, while the intelligence and vital energies were on high"; ch. 48, "Ji yi," p. 14a: "Vital energies are what fill the spirit [*shen* 神]; the *po* is what fills a ghost [*gui* 鬼]." The pairing of intelligence with the vital energies in

the preceding passage also figures in *Lun heng ji jie*, ch. 23, "Bo zang," p. 463. Given the hierarchical relation between the *shen*—more ethereal, refined, and linked to Heaven—and *gui*—coarser and linked with dead bodies or the tomb—all these passages share a common repertoire of associations in their images of the division of the body's elements between the two vertical poles of the cosmos. The same opposition between *shen*, on the one hand, and *gui* or the body, on the other, also figures in the passages quoted in note 160. Brashier also points out that this contrast between the *hun*, now paired with the essential energies [*jing*], and the body also figures in the Eastern Han divinatory text, the *Yilin*. In addition, see *Lun heng ji jie*, ch. 22, "Ji yao," pp. 440: "Even when the *hun* and the bodily form are united, they still cannot move quickly. How much less could the *hun* move rapidly when it was all alone?" See also *Hou Han shu* 52, p. 1724.

163. Brashier, "Han Thanatology," pp. 155–157. However, in some texts the energies that linger with the corpse in the tomb are also called the "spirit [*shen*]." See, for example, *Lun heng ji jie*, ch. 21, "Si wei 死偽," p. 433. In this case, however, the spirit of the recently deceased is called *shen*, while that of one dead in the tomb for some time is called *hun* or *jing*. See p. 434.

164. *Huainanzi*, ch. 14, "Quan yan," p. 249. Creating the body through the fusion of spirit and physical form is also described in *Huainanzi*, ch. 20, "Tai zu," p. 356: "For putting the body [*shen* 身] in order, the highest way is to nourish the spirit [*shen* 神]. Next best is to nourish the physical form [*xing* 形]. . . . When the spirit is clear and the intent equable, then all the joints are at ease. This is the root of nourishing life/nature [*xing* 性]. To make the flesh fat, fill the stomach and intestines, and provision the desires is merely the peripheral branch of nourishing life [*sheng* 生]."

165. *Chu ci bu zhu*, ch. 2, "Guo shang 國殤," p. 23b.

166. *Lun heng ji jie*, ch. 4, "Shu xu," p. 86; ch. 25, "Jie chu 解除," pp. 504–505.

167. See the story cited in note 156.

168. *Huang Di nei jing ling shu jiao zhu yu yi* 54, pp. 375, 377. For discussions of fetal development as a reverse process of accumulation, see Kinney, *Representations*, pp. 154–158.

169. *Chu ci bu zhu*, ch. 5, "Yuan you," pp. 1b–2a.

170. Paul W. Kroll, "On 'Far Roaming'," *Journal of the American Oriental Society* 116:4 (October–December 1996), p. 653.

171. *Hou Han shu* 39, p. 1314.

172. The *Huainanzi* describes a program of perfecting the self through disciplining the senses [*er mu* 耳目], the energy and intent [*qi zhi* 氣志], the five depots [*wu zang* 五藏], and the refined spirit energies [*jing shen* 精神]. See ch. 7, "Jing shen," p. 101. A reversed hierarchy of less and less refined substances is suggested in Wang Chong's account of how he ruined his health in writing the *Lun heng*: "Grieving my refined spirit energies and isolating my *hunpo*, agitating the tranquil energies in my breast, I thereby reduced my years, damaged my longevity, and provided no benefit to my nature/vitality. . . . I turned my back on the teachings of Huang-Lao [here techniques of longevity]." See *Lun heng ji jie*, ch. 29, "Dui zuo 對作," pp. 575–576.

173. *Li ji zhu shu*, ch. 10, "Tan gong xia," p. 19b; ch. 47, "Ji yi 祭義," p. 14b. See also ch. 26, "Jiao te sheng," p. 31b: "The *hun* energies [or '*hun* and energies'] return to Heaven, and the bodily *po* [or 'body and *po*'] return to Earth"; *Huainanzi*, ch. 7,

"Jing shen," p. 99; *Shuo yuan*, ch. 19, "Xiu wen 脩文," p. 12a; *Feng su tong yi jiao shi*, p. 345; *Han shu* 67, p. 2908; *Hou Han shu* 52, p. 1724.

174. *Huainanzi*, ch. 11, "Qi su," p. 175.

175. For criticisms of burials because they delayed the process of decay, see *Han shu* 67, p. 2908; *Hou Han shu* 39, p. 1314; *Guanzi jiao zheng*, ch. 17, "Jin zang," p. 290. On the inevitability of the fact that even bones would rot, see *Lun heng ji jie*, ch. 11, "Tan tian 談天," p. 216; ch. 20, "Lun si," p. 420.

176. *Lun heng ji jie*, ch. 7, "Dao xu," p. 154.

177. *Lun heng ji jie*, ch. 2, "Wu xing 無形," p. 32. The *Huang Di nei jing ling shu* argues that the size of the bones determines the time of death. See *Ling shu jiao zhu yu yi* 6, p. 68; 46, p. 327; 54, p. 376. Similarly the *Lü shi chun qiu* argues that if the bones develop to full maturity early, the body remains small and weak. Once again it is the bones that are least changeable and consequently fix the limits of the body. See *Lü shi chun qiu jiao shi*, ch. 26, "Shi rong 士容," p. 1690.

178. *Lü shi chun qiu jiao shi*, ch. 10, "Yi yong 異用," p. 560; *Jiazi xin shu jiao shi* 賈子新書校釋, annotated by Qi Yuzhang 祁玉章 (Taipei: Qi Yuzhang, 1974), ch. 7, "Shu cheng 輸誠," p. 865; *Shuo yuan* 説苑, in *Han Wei cong shu*, vol. 1 (Taipei: Xinxing, 1977), ch. 18, "Bian wu 辨物," p. 19b; *Lun heng ji jie*, ch. 21, "Si wei," p. 430; ch. 26, "Shi zhi 實知," p. 523.

179. *Guo yu*, 國語 (Shanghai: Gu ji, 1978), ch. 14, "Jin yu 8," p. 463; ch. 20, "Chu yu shang," p. 634; *Zuo zhuan zhu*, Xi 32, p. 491; Xuan 12, p. 746; Xiang 9, p. 968; Xiang 26, p. 1111; Ding 5, p. 1552; Ai 1, p. 1608; *Mozi jian gu*, ch. 6, "Jie zang xia 節葬下," p. 116: this describes people who in an early version of "sky burials" allowed the flesh to rot away before burying the bones; *Zhuangzi ji shi*, ch. 29, "Dao Zhi 盜跖," p. 421; *Han Feizi ji shi*, ch. 20, "Zhong xiao 忠孝," p. 1109; *Lü shi chun qiu jiao shi*," ch. 7, "Jin se 禁塞," p. 402; *Zhan guo ce* (Shanghai: Guji, 1978), ch. 6, "Qin si," p. 248; *Shi ji* 78, p. 2391; 92, p. 2623; 99, p. 2716; *Shuo yuan*, ch. 8, "Zun gui 尊貴," p. 8b; ch. 11, "Shan shui 善説," p. 2b; ch. 12, p. 13b; *Xin xu shu zheng* 新序疏證, compiled by Liu Xiang 劉向, annotated by Zhao Shanyi 趙善詒 (Shanghai: Huadong Shifan Daxue, 1989), ch. 9, p. 254; ch. 10, p. 287; ch. 11, p. 310; *Lun heng ji jie*, ch. 6, "Huo xu 禍虛," p. 128; ch. 20, "Lun si," p. 418; *Hou Han shu* 9, p. 376; Lu Qinli 逯欽立, ed., *Xian Qin Han Wei Jin Nanbeichao shi* 先秦漢魏晉南北朝詩 (Beijing: Zhonghua, 1983), vol. 1, p. 365.

180. *Zhou li zhu shu*, ch. 36, "Zha shi 蜡氏," p. 21a; *Li ji zhu shu*, ch. 14, "Yue ling," p. 23b; *Lü shi chun qiu jiao shi*, ch. 1, "Meng chun," p. 2: this says "cover the bones and bury the bones with flesh still attached [*ci* 骴 = 胔]"; *Huainanzi*, ch. 5, "Shi ze 時則," p. 70: this agrees with the *Lü shi chun qiu*.

181. *Zhou li zhu shu*, ch. 36, "Zha shi," p. 21a; *Han shu* 10, p. 310; 11, p. 337; 12, p. 353; *Hou Han shu* 1b, p. 74; 5, pp. 230, 236; 6, pp. 256, 267, 278: concludes that state-sponsored burials "consoled the orphaned *hun*," p. 281 (2): the first passage on this page cites the "Yue ling" on burying skeletons and commands "collect the dried skeletons, and work at burying and comforting them"; 7, p. 294: the state also offers burial on unused public lands and sacrifices to those buried there, p. 301.

182. See, for example, *Hou Han shu* 82a, p. 2720: "[Liao] Fu knew in advance which years would have calamitous harvests, so he gathered large amounts of grain which he gave to members of his patriline and relatives by marriage. He also collected

and buried those who perished in plagues and who could not be gathered in by their own people."

183. *Hou Han shu* 64, p. 2117: "Moreover the skeletons and corpses of the innocent are strewn about. If one is not able to gather and bury them, the coming of the plague will be due to this."

184. *Guanzi jiao zheng*, ch. 18, "Duo di," p. 306; *Chun qiu fanlu yi zheng*, ch. 16, "Qiu yu 求雨," p. 430.

185. *Hou Han shu* 46, p. 1553; *Lun heng ji jie*, ch. 20, "Lun si," pp. 418–419.

186. Tales of such creatures appear in *Feng su tong yi jiao shi*, ch. 9, pp. 348–349: here an unburied corpse is possessed by the spirit of a dog, p. 353: here the corpse of a dead woman flies off before it is buried, engages in sex with a living man, and thus kills him. References to murderous corpses produced by incorrect burials also appear in *Lun heng ji jie*, ch. 21, "Si wei," p. 434; ch. 22, "Ding gui," p. 451: "In homes that suffer calamities, some see flying corpses, some see walking malevolences, and some see human forms. All of these are ghosts"; ch. 24, "Ji ri 譏日," p. 477: "If you do not accord with these calendrical [taboos for burial], the corpse will turn into a malevolent evil [*xiong e* 凶惡]"; "Bian sui 辨祟," p. 489: "If deaths accumulate with burials and coffins reaching as many as ten, they do not say, 'The bodily energies declined.' Instead they say, 'The day of the burial was inauspicious.' If events occur they attribute it to violations of calendrical taboos; if they achieve nothing they attribute it to an incorrect choice of dwelling. When the dwelling declines and the house dilapidates, they say that flying malevolences and flowing corpses [*fei xiong liu shi* 蜚 = 飛凶流尸] have gathered in the house, and pray to their ancestors to expel the calamities"; ch. 25, "Jie chu," p. 505: "Flying corpses and flowing malevolences would not dare to gather." See also *Qian fu lun jian* 潛夫論箋, by Wang Fu 王符, annotated by Wang Jipei 汪繼培 (Beijing: Zhonghua, 1979), ch. 6, "Wu lie 巫列," p. 306.

187. *Sou shen ji* 搜神記, compiled by Gan Bao 干寶, annotated by Wang Shao-ying 汪紹楹 (Beijing: Zhonghua, 1979), ch. 3, p. 34; ch. 16, pp. 193, 194–195, 206.

188. See, for example, *Yanzi chun qiu ji shi*, ch. 2, pp. 148–149.

189. The propriety of offspring viewing the rotting remains of their parents is discussed in *Hou Han shu* 32, p. 1121. Opening up an imperial tomb to inter an empress with her husband is recorded in *Hou Han shu* 56, pp. 1832–1833. Reopening a father's tomb for the mother's burial also figures in Gan Bao's justification for writing the *Sou shen ji*. See *Jin shu* 晉書 (Beijing: Zhonghua, 1974) 82, pp. 2150–2151.

190. *Zuo zhuan zhu*, Xiang 22, p. 1070; Zhao 25, p. 1466; *Guo yu*, ch. 19, "Wu yu," p. 593; *Jiazi xin shu jiao shi*, ch. 1, "Fan shang 藩傷," p. 111.

191. *Huang Di nei jing su wen ji zhu* 14, p. 55; *Huang Di nei jing ling shu jiao zhu yu yi* 10, p. 125: "If the bones and flesh are not close, then the flesh grows soft and retracts"; 71, p. 456.

192. *Chu ci bu zhu*, ch. 10, "Da zhao 大招," p. 5b. The Chinese says "*feng rou wei gu* 豐肉微骨." *Wei* 微 means "without" in such cases as *Lun yu zheng yi*, ch. 14, "Xian wen 憲問," p. 314: "Without [*wei*] Guan Zhong we would all wear our hair loose and button our collars on the left [be barbarians]"; or that in *Zuo zhuan zhu*, Zhao 1, p. 1220: "Without [*wei*] Yu wouldn't we all be fish?"

193. *Mozi jian gu*, ch. 2, "Shang xian xia 尚賢下," pp. 40 (3), 41, 42 (4); *Han Feizi ji shi*, ch. 4, "Jian jie shi chen 姦劫弒臣," p. 247; ch. 5, "Bei nei 備內," p. 289 (2); ch.

19, "Wu du 五蠹," p. 1041; *Yan zi chun qiu ji shi*, ch. 2, p. 145; *Guanzi jiao zheng*, ch. 24, "Qing zhong ding 輕重丁," p. 411; *Zhan guo ce*, ch. 5, "Qin san," p. 185; ch. 14, "Chu yi," p. 488; ch. 21, "Zhao si," p. 772; *Li ji zhu shu*, ch. 48, "Ji yi," p. 5a; ch. 20, "Wen Wang shi zi 文王世子," p. 26a; *Jiazi xin shu jiao shi*, ch. 1, "Zong shou 宗首," p. 78; "Fan jiang 藩將," p. 121; ch. 2, "Zhi bu ding 制不定," p. 209; *Shi ji* 5, p. 219; 6, p. 290; 17, p. 802; 38, p. 1610; 40, p. 1713; 43, p. 1824; 52, p. 2008; 55, p. 2045; 60, pp. 2114, 2117, 2118, 2119 (2); 66, p. 2172; 71, p. 2321; 83, p. 2473; 87, p. 2552; 101, p. 2747; 104, p. 2782; 105, p. 2814; 106, pp. 2821, 2828; 107, p. 2851; 112, pp. 2961, 2967; 118, pp. 3080, 3098; *Huainanzi*, ch. 6, "Lan ming 覽冥," p. 96 (2); ch. 9, "Zhu shu," pp. 137, 145; ch. 11, "Qi su," p. 169; ch. 17, "Shuo lin 説林," pp. 290, 291; ch. 20, "Tai zu," p. 359; *Shuo yuan*, ch. 2, p. 2b; ch. 3, p. 7a; *Xin xu shu zheng*, ch. 3, p. 80; ch. 10, pp. 290–291, 299; *Han shu* 8, pp. 257, 266; 9, p. 292; 99c, p. 4185; *Lun heng ji jie*, ch. 3, "Gu xiang," p. 56; ch. 4, "Shu xu," p. 87; ch. 19, "Hui guo 恢國," p. 397; ch. 26, "Zhi shi 知實," p. 531; *Chun qiu fan lu yi zheng*, ch. 9, "Guan de 觀德," p. 273; ch. 13, "Wu xing xiang sheng 五行相勝," p. 368; "Wu xing shun ni 五行順逆," p. 373; ch. 15, "Shun ming 順命," p. 411; *Qian fu lun jian*, ch. 3, "Zhong gui 忠貴," p. 113; ch. 7, "Shi nan 釋難," p. 327; *Feng su tong yi jiao shi*, ch. 3, p. 116; *Hou Han shu* 47, p. 1584.

194. *Lun heng ji jie*, ch. 19, "Hui guo," p. 397.

195. *Lü shi chun qiu jiao shi*, ch. 9, "Jing tong 精通," p. 508. Quoted by Cao Zhi in his "Qiu zi shi biao 求自試表" in A.D. 228, in the commentary to "Song Xiaowu Xuan Guifei hao 宋孝武宣貴妃誄," by Xie Zhuang in A.D. 462, and in a sixth-century commentary to *Wen Xuan*, the line is "one body in two forms [*yi ti er liang xing* 一體而兩形]." See *Wen xuan*, ch. 37, p. 809; ch. 57, p. 1244. The *Lü shi chun qiu* also states, "It is natural that the filial son's honoring of his parents and the tender parents' love for their child should penetrate into their skin and bone." See ch. 10, "Jie sang 節喪," p. 524.

196. *Lun heng ji jie*, ch. 2, "Wu xing," p. 29: "The body's energies and the skeleton cling to one another [*ti qi yu xing hai xiang bao* 體氣與形骸相抱]."

197. See, for example, *Hou Han shu* 2, p. 95.

198. *Han Feizi ji shi*, ch. 5, "Bei nei," p. 289: "Wives do not enjoy the favor of being 'bone and flesh'. When loved, then they are near; when not loved, then they become distant."

199. *Han shu* 11, p. 339.

200. See, for example, *Shi ji* 56, pp. 2054, 2056; 96, p. 2688; 103, p. 2768; 112, pp. 2952 (2), 2964; *Hou Han shu* 43, p. 1461: this uses the synonymous *qi shen* 乞身; 44, pp. 1495, 1504; 46, p. 1547; 48, p. 1619; 51, p. 1694; 57, p. 1841. The inversion of this phrase is "present one's skeleton [*ci hai gu* 賜骸骨]" in which one offered service to one's lord just before dying. See *Shi ji* 7, p. 325; 8, p. 375; 70, p. 2287; *Chun qiu fan lu yi zheng*, ch. 15, "Jiao shi 郊事," p. 417.

201. Thus biographies often noted whether an individual died in office [*guan* 官] or at home [*jia* 家]. See *Hou Han shu* 43, p. 1487; 44, pp. 1499, 1504; 47, p. 1590; 48, pp. 1601, 1605, 1617, 1622; 49, p. 1643; 51, pp. 1686, 1691; 53, p. 1741; 56, p. 1826.

202. See Li Jianmin, "Shiti, kulou, hunpo: chuantong linghun guan xin kao 屍體，骷髏，魂魄；傳統靈魂觀新考," in *Fangshu, yixue, lishi*, pp. 2–24. Originally published in *Dang dai* 90 (1993).

203. *Han shu* 53, pp. 2428–2430. In the seventh century A.D. the Empress Wu supposedly also killed two former rivals, chopped up their bodies, and pickled their bones, but was still haunted by their ghosts. See Sima Guang 司馬光, *Zi zhi tong jian* 資治通鑑 (Beijing: Zhonghua, 1956), pp. 6294–6295.

204. On rendering Chi You's flesh and bones into a stew, see *Jing fa* 經法 (Beijing: Wenwu, 1976), p. 61. On stories of Chi You returning to life, see *Taiping yu lan* 太平御覽, compiled by Li Fang 李昉 et al. (Taipei: Shangwu, 1935), ch. 79, p. 3b; ch. 694, p. 4a; ch. 736, pp. 6a–b; ch. 872, p. 11b. On Wu Zixu's corpse being boiled, see *Lun heng ji jie*, ch. 4, "Shu xu," pp. 83–84; ch. 10, "Ci Meng 刺孟," p. 214; ch.21, "Si wei," p. 434.

205. *Han shu* 99c, p. 4185. On using the annual military training sessions to rebel, see Mark Edward Lewis, "The Han Abolition of Universal Military Service," in *Warfare in Chinese History*, ed. Hans van de Ven (Leiden: E. J. Brill, 2000), p. 41.

206. *Zhuangzi ji shi*, ch. 18, "Zhi le 至樂," p. 273.

207. Li Xueqin 李學勤, "Fangmatan jian zhong de zhiguai gushi 放馬灘簡中的志怪故事," *Wenwu* (1990:4), pp. 43–47; Donald Harper, "Resurrection in Warring States Popular Religion," *Taoist Resources* 5:2 (December 1994), pp. 13–28. On links between the skull and the *hun*, see Ōgata Osamu 大形徹, "Hihatsu kō: hakkei to reikon no kanren ni tsuite 被髮考：髮型と靈魂の關連について," *Tōhō shūkyō* 86 (Nov. 1995), pp. 4–10.

208. See Li Jianmin, "Shiti, kulou, hunpo: chuantong linghun guan xin kao," pp. 15–21.

209. Lewis, *Sanctioned Violence*, ch. 6; Shigehisa Kuriyama, "The Imagination of Winds and the Development of the Chinese Conception of the Body," in *Body, Subject and Power in China*, pp. 23–41; Kuriyama, *The Expressiveness of the Body*, ch. 6.

210. Porkert, *The Theoretical Foundations of Chinese Medicine*, ch. 3.

211. John Hay, "The Human Body as Microcosmic Source for Macrocosmic Values in Calligraphy," in *Theories of the Arts in China*, ed. Susan Bush and Christian Murck (Princeton: Princeton University, 1983), pp. 89–92. See also Angela Zito, "Silk and Skin: Significant Boundaries," in *Body, Subject and Power in China*, pp. 110–111.

212. Carolyn Korsmeyer, *Making Sense of Taste: Food and Philosophy* (Ithaca: Cornell University, 1999), ch. 1–2; Susan Stewart, *Poetry and the Fate of the Senses* (Chicago: University of Chicago, 2002), pp. 17–38 and passim. In a meditation on the five senses, Michel Serres both affirms and challenges this hierarchy. See Serres, *Les cinq sens: Philosophie des corps mêlés* (Paris: Grasset, 1985), pp. 45–47, 51–56, 71–72, 80–83, 100–101, 146, 148–149, 184–185, 322.

213. Kuriyama, *The Expressiveness of the Body*, ch. 1–2.

214. Kuriyama, *Expressiveness of the Body*, pp. 25, 51–54, 103–104, 164–166. For passages distinguishing the "floating *fu* 浮" point of the pulse site from the "sinking *chen* 沉" point as a means of diagnosis, see *Huang di nei jing su wen ji zhu* 5, p. 28; 18, p. 72; *Huang di nei jing ling shu jiao zhu yu yi* 49, pp. 352, 357; 59, p. 395; 74, p. 482.

215. In addition to the works by Lewis and Kuriyama cited earlier, see Unschuld, *Medicine in China*, pp. 6–7, 25, 67–73, 84, 87, 151, 169, 173–174, 176, 204–205, 222, 231; Unschuld, "Der Wind als Ursache des krankseins," *T'oung Pao* 68 (1982), pp. 91–131; Ishida Hidema 石田秀實, "Kaze no byōinron to chūgoku dentō igaku shisō

no keisei 風の病因論と中國傳統醫學思想の形成," *Shisō* 799 (1991), pp. 105–124; Sakade Yoshinobu 坂出祥伸, "Kaze no kannen to kaze uranai 風の觀念と風占い," in *Chūgoku kodai no senpō: Gijutsu to jujutsu no shūhen* 中國古代の占法：技術と咒術の週邊 (Tokyo: Kenbun Shuppan, 1991), pp. 45–127; Yamada Keiji 山田慶兒, "Kyūkyū happū setsu to Shōshi ha no tachiba 九宮八風説と少師派の立場," *Tōhō gakuhō* 52 (1980), pp. 199–242.

216. In the medical literature see *Huang di nei jing su wen ji zhu* 5, pp. 27–28; *Huang di nei jing ling shu jiao zhu yu yi* 4, p. 39; 59, pp. 393, 395; 66, p. 436; 67, p. 444 (3). A story tells of the physician Bian Que's repeated visits to Lord Huan of Qi. Each time he announced the inward march of the disease till it reached the bone marrow, where it became impossible to cure. See *Shi ji* 105, p. 2793.

217. Kuriyama, *Expressiveness of the Body*, pp. 167–192; Zito, "Silk and Skin," pp. 119–120.

218. See, for example, *Huang di nei jing su wen ji zhu* 5, p. 28; 10, pp. 46, 47; 13, pp. 52 (2), 53; 17, pp. 65–66, *Huang di nei jing ling shu jiao zhu yu yi* 4, pp. 39–40, 41.

219. *Lun yu zheng yi*, ch. 1, "Xue er," p. 5; ch. 2, "Wei zheng," p. 27; ch. 6, "Gongye Chang," p. 108; ch. 9, "Tai Bo," p. 157; ch. 11, "Xiang dang," pp. 203, 204; ch. 15, "Yan Yuan," p. 276; ch. 19, "Ji shi," p. 359; *Shang shu zheng yi*, "Gao Yao mo 皋陶謨," ch. 4, p.18a; "Jiong ming 冏命," ch. 19, p. 15a; *Mengzi zheng yi*, IIA, "Gongsun Chou shang," pp. 114, 123; IIIA, "Teng Wen Gong shang," p. 195; IVA, "Li Lou shang," p. 305; VIB, "Gaozi xia," pp. 508, 514; VIIA, "Jin xin shang," p. 535; *Mozi jian gu*, ch. 4, "Jian ai xia 兼愛下," p. 75; ch. 15, "Hao ling 號令," p. 352; *Xunzi ji jie*, ch. 2, "Bu gou 不苟," p. 29; ch. 3, "Fei shier zi," p. 66; ch. 13, "Li lun," p. 242; ch. 19, "Da lüe 大略," p. 332; *Zhuangzi ji shi*, ch. 11, "Zai you 在宥," p. 167; ch. 12, "Tian di 天地," pp. 195, 203; ch. 13, "Tian dao 天道," p. 217; *Qian fu lun jian*, ch. 6, "Xiang lie 相列," p. 310. See also Geaney, *On the Epistemology of the Senses in Early Chinese Thought*, ch. 2, esp. 65–67. The recognition of character in speech also figured prominently in early theories of poetic performance. See Lewis, *Writing and Authority*, pp. 155–176.

220. *Lun heng ji jie*, ch. 26, "Zhi shi," pp. 532–534. This refutes the idea that sages such as Confucius had prophetic powers. It rationally explains seemingly magical fore-knowledge. In the cases cited, knowledge derives from "observing the expression to glimpse the heart/mind." One of the stories appeared earlier in *Guanzi jiao zheng*, ch. 18, "Xiao wen 小問," p. 278; *Lü shi chun qiu jiao shi*, ch. 18, "Zhong yan 重言," pp. 1156–1157; *Shuo yuan*, ch. 13, "Quan mou 權謀," pp. 3a–4a.

221. *Mengzi zheng yi* IA, "Liang Hui Wang shang," p. 37; IB, "Liang Hui Wang xia," p. 62; IIIB, "Teng Wen Gong xia," p. 269; *Xunzi ji jie*, ch. 6, "Fu guo," p. 126.

222. Kuriyama, *Expressiveness of the Body*, p. 180. He cites *Mengzi zheng yi* VIIA, "Jin xin shang," p. 552: "The physical form and color/expression are our Heaven-endowed nature. Only the sage can fully put into practice the capacities of his form." See also *Zhuangzi ji shi*, ch. 12, "Tian di," p. 203; *Xunzi ji jie*, ch. 16, "Zheng ming," p. 277.

223. *Huang di nei jing ling shu jiao zhu yu yi* 73, p. 473.

224. On the link of physiognomy and the examination of expressions, see *Xunzi ji jie*, ch. 3, "Fei xiang," p. 46; *Shi ji* 92, p. 2623; *Qian fu lun jian*, ch. 6, "Xiang lie," pp. 310, 314. On the different parts of the body that could be used for physiognomy, see *Qian fu lun*, ch. 6, "Xiang lie," p. 310.

225. See John Knoblock's introduction to the chapter "Contra Physiognomy" in *Xunzi: A Translation and Study of the Complete Works*, vol. 1 (Stanford: Stanford University, 1988), pp. 196–197.

226. *Xunzi ji jie*, ch. 4, "Ru xiao," p. 79. See also *Feng su tong yi jiao shi*, p. 417.

227. Knoblock, *Xunzi*, vol. 1, pp. 196–200.

228. *Shi ji* 8, pp. 344, 346; 20, p. 1064; 57, pp. 2073–2074; 79, p. 2418 (2); 91, p. 2597; 92, p. 2623; 96, p. 2686; 111, p. 2922; 125, p. 3192: here Emperor Wen employs a physiognomist to evaluate a friend and attempts to alter the poverty that is foretold, but the prediction is fulfilled; *Han shu* 8, p. 237; 40, p. 2057; 55, p. 2471; *San guo zhi* 29, pp. 808–809; *Lun heng ji jie*, ch. 3, "Gu xiang," pp. 53–54.

229. *Song shu* 宋書 (Beijing: Zhonghua, 1974) 2, p. 48; *Nan Qi shu* 南齊書 (Beijing: Zhonghua, 1972) 1, p. 21. Examining the body to predict destiny also figures in the Age of Disunion's fascination with methods of recognizing character. See Nanxiu Qian, *Spirit and Self in Medieval China: The Shih-shuo hsin-yü and Its Legacy* (Honolulu: University of Hawai'i, 2001), ch. 5.

230. *Lun heng ji jie*, ch. 3, "Gu xiang," p. 57.

231. Wang Chong makes similar remarks in other chapters. See *Lun heng ji jie*, ch. 2, "Ming yi 命義," p. 23; ch. 16, "Jiang rui 講瑞," pp. 340–341; ch. 18, "Zi ran 自然," p. 371; ch. 30 "Zi ji 自紀," p. 584.

232. See the positive remarks in *Qian fu lun jian*, ch. 6, "Xiang lie," pp. 308–314.

233. *Lun heng ji jie*, ch. 2, "Wu xing," p. 29.

234. *Lun heng ji jie*, ch. 2, "Wu xing," pp. 31–32. On altering bodies to extend lifespan, see also *Baopuzi nei pian jiao shi* 抱朴子內篇校釋, annotated by Wang Ming 王明 (Beijing: Zhonghua, 1980), p. 77.

235. *Lun heng ji jie*, ch. 2, "Wu xing," p. 32.

236. My discussion borrows from Li Jianmin 李建民, "Zhongguo fangshu shi shang de xing ying guan 中國方術史上的形影觀, in *Fangshu yixue lishi*, pp. 34–57.

237. A. C. Graham and N. Sivin, "A Systematic Approach to the Mohist Optics," in *Chinese Science*, ed. Shigeru Nakayama and N. Sivin (Cambridge: MIT Press, 1973), pp. 105–152; Graham, *Later Mohist Logic, Ethics and Science* (Hong Kong: Chinese University of Hong Kong, 1978), pp. 369–385.

238. *Zhuangzi ji shi*, ch. 27, "Yu yan 寓言," pp. 412–413. This elaborates a passage from an earlier chapter: "The penumbra asked the shadow, 'Previously you were walking, but now you have stopped. Previously you were sitting, but now you have stood up. Whey do you have no independent actions?' The shadow said, 'Am I dependent on something that I am thus? Does that on which I depend also depend on something to be thus? Am I dependent on the snake's scales and the cicadas wings? How can I know why it is thus? How can I know why it is not thus?'" See *Zhuangzi ji shi*, ch. 2, "Qi wu lun," pp. 52–53.

239. *Lie xian zhuan* 列仙傳, in *Zheng tong dao zang* 正統道藏, vol. 8 (rep. ed., Taipei: Yiwen, 1976), ch. 2, p. 16. On dating the text, see Max Kaltenmark, *Le Lie-sien Tchouan* (Beijing: Université de Paris, Publications du Centre d'études sinologiques de Pékin, 1953), pp. 1–6.

240. *Baopuzi nei pian jiao shi*, pp. 73, 77; *Shi yi ji* 拾遺記, compiled by Wang Jia 王嘉, in *Han Wei Liuchao biji xiaoshuo daguan* 漢魏六朝筆記小説大觀 (Shanghai:

Shanghai guji, 1999), pp. 496–497: "To the north of the Bin Sea is the state of Boti. Its people all wear feathers and fly without wings. In the sunlight they have no shadows. They live to be a thousand years."

241. Ma, *Mawangdui gu yi shu kaoshi*, pp. 879, 882: here the drinking of special animal products "repels age and restores youthful vigor, so one becomes lustrous and glowing," pp. 892, 914, 969, 989, 1025; Harper, *Early Chinese Medical Literature*, pp. 388, 391, 405, 410, 418, 427.

242. Ma, *Mawangdui gu yi shu kaoshi*, pp. 930–931; Harper, *Early Chinese Medical Literature*, p. 398; *Shi ji* 28, pp. 1368–1369.

243. *Feng su tong yi jiao shi*, pp. 348–349, 349, 353–354.

244. *Baopuzi nei pian jiao shi*, p. 274.

245. Wen Yiduo 聞一多, *Zhuangzi yanjiu* 莊子研究 (rep. ed., Shanghai: Fudan Daxue, 1986), p. 486.

246. *Han shu* 97a, p. 3952; *Shi ji* 28, p. 1387; *Han shu* 25a, p. 1219; Huan Tan 桓譚, *Xin lun* 新論, quoted in the commentary to *Wen xuan* 文選 (Hong Kong: Shangwu, 1936), ch. 23, p. 501; *Sou shen ji*, ch. 2, p. 25; *Shi yi ji*, pp. 524–525. This last version is distinct, involving carving an image of the deceased concubine from a magical stone which could not be approached because it was poisonous.

247. Scholars argued this as early as the Song dynasty. See Gao Cheng 高承, *Shi wu ji yuan* 事物紀原 (Taipei: Zhonghua, 1989), p. 495. See also Gu Jiegang 顧頡剛, "Zhongguo yingxi lüe shi ji qi xianzhuang 中國影戲略史及其現狀," *Wen shi* 19 (1983), pp. 109–136; Jiang Yuxiang 江玉祥, "Zhongguo yingxi tanyuan 中國影戲探源," *Minjian wenxue luntan* 2 (1988), pp. 85–92.

248. Derk Bodde, *Festivals in Classical China: New Year and Other Annual Observances During the Han Dynasty* (Princeton: Princeton University, 1975), pp. 289–316.

249. *You yang za zu*, compiled by Duan Chengshi 段成式 (Beijing: Zhonghua, 1981), p. 104.

250. Ma Changyi 馬昌儀, *Zhongguo linghun xinyang* 中國靈魂信仰 (Taipei: Hanzhong, 1996), p. 134.

251. *Li ji zhu shu*, ch. 16, "Yue ling," p. 6a; *Si min yue ling ji shi* 四民月令輯釋, compiled by Cui Shi 崔寔, annotated by Miao Qiyu 繆啓愉 and Wan Guoding 萬國鼎 (Beijing: Nongye, 1981), p. 54.

252. Li, "Zhongguo fangshu shi shang de xing ying guan," p. 46.

253. *Bo wu zhi jiao zheng* 博物志校證, compiled by Zhang Hua 張華, annotated by Fan Ning 范寧 (Beijing: Zhonghua, 1980), p. 109. I have amended the passage in light of a version quoted in the later *Yi yuan*, compiled during the fifth-century Liu-Song dynasty. See *Yi yuan* 異苑, compiled by Liu Jingshu 劉敬叔, in *Han Wei Liuchao biji xiaoshuo daguan*, p. 672.

254. *Feng su tong yi jiao shi*, p. 420.

255. A similar belief is suggested in the *You yang za zu*'s account of a man who "physiognomized shadows." According to this man, shadows should be "deep," which indicated that the person would be noble and long-lived. Thus, the density of the shadow indicated the body's energetic endowment. The same passage speaks of several animals that could harm the body by striking its shadow, and of a therapeutic method applied to the shadow to heal the body. See *Yu yang za zu*, p. 108.

256. E. R. Leach, "Magical Hair," *Journal of the Royal Anthropological Institute* 88 (1958), pp. 147–164; Christopher R. Hallpike, "Social Hair," *Man* (N.S.) 4 (1969), pp. 256–264; Gananath Obeyesekere, *Medusa's Hair: An Essay on Personal Symbols and Religious Experience* (Chicago: University of Chicago, 1981); Alf Hiltebeitel and Barbara D. Miller, eds., *Hair: Its Power and Meaning in Asian Cultures* (Albany: State University of New York, 1998).

257. *Huang Di nei jing su wen ji zhu* 1, pp. 2–3; 10, p. 43 (3); 19, p. 76; *Huang Di nei jing ling shu jiao zhu yu yi* 8, pp. 83–84; 10, pp. 102, 123–124; 21, p. 192; 54, pp. 376–377; 66, p. 436; 74, p. 482; 79, p. 531; *Shi ji* 105, p. 2805.

258. *Huang Di nei jing su wen ji zhu* 21, p. 91; 56, pp. 204–205; *Huang Di nei jing ling shu jiao zhu yu yi* 7, p. 74; 9, pp. 96–97; 66, p. 436.

259. *Huang Di nei jing ling shu jiao zhu yu yi* 50, p. 363.

260. *Shi ji* 6, p. 313.

261. *Shi ji* 81, p. 2440.

262. *Shi ji* 86, p. 2534; See also Zuo Si 左思 "Wu du fu 吳都賦," in *Wen xuan*, ch. 5, p. 107.

263. Wu Hung, *The Wu Liang Shrine: The Ideology of Early Chinese Pictorial Art* (Stanford: Stanford University, 1989), p. 54, figure 29.

264. Ōgata, "Hihatsu kō: hakkei to reikon no kanren ni tsuite, pp. 12–19. Southern barbarians leaving their hair unbound will be discussed in chapter four. On men leaving hair unbound to feign madness, see *Shi ji* 38, p. 1609; 79, p. 2407 (2); 84, p. 2486; 128, p. 3234. See also *Han Feizi ji shi*, ch. 10, "Nei chu shuo xia 內儲説下," p. 579, where hair is untied to feign being a ghost. In *Shi ji* 127, p. 3217, unbound hair indicated young boys.

265. *Yunmeng Shuihudi Qin mu* 雲夢睡虎地秦墓 (Beijing: Wenwu, 1981), ill. 133, strip 850 verso.

266. *Xunzi ji jie*, ch. 1, "Xiu shen," pp. 13–14; ch. 5, "Wang zhi," p. 101; ch. 7, "Wang ba," p. 144; ch. 8, "Jun dao," p. 156; *Bo hu tong de lun* 白虎通德論, in *Han Wei cong shu*, vol. 1, ch. 2, pp. 43a, 55a; Wang Yanshou 王延壽, "Lu Lingguangdian fu 魯靈光殿賦," in *Wen xuan*, ch. 11, p. 235.

267. Marcel Granet, *Danses et légendes de la Chine ancienne* (rep. ed., Paris: Presses Universitaires de France, 1994), pp. 259–264.

268. *Hou Han shu, zhi* 13, p. 3661. A similar passage appears in *Jin shu* 25, p. 751. See Roel Sterckx, *The Animal and the Daemon in Early China* (Albany: State University of New York, 2002), pp. 53, 97–98, 159–161.

269. *Guo yu*, ch. 5, "Lu yu xia," p. 195.

270. Sterckx, *The Animal and the Daemon*, pp. 192–193.

271. *Shang shu zheng yi*, ch. 5, "Yi ji 益稷," p. 4b; Schuyler Cammann, *China's Dragon Robes* (New York: Ronald Press, 1952), pp. 87–88; Zito "Silk and Skin," pp. 115–117.

272. John Hay, "The Body Invisible in Chinese Art," in *Body, Subject & Power*, pp. 42–77, esp. 61–63.

273. Audrey Spiro, *Contemplating the Ancients: Aesthetic and Social Issues in Early Chinese Portraiture* (Berkeley: University of California, 1990), esp. ch. 2.

274. Nagahiro Toshio 長廣敏雄, *Kandai gazō no kenkyū* 漢代畫像の研究 (Chūō kōron no bijutsu, 1965), p. 10.

CHAPTER TWO

1. Peter Murdock defined the family through shared residence, economic cooperation, and transgenerational reproduction. See *Social Structure* (New York: Macmillan, 1960), pp. 1–16. Christopher Harris defined it as a social group that carries out biological and cultural reproduction, shares a residence, and performs the economic functions to sustain itself. The family is thus a *process* whose participants change over time. See *Kinship* (Milton Keynes: Open University, 1990), p. 70; *The Family* (London: George Allen and Unwin, 1969), pp. 62–92; A. R. Radcliffe-Brown, *The Social Anthropology of Radcliffe-Brown* (Harmondsworth: Penguin, 1977), p. 16; Robin Fox, "Kinship, Family, and Descent," in *Kinship and Marriage: An Anthropological Perspective* (Harmondsworth: Penguin, 1967), pp. 27–53. Richard Wilk and Robert Netting argue that the makeup of the household changes in relation to five types of activity: reproduction, co-residence, production, distribution, and transmission of property. See "Changing Forms and Functions," in *Household: Comparative and Historical Studies of the Domestic Group*, ed. Robert Netting, Richard Wilk, and Eric Arnould (Berkeley: University of California, 1984), pp. 1–28. Peter Laslett says that a family consists of those related by blood or marriage, who sleep habitually under the same roof, and who share activities related to production, distribution, and transmission of material goods. See Laslett, "Introduction: The History of the Family," in *Household and Family in Past Time*, ed. Peter Laslett (Cambridge: Cambridge University, 1972), pp. 1–89.

2. Lewis, *Sanctioned Violence in Early China*, ch. 2 and passim.

3. *Mao shi zheng yi*, ch. 2.2, #35, "Gu feng 谷風," pp. 7b–8a: a woman laments that she must now feast affines as she feasted her brothers; ch. 2.3, #39, "Quan shui 泉水," p. 6b: consulting aunts and sisters, and leaving father, mother, and brothers; ch. 3.2, #51, "Di dong 蝃蝀," pp. 1a, 1b; ch. 3.3, #59, "Zhu gan 竹竿," p. 7b; ch. 4.1, #71, "Ge lei 葛藟," pp. 14b–15a: being far from brothers, and having to call new people "father," "mother," and "elder brother"; ch. 5.3, #110, "Zhi hu 陟岵," pp. 7b–8b: a soldier on expedition who gazes longingly back toward his father, mother, and elder brother.

4. *Mao shi zheng yi*, ch. 6.2, #121, "Bao yu 鴇羽," pp. 7b–8a.

5. *Mao shi zheng yi*, ch. 8.1, #154, "Qi yue 七月," p. 18a: a man calls on his wife and children to dwell in a newly repaired house. See also ch. 19.4, #291, "Liang si 良耜," pp. 9b, 11a.

6. *Mao shi zheng yi*, ch. 14.1, #211, "Fu tian 甫田," p. 9b; #212, "Da tian 大田," p. 17b.

7. *Mao shi zheng yi*, ch. 9.2, #164, "Chang di 常棣," pp. 13a–17a: brothers attending the feast accompanied by their own wives and children; ch. 9.3, #165, "Fa mu 伐木," pp. 3a–5b; ch. 14.2, #217, "Que bian 頍弁," pp. 11a–12b. See also ch. 13.2, #209, "Chu ci 楚茨," p. 14a: the master of the house and his wife are placed in syntactic and ritual opposition to the brothers and uncles.

8. *Mao shi zheng yi*, ch. 5.3, #112, "Fa tan 伐檀," pp. 9b–11b; ch. 8.1, #154, "Qi yue," pp. 9a–22a; ch. 10.3, #179, "Che gong 車攻," p. 6a; ch. 11.2, #190, "Wu yang

無羊," pp. 12b–13b; ch. 13.2, #210, "Xin nan shan 信南山," pp. 17a–22b; ch. 14.1, #211, "Fu tian," pp. 1a–12a; #212, "Da tian," pp. 13b–17b; ch. 19.2, #276, "Chen gong 臣工," pp. 15b–17a; #277, "Yi xi 噫嘻," pp. 18a–19b; ch. 19.4, #290, "Zai shan 載芟," pp. 4b–8b; #291, "Liang si," pp. 9a–11b.

9. On the ideal of the Homeric *oikos* as the autarkic center of political society, with its life of leisured cultivation for the nobles, see M. M. Austin and Pierre Vidal-Naquet, *Economic and Social History of Ancient Greece*, tr. and rev. M. M. Austin (Berkeley: University of California, 1977), pp. 16, 40–46; Moses Finley, *The Ancient Economy* (Berkeley: University of California, 1973), pp. 17–21; Louis Gernet, "Les nobles dans la Grèce antique," in *Droit et institutions en Grèce antique* (paperback ed., Paris: Flammarion, 1982), pp. 215–228; William James Booth, *Households: On the Moral Architecture of the Economy* (Ithaca: Cornell University, 1993), pp. 17–34; Georges C. Vlachos, *Les sociétés politiques homériques* (Paris: Presses Universitaires de France, 1974), pp. 98, 258; Edouard Will, *Le monde grecque et l'orient* (Paris: Presses Universitaires de France, 1974), vol. 1, p. 632; Elisabeth Welskopf, *Probleme der Musse im alten Hellas* (Berlin: Rütten & Loening, 1962), pp. 46–47. On the horizontal division of labor and the role of elite women in production, see Gisela Wickert-Micknat, *Unfreiheit im Zeitalter der homerischen Epen* (Wiesbaden: Franz Steiner Verlag, 1983), pp. 151–154; Andre Aymard, "Hiérarchie du travail et autarcie individuelle dans la Grèce archaïque," *Revue d'histoire de la philosophie et d'histoire générale de la civilisation* 2 (1943), pp. 124–146; Moses Finley, *The World of Odysseus* (London: Penguin, 1979), p. 73.

10. Lewis, *Sanctioned Violence*, pp. 28–35. See also *Mao shi zheng yi*, ch. 16.3, #240, "Si qi 思齊," pp. 11b–12b. This refers to the Zhou ruling house as the "great household [*jing shi* 京室]" and states that King Wen "provided laws for his wife, extended these to his brothers, and thereby controlled his family and state [or 'family/state *jia bang* 家邦']." Quoted in *Zuo zhuan zhu*, Xuan year 19, p. 384.

11. *Zuo zhuan zhu*, Huan year 2, p. 94.

12. The Harvard-Yenching concordance of the *Zuo zhuan*, *Gu liang*, and *Gongyang* commentaries lists thirty-six uses of the phrase *guo jia*, and thirty-two of these are from the *Zuo zhuan*. See William Hung et al., eds., *Harvard-Yenching Institute Sinological Index Series Supplement #11: Combined Concordances to Ch'un-Ch'iu, Kung-yang, Ku-liang, and Tso-chuan* (rep. ed., Taipei: Chengwen, 1966), p. 864. One example of the phrase *jia bang* 家邦 would mean the same thing, but it is a quote from the *Shi jing*. See *Zuo zhuan zhu*, Xi year 19, p. 384. For examples of parallels between *guo* and *jia* or their contrast as competing political units see *Zuo zhuan zhu*, Zhuang year 30, p. 247; Wen year 4, p. 534; Wen year 14, p. 602; Xiang year 24, p. 1089; Xiang year 31, pp. 1192–1193; Zhao year 5, p. 1266; Zhao year 16, p. 1377; Zhao year 26, p. 1480; *Gongyang zhuan zhu shu*, Zhuang year 4, ch. 6, pp. 10b–12b. This pairing also appears in *Yi Zhou shu hui jiao ji zhu* 逸周書彙校集注, annotated by Huang Huaixin 黃懷信, Zhang Maorong 張懋鎔, and Tian Xudong 田旭東 (Shanghai: Shanghai gu ji, 1995), ch. 2, "Da kuang 大匡," p. 159; ch. 5, "Zuo Luo 作雒," p. 566; "Huang men 皇門," pp. 584, 590, 593; ch. 9, "Zhou zhu 周祝," p. 1134 (2). The *Yi jing* also lists *guo* and *jia* in parallel, the former referring to a feudatory state, the latter to a ministerial house. See *Zhou yi zheng yi*, ch. 2, p. 10b. *Li ji zhu shu*, ch. 21, "Li yun," p. 20a, states, "So one who serves a lord [*gong* 公] is called a minister [*chen* 臣]; one who serves a household [*jia* 家] is called a servant [*pu* 僕]." This opposition informs the chapter's opening passage, which traces the descent from *tian xia wei gong* 天下為公 to *tian xia wei jia* 家. See pp. 3a–5a. *Xunzi ji jie*, ch. 20, "Zi dao 子道," p. 348, lists

a state with ten thousand chariots, a state with one thousand chariots, and a household (*jia* 家) with one hundred chariots. Closely related is the phrase *guo zu* 國族, although the *zu* is a larger kin grouping than the household. See *Li ji zhu shu*, ch. 10, "Tan gong xia 檀弓下," p. 24a.

13. In addition to pages cited in the previous note see *Zuo zhuan zhu*, Cheng year 14, p. 869; Xiang year 4, p. 937: this tells how the "household masses [*jia zhong* 家眾]" engage in armed rebellion; Xiang year 23, p. 1083; Xiang year 27, pp. 1135–1137; Xiang year 29, pp. 1158–1159; Xiang year 31, pp. 1192–1194: this tells of a *jia* that possessed numerous towns [*yi* 邑] and also places the *guo* and *jia* of the ruler in opposition to the "lineage [*zu* 族]" and *jia* of the ministerial houses; Zhao year 2, p. 1228: this refers to ministers of a *jia*; Zhao year 3, p. 1236: this passage states that Lu's government was located within the ministerial households; Zhao year 5, pp. 1266, 1268–1269: these repeat that the government lies in the *jia*, give a list of powerful *jia* including the numbers of towns and administered districts [*xian* 縣] that they controlled and could mobilize for their armies, and refer to the "household masses [*jia zhong*]"; Zhao year 12, pp. 1335–1336: this tells of a minister of a *jia* who leads his own town in rebellion; Zhao year 14, p. 1364: a minister of a *jia* swears a blood oath to raise some towns in rebellion; Zhao year 25, pp. 1460, 1464: a minister of a *jia* is responsible for its armies and gives a formal address to their assembled masses; Ding year 10, p. 1581: the masses of a ministerial house in Lu are alarmed over rumors that they will be moved. The *Guliang zhuan* tells how the rising power of the ministerial houses of Lu led to the capital being divided into walled districts. See *Guliang zhuan zhu shu*, Ding year 6, ch. 19, p. 10b.

14. *Mengzi zhengyi* IA, "Liang Hui Wang shang," pp. 22–25.

15. *Guanzi jiao zheng*, ch. 21, "Ming fa," pp. 345, 348.

16. *Zuo zhuan zhu*, Huan year 18, p. 152; *Guliang zhuan zhu shu*, Yin year 2, ch. 1, p. 10b; Cheng year 9, ch. 14, p. 1b.

17. *Zuo zhuan zhu*, Ding year 9, p. 1575: a noble receives five households for service in battle; Ding year 10, p. 1581; Ding year 13, p. 1589: five hundred households are presented as a reward.

18. See *Zuo zhuan zhu*, Huan year 15, p. 143; Xi year 26, p. 439; Xuan year 15, p. 761; Xiang year 15, p. 1023 (2); year 23, p. 1084; Zhao year 12, p. 1331; year 18, p. 1396; year 26, p. 1480; Ding year 8, p. 1569; *Gongyang zhuan zhu shu*, Yin year 5, ch. 3, p. 2b; Ding year 4, ch. 25, p. 17b; Ai year 1, p. 1608; year 25, p. 1726.

19. On *shi* as the inner chamber, see *Zuo zhuan zhu*, Cheng year 10, p. 849. "The Marquis of Jin dreamt of a huge evil spirit. With its hair unbound it descended to the earth, beating its chest and hopping about. It said, 'To have killed my descendants was unrighteous. I have obtained my request from Heaven [to punish you].' Destroying the great gate of the compound and then the gate of the sleeping chambers, it entered. The marquis was afraid and retreated into his *shi*. The spirit further destroyed the window and then the marquis awoke." See also Xiang year 25, p. 1097; *Han Feizi ji shi*, ch. 4, "Jian jie shi chen," p. 251; *Li ji zhu shu*, ch. 51, "Fang ji 坊記," p. 19b.

20. The *Zuo zhuan* makes forty-seven references to the "royal house [*wang shi* 王室]," seven to the "Zhou house [*zhou shi* 周室]," and thirty-four to the "lord's house [*gong shi* 公室]." See *Combined Concordances*, pp. 562, 826, 933–934. *Zhou shi* also appears in *Yi Zhou shu hui jiao ji zhu*, ch. 5, "Zuo Luo," pp. 559, 571; ch. 10, "Zhou

shu xu 周書序," p. 1214. There are no references to ministerial *shi*, just as there are no references to royal *jia* or the lord's *jia*.

21. *Yi Zhou shu hui jiao ji zhu*, ch. 5, "Huang men," p. 590; ch. 7, "Ji gong 祭公," p. 1001; *Zuo zhuan zhu*, Zhao year 3, p. 1236; year 12, 1335. The *Zuo zhuan* also describes conflicts between royal or ducal *shi* and the lesser nobility, without using the term *jia*. See Zhuang year 20, p. 214; Xi year 5, pp. 307–308; year 28, p. 466; Wen year 14, p. 604; Xuan year 16, p. 769; Cheng year 2, p. 809; Xiang year 10, p. 983; Xiang year 11, p. 989; year 21, p. 1062; year 29, p. 1157; Zhao year 1, pp. 1212–1213; year 15, p. 1371; year 22, pp. 1435–1437; year 24, pp. 1451–1452; year 26, pp. 1476–1478; year 27, p. 1486; year 28, pp. 1493–1494; Ding year 4, pp. 1539–1540; year 8, p. 1564; Ai year 16, p. 1703; *Han Feizi ji shi*, ch. 1, "Ai chen 愛臣," p. 60 (2): this refers both to a "house [*jia*] of one thousand chariots" toppling the ruler; and to "ministers who manipulate their ruler to aggrandize their own households [*long jia* 隆家]."

22. *Zuo zhuan zhu*, Xiang year 31, p. 1192: refers to an official who administers a village that belongs to a noble household; *Han Feizi ji shi*, ch. 7, "Shuo lin shang 説林上," p. 443.

23. *Zuo zhuan zhu*, Wen year 1, p. 515: the heir apparent gives his *shi* to another man to provide him with income for the posts to which he is appointed; Cheng year 7, p. 834: a *shi* is divided up by rival nobles; Cheng year 16, p. 890; Xiang year 14, p. 1008: the story of renouncing a *shi*; year 17, p. 1031; year 19, pp. 1049, 1050 (3); year 21, p. 1058; year 30, p. 1178; Zhao year 4, p. 1247; year 5, p. 1266: refers to the division of the ducal *shi* between the ministerial houses; year 8, p. 1302; year 10, p. 1317; year 12, p. 1335; year 13, p. 1344; year 25, p. 1460; Ding year 10, p. 1582; Ai year 8, p. 1650; year 11, p. 1658: on the military balance between households of ministerial houses of Lu and the armies of Qi.

24. *Houma meng shu* 侯馬盟書, ed. Shanxisheng Wenwu Gongzuo Weiyuanhui 山西省文物工作委員會 (Shanghai: Wenwu, 1976), pp. 73–74, 320.

25. *Zuo zhuan zhu*, Zhuang year 26, p. 439: describes the households of poor people as *shi*; Xuan year 15, p. 764: tells of an official granted 1,000 *shi*; Cheng year 17, p. 898: a household official possesses a town of one hundred *shi*; *Guliang zhuan zhu shu*, Zhuang year 9, ch. 5, p. 15a. See also *Xunzi ji jie*, ch. 19, "Da lüe 大略," p. 325. The *Yi Zhou shu* measures income for offices in terms of the number of *shi*— clearly peasant households—and measures villages in terms of the numbers of *shi*. See *Yi Zhou shu hui jiao ji zhu*, ch. 4, "Da ju 大聚," p. 417; ch. 5, "Zuo Luo," p. 566. The same text uses *shi jia* 室家 to refer to the households of the common people. See ch. 6, "Shi xun 時訓," p. 642.

26. *Shi ji* 68, pp. 2232, 2236–2337; 85, pp. 2512–2513.

27. "Lodging" guests was not limited to powerful figures. The *Li ji* discusses etiquette when one person lodges at another's house. It also describe how states lodged emissaries and other visitors who were housed and fed at state expense. It stipulates how they were to be treated, and how funerals were to be staged if they died as guests. There were even rules for housing visiting rulers. See *Li ji zhu shu*, ch. 2, "Qu li 曲禮," pp. 1b–2a: discusses the etiquette of going to stay (*she*) at another person's house; ch. 8, "Tan gong shang," p. 16a: refers to a guest who stayed at Zi Xia's house; ch. 9, "Tang gong xia," p. 5a: states that a guest could perform the ceremony of greeting a visiting ruler if his host was absent; ch. 19, "Zengzi wen 曾子問," p. 19b: discusses pro-

cedure when a foreign emissary dies in state-provided lodging, p. 22a: discusses where visiting officials were lodged if the ruler's house was in mourning; ch. 21, "Li yun," p. 21a: states that the Son of Heaven when visiting a feudal lord lodges in the ancestral temple; ch. 42, "Za ji xia 雜記下," p. 4a; ch. 54, "Biao ji 表記," p. 24a: stipulates that one cannot inquire about the place of lodging of a guest whom one cannot oneself lodge; p. 28a: indicates that the Son of Heaven while visiting a feudal lord should not divine about his lodging, but should lodge in the ancestral temple; ch. 59, "Ru xing 儒行," p. 13b; ch. 63, "Pin yi 聘義," p. 6a: describes the prince's providing food for emissaries who lodge in his state. *Shi ji* 68, p. 2236: refers to a building to house guests at Qin's frontiers.

28. On the forms and significance of these personal ties, see Lewis, *Sanctioned Violence*, pp. 67–80.

29. *Zhan guo ce* 戰國策 (Shanghai: Guji, 1985), ch. 9, "Qi 2," p. 352: a lodger goes on a mission as a diplomatic representative; p. 356: lodgers participate in their host's rituals and receive food; ch. 10, "Qi 3," pp. 381–382: lodgers have social contact with the host's wives, p. 384; ch. 11, "Qi 4," pp. 395–397: a guest who has not done anything for the hosts receives lodging, food, clothing, a chariot, and support for his family; pp. 402–403: speaker lists the talents of several of Prince Mengchang's guests as a key to his power; p. 421: inadequate regular feeding of guests is a reason for a lack of loyalty; ch. 13, "Qi 6," p. 473: guests are sent on political missions; ch. 16, "Chu 3," p. 537: lodgers travel with their host on political business; ch. 17, "Chu 4," p. 573: retainers are recorded in a register which also provides a schedule for their meetings with the host, pp. 575–576; ch. 18, "Zhao 1," pp. 605, 627–628: a lodger is sent as an emissary; ch. 30, "Yan 2," p. 1104: rulers are praised for selecting men for office and establishing social links with them (*jiao jie* 交結) rather than relying on kin; ch. 31, "Yan 3," p. 1132: a hierarchy of lodgings for guests, p. 1137; *Shi ji* 41, p. 1742; 46, p. 1885: one member of the Tian clan in Qi allowed his guests and lodgers to freely enter and exit the rear quarters where his wives lived; 76, p. 2355: lists the unusual talents of several guests; 77, p. 2377: guests infiltrated the court of a foreign ruler and provided military intelligence; p. 2378: a host stages a great banquet for his guests and his blood kin; 78, p. 2395: describes the fabulous attire of guests of Prince Chunshen that humbled emissaries from Zhao; 81, p. 2443; 89, p. 2571: guests persuade the daughter of their deceased patron to marry; 112, p. 2962: lumps guests together with the brothers of the household, and refers to how guests prevented an unsuccessful brother from entering the house; 118, p. 3096: states that the younger sister of the heir to a Han king had sex with guests as well as servants.

On the structural tensions within the lord's household between guests and women, see Lewis, *Sanctioned Violence*, pp. 74–75. See also *Shi ji* 76, p. 2369; 82, p. 2455.

30. *Zhan guo ce*, ch. 19, "Zhao 2," p. 635: the death of a chief minister is called "leaving the palace [*sun guan she* 損館舍]," where the words for "palace" are the same as those for the lodgings of guests; ch. 20, "Zhao 3," p. 707: when the Son of Heaven visits the feudal lords, they must "vacate their palaces [*bi she* 避舍]" for him, and again the "palace" is called a *she*; ch. 22, "Wei 1," p. 787: pairs the "galleried palaces [*wu she* 廡舍]" of the nobles with the "field huts [*tian lu* 田廬]" of the peasants; ch. 25, "Wei 4," p. 903: refers to the hostels provided for foreign emissaries as *zhuan she* (傳舍). The term *she* also refers to the dwelling of the master in a Han poem, but here it is the house of a poor man. See "Dong men xing 東門行," in Lu, *Xian Qin Han Wei Jin Nanbeichao shi*, vol. 1, p. 269.

31. *Shi ji* 5, p. 193; 12, pp. 458, 462; 28, pp. 1387, 1390; 120, p. 3112.

32. *Shi ji* 75, pp. 2354, 2359–2360, 2362: Prince Mengchang had either "several thousand" or "more than 3,000" guests and resorted to moneylending to house and feed them; a multitude of guests is essential to the rich and noble, p. 2363: the mores of Prince Mengchang's fiefs declined because he gathered 60,000 households devoted to the way of the "swordsmen"; 76, p. 2365: Prince Pingyuan loved guests and attracted several thousand, p. 2368: their number varied from the hundreds to the thousands, p. 2369: he exhausted his household's wealth entertaining guests; 77, p. 2377: Prince Xinling had 3,000 guests, so that other states feared him, p. 2379: more than one hundred chariots driven by guests joined Zhao's army; 78, p. 2395: Prince Chunshen had more than 3,000 guests; 130, p. 3314. See also *Xin xu shu zheng* 新序疏證, annotated by Zhao Shanyi 趙善詒 (Shanghai: Huadong Shifan Daxue, 1989), p. 22: Lord Ping of Jin claims to feed more than 3,000 resident guests. *Han shi wai zhuan ji shi* 韓氏外傳集釋, annotated by Xu Weiyu 許維遹 (Beijing: Zhonghua, 1980), p. 236; *Shuo yuan* 數苑, ch. 8, "Zun xian 尊賢," p. 11a: a man claims to have 2,000 guests in his household. The figure of 3,000 guests became so standard that the *Shi ji* stated that Confucius had 3,000 disciples. *Huainanzi*, ch. 20, "Tai zu 泰族," p. 357 described these as *yang tu* 養徒, "followers whom he nourished" like the guests who were fed by their host (*shi ke*). On guests as private armies see *Han Feizi ji shi*, ch. 1, "Ai chen," p. 60; ch. 4, "Gu fen 孤憤," p. 207; "Jian jie shi chen," p. 251; ch. 19, "Wu du," p. 1058; ch. 20, "Ren zhu 人主, p. 1119; *Shi ji* 7, p. 296: guests and brothers are drilled together; 77, p. 2379; 78, p. 2395; *Guanzi jiao zheng*, ch. 21, "Ming fa 明法," p. 348.

33. *Han Feizi ji shi*, ch. 2, "Yang quan 揚權, p. 124: "The private households will be full and the lord's court empty." Ch. 4, "Gu fen," p. 207: "Therefore they avoid the ruler and hasten to the private households." Ch. 14 "Wai chu shuo you xia 外儲說右下," p. 775: "The means by which the ruler can be illumined are the noble followers of the feudal lords. Now the noble followers of the feudal lords are all the factions of private households. The means by which the ruler provides himself with wings are the recluses. Now the recluses are all the lodgers of private households." P. 776; ch. 19, "Wu du," p. 1075.

34. *Shi ji* 85, pp. 2507, 2510.

35. *Han Feizi ji shi*, ch. 7, "Shuo lin shang," p. 426. See also ch. 7, "Shuo lin shang," p. 440: refers to an official's crowd of followers; ch. 8, "Shuo lin xia," p. 476.

36. *Shi ji* 76, p. 2362. The same argument appears in *Shi ji* 120, pp. 3113–3114; 129, pp. 3255–3256. Stories of competition between leading political figures to secure the greatest number of retainers and to lure away each others guests appear in *Shi ji* 77, pp. 2383, 2384; 78, p. 2395; 124, p. 3183.

37. *Shi ji* 49, p. 1974; 55, p. 2045: the ability of the heir apparent to attract four hermits as guests persuades Gaozu not to replace him; 89, p. 2571, 2572, 2583, 2584, 2586; 93, pp. 2640, 2642: a man under Gaozu gathered more than 1,000 guests and admired one of the Four Princes; 107, p. 2839: an important official under Emperors Wen and Jing collected guests, pp. 2842, 2847: a local magnate from the same period daily fed up to 100 guests and employed them and his kin to maintain power, pp. 2849, 2850; 117, p. 3000: the wealthy merchant Zhuo's household had eight hundred servants [*jia tong* 家僮] and hundreds of guests, and Sima Xiangru was ultimately reconciled with him because of his ability to command guests; 118, p. 3082 and *Huainanzi* quoted in note 2, 3093, 3095, 3096; 120, p. 3112: a man acted as a bravo and spent

his nights chatting with guests; 121, p. 3121: a man distinguished himself by not gathering guests, although he gathered more than a hundred "disciples"; 122, p. 3138: a high legal official refuses to lodge and feed guests and rejects requests from high officials and guests, pp. 3139, 3142: a leading "cruel clerk" collects guests with whom he regularly dines, p. 3146: several hundred guests and brothers of imprisoned men are executed by a cruel clerk, p. 3153: another cruel clerk with retainers; 124, pp. 3184, 3186, 3187, 3188: the relations of bravoes with their guests.

38. *Han Feizi ji shi*, ch. 1, "Ai chen," p. 60 (2): a "household (*jia*) of one thousand chariots" menacing the ruler, and generals and ministers manipulating the ruler to "aggrandize their households [*long jia* 隆家];" ch. 2, "You du 有度," p. 88; "Yang quan," p. 123: the ruler "only fears there will be many men in the households of the great ministers," p. 124: "A prince who has the Way will not enlarge his capital; ministers who have the way will not enrich their families"; "decrease those who have much and increase those who have little; when decrease and increase are in balance this will not allow the people to join together in larger groups"; "Ba jian 八姦," p. 152: one of the eight paths of treachery, which begin in the prince's bedchamber and then move spatially, is the existence of overly strong households among the people; ch. 4, "Gu fen," p. 207 (2): men who "obscure the ruler and hasten to the private households" and "the ruler is increasingly debased while the private households are increasingly honored"; p. 208: the transfer of power in Qi and the partition of Jin as a result of one family (*shi* 氏) supplanting another; "He shi 和氏," pp. 238–239: Wu Qi states that in Chu the great ministers are too powerful and their fiefs too numerous; "Jian jie shi chen," p. 245: men who obscure the ruler and serve the important ministers are "persons honored and families enriched, whose fathers and sons enjoy their blessings"; ch. 5, "Wang zheng 亡徵," p. 267: "In all cases when the ruler's state [*guo* 國] is small and the ministerial houses [*jia* 家] great, when the authority is weak and the ministers important, it ought to perish;" p. 269; ch. 8, "Yong ren 用人," p. 499: the ruler's fear that the power of punishments, and by extension military action, will be seized by the private households; ch. 20, "Ren zhu," p. 1119. References to households of a thousand chariots or other military force echo the passage in the *Mencius* in which it is the vassal with a thousand chariots who will destroy the lord of ten thousand, or the vassal with a hundred chariots who will destroy the lord with a thousand. See *Mengzi zhengyi* IA, "Liang Hui Wang shang," p. 22–25. It is significant that in this passage the hereditary officials are said to ask, "How can I profit my household [*jia*]?" See p. 22.

39. Du Zhengsheng 杜正勝, "Bian hu qi min de chuxian ji qi lishi yiyi: bianhu qimin de yanjiu zhi yi 編戶齊民的出現及其歷史義意：編戶齊民的研究之一," *Zhongyang Yanjiuyuan Lishi Yuyan Yanjiushuo jikan* 54:3 (1983), pp. 77–111; Du, *Bian hu qi min: chuantong zhengzhi shehui jiegou zhi xingcheng* 編戶齊民：傳統政治社會結構之形成 (Taipei: Lianjing, 1989), pp. 1–10, 188–196.

40. *Zhou yi zheng yi*, ch. 4, pp. 16a–b.

41. *Li ji zhu shu*, ch. 21, "Li yun," p. 4b; ch. 22, "Li yun," p. 4a.

42. *Mengzi zhengyi* IA, "Liang Hui Wang shang," p. 57.

43. *Mengzi zhengyi* IA, "Liang Hui Wang shang," p. 35; VIIA, "Jin xin shang," p. 537.

44. *Han Feizi ji shi*, ch. 19, "Wu du," p. 1041.

45. *Mengzi zhengyi* IA, "Liang Hui Wang shang," p. 57. See also *Mengzi zhengyi* IA, "Liang Hui Wang shang," p. 41: "Other [rulers] deprive the people of their time for agricultural labor, making it so they cannot plough and weed in order to nourish their parents. The parents freeze and starve, and brothers, wives, and children scatter." IB "Liang Hui Wang xia," p. 61: "Now how could our king's love of hunting cause us to reach this extremity. Fathers and sons can no longer see each other. Brothers, wives, and children are scattered." IVB, "Li Lou xia," pp. 353–354: "How could it be that Master Zhang did not desire to have the links between husband and wife or son and mother? Because he offended his father, he could not approach him. So he drove away his wife and son and to the end of his life did not nourish them." VA, "Wan Zhang shang," p. 376: "Toiling in the king's service, they were unable to nourish their parents."

46. *Mengzi zhengyi* VIIA, "Jin xin shang," p. 533.

47. Emile Durkheim, *The Division of Labor in Society*, tr. George Simpson (New York: The Free Press, 1933), ch. 2.

48. Moriya Mitsuo 守屋美都雄, "Kandai kazoku no keitai ni kan suru kōsatsu 漢代家族の形態に關する考察," "Kandai kazoku no keitai ni kan suru sai kōsatsu 漢代家族の形態に關する再考察," and "Kandai no kazoku 漢代の家族," in *Chūgoku kodai no kazoku to kokka* 中國古代の家族と國家 (Kyoto: Tōyōshi Kenkyūkai, 1968), pp. 297–415: argues that a typical Han family had three generations: the parents, the eldest son, his wife and children, and unmarried siblings; Makino Tatsumi 牧野巽, "Kandai ni okeru kazoku no ōkisa 漢代における家族の大きさ" and "Kandai no kazoku keitai 漢代の家族形態," reprinted in *Makino Tatsumi Chosaku shū*, vol. 1, *Chūgoku kazoku kenkyū* 著作集: 中國家族研究 (Tokyo: Ochanomizu, 1980), pp. 119–250: argues that a typical Han family was the nuclear family, and that brothers generally lived apart after their marriages; Utsunomiya Kiyoyoshi 宇都宮清吉, "Kandai gōzoku kenkyū 漢代豪族研究," in *Chūgoku kodai chūsei shi kenkyū* 中國古代中世史研究 (Tokyo: Sōbunsha, 1977), pp. 351–388; Utsunomiya, *Kandai shakai keizai shi kenkyū* 漢代社會經濟研究 (Tokyo: Kōbundō, 1955), pp. 405–472; Ochi Shigeaki 越智重明, "Kan jidai no ko to ie 漢時代の戶と家," *Shigaku zasshi* 78.8 (1969), pp. 1–44; Ochi, "Kan jidai no ie o megutte 漢時代の家おめぐつて," *Shigaku zasshi* 86.6 (1977), pp. 1–36: argues that division into nuclear households was standard, with the parents living with one son, but he also posits another form in which sons lived with their father; Inaba Ichiro 稻葉一郎, "Kandai no kazoku keitai to keizai hendō 漢代の家族形態と經濟變動," *Tōyōshi kenkyū* 43.1 (1984), pp. 88–117: argues that the nuclear family was predominant through the reign of Emperor Wu, but that the rise of landlordism and Confucianism encouraged wealthy families to have several generations and numerous siblings dwell together; Rui Yifu 芮逸夫, "Zhongguo jia zhi de yanbian 中國家制的演變," and "Changing Structure of the Chinese Family," in *Zhongguo minzu ji qi wenhua lungao* 中國民族及其文化論稿 (Taipei: Yiwen, 1972), pp. 747–777: argues that over the course of the Han the "stem family" with parents, one married son and his spouse, and unmarried siblings became increasingly common; Xu Zhuoyun [Hsü Cho-yün] 許倬雲, "Handai jiating de daxiao 漢代家庭的大小," in *Qiu gu pian* 求古篇 (Taipei: Lianjing, 1982), pp. 515–541: argues that the nuclear family was predominant in the Western Han, but the stem family became important in the Eastern; Ma Xin 馬新, "Handai xiao nong jiating lüe lun 漢代小農家庭略論," *Wen shi zhe* (1986:4), pp. 14–18: argues that the nuclear family was predominant in the Western Han but that siblings living together became common in the Eastern;

Huang Jinshan 黃金山, "Lun Handai jiating de ziran goucheng yu dengji goucheng 論漢代家庭的自然構成與等級構成," *Zhongguo shi yanjiu* (1987:4), pp. 81–89: argues that the nuclear family was most common throughout the Han, but that families with married siblings living together and fragmentary families (missing a parent) were not uncommon; Lai Ming-chiu, "Familial Morphology in Han China: 206 B.C.–A.D. 220" (Ph. D. dissertation, University of Toronto, 1995): argues that there was no single characteristic type, but that Han families were adaptive units that varied across the regions and the centuries, and shifted depending on what economic "niches" were available. On "niche" see Richard R. Wilk, *Household Ecology: Economic Change and Domestic Life among the Kekchi Maya in Belize* (Tucson: University of Arizona, 1991). The three categories of households employed by most scholars derive from Olga Lang, *Chinese Family and Society* (New Haven: Yale University, 1946). With the addition of a category composed of domestic groups with no family structure these categories would roughly correspond to those suggested by the Cambridge Group for the History of Population and Social Structure. See Laslett, "Introduction: The History of the Family," pp. 36–39; and Martine Segalen, *Historical Anthropology of the Family*, tr. J. C. Whitehouse and Sarah Matthews (Cambridge: Cambridge University, 1986), pp. 23–24.

49. *Jiazi xin shu jiao shi*, pp. 303, 315, 317. See also *Han shu* 48, p. 2244.

50. *Shuihudi Qin mu zhu jian* 睡虎地秦墓竹簡 (Beijing: Wenwu, 1978), p. 159. "Those who dwell together" is defined on another strip as equivalent to "household (*hu* 戶)." See *Shuihudi Qin mu zhu jian*, p. 160. *Shuihudi Qin mu zhu jian*, pp. 197–198 posits father and son dwelling together as a possible, but not a necessary practice.

51. *Jin shu* 30, p. 925.

52. The cases are presented in a table in Lai, "Familial Morphology in Han China," pp. 90–93, 259.

53. *Shuihudi Qin mu zhu jian*, pp. 209 (2), 249.

54. *Shuihudi Qin mu zhu jian*, pp. 3–7; Gao Min 高敏, "Bian nian ji de xingzhi yu zuozhe zhiyi 編年記的性質與作者質疑," in *Yunmeng Qin jian chutan* 雲夢秦簡初探 (Henan: Renmin, 1979), pp. 10–16.

55. *Yunmeng Shuihudi Qin mu* 雲蒙睡虎地秦墓 (Beijing: Wenwu, 1981), strips recto 776–781. On this passage and its unusual physical arrangement, see Li Xueqin 李學勤, "Shuihudi Qin jian de *gen shan tu* 睡虎地秦簡的艮山圖," *Wenwu tiandi* (1991:4), pp. 30–32. The term I have translated as "slave" is *ren min* 人民. For evidence of this sense of the term, see *Shuihudi Qin mu*, strips recto 743, 746, 752, 765, 779–780, 810, 874, 939, 948, 952: refers to buying and selling *renmin*, 955, 957: also refers to buying and selling; Wu Jiulong 吳九龍, *Yinqueshan Han jian shi wen* 銀雀山漢簡釋文 (Beijing: Wenwu, 1988), slips 0273: refers to buying and selling, 0916, 4941: refers to buying them. See also Li Xueqin, "Shuihudi Qin jian 'Ri shu' yu Chu Qin shehui 睡虎地秦簡日書與楚秦社會," *Jiang Han kaogu* (1985:4), pp. 60–64; M. C. Lai, "Familial Morphology," p. 59, note 91.

56. Wu Jiulong, *Yinqueshan Han jian shi wen*, slips #0050, 0862, 0888, and 0892.

57. *Shi ji* 97, p. 2699; *Hou Han shu* 39, pp. 1294–1295: an exemplar of filial piety has to accept the request of a nephew to divide their property; 76, p. 2471: division of property is described as a ritual duty, although the instigator is criticized for giving himself the lion's share; 81, pp. 1685–1686: the division is instigated by the brothers' wives, anticipating a theme of later family instructions.

58. *Han shu* 43, p. 2114; 58, p. 2624; 66, p. 2890; 76, p. 3213; 83, p. 3369; *Hou Han shu* 10a, p. 402; 14, pp. 557, 560; 27, p. 941; 31, p. 1100; 32, pp. 1119, 1125, 1132; 39, pp. 1294–1295; 45, p. 1534; 76, p. 2472; 81, pp. 2684, 2685–2686; 84, pp. 2793–2794; *Feng su tong yi jiao shi*, pp. 155–156 (2); *Xie Cheng shu* 謝承書, quoted in *Hou Han shu*, ch. 76, p. 2472; *Li shi* 隸釋, compiled by Hong Gua 洪适, in *Shike shiliao congshu* 石刻史料叢書, vol. 1–3 (Taipei: Yiwen, 1966), ch. 6, pp. 9a–10b; ch. 9, pp. 18b–19b; ch. 15, pp. 10b–11b, 17a–19a; *Dong guan Han ji jiao zhu* 東觀漢記校注, compiled by Liu Zhen 劉珍 et al., annotated by Wu Shuping 吳樹平 (Zhongzhou: Zhongzhou gu ji, 1987), ch. 14, p. 531; *Xu Qi xie ji* 續齊諧記, quoted in *Tai ping yu lan*, ch. 421, p. 9a; *Lie nü zhuan*, quoted in *Tai ping yu lan*, ch. 516, p. 6b. For a study of the anecdote from the *Xu Qi xie ji*, see Wang Guoliang 王國良, *Xu Qi xie ji yanjiu* 續齊諧記研究 (Taipei: Wen shi zhe, 1987), pp. 24–26.

59. *Hou Han shu* 32, p. 1119: a family is praised for devotion to rites because three generations share property; 43, p. 1487: a virtuous official's benevolent government and propagation of morality leads many people to move back with their parents (see also *Dong Guan Han ji* 16, p. 681); 60b, p. 1980: the family of Cai Yong is praised because three generations lived together without dividing property; 81, p. 2471: the eldest brother insists on not dividing the family property with his brothers in order to correct local custom.

60. See chapter four, note 101.

61. In contrast, Moriya Mitsuo and Utsunomiya Kiyoyoshi argued that the standard family in the Han consisted of three generations: parents, married children, and children's children. See Utsunomiya, *Kandai shakai keizai shi kenkyū*, pp. 405–437; Moriya Mitsuo, "Kandai kazoku no keitai ni kansuru kōsatsu" and "Kandai kazoku no keitai ni kansuru sai kōsatsu," pp. 297–353, 354–377. They argue that the most common form of collective legal familial responsibility was the punishment of these three generations, and that ritualists declared three generations to be the standard and criticized division of property among brothers. Makino Tatsumi pointed out that there is no reason to equate mutual liability with common residence, and that different degrees of collective responsibility were applied in different cases. Three generations was simply the most common figure. See Makino Tatsumi, "Kandai ni okeru kazoku no ōkisa" and "Kandai no kazoku keitai," reprinted in *Makino Tatsumi Chosaku shū*, vol. 1, *Chūgoku kazoku kenkyū*, pp. 119–142, 143–250. A notable example is a protest by He Hai regarding the "Great Proscription" on officeholding from A.D. 169 to 184. He points out that the ban was extended to kin sharing a common ancestor up to five generations earlier, while brothers lived apart and divided property in the third generation, that is, typical families were two generations. See *Hou Han shu* 67, p. 2189; 8, p. 330. As for the second argument, even Moriya and Utsunomiya admit that division between brothers was common, and that the three-generation household was only the "model" form (*tenkei* 典型). Although the three-generation household was "normative," it was not "normal."

62. "Jiangsu Yizheng Xupu 101 hao Xi Han mu 江蘇儀征胥浦101號西漢墓," *Wenwu* (1987:1), pp. 1–16. Photographs of the strips are plates one and two. A drawing appears on p. 10 and a transcription on pp. 11–12. For another transcription and more detailed philological study, see Chen Ping 陳平 and Wang Qinjin 王勤金, "Yizheng Xupu 101 hao Xi Han mu 'xian ling quan shu' chu kao 儀征胥浦101號西漢墓 '先令券書' 初考," *Wenwu* (1987:1), pp. 20–25, 36. For studies, see Chen Ping, "Yizheng Xupu 'Xian ling quan shu' xu kao 儀征胥浦 '先令券書' 續考,"

Kaogu (1992:2), pp. 84–92, 83; Chen, "Zai tan Xupu 'Xian ling quan shu' zhong de jige wenti 再談胥浦'先令券書'中的幾個問題," *Wenwu* (1992:9), pp. 62–65; Nishikawa Motoharu 西川素治, "Kandai no igenjō—Kōso Gicho Shoho 101 gō Zenkan shutsudo 'Senrei kensho' ni tusite 漢代の遺言書—江蘇儀征胥浦一零一號前漢出土先令券書について," in *Chūgoku kodai no hō to shakai* 中國古代の法と社會, ed. Hori Toshikazu 崛敏一 (Tokyo: Kyūko Shoin, 1988), pp. 77–97; Lai, "Familial Morphology in Han China," Appendix One; Bret Hinsch, "Women, Kinship, and Property as Seen in a Han Dynasty Will," *T'oung Pao* 84 (1998), pp. 1–21.

63. *Shi ji* 68, p. 2230.

64. On uxorilocal marriages in different periods of Chinese history and different social strata, see Patricia Buckley Ebrey, *The Inner Quarters* (Berkeley: University of California, 1994), pp. 211–212, 235–249; Margery Wolf, *Woman and the Family in Rural Taiwan* (Stanford: Stanford University, 1972), pp. 191–204; Burton Pasternak, "On the Causes and Demographic Consequences of Uxorilocal Marriage in China," in *Family and Population in East Asian History*, ed. Susan B. Hanley and Arthur P. Wolf (Stanford: Stanford University, 1985), pp. 309–336; Hinsch, "Women, Kinship, and Property," pp. 5–8; Lai, "Familial Morphology in Han China," pp. 234–236.

65. Most scholars believe that sons usually received equal shares. See Niida Noboru 仁井田陞, "Chūgoku no ie ni tsuite 中國の家について," in *Chūgoku no hō to shakai to rekishi* 中國の法と社會と歷史 (Tokyo: Iwanami Shoten, 1967), pp. 159–162; Morioka Kiyomi, "Life Cycle Patterns in Japan, China, and the United States," *Journal of Marriage and the Family* 29 (1967), p. 602; Ma Xin 馬新 and Qi Tao 齊濤, "Lüe lun Zhongguo gudai de jiachan jicheng zhidu 略論中國古代的家產繼承制度," *Renmin zazhi* (1987:5), pp. 101–104, 110.

66. "Yinqueshan zhu shu 'Shou fa', 'Shou ling', deng shisan pian 銀雀山竹書'守法','守令'等十三篇," *Wenwu* (1985:4), p. 35.

67. *Zhou li zhu shu*, ch. 11, "Xiao situ 小司徒," p. 4a. This same system of linking service quotas to quality of land, with no reference to family size, is sketched in ch. 29, "Da sima 大司馬," pp. 6a–b.

68. *Han Feizi ji shi* 49 "Wu du," p. 1041; *Qian fu lun jian* 7 "Kao ji 考績," p. 63. The *Han Feizi* states that five sons "would not be many," but this is only in contrast with the twenty-five grandsons in the next generation, if each son reproduced in the same manner as his father.

69. *Han shu* 24a, pp. 1124–1125, 1132. Chao Cuo refers to the average household having "two people (*er ren* 二人)" liable for corvee labor. As there are records of women mobilized for corvee labor both for building city walls and for the transport of grain, this reference to "two people" probably indicates the married couple. For evidence of women's liability for corvee, see Qian Jianfu 錢劍夫, *Qin Han fu yi zhidu kao lüe* 秦漢賦役制度考略 (Hubei: Renmin, 1988)," pp. 162–163; *Han shu* 2, pp. 89–90.

70. *Fengsu tong yi*, p. 406, in a commentary in *Hou Han shu* 76, p. 2478; *Gongyang zhuan zhushu*, Xuan 15, ch. 16, p. 15b; *Guliang zhuan zhu shu* 穀梁傳注疏, in *Shisan jing zhu shu*, vol. 7. (Taipei: Yiwen, 1976), Xuan 15, ch. 12, p. 15b.

71. Lao Gan 勞榦, *Juyan Han jian kaoshi* 居延漢簡考釋 (Taipei: Zhongyang Yanjiuyuan Lishi Yuyan Yanjiusuo zhuankan 40, 1960), pp. 26 (1274), 55 (2745), 65 (3281), 65 (3282), 66 (3287), 66 (3289), 66 (3295), 82 (4069), 83 (4085), 86 (4207), 92 (4468), 102 (4963), 108 (5242), 111 (5345), 113 (5461), 113–114 (5462), 198 (9903).

72. Hong Yi 弘一, "Jiangling Fenghuangshan 10 hao Han mu jiandu chu tan 江陵鳳凰山十號漢墓簡牘初談," *Wenwu* (1974:6), pp. 78–84; Huang Shengzhang 黃盛璋, "Jiangling Fenghuangshan Han mu jiandu ji qi zai lishi dili yanjiu shang de jiazhi 江陵鳳凰山漢墓簡牘及其在歷史地理研究上的價值," *Lishi dili yu kaogu luncong* 歷史地理與考古論叢 (Ji'nan: Qilu, 1982), pp. 116–193; Qiu Xigui 裘錫圭, "Hubei Jiangling Fenghuangshan 10 hao Han mu chutu jiandu kaoshi 湖北江陵鳳凰山十號漢墓出土簡牘考釋," *Wenwu* (1987:7), pp. 49–62.

73. Lao Gan, "Liang Han huji yu dili zhi guanxi 兩漢戶籍與地理之關係, "*Zhongyang Yanjiu Yuan Lishi Yuyan Yanjiusuo jikan* 5:2 (1935), pp. 179–214; Lao Gan, "Liang Han jun guo mianji zhi guji ji koushu zengjian zhi tuice 兩漢郡國面積之估計及口數增減之推測," *Zhongyang Yanjiu Yuan Lishi Yuyan Yanjiusuo jikan* 5:2 (1935), pp. 215–240; Hans Bielenstein, "The Census of China during the Period 2–742 A.D.," *Bulletin of the Museum of Far Eastern Antiquities* 19 (1946), pp. 125–145; Bielenstein, "Chinese Historical Demography A.D. 2–1982," *Bulletin of the Museum of Far Eastern Antiquities* 59 (1987), pp. 11–15; Feng Chengji 馮承基, "Fu Wuji suo ji Dong Han hukou shuzi zhi jiantao 伏無忌所記東漢戶口數字之檢討," *Dalu zazhi* 27.2 (1963), pp. 9–15; Liang Fangzhong 梁方仲, *Zhongguo lidai hukou tiandi tianfu tongji* 中國歷代戶口地田賦統計 (Shanghai: Renmin, 1980), pp. 14–20. A summary is given in Lai, "Familial Morphology in Han China," table 5, p. 263.

74. On the rare "communal families" in the Tang, the attention they attracted, and their relation to the ideological program of certain scholars, see Patricia Ebrey, "The Early Stages in the Development of Descent Group Organization," in *Kinship Organization in Late Imperial China: 1000–1940* (Berkeley: University of California, 1986), pp. 29–39.

75. *Shuo wen jie zi zhu*, ch. 7b, pp. 5b, 6a. In some editions the character is *ju* 居. Duan Yucai argues that this is a mistake, but either reading would support the present argument. For examples of *jia* and *shi* as a synonym compound in Han sources, see *Shi ji* 48, p. 1955: refers to collective punishment; 71, p. 2317; 118, p. 3077 (2): refers to the physical construction of houses. The supplemental section of the *Shi ji* chapter on diviners has dozens of examples. See *Shi ji* 128, pp. 3242–3247. See also *Li ji zhu shu*, ch. 50, "Jing jie 經解," p. 4b; *Da Dai li ji jie gu* 大戴禮記解詁, annotated by Wang Pinzhen 王聘珍 (Beijing: Zhonghua, 1983), ch. 9, p. 159. For examples from the Qin see *Lü shi chun qiu jiao shi*, ch. 17, "Shen shi 慎勢," p. 1109; ch. 24, "Gui dang 貴當," p. 1629; ch. 25, "Bie lei 別類," p. 1643: building a house. Two wooden planks discovered at Shuihudi contain letters home from two brothers. In the second letter they used the term *jia shi* 家室 to address their family. See "Hubei Yunmeng Shuihudi 11 zuo Qin mu fajue jianbao 湖北雲蒙睡虎地十一座秦墓發掘簡報," *Wenwu* (1976:9), pp. 51–61; Huang Shengzhang 黃盛璋, "Yunmeng Qin mu liang feng jia shu zhong you guan lishi dili de wenti 雲蒙秦墓兩封家書中有關歷史地理的問題," *Wenwu* (1980: 8), pp. 74–77; Li Junming 李均明 and Ho Shuangquan 何雙全, ed., *San jian jiandu ho ji* 散見簡牘合集 (Beijing: Wenwu, 1990), pp. 83–84. On the manner in which the characters *jia* 家, *shi* 室, and *hu* 戶 formed synonym compounds, see Hori, "Chūgoku kodai no ie to ko," pp. 307–310.

76. *Shuo wen jie zi zhu*, ch. 14b, pp. 44a–b. See also Shao Junpu 邵君樸, "Shi jia 釋家," *Zhongyang Yanjiuyuan Lishi Yuyan Yanjiusuo jikan* 5:2 (1935), pp. 279–281; Hori Toshikazu, "Chūgoku kodai no ie to ko 中國古代の家と戶," *Chūgoku kankei ronsetsu shiryō* 31:3 (1989), pp. 306–331, esp. p. 307. One modern scholar who argues that the character *jia* originally referred to a dwelling for pigs or dogs is Wang Liqi 王利器,

"Jia, ren dui wen jie 家, 人對文解*"* in *Xiao chuan shuzhai wen shi lun ji* 曉傳書齊文史論集 (Hong Kong: Zhongwen Daxue, 1989), pp. 238–239. The close resemblance of the seal forms "pig *shi* 豕*"* and "child *hai* 亥*"* is the subject of a story in the *Lü shi chun qiu:*

> Zi Xia was going to Jin and passed through Wei. Someone reading a historical chronicle said, "The Jin army, three pigs, forded the Yellow River." Zi Xia said,"That is wrong. This says *ji hai.* [已亥, one of the sexagenary cycle used to indicate the day] The character '*ji* 已' is close to 'three [*san* 三]' and the character 'pig [*shi* 豕]' resembles 'child [*hai* 亥]'."

See *Lü shi chun qiu jiao shi,* ch. 22, "Cha zhuan 察傳*,"* p. 1527.

77. *Shuihudi Qin mu zhu jian,* pp. 160, 238. In the second passage, I follow Satake Yasuhiko 佐竹靖彥 in amending the printed transcription of a character as *mu* 母 to *guan* 貫. See "Shin koku no kazoku to Shō Yō no bun'i rei 秦國の家族と商鞅の分異令*,"* *Shirin* 63 (1980), p. 13. Hulsewe rejects this because the term "*hu guan*" is not attested until a memorial written in 487 A.D. See Hulsewe, *Remnants of Ch'in Law* (Leiden: E. J. Brill, 1985), p. 179. However, the Chinese editors' gloss as "persons in the household with the same mother" ignores the Chinese. His own reading as "only the mother of the household" is incoherent (how could a single person "dwell together"?), posits a phrase (*hu mu* "mother of the household") that appears nowhere else, and contradicts the other gloss on *tong ju* cited earlier. Consequently Hulsewe's appeal to an argument from silence is unconvincing.

78. *Shuihudi Qin mu zhu jian,* pp. 197, 197–198.

79. *Shui hudi Qin mu zhu jian,* p. 63.

80. *Han shu* 2, p. 85: lists "father, mother, wife, children, and those who dwell together [*tong ju*]" of one category of official in parallel with the "family [*jia*]"of another category. Yan Shigu suggests that *tong ju* refers to brothers, brothers' wives, and brothers' children also living in the same household. For examples of its application to people living together with brothers, a father's brother, and his sons, see *Han shu* 50, p. 1307; *Hou Han shu* 25, p. 886; 52, p. 1722; 60b, p. 1980.

81. See the preceding note. See also Hiranaka Reiji 平中苓次, *Chūgoku kodai no densei to zeihō* 中國古代の田制と税法 (Kyoto: Tōyōshi kenkyūkai, 1967), pp. 320–336, 341.

82. Chen Pan 陳槃, "You Han jian zhong zhi jun li mingji shuo qi 由漢簡中之軍吏名籍説起*,"* *Dalu zazhi* 2:8 (1951), pp. 15, 19, 32–33; Hiranaka, *Chūgoku kodai no densei to zeihō,* pp. 205–236; He Changqun 賀昌群, *Lun Liang Han tudi zhanyou xingtai de fazhan* 論兩漢土地佔有形態的發展 (Shanghai: Renmin, 1956), pp. 18–19; Michael Loewe, *Records of Han Administration* (Cambridge: Cambridge University, 1967), vol. 1, pp. 71–72; Hsu Cho-yun, *Han Agriculture: The Formation of Early Chinese Agrarian Economy* (Seattle: University of Washington, 1980), pp. 230–231.

83. *Li ji zhu shu,* ch. 30, "Yu zao 玉藻*,"* p. 17a. Here "*yi shi zhi ren* 一室之人*"* means "all those dwelling in a household" as opposed to guests. In one *Shi jing* ode *shi ren* also refers to all those living in the household. See *Mao shi zheng yi,* ch. 2.3, #40, "Bei men 北門*,"* pp. 10a, 10b.

84. *Gong shi* 宮室 appears frequently. For *wu shi* 屋室 see *Lü shi chun qiu jiao shi,* ch. 7, "Huai chong 懷寵*,"* p. 412: an invading army is told not to burn houses; ch.

11, "Zhong dong 仲冬," p. 567: *fang shi* 房室 refers to houses sealed in the winter; *Shi ji* 56, p. 2058; 123, p. 3160.

85. *Zuo zhuan zhu*, Huan year 18, p. 152.

86. The links of *shi* with the wife are as early as the *Shi jing*. See *Mao shi zheng yi*, ch. 4.2, #73, "Da che 大車," p. 18b; ch. 7.2, #148, "Xi you changchu 隰有萇楚," pp. 8b–9a; 9.2; #164, "Chang di 常棣," p. 17a. "Zhong yong" cites this poem to show that ordering the state begins with ordering the household. See *Li ji zhu shu*, ch. 52, "Zhong yong," p. 11b. *Zuo zhuan zhu*, Huan year 6, p. 114; Xi year 15, p. 364: refers to a wife as *jia* 家; Xuan year 14, p. 754; Xiang year 4, p. 937; Zhao year 1, p. 1199; year 2, p. 1230; year 19, p. 1401; year 28, p. 1491; Ding year 9, p. 1574; Ai year 11, p. 1666; *Mengzi zheng yi* IIIB, "Teng Wen Gong xia," p. 251; *Li ji zhu shu*, ch. 1, "Qu li shang 曲禮上," pp. 14b, 23b; ch. 28, "Nei ze 內則," p. 20b; *Da Dai li ji jie gu*, ch. 13, "Ben ming 本命," p. 251; *Chun qiu fan lu yi zheng*, ch. 16, "Xun Tian zhi dao 循天之道, p. 445; "Chang'an you xia xie xing 長安有狹斜行," in *Xian Qin Han Wei Jin Nan Bei Chao shi*, vol. 1, p. 266; *Hou Han shu* 42, p. 1715. On *shi* as the dwelling of a man and his wife, see also *Mengzi zheng yi* IVB, "Li Lou xia," p. 357; VA, "Wang Zhang shang," p. 364: "For man and woman to dwell in a house [*shi*] is one of the great human relations." The use of *shi* as "marriage" also figures in *Yi Zhou shu hui jiao ji zhu*, ch. 3, "Wu shun 武順," p. 329; *Lie nü zhuan jiao zhu* 列女傳校注, Si bu bei yao ed., ch. 2, p. 5a. In another *Li ji* passage *zheng shi* 正室 designates the eldest son of the primary wife, that is, the heir. See *Li ji zhu shu*, ch. 20, "Wen Wang shi zi 文王世子," p. 20b. See also *Guo yu*, ch. 20, "Yue Yu shang," p. 635. As in the *Zuo zhuan*, *jia* can also refer to a wife. See also *Gu Liang zhuan zhu shu*, Xuan year 9, ch. 12, p. 11a.

87. Chang Kwang-chih, *Shang Civilization* (New Haven: Yale University, 1980), pp. 161–165; Ding Shan 丁山, *Jiaguwen suojian shizu ji qi zhidu* 甲骨文所見氏族及其制度 (Beijing: Kexue, 1956); Shirakawa Shizuka 白川靜, "Yin no kiso shakai 殷の基礎社會," in *Ritsumeikan sōritsu gojū shūnen kinen ronbun shū Bungaku hen* 立命館創立五十週年紀年論文集文學篇 (Kyoto: Ritsumeikan, 1958), pp. 260–296; Shirakawa, "In no ōzoku to seiji no keitai 殷の王族と政治の形態," *Kodaigaku* 3 (1954), pp. 19–44; Shirakawa, "Indai yūzoku kō, sono ni, Jaku 殷代雄族考，其二，雀," *Kōkotsu kin-bungaku ronsō* 6 (1957), pp. 1–62.

88. Lewis, *Sanctioned Violence*, pp. 49–50.

89. *Zuo zhuan zhu*, Zhao year 3, pp. 1236–1237.

90. *Lun yu zheng yi*, ch. 16, "Zi Lu 子路," p. 293: *zong zu* parallels *xiang dang* 鄉黨 "village coterie." These form a second level—below serving at court and going on foreign missions—in the actions that define a "man of service [*shi* 士]." See also *Zuo zhuan zhu*, Xi year 24, p. 423; Zhao year 3, p. 1237; Ding year 4, p. 1536: parallel of commanding the *zong shi* 宗氏 [the ruling house], and assembling the "separate lineages [*fen zu* 分族 of hereditary officials]"; *Yi Zhou shu hui jiao ji zhu*, ch. 10, "Wu ji 武紀," p. 1163: *zong zu* parallels *she ji* 社稷 "altars of grain and soil," *zong miao, fen mu* 墳墓 "graves," and *gui shen* 鬼神 "[ancestral] spirits" as aspects of a ruling house.

91. *Er ya zhu shu* 爾雅注疏, in *Shisan jing zhu shu*, vol. 8 (Taipei: Yiwen, 1976), ch. 4 "Shi qin 釋親," pp. 14a–19a. The statement that the *zong zu* is the father's group is on page 19a. The enumeration of its members appears on pp. 14a–15b.

92. For other examples see *Li ji zhu shu*, ch. 4, "Qu li xia 曲禮下," p. 7b; ch. 27, "Nei ze," p. 12b; ch. 50, "Ai Gong wen 哀公問," p. 7b; ch. 51, "Fang ji 坊記," p. 19b.

93. Han-yi Feng, *The Chinese Kinship System* (Cambridge: Harvard University, 1967), p. 95.

94. *Bo hu tong de lun*, ch. 2 "Zong zu 宗族," p. 33b. The phonetic gloss of *zong* with *zun* was also adopted in the *Shuo wen jie zi*. See *Shuo wen jie zi zhu*, ch. 7b, p. 14b. See also *Bo hu tong*, ch. 1, "Feng gong hou 封公候," p. 32b.

95. The overlap of *zong* and *zu* also figures in the *Li ji*:

> By treating those close to one as intimate [*qin qin* 親親], one learns to honor the ultimate ancestor [*zun zu* 尊祖]. By honoring the ultimate ancestor, one learns to revere the head of the lineage [*jing zong* 敬宗]. By revering the head of the lineage, one gathers the kin [*shou zu* 收族]. By gathering the kin, one solemnizes the ancestral temple [*yan zong miao* 嚴宗廟].

See *Li ji zhu shu*, ch. 34, "Da zhuan," p. 13a. Here *zu* are kin who gather at the ancestral temple under the guidance of the elder of the lineage to worship the ancestors, particularly the founding ancestor.

96. *Bo hu tong de lun*, ch. 2, "Zong zu," p. 34a.

97. *Shuo wen jie zi zhu*, ch. 7a, p. 21b. This gloss is wrong, but it shows understanding of the term during the Han period. Moreover, it concurs with the *Bo hu tong* without simply copying it.

98. *Xin xu shu zheng*, p. 317; *Lun heng ji jie*, ch. 13, "Chao qi 超奇," p. 285. Ch. 19, "Hui guo," p. 397 uses *ta zu* "other *zu*" in parallel to *gu rou* 骨肉 "bone and flesh," that is, those descended from a common ancestor. *Yi Zhou shu hui jiao ji zhu*, ch. 21, "Feng bao 酆保," p. 21 also pairs *xing* 姓 and *zu*. Some texts describe kin scattered, lineage temples destroyed, and spirits lacking sacrifice as *zu lei li san* 族類離散 "those of the *zu* category being dispersed." See *Zhan guo ce*, ch. 6, "Qin 4," p. 248; *Xin xu shu zheng*, ch. 9, "Shan mou shang 善謀上," p. 254. These treat *zu* as equivalent to kin in the broadest sense. Linking *zu* and *lei* to indicate kin in the broad sense echoes *Zuo zhuan zhu*, Xi year 10, p. 334: "Spirits do not enjoy offerings from those who are not of their kind, and the people do not sacrifice to those who are not of their kin [*shen bu xin fei lei, min bu si fei zu* 神不歆非類，民不祀非族]." This is quoted in *Lun heng ji jie*, ch. 21, "Si wei 死偽," p. 424. *Li ji zhu shu*, ch. 46, "Ji fa 祭法," p. 15b treats *zu* as a synonym of *lei*.

99. *Lun heng ji jie*, ch. 25, "Jie shu 詰術," p. 502.

100. *Xin xu shu zheng*, ch. 7, "Jie shi 節士," pp. 213–214; *Shuo yuan*, ch. 6, "Fu en 復恩," p. 12a; *Shi ji* 43, pp. 1783–1785; *Lie nü zhuan*, ch. 7, "Chen nü Xia Ji 陳女夏姬," p. 7b: refers to destroying a person's *zu* and dividing his household (*shi* 室).

101. It refers to kin one step beyond the degree of closeness for which one would observe some form of mourning as "cut-off kin [*jue zu* 絕族]." See *Li ji zhu shu*, ch. 34, "Da zhuan," p. 13a.

102. *Lun heng ji jie*, ch. 8, "Yi zeng 藝增," p. 176.

103. *Li ji zhu shu*, ch. 20, "Wen Wang shizi," p. 21; p. 25b elaborates on this passage and explains that it demonstrates that people "do not forget those close to them [*bu wang qin* 不忘親]."

104. *Li ji zhu shu*, ch. 34, "Da zhuan," pp. 3a–b, 10a–b. On the ruler dining with his *zu* see also *Li ji zhu shu*, ch. 20, "Wen Wang shizi," pp. 19a, 24a.

105. *Li ji zhu shu*, ch. 46, "Ji fa," p. 12b. On *li* as the potent spirits of major lineages, often spirits that harm the living, see *Zuo zhuan zhu*, Zhao year 7, pp. 1289–1290; 1291–1293. This second story links the power of the ghost to the size of his *zu* kin group. Another passage indicating that the noble *zu* was the lesser *zong* is *Li ji zhu shu*, ch. 20, p. 17a: this contrasts the manner in which *zu* are arranged in the inner court by age, that is, on the basis of their kin ties, and in the outer court by rank.

106. *Li ji zhu shu*, ch. 39, "Yue ji," p. 20b.

107. *Li ji zhu shu*, ch. 4, "Qu li xia," p. 7b; ch. 20, "Wen Wang shizi," p. 19a; ch. 34, "Da zhuan," pp. 3a–b: "Above one puts in order the temple of the ultimate ancestor in order to honor the honorable. Below one puts in order one's sons and grandsons in order to treat those close to one as intimate. To the side one puts in order one's brothers, and assembles the *zu* to eat."

108. *Li ji zhu shu*, ch. 43, "Za ji xia 雜記下," p. 1b.

109. *Li ji zhu shu*, ch. 20, "Wen Wang shizi," p. 19b. Commentators state that the roles of host and guest are marked by clear separation. Since the banquet is intended to draw the ruler close to his *zu*, the roles of guests and host are assigned to the people of different surnames and the chief cook.

110. *Li ji zhu shu*, ch. 34, "Da zhuan," p. 5a.

111. Shen Jiaben 沈家本, *Lidai xingfa kao* 歷代刑法攷, 4 vols. (Beijing: Zhonghua, 1985), vol. 1, pp. 71–79; Qiao Muqing 喬木青, "Zu xing lianzuo fa de chubu tantao 族形連坐法的初步探討," *Falü shi luncong* (1981:1), pp. 68–85; Lai Ming-chiu [Li Mingjian], "Qin dai shi wu lianzuo zhidu zhi yuan yuan wenti 秦代什伍連坐制度之淵源問題," *Dalu zazhi* 79:4 (1989), pp. 27–44. On the significance of the shifting range of collective punishments, see Lewis, *Sanctioned Violence*, pp. 80–94.

112. *Jin shu* 30, p. 925.

113. *Li ji zhu shu*, ch. 50, "Zhongni yan ju," pp. 17a, 18a. In these two passages harmony or disorder among the "three *zu*" derive from ritual in the "private chambers [*gui zhong* 閨中]." This term usually indicates the women's quarters and suggests that the "three *zu*" shared a household. However, it is perhaps significant that *gui zhong* in this passage is the second term in a series. It is preceded by a "dwelling place [*ju chu* 居處]" that is ritually linked to the proper order of elder and younger, and is followed by the court, the hunt, and the army. This list thus proceeds from smallest and most inward to largest and most outward, in which case the *gui zhong* might not have its usual limited sense, and "three *zu*" would indicate a kin group one step above the household. It is possible that the "three *zu*" referred to here is the "three *zu*" of the mother cited earlier in the listing of the "nine *zu*." This would explain their links to order in the women's quarters, and their placement second in a series moving out from individual household to the next larger group formed through ties established by marriage. Such links between the *zu* and relations with relatives by marriage are discussed in *Li ji zhu shu*, ch. 51, "Fang ji," p. 27a.

114. *Shi ji* 5, p. 180; *Han shu* 1b, p. 67.

115. *Han shu* 49, p. 2302: the penalty included Chao Cuo, his father, mother, wife, children, and all his siblings and half-siblings; 64a, p. 2804; 66, p. 2878: only the house-

hold (*jia*) of the criminal was executed; 90, p. 3658: five households, including that of the main criminal, two of his brothers, and two of his brothers-in-law were executed. An official of the period refers to these as "five *zu*."

116. *Jin shu* 30, p. 925.

117. *Hou Han shu* 34, p. 1186; 78, p. 2520. For translations involving the three *zu*, see T'ung-tsu Ch'ü, *Han Social Structure* (Seattle: University of Washington, 1972), pp. 251, 265, 266, 355, 402, 410.

118. Yan Zhitui 顏之推, writing centuries after the Han, said, "Only after there were people were there husbands and wives. Only after there were husbands and wives were there fathers and sons. Only after there were fathers and sons were there brothers. The kin of a household consist only of these three relations. Proceeding outward from this, reaching to the nine *zu*, everything is based on the three kin relations." *Yan shi jia xun hui zhu* 顏氏家訓彙注, annotated by Zhou Fagao 周法高 (Taipei: Zhong Yang Yanjiuyuan Lishi Yuyan Yanjiusuo, Zheng Kan 41), ch. 3, p. 6b.

119. Rui Yifu 芮逸夫, "Jiu zu zhi yu *Er ya* 'Shi qin' 九族制與爾雅釋親," in *Zhongguo minzu ji qi wenhua lungao* 中國民族及其文化論稿, 3 vols. (Taipei: Yiwen, 1972), pp. 723–745; Makino Tatsumi, "Kyūzoku shō kō 九族小考, in *Makino Tatsumi chosaku shū*, vol. 7, pp. 133–158; Ochi Shigeaki, "Kyūzoku to sanzoku 九族と三族," *Kurume Daigaku hikaku bunka kenkyūsho kiyō* 13 (1993), pp. 1–61; Ch'ü, *Han Social Structure,* pp. 251 note 1, 294 note 198, 317 note 276. For a recent debate on the significance of the supposed disputes between the "Old Text" and "New Text" traditions in the Eastern Han, see Michael Nylan, "The Chin Wen/Ku Wen Controversy in Han Times," *T'oung Pao* 80 (1994), pp. 83–144; Hans van Ess, "The Old Text/New Text Controversy: Has the 20th Century Got It Wrong?" *T'oung Pao* 80 (1994), pp. 146–170; Nylan, "The Ku Wen Documents in Han Times," *T'oung Pao* 81 (1995), pp. 25–50.

120. See Jack L. Dull, "Marriage and Divorce in Han China: A Glimpse at 'Pre-Confucian' Society," in *Chinese Family Law and Social Change in Historical and Comparative Perspective*, ed. David C. Buxbaum (Seattle: University of Washington, 1978), pp. 23–74.

121. Makino, "Kyūzoku shō kō," p. 157.

122. Jack Goody, Joan Thirsk, and E. P. Thompson, eds., *Family and Inheritance: Rural Society in Western Europe 1200–1800* (Cambridge: Cambridge University, 1976); Goody, *The Development of the Family and Marriage in Europe* (Cambridge: Cambridge University, 1983); Goody, *The Oriental, the Ancient and the Primitive: Systems of Marriage and the Family in the Pre-Industrial Societies of Eurasia* (Cambridge: Cambridge University, 1990).

123. *Hou Han shu* 26, pp. 903–904: "All the income from his fief he distributed among his nine *zu*, so his own household had no accumulated property"; 31, p. 1093: "[The emperor] gave him a dwelling, with curtains, cash, and grain to fill his house. He immediately distributed all this among his lineage [*zong qin* 宗親] and his nine *zu*, so that nothing was left." Also relevant is *Hou Han shu* 34, p. 1171: "[Liang Song] by nature was charitable and did not devote himself to family financial affairs. His elder brother's wife, the Princess of Wuyin, financially supported all the Liang in proportion to their degree of closeness to her [*qin shu you xu* 親疏有序]. She particularly honored Song. Even if it were only clothing, food, or household utensils what he received was invariably more and better. Song distributed all this to his kin [*qin zu*

親族] and used nothing himself." This treats the woman as a member of the kin group with clearly defined degrees of relationship to her relatives by marriage.

124. This document has received little attention in the secondary literature. See Zhou Shirong 周世榮, "Luetan Mawangdui chutu de boshu zhujian 略談馬王堆出土的帛書竹簡," in *Mawangdui yishu yanjiu zhuankan* 馬王堆醫書研究專刊 2 (1981); Fu Juyou 傅舉有 and Chen Songchang 陳松長, *Mawangdui Han mu wenwu* 馬王堆漢墓文物 (Changsha: Hunan, 1992), p. 36; Liu Xiaolu 劉曉路, *Zhongguo bo hua* 中國帛書 (Beijing: Zhongguo Shudian, 1994); Cao Xuequn 曹學群, "Mawangdui Han mu Sangfutu jian lun 馬王堆漢墓喪服圖簡論," *Hunan kaogu jikan* 6 (1994), pp. 226–229, 225.

125. Lai Guolong, "The Diagram of Mourning System [sic] from Mawangdui: Numerology, Kinship, and Women in Early China," presented at "From Image to Action: The Dynamics of Visual Representation in Chinese Intellectual and Religious Culture," Collège de France, Paris, France, September 3–5, 2001.

126. *Yi li zhu shu* 儀禮註疏, in *Shi san jing zhu shu*, vol. 4, ch. 28–34.

127. Ch'ü, *Han Social Relations*, p. 294 note 198; Rui, "Jiu zu zhi yu *Er ya* 'Shi qin'," pp. 723–745. Shi Lei argued that the kinship structure in the *Yi li* should logically include the female relatives on the father's side as well as their children. See Shi Lei 石磊, "*Yi li* 'Sangfu' pian suo biaoxian de qinshu jiegou 儀禮喪服篇所表現的親屬結構," *Minzuxue Yanjiusuo jikan* 53 (1982), pp. 24–26.

128. *Mengzi zheng yi* IIIA, "Teng Wen Gong shang," pp. 216–229. The idea that the social hierarchy was based on a differential breadth of vision also appears in VIA, "Gaozi shang 告子上," p. 467. On the necessity of dividing labor, explicitly linking the social division of labor to the division of labor between men and women in the household, see also IIIB, "Teng Wen gong xia," p. 252.

129. *Xunzi ji jie*, ch. 15, "Jie bi," p. 266.

130. *Xunzi ji jie*, ch. 2, "Rong ru," p. 40: "One who becomes a Yao or Yu will always be happy and at ease. One who becomes a craftsman, farmer, or merchant will always be troubled and toiling. But most men become the latter and few the former. Why? I say, 'Because they are narrow [*lou* 陋; see chapter four]. Yao and Yu were not born complete. It arose from difficulties and was completed through cultivation. Only after this cultivation had been exhaustively carried out were they comprehensive'"; p. 44: "[The former kings] caused everyone to take up their own tasks, so that each obtained the appropriate position, and only then allocated them corresponding quantities of grain or salary. This is the Way of causing the populace to live in harmony and unity. So when a humane man is in authority, then the farmers use their strength to get full productivity from the land, merchants use their discernment to get full value from goods, craftsmen use their skill to make the finest tools and utensils, and the men of service from the lowest to the highest all use humanity, generosity, wisdom, and skill to fully carry out their offices"; ch. 4, "Ru xiao 儒效," p. 78: "At assessing the lay of the land, examining its fertility, or rating the five grains, the gentleman is no match for a farmer. At fully comprehending goods, assessing their quality, and distinguishing the costly from the cheap, the gentleman is no match for a merchant. At applying the square and compass, laying out the inked cord as a straight edge, and facilitating the complete use of things, the gentleman is no match for a craftsman. At ignoring considerations of right and wrong or what is truly so, in order to bully, insult, and deceive one another, the gentleman is no match for sophists like Hui Shi or Deng Xi. But as

for assessing virtues to establish rankings, measuring talents to bestow offices, causing the worthy and unworthy to each obtain their proper places, and the capable and talentless to each obtain their proper post, having all objects obtain what is suited to them, and all changes meet their proper response, to prevent Shen Dao and Mo Di from advancing their arguments, and Hui Shi and Deng Xi from slipping in their specious discernment, to make words invariably appropriate to proper reasoning and tasks appropriate to those responsible, this and only this is that for which the gentleman is best"; pp. 91–92: "Being a sage is a matter of what a person accumulates. If he accumulates plowing and weeding he will be a farmer. If he accumulates chopping and carving he will be a carpenter. If he accumulates circulating commodities he will be a merchant. If he accumulates ritual and duty he will be a gentleman"; ch. 5, "Wang zhi 王制," p. 103: "So people who live near marshes can have enough wood, while people who live on mountains can have enough fish. The farmer does not chop and carve, nor does he fire pots or forge metals, but he has enough tools and utensils. Craftsmen and merchants do not till fields yet they have enough beans and grains. Even though the tiger and wolf are ferocious, the gentleman skins and employs them;" ch. 6, "Fu guo 富國," pp. 113–114: "The products of all the arts are used to nourish a single individual, but even the most capable cannot possess all the arts, and a person cannot hold all posts. If they dwell apart and do not rely on one another then they will be impoverished. If they dwell together without proper divisions then they will fight. Poverty is a calamity and fighting a disaster. To rescue people from calamity and eliminate disaster, the best solution is to make clear the social divisions and allow them to dwell together;" ch. 7, "Wang ba 王霸," p. 139: "If the farmers divide up the fields and till them, the merchants divide up the commodities and deal in them, all the craftsmen divide up the tasks and work hard at them, the officials divide up the offices and pay heed to them, the nobility and princes who are established in fiefs divide up the land and protect it; the Three Lords combine all these aspects and evaluate them, then the Son of Heaven does nothing but hold himself respectful."

131. *Mozi jian gu*, ch. 3, "Shang xian shang, zhong, xia 尚賢上中下," esp. pp. 32–33; *Han Feizi ji shi*, ch. 1, "Zhu dao 主道," pp. 67–68; ch. 2, "You du 有度," p. 87; "Er bing 二柄," p. 112; "Yang quan 揚權," pp. 121, 123; ch. 4, "He Shi 和氏," p. 238.

132. *Shi ji* 129, pp. 3253–3255.

133. See Utsunomiya, *Kandai shakai keizai shi kenkyū*, ch. 5 on this chapter's economic thought.

134. *Han shu* 24a, pp. 1117–1118. For the *Yi jing* quote, see *Zhou yi zheng yi*, ch. 8, "Xi ci xia," pp. 3b–4a. For a related passage quoted in the *Han shu* monograph, see p. 5a: "When the sun reached noon [Shen Nong] created a market. He assembled the world's people and gathered the world's commodities. Having exchanged the goods, the people withdrew. Each obtained what was proper to his place." The same model of society is described in *Guanzi jiao zheng*, ch. 8, "Xiao kuang 小匡, pp. 121–122.

135. Francesca Bray, *Technology and Gender: Fabrics of Power in Late Imperial China* (Berkeley: University of California, 1997), part 1, ch. 1–3.

136. Elizabeth Wayland Barber, *Women's Work: The First 20,000 Years; Women, Cloth, and Society in Early Times* (New York: W. W. Norton, 1994); Barber, *Prehistoric Textiles* (Princeton: Princeton University, 1991). On the links between women and weaving in the *political* mythology of weaving in ancient Greece, see John Scheid and Jesper

Svenbro, *Le métier de Zeus: Mythe du tissage et du tissu dans le monde gréco-romaine* (Paris: Editions La Découverte, 1994). On the changing relation between gender and weaving in late imperial China, see Bray, *Technology and Gender*, part 2, ch. 4–6.; Li Bozhong, *Agricultural Development in Jiangnan, 1620–1850* (London: Macmillan, 1998), pp. 89–97, 141–155.

137. *Mao shi zheng yi*, ch. 1.2, #2, "Ge tan 葛覃," p. 2b; ch. 2.1, #27, "Lu yi 綠衣," p. 4b; ch. 4.2, #75, "Zi yi 緇依," p. 4b; ch. 5.3, #107, "Ge lü 葛履," p. 2b: this poem specifically states that women's slender figures are good for weaving; ch. 8.1, #154, "Qi yue," pp. 11b–14a; ch. 8.2, #156, "Dong shan 東山," p. 7a; ch. 15.2, #226, "Cai lu 采綠," pp. 6a–b.

138. *Zuo zhuan zhu*, Wen 2, p. 525; Zhao 24, p. 1451; *Guo yu*, ch. 5, "Lu yu xia," pp. 205, 208; ch. 13, "Jin yu qi," p. 443; ch. 20, "Yue yu shang," p. 635; *Mozi jiangu*, ch. 1, "Ci guo 辭過," pp. 18–19, 21; ch. 8, "Fei yue shang 非樂上," p. 159; ch. 9, "Fei ming xia 非命下," p. 176; ch. 11, "Geng zhu 耕柱," p. 260; ch. 13. "Lu wen 魯問," p. 287; *Mengzi zheng yi*, IIIB, "Teng Wen Gong xia," p. 275; *Zhuangzi ji shi*, ch. 9, "Ma ti 馬蹄," p. 151; ch. 29, "Dao Zhi," p. 429; *Yanzi chun qiu ji shi*, ch. 2, p. 97 *Shang Jun shu zhu yi* 商君書注譯 (Beijing: Zhonghua, 1974), ch. 18, "Hua ce 畫策," p. 372; *Han Feizi ji shi*, ch. 8, "Shuo lin xia 説林下," p. 453; ch. 13, "Wai chu shuo you shang 外儲説右上," p. 748; ch. 15 "Nan er 難二," p. 835; ch. 19, "Wu du," p. 1040; *Zhou li zhu shu*, ch. 2, p. 8b; ch. 8, pp. 3b, 12b; ch. 13, p. 17b; ch. 15, p. 25a; *Huainanzi*, ch. 2, "Chu zhen," p. 27: refers to the Weaver Girl star; ch. 9, "Zhu shu," pp. 146, 151; ch. 11, "Qi su," p. 185; ch. 15, "Bing lüe," p. 266; ch. 16, "Shuo shan," p. 280; 17, "Shuo lin 説林," pp. 301, 303; *Guanzi jiao zheng*, ch. 1, "Li zheng 立政," p. 10: opposes women's work on cloth to the carving of wood by craftsmen; ch. 3, "You guan 幼官," p. 39; "Wu fu 五輔," pp. 49–50; ch. 5, "Zhong ling 重令," p. 80: pairs women's weaving with craftsmen's carving; ch. 17, "Qi chen qi zhu 七臣七主," p. 286 (2); ch. 20, "Xing shi jie 形勢解," p. 330; ch. 21, "Chen cheng ma 臣乘馬," p. 350; ch. 22, "Hai wang 海王," pp. 358–359; "Shan guo gui 山國軌," pp. 362, 363, 364; ch. 23, "Kui du 揆度," p. 388 (2); "Qing zhong jia 輕重甲," pp. 389, 392, 393; ch. 24, "Qing zhong yi 乙," pp. 404, 407; *Lü shi chun qiu jiao shi*, ch. 9, "Shun min 順民," p. 479; ch. 21, "Ai lei 愛類," p. 1462: this passage cites Shen nong; ch. 26, "Shang nong 上農," p. 1711: refers to the queen and her palace ladies producing silk; *Jiazi xin shu jiao shi*, ch. 1, "Guo Qin shang 過秦上," p. 1; ch. 4, "Wu xu 無蓄," p. 517; *Zhan guo ce*, ch. 4, "Qin er," p. 150; ch. 29, "Yan yi," p. 1071; *Da Dai li ji jie gu*, ch. 2, "Xia xiao zheng 夏小正," pp. 42, 46: the Weaver Girl star; *Shi ji* 5, p. 173; 27, p. 1311: the Weaver Girl star; 41, p. 1742; 49, pp. 1970–1971: palace ladies having a room for their weaving; 66, p. 2174; 110, p. 2902; 112, p. 2954; 118 p. 3086; 129, p. 3255; *Han shu* 24a, pp. 1126, 1128; 28b, pp. 1660, 1670; 59, p. 2652: a nobleman's wife with hundreds of slaves who still personally weaves; *Hou Han shu* 18b, p. 1003: the commentary quotes a letter from a man to his brother-in-law complaining because his wife employs no female servants to produce clothing and rugs for the household; 71, p. 2308; 84, pp. 2783, 2792–2793; *Li ji zhu shu*, ch. 16, "Yue ling," pp. 10a–b; ch. 28, "Nei ze," pp. 21a–b; ch. 49, "Ji tong," pp. 3b–4a: the wives of the Son of Heaven and the feudal lords all personally produce clothing for sacrificial rituals; *Han shi wai zhuan ji shi*, ch. 5, p. 185; ch. 9, p. 306; *Shuo yuan*, ch. 3, p. 7a; ch. 11, p. 6b; ch. 19, p. 5b; ch. 20, pp. 6b, 9a; *Yan tie lun* 鹽鐵論 (Shanghai: Renmin, 1974), ch. 5 "Xiang ci 相刺," p. 46 (2); "Guo ji 國疾," pp. 63–64; ch. 6 "Shou shi 授時," p. 78 (2); *Lie nü zhuan*, ch. 1, pp. 7b, 8a, 8b, 10b, 11a; ch. 2, p. 5a; ch. 4, p. 8a; ch. 5, p. 7a; Lu, *Xian Qin Han Wei Jin Nanbei-*

chao shi, vol. 1, p. 259: a woman gathers mulberry leaves, pp. 265, 266: these two versions of the same poem describe the wives in a rich household in terms of the cloth that they weave, pp. 283, 284, 331: the Weaver Girl star's action as it weaves, p. 334: a husband compares his first and second wives in terms of the quality and quantity of the cloth they produce; *Lun heng ji jie*, ch. 12, "Cheng cai 程材, p. 248; "Liang zhi 量知," p. 252; *Wu yue chun qiu* 吳越春秋 (Si bu bei yao ed.), ch. 8, "Gou Jian gui guo wai zhuan 勾踐歸國外傳," pp. 2b, 3b–4a; *Yue jue shu* 越掘書 (Shanghai: Shangwu, 1956), ch. 4, "Ji Ni nei jing 計倪內經," p. 33a; ch. 10, "Wai zhuan ji di 外傳記地," p. 72a; *Qian fu lun jian*, ch. 1 "Zan xue 讚學," p. 3; ch. 3, "Fu chi 浮侈," pp. 120 (2), 125. On ritual pertaining to sericulture performed by the women of the ruling house, see Bodde, *Festivals in Classical China*, pp. 263–272. For depictions in Han tomb art of women gathering mulberry leaves and producing cloth, see Lucy Lim, ed., *Stories from China's Past: Han Dynasty Pictorial Reliefs and Archaeological Objects from Sichuan Province, People's Republic of China* (San Francisco: Chinese Culture Foundation, 1987), pp. 95–98, 152, 155; Käte Finsterbusch, *Verzeichnis und Motivindex der Han-Darstellungen* (Wiesbaden; Otto Harrasowitz, 1971), vol. 2, figures #33, 594, nachtrag 5; Hayashi Minao 林巳奈夫, *Ishi ni kizamareta sekai 石に刻れた世界* (Tokyo:Tōhō shoten, 1992), pp. 29, 99; Hayashi Minao, *Chūgoku kodai no seikatsu shi 中國古代の生活史* (Tokyo: Yoshikawa Kōbunkan, 1992), pp. 75–78; Hayashi Minao, *Kandai no bunbutsu 漢代の文物* (Kyoto: Kyoto Daigaku Jinbun Kagaku Kenkyushō, 1977), illustrations on pp. 41–53; Satō Taketoshi 佐藤武敏, *Chūgoku kodai kinu orimono shi kenkyū 中國古代絹織務史研究* (Fūkan shobō, 1978), vol. 1, illustrations 1–7; Wu Hung, *Monumentality in Early Chinese Art and Architecture* (Stanford: Stanford University, 1995), p. 233.

139. *Yanzi chun qiu ji shi*, ch. 8, pp. 509–510: "As for governing in ancient times, men of service, farmers, craftsmen, and merchants dwelt apart, and men and women were separated. Therefore men were without deviant conduct and women without lascivious affairs." *Mozi jiangu*, ch. 8, "Fei yue shang," p. 159 "enumerates the world's division of labor [*shu tian xia fen shi* 數天下分事]" under four headings: the work of rulers, the work of ministers, the work of farmers, and the work of women. An identical model, without reference to division of labor appears in ch. 9, "Fei ming xia," p. 176.

140. See, for example, *Li ji zhu shu*, ch. 50, "Jing jie 經解," p. 4b.

141. *Li ji zhu shu*, ch. 37, "Yue ji," pp. 11b–12a; *Shi ji* 24, p. 1187. *Li ji zhu shu*, ch. 37, p. 14a: "Ritual differentiates types of service but joins together the reverent"; p. 19a: "Heaven is high and Earth low. The myriad objects having dispersed and divided, the ritual institutions are carried out. Flowing without cease, joining together in identity and transforming, music arises. . . . Music makes harmony sincere. Guiding the spirits, it follows Heaven. Ritual distinguishes local characteristics [*bie yi* 別宜]. Giving ghosts a place to dwell, it follows Earth. . . . Ritual is the separation of Heaven and Earth."

142. *Xunzi ji jie*, ch. 2. "Rong ru," p. 44: the statement that former kings created ritual and duty to divide people and hierarchize them leads to a discussion of the division of labor as the basis of social order; ch. 5, "Wang zhi," p. 96: if people are equal in position and desires there will be chaos, so they must be divided by rituals into hierarchies; ch. 13, "Li lun," p. 231: ritual was created to divide people in order to maintain order. P. 232: rituals devoted to ancestors are the origins of *lei* 類 "categories." On the separation of men from beasts being due to rituals and duty, see ch.1, "Quan xue," p. 7; ch. 3, "Fei xiang," p. 50; ch. 5, "Wang zhi," p. 104. In addition to

general statements, the *Xunzi* also describes specific social divisions created by ritual, including those between husband and wife. See ch. 6, "Fu guo," p. 114. See also *Guanzi jiao zheng*, ch. 17, "Jin zang," p. 290; *Huainanzi*, ch. 11, "Qi su," p. 169. Discussions of the role of ritual in creating divisions are even more common in *Li ji*. On the separation between husband and wife, or man and woman, see *Li ji zhu shu*, ch. 13, "Wang zhi 王制," p. 23b; ch. 26, "Jiao te sheng," pp. 18b, 19a: without separation (*bie*) humans are beasts; ch. 32, "Sang fu xiao ji 喪服小記," p. 11a: the separation of men and women is the greatest principle of the human Way; ch. 34, "Da zhuan," pp. 3b, 4a: the separation of men and women is one of the unchangeable principles of the sage; ch. 37, "Yue ji," p. 11a; ch. 49, "Ji tong," pp. 10b, 14b; ch. 50, "Jing jie," p. 5a; ch. 51, "Ai Gong wen," pp. 7a, 9b; "Fang ji," pp. 24b, 25a; ch. 61, "Hun li 昏禮," p. 6b: the separation of men and women is the essence of ritual, and betrothal rites the root of all ritual. See also *Mozi jian gu*, ch. 1, "Ci guo," p. 18; *Huainanzi*, ch. 20, "Tai zu," p. 350. The *Zuo zhuan* asserts that "the distinction of the surnames of men and women [i.e., no marriage between people of the same surnames] is the great rule of ritual." See Zhao year 1, pp. 1220–1221.

143. The priority of age (referred to as *chi* 齒 or *zhang* 長) in the household and in all kin-related affairs is announced in several chapters in the *Li ji*, notably "Ji yi 祭義" See also Xing Yitian 形義田, "Mu quan, waiqi, rusheng: Wang Mang chuan Han de jidian jieshi 母權，外戚，儒生：王莽篡漢的幾點解釋," *Lishi yuekan* 14.3 (1989), pp. 36–44.

144. *Li ji zhu shu*, ch. 26, "Jiao te xing," p. 19b: "Men lead women; women obey men. . . . A woman obeys others. When young she obeys her father and elder brothers. When she marries she obeys her husband. When her husband dies she obeys her son." See also *Da Dai li ji jie gu*, ch. 13, "Ben ming," p. 254. On Mencius's mother see *Lie nü zhuan*, ch. 1, pp. 10a–11b.

145. *Li shi*, ch. 15, pp. 10b–11b. On mothers denouncing their children see Kinney, *Representations of Childhood*, pp. 92–93; *Zhangjiashan Hanmu zhujian* p. 227 (strips 180–196); *Han Shu* 76, p. 3227; *Hou Han shu* 76 pp. 2479–2480.

146. Lu, *Xian Qin Han Wei Jin Nanbeichao chi*, pp. 283–286.

147. Lu, *Xian Qin Han Wei Jin Nanbeichao chi*, p. 268.

148. *Yan shi jia xun hui zhu*, pp. 1a–b.

149. "The Republic" 377c, 380e, in *Plato: The Collected Dialogues* (Princeton: Princeton University, Bollingen, 1961), pp. 624, 628. On writing versus speech as a ground of gender distinction in late imperial China, see Brigitte Berthier, *La Dame-du-bord-de-l'eau* (Société d'ethnologie: Nanterre, 1988), pp. 8–10, 161–181. This association of writing with the masculine and oral stories with the feminine is also indicated in the English idiom referring to "old wives' tales" and the French "commérage."

150. Lu Qinli, *Xian Qin Han Wei Jin Nanbeichao shi*, pp. 270–271.

151. *Yan shi jia xun hui zhu*, pp. 8b–10a. The line quoted occurs on p. 9a.

152. Wu Hung, "Private Love and Public Duty: Images of Children in Early Chinese Art," in *Chinese Views of Childhood*, ed. Anne Behnke Kinney (Honolulu: University of Hawai'i, 1995), pp. 79–110; Wu Hung, *The Wu Liang Shrine: The Ideology of Early Chinese Pictorial Art* (Stanford: Stanford University, 1989), pp. 256–258, 264–266, 278–280. 291–292.

153. *Lie nü zhuan*, ch. 5, pp. 6a–b. Note that the man treats only the son of his first marriage as his heir.

154. *Lie nü zhuan*, ch. 5, p. 5a.

155. *Lie nü zhuan*, ch. 5, pp. 9a–b.

156. Yang Shuda 楊樹達, *Han dai hunsang li su kao* 漢代婚喪禮俗考 (Shanghai: Shangwu, 1933), pp. 53–64.

157. *Li ji zhu shu*, ch. 26, "Jiao te sheng," pp. 18b–19a.

158. *Lie nü zhuan*, ch. 4, p. 9a.

159. Yang Shuda, *Han dai hunsang li su kao*, pp. 56–62. See also *Hou Han shu* 84, p. 2797; *Huayang guo zhi jiao zhu* 華陽國志校注, compiled by Chang Qu 常璩, annotated by Liu Lin 劉琳 (Taipei: Xin Wen Feng, 1988), ch. 10, p. 537.

160. *Yan shi jia xun hui zhu*, ch. 4, pp. 9a–b.

161. *Li ji zhu shu*, ch. 63, "Sangfu si zhi," p. 12b; *Da Dai li ji jie gu*, ch. 13, "Ben ming," p. 253.

162. *Lie nü zhuan*, ch. 5, p. 5a.

163. Wu Hung, "Private Love and Public Duty," pp. 86, 90–91, 94.

164. Lewis, *Sanctioned Violence*, pp. 70–78.

165. This is nearly a direct quote from Wu Hung's article, which, as he says in note 31, came from an anonymous reader. As that anonymous reader, I here reincorporate my own argument.

166. *Han shu* 40, p. 2038; *Hou Han shu* 81, pp. 2684, 2685–2686.

167. *Yan shi jia xun hui zhu*, ch. 3, pp. 6b–7b. The idea of kin as "shared substance in separate bodies," a shared substance identified with bones and flesh, was discussed in chapter one.

168. Ch'ü, *Han Social Structure*, pp. 57–62, 77–83, 168–174, 210–229, 237–240.

169. Lao Gan 勞榦, "Lun Han dai de nci chao yu wai chao 論漢代的內朝與外朝," *Lishi Yuyan Yanjiusuo jikan* 13 (1948), pp. 227–267; Wang Yü-ch'üan, "An Outline of the Central Government of the Former Han Dynasty," *Harvard Journal of Asiatic Studies* 12 (1949), pp. 166–173; Ch'ü, *Han Social Structure*, pp. 168–174, 216–217, 234–235.

170. *Li ji zhu shu*, ch. 2, "Qu li shang," p. 13a: "Men and women do not sit together. They do not place their clothing on the same tables or hooks, nor do they share napkins or combs. They do not pass anything directly from one to the other. Sisters-in-law and brothers-in-law do not ask after each other's health. . . . Words about the outside do not pass the door jamb [to the inner chambers]. Words about the inside do not pass the door jamb [to the outer world]"; ch. 18, "Zengzi wen," p. 16b: "Confucius said, 'The man does not enter, but changes his clothing outside the house. The woman enters and changes her clothing in the house'"; p. 22a: "Confucius said, 'In ancient times a man on the outside had a tutor and on the inside a wetnurse'"; ch. 27, "Nei ze," p. 8a: "Men do not speak of the inside; women do not speak of the outside. Except in sacrifices or rituals of mourning they do not hand each other vessels. . . . The inside and outside do not share a well nor a bathing place. . . . Men and women do not share any clothing. Words from the inside do not go out, and words from the outside do not come in"; ch. 28, "Nei ze," p. 10a: "Ritual begins with

caution in the relation of husband and wife. One creates a house and distinguishes an inside and an outside. The men stay on the outside and the women stay on the inside. A deep dwelling with solid gates and eunuchs to guard it, men do not enter; women do not go out"; ch. 45, "Sangfu da ji," p. 15a: "When the gentleman retires, the primary wife sees him off inside the gate. She bows and strikes her forehead on the ground. The master sees him off outside the main gate. He does not bow"; ch. 49, "Ji tong," p. 3a: "As for sacrifices, husband and wife must personally perform them. This is the means of completing the outer and inner offices. When the outer and inner offices are complete, then the offerings will be complete"; ch. 50, "Zhong Ni yan ju," p. 24b: "Long ago the sage emperors, enlightened kings, and feudal lords distinguished noble from base, elder from younger, distant from near, man from woman, and outer from inner"; ch. 61, "Hun yi," p. 8b: "Therefore only after the wife's obedience is complete is the inside harmonious and ordered. Only after the inside is harmonious and ordered will the household endure a long time."

171. *Li ji zhu shu*, ch. 61, "Hun yi," p. 10a: "In ancient times the wife of the Son of Heaven had six buildings, within which lived three second-degree wives, nine third-degree ones, twenty-seven fourth-degree ones, and eighty-one fifth-degree ones. Thereby she governed the interior of the whole realm, and made clear the obedience of the wives. Therefore the interior of the whole realm was harmonious and the households orderly. . . . The Son of Heaven handles the instruction of men; his wife handles the obedience of women. The Son of Heaven orders the way of *yang*; his wife regulates the virtue of *yin*. The Son of Heaven handles the regulation of the exterior; his wife handles the regulation of the interior. When instruction and obedience become custom, outer and inner are harmonious and obedient, and the state and the households are regulated"; *Guo yu*, "Jin yu xia," pp. 203–204, 209: "Have you not heard? The Son of Heaven and the feudal lords bring together the people's business in the outer court and the spirits' business in the inner court. From the hereditary officials down, they gather the business of the government offices in the outer court, and their family business in the inner court. Within the gate to the private quarters, the women administer their affairs"; *Da Dai li ji jie gu*, ch. 13, "Ben ming," p. 254.

This idea survived into later imperial China, as demonstrated in the writings of Sima Guang: "The men are in charge of all affairs on the outside; the women manage the inside affairs. During the day, without good reason the men do not stay in their private rooms nor the women go beyond the inner door." Quoted in Dorothy Ko, "Pursuing Talent and Virtue: Education and Women's Culture in Seventeenth- and Eighteenth-Century China," *Late Imperial China* 13:1 (June 1992), p. 15. The establishment of a hierarchy of titles and offices within the emperor's harem also follows from the idea of the interior of the household as a separate zone with its own patterns of authority.

172. Boyd, *Chinese Architecture and Town Planning: 1500 B.C.—A.D. 1911* (Chicago: University of Chicago, 1962), p. 48. This point is also discussed in Bray, *Technology and Gender*, pp. 52–53.

173. Robert L. Thorp, "Origins of Chinese Architectural Style: The Earliest Plans and Building Types," *Archives of Asian Art* 36 (1983), pp. 26–31; Chen Quanfang 陳全方, *Zhouyuan yu Zhou wenhua* 周原與周文化 (Shanghai: Renmin, 1988), pp. 37–69; Yang Hongxun 楊鴻勛, "Zhongguo zaoqi jianzhu de fazhan 中國早期建築的發展", in *Jianzhu lishi yu lilun* 建築歷史與理論 (Jiangsu: Jiangsu

Renmin, 1981), pp. 128–130; Tanaka Tan 田中淡, *Chūgoku kenchiku shi no kenkyū* 中國建築史の研究 (Tokyo: Kōbundō, 1995), pp. 93–146; Hayashi, *Chūgoku kodai no seikatsu shi*, pp. 22–24; Cho-yun Hsu and Katheryn M. Linduff, *Western Zhou Civilization* (New Haven:Yale University, 1988), pp. 289–296; Kwang-chih Chang, *The Archaeology of Ancient China* (4th ed., revised and enlarged; New Haven:Yale University, 1986), pp. 353–357; Jessica Rawson, "Western Zhou Archaeology," in *The Cambridge History of Ancient China*, pp. 390–393; Wu Hung, *Monumentality*, pp. 84–88; Ronald G. Knapp, *China's Old Dwellings* (Honolulu: University of Hawai'i, 2001), pp. 30–32.

174. This linkage of the interior, the ancestors, and state power in Zhou political ritual is also described in Lothar von Falkenhausen, "Issues in Western Zhou Studies: A Review Article," *Early China* 18 (1993), pp. 148–150, 157–158, 162, 166, 170–171.

175. For images in Han art see Finsterbusch, *Verzeichnis und Motivindex der Han-Darstellungen*, vol. 2, figs. #34, 311, 508s–t, 593, 594; *Stories from China's Past*, pp. 104–105; Hayashi, *Kandai no bunbutsu*, plates, pp. 57, 66–67, 71; Hayashi, *Ishi ni kizamareta sekai*, pp. 28, 126, 131; Liu Zenggui 劉增貴, "Menhu yu Zhongguo gudai shehui 門戶與中國古代社會," *Lishi Yuyan Yanjiusuo jikan* 68:4 (1997), pp. 891–892, 895. For discussions of this as the classic form of the Chinese house, see Knapp, *Chinese Old Dwellings*, ch. 2, esp. pp. 27–54; Knapp, *China's Vernacular Architecture: House Form and Culture* (Honolulu: University of Hawai'i, 1989), pp. 38–40; Knapp, *China's Traditional Rural Architecture: A Cultural Geography of the Common House* (Honolulu: University of Hawai'i, 1986), pp. 10–17; Rolf A. Stein, *Le monde en petit: Jardins en miniature et habitations dans la pensée religieuse d'Extrême-Orient* (Paris: Flammarion, 1987), pp. 120–167.

176. *Lun yu zheng yi*, ch. 20, "Yang Huo," pp. 363–364.

177. *Li ji zhu shu*, ch. 51, "Fang ji," pp. 19a–b. See also ch. 2, "Qu li xia," pp. 1b–2a, 6a; ch. 9, "Tan gong xia," pp. 15b–16a; ch. 21, "Li yun," p. 12a; ch. 27, "Nei ze," p. 5b; ch. 33, "Sangfu xiao ji," p. 1a; ch. 35, "Shao yi 少儀," p. 14a; ch. 50, "Zhong Ni yan ju," p. 24a; ch. 51, "Fang ji," p. 21a; ch. 56, "Wen sang 問喪," p. 15a; ch. 58, "Tou hu 投壺," p. 16a; *Zuo zhuan zhu*, Cheng year 10, p. 849; Zhao year 28, p. 1493; *Gongyang zhuan zhu shu*, ch. 15, Xuan year 6, p. 12b; *Guliang zhuan shu zhu*, ch. 3, Huan year 3, p. 7b; *Lie nü zhuan*, ch. 1, p. 11a. In the *Lun yu* the progression from gate to hall to chamber marks advancement in musical mastery. See *Lun yu zheng yi*, ch. 14, "Xian jin 先進," p. 245.

178. *Li ji zhu shu*, ch. 24, "Li qi," pp. 12a: lists the courtyard, outer hall, and inner chamber in the temple, 17b; ch. 26, "Jiao te sheng," p. 22a: in addition to the inner chamber and outer hall in the temple, this also refers to the door that connects them, and the steps that lead to the courtyard. For reconstructions from texts and art of Warring States and Han housing and temple complexes, see Liu, "Menhu yu Zhongguo gudai shehui," pp. 825–835. See also *Lun yu zheng yi*, ch. 22, "Zi Zhang," p. 409.

179. Donald Harper, "Warring States Natural Philosophy and Occult Thought," in *The Cambridge History of Ancient China*, ed. Michael Loewe and Edward L. Shaughnessy (Cambridge: Cambridge University, 1999), pp. 841, 847–852; Marc Kalinowski, "Mawangdui boshu Xingde shitan 馬王堆帛書刑德試探," *Huaxue* 1 (1995), pp. 82–110; Kalinowski, " Astrologie calendaire et calcul de position dans la Chine ancienne: Les mutations de l'hémérologie sexagésimale entre le IVe et le IIe siècle avant notre ère," *Extrême-Orient, Extrême-Occident* 18 (1996), pp. 81–101; Kalinowski, "The *Xingde* 刑德 Text from Mawangdui," *Early China* 23–24 (1998–1999),

pp. 125–202; Robin Yates, "The Yin-Yang Texts from Yinqueshan: An Introduction and Partial Reconstruction with Notes on their Significance in Relation to Huang-Lao Taoism," *Early China* 19 (1994), pp. 82–84, 88–90, 93; John Major, "The Meaning of *Hsing-te* [*Xingde*]," in *Chinese Ideas about Nature and Society*, ed. Charles Le Blanc and Susan Blader (Hong Kong: Hong Kong University, 1987), pp. 281–291; Li Ling 李零, *Zhongguo fangshu kao* 中國方術考 (revised and expanded; Beijing: Dongfang Chubanshe, 2000), pp. 47–51; Li Ling, "Du ji zhong chutu faxian de xuanze lei gu shu 讀幾種出土發現的選擇類古書," *Jianbo yanjiu* 3 (1998), pp. 96–104; Fu Juyou and Chen Songchang, *Mawangdui Han mu wenwu*, pp. 132–143; Chen Songchang, "Boshu *Xingde* lüe shuo 帛書刑德略説," *Jianbo yanjiu* 1 (1993), pp. 96–107; Chen Songchang, "Boshu *Xingde* yi ben shiwen jiaodu 帛書刑德乙本釋文校讀," *Hunansheng Bowuguan sishi zhounian jinian lunwen ji* 湖南省博物館四十週年紀念論文集 (Changsha: Hunan jiaoyu, 1996), pp. 83–97; Chen Songchang, "Boshu *Xingde* bing pian shitan 帛書刑德丙篇試探," *Jianbo yanjiu* 3 (1998), pp. 242–247; Chen Songchang, "Mawangdui boshu *Xingde* jia yi pian de bijiao yanjiu 馬王堆帛書刑德甲乙篇的比較研究," *Wenwu* (2000:3), pp. 75–84; Li Xueqin 李學勤, "Mawangdui boshu *Xingde* zhong de junli 馬王堆帛書刑德中的軍吏," *Jianbo yanjiu* 2 (1996), pp. 156–159; Liu Lexian 劉樂賢, "Mawangdui Han mu xingzhan shu chutan 馬王堆漢墓星占書初探," *Huaxue* 1 (1995), pp. 111–121; Rao Zongyi 饒宗頤, "Mawangdui *Xingde* yi ben jiugongtu zhu shen shi, jianlun chutu wenxian zhong de Zhuanxu yu Sheti 馬王堆刑德乙本九宮圖諸神釋, 兼論出土文獻中的顓頊與葉提," *Jiang Han kaogu* (1993:1), pp. 84–87; Rao Zongyi and Zeng Xiantong 曾憲通, *Yunmeng Qin jian ri shu yanjiu* 雲蒙秦簡日書研究 (Hong Kong: Zhongwen Daxue, 1982), pp. 63–65, 81–87. On the "seven dwellings version," see Kalinowski, "The *Xingde* Texts from Mawangdui," pp. 158–159, 175; Rao Zongyi and Zeng Xiantong, *Yunmeng Qin jian ri shu yanjiu*, pp. 81–95; John Major, *Heaven and Earth in Early Han Thought: Chapters Three, Four, and Five of the Huainanzi* (Albany: State University of New York, 1993), pp. 86–88.

180. *Huainanzi*, ch. 3, "Tian wen," p. 40.

181. *Juyan xin jian: Jiaqu hou guan* 居延新簡：甲渠侯官 (Beijing: Zhonghua, 1994), pp. 47, 186, 249.

182. *Shuo wen jie zi zhu*, ch. 14b, pp. 29b, 33a-b.

183. *Li ji zhu shu*, ch. 14, "Yue ling," p. 9b; ch. 15, "Yue ling," pp. 2a, 10a; ch. 16, "Yue ling," pp. 17b, 20a; ch. 17, "Yue ling," p. 1a; *Lü shi chun qiu jiao shi*, ch. 1, "Meng chun ji," p. 1; ch. 2, "Zhong chun ji," p. 63; ch. 3, "Ji chun ji," p. 121; ch. 7, "Meng qiu ji," p. 375; ch. 8, "Zhong qiu ji," p. 421; ch. 9, "Ji qiu ji," p. 467; *Huainanzi*, ch. 5, "Shi ze 時則," pp. 69, 70, 71, 76, 77, 79. Sacrifices to the doorway and the gate were incorporated into Han theories of the "five sacrifices" or "seven sacrifices" made to the powers of the household. See Robert Chard, "The Imperial Household Cults," in *State and Court Ritual in China*, ed. Joseph P. McDermott (Cambridge: Cambridge University, 1999), pp. 237–251.

184. On the manner in which household structure mapped out the cosmos among certain villages of the Yi people in contemporary Yunnan, see Erik Mueggler, *The Age of Wild Ghosts: Memory, Violence, and Place in Southwest China* (Berkeley: University of California, 2001), ch. 2, "An Empty Frame."

185. Pu Muzhou, *Muzang yu shengsi*: Pu, "Lun Zhongguo gudai muzang xing zhi 論中國古代墓葬形制," *Guoli Taiwan Daxue wen shi zhe xuebao* 37 (1989), pp. 235–279; Poo Mu-chou, *In Search of Personal Welfare: A View of Ancient Chinese Religion* (Albany:

State University of New York, 1998), pp. 165–167; Wang Zhongshu, *Han Civilization*, tr. K. C. Chang and collaborators (New Haven: Yale University, 1982), ch. 8–9; Wu Hung, "Art and Architecture of the Warring States Period," in *The Cambridge History of Ancient China* (Cambridge: Cambridge University, 1999), pp. 707–744; Wu, *Monumentality*, pp. 110–121; Lothar von Falkenhausen, "Grabkult und Ahnenkult im Staat Qin: Der religiöe Hintergrund der Terrakotta-Armee," in *Jenseits der Grossen Mauer: Der Erste Kaiser von China und seine Terrakotta-Armee*, ed. Lothar Ledderose and Adele Schlombs (Munich: Bertelsmann Lexikon Verlag, 1990), pp. 35–48; von Falkenhausen, "Sources of Taoism: Reflections on Archaeological Indicators of Religious Change in Eastern Zhou China" *Taoist Resources* 5.2 (1994), pp. 1–12; Alain Thote, "I Zhou orientali," in *La Cina*, ed. Michèle Pirazzoli-t'Serstevens (Turin: UTET; Storia Universale dell'Arte, 1996), vol. 1, pp. 95–165; Robert L. Thorp, "The Mortuary Art and Architecture of Early Imperial China," (Ph.D. diss., University of Kansas, 1980). One important early example of this development not much discussed in these articles is the Chu tomb from Baoshan, whose occupant died in 316 B.C. See *Baoshan Chu mu* 包山楚墓 (Beijing: Wenwu, 1991), vol. 1, p. 336; vol. 2, plate 47, nos. 10–14.

186. *Zeng Hou Yi mu* 曾侯乙墓, 2 vols. (Beijing: Wenwu, 1989); *Zeng Hou Yi mu wenwu yishu* 文物藝術 (Wuhan: Hubei meishu, 1992); Robert L. Thorp, "The Sui Xian Tomb: Re-thinking the Fifth Century," *Artibus Asiae* 43:5 (1981), pp. 67–92; Alain Thote, "Une tombe princière du Ve siècle avant notre ère," *Comptes rendus de l'académie des inscriptions et belles-lettres* (Avril-Juin 1986), pp. 393–413; Thote, "The Double Coffin of Leigudun Tomb No. 1: Iconographic Sources and Related Problems," in *New Perspectives on Chu Culture During the Eastern Zhou Period*, ed. Thomas Lawton (Washington, DC: Arthur M. Sackler Gallery, 1991), pp. 23–46.

187. "Hebei sheng Pingshan xian Zhanguo shiqi Zhongshan guo muzang fajue jianbao 河北省平山縣戰國時期中山國墓葬發掘簡報," *Wenwu* (1979:1), pp. 1–31; Wu, *Monumentality*, pp. 112–113.

188, Yu Weichao 俞偉超, *Xian Qin Liang Han kaoguxue lunji* 先秦兩漢考古學論集 (Beijing: Wenwu, 1985), pp. 187–188; Xie Duanju 謝端琚, "Shilun wo guo zaoqi tudongmu 試論我國早期土洞墓," *Kaogu* (1987:12), pp. 1097–1104; Han Wei 韓偉, "Lüe lun Shaanxi Chunqiu Zhanguo Qin mu 略論陝西春秋戰國秦墓," *Kaogu yu wenwu* (1981:1), pp. 83–93; von Falkenhausen, "Grabkult und Ahnenkult," pp. 45–46.

189. See Knapp, *China's Old Dwellings*, pp. 192–220. For critical observations on this argument, see Pu, *Muzang yu shengsi*, p. 49.

190. *Xunzi ji shi*, ch. 13, "Li lun," pp. 243–246.

191. *Mancheng Han mu* 滿城漢墓 (Beijing: Wenwu, 1978), pp. 14–17, plate 3; *Mancheng Han mu fajue baogao* (Beijing: Wenwu, 1980); "Qufu Jiulongshan Han mu fajue jianbao 曲阜九龍山發掘簡報," *Wenwu* (1975:5), pp. 39–41.

192. *Luoyang Shaogou Han mu* 洛陽燒溝漢墓 (Beijing: Kexue, 1959), p. 30, plate 6; "Luoyang Xi Han Bu Qianqiu bihua mu fajue jianbao 洛陽西漢卜千秋壁畫墓發掘簡報," *Wenwu* (1977:6), pp. 8–12, plates 1–3; Guo Moruo 郭沫若, "Luoyang Han mu bihua shitan 洛陽漢墓壁畫試探," *Kaogu xuebao* (1964:2), pp. 1–5.

193. "Hebei Ding xian Beizhuang Han mu fajue baogao 河北定縣北庄漢墓發掘報告," *Kaogu xuebao* (1964:2), pp. 127–133; *Wangdu er hao Han mu* 望都二號漢墓 (Beijing: Wenwu, 1959); *Wangdu Han mu bihua* 望都漢墓壁畫 (Beijing: Chinese Classic Art, 1955), pp. 3–14, plates 8,9; An Jinhuai 安金槐, et al., "Mi xian Dahuting Han dai huaxiangshi mu he bihua mu 密縣打虎亭漢代畫像石墓和壁畫墓," *Wenwu* (1972:10),

p. 52, plate 1; *Helin'geer [Holingor] Han mu bihua* 和林格爾漢墓壁畫 (Beijing: Wenwu, 1978).

194. Zeng Zhaoyu 曾昭燏, Jiang Baogeng 蔣寶庚, and Li Zhongyi 黎忠義, *Yinan gu huaxiangshi mu fajue baogao* 沂南古畫像石墓發掘報告 (Beijing: Wenhuabu Wenwu Guanliju, 1956); Zhou Dao 周到 and Li Jinghua 李京華, "Tanghe Zhenzhichang Han huaxiangshi mu de fajue 唐河針織廠漢畫像石墓的發掘," *Wenwu* (1973:6), pp. 26–27, 33–36; Yin Ruzhang 殷汝章, "Shandong Anqiu Moushan Shuiku faxian daxing shike Han mu 山東安邱牟山水庫發現大型石刻漢墓," *Wenwu* (1960:5), pp. 55–59; "Shandong Cangshan Yuanjia yuan nian huaxiangshi mu 山東蒼山元嘉元年畫像石墓," *Kaogu* (1975:2), pp. 124, 125.

195. *Lun heng ji jie*, ch. 23, "Si hui," p. 467.

196. Von Falkenhausen, "Ahnenkult und Grabkult," pp. 35–38; von Falkenhausen, "Sources of Taoism," pp. 3–5; Rawson, "Western Zhou Archaeology," pp. 364–375, 433–440; Pu, *Muzang yu shengsi*, pp. 198–199.

197. Pu, *Muzang yu shengsi*, pp. 139–191, 198–201; Wang, *Han Civilization*, pp. 206–210.

198. Wu Hung, "From Temple to Tomb: Ancient Chinese Art and Religion in Transition," *Early China* 13 (1988), pp. 78–115; Wu, *Monumentality*, pp. 79–121.

199. Lothar von Falkenhausen, "Review of Wu Hung, *Monumentality in Early Chinese Art and Architecture*," *Early China* 21 (1996), p. 193.

200. von Falkenhausen, "Review," pp. 193–195.

201. *Li ji zhu shu*, ch. 8, "Tan gong shang," p. 5b: "To treat the dead as dead would be inhuman; it cannot be done. To treat the dead as living would be unwise; it cannot be done. Thus the bamboo utensils cannot be used, the clay utensils have no lustre, wooden utensils are not carved, the lutes are strung but not in balance, the pipes are complete but not harmonized, there are bells and musical stones, but no frame on which to hang them. They are called *ming qi* [brilliant vessels] in order to treat the dead as spirit brilliance [*shen ming*];" ch. 9, "Tan gong xia," p. 20a: "Confucius said, 'The one who created *ming qi* understood the Way of funerals. All objects were present, but they could not be used [by the living]. If the dead used the vessels of the living, would there not be a danger of introducing human sacrifice [to accompany the dead]? They are called brilliant vessels in order to treat the dead as spirit brilliance.'"

202. *Li ji zhu shu*, ch. 9, "Tan gong xia," p. 18b.

203. Anna Seidel, "Post-mortem Immortality—or the Taoist Resurrection of the Body," in *Gilgul: Essays on Transformation, Revolution and Permanence in the History of Religions* (Leiden: E. J. Brill, 1987), pp. 223–237; Seidel, "Traces of Han Religion in Funeral Texts Found in Tombs," in *Dōkyō to shūkyō bunka* 道教と宗教文化, ed. Akizuki Kan'ei 秋月觀暎 (Tokyo: Hirakawa, 1987), pp. 21–57.

204. Ikeda On 池田溫, "Chūgoku rekidai boken ryakkō 中國歷代墓券略考," *Tōyō bunka kenkyōsho kiyo* 86 (1981), p. 273, no. 7.

205. "Jiangsu Gaoyou Shaojiagou Han dai yizhi de qingli 江蘇高郵邵家沟漢代遺址的清理," *Kaogu* (1960:10), pp. 20–21.

206. Wu Hung, "Beyond the 'Great Boundary': Funerary Narrative in the Cangshan Tomb," in *Boundaries in China* (London: Reaktion Books, 1994), pp. 93–98.

207. Lewis, *Writing and Authority*, pp. 49–51.

208. On spirit bureaucracy and the afterlife in early China, see Li Xueqin 李學勤, "Fangmatan jian zhong de zhiguai gushi 放馬灘簡中的志怪故事," *Wenwu* (1990:4), pp. 43–47; Donald Harper, "Resurrection in Warring States Popular Religions," *Taoist Resources* 5:2 (December 1994), pp. 13–28; *Huainanzi*, ch. 3, "Tian wen," p. 39; ch. 8, "Ben jing 本經," p. 119; Jeffrey K. Riegel, "Kou-mang and Ju-shou," *Cahiers d'Extrême-Asie: Special Issue, Taoist Studies II* 5 (1989–90), pp. 57–66; Noel Barnard, *The Ch'u Silk Manuscript* (Canberra: Australian National University, 1973), pp. 207–210. The emergence of the tomb as a household as linked to the dissolution of the old Zhou order based on a spirit-sanctioned nobility, and the emergence of bureaucratic forms that took the peasant household as their basis is argued in Pu, *Muzang yu shengsi*, esp. pp. 273–275; Du Zhengsheng 杜正勝, "Zhou li shenfen de xiangzheng 周禮身分的象徵," in *Zhongyang Yanjiuyuan di er jie guoji Han xue huiyi lunwenji* 中央研究院第二屆國際漢學會議論文集 (Taipei: Zhongyang Yanjiuyuan, 1989), pp. 295–306.

209. *Mozi jian gu*, ch. 8, "Ming gui xia 明鬼下," pp. 139–141, 142–143, 143–144.

210. *Lun heng ji jie*, ch. 23, "Bo zang 薄葬," pp. 461 (3), 464 (4).

211. Alvin Cohen, "Avenging Ghosts and Moral Judgment in Ancient Chinese Historiography: Three Examples from *Shi-chi*," in *Legend, Lore, and Religions in China: Essays in Honor of Wolfram Eberhard on His Seventieth Birthday*, ed. Sarah Allan and Alvin P. Cohen (San Francisco: Chinese Materials Center, 1979), pp. 97–108; Cohen, "The Avenging Ghost: Moral Judgment in Chinese Historical Texts" (Ph.D. dissertation, University of California at Berkeley, 1971).

212. *Lun heng ji jie*, ch. 22, "Ding gui 訂鬼," pp. 449–450; ch. 23, "Bo zang," p. 461; ch. 25 "Jie chu," p. 505.

213. The separation of the dead and the living became a maxim in Chinese writings about the afterlife. Already in the Eastern Han, Wang Chong argued that the dead "had a different road from the living [*yu ren shu tu* 與人殊途]." See *Lun heng ji jie* 23, "Bo zang," p. 462. This idea soon became a cliché, as exemplified by the *Sou shen ji*, which repeats that "the dead and the living have different roads [*si sheng yi lu* 死生異路]." See *Sou shen ji* 搜神記 (Beijing: Zhonghua, 1979), pp. 145, 178 [this says *sheng si yong jue* 生死永訣 = 絕] "the living and the dead are eternally separated"], 181, 190, 200 (2): here after repeating the maxim, the deceased girl says to her beloved, "Do you fear that I, being a ghost, will harm you?," 201: this story states that a human would be harmed by spending time with a ghost, 206: when a man realizes that the woman with whom he is having an affair is a ghost, he must kill her to save himself.

214. *Shi ji* 6, p. 265.

215. *Lü shi chun qiu jiaoshi*, ch. 10, "An si 安死," pp. 535–536.

216. Wu Hung, "Art in Ritual Context: Rethinking Mawangdui," *Early China* 17 (1992), pp. 111–144.

217. Sōfukawa Hiroshi 曾布川寬, "Konronzan to shōsenzu 崑崙山と昇仙圖," *Tōhō gakuhō* 51 (1979), pp. 87–102.

218. See the early Western Han banner found at Jinque shan, published on the inner cover of *Wenwu* (1977:11), with the article "Shandong Linyi Jinque shan jiu hao Han mu fajue jianbao 山東臨沂金雀山九號漢墓發掘簡報," pp. 24–27. On these banners, see Jean James, *A Guide to the Tomb and Shrine Art of the Han Dynasty* (Lewiston, NY: Edwin Mellen, 1996), pp. 4–13, 23–27.

219. Lei Jianjin 雷建金, "Jianyang xian Guitou shan faxian bangti huaxiangshi guan 簡陽縣鬼頭山發現榜題畫像石棺," *Sichuan wenwu* (1988:6), p. 65; "Sichuan Jianyang xian Guitou shan Dong Han yamu 四川建陽縣鬼頭山東漢崖墓," *Wenwu* (1991:3), pp. 20–25; Zhao Dianzeng 趙殿增, " 'Tianmen' kao—jianlun Sichuan Han huaxiang zhuan de zuhe yu zhuti 天門考—兼論四川漢畫像磚的組合與主題," *Sichuan wenwu* (1990:6), pp. 3–11.

220. Finsterbusch, *Verzeichnis und motivindex*, figures 32a, 45, 101–102, 106, 127, 137, 150, 158, 161, 167, 172, Hebei appendix 3–4; "Sichuan Pi xian Dong Han zhuan mu de shi guan huaxiang 四川郫縣東漢磚墓的石棺畫象," *Kaogu* (1979:6), pp. 497, 499: this also refers to two other coffin-lid images of Fu Xi and Nü Gua that are not reproduced; Li Fuhua 李復華 and Guo Ziyou 郭子游, "Pi Xian chutu Dong Han huaxiang shi guan tuxiang lüe shuo 郫縣出土東漢畫象石棺圖象略説," *Wenwu* (1975:8), p. 63; "Hechuan Dong Han huaxiang shi mu 合川東漢畫像石墓," *Wenwu* (1977:2), p. 67 (figures 15 and 16); Xie Li 謝荔 and Xu Lihong 徐利紅, "Sichuan Hejiang xian Dong Han zhuan shi mu qingli jian bao 四川合江縣東漢磚室墓清理簡報," *Wenwu* (1991:4), p. 47; "Sichuan Changning 'qi ge dong' Dong Han jinian huaxiang ya mu 四川長寧七個洞東漢紀年畫像崖墓," *Kaogu yu wen wu* (1985:5), p. 47; Cui Chen 崔陳, "Yibin diqu chutu Han dai huaxiang shi guan 宜賓地區出土漢代畫像石棺," *Kaogu yu wen wu* (1991:1), p. 37 (figures 3 and 5); Gao Wen 高文 and Gao Chengying 高成英, "Han hua guibao—Sichuan xin chutu de ba ge huaxiang shi guan 漢畫瑰寶—四川新出土的八個畫像石棺," *Wen wu tian di* (1988:3). The pair of snake-bodied creatures with the sun and moon also appears on stones from the walls of Shandong tombs. See "Shandong Zao zhuang huaxiang shi diaocha ji 山東棗莊畫像石調查記," *Kaogu yu wen wu* (1983:3), p. 28 (figures 13 and 14).

221. *Stories from China's Past*, pp. 20–21, 34–35, 155–156, 158–181; Hayashi, *Ishi ni kizamareta sekai*, pp. 147–195; Hayashi Minao, *Kan dai no kamigami* 漢代の神神 (Kyoto: Nozokawa, 1989), ch. 5, 7–8; Li Song 李淞, *Lun Han dai yishu zhong de Xi Wang Mu tuxiang* 論漢代藝術中的西王母圖像 (Hunan: Hunan jiaoyu, 2000); James, *Guide*, passim; Michael Loewe, *Ways to Paradise*, ch. 2, 4, and 5; Wu, *The Wu Liang Shrine*, ch. 3–4. For tabular inventories of the images in many Han tombs, see Tanaka, *Chūgoku kenchiku shi*, pp. 302–305; Pu, *Muzang yu shengsi*, p. 137.

222. Brashier, "Han Thanatology and the Division of 'Souls'," pp. 152–153, note 100.

223. *Hou Han shu* 4, p. 167; 5, p. 205; 6, p. 250; 7, p. 288; 61, pp. 2029–2030; *zhi* 9, p. 3197; Cai Yong 蔡邕, *Du duan* 獨斷, in *Han Wei cong shu*, vol. 1 (Taipei: Xin xing, 1977), ch. 2, pp. 5a–7b; *Dong Guan Han ji jiao zhu*, pp. 165–166; Cai Yong, *Cai Zhonglang wen ji* 蔡中郎文集 (Si bu cong kan ed.), ch. 8, pp. 4a–5a. On Eastern Han debates over the ancestral temple and the policies in which they resulted, see K. E. Brashier, "Evoking the Ancestor: The Stele Hymn of the Eastern Han Dynasty" (Ph.D. dissertation, Cambridge University, 1997), ch. 1.

224. Cui Shi 崔寔, *Si min yue ling ji shi* 四民月令輯釋, annotated by Miao Qiyu 繆啟愉 and Wan Guoding 萬國鼎 (Beijing: Nongye, 1981), p. 1.

225. *Si min yue ling ji shi*, pp. 3, 25, 53, 68 (2), 84, 98, 104, 109.

226. *Si min yue ling ji shi*, pp. 25, 53, 84. P. 109 refers to grave offerings after temple offerings, but they do not occur on the next day and the recipients are not close kin but rather local officials, teachers, distant kin [*jiu zu* 九族], and friends who received calls of respect on New Year's Day when still alive.

227. *Hou Han shu zhi* 9, p. 3197. See also *Du duan*, ch. 2, p. 7a.

228. *Du duan*, ch. 2, p. 7a. *Hou Han shu zhi* 9, p. 3197: "Emperor Shang died after living just over three hundred days, and Dowager Empress Deng ruled as regent. Because he had still been an infant he was not placed in the temple, so they simply made offerings to him at his graveside mausoleum. . . . Emperors Chong and Zhi had both died when young, and Dowager Empress Liang had ruled as regent. On the basis of the precedent of Emperor Shang, they received offerings at their mausolea."

229. Wu Hung, *The Wu Liang Shrine*, pp. 30–37.

230. Cai Yong, *Du duan*, ch. 2, pp. 5a–b.

231. *Lun heng ji jie*, ch. 23, "Si hui," p. 467.

232. *Lun heng ji jie*, ch. 23, "Bo zang," pp. 463–464.

233. *Lun heng ji jie*, ch. 25, "Jie chu," p. 507.

234. Hayashi, *Ishi ni kizamareta sekai*, pp. 18–26. For scenes of couples and intimacy, see *Stories from China's Past*, pp. 126–131. For sex scenes, see Jessica Rawson, ed., *Mysteries of Ancient China: New Discoveries from the Early Dynasties* (London: British Museum Press, 1996), pp. 201–203; Liu Dunyuan 劉敦愿, "Han huaxiangshi shang de yinshi nannü—Pingyin Meng Zhuang Han mu shizhu jisi gewu tusiang fenxi 漢畫像石上的飲食男女——平陰孟莊漢墓石柱祭祀歌舞圖像分析," *Gu Gong wenwu yuekan* 141 (December 1994), pp. 122–135, esp. figures 3:1–12, 4:1–2; James, *Guide*, pp. 163, 202, 226–227, 230; Martin J. Powers, *Art and Political Expression in Early China* (New Haven: Yale University, 1991), pp. 51, 288, 291, 306; Finsterbusch, *Verzeichnis und Motivindex*, vol. 2, #261, 310, 338, 508a, 508q, 508s, 508t, 594.

235. *Stories from China's Past*, pp. 109 (figure 3), 138, 139 (photo at bottom center), 141, 143, 144, 189, 190; Powers, *Art and Political Expression*, p. 293; James, *Guide*, pp. 228–229; Finsterbusch, *Verzeichnis und Motivindex*, vol. 2, #212, 268, 277, 363, 508q, 538, 552, 641, 786, 793.

236. Wu, "Beyond the Great Boundary," pp. 90, 101; Hayashi, *Ishi ni kizamareta sekai*, pp. 156–157.

237. Li, *Lun Han dai yishu zhong de Xi Wang Mu tuxiang*.

238. On their mythology as individuals, see Lewis, *Writing and Authority*, pp. 197–209.

239. Hayashi, *Kandai no kamigami*, p. 294.

240. Wu Hung, *The Wu Liang Shrine*, pp. 246–247.

241. Li Chenguang 李陳廣 argues that as depicted in Han funerary art they are the chief gods of the Han pantheon. See "Han hua Fu Xi Nü Gua de xingxiang tezheng ji qi yiyi 漢畫伏羲女媧的形象特徵及其意義," *Zhongyuan wen wu* 1992:1, p. 37.

CHAPTER THREE

1. Norman Crowe, *Nature and the Idea of a Man-made World: An Investigation into the Evolutionary Roots of Form and Order in the Built Environment* (Cambridge: MIT, 1995).

2. K. C. Chang, *The Archaeology of Ancient China*, 4th ed. rev. (New Haven: Yale University, 1986), pp. 114–120, 248–249, 286–288, 303, 322–339, 362–363.

3. David Keightley, "The Late Shang State: When, Where, and What?" in Keightley, ed., *The Origins of Chinese Civilization* (Berkeley: University of California, 1983), pp. 523–558.

4. Chang, *Shang Civilization*, pp. 158–165.

5. Keightley, "The Late Shang State," pp. 529–532, 543, 545; Hsu and Linduff, *Western Zhou Civilization*, pp. 41–49.

6. Hsu and Linduff, *Western Zhou Civilization*, pp. 48–49.

7. Akatuska Kiyoshi 赤塚忠, *Chūgoku kodai no shūkyō to bunka: In ōchō no saishi* 中國古代の宗教と文化 ： 殷王朝の祭祀 (Tokyo: Kadokawa, 1977); Keightley, "Akatsuka Kiyoshi and the Culture of Early China: A Study in Historical Method," *Harvard Journal of Asiatic Studies* 42.1 (1982), pp. 267–320.

8. Itō Michiharu 伊籐道治, *Chūgoku kodai ōchō no keisei* 中國古代王朝の形成 (Tokyo: Sōbunsha, 1975), pp. 225–246; Itō Michiharu, *Chūgoku kodai kokka no shihai kōzō* 中國古代國家の支配構造 (Tokyo: Chuō kōron, 1987), pp. 77–153; Hsu and Linduff, *Western Zhou Civilization*, pp. 151–185; Lewis, *Sanctioned Violence in Early China*, pp. 33–36, 54.

9. Lewis, *Sanctioned Violence*, pp. 54–58; Du Zhengsheng 杜正勝, *Zhou dai chengbang* 周代城邦 (Taipei: Lianjing, 1979), pp. 21–46; Yang Kuan 楊寬, *Gu shi xin tan* 古史新探 (Beijing: Zhonghua, 1965), pp. 135–165; He Ziquan 何茲全, "Zhou dai tudi zhidu he ta de yanbian 周代土地制度和它的演變," *Lishi yanjiu* 1964 (3), pp. 145–162; Li Ling 李零, "Zhongguo gudai jumin zuzhi de liang da leixing ji qi butong laiyuan 中國古代居民組織的兩大類型及其不同來源," *Wen shi* 28 (March, 1987), pp. 59–78; Ying Yongchen 應永深, "Lun Chunqiu shidai Lu guo he Jin guo de shehui tedian jian ji rujia he fajia chansheng de lishi beijing 論春秋時代魯國和晉國的社會特點兼及儒家和法家產生的歷史背景," *Lishi yanjiu* 1964 (1), pp. 151–168.

10. Hsu and Linduff, *Western Zhou Civilization*, pp. 278–286; Edward L. Shaughnessy, 1999. "Western Zhou History," in M. Loewe and E. L. Shaughnessy, eds., *The Cambridge History of Ancient China* (Cambridge: Cambridge University, 1999), pp. 322–331.

11. Tong Shuye 童書業, *Chun qiu shi* 春秋史 (Shanghai: Kaiming, 1946), pp. 82–84; Tong, *Chun qiu Zuo zhuan yanjiu* 春秋左傳研究 (Shanghai: Renmin, 1980), pp. 177–184, 366–368; Du, *Zhou dai chengbang*; Miyazaki Ichisada 宮崎市定, "Chūgoku ni okeru shuraku keitai no hensen ni tsuite 中國における聚落形體の變遷について," in *Ajia shi ronkō*, vol. 2 (Tokyo: Asahi Shimbun, 1978), pp. 3–30; Miyazaki, "Chūgoku jōdai wa hōkensei ka toshi kokka ka中國上代は封建制か都市國家か," in *Ajia shi kenkyū*, vol. 3 (Kyoto: Dōshōsha, 1957), pp. 63–86; Miyazaki, "Chūgoku jōdai no toshi kokka to sono bōchi 中國上代の都市國家とその墓地," in *Ajia shi ronkō*, vol. 2, pp. 31–55; Kaizuka Shigeki 貝塚茂樹, *Chūgoku no kodai kokka* 中國の古代國家, in *Kaizuka Shigeki chosaku shū* 貝塚茂樹著作集, vol. 1 (Tokyo: Chuō Kōron, 1978), pp. 255–382; Kaizuka Shigeki, "Chūgoku kodai toshi kokka no seikaku 中國古代都市國家の性格," in *Kaizuka Shigeki chosaku shū*, vol. 2, pp. 119–132; Itō, *Chūgoku kodai ōchō no keisei*, pp. 172–224; Kimura Masao 木村正雄, *Chūgoku kodai teikoku no keisei* 中國古代帝國の形成 (Tokyo: Fumeito, 1979), pp. 60–81; Masabuchi Tatsuo 增淵龍夫, *Chūgoku kodai no shakai to kokka* 中國古代の社會と國家 (Tokyo: Kōbundō, 1962), pp. 421–435; Mark Edward Lewis, "The City-State in Spring-and-Autumn China," in *A Comparative Study of Thirty City-State Cultures*, ed. Mogens Herman Hansen (Copenhagen: C. A. Reitzels Forlag, 2000),

pp. 359–373; Robin D. S. Yates, "The City-State in Ancient China," in *The Archaeology of City-States: Cross-Cultural Approaches*, ed. Deborah L. Nichols and Thomas H. Charlton (Washington, DC: Smithsonian Institution, 1997), pp. 71–90.

12. Nancy S. Steinhardt, *Chinese Imperial City Planning* (Honolulu: University of Hawai'i, 1990), pp. 43–50; Yang Kuan 楊寬, *Zhan guo shi* 戰國史, 2nd ed. rev. (Shanghai: Renmin, 1980), pp. 95–98.

13. Lothar von Falkenhausen, "The Waning of the Bronze Age: Material Culture and Social Developments, 770–481 B.C." in M. Loewe and E. L. Shaughnessy, eds., *The Cambridge History of Ancient China* (Cambridge: Cambridge University, 1999), pp. 453–463.

14. *Di wang shi ji ji cun* 帝王世紀輯存, annotated by Xu Zongyuan 徐宗元 (Beijing: Zhonghua 1964), p. 119.

15. *Zuo zhuan zhu*, Ai year 7, p. 1642; *Shang shu zheng yi*, ch. 5 "Yi ji," p. 10b; *Xunzi ji jie*, ch. 6, "Fu guo," p. 127; ch. 8, "Jun dao," p. 160.

16. *Zhan guo ce*, ch. 20, "Zhao 3," p. 678.

17. Gu Donggao 顧東高, *Chun qiu da shi biao*, 春秋大事表, in *Huang Qing jing jie xu bian, ce 67–133*, (Nanqing Shuyuan, 1888); Kaizuka, *Chūgoku no kodai kokka*, pp. 277–279.

18. Miyazaki, "Chūgoku ni okeru shuraku keitai no hensen ni tsuite," pp. 6–15.

19. Miyazaki, "Chūgoku jōdai wa hōkensei ka toshi kokka ka," p. 73.

20. *Mengzi zheng yi* IA "Liang Hui Wang shang," p. 40; IIA "Gongsun Chou shang," pp. 105, 128, 130; IIIA "Teng Wen Gong shang, " p. 189; VB "Wan Zhang xia," p. 402; VIB "Gaozi xia," p. 502; *Shang jun shu zhu yi*, ch. 15, "Lai min 來民," p. 308; *Guanzi jiao zheng*, ch. 1, "Sheng ma 乘馬," p. 17.

21. The existence of such lands is indicated in *Zuo zhuan zhu*, Ai year 12, p. 1673.

22. Victor Ehrenberg, *The Greek State* (New York: W. W. Norton, paperback edition, 1960), p. 29.

23. *Mengzi zheng yi* IA "Liang Hui Wang shang," p. 54; VIB "Gaozi xia," p. 502.

24. Henri Maspero, *China in Antiquity*, tr. Frank A. Kierman, Jr. (Amherst: University of Massachusetts, 1978), pp. 175–176, 194, 203–204, 212–213, 225–232.

25. Maspero, *China in Antiquity*, pp. 207, 245.

26. *Mengzi zheng yi* VIB "Gaozi xia," p. 502.

27. Maspero, *China in Antiquity*, pp. 185–186, 204–205, 215–216; Hsu Cho-yun, "The Spring and Autumn Period," in M. Loewe and E. L. Shaughnessy, eds. *The Cambridge History of Ancient China*, p. 574.

28. Hsu, "The Spring and Autumn Period," p. 571.

29. Mark Edward Lewis "Warring States Political History," in M. Loewe and E. L. Shaughnessy, eds., *The Cambridge History of Ancient China*, p. 639.

30. Maspero, *China in Antiquity*, pp. 172–174.

31. Maspero, *China in Antiquity*, pp. 180–185.

32. Lewis, *Sanctioned Violence*, pp. 17–36.

33. Kaizuka, *Chūgoku no kodai kokka*, pp. 260–268.

34. Lewis, *Sanctioned Violence*, pp. 34–37.

35. Lewis, *Sanctioned Violence*, pp. 35–37.

36. Lewis, *Sanctioned Violence*, pp. 22, 29, 44, 48; Masubuchi Tatsuo 増淵龍夫, "Shunjū Sengoku jidai no shakai to kokka 春秋戰國時代の社會と國家," in *Iwanami kōza sekai rekishi*, vol. 4 (Tokyo: Iwanami, 1970), pp. 139–179; Du, *Zhou dai chengbang*, pp. 76–84, 132–138; Du Zhengsheng, *Bian hu qi min*, pp. 38–40, 47–50, 56–61; Ri Zhi 日知, "Chengbang shi zong lun 城邦史總論," in Ri Zhi, ed., *Gu dai chengbang shi yanjiu* 古代城邦史研究 (Beijing: Renmin, 1989), pp. 27–35.

37. Kaizuka, "Chūgoku kodai toshi ni okeru minkai no seido 中國古代都市にお ける民會の制度," in *Kaizuka Shigeki chosaku shū*, vol. 2, pp. 97–118; Kaizuka, *Chūgoku no kodai kokka*, p. 325.

38. Ri, "Chengbang shi zong lun," pp. 32–36.

39. Lewis, *Sanctioned Violence*, p. 48.

40. J. F. McGlew, *Tyranny and Political Culture in Ancient Greece* (Ithaca: Cornell University, 1993).

41. Ri, "Chengbang shi zong lun," pp. 93–95; Lewis, *Sanctioned Violence*, pp. 54–56, 76.

42. Ri, "Chengbang shi zong lun," pp. 96–97.

43. *Zuo zhuan zhu*, Xiang year 31, pp. 1191–1192.

44. Lewis, *Sanctioned Violence*, p. 59; François Martin, "Le cas Zichan: Entre légistes et confucianistes," in J. Gernet and M. Kalinowski, eds., *En suivant la Voie Royale: Mélanges en hommage à Léon Vandermeersch* (Paris: École Française d'Extrême-Orient, 1997), pp. 69–83.

45. Lewis, *Sanctioned Violence*, pp. 48, 76.

46. Kaizuka, *Chūgoku no kodai kokka*, pp. 313–318.

47. Lester Bilsky, *The State Religion of Ancient China* (Taipei: The Chinese Association for Folklore, 1975), pp. 14–16, 58–60, 66, 126–127, 162–169, 183–190, 235–246, 274–276, 297–308, 318–324; Lewis, *Sanctioned Violence*, p. 162; Lewis, "The *Feng* and *Shan* Sacrifices of Emperor Wu of the Han," in McDermott, ed., *State & Court Ritual in China* (Cambridge: Cambridge University, 1999), pp. 55–58, 74–76.

48. Ikeda Suetoshi 池田末利, *Chūgoku kodai shūkyō shi kenkyū* 中國古代宗教史研 究 (Tokyo: Tōkai Daigaku, 1983), pp. 108–121, 696–699.

49. Kaizuka, *Chūgoku no kodai kokka*, pp. 337–341.

50. *Zuo zhuan zhu*, Ding year 6, p. 1559.

51. Kaizuka, *Chūgoku no kodai kokka*, pp. 330–336.

52. Lewis, *Sanctioned Violence*, pp. 49–50; *Writing and Authority in Early China*, p. 19.

53. Wolfram Eberhard, *Social Mobility in Traditional China* (Leiden: E. J. Brill, 1962), pp. 228, 267; Mark Elvin, *The Pattern of the Chinese Past* (London: Eyre Methuen, 1973), pp. 22, 177; Jacques Gernet, "Note sur les villes chinoises au moment de l'apogée islamique," in A. H. Hourani and S. M. Stern, eds., *The Islamic City* (Oxford: Bruno Cassirer, 1970), pp. 77–85; F. W. Mote, "The City in Traditional China," in J. T. C. Liu and Tu Wei-ming, eds., *Traditional China* (New York: Prentice-Hall, 1970), pp. 42–43; Mote, "A Millenium of Chinese Urban History: Form, Time, and Space Concepts in Soochow," *Rice University Studies* 59:4 (Fall 1973), pp. 37–38; Mote, "The Transformation of Nanking, 1350–1400," in G. William Skinner, ed., *The City in Late*

Imperial China (Stanford: Stanford University, 1977), pp. 102–110; Rhoads Murphey, "The City as a Center of Change: Western Europe and China," *Annals of the Association of American Geographers* 44:4 (December 1954), pp. 349–362; Murphey, "The City as a Mirror of Society: China, Tradition, and Transformation," in John A. Agnew, John Mercer, and David E. Sopher, eds., *The City in Cultural Context* (Boston: Allen & Unwin, 1984), pp. 186–204; Joseph Needham, *Science and Civilisation in China*, vol. 4, Part III (Cambridge: Cambridge University, 1971), pp. 71–72; Yinong Xu, *The Chinese City in Space and Time: The Development of Urban Form in Suzhou* (Honolulu: University of Hawai'i, 2000), pp. 65–85.

54. Mote, "The Transformation of Nanking," pp. 101–105. Du, *Zhou dai chengbang*, pp. 138–156, also argues that dissolving the legal distinction between urban and rural populations marked a major shift in Chinese history.

55. Sylvie Vilatte, *Espace et Temps: La cité aristotélicienne de la Politique* (Paris: Les Belles Lettres, 1995); Louis Gernet, "Droit et ville dans l'Antiquité greque," and "Sur le symbolisme politique: le Foyer commun," reprinted in *Droit et institutions en Grèce antique* (paperback ed., Paris: Flammarion, 1982), pp. 265–278, 279–305.

56. On urban autonomy and the city as the realm of human perfection in Renaissance Italy see Hans Baron, *The Crisis of the Early Italian Renaissance* (Princeton: Princeton University, 1955); Lauro Martines, *Power and Imagination: City-States in Renaissance Italy* (New York: Random House, 1979).

57. Yang, *Zhan guo shi*, pp. 88–105; Wu Hung, "The Art and Architecture of the Warring States Period," in M. Loewe and E. L. Shaughnessy, eds., *The Cambridge History of Ancient China*, pp. 653–665; Ye Xiaojun 葉曉軍, *Zhongguo ducheng fazhan shi* 中國都城發展史 (Xi'an: Shaanxi Renmin, 1988), pp. 61–76; Heather Peters, "Towns and Trade: Cultural Diversity in Chu Daily Life," in Constance A. Cook and John S. Major, eds., *Defining Chu: Image and Reality in Ancient China* (Honolulu: University of Hawai'i, 1999), pp. 99–117.

58. *Shi ji* 69, p. 2257: this describes the size of the Qi capital Linzi as "70,000 households"; 85, p. 2511; 129, p. 3272; *Zhan guo ce*, ch. 20, "Zhao 3," p. 678; ch. 19, "Zhao 1," pp. 587, 591, 619; ch. 21, "Zhao 4," pp. 748–749; ch. 22, "Wei 1," p. 775; ch. 27, "Han 2," p. 989, etc; *Han shu* 91, p. 3686.

59. Steinhardt, *Chinese Imperial City Planning*, pp. 46–53; Qu Yingjie 曲英傑, *Xian Qin ducheng fuyuan yanjiu* 先秦都城復原研究 (Harbin: Heilongjiang Renmin, 1991); Wu, "The Art and Architecture of the Warring States Period," pp. 653–665.

60. Lewis, "Warring States Political History," pp. 603–619.

61. Lewis, *Sanctioned Violence*, pp. 31–33.

62. Lewis, *Writing and Authority*, pp. 358, 495 n. 60–62; Xu Fuguan 徐復觀, *Liang Han sixiang shi* 兩漢思想史, vol. 3 (Taipei: Xuesheng, 1979), pp. 34–42.

63. Lewis, *Writing and Authority in Early China*, pp. 79–83, 287–336.

64. *Shi ji* 30, pp. 1418, 1430.

65. This contrast between the divided and the undivided city defines the analysis of the Greek polis in Stephen Scully, *Homer and the Sacred City* (Ithaca: Cornell University, 1990), pp. 9, 14–15, 16–32, 82–83, 112–113. In contrast with Mycenean "cities" and those of ancient Mesopotamia, the polis as adumbrated in Homer's account of Troy and fully developed in the fifth century included the entire population within

the city walls. Thus, the Warring States city moved away from the model of the polis or city-state and toward the type found in the temple-dominated cities of the ancient Middle East.

66. Neimenggu Zizhiqu Bowuguan Wenwu Gongzuo Dui 內蒙古自治區博物館文物工作隊, *Helin'ge'er Han mu bihua* 和林格爾漢墓辟畫 (Beijing: Wenwu, 1987), pp. 17, 82, 84–89, 99, 130–135, 145. On this tomb, and the evidence it provides regarding society and architecture, see also Neimenggu Zizhiqu Bowuguan Wenwu Gongzuo Dui, "Helin'ge'er faxian yi zuo zhongyao de Dong Han mu bihua mu 和林格爾發現一坐重要的東漢壁畫墓," *Wenwu* 1974 (1), pp. 8–23; Wu Rongzeng 吳榮曾, "Helin'ge'er Han mu bihua zhong fanying de Dong Han shehui shenghuo 和林格爾漢墓壁畫中反映的東漢社會生活," *Wenwu* 1974 (1), pp. 24–30; Luo Zhewen 羅哲文, "Helin'ge'er Han mu bihua zhong suo jian de yixie gu jianzhu 和林格爾漢墓壁畫中所見的一些古建築," *Wenwu* 1974 (1), pp. 31–37.

67. Wu, "Art and Architecture," pp. 665–675; Wu, *Monumentality*, pp. 102–110.

68. *Lun heng ji jie*, ch. 13, "Bie tong 別通," p. 273.

69. *Tai ping yu lan*, ch. 177; *Shi ji* 5, p. 192; *Han Feizi ji shi*, ch. 7, "Shuo lin shang," p. 443; Lu Jia 陸賈, *Xin yu jiaozhu* 新語校注, annotated by Wang Liqi 王利器 (Beijing: Zhonghua, 1986), p. 134; *Wen xuan* (Hong Kong: Shangwu, 1978) 1 "Xi du fu 西都賦," p. 10; "Xi jing fu," pp. 31, 32, 33; *Han shu* 90, p. 3658; *Huang Di nei jing ling shu jiao zhu yu yi* 80, p. 537.

70. Shandong Sheng Wenwu Guanli Chu 山東省文物管理處, "Shandong Linzi Qi gu cheng shijue jianbao 山東臨淄齊故城試掘簡報," *Kaogu* 1961 (6), pp. 289–297; Qun Li 群力, "Linzi Qi gu cheng kantan jiyao 臨淄齊故城勘探紀要," *Wenwu* 1972 (5), pp. 45–54; Liu Dunyuan 劉敦願, "Chunqiu shiqi Qi guo gu cheng de fuyuan yu chengshi buju 春秋時期齊國故城的復原與城市佈局," *Lishi dili* 1981 (1), pp. 148–59; Zhang Longhai 張龍海 and Zhu Yude 朱玉德, "Linzi Qi gu cheng de paishui xitong 臨淄齊故城的排水系統," *Kaogu* 1988 (9), pp. 784–787; Chang Wenzhai 暢文齋, "Houma diqu gu cheng zhi de xin faxian 候馬地區古城址的新發現," *Wenwu* 1958 (12), pp. 32–33; Ma Xianxing 馬先醒, *Han jian yu Han dai chengshi* 漢簡與漢代城市 (Taipei: Jiandu She, 1976), pp. 195–211; Charles D. Weber, *Chinese Pictorial Bronze Vessels of the Late Zhou Period* (Ascona: Artibus Asiae, 1968), figure 25.

71. *Shi ji* 129, p. 3260.

72. *Shi ji* 8, p. 385; 68, p. 2232. The *Shi ji* indicates that building this gate figured prominently in Shang Yang's estimate of his own achievements, and in attacks by his critics. See p. 2234 (2).

73. *Chun qiu Gongyang zhuan zhu shu*, ch. 24, Zhao year 24, pp. 7a–b; *Li ji zhu shu*, ch. 23 "Li qi 禮器," p. 13a; ch. 25 "Jiao te sheng," p. 15a; *Bo hu tong* 白虎通, quoted in Li Daoyuan 酈道元, *Shui jing zhu* 水經注 (Shanghai: Shijie, 1936), p. 215. Han imperial gate towers are also described in *Wen xuan* 1"Xi du fu," pp. 7, 10; 2 "Xi jing fu," pp. 28, 31, 34; 3 "Dong jing fu," p. 53. For a poem that links lofty towers with high status, see Lu, *Xian Qin Han Wei Jin Nanbeichao shi*, vol. 1, p. 277.

74. *Zuo zhuan zhu*, Zhuang year 19, p. 211; Xuan year 4, p. 756.

75. Lewis, *Writing and Authority*, pp. 43, 379 n. 105; *Guo yu*, "Qi yu," pp. 223, 225, n. 17.

76. *Er ya zhu shu*, ch. 5 "Shi gong 釋宮," p. 5a; *Shuo wen jie zi zhu*, ch. 12, p. 9a.

77. *Li ji zhu shu* 10 "Tan gong xia," p. 25b; Finsterbusch, *Verzeichnis und Motivindex der Han-Darstellungen*, plates #34, 103, 124, 128, 141, 151, 155, 164, 179, 198, 223, 240, 459, 625, 639, 652, 1016, 1017, 1018; *Stories from China's Past*, pp. 105–107. Pages 110–113 depict multistory granaries to express landlord power. See also *Tai ping yu lan*, ch. 179; Marcel Granet, *La Civilisation chinoise* (Paris: Renaissance du Livre, 1929), pp. 279–280. On the gate as a symbol for the city in medieval Europe see Paul Zumthor, *La Mesure du monde: représentation de l'espace au Moyen Âge* (Paris: Seuil, 1993), p. 129.

78. Wu, *Monumentality*, p. 106. Qin du Xianyang kaogu gongzuo zhan 秦都咸陽考古工作站," Qin du Xianyang de yi hao gongdian jianzhu jianbao 秦都咸陽的一號宮殿建築簡報," *Wenwu* 1976 (11), pp. 12–24.

79. Even in medieval China the major cities, such as Tang Chang'an, had only a few multistory buildings and vertical elements such as gate towers, pavilions, and—from the fifth century—pagodas. See Heng Chye Kiang, *Cities of Aristocrats and Bureaucrats: The Development of Medieval Chinese Cityscapes* (Honolulu: University of Hawai'i, 1999), pp. 9, 33–34.

80. *Laozi dao de jing zhu* #14, pp. 7–8; #15, p. 8; #20, p. 11; #21, p. 12; #22, p. 12, #27, p. 15; #41, p. 26. Only passage #15 appears in the proto-*Laozi* discovered at Guodian. See *Guodian Chu mu zhu jian*, p. 21. This suggests that the idea developed largely in the third century B.C.

81. *Xunzi ji jie*, ch. 1 "Quan xue 勸學," p. 5. *Xunzi ji jie*, ch. 12, "Zheng lun 正論," p. 214, attributes the doctrine that the ruler benefits from secrecy to the "conventional persuaders of this age" whom it then refutes. Ch. 15, "Jie bi," p. 273, states that the wicked ruler succeeds through reliance on secrecy.

82. *Shi yi jia zhu Sunzi* 十一家註孫子 (Shanghai: Guji, 1978), "Xushi 虛實," pp. 132–133, 139, 149, 150, 152; *Huainanzi*, ch. 15, "Bing lüe," pp. 253 (2), 258, 260 (2), 261, 262, 267.

83. *Han Feizi ji shi*, ch. 1, "Zhu dao," pp. 67, 68 (2); ch. 2, "Yang quan," pp. 121, 122 (2); "Ba jian 八姦," p. 151; ch. 4, "Shui nan 説難," p. 221; ch. 5, "Bei nei," p. 289; "Nan mian 南面," p. 298; ch. 6, "Jie Lao 解老," p. 377; ch. 13, "Wai chu shuo you shang 外儲説右上," p. 728.

84. *Lun heng ji jie*, ch. 26, "Shi zhi 實知," p. 521.

85. Graham, *Disputers of the Tao*, pp. 215–217. He explains the practice by imagining the authors/editors as a "disregarded, unsuccessful man, withdrawn and timid, fantasising as [*sic*] a secret power in history who disdained public notice." However, to explain through a quirk of psychology a widespread phenomenon involving the collective authorship of several works is not persuasive. It is more plausible to explain it as the intellectual version of the widespread association of invisibility with power. On how the *Dao de jing* was attributed to Lao Dan, see Graham, "The Origins of the Legend of Lao Dan," in *Studies in Chinese Philosophical Literature* (Singapore: Institute of East Asian Philosophies, 1986), pp. 111–124. On the *He guanzi*, see Graham, "A Neglected Pre-Han Philosophical Text: *Ho Kuan-tzu*," *Bulletin of the School of Oriental and African Studies* 52.3 (1989), pp. 497–532; Carine Defoort, *The Pheasant Cap Master: A Rhetorical Reading* (Albany: State University of New York, 1997). On the *Gui guzi*, see Chen Yinglüe 陳英略, *Gui guzi shen ji bingfa* 鬼谷子神機兵法 (Taipei: Xin Dongli Zazhi, 1972) and Chen, *Gui guzi douzhi mijue* 鬼谷子鬥智秘訣 (Taipei: Xin Dongli Zazhi, 1972).

86. The so-called Four Canons of the Yellow Emperor from Mawangdui asserts that only the formless can govern the world. Similarly, the Way that guides all things in its "Dao yuan" chapter is described as formless and invisible. See *Jing fa*, pp. 1, 3, 101. The *Huainanzi*, cited in note 82 for references to the military uses of invisibility, and the *Lü shi chun qiu* also link the power of the ruler, the Way, and Heaven to their formlessness. See *Huainanzi*, ch. 9, "Zhu shu," pp. 129, 143; *Lü shi chun qiu jiao shi*, ch. 17, "Jun shou 君守," p. 1049; "Wu gong 勿躬," p. 1078; ch. 21, "Qi xian 期賢," p. 1447. This last passage again refers to a military context.

87. *Shi ji* 6, pp. 239, 241 (the commentary states that walled roads let the emperor travel invisibly), 251, 256, 257, 264. The Second Emperor's being rarely seen was justified as an aspect of rulership by Zhao Gao. See *Shi ji* 6, p. 271; 87, p. 2558. On Xiang Yu and Liu Bang viewing the First Emperor, see *Shi ji* 7, p. 296; 8, p. 344. Their distinctive responses were used by Sima Qian to contrast their characters. See Grant Hardy, *Worlds of Bronze and Bamboo: Sima Qian's Conquest of History* (New York: Columbia University, 1999), pp. 90–92, and ch. 4.

88. *Wen xuan* 1 "Xi du fu," pp. 10, 11; 2, "Xi jing fu," p. 30.

89. The term "forbidden (*jin* 禁)" was already an epithet for imperial parks and forests in the Han. See *Wen xuan* 1 "Xi du fu," pp. 6, 12; 2 "Xi jing fu," p. 35; 6 "Wei du fu," pp. 121, 123.

90. Lewis, "The *Feng* and *Shan* Sacrifices," pp. 55–57, 68–69; Yoshinami Takeshi 好並隆司, *Shin Kan teikoku shi kenkyū* 秦漢帝國史研究 (Tokyo: Mirai, 1978), pp. 315–361.

91. *Shi ji* 28, pp. 1388, 1396 (this refers to a spirit on top of a city wall), 1400; 117, p. 3026.

92. *Stories from China's Past*, pp. 105–106, 108, 111; Finsterbusch, *Verzeichnis*, #15, 34, 128, 160, 188, 275, 507a, 508a, 508q, 508s, 512, 542, 543; Wen You 聞宥, *Sichuan Handai huaxiang xuan ji* 四川漢代畫象選集 (Shanghai: Qunlian, 1955), pl. 80. On bronze phoenixes used as weather vanes on gates, see [*Jiao zheng*] *Sanfu huang tu* 三輔黃圖 (Taipei: Shijie, 1974), pp. 15–16; *Wen xuan* 2 "Xi jing fu," p. 31; 6 "Wei du fu," p. 123; Needham, *Science and Civilisation in China*, vol. 3, pp. 478–479.

93. Xi'an Shi Wenwu Guanli Weiyuanhui 西安市文物管理委員會, "Xi'an shi faxian yi pi Han dai tongqi yu tong yu ren 西安市發現一批漢代銅器和銅羽人," *Wenwu* 1966 (4), pp. 7–8; Rawson, ed., *Mysteries of Ancient China*, p. 176; *Lun heng ji jie* "Wu xing," p. 33. In a secular context, "to sprout down and feathers" meant to become famous. See *Wen xuan* 2 "Xi jing fu," p. 35.

94. *Shi ji* 6, pp. 241, 242 n. 6; Liu Xinfang 劉信芳 and Liang Zhu 梁柱, ed., *Yunmeng Longgang Qin jian* 云夢龍崗秦簡 (Beijing: Kexue, 1997), p. 34.

95. For discussions in the Eastern Han *Bo hu tong* of trees on altars and tombs, see Susan N. Erickson, "Money Trees of the Eastern Han Dynasty," *Bulletin of the Museum of Far Eastern Antiquities* 11 (1994), pp. 33–34. See also *Lü shi chun qiu*, ch. 10 "An si," pp. 535–536: "When making tumuli in the present age, they are as tall as mountains and their trees are thick as forests."; *Shi ji* 6, p. 275. *Li ji zhu shu*, ch. 12, "Wang zhi," p. 10b stipulates that commoners' tombs have no tumuli or trees over them, showing that those of rulers or high officials did. Trees at local altars of the soil are mentioned in *Zhuangzi ji shi*, ch. 4, "Ren jian shi 人間世," pp. 77, 80.

96. Lu, *Xian Qin Han Wei Jin Nanbeichao shi*, vol. 1, pp. 259, 329, 332 (2), 335. *Qian fu lun jian*, ch. 3, "Fu chi," p. 134, insists that trees were as important in Han burials as the tomb mound. The same point is made in *Yan tie lun*, p. 69.

97. *Hou Han shu* 81, p. 2684.

98. Major, *Heaven and Earth in Early Han Thought*, pp. 102, 158, 196, 204.

99. Hebei Sheng Wenwu Guanlichu 河北省文物管理處, "Hebei sheng Pingshan xian Zhanguo shiqi Zhongshan guo muzang fajue jianbao 河北省平山縣戰國時期中山國墓葬發掘簡報," *Wenwu* 1979 (1), p. 9 and pl. 1, no. 1; Danielle and Vadime Elisseeff, *New Discoveries in China* (Seacaucus: Chartwell, 1983), p. 91.

100. Guo Moruo 郭沫若, "Chutu wenwu er san shi: Fusang mu yu Guanghan gong 出土文物二三事:扶桑木與廣寒宮," *Wenwu* 1972 (3), pp. 7–10; Henan Sheng Bowuguan 河南省博物館, "Jiyuan Sijiangou san zuo Han mu de fajue 濟源泗澗溝三坐漢墓的發掘," *Wenwu* 1973 (2):, pp. 46–53 (illustration on page 51); Rawson, *Mysteries*, pp. 190, 192.

101. Erickson, "Money Trees," pp. 9–27; Rawson, *Mysteries*, pp. 177–178; Wu Hung, "Mapping Early Taoist Art: The Visual Culture of Wudoumi Dao," in *Taoism and the Arts of China*, ed. Stephen Little (Chicago: The Art Institute of Chicago, 2000), pp. 84–88; Robert Bagley, ed., *Ancient Sichuan: Treasures from a Lost Civilization* (Seattle: Seattle Art Museum, 2001), pp. 272–277.

102. Two related images on Eastern Han tomb tiles depict a human pair engaging in sex beneath a tree. Above the earthbound humans in the first tile, monkeys and birds cavort in the tree. Whether or not this is a parody or adapatation of a known theme remains unclear. See Rawson, *Mysteries*, pp. 201–203.

103. *Li He shi ji* 李賀詩集 (Beijing: Remin Wenxue, 1984), p. 77. Translated in A. C. Graham, *Poems of the Late T'ang* (Harmondsworth: Penguin, 1965), p. 106.

104. *Mengzi zheng yi* VIIA, "Jin xin shang," p. 538.

105. Yang Xuanzhi 楊衒之, *Luoyang qielan ji jiao zhu* 洛陽伽藍記校注, annotated by Fan Xiangyong 范祥雍 (Shanghai: Guji, 1958), pp. 1, 5. This book is particularly relevant here because it is a meditation on the evanescence of the splendors of an earthly capital.

106. F. Scott Fitzgerald, "My Lost City," in *The Crack-up* (New York: New Directions, 1945), p. 32.

107. Nishijima Sadao, "The Economic and Social History of Former Han," in Michael Loewe, ed., *The Cambridge History of China*: Vol. 1, *The Ch'in and Han Empires* (Cambridge: Cambridge University: 1986), pp. 574–585; Nishijima Sadao 西島定生, *Chūgoku kodai no shakai to keizai* 中國古代の社會と經濟 (Tokyo: Tōkyō Daigaku, 1981), pp. 137–165; Utsunomiya, *Kandai shakai keizai shi kenkyū*, pp. 107–140.

108. On using the grid for police patrols, see "*Wen xuan* 1"Xi du fu," p. 10. The Chinese system recalls the French word *quadriller*, which means to divide a territory into regular segments through which one distributes police or troops to impose public order.

109. On using grids in cities to impose an ordered space on landscape, see Richard Sennett, *The Conscience of the Eye: The Design and Social Life of Cities* (New York: Alfred A. Knopf, 1991), pp. 46–68, 169–174, 244–248.

110. Lu, *Xian Qin Han Wei Jin Nanbeichao shi*, vol. 1, p. 329; *Wen xuan* 2 "Xi jing fu," pp. 33–34.

111. *Zhuangzi ji shi*, ch. 32, "Lie Yukou 列禦寇," p. 454; ch. 28, "Rang wang 讓王," pp. 417–418: Yuan Xian lives in poverty in an alley so small that Zi Gong's carriage cannot fit into it. See also *Mozi jiangu*, ch. 15, "Hao ling 號令," p. 348: contrasts thoroughfares with lesser streets inside the wards; 349; *Shi ji* 87, p. 2563; *Han shu* 40, p. 2038; 64a, p. 2796; *Mengzi zheng yi* IVB "Li Lou xia," p. 351: shows the frugality of Yan Hui by pointing out that he lived in an alley; *Huainanzi*, ch. 19 "Xiu wu 脩務," p. 344; *Da Dai li ji jie gu* 49 "Zengzi li shi 曾子立事," p. 75: those in the alleys are paired with villagers for being fond of wine and song, that is, low class; 50 "Zengzi ben xiao 曾子本孝," p. 79; *Xunzi ji jie*, ch. 4, "Ru xiao," p. 87; ch. 6, "Fu guo," p. 127; *Chun qiu fan lu yi zheng*, ch. 15, "Jiao shi 郊事," p. 417; *Yan tie lun*, p. 64; *Lie nü zhuan*, ch. 1, p. 7a. For a passage that links drinking and singing not with alleys, but with butchers and assassins in the marketplace, see *Shi ji* 86, p. 2528. On the men of the alleys as criminals, see *Xunzi ji jie*, ch. 1, "Quan xue," p. 11. On alleys so narrow that carriages cannot move through them, see Lu, *Xian Qin Han Wei Jin Nanbeichao shi*, vol. 1, pp. 263–264.

112. Hans Bielenstein, "Lo-yang in Later Han Times," *Bulletin of the Museum of Far Eastern Antiquities* 48 (1976), pp. 58–59.

113. *Wen xuan* 2 "Xi jing fu," p. 34; *Stories from China's Past*, p. 101.

114. Steinhardt *Imperial City Planning*, p. 90. On interpreting it as a market, see Zhao Liying 趙立瀛, "Lun Tang Chang'an de guihua sixiang ji qi lishi pingjia 論唐長安的規劃思想及其歷史評價," *Jianzhushi* 29 (June 1988), pp. 41–50. These arguments have been widely accepted.

115. Heng, *Cities of Aristocrats*, p. 20; Denis Twitchett, "The T'ang Market System," *Asia Major* 12:2 (1966), p. 209; Victor Cunrui Xiong, *Sui-Tang Chang'an: A Study in the Urban History of Medieval China* (Ann Arbor: Center for Chinese Studies, University of Michigan, 2000), pp. 166–170.

116. *Wen xuan* 1 "Xi du fu 西都賦," p. 4; 4 "Shu du fu," p. 89; 6 "Wei du fu," p. 126; *Huainanzi*, ch. 11, "Qi su," pp. 175–176; *Shi ji* 6, p. 289; 30, p. 1442; 76, p. 2362: the market is called "market-court [*shi chao* 市朝]" because the lines of stalls resembled the ranks of courtiers; 119, p. 3100; *Shuihudi Qin mu zhu jian*, p. 57: the market stalls form *lie* 列 "lines." *Shuihudi*, p. 90, states that convict laborers could not enter the markets. For Han tomb tiles depicting lines of stalls and shops, see Finsterbusch, *Verzeichnis*, #160, 187; Rawson, *Mysteries*, pp. 199–201; *Stories from China's Past*, pp. 102–103. On the physical layout of markets in the context of state attempts to regulate trade, see Kageyama Tsuyoshi 影山剛, *Chūgoku kodai no shōkōgyō to sembaisei* 中國古代の商工業と專賣制 (Tokyo: Tōkyō Daigaku, 1984), pp. 73–81.

117. *Li ji zhu shu*, ch. 10, "Tan gong xia," p. 12a; ch. 11, "Wang zhi," p. 36a; *Sima fa zhi jie* 司馬法直解, in *Ming ben wu jing qi shu zhi jie* 明本武經七書直解, vol. 1 (Taipei: Shi di jiaoyu, 1972), p. 21a. See also *Lun yu zheng yi*, ch. 17, "Xian wen," p. 322; *Shi ji* 6, p. 255; 8, pp. 362, 377; 10, p. 426; 14, p. 615; 15, p. 748; 18, pp. 887, 909, 921, 925–926, 926, 954, 960; 19, p. 982, 1012; 20, p. 1065; 21, pp. 1071, 1077, 1078, 1091, 1097; 22, p. 1135; 32, p. 1503; 41, p. 1753; 42, p. 1762; 56, p. 2062; 58, p. 2088; 67, p. 2214; 69, p. 2265; 70, pp. 2292, 2296; 86, pp. 2525, 2526; 87, pp. 2552, 2557, 2562; 91, p. 2600; 97, p. 2696; 101, p. 2747; 102, p. 2755; 107, pp. 2850, 2853 (2); 115, p. 2989; 118, pp. 3077, 3078, 3080, 3084, 3097 (2); 122, pp. 3136, 3146–3147;

129, p. 3256; *Han shu* 6, p. 164; 7, p. 222; 8, p. 265; 9, p. 294; 11, p. 342; 53, p. 2432; 64a, pp. 2790–2791; 71, p. 3038; 76, pp. 3199, 3223; 81, p. 3355; 99c, pp. 4157, 4158; *Hou Han shu* 5, p. 229; 6, pp. 257, 279; 7, pp. 311, 315, 318; 8, p. 338; 15, p. 575; 43, p. 1470; 47, p. 1586; *Mengzi zheng yi* IIA "Gongsun Chou shang," p. 111; *Xunzi ji jie*, ch. 3, "Fei xiang," p. 48; *Mozi jian gu* 15 "Hao ling," p. 364; *Zhou li zhu shu*, ch. 14, "Si shi 司市," pp. 18a, 21b, 24a–b; *Jiazi xin shu jiaoshi* 2 "Jie ji 階級," p. 249; 4 "Zhu qian 鑄錢," p. 543; *Huainanzi*, ch. 13 "Fan lun 氾論," p. 230; ch. 16 "Shuo shan," p. 274; *Zhan guo ce*, ch. 13, "Qi 6," pp. 447, 449; ch. 14, "Chu yi," p. 509; ch. 19, "Zhao er," p. 651; *Baopuzi nei pian jiaoshi*, p. 157. The corpse that was cited in Chapter One of the man who died and then returned to life also was exposed in the marketplace after his death.

118. *Shi ji* 85, p. 2510; 68, p. 2231.

119. Ban Gu states that Chang'an's markets were so crowded that people could not turn their heads, or chariots turn around. The crowds overflowed the city walls and spilt into the suburbs. See *Wen xuan* 1 "Xi du fu," p. 4.

120. Lewis, *Sanctioned Violence*, ch. 2: Nishijima, *Chūgoku kodai teikoku no keisei to kōzō—nijū tō shakusei no kenkyū* 中國古代帝國の形成と構造―二十等爵制の研究 (Tokyo: Tōkyō Daigaku, 1961). This is discussed in the *Han Feizi*, *Shang Jun shu*, and *Shi ji* 129, pp. 3271, 3274, 3282–3283.

121. See *Zhan guo ce*, ch. 3, "Qin ce 1," p. 115: "I have heard it said, 'Battling for fame (*ming* 名) is in the court; battling for profit (*li* 利) is in the market.'"

122. *Wen xuan* 1 "Xi du fu," p. 5; 2 "Xi jing fu," p. 34; *Han shu* 48, 3 p. 2242; *Jiazi xin shu*, 3 p. 335.

123. *Guanzi jiao zheng*, ch. 22, "Guo xu 國蓄," p. 360.

124. *Qian fu lun jian*, ch. 12, "Fu chi," pp. 120, 130, 133–134. See Ann Behnke Kinney, *The Art of the Han Essay: Wang Fu's Ch'ien-fu Lun* (Tempe: Center for Asian Studies, Arizona States University, 1990). On the debate over lavish burials, see Poo Mu-Chou, "Ideas Concerning Death and Burial in Pre-Han China," *Asia Major*, 3rd series, 3:2 (1990), pp. 25–62.

125. *Shi ji* 41, p. 1753; 129, p. 3256.

126. Lewis, *Writing and Authority*, pp. 357–358. On merchant wealth forming a hierarchy that paralleled the state, see *Guanzi jiao zheng*, ch. 23, "Qing zhong 輕重," pp. 392–393.

127. *Hou Han shu* 41, p. 1396; *Dong guan Han ji jiao zhu*, p. 664.

128. Miyazaki, "Sengoku jidai no toshi 戰國時代の都市," in *Ajia shi ronkop8*, vol. 2, pp. 61–65.

129. *Lun heng ji jie*, ch. 25, "Jie chu," p. 504; Lu, *Xian Qin Han Wei Jin Nanbeichao shi*, vol. 1, p. 258; *Han shu* 71, p. 3037.

130. Lu, *Xian Qin Han Wei Jin Nanbeichao shi*, vol. 1, p. 135.

131. *Han Feizi ji shi*, ch. 11, "Wai chu shuo zuo shang," pp. 655, 661.

132. *Shi ji* 86, p. 2525.

133. *Hou Han shu* 63, p. 2087.

134. *Zuo zhuan zhu*, Wen year 18, p. 632; *Shi ji* 33, p. 1536.

135. *Shi ji* 77, pp. 2378–2379.

136. Lewis, *Sanctioned Violence*, pp. 74, 77, 80, 89.

137. *Shi ji* 92, p. 2610.

138. *Shi ji* 124 and *Han shu* 92; Lewis, *Sanctioned Violence*, pp. 80, 88–91; Masubuchi, *Chūgoku kodai no shakai to kokka*, pp. 49–136; Miyazaki Ichisada, "Yūkyo ni tsuite 游俠について," in *Ajia shi kenkyū*, vol. 1, pp. 131–150; James J. Y. Liu, *The Chinese Knight Errant* (London: Routledge & Kegan Paul, 1967); Ch'ü *Han Social Structure*, pp. 161, 188–198, 232, 245–247; Lao Gan 勞榦, "Lun Han dai de youxia 論漢代的游俠," in *Lao Gan xueshu lunwen ji* 勞榦學術論文集, vol. 2 (Taipei: Yiwen, 1976), pp. 1021–1036; Tao Xisheng 陶希聖, *Bianshi yu youxia* 辯士與游俠 (Shanghai: Shangwu, 1933); Chen Shan 陳山, *Zhongguo wuxia shi* 中國武俠史 (Shanghai: Sanlian, 1992), ch. 1.

139. *Wen xuan* 1 "Xi du fu," p. 5; 2 "Xi jing fu," pp. 34–35; *Shi ji* 124, p. 3183; *Han shu* 94, pp. 3698, 3699. On the profit motive for gangsters and assassins, see *Shi ji* 129, p. 3271.

140. See Lewis, *Sanctioned Violence*, p. 281 n. 137 for a list of the relevant passages.

141. *Han Feizi ji shi*, ch. 19, "Wu du," pp. 1057, 1058; "Xian xue 顯學," pp. 1091, 1095 (2); *Shi ji* 124, pp. 3181, 3184; *Hou Han shu* 28a, p. 958; 67, p. 2184.

142. Zhu Hai, in the story of Prince Xinling cited earlier, was found among the butchers, as were Nie Zheng, Jing Ke, and Gao Jianli in Sima Qian's chapter on assassins. See *Shi ji* 86, pp. 2522, 2523, 2525, 2528. For butchers involved in rebellion and killing, see *Shi ji* 95, pp. 2651, 2673. The young butcher who threatened to kill Han Xin is another example of the violence found in this trade.

143. Lewis, *Sanctioned Violence*, pp. 147, 154, 155, 224, 321 n. 49. In *Shi ji* 106, p. 2832, a reckless, dangerous plan is described as "the plan of a youth pushing against a blade."

144. *Shi ji* 124 pp. 3184, 3185, 3186; *Hou Han shu* 76, p. 2468.

145. *Shi ji* 129, p. 3271. When an emissary sent by the Han was a youth, the Xiongnu assumed that he was intent on assassination, and sought to curb his violent energy (*qi* 氣). See *Shi ji* 105, p. 2913.

146. *Shi ji* 58, p. 2089.

147. *Shi ji* 122, pp. 3144, 3149.

148. *Shi ji* 123, pp. 3174, 3176.

149. Masubuchi, *Chūgoku kodai no shakai to kokka*, pp. 69–71; Yang, *Zhanguo shi*, pp. 514–515. Cao Zhi's "The Famous Capital" in Lu, *Xian Qin Han Wei Jin Nanbeichao shi*, vol. 1, p. 431, depicts the violence of an urban youth. See also *Yan tie lun*, p. 77. For images in Han art of cock fighting and setting hounds on hares, see Hayashi, *Chūgoku kodai no seikatsu shi*, pp. 110–111.

150. *Shi ji* 7, p. 298; 55, p. 2036; 56, p. 2053; 89, pp. 2574, 2575 (2); 90, p. 2591 (3); 95, p. 2660; 100, p. 2732.

151. *Shi ji* 8, pp. 342, 350, 387; 50, p. 1987; *Han shu* 36, p. 1922; *Hou Han shu* 11, p. 477 (3).

152. *Shi ji* 124, pp. 3182–3183, describes some *you xia* as ordinary men surviving in chaotic times. See also the physiognomic account of Cao Cao: "You would be a talented minister in an orderly age, but a treacherous hero in a disorderly one." As a

youth, he "worked as a swordsmen/gangster and pursued no regular occupation." *San guo zhi* 1, pp. 2, 3 n. 2.

153. *Shi ji* 127. For a brief discussion of this text, see Lewis, *Writing and Authority*, pp. 250–251.

154. See Harper, "Warring States Natural Philosophy and Occult Thought," p. 825; Li Ling, *Zhongguo fangshu kao*.

155. *Lun heng ji jie*, ch. 26, pp. 519–536, especially, pp. 521, 524–525, 526, 534–535. The identification of those skilled in techniques as diviners is reiterated in *Lun heng ji jie*, ch. 23, "Si hui," p. 466.

156. Lewis, *Writing and Authority*, ch. 2, esp. pp. 63–83.

157. *Shi ji* 46, p. 1893; *Han shu* 72, pp. 3056–3057; *Hou Han shu* 30b, p. 1053; 81, p. 2689; 82b, pp. 2710, 2743; *Lun heng ji jie*, ch. 23, "Bo zang," p. 463; *Sanfu jue lu* 三輔決錄, in *Guanzhong cong shu* 關中叢書 (Taipei: Yiwen, 1972) ch. 1, pp. 5a, 8b; Huangfu Mi 皇甫謐, *Gao shi zhuan* 高士傳, in *Tai ping yu lan*, ch. 508, p. 1b; Xie Cheng 謝承, *Hou Han shu*, in *Taiping yu lan*, ch. 725, pp. 11a–b, 11b.

158. *Han shu* 24b, p. 1181.

159. The *Zhuangzi* tells of a "daemonic shaman" who predicted deaths. See *Zhuangzi ji shi*, ch. 7, "Ying di wang," p. 134. A fragment of Gao You's late Han commentary to the *Huainanzi* in *Taiping yu lan*, ch. 735, p. 3a, discusses this story. Predicting the time of death was central to the physician's art. See *Lü shi chun qiu jiao shi*, ch. 16, "Zhi jie 知接," pp. 968–969, and the records of Chunyu Yi's cases in *Shi ji* 105, pp. 2797–2813. A section in an almanac found at Yunmeng predicts diseases' course by fixing the day on which they arose. See *Shuihudi Qin mu zhujian*, p. 193; Donald Harper, "Iatromancy, Diagnosis, and Prognosis in Early Chinese Medicine," in *Innovation in Chinese Medicine*, ed. Elizabeth Hsu (Cambridge: Cambridge University, forthcoming). Texts from the fourth-centry B.C. tomb at Baoshan include divinations on disease. See *Baoshan Chu jian* 包山楚簡 (Beijing: Wenwu, 1991), pp. 32–37; Harper, "Warring States Natural Philosophy," pp. 854–857; Li Ling, "Formulaic Structure of Chu Divinatory Bamboo Slips," *Early China* 15 (1990), pp. 71–86; Li, *Zhongguo fangshu kao*, pp. 272–296. On shaman/doctors or physicians using spirits, see *Shi ji* 28, p. 1388; *Hou Han shu* 71, p. 2299: the Yellow Turbans cured diseases through ritual confession and ingesting ashes from burned tallies; 82a, p. 2710; 82b, pp. 2741, 2744; *Tai ping yu lan*, ch. 508, p. 1b; *San guo zhi* 8, p. 264; *Baopuzi nei pian*, ch. 9, "Dao yi 道意," p. 159. On shamans as diviners, see *Han Feizi ji shi*, ch. 13, "Wai chu shuo you shang," p. 745; *Shi ji* 28, p. 1400; *Hou Han shu* 41, p. 1397; *Tai ping yu lan*, ch. 735, p. 4b. In the *Shi ji* chapter "Diviners of Auspicious Days," Jia Yi says that diviners falsely attribute their words to ghosts and spirits.

160. *Lü shi chun qiu jiao shi*, ch. 3, "Jin shu 盡數," p. 137; ch. 17, "Wu gong," p. 1078; Harper, "Warring States Natural Philosophy," pp. 874–875; Harper, *Early Chinese Medical Literature*, pp. 43–44, 152–153, 155–159, 166, 168, 174–175, 177; Harper, "The *Wu Shih Erh Ping Fang*: Translation and Prolegomena" (Ph.D. dissertation, University of California at Berkeley, 1982), pp. 42–47.

161. *Yan tie lun*, p. 68.

162. "Many women do not prepare food for their households, give up caring for silkworms and weaving, and go to study with shamans and invocators. Drumming and dancing they serve the spirits, in order to cheat humble people and delude peasants.

Women grown thin and weak, or households afflicted with disease are thrown into turmoil by worries and are easy to frighten. . . . Some abandon their medicines, go out to serve the spirits, and so die without recognizing they have been cheated by the shamans. Instead they regret that they began to serve the shamans too late." See *Qian fu lun jian*, ch. 3, "Fu chi," p. 125; *Baopuzi nei pian*, ch. 9, "Dao yi," p. 159.

163. The character *shi* 事 translated earlier as "work" referred to corvee labor. See *Han shu* 8, pp. 249, 250 n. 7. While these passages describe transmission from teacher to disciple, others note that shamanism was hereditary, or used powers obtained in an experience allowing contact with spirits. See *Shi ji* 28, p.1379 n.6. Page 1388 tells of a woman who gained the power to be possessed by spirits after recovering from an illness.

164. *Xunzi ji jie*, ch. 1, "Xiu shen 修身," p. 20. Idle youths also threaten social order through their feminine bearing and appearance, and so are to be executed and exposed in the market. See ch. 3, "Fei xiang," p. 48.

165. Liu Bang refused to work in his family's business or any ordinary job, as did Cao Cao, founder of the Wei dynasty. See *Shi ji* 8, pp. 342, 387; 50, p. 1987; *San guo zhi* 1, pp. 2, 3 n. 2. The *Lü shi chun qiu jiao shi*, ch.10 "An si," p. 537, writes: "The ruler's wicked people, the father's unfilial sons, the unloving younger brothers are all driven from their villages with pots and pans. They dread (*dan* 憚) the toil of plowing, harvesting, and gathering firewood, and are unwilling to do this work (*shi* 事), but seek the pleasures of fine clothes and rich foods. With all their cunning they cannot achieve it. So they gather groups of their fellows, and from the forest thickets of the deep mountains and vast wastelands they attack and rob. They observe the richest of the famous tumuli and great tombs . . . so they can secretly break into them." This is a rural version of the "wicked youths" whose dread of labor leads them to form bandit gangs. At the end of the Eastern Han, Xun Yue blamed the world's troubles on three types of "villainous people" who did not follow the occupations of the common people: swordsmen, persuader/philosophers, and displayers of hypocritical conduct. See Xun Yue 荀悅, *Han ji* 漢紀 (Taipei: Shangwu, 1971) "Qian Han ji 前漢紀," ch. 10, p. 96.

166. *Han shu* 90, p. 3673.

167. *Fengsu tongyi jiaoshi*, ch. 9, "Guai shen 怪神," pp. 333–334, 339; *Hou Han shu* 11, p. 479; 12, p. 491; *San guo zhi* 8, p. 285.

168. *Baopuzi nei pian*, ch. 9, "Dao yi," p. 158.

169. See references to the *Fengsu tongyi* in note 167. See also *Hou Han shu* 18, p. 694; 24, p. 838.

170. *Shi ji* 75, p. 2362. On the mob in Western political thought, see J. S. McClelland, *The Crowd and the Mob* (London: Unwin Hyman, 1989); Serge Moscovici, *L'âge des foules* (Paris: Fayard, 1981).

171. *Shi ji* 129, pp. 3263, 3274: "For the poor to seek wealth, being a farmer is not as good as being a craftsman, being a craftsman is not as good as being a merchant, and embroidering patterns is not as good as leaning against the market gate. This says that peripheral occupations are the resource of the poor." Since those who embroidered were by convention women, earning money by the alternative of "leaning against the market gate" clearly refers to prostitution. Again the rejection of assigned occupations is associated with the market.

172. *Shi ji* 79, p. 2407; 86, p. 2520.

173. A classic example is Arthur F. Wright, "The Cosmology of the Chinese City," in *The City in Later Imperial China*, pp. 33–74, which is actually about the cosmology of the Chinese imperial *capital*.

174. Xu, *The Chinese City in Space and Time*, pp. 56–66.

175. The imperial Chinese capital is thus comparable to Western capitals erected by ambitious rulers: imperial Rome, Versailles, St. Petersburg, and the unbuilt Germania of Hitler and Albert Speer. A valuable comparison is Versailles, which was celebrated as a city created out of nothing by royal will, where nature had been replaced by artifice. "The very significance of Versailles was to make power visible to all, and to show that the king's residence was also the seat of state power, which merged with the king, and with the nation of which he exalted the supremacy." Édouard Pommier, "Versailles, l'image du souverain," in Pierre Nora, ed., *Les lieux de mémoire* (paperback ed., Paris: Gallimard, 1997), vol. 1, pp. 1253–1281, esp. pp. 1253, 1258, 1259–1260, 1274; Chandra Mukerji, *Territorial Ambitions and the Gardens of Versailles* (Cambridge: Cambridge University, 1997); Gérard Sabatier, *Versailles ou la figure du roi* (Paris: Albin Michel, 1999).

176. Wang Xueli 王學理, *Xianyang di du ji* 咸陽帝都記 (Xi'an: San Qin, 1999).

177. *Shi ji* 6, p. 241. On the symbolism of this star, see *Shi ji* 27, pp. 1289–1290.

178. *Shi ji* 6, p. 256.

179. Fragments of the *Sanfu huang tu* contains a list of eighteen palaces. See *Sanfu huang tu*, pp. 4–7.

180. *Wen xuan* 2 "Xi jing fu," pp. 27, 28, 29 (2), 31.

181. *Shi ji* 6, p. 239; *Wen xuan* 2, "Xi jing fu," p. 28.

182. Wu, *Monumentality*, pp. 102–108.

183. *Shi ji* 6, p. 239. *Sanfu huang tu* p. 5 states that the statues had inscriptions on the achievements of the First Emperor, and notes the manifestation of the giants as a consequence of those achievements.

184. *Shi ji* 6, p. 239.

185. *Shi ji* 6, pp. 244, 256.

186. *Lü shi chun qiu jiaoshi*, ch. 10, "An si," pp. 535–536; Wu, "Art and Architecture," pp. 709–717; Yang Hongxun 楊鴻勛, "Zhanguo Zhongshan wangling ji zhaoyu tu yanjiu 戰國中山王陵及兆域圖研究," *Kaogu xuebao* 1980 (1), pp. 119–137; Fu Xinian 傅熹年, "Zhanguo Zhongshan wang Cuo mu chutu de zhaoyu tu ji qi lingyuan guizhi de yanjiu 戰國中山王𰻞墓出土的兆域圖及其陵園規制的研究," *Kaogu xuebao* 1980 (1), pp. 97–119.

187. *Shi ji* 6, p. 265.

188. "Qin Shihuang ling dong ce di er hao bing ma yong keng zuantan jianbao 秦始皇陵東側第二號兵馬俑坑鑽探簡報," *Wenwu* 1978 (5), pp. 1–19; "Qin Shihuang ling dong ce di san hao bing ma yong keng qingli jianbao 秦始皇陵東側第三號兵馬俑坑清理簡報," *Wenwu* 1979 (12), pp. 1–12; "Qin Shihuang ling majiu keng zuantan jianbao 秦始皇陵馬廄坑鑽探簡報," *Kaogu yu Wenwu* 1980 (4), pp. 31–41; "Qin Shihuang ling yuan peizang zuantan qingli jianbao 秦始皇陵園陪葬鑽探清理簡報," *Kaogu yu Wenwu* 1982 (1), pp. 25–29; "Qin Shihuang ling xi ce Zhaobeihucun Qin

xingtu mu 秦始皇陵西側趙背戶村秦刑徒墓," *Wenwu* 1982 (3), pp. 1–11; "Qin Shi-huang ling er hao tong chema qingli jianbao 秦始皇陵二號銅車馬清理簡報," *Wenwu* 1983 (7), pp. 1–16; Yuan Zhongyi 袁仲一, *Qin Shihuang bing ma yong* 秦始皇兵馬俑 (Beijing: Wenwu, 1983); Yuan Zhongyi, *Qin Shihuang ling bing ma yong yanjiu* 秦始皇陵兵馬俑研究 (Beijing: Wenwu, 1990); *Qin Shihuang ling bing ma yong keng yi hao keng fajue baogao* 秦始皇陵兵馬俑坑一號坑發掘報告 (Beijing: Wenwu, 1988); *Qin Shihuang ling tong chema fajue baogao* 秦始皇陵銅車馬發掘報告 (Beijing: Wenwu, 1998); *Qin Shihuang ling tong chema xiufu baogao* 秦始皇陵銅車馬修復報告 (Beijing: Wenwu, 1998); Wu Ge 無戈, *Qin Shihuang ling yu bing ma yong* 秦始皇陵與兵馬俑 (Xi'an: Shaanxi Renmin, 1982); Wang Xueli 王學理, *Qin Shihuang ling yanjiu* 秦始皇陵研究 (Shanghai: Shanghai Renmin, 1994); *Qin yong xue yanjiu* 秦俑學研究 (Xi'an: Shaanxi Renmin Jiaoyu, 1996).

189. *Shi ji* 28, pp. 1358–1360, 1364, 1375–1377.

190. *Shi ji* 28, pp. 1367–1368, 1377.

191. *Shi ji* 28, pp. 1371–1374. This may be the target of a rhapsody that says that the rivers of Guanzhong did *not* merit comparison with the Yellow River and the Luo: *Wen xuan* 1 "Dong du fu," p. 22.

192. *Shi ji* 6, pp. 282–283; *Jiazi xin shu jiaoshi*, pp. 33–41: "Taking and keeping use different methods. Qin had left the Warring States period and become king of the world, but its Way did not change and its policies were not altered."

193. Mao Zedong, an admirer of the First Emperor, evinced a similar attitude. See Judith Shapiro, *Mao's War Against Nature* (Cambridge: Cambridge University, 2001).

194. *Shi ji* 6, pp. 280–281; *Jiazi xin shu jiaoshi*, pp. 15, 18–19. For the word "moat" I follow *Xin shu*.

195. *Shi ji* 6, pp. 242, 248, 256.

196. *Shi ji* 6, pp. 245, 250, 252, 263.

197. Later texts told how the First Emperor learned that the topography of the Nanjing region indicated a future capital. To thwart this prophecy of the fall of his own dynasty, he had the top of a mountain lopped off. See *Wu lu* 吳錄, in *Tai ping yu lan*, ch. 156, p. 3a; *San guo zhi* 53, p. 1246 n. 2; *Jin shu* 6, p. 157; 53, p. 1457. Jiang Yan's sixth-century A.D. "Rhapsody on Resentment" tells how he constructed a bridge of sea turtles across the Eastern Sea to reach the isles of the immortals. See *Liang Jiang Wentong wenji* 梁江文通文集 (Si bu cong kan ed.) ch. 1, p. 5. A century later Li Bo told of a sorcerer who brought stones to life, and the First Emperor whipped them to make them march into the sea to form his bridge. See *Li Bo ji jiaozhu* 李白集校注 (Shanghai: Gu ji, 1980), vol. 1, p. 97. Li He's ninth-century A.D. "The King of Qin Drinks Wine" tells how he rode a tiger, flogged the sun to make night fall sooner for his banquet, and then shouted at the moon to make it retreat, so that the night would last longer. At the banquet he entertains the Wine Star. See *Li He shi ji*, p. 53.

198. Lewis, *Sanctioned Violence*, pp. 150, 152, 160, 175–176, 200–201, 298 n. 24; Sterckx, *The Animal and the Daemon in Early China*, ch. 2, 5; *Wen xuan* 3 "Dong jing fu," p. 65.

199. *Shi ji* 117, pp. 3058–3060; *Wen xuan* 2, "Xi jing fu," pp. 38, 39. Here the emperor commands constellations and gods when he hunts, and his hunters cause the seas to shake and mountains to topple.

200. Steinhardt, *Chinese Imperial City Planning*, ch. 3; Wu, *Monumentality*, ch. 3; Wang Zhongshu, *Han Civilization*, ch. 1–2; Xiong, *Sui-Tang Chang'an*, ch. 1; E. R. Hughes, *Two Chinese Poets: Vignettes of Han Life and Thought* (Princeton: Princeton University, 1960); Stephen Hotaling, "The City Walls of Han Ch'ang-an," *T'oung Pao* 64 (1978), pp. 1–36; Bielenstein, "Lo-yang in Later Han Time"; Wang Zhongshu 王仲殊, "Han Chang'an cheng kaogu gongzuo de chu bu shouhuo 漢長安城考古工作的初步收穫," *Kaogu* 1957 (5), pp. 102–110; Wang Zhongshu, "Han Chang'an cheng kaogu gongzuo shouhuo xu ji 漢長安城考古工作收穫續記," *Kaogu* 1958 (4), pp. 23–32; Wang Zhongshu, "Chūgoku kodai tojōsei gairon 中國古代都城制概論," in Nishijima Sadao, ed., *Nara Heian no miyako to Chōan* 奈良平安の都と長安 (Tokyo: Shōgakukan, 1983); Ma Xianxing, *Han jian yu Han dai chengshi*, pp. 212–297; Liu Yunyong 劉運勇, *Xi Han Chang'an* 西漢長安 (Beijing: Zhonghua, 1982); Koga Noboru 古賀登, "Kan Chōanjō no kensetsu puran: Sempaku kenkyō seido to no kankei o chūshin to shite 漢長安城の建設ぷらん：阡陌縣鄉制度との關係を中心として," *Tōyō shi kenkyū* 31:2 (September 1972), pp. 28–60; Koga Noboru, *Kan Chōanjō to sempaku, kenkyōteiri seido* 漢長安城と阡陌縣鄉亭里制度 (Tokyo: Yūsankaku, 1980); Utsunomiya, *Kan dai shakai keizai shi kenkyū*, pp. 141–167.

201. *Shi ji* 99, p. 2723; *Han shu* 43, pp. 2126–2128.

202. On Chu culture in the Guanzhong court, see David Knechtges, "The Emperor and Literature: Emperor Wu of the Han," in Frederick Brandauer and Chun-chieh Huang, eds., *Imperial Rulership and Cultural Change in Traditional China* (Seattle: University of Washington, 1994), pp. 51–76; Gopal Sukhu, "Monkeys, Shamans, Emperors, and Poets: The *Chuci* and Images of Chu during the Han Dynasty," in Cook and Major, eds., *Defining Chu*, pp. 145–169.

203. *Shi ji* 8, p. 341. On the divine paternity of sages in Warring States and Han myth, see Xu Shen 許慎 (d. ca. A.D. 120) and Zheng Xuan 鄭玄 (127–200 A.D.), *Bo wu jing yi yi* 駁五經異義, in *Hou zhi bu zu zhai congshu* 後知不足齋叢書 (Chang Shubao Shi, 1884), *tao* 1, *ce* 1, ch. 1, pp. 19a–b; Yasui Kōzan 安居香山, *Isho no seiritsu to sono tenkai* 緯書の成立とその展開 (Tokyo: Kokusho Kankō, 1981), pp. 413–444; Lewis, *Writing and Authority*, pp. 219, 447 n. 117.

204. *Shi ji* 7, pp. 311, 322, 327–328: Xiang Yu's adviser says, "One who is acting for the whole world pays no heed to his family"; 8, pp. 341, 342, 347, 350, 358, 371, 372, 381, 382, 386–387; 50, p. 1987.

205. *Shi ji* 7, p. 315: Xiang Yu's "heart was filled with longing to return to his home in the east." Sima Qian lists his "turning his back on the passes and longing for Chu" as the first reason for his defeat. See *Shi ji* 7, p. 359.

206. *Shi ji* 8, p. 385–386.

207. *Shi ming shu zheng bu* 釋名疏証補, annotated by Wang Xianqian 王先謙 (Shanghai: Guji, 1984), ch. 2, p. 10b; *Zuo zhuan zhu*, Zhuang year 28, p. 242.

208. *Zhou li zhushu*, ch. 41, pp. 24b–25a. On this passage, see Steinhardt, *Chinese Imperial City Planning*, pp. 33–36; Xu, *The Chinese City in Space and Time*, pp. 31–39; Paul Wheatley, *The Pivot of the Four Quarters* (Edinburgh: Aldine, 1971), pp. 411–419. The same official creates the grid of water channels that define the "well-field," a rural equivalent of the capital's grid. See ch. 42, p. 1b.

209. Wu, *Monumentality*, pp. 157–162.

210. Liu Qingzhu 劉慶柱 and Li Yufang 李毓芳, *Xi Han shiyi ling* 西漢十一陵 (Xi'an: Shaanxi Renmin, 1987), pp. 24, 32, 225.

211. Yoshinami, *Xin Kan teikoku shi kenkyū*, pp. 191–262.

212. *Shi ji* 28, pp. 1378–1380.

213. *Shi ji* 28, pp. 1382, 1384, 1386, 1387, 1388, 1389, 1393–1395, 1397–1398, 1402–1404.

214. Powers, *Art and Political Expression in Early China*, pp. 160–161, 171–180.

215. *Wen xuan* 1 "Liang du fu," pp. 1–3. See also *Han shu* 30, p. 1756.

216. *Wen xuan* 1 "Xi du fu," p. 3. On the quote from Wu Qi, see *Zhan guo ce*, ch. 22, "Wei yi," pp. 781–782; *Shi ji* 65, pp. 2166–2167; *Shuo yuan*, ch. 5, pp. 3a–b. See also *Mengzi zheng yi* IIB "Gongsun Chou xia," pp. 149–150.

217. *Wen xuan* 1 "Xi du fu," pp. 4–5. On merchants as a threat to the sumptuary order see *Shi ji* 129, p. 3274; *Jiazi xin shu*, p. 335; *Han shu* 48, p. 2242; *Zhan guo ce*, ch. 3, "Qin 1," p. 115; *Qian fu lun jian*, ch. 3, "Fu chi," pp. 120, 130, 133–134; *Yan tie lun*, pp. 3, 5–6, 7, 7–8, 9, 20, 64, 66–67.

218. *Wen xuan* 1 "Xi du fu," p. 5. For memorials from the first century A.D. criticizing the *you xia* and linking them to the Western Han, see Lewis, *Sanctioned Violence*, pp. 89–90.

219. *Wen xuan* 1 "Xi du fu," p. 16; 2, "Xi jing fu," p. 28. Wu Hung cites only the second statement, contrasting it with the later rhapsody of Zhang Heng, which describes Gaozu measuring out diameter and circumference and establishing the wall and moats. He argues that Ban Gu approaches the city as a *historian*, tracing its evolution, while Zhang Heng approaches it as a *classicist*, seeking an eternal image of the city based on the classical texts. See *Monumentality*, pp. 145–148. This misreads Ban Gu. In the rhapsody some positions are established only to be demolished. The Western Guest, whom Wu Hung cites as speaking for Ban Gu, is a straw man whose positions are stated only to be refuted. In the prose transition to the second rhapsody, the Eastern Host says that his guest is "dazzled by the peripheral creations of later successors." See *Wen xuan* 1 "Dong du fu," p. 15. The position that Wu Hung attributes to Ban Gu is thus in fact denounced by him.

220. *Wen xuan* 1 "Xi du fu," p. 9; *Han shu* 30, p. 1723.

221. *Wen xuan* 1 "Xi du fu," pp. 10–11.

222. *Wen xuan* 1 "Xi du fu," pp. 11–14.

223. *Wen xuan* 1 "Dong du fu," pp. 15–17.

224. *Wen xuan* 1, "Dong du fu," p. 15: "The Eastern-Capital Host deeply sighed, 'It is indeed painful how customs can affect people. You are indeed a man of Qin.'"

225. *Wen xuan* 1, "Dong du fu," pp. 18–21.

226. *Wen xuan* 1, "Dong du fu," pp. 22–24.

227. *Zuo zhuan zhu*, Xuan year 3, pp. 669–672. The failure of the First Emperor to retrieve the tripods was depicted both in Han texts and in art. See Wu Hung, *Monumentality*, pp. 4–10, 24, 72–75, 78, 82.

228. Lewis, *Writing and Authority*, pp. 319, 322–323.

229. On the historical significance of establishing the cult of Heaven, see also Marianne Bujard, *Le sacrifice au ciel dans la Chine ancienne: théorie et pratique sous les Han occidentaux* (Paris: Ecole Française d'Extrême-Orient, 2000); Michael J. Puett, *To Become a God: Cosmology, Sacrifice, and Self-Divination in China* (Cambridge: Harvard University, 2002), ch. 8.

230. On the *jue di*, see *Wen xuan* 2, "Xi jing fu," pp. 42–44. On imperial debauchery, see pp. 44–45.

231. *Stories from China's Past*, pp. 64–71, 132–148; Finsterbusch, *Verzeichnis*, #12, 13, 23, 185, 191, 206, 309 (left and right), 363, 508a, 508j, 594, 701, 717, 718, 719a, 720a–b, 730, 731, 786, 793, Nachtrag Shantung 6, Nachtrag Honan 11–12.

232. *Wen xuan* 3 "Dong jing fu," pp. 49–50 (on Western Han emperors), 51–52 (on Luoyang's natural setting), 53–54 (on towers and palaces in Luoyang).

233. *Wen xuan* 3 "Dong jing fu," pp. 55–66.

234. *Wen xuan* 3 "Dong jing fu," pp. 68–70 (on difficulty of rule), 71–72 (on failures of verse).

235. *Wen xuan* 3 "Dong jing fu," p. 67.

236. *Han shu* 99b, p. 4193.

237. Lu Qinli, *Xian Qin Han Wei Jin Nanbaichao shi*, vol. 1, p. 454. On meditations on vanished capitals, see Stephen Owen, *Remembrances: The Experience of the Past in Classical Literature* (Cambridge: Harvard University, 1986), pp. 58–65.

CHAPTER FOUR

1. R. E. Dickinson, *The Regions of Germany* (London: Kegan Paul, Trench, Trubner & Co., 1945), p. 23; Dickinson, *The City Region in Western Europe* (London: Routledge, 1967); Josiah Cox Russell, *Medieval Regions and their Cities* (Bloomington: Indiana University, 1972), ch. 1. On regions and political authority, see Pierre Bourdieu, *Ce que parler veut dire: l'économie des échanges linguistiques* (Paris: Fayard, 1982), ch. 3; Anthony Giddens, "Time, Space, and Regionalisation," in *Social Relations and Spatial Structures*, ed. Derek Gregory and John Urry (London: Macmillan, 1985), pp. 265–295; Allan Pred, "The Social Becomes the Spatial, the Spatial Becomes the Social," *Social Relations and Spatial Structures*, pp. 337–365.

2. Skinner, "Marketing and Social Structures in Rural China," 3 parts, *Journal of Asian Studies* 24.1 (1964), pp. 3–44; 24.2 (1964), pp. 195–228; 24.3 (1965), pp. 363–399; "Regional Urbanization in Nineteenth-Century China," in *The City in Late Imperial China*, ed. G. William Skinner (Stanford: Stanford University, 1977), pp. 211–252; "Cities and the Hierarchy of Local Systems," in *The City in Late Imperial China*, pp. 275–351. On the impact of Skinner's model and a modification of it, see Philip C. C. Huang, *The Peasant Economy and Social Change in North China* (Stanford: Stanford University, 1985), pp. 24–30, 65, 220–240, 244, 246.

3. Lewis, *Writing and Authority in Early China*, pp. 309–313.

4. Lewis, *Sanctioned Violence in Early China*, pp. 215–219.

5. *Han shu* 28b, p. 1640.

6. *Feng su tong yi jiao shi*, p. 1.

7. Lewis, *Writing and Authority in Early China*, ch. 8. See also chapter three.

8. *La coutume et la norme en Chine et au Japon, Extrême-Orient Extrême-Occident* 23 (2001).

9. Lewis, *Writing and Authority*, pp. 358–365.

10. Lewis, *Writing and Authority in Early China*, pp. 63–83.

11. On the *ru* as a broader social category, see Feng Youlan 馮友蘭, *Zhongguo zhexue shi bu* 中國哲學史補 (Shanghai: Shangwu, 1936), pp. 1–61; Hu Shi 胡適, "Shuo ru 說儒," in *Hu Shi lun xue jin zhu* 胡適論學今注, vol. 1 (Shanghai: Shangwu, 1935), pp. 3–81; Robert Eno, *The Confucian Creation of Heaven* (Albany: State University of New York, 1990); Graham, *Disputers of the Tao*, pp. 31–33.

12. *Laozi dao de jing zhu, zhang* 20, p. 11.

13. *Zhuangzi ji shi*, ch. 4, "Ren jian shi 人間世," p. 79; ch. 6, "Da zong shi 大宗師," pp. 122–123; 8 "Pian mu 駢拇," p. 147; ch. 10, "Qu qie 胠篋," pp. 155, 156; ch. 11, "Zai you 在宥," p. 177; ch. 12, "Tian di 天地," pp. 199–200, 201: "customary words" are linked with the stupidity of "villagers" and "the masses"; ch. 17, "Qiu shui 秋水," p. 253: the conduct of the "Great Man" is contrasted with "custom," pp. 257–258; ch. 18, "Zhi le 至樂," p. 270; ch. 20, "Shan mu 山木," p. 295: a ruler is urged to attain the Way by leaving his state and abandoning its customs; ch. 24, "Xu Wugui 徐無鬼," p. 371; ch. 28, "Rang wang," p. 415: contrasts "those who have the Way" with "those who follow custom," p. 418; ch. 29, "Dao Zhi," p. 436: those who "join with custom" are said to "eliminate the most important" and "cast aside the most honored"; ch. 31, "Yu fu 漁父," p. 447: "The sage imitates Heaven, values the True (*zhen*), and is not constrained by custom. Stupid people are the opposite of this. They cannot imitate Heaven, but are concerned only with the human. They are unable to value the True, but being conventional they are altered by custom and thus are never satisfied"; ch. 33, "Tian xia 天下," p. 468.

14. *Zhuangzi ji shi*, ch. 16, "Shan xing 繕性," pp. 242, 247.

15. *Zhuangzi ji shi*, ch. 10, "Qu qie," p. 164; ch. 12, "Tian di," p. 200.

16. *Zhuangzi ji shi*, ch. 10, "Qu qie," pp. 162, 164; ch. 12, "Tian di," p. 193.

17. *Zhuangzi ji shi*, ch. 12, "Tian di," p. 196; ch. 15, "Ke yi 刻意," p. 237; ch. 20, "Shan mu," p. 305; ch. 33, "Tian xia," p. 475.

18. Graham, *Disputers of the Tao*, pp. 244–251; Knoblock, *Xunzi*, vol. 3, pp. 139–150.

19. *Xunzi ji jie*, ch. 4, "Ru xiao," pp. 89–91; ch. 17, "Xing e 性惡," pp. 289, 290.

20. *Xunzi ji jie*, ch. 2, "Rong ru 榮辱," p. 40. See also *Lun heng ji jie*, ch. 29, "Dui zuo," p. 574: "The sages' raising up of the canonical arts and composing of commentaries and records was in order to correct depleted customs, to drive the people to return to the substantial and the sincere."

21. On "chaotic" customs, see also *Xunzi ji jie*, ch. 3, "Fei xiang," p. 48. Elsewhere, damaging customs are described as "treacherous (*jian*)" and "weird (*guai*)." See ch. 17, "Junzi 君子," p. 300.

22. *Xunzi ji jie*, ch. 2, "Bu gou 不苟," p. 31. The adjective "conventional" or "mediocre" (*yong*) that characterizes the man of custom contrasts with knowledge of the classics in ch. 2, "Rong ru," p. 43.

23. *Xunzi ji jie*, ch. 4, "Ru xiao," pp. 91–92. See also ch. 2, "Rong ru," p. 39: "It is like the people of Yue being at ease in Yue, the people of Chu being at ease in Chu, but the gentleman being at ease in the refined [*ya* 雅]. . . . They are divided by their focus on actions and habituation to custom." The character *xia* 夏, translated as "Chinese" in the passage previously cited, was homophonous and interchangeable with the character *ya* in this passage, so the two arguments are virtually identical. "One can be a Yao or a Yu; one can be a Jie or Robber Zhi; one can be a craftsman or carpenter; one can be a farmer or merchant. It depends on the tendencies which they accumulate in focusing on their actions and habituating to their customs."

This idea is closely related to the Mencian doctrine in which social hierarchy is established by the parts of the body to which different individuals give precedence and on which they rely. See *Mengzi zheng yi* IIIA "Teng Wen Gong shang," pp. 318–319; VIA "Gaozi shang," p. 467.

24. *Hou Han shu* 79a, p. 2558. This contrast also appears in Yang Ce's account of the scholars who were barred from holding office in the "Great Proscription" of A.D. 169–184. These men "remained hidden amid the fields, reciting from memory the words of Yao and Shun, and practicing conduct that separated them from custom." See *Hou Han shu* 54, p. 1780. In the *Chun qiu fan lu* "custom" contrasts with the "royal transformation [*wang hua*]" that is achieved by the *Spring and Autumn Annals*. See *Chun qiu fan lu yi zheng*, "Yu xu 俞序," ch. 17, p. 162. Wang Chong uses the contrast to justify his style of writing: "Hoping that people bound by custom would read the text and awaken, I wrote it in a direct style with no hidden meanings, and gathered in many common expressions [*su yan*]. Some might dismiss it as shallow, but I reply, 'If one used the sagely classics to demonstrate things to those of little refinement [*ya*], or used refined language to explain things to [people of] the hills and fields, one would achieve no enlightenment.' " See *Lun heng ji jie*, ch. 30, "Zi ji 自紀," p. 582.

25. *Mengzi zheng yi* IB "Liang Hui wang xia," p. 59; *Xunzi ji jie*, ch. 3, "Fei xiang," p. 48. See note 13 on the *Zhuangzi*'s negative use of *shi su*. See also *Shi ji* 28, p. 1389; 43, p. 1809; 65, p. 2168; 68, p. 2229; 74, p. 2345; 83, p. 2468; 84, p. 2486: this quotes "Yu fu"; 87, p. 2557; 96, p. 2688; 110, p. 2919; 117, p. 3056: this quotes "Da ren fu 大人賦"; 124, p. 3183; 127, p. 3216; 130, p. 3318.

26. *Mengzi zheng yi* IIA "Gongsun Chou shang," p. 105; VIB "Gaozi xia," p. 490; *Xunzi ji jie*, ch. 3, "Fei xiang," p. 48; *Zhuangzi ji shi*, ch. 20, "Shan mu," p. 295.

27. Lewis, *Writing and Authority*, pp. 111–112, 114, 120, 122.

28. *Xunzi ji jie*, ch. 12, "Zheng lun 正論," pp. 214, 215, 218, 219, 224, 225.

29. *Xunzi ji jie*, ch. 15, "Jie bi," p. 260. The reference to "all forms of palace" is of interest in light of the First Emperor's policy of building replicas of the palaces of conquered states and the Han incorporation of diverse regional features into their palaces.

30. There are two nearly identical passage in the *Lü shi chun qiu*. One refers to "being king of all within the seas," while the second substitutes the phrase "correcting divergent customs." This text thus identifies world rulership with the establishment of a body of universal custom. See *Lü shi chun qiu jiao shi*, ch. 13, "Lun da 論大," p. 722; ch. 26, "Wu da 務大," p. 1706. See also ch. 19, "Wei yu 為欲," pp. 1293–1294: the sage kings can follow Heaven, in contrast with the evil kings of antiquity who went against Heaven because they were "immersed in custom"; ch. 20, "Zhao lei 召類," p. 1360. For a discussion of the sage being able to reconcile or correct diverse

customs by transcending the limits of his own sense experience, see ch. 17, "Ren shu 任數," p. 1065. The use of the "Way" to transform customs and unite diverse regions is also described in *Sima fa zhijie*, p. 50b.

31. Sterckx, *The Animal and the Daemon*, pp. 101–122. On the interlinking of people, animals, and landscape during the Shang, see David Keightley, *The Ancestral Landscape: Time, Space, and Community in Late Shang China* (Berkeley: Institute of East Asian Studies, University of California at Berkeley, 2000), pp. 107–113.

32. *Mengzi zheng yi* IIIA "Teng Wen Gong shang," pp. 230–231, 232, 233; IIIB "Teng Wen Gong xia," pp. 264, 271, 272.

33. *Mengzi zheng yi* IVB "Li Lou xia," pp. 317–318.

34. *Mengzi zheng yi* IB "Liang Hui wang xia," p. 90; IIA "Gongsun Chou shang," p. 131.

35. *Xunzi ji jie*, ch. 3, "Fei xiang," p. 53.

36. *Xunzi ji jie*, ch. 17, "Junzi," p. 300.

37. *Xunzi ji jie*, ch. 4, "Ru xiao," pp. 82–83.

38. Ch. 4, "Ru xiao," p. 88 describes the *su ru* as those who invoke the Former Kings to cheat the stupid, but are also "at one with the customs of the age." They are contrasted with the "refined" (*ya*) in the opposition that figured earlier in discussions of music and regional cultures. On the doctrine that the sage is defined by his ability to change, see Mark Edward Lewis, "Les rites comme trame de l'histoire," in *Notions et perceptions du changement en Chine*, ed. Viviane Alleton and Alexei Volkov (Paris: Collège de France, 1994), pp. 29–39.

39. *Xunzi ji jie*, ch. 3, "Fei xiang," p. 48. The notes list editions that use the character *min* 民, rather than *jun* 君. "Custom" and "villages" are also linked in *Zhuangzi ji shi*, ch. 12, "Tian di," p. 201.

40. *Mengzi zheng yi* VIIB "Jin xin xia," pp. 605–606; *Lun yu zheng yi*, ch. 20, "Yang huo," p. 377.

41. *Xunzi ji jie*, ch. 2, "Rong ru," p. 41; ch. 13, "Li lun 禮論," p. 247. These passages use *lou* with the adjectives "stupid (*yu* 愚)" and "blocked (*se* 塞)." See also ch. 2 "Xiu shen 修身," p. 14; ch. 3, "Fei xiang," p. 52.

42. *Xunzi ji jie*, ch. 4, "Ru xiao," p. 88. The final passage from the *Zhuangzi* cited in note 14 also places in parallel the "loss of self in objects" with the "loss of [one's] nature in custom."

43. *Xunzi ji jie*, ch. 1, "Quan xue." The link of study and change is already articulated in *Lun yu*, ch. 1, "Xue er 學而," p. 8: "If he [the gentleman] studies then he will not be fixed or rigid."

44. On the tyranny of the senses and their desire for objects see, *Xunzi jijie* ch. 7, "Wang ba," pp. 137, 141: both passages note that the individual senses are partial, and only the ruler combines them; ch. 11, "Tian lun 天倫," p. 206; ch. 12, "Zheng lun," p. 230; ch. 13, "Li lun," p. 231; ch. 14, "Yue lun 樂論," p. 254; ch. 15, "Jie bi," pp. 263–266. This cites the contrast between ordinary occupations and the ruler in their different relation to objects.

45. *Xunzi ji jie*, ch. 1, "Xiu shen," p. 16; *Guanzi jiao zheng*, ch. 16, "Nei ye," p. 270: "The gentleman commands things; he is not commanded by things"; *Zhuangzi ji shi*, ch. 7, "Ying di wang," p. 138: "The ultimate man uses his mind like a mirror. He

does not see off or welcome; he responds without storing. Therefore he can conquer things and not be harmed"; ch. 20, "Shan mu," p. 293: "Floating and wandering through the ancestor of the myriad things, treating things as things and not being turned into a thing by things, then what would be able to bind you?" *Jing fa*, p. 88.

46. *Lü shi chun qiu jiao shi*, ch. 26, "Shi rong 士容," p. 1689.

47. *Lü shi chun qiu jiao shi*, ch. 1, "Ben sheng," p. 20: "People's nature is to be longlived, but things encumber them, so they are unable to live long. Things are the means to nourish life; they are not that which is nourished with one's life." ch. 2, "Gui sheng," p. 75: "Now the 'gentlemen' controlled by custom in the present age endanger themselves and abandon their lives to pursue objects."

48. *Lü shi chun qiu jiao shi*, ch. 2, "Qing yu 情欲," p. 85: "The ruler controlled by custom harms his essential nature. . . . His ears cannot be satisfied; his eyes cannot be satiated; his mouth cannot be filled"; ch. 10, "Jie sang 節喪," p. 525: "Now disordered rulers controlled by custom in the present age make their burials excessively lavish"; "Yi bao 異寶," p. 551: "As for this state, its terrain is difficult and its people cunning. Its ruler is controlled by custom. He is not worthy of joining with for any action;" ch. 13, "Wu ben 務本," p. 714: the advisers of the *su zhu* are contrasted with those of the sage kings because the former are partial and limited, interested only in themselves and their family. See also ch. 26, "Wu da," p. 1705. Ch. 15, "Shun shui 順説," p. 906; ch. 17, "Zhi du 知度," p. 1094; ch. 19, "Wei yu," p. 1294. In a brief span in the final chapter of *Lun heng* Wang Chong uses *su* as a term of contempt for "talents," "innate nature," "people," and "true nature." He defines his writings as a "text to attack custom." See *Lun heng ji jie* 30 "Zi ji 自紀," pp. 580 (2), 582 (2), 583, 585.

49. *Hou Han shu* 3, pp. 133, 148, 155. See also *Hou Han shu* 43, pp. 1460: Emperor Zhang praises an official of integrity, and contrasts him with the *su li*, p. 1468.

50. *Lü shi chun qiu jiao shi*, ch. 10, "Yi bao," p. 551; ch. 12, "Jie li," p. 618; ch. 13, "Qu you 去尤," p. 689; ch. 14, "Bi ji 必己," p. 829; ch. 15, "Xia xian 下賢," p. 878; ch. 16, "Guan shi 觀世," p. 958; ch. 17, "Jun shou 君守," p. 1050; ch. 19, "Gao yi 高義," p. 1245; ch. 24, "Zan neng 贊能," p. 1592; ch. 24, "Bo zhi 博志," p. 1618.

51. See *Wuzi zhi jie* 吳子直解, annotated by Liu Yin, *Ming ben wu jing qi shu*, vol. 1, ch. 2 "Liao di 料敵," pp. 17a–20a. The link of "nature" and "custom" also appears in *Sima fa zhi jie*, p. 50b.

52. Anne Behnke Kinney, "Dyed Silk: Han Notions of the Moral Development of Children," in *Chinese Views of Childhood*, ed. Kinney (Honolulu: University of Hawai'i, 1995), pp. 20, 27–32; Kinney, *Representations of Childhood and Youth in Early China* (Stanford: Stanford University, 2004), ch. 6, (see "Works Cited").

53. Jia Yi's essays on fetal instruction and the education of the heir apparent survive in three versions: as chapters in the *Xin shu*—see *Jiazi Xin shu jiao shi*, pp. 583–630, 1115–1165; as a chapter in the *Da Dai li ji*—see *Da Dai li ji jie gu* 48 "Bao fu 保傅," pp. 49–67; and in Jia Yi's biography in the *Han shu*—see *Han shu*, pp. 2248–2252. See also *Han shi wai zhuan ji shi*, ch. 9, p. 306, which attributes a brief discussion of fetal education to Mencius's mother. The idea also figures in a manual discovered at Mawangdui, and in Liu Xiang's *Lie nü zhuan*.

54. *Jiazi xin shu*, pp. 586–587. On the identity of human nature, see pp. 583, 621, 626, 1138.

55. *Jiazi xin shu*, pp. 584, 593–594, 597, 608–609, 615–616, 1121, 1126–1127, 1132. See also pp. 1138–1139, 1148, 1157.

56. *Jiazi xin shu*, pp. 1115, 1121.

57. *Jiazi xin shu*, pp. 621, 626. Linking the brutality of Qin law and the dynasty's failure to "custom" is a regular topos in Han writing. On the difference between the Chinese and the barbarians as one based on custom see also the "Wang zhi" chapter of the *Li ji*: "Whenever giving people a place and the material goods to live, you must accord with the warmth and humidity of Heaven and Earth. The bodies of those dwelling in broad valleys or at the edge of great rivers differ, and the customs of those dwelling there are also distinct. Their firmness or softness, lightness or heaviness, slowness or speed are all different. They mix the flavors differently, manufacture different types of implements, and wear different clothing. One cultivates their education without altering their customs, and equalizes their government without changing their local products. The middle kingdom and the barbarians are the people of the five regions. They all have a human nature which cannot be changed. Those in the east are called Yi. They leave their hair loose and tattoo their bodies. Some eat raw food. Those in the south are called Man. They tattoo their foreheads and cross their legs. Some eat raw food. Those in the west are called Rong. They leave their hair loose and wear animal hides. Some do not eat grains. Those in the north are called Di. They wear feathers and furs, and dwell in caves. Some do not eat grains. All these peoples have dwellings that suit them, seasoned foods, suitable clothing, implements that meet their needs. Nevertheless, their languages are mutually unintelligible and their tastes and desires are different." See *Li ji zhu shu*, ch. 12, pp. 26a–27a.

58. *Wuzi zhi jie*, ch. 2, "Liao di," pp. 19a–b. See *Guanzi jiao zheng*, ch. 14, "Shui di 水地," pp. 237–238.

59. *Xunzi ji jie*, ch. 10, "Yi bing," p. 181.

60. Lewis, "Custom and Nature in Early China," *Philosophy East and West* 53:3 (July 2003).

61. *Shang Jun shu zhu yi*, ch. 1, "Geng fa 更法," pp. 5, 10.

62. *Shang Jun shu zhu yi*, ch. 3, "Nong zhan 農戰," p. 83; ch. 7, "Kai se 開塞," p. 194; ch. 13, "Jin ling 靳令," p. 277; ch. 25, "Shen fa 慎法," p. 518.

63. *Shang Jun shu zhu yi*, ch. 8, "Yi yan 壹言," pp. 205–206; ch. 11, "Li ben 立本," p. 248.

64. *Shang Jun shu zhu yi*, ch. 6, "Suan di 算地," p. 170; ch. 8, "Yi yan," p. 215.

65. *Han Feizi ji shi*, ch. 14, "He shi 和氏," pp. 238–239.

66. *Han Feizi ji shi*, ch. 4, "Jian jie shi chen," p. 247; ch. 9, "Nei chu shuo shang 內儲說上," p. 533.

67. *Han Feizi ji shi*, ch. 7, "Yu lao 喻老," p. 390; *Huainanzi*, ch. 18, "Ren jian 人間," p. 306.

68. *Shuihudi Qin mu zhu jian*, p. 15.

69. Steven F. Sage, *Ancient Sichuan and the Unification of China* (Albany: State University of New York, 1992), ch. 5, "Sichuan's Century under Qin." The use of written laws to change local practice is exemplified by a text found in the tomb of a Qin official that dictates the imposition of a Qin-style grid on the fields of the recently conquered state of Shu. See Sichuan Sheng Bowuguan 四川省博物館, "Qingchuan xian chutu Qin geng xiu tian lü mu du 青川縣出土秦更修田律木牘," *Wenwu* 1982 (1), pp. 1–21; Li Zhaohe 李昭和, "Qingchuan xian chutu mu du wenzi jian kao 青川縣出土木牘文字簡考," *Wenwu* 1982 (1), pp. 24–27; Yu Haoliang 于豪亮, "Shi Qingchuan Qin mu mu du 釋青川秦墓木牘," *Wenwu* 1982 (1), pp. 22–24.

70. *Han shu* 64b, p. 2821.

71. *Shi ji* 6, p. 277.

72. *Shi ji* 6, p. 278.

73. *Jiazi xin shu jiao shi*, pp. 303, 315, 317. For another version, see *Han shu* 48, p. 2244.

74. *Huainanzi*, ch. 21, "Yao lüe," p. 376.

75. *Shi ji* 15, p. 685.

76. *Shi ji* 122, p. 3149.

77. *Shi ji* 68, p. 2234.

78. *Han shu* 56, pp. 2510–2511.

79. Several other Western Han writers touch on this topos. Under Emperor Jing, Zou Yang argued that Zhou had flourished and Qin perished because the former had brought in advisers from distant regions while Qin was trapped in its own local practices and did not listen to "advice from outside the region." (This argument is historically wrong, but it extends the discourse on Qin previously discussed.) See *Han shu* 51, p. 2351. Mei Cheng stated that Qin had conquered because of its geographic setting, and that Han was now based in the same region. See *Han shu* 51, p. 2362. Lu Wenshu argued that Han law was still under the influence of Qin's customs. He also gives a variant of Jia Yi's remarks about Qin's taboo on criticism. See *Han shu* 51, pp. 2369–2370.

80. *Hou Han shu* 41, p. 1400. On the links between Qin and Wang Mang, see also *Han shu* 99b, p. 4154. "Clerks dominated by custom" as a negative category, without special reference to Qin, also appears in *Hou Han shu* 3, pp. 133, 148.

81. *Han shu* 30, pp. 1097, 1112.

82. Qin's customs also figure in Ban Gu's "Two Capitals Rhapsody." After the Western Capital guest has completed his praise of Chang'an—in the Qin capital region—the Eastern Capital host replies, "How grievous is custom's influence on people. You are truly a man of Qin." See *Wen xuan* 1, p. 15.

83. One passage in the *Xunzi* links "custom" not with laws but criminality. "The masses of the common people will have no treacherous, abnormal customs, and thus no crimes of banditry or robbery." See *Xunzi ji jie*, ch. 17, "Junzi," pp. 300–301.

84. *Xunzi ji jie*, ch. 5, "Wang zhi," pp. 102–103; ch. 15, "Jie bi," p. 260; ch. 12, "Zheng lun," pp. 219–220.

85. *Shi ji* 129, pp. 3261–3270, esp. pp. 3264, 3266. See a related passage in *Han shu* 28b, pp. 1640–1671.

86. *Shi ji* 6, pp. 282–283.

87. *Shi ji* 6, p. 281; 129, p. 3267. See also *Han shu* 28b, p. 1663: "[Lu's] customs are stingy and fond of wealth, so they hasten to be merchants. They love slander and are often cunning and deceitful. Their rituals of mourning and sacrifice are complete in their form but lacking in substance. However, their love of learning is still greater than that in the customs of other regions." The use of the term "diverse customs" to indicate all the regions of the empire also appears in *Hou Han shu* 4, p. 167.

88. *Han shu* 64b, p. 2818.

89. The people of Zhong and Dai, whose customs had intermingled with those of the Xiongnu, were proud and stubborn, prone to violence, acted as bravoes/gang-

sters, and engaged in neither agriculture nor trade. Since the eighth century they caused trouble, and King Wuling's introduction of cavalry and barbarian attire had made things worse. The people of Zhongshan, under the influence of the evil King Zhou, were impetuous and looked for opportunities for easy profit. They were given to games, singing, and dancing. They often engaged in banditry and grave robbing. The women learned to perform music and became prostitutes or concubines. The people of Yan, which bordered on the Xiongnu, were fierce and little given to reflection. The people of Linzi were adept at single combat and prone to become highway robbers. The people of Western Chu were volatile and prone to anger. Those of Southern Chu were similar, but their customs had mixed with those of the Min and Yue, so they tended to be glib and untrustworthy. Although the customs of Nanyang and Yingchuan were basically good due to the influence of the Xia kings, Qin had deported many criminals to the region, so they had a tendency toward meddling and acting as bravoes/gangsters. *Shi ji* 129, pp. 3263, 3265, 3267–3268.

90. *Hou Han shu* 3, p. 155.

91. The *Guliang zhuan* contrasts "the Way of the ancients" employed by Confucius and Lu, with "the customs of the barbarians" used by Qi. See *Guliang zhuan zhu shu*, ch. 19, Ding year 10, p. 13a.

92. *Han shu* 76, p. 3210. Linking songs and customs here refers to the idea that officials collected local music as an indication of the moral condition of the people, a practice that in Han times was presumed to have led to the collection of the Zhou odes. See Jean-Pierre Diény, *Aux origines de la poésie classique en Chine: étude de la poésie lyrique à l'époque des Han* (Leiden: E. J. Brill, 1968), ch. 1.

93. Ch'ü, *Han Social Structure*, pp. 160–247. Translations from primary sources appear on pp. 393–506. The most valuable Japanese study remains Utsunomiya, *Kan dai shakai keizai shi kenkyū*, ch. 9–11. The classic articles by Yang Liansheng [Yang Lien-sheng] and He Changqun [Ho Ch'ang-ch'ün], cited in Ch'ü's work, also remain useful.

94. Lewis, *Sanctioned Violence*, ch. 2; Nishijima, *Chūgoku kodai teikoku no keisei to kōzō—nijū tō shakusei no kenkyū.*

95. Lewis, "Warring States Political History," pp. 593–597.

96. Yan Gengwang 嚴耕望, *Zhongguo difang xingzheng zhidu shi*, vol. 1, *Qin Han difang xingzheng zhidu* 中國地方行政制度史：秦漢地方行政制度 (Taipei: Zhongyang Yanjiuyuan Lishi Yuyan Yanjiusuo Zhuankan 45, 1974), pp. 37–38.

97. *Han shu* 64a, p. 2802; *Jiazi xin shu* 1 "Fan qiang 藩強," pp. 117–123; 2 "Wu mei 五美," pp. 195–207; *Han shu* 48, p. 2237.

98. Matsumoto Yoshimi 松木善海, *Chūgoku sonraku seido no shiteki kenkyū* 中國村落制度の史的研究 (Tokyo: Iwanami Shoten, 1977), part 1.

99. Yan, *Zhongguo difang xingzheng*, vol. 1, pp. 345–359. See the table on pp. 359–382. On the documents from Donghai Commandery, see Li Jiemin 李解民, "'Donghai jun xia xia zhangli ming ji' yanjiu 東海郡下轄長吏名藉研究," in *Yinwan Han mu jian du zong lun* 尹灣漢墓簡牘綜論, ed. Lianyungang Shi Bowuguan 連雲港市博物館 and Zhongguo Wenwu Yanjiusuo 中國文物研究所 (Beijing: Kexue, 1999), pp. 46–75, esp. pp. 55–57; Lai Mingchiu [Li Mingjian] 黎明劍, "Xi Han zhongqi zhi 'San lao' yu haoqiang 西漢中期之三老與豪彊," *Xin shi xue* 8:2 (1997), pp. 59–91; Lai, "Han dai difang guanliao jiegou: Jun gong cao zhi zhizhang yu Yinwan Han mu jiandu zhi guanxi 漢代地方官僚結構：郡功曹之職掌與尹彎漢墓簡牘之關

係," *Zhongguo Wenhua Yanjiusuo xue bao* 8 (1999), pp. 35–72; Lai, "Han dai Donghai jun de hao zu da xing: yi 'Donghai jun xia xia zhang li ming ji' ji 'Zeng qian ming ji' wei zhong xin 漢代東海郡的豪族大姓：以 "東海郡下轄長吏名籍" 及 "贈錢名籍" 為中心," *Zhongguo Wenhua Yanjiusuo xue bao* 9 (2000), pp. 47–96.

100. *Shuihudi Qin mu zhu jian*, pp. 30, 30–32, 35–38, 60–61, 76–80, 84–87, 98–99, 99–100, 123, 125, 125–126, 143–144, 144–145, 152–153, 154, 163–164, 173, 178, 183, 184, 185, 186, 187, 188, 189, 193–194, 194–195, 195, 197–198, 213–214, 214, 218, 219, 221–222, 223, 224, 225, 231, 237, 249–250, 263–264, 267–270. On the *sefu* in the Han, see Ōba Osamu 大庭脩, "Kan no shokufu 漢の嗇夫," in *Shin kan hōseishi no kenkyū* 秦漢法制史の研究 (Tokyo: Sōbunsha, 1982), pp. 497–523.

101. *Lun heng ji jie*, ch. 27, "Ding xian 定賢," p. 543; *Hou Han shu* 52, p. 1722: "[Cui Yuan's] family was poor, so the brothers lived together for several decades." Utsunomiya cites the family of Gaozu's father, which had around ten people on a single property, but hardly any kin elsewhere. See *Kandai shakai keizai shi*, p. 435 n. 64.

102. *Wei lüe* 魏略, quoted in *San guo zhi* 15, p. 473: Zhang Ji, although his family was rich, could not go beyond appointment as a menial clerk because his ancestors for generations were a "lone family" and a "cold gate"; *Sanfu jue lu* 三輔決錄, in *Guanzhong cong shu* 關中叢書, compiled by Song Liankui 宋聯奎 (reprint of 1934 edition, Taipei: Yiwen, 1970), ch. 2, p. 19b: Wang Bao came from a "lone gate"; *Dian lüe* 典略, quoted in *Hou Han shu ji jie* 集解, annotated by Wang Xianqian 王先謙 (Taipei: Yiwen, 1956), ch. 53, p. 4a: Huang Xian's family was "orphaned and provincial"; *Hou Han shu* 80b, p. 2649: Gao Biao's family was "originally lone and cold"; 62, p. 2065: Chen Shi's family was "lone and obscure"; 53, p. 1743: Zhou Liang's family was "orphaned and obscure"; *San guo zhi* 11, p. 357: here "orphaned and obscure" is a humble self-description; *Lun Heng ji jie*, ch. 30 "Zi ji 自紀," p. 590: Wang Chong's family was a "petty lineage, an orphaned gate"; *Hou Han shu* 81, p. 2689: a man who "goes against the times and cuts himself off from custom" lives isolated in a thatched hut and is described as "lone and boorish (*dan lou* 單陋)." On the later application of these terms to less eminent, although often wealthy families, see Tang Zhangru 唐長孺, "Nanchao han ren de xingqi 南朝寒人的興起," in *Wei Jin Nanbeichao shi luncong xu bian* 魏晉南北朝史論叢續編 (Beijing: San lian, 1959), pp. 93–123. Similar terms are used in parts of contemporary China to describe families that lack networks of friends and kin. Thus in Xiajia in Heilongjiang, families that lack such networks are described as "isolated-door small households (*du men xiao hu* 獨門小戶)" or "dead doors (*si menzi* 死門子)." The description of people or households without networks as "dead" is also used in other parts of China. See Yunxiang Yan, *The Flow of Gifts: Reciprocity and Social Networks in a Chinese Village* (Stanford: Stanford University, 1996), pp. 38, 103.

103. *Yan tie lun*, p. 118.

104. See *Hou Han shu* chapters 81 and 83, the collective biographies of those whose unique conduct set them apart or who withdrew from the world. See also 41, p. 1395. There are also phrases such as "had no dealings with human affairs." See *Hou Han shu* 63, p. 2078; 83, p. 2774; *Dong guan Han ji jiao zhu*, ch. 10, p. 379; ch. 18, p. 804. For criticisms of such behavior, see *Hou Han shu* 43, p. 1459; 62, p. 2069; 81, p. 2665. On Han eremitism, see Aat Vervoorn, *Men of the Cliffs and Caves: The Development of the Chinese Eremitic Tradition at the End of the Han Dynasty* (Hong Kong: The Chinese

University, 1990); Alan J. Berkowitz, *Patterns of Disengagement: The Practice and Portrayal of Reclusion in Early Medieval China* (Stanford: Stanford University, 2000), ch. 1–3. Note 1 on p. 101 lists the major Japanese scholarship on Han eremitism.

105. *Hou Han shu* 27, p. 931 (3). Cai Yong argued that in antiquity links were based on "oaths that were trustworthy and solid." See *Hou Han shu* 43, p. 1474, note 2. The use of these terms to indicate a formal relation also appears in *Hou Han shu* 32, p. 1122; 81, p. 2692.

106. *Han shu* 71, p. 3036: Liu Ze links up with (*jiao jie*) the powerful clans of the commanderies and starts to plan a rebellion; *Hou Han shu* 11, p. 467: Liu Xuan links up with a retainer (*jie ke*) to avenge a murdered brother; 15, p. 574: Li Tong forms an alliance with Liu Xiu against Wang Mang; 20, p. 738: Ji Zun links up with a retainer to kill government clerks who damaged his mother's tomb mound; 21, p. 760; 31, pp. 1102, 1114; 34, p. 1169: bandits from three regions traverse rivers and cross commanderies "to link up across ten thousand *li*"; p. 1175: Liang Shang attempts to "link as friends (*jie you*)" with leading eunuchs; 67, p. 2187: Li Ying is accused of forming links (*jiao jie*) with the students at the Imperial Academy to establish a clique (*bu dang* 部黨).

107. *Han shu* 83, p. 3398; *Hou Han shu* 14, p. 556; 32, p. 1130; 42, pp. 1428, 1431; 76, p. 2468. On p. 1427 in chapter 42 the verb employed is *li* 禮 "to treat with proper ritual."

108. *Han shu* 45, p. 2163; *Hou Han shu* 43, p. 1459; 53, p. 2073: Li Gu travels great distances to seek out teachers and thus "establishes links with heroic worthies"; 67, p. 2201–2202: Xia Fu rejects all contact with the powerful lineages in his commandery; *Chu guo xian xian zhuan* 楚國先賢傳, quoted in *Hou Han shu* 63, p. 2089: Dong Ban had "no contact with those not of his kind (*bu jiao fei lei* 不交非類)"; *Dong guan Han ji jiao zhu*, ch. 15, p. 598: Liu Shang's "brilliance and trustworthiness linked him to the party of his friends"; *San guo zhi* 37, p. 953: one forms a "profound alliance" on the basis of a shared appreciation of true scholars.

109. *Shi ji* 107, p. 2847; *Hou Han shu* 18, p. 675; 67, p. 2187: the diviner Zhang Cheng "by means of his arts established communication with the eunuchs" to gain the emperor's ear; p. 2217: wherever he travelled, He Yong formed intimate ties (*qin* 親) with the powerful lineages.

110. *Hou Han shu* 14, p. 549; 41, p. 1398. See also 52, p. 1732; 80b, p. 2627.

111. *Hou Han shu* 43, pp. 1467–1468, note 1. The distinction between proper associations based on public spirit and corrupt ones based on selfish interest also figures in *Lun heng ji jie*, ch. 27, "Ding xian," p. 537.

112. *Hou Han shu* 43, pp. 1474–1475, note 2.

113. *Hou Han shu, zhi* 28, pp. 3625–3626, quoting the *Tai Gong yin fu* (太公陰符); *Hou Han shu* 41, pp. 1398–1399.

114. *Shi ji* 8, pp. 344–345. Zhuo Wangsun's friends tried to reconcile him to his daughter's elopement by pointing out Sima Xiangru's talents and contacts with officials. See *Shi ji* 117, pp. 3000–3001.

115. *Han shu* 71, p. 3038; 76, p. 3199: major surnames of Yingchuan intermarry; 89, p. 3635: a rising official marries a shaman's daughter, due to her physiognomy; 99c, pp. 4180–4181: a rebel against Wang Mang mobilizes both his own lineage and relatives by marriage; *Hou Han shu* 14, p. 561; 15, p. 575; 26, p. 909; 28b, p. 1003; 60a,

p. 1953; 81, p. 2676, 83, p. 2766; 84, pp. 2781, 2796, 2798; *Dong guan Han ji jiao zhu*, ch. 7, p. 230; ch. 13, p. 471; *Sanfu jue lu*, ch. 1, p. 5b; 2, p. 10b; *Dian lüe* quoted in *San guo zhi* 10, p. 309; *San guo zhi* 11, pp. 336–337; *Dian lüe*, quoted in *San guo zhi* 36, p. 946.

116. David Wakefield, *Fenjia: Household Division and Inheritance in Qing and Republican China* (Honolulu: University of Hawai'i, 1998); Yan, *The Flow of Gifts*, pp. 39–42, 109, 115–119, 178–209, esp. p. 196; Andrew B. Kipnis, *Producing Guanxi: Sentiment, Self, and Subculture in a North China Village* (Durham: Duke University, 1997), pp. 87–90, 99, 138.

117. Ma, *Mawangdui gu yi shu kaoshi*, p. 1008; Harper, *Early Chinese Medical Literature*, p. 423. Quarrels between mothers-in-law and daughters-in-law were also cited in the passage on Qin from Jia Yi quoted earlier.

118. Ebrey, "Early Stages," pp. 18–29; Donald Holzman, "The Cold Food Festival in Early Medieval China," *Harvard Journal of Asiatic Studies* 46:1 (1986), pp. 51–79; Wu, *The Wu Liang Shrine*, pp. 30–37. The Han patriline was sufficiently undeveloped, in cultic terms, that lineages would sometimes leave their ancestral tombs attended by only a single household. See *Han shu* 73, p. 3107; *Sanfu jue lu* 2, p. 6a.

119. *Hou Han shu* 32, pp. 1119–1120. The largest estates in Han texts are 4,500 hectares. In his study of the Nanyang region, which Chinese sources treat as the leading region for large-scale landlordism, Utsunomiya has shown that the major estates were a few hundred *qing*, that is, 1,200–1,600 hectares. See *Shi ji* 122, p. 3135; *Hou Han shu* 42, p. 1431; Utsunomiya, *Kandai shakai keizai shi kenkyū*, pp. 384–395. On the size of *latifundia* in imperial Rome and estates in the golden age of the manorial economy, see A. H. M. Jones, *The Later Roman Empire, 284–602: A Social, Economic and Administrative Survey* (Norman: University of Oklahoma, 1964), pp. 782–785; B. H. Slicker van Bath, *The Agrarian History of Western Europe*, A.D. *500–1850* (London: Edward Arnold, 1963), pp. 42–43; Georges Duby, *Rural Economy and Country Life in the Medieval West*, tr. Cynthia Postan (London: Edward Arnold, 1968), pp. 34–35. These indicate that a large Roman estate could have been about 30,000 hectares, while large monastic and lay estates varied between 10,000 and 35,000 hectares.

120. *Hou Han shu* 8, p. 330; 67, p. 2189. On punishments reaching to the *wu shu*, *jiu zu*, *zong zu*, and clients, see cases listed in Makino Tatsumi, *Chūgoku kazoku kenkyū*, pp. 189–216.

121. *Hou Han shu*, *zhi* 10, p. 3221; 48, pp. 1598–1599. On the similar reach of collective responsibility and mutual implication in the actions of the "cruel clerks" under Emperor Wu, see *Han shu* 60, p. 2660.

122. *Shi ji* 107, p. 2847; *Han shu* 66, p. 2879; 84, p. 3416; 99c, pp. 1480–1481; *Hou Han shu* 21, p. 762; *San guo zhi* 16, p. 489.

123. *Hou Han shu* 21, pp. 760, 762 (2); 31, p. 1093; 32, p. 1129; 62, p. 2049; 76, pp. 2481–2482; *Si min yue ling ji shi*, pp. 1, 109. On modern New Year greetings to widening circles of kin and friends, see Kipnis, *Producing Guanxi*, p. 33.

124. *Hou Han shu* 15, pp. 573–575; 32, p. 1129. On *men zong* as more distant kin who are not members of the same household, see *Hou Han shu* 81, p. 2692. Two other lists linking patriline and village occur in *Hou Han shu* 43, p. 1459. Those among whom Zhu Hui divided his wealth during a famine are the "starving among his patriline, village, and old acquaintances." Following this act of generosity the "village and

lineage all submitted to him." On "old acquaintances" (*gu jiu* or *jiu gu*) as a category, see *Hou Han shu Hou* 25, p. 869; 43, p. 1457. *Han shu* 21, p. 792 lists "patriline and retainers." *Hou Han shu* 81, pp. 2690, 2696, lists "villagers and patriline" and "villagers and lineage." Liao Fu "knew in advance which years would have calamitous harvests, so he gathered large amounts of grain which he gave to members of his patriline and relatives by marriage. He also collected and buried those who perished in plagues and who could not be gathered in by their own people." Again the charity moves outward from blood kin, through relatives by marriage, to the community at large. See *Hou Han shu* 81a, p. 2720. On the continued importance of such radiating circles of kin and allies in contemporary rural China, see Yan, *The Flow of Gifts*, pp. 99–102, 108–109; Kipnis, *Producing Guanxi*, pp. 80–81.

125. Ch'ü, *Han Social Structure*, pp. 161–165, 393–394, 403–407, 410–413, 419–420.

126. *Han shu* 28b, pp. 1642–1643, 1645, 1647, 1651, 1655, 1656, 1661, 1665. See also *Han shu* 10, pp. 324–325; 76, pp. 3200, 3206, 3210; 90, p. 3669; *Hou Han shu* 2, p. 115; 3, p. 134; 5, p. 207; 41, p. 1398; 51, pp. 1689, 1692; 64, pp. 2103–2104; 67, p. 2214; 77, p. 2492; *San guo zhi* 13, p. 421; *Taiping huan yu ji* 太平寰宇記 (n.p.: Hongxing Shan fang, 1803) ch. 25, pp. 5b–6a. Most districts discussed in the *Huayang guo zhi* list their major surnames or lineages. See Chang Qu 常璩 *Huayang guo zhi jiao zhu* 華陽國志校注 (Chengdu: Ba Shu shu she, 1984), pp. 65, 66, 67, 69, 78, 83, 93, 94, 95, 100, so on.)

127. *Han shu* 90, p. 3647. Another account of the same lineage treats them as a type of *you xia* or gangster. See *Han shu* 92, p. 3700. See also *Shi ji* 122, p. 3133.

128. *Hou Han shu* 33, p. 1155, note 2 quotes Xie Cheng's history. Even if the attribution of such a decree to Emperor Wu is incorrect, it shows that, by the Eastern Han, writers recognized that having households live close together was a basis of the power of the major surnames or lineages.

129. *Hou Han shu* 70, p. 2281. A later account speaks of another patriline with three hundred families. See *San guo zhi* 11, p. 343. Moreover, where people number in the hundreds it is clear that many households were involved. See, for example, *Hou Han shu* 31, p. 1114; *San guo zhi* 36, p. 947.

130. *Shi ji* 117, pp. 3000–3001.

131. *Shi ji* 129, pp. 3277–3280; *Han shu* 66, p. 2883. The Tian were divided into so many households that they are called "the various Tian (*zhu tian* 諸田)." On the significance of this usage see the commentary of Yan Shigu in *Han shu* 43, p. 2124; 92, p. 3700.

132. *Han shu* 1b, p. 66; 90, p. 3668: a Gao lineage is divided into eastern and western branches whose retainers acted as bandits; *Shi ji* 8, p. 386; 99, p. 2720; 122, p. 3145 (3); 124, pp. 3184 (2), 3188 (2), 3189 (2). One of these lineages may be related to the merchant Kong Jin who helped establish the salt and iron monopolies. See *Hou Han shu* 41, pp. 1398–1399 (3); 60b, p. 1972; 67, p. 2201; 83, p. 2766; *Sanfu jue lu*, ch. 2, pp. 7a–8a, 10b.

133. Ebrey, "The Economic and Social History of the Later Han," in *The Cambridge History of China, Vol. 1: The Ch'in and Han Empires*, ed. Denis Twitchett and Michael Loewe (Cambridge: Cambridge University, 1986), pp. 637–640; Ebrey, "Later Han Stone Inscriptions," *Harvard Journal of Asiatic Studies* 40:2 (1980), pp. 325–353.

134. In contemporary China social networks enable limited opposition to the state's formal authority. See Kipnis, *Producing Guanxi*, pp. 78–79, 149–153, ch. 9; Mayfair Mei-hui Yang, *Gifts, Favors, and Banquets* (Ithaca: Cornell University, 1994), ch. 5, 7, 8; Yan, *The Flow of Gifts*, pp. 96–97.

135. *Han shu* 76, pp. 3200, 3210; 83, p. 3402; 100a, p. 4199; *Hou Han shu* 18, p. 680: a rebellion by an alliance of five leading surnames of a district; 21, pp. 755, 761; 26, p. 912; 31, p. 1100; 32, p. 1119; 51, p. 1692; 62, p. 2064; 67, pp. 2201–2202: two lineages that control a commandery, 2214; 76, p. 2463; 77, p. 2492; *Dong guan Han ji jiao zhu*, ch. 1, p. 2; *San guo zhi* 13, p. 421.

136. On Qin *fu lao*, see *Shuihudi Qin mu zhu jian*, pp. 143, 193, 230. On Han, see *Shi ji* 8, p. 362: a bond with Gaozu to establish Han law; *Han shu* 24a, p. 1139: receiving tools produced in state workshops and disseminating new techniques; 40, p. 2039: supervising the local altar of the soil; 71, p. 3046: supervising repairs of the village gate; 89, p. 3629: assisting in charity organized by local officials and supervising the squads of five. For modern studies, see Moriya Mitsuo 守屋美都雄, "Furō 父老," *Tōyōshi kenkyū* 14 (1955), pp. 43–60; Xing Yitian 邢義田, "Han dai de Fulao Dan yu ju zu li ju—'Han Shiyan li Fulao Dan mai tian yueshu shi quan duji 漢代的父老與聚族里居—漢侍延里父老僤買田約束石券讀記," *Hanxue yanjiu* 1:2 (December 1983), pp. 355–377; Lai, "Xi Han zhong qi zhi san lao yu haoqiang, pp. 59–91.

137. *Han shu* 45, p. 2166; *Hou Han shu* 43, p. 1457.

138. *Lun heng ji jie*, ch. 7, "Yu zeng 語增," p. 164.

139. *Han shu* 71, p. 3040. See also *Dong guan Han ji jiao zhu*, ch. 15, pp. 598–599: "Much accumulation increases losses and is a burden to one's descendants"; *Hou Han shu* 82a, pp. 2720–2721. For lists joining villagers and patriline as a group, and sometimes including retainers or dependants, see *Han shu* 21, p. 792; *Hou Han shu* 41, p. 1395; 81, pp. 2690, 2696; *San guo zhi* 11, p. 341.

140. Okazaki Fumio 岡崎文夫, *Gi Kin Nambokuchō tsū shi* (Tokyo: Heibonsha, 1989), pp. 426–427.

141. *Shi ji* 129, pp. 3271–3272: "If you are to live in a place for one year, seed it with grain. If for ten years, plant it with trees. If for one hundred years, cause people to come through virtue/generosity [*de*]. *De* means being a local eminence. Now there are men who have no rank or salary from the government, nor any noble title with income from towns, yet their enjoyments are equal to those who do. They are called the 'untitled nobility'."

142. James Scott, *The Moral Economy of the Peasant* (New Haven: Yale University, 1976), ch. 6.

143. Landlords may have profitably assisted the work of their tenants by loaning oxen and expensive tools such as high-quality ploughs and seeders. Such actions, however, would have simply substituted for the role of the state as demonstrated in the Shuihudi documents. See *Shuihudi Qin mu zhu jian*, pp. 30–31, 33, 60, 81.

144. This idea is accepted as a fundamental premise in Sima Qian's exposition of the social roles of wealth and trade. It is the power of wealth to attract men, to guide their actions, and to cause them to serve the rich that makes it a value both to society as a whole and to those who can accumulate it. See *Shi ji* 129, pp. 3271–3274. It is also this power that makes it feared by the imperial order. The one modern scholar who has suggested that the strategy of the great Han lineages was to increase

social networks and local influence, rather than to accumulate wealth and land for their households, was Moriya Mitsuo. See Moriya, "Kan no Kōso shūdan no seikaku ni tsuite 漢の高祖集團の性格について," in *Chūgoku kodai no kazoku to kokka* 中國古代の家族と國家 (Kyoto: Tōyōshi Kenkyūkai, 1986), pp. 177–182.

145. *Hou Han shu* 27, pp. 930–931. *Xia* and conspicuous generosity are also linked in *Hou Han shu* 83, p. 2773.

146. *Sanfu jue lu*, ch. 1, p. 5a: a man shared his fortune among his patriline, beginning with the poorest; pp. 8a–b: a man who expended all his wealth supporting a wastrel nephew was rewarded by the emperor; *Hou Han shu* 18, p. 683: Wu Han's wife accumulated land while he was on campaign, but he distributed it among his brothers and his wife's family; 26, p. 920: an official distributed his salary and gifts from the ruler among his patriline, so that his own household had no wealth; 31, p. 1093; 34, p. 1171: an imperial princess provided gifts to the Liang clan, but her favorite recipient distributed everything among his patriline; 62, p. 2049; 67, p. 2215: a child refused to accept the charity of his village; 76, pp. 2480, 2481.

147. *Si min yue ling ji shi*, pp. 37, 94, 98, 109.

148. *Han shu* 89, p. 3629; *Hou Han shu* 31, p. 1114; 34, p. 1175: Liang Shang regularly distributed state grain during famines. *Dong guan Han ji jiao zhu*, ch. 15, pp. 598–599: he also distributed grain to his kin. Some accounts treat remission of taxes by local officials to people in dire straits as a form of benevolence or charity.

149. *Hou Han shu* 43, pp. 1458, 1459; *Sanfu jue lu*, ch. 2, pp. 11a–12a.

150. See *Stories from China's Past*, pp. 110–111, plate 25.

151. *Hou Han shu* 6, p. 259. The "Fundamental Chronicles" of the Han dynastic histories are filled with references to the emperor's gifts to his officials and to the poor.

152. *Li shi*, ch. 9, p. 3b. See also *Li shi* 5, pp. 5b, 9a, 11b; 7, p. 19a; 10, p. 22b; *Liang Han jin shi ji* 兩漢金石記, in *Shike shiliao congshu*, vol. 4–5; ch. 11, p. 12b.

153. *Hou Han shu* 20, pp. 741, 742. This action is significant in an age when the personal ties between a general and his men were becoming increasingly important. See Lewis, "The Han Abolition of Universal Military Service," pp. 71–73.

154. *Hou Han shu* 81, pp. 2680, 2687, 2695, 2696.

155. *Hou Han shu* 43, p. 1459; *San guo zhi* 11, pp. 334–335, 338.

156. *Hou Han shu* 43, p. 1457.

157. The scholastic tradition of the Eastern Han classicist Ma Rong was carried on by a "younger member [of a collateral branch] of the patriline." See *Hou Han shu* 60b, p. 1972; *Sanfu jue lu*, ch. 2, p. 8a. The transmission of scholarly traditions through a lineage is also mentioned in *Hou Han shu* 19, p. 703; 36, pp. 1223, 1224, 1226, 1235, 1241; 37, pp. 1254, 1258; 76, p. 2477; 79b, p. 2573; *Sanfu jue lu*, ch. 2, p. 12a. Such ties could also be artificially created through marrying a daughter to a prize disciple. See *Hou Han shu* 60a, p. 1953.

158. *Han shu* 92, p. 3709; 99a, p. 4039; *Hou Han shu* 14, p. 553; 20, p. 744; 22, p. 769, 25, p. 873: fellow villagers care for orphans of a deceased official, p. 886; 27, pp. 944, 947; 31, p. 1100; 36, p. 1226; 39, pp. 1295–1296, 1300, 1301; 43, p. 1459; 63, pp. 2089–2090: an elder sister entrusts the eldest son of an executed official to a retainer; 51, p. 1689; 76, p. 2475; 80b, pp. 2635, 2649; 81, pp. 2671, 2679; 83, p. 2765; *Dong guan Han ji jiao zhu*, ch. 7, p. 239; ch. 13, p. 471; ch. 14, p. 531; ch. 15, pp. 629, 643;

ch. 16, p. 663; *San guo zhi* 11, p. 354. On the theme in Han art, see Wu Hung, "Private Love and Public Duty," pp. 83–91.

159. *Hou Han shu* 32, p. 1133; 43, p. 1480; *Sanfu jue lu*, ch. 1, pp. 5a–7b; *Sou shen ji*, quoted in *Taiping yu lan*, ch. 921, pp. 5b–6a. In another version of He Bigan's story there was only a single woman who was "more than eighty years old." Bigan had six sons at the time of the incident, and in the three years following the old woman's gift and prophecy three further sons were born. When the family moved, one of the nine sons stayed behind to perform regular sacrifices to the old woman.

160. *Han shu* 91, p. 3690; *Hou Han shu* 25, pp. 869–870.

161. *Hou Han shu* 27, pp. 945–946; 41, pp. 1398, 1399.

162. *Han shu* 91, p. 3690.

163. *Sanfu jue lu*, ch. 2, pp. 4b, 14a–b. In Fan Ye's *Hou Han shu* the accusation of taking bribes is made by Liang Ji, whom Ma Rong had previously offended. See *Hou Han shu* 60a, p. 1972. For another story of a gift at a funeral leading to an appointment, with criticism of this apparent bribery, see *Hou Han shu* 43, p. 1458.

164. *Li shi*, ch. 7, pp. 5b–7b; 11, pp. 4a–6a; *Li xu*, ch. 12, pp. 5b–18b. Modern Chinese still emphasize the distance over which links are established, or from which a guest comes. See Kipnis, *Producing Guanxi*, p. 45.

165. *Hou Han shu* 36, pp. 1226, 1240, 1241, 1242; 79a, p. 2550; 79b, pp. 2572, 2573; 81, pp. 2671, 2675; 83, p. 2774; *Sanfu jue lu*, ch. 1, pp. 10a–b; *Dong guan Han ji jiao zhu*, ch. 18, p. 803.

166. *Hou Han shu* 53, p. 2073; 79b, p. 2572.

167. *Hou Han shu* 35, p. 1207.

168. *Hou Han shu* 60a, p. 1953.

169. *Li ji zhu shu*, "Wang zhi," ch. 12, pp. 16a–b. For an application of this passage to local cults at the end of the Han, see *Feng su tong yi jiao shi*, p. 325.

170. *Feng su tong yi jiao shi*, pp. 291, 334. The criteria were derived from *Guo yu*, ch. 4, "Lu yu shang 魯語上," p. 166. This lists five categories as potential recipients of state sacrifice: those who bestowed laws on the people, those who died in service, those who brought order to the state, those who warded off great calamities, and those who prevented disasters. The principle that people should sacrifice only to their own ancestors is based on *Lun yu*, ch. 2, "Wei zheng 為政," p. 41: "To sacrifice to one who is not one's own ghost is flattery."

171. For a sketch of Han official religion, see Mu-chou Poo, *In Search of Personal Welfare*, ch. 5.

172. *Shi ji* 77, p. 2385: Gaozu established regular sacrifices at the tomb of Gongzi Wuji because he had been a "worthy"; *Hou Han shu* 7, p. 313 and *Dong guan Han ji jiao zhu*, ch. 3, p. 126: Emperor Huan reestablished state sacrifices to kin of Liu Xiu who had died in the rebellion against Wang Mang; ch. 20, p. 741: the emperor sacrificed to deceased generals; ch. 28, p. 962: the emperor made an individual sacrifice to the scholar Huan Tan.

173. *Shi ji* 47, p. 1945; 66, p. 2180; 103, p. 2767; *Han shu* 71, p. 3041; *Hou Han shu* 16, p. 612; 62, p. 2049; 76, pp. 2462, 2470; 81, p. 2676.

174. *Hou Han shu* 11, pp. 479, 480; *Dong guan Han ji jiao zhu*, ch. 21, p. 863.

175. *Fengsu tong yi jiao shi*, pp. 333–334.

176. *Sanfu jue lu*, ch. 1, pp. 4a–b, 7a.

177. Kristofer Schipper, "Le culte de l'immortel Tang Gongfang," in *Cultes populaires et sociétés asiatiques*, ed. Alain Forest, Yoshiaki Ishizawa, and Léon Vandermeersch (Paris: L'Harmattan, 1991), pp. 59–72; Chen Huan 陳歡, *Daojia jin shi lüe* 道家金石略 (Beijing: Wenwu, 1988), p. 2. For transcriptions of the stele, see *Li shi*, ch. 3, pp. 9b–11a; Yuan Weichun 袁維春, *Qin Han bei shu* 秦漢碑述 (Beijing: Gongyi meishu, 1990), pp. 589–600. A reproduction of the original is in Li Yuzheng 李域錚, Zhao Minsheng 趙敏生, and Lei Bing 雷冰, *Xi'an beilin shufa yishu* 西安碑林書法藝術 (Xi'an: Shaanxi Renmin, 1983), p. 38. For Ouyang Xiu's assessment, see *Ji gu lu* 集古錄, in *Shi ke shi liao cong shu*, vol. 77, ch. 2, pp. 6b–7b. On temples, associated placenames, and versions of the story, see *Huayang guo zhi jiao zhu*, p. 124; *Taiping huanyu ji*, ch. 138, p. 4b; Li Daoyuan 酈道元, *Shui jing zhu* 水經注 (Shanghai: Shijie, 1936), ch. 27, p. 553; *Liangzhou ji* 梁州記, cited in *Yi wen lei ju* 藝文類聚 (Taipei: Wenguang, 1974), ch. 95, p. 1654; Zhang Hua 張華, *Bo wu zhi jiao zheng* 博物志校證 annotated by Fan Ning 范寧 (Beijing: Zhonghua, 1980), p. 125; Ge Hong 葛洪, *Shen xian zhuan* 神仙傳, abridged version in *Yun ji qi qian* 雲笈七籤, in *Zheng tong Dao zang* 正統道藏 (Shanghai: Shangwu, 1923–26), ch. 109, pp. 8–9.

178. The tale about killing the rat figures prominently in later references to Tang Gongfang's career. As Schipper has shown, this links him to certain alchemical practices which used substances also used to poison rats. It also helps to explain his role as an exterminator of pests in local mythology.

179. Kristofer Schipper, "Une stèle taoiste des Han orientaux récemment découverte," in *En suivant la voie royale: Mélanges en hommage à Léon Vandermeersch*, ed. Jacques Gernet and Marc Kalinowski (Paris: Ecole Française d'Extrême Orient, 1997), pp. 239–247; Stephen Little with Shawn Eichman, *Taoism and the Arts of China* (catalogue published in conjunction with an exhibition of the same name; Chicago: Art Institute of Chicago, 2000), pp. 150–151.

180. Max Kaltenmark, *Le Lie-sien Tchouan* (Beijing: Université de Paris, Publications du Centre d'études sinologiques de Pékin, 1953), pp. 1–6.

181. *Lie xian zhuan*, in *Zheng tong Dao zang*, ch. 1, p. 6. The manufacture or repair of sandals in early China was associated with extreme poverty. See chapter three, note 111.

182. *Lie xian zhuan*, ch. 1, p. 8: an immortal who supposedly received sacrifice from King Wu of Zhou; pp. 10, 11, 13, 14, 14–15: Master Anqi, who thwarted Qin Shihuang's attempts to reach the Isles of the Immortals; pp. 17, 18: an immortal who refuses to divulge his arts to a ruler; p. 19: Jiqiu Jun, who thwarts Emperor Wu's attempt to ascend Mt. Tai but has a cult established by the emperor; ch. 2, pp. 4, 5, 6–7, 8, 10: the shrine is established by the king to assuage the immortal whom he had offended; pp. 12, 13: the cult is established out of gratitude to the immortal who warned the people of the imminent collapse of a mountain; p. 15: people from an area of one thousand *li* collectively pay for the maintenance of a cult. Similar cults in Sichuan are described in the *Huayang guo zhi jiao zhu*. See, for example, pp. 64, 77, 96–97, 124, 145, 181, 182, 200, 201, 242, 244, 279, and so on.

183. *Lie xian zhuan*, ch. 1, p. 14.

184. Yan Kejun 嚴可均, *Quan shanggu sandai Qin Han Sanguo Liuchao wen* 全上古三代秦漢三國六朝文 (Beijing: Zhonghua, 1965), *Quan Hou Han wen* 全後漢文, pp. 824, 879, 1030.

185. The inscription, written by the celebrated calligrapher and composer of inscriptions Cai Yong, is in *Quan Hou Han wen*, p. 879. A partial transcription also is in *Hou Han shu*, *zhi* 13, p. 3280. A sacrifice for rain mentioned in the inscription appears in *Hou Han shu* 8, pp. 337–338. The cult and its shrine are mentioned in Li Daoyuan, *Shui jing zhu*, p. 55. On this inscription and its location, see Shi Zhicun 施蟄存, *Shui jing zhu bei lu* 水經注碑錄 (Tianjin: Tianjin Guji, 1987), pp. 17–18.

186. *Hou Han shu* 41, pp. 1397, 1413; *Feng su tong yi jiao shi*, pp. 338–339.

187. Li Ling, "Qin Yin dao bing yu ban de yanjiu 秦駰禱病玉版的研究," *Guoxue yanjiu* 6 (1991), pp. 525–548, reprinted in *Zhongguo fang shu xu kao*; Li Xueqin, "Qin yu du suoyin 秦玉牘索隱," *Gu gong bowuyuan yuan kan* (2000:2), pp. 41–45; Wang Hui 王輝, "Qin zeng sun yin gao Hua Shan da shan ming shen wen kaoshi 秦曾孫駰告華山大山明神文考釋," *Kaogu xue bao* 2001 (2), pp. 143–158; Zeng Xiantong, Yang Zesheng, Xiao Yi 曾憲通，楊澤生，肖毅, "Qin yin yu ban chutan 秦駰玉版初探," *Kaogu yu wenwu* 2001 (1), pp. 49–53; Li Jiahao 李家浩, "Qin Yin yu ban mingwen yanjiu 秦駰玉版銘文研究," *Beijing Daxue Zhongguo guwenxian yanjiu zhongxin jikan* (2001), pp. 99–128; Zhou Fengwu 周鳳五, "Qin Huiwen Wang daoci Hua Shan yu ban xin tan 秦惠文王禱辭華山玉版新探," *Lishi yuyan yanjiusuo jikan* 72:1 (2001), pp. 217–231; Lian Shaoming 連劭名, "Qin Huiwen Wang daoci Hua Shan yu jian wen yanjiu 秦惠文王禱辭華山玉簡文研究," *Zhongguo lishi bowuguan guan kan* (2001:1), pp. 49–57; Lian, "Qin Huiwen Wang daoci Hua Shan yu jian wen yanjiu buzheng 補正," *Zhongguo lishi bowuguan guan kan* (2001:2), pp. 52–54.

188. Mount Baishi—see Gao Wen 高文, *Han bei ji shi* 漢碑集釋 (Kaifeng: Henan Daxue, 1985), p. 471; *Qin Han bei shu*, p. 509; Mount Fenglong—*Han bei ji shi*, p. 251; *Qin Han bei shu*, p. 252; Mount Sangong I—*Han bei ji shi*, p. 32; *Qin Han bei shu*, p. 102; Mount Sangong II—*Li shi* 3, p. 15a; *Quan Hou Han wen*, p. 1030; Mount Wuji—*Li shi* 3, p. 18b; *Quan Hou Han wen*, p. 1032; Mount Hua temple—*Han bei ji shi*, p. 275; *Qin Han bei shu*, p. 275; *Li shi* 2, p. 1a; *Quan Hou Han wen*, p. 1012; Mt. Hua hall and gateposts—*Quan Hou Han wen*, p. 824; Mount Hua pavilion—*Li shi* 2, p. 4a; Mount Hua restoration I—*Li shi* 2, p. 7b; *Quan Hou Han wen*, p. 1029; Mount Hua restoration II—*Li shi* 2, p. 6a; Mount Song Greater Hall Peak—*Han bei ji shi*, p. 37; *Qin Han bei shu*, p. 111; Mount Song Lesser Hall Peak—*Han bei ji shi*, p. 42; *Qin Han bei shu*, p. 116; Mount Song inscription to Kai's mother [the wife of Yu]—*Han bei ji shi*, p. 46; *Qin Han bei shu*, p. 121; Mount Song request for rain—*Han bei ji shi*, p. 433; *Qin Han bei shu*, p. 46; Mount Jiuyi—*Quan Hou Han wen*, p. 879; Inscription to Bo Yi and Shu Qi—*Quan Hou Han wen*, p. 879; Mount Tongbo—*Li shi* 2, p. 12a; *Qin Han bei shu*, p. 258; Yao Gully—*Li shi* 2, p. 14a; *Quan Hou Han wen*, p. 103; K. E. Brashier, "The Spirit Lord of Baishi Mountain: Feeding the Deities or Heeding the Yinyang," *Early China* 26–27 (2001–2002), pp. 159–231.

189. Marianne Bujard, "Célébration et Promotion des Cultes Locaux: Six Stèles des Han Orientaux," *Bulletin de l'École Française d'Extrême-Orient* 87 (2000), pp. 262–263.

190. There are also references to about twenty major official mountain sacrificial sites in the *Han shu* "Treatise on Geography." See *Han shu* 28, pp. 1543–1544, 1547, 1550, 1560, 1569, 1576, 1581, 1582, 1583, 1585, 1586, 1591, 1611, 1617, 1635.

191. Matsumoto, *Chūgoku sonraku seido*, part 1; Hattori Katsuhiko 服部克彦, *Kodai Chūgoku no gun ken to sono shūhen* 古代中國の郡縣とその周邊 (Kyoto: Mineruba [Minerva], 1969), ch. 1–2.

192. Lewis, *Writing and Authority*, pp. 308–325.

193. Lewis, *Writing and Authority*, pp. 325–351.

194. Ebrey, "Economic and Social History of Later Han," p. 645. *Sanfu jue lu* told of eminent people from the capital region. An essay by Kong Rong (d. 208) compared gentlemen of Yingchuan with those of Runan. See *Quan Hou Han wen*, pp. 923–924. Another collection, preserved only in fragments, gave biographies of men from the Chu region. See *Chu guo xian xian zhuan*, cited in *Hou Han shu* 63, p. 2089. The *Qian fu lun* of Wang Fu also takes on a strong regional character in its discussions of the Qiang wars. See Lewis, "The Han Abolition of Universal Military Service," pp. 65–66, 68–69.

195. Sage, *Ancient Sichuan and the Unification of China*.

196. *Wen xuan* 4 "San du fu xu 三都賦序," p. 82.

197. *Wen xuan* 42 "Yu Wu Zhi shu 與吳質書," p. 925.

198. Audrey Spiro, *Contemplating the Ancients: Aesthetic and Social Issues in Early Chinese Portraiture* (Berkeley: University of California, 1990).

199. Morino Shigeo 森野繁夫, *Rikuchō shi no kenkyū: shūdan bungaku to kojin bungaku* 六朝詩の研究：集團文學と個人文學 (Tokyo: Daiichi Gakushū, 1976); Thomas Jansen, *Heimische Öffentlichkeit in frühmitteralterliche China: Debatten im Salon des Prinzen Xiao Ziliang* (Rombach: Freiburg in Breisgau, 2000).

200. *Wen xuan* 2 "Xi jing fu," pp. 25–26.

201. *Wen xuan* 3 "Dong jing fu," p. 51.

202. Major, *Heaven and Earth in Early Han Thought*, pp. 84–86.

203. *Wen xuan* 4 "San du fu xu," pp. 81–82. On changing attitudes to depiction of nature in Sima Xiangru, Zhang Heng, and Zuo Si, see Obi Kōichi 小尾郊一, *Chūgoku bungaku ni okeru shizen to shizenkan* 中國文學における自然と自然觀 (Tokyo: Iwanami, 1963), pp. 30–41, 233–240.

204. *Wen xuan* 4, pp. 81–82.

205. *Wen xuan* 4 "Shu du fu 蜀都賦," pp. 83–87.

206. *Wen xuan* 4 "Shu du fu," pp. 88–90.

207. *Wen xuan* 4 "Shu du fu," pp. 90–92.

208. *Wen xuan* 5 "Wu du fu 吳都賦," p. 94.

209. *Wen xuan* 5 "Wu du fu," pp. 103–104.

210. *Wen xuan* 5 "Wu du fu," pp. 97, 102.

211. *Wen xuan* 5 "Wu du fu," pp. 102 (3), 105 (2), 106, 112 (3).

212. *Wen xuan* 5 "Wu du fu," pp. 104, 106, 110.

213. *Wen xuan* 5 "Wu du fu," p. 112.

214. *Wen xuan* 5 "Wu du fu," pp. 115–116.

215. *Wen xuan* 6 "Wei du fu 魏都賦," pp. 115–117.

216. *Wen xuan* 6 "Wei du fu," pp. 117–119.

217. *Wen xuan* 6 "Wei du fu," pp. 129–132.

218. *Wen xuan* 6 "Wei du fu," pp. 133–134.

219. *Wen xuan* 6 "Wei du fu," pp. 135–138. The two speakers describe themselves with the image of the "smartweed bug" that is oblivious to the bitter taste of the plant on which it lives, quoting a soldier describing his life at the frontier in a poem by Wang Can (A.D. 177–217). See Lu, *Xian Qin Han Wei Jin Nanbeichao shi*, vol. 1, p. 366. This reiterates the theme of Wu and Shu as frontier regions.

220. For an interesting discussion of regional literature at the end of the empire, see Prasenjit Duara, *Sovereignty and Authenticity: Manchukuo and the East Asian Modern* (Oxford: Rowman & Littlefield, 2003), ch. 6 "Local Worlds: The Poetics and Politics of the Native Place."

CHAPTER FIVE

1. D. Lowenthal and M. J. Bowden, eds., *Geographies of the Mind: Essays in Honor of Historical Geosophy* (Oxford: Oxford University, 1976); James S. Romm, *The Edges of the Earth in Ancient Thought* (Princeton: Princeton University, 1992); François Hartog, *Le miroir d'Hérodote: Essai sur la représentation de l'autre* (Paris: Gallimard, 1980); Hartog, *Mémoire d'Ulysse: Récits sur la frontière en Grèce ancienne* (Paris: Gallimard, 1996), especially ch. 3; Irad Malkin, *The Returns of Odysseus: Colonization and Ethnicity* (Berkeley: University of California, 1998); Claude Nicolet, *Space, Geography, and Politics in the Early Roman Empire* (Ann Arbor: University of Michigan, 1991); Zumthor *La mesure du monde*, ch. 11–14; Frank Lestringant, *L'atelier du cosmographe ou l'image du monde à la Renaissance* (Paris: Albin Michel, 1991); Lestringant, *Écrire le monde à la Renaissance: Quinze études sur Rabelais, Postel, Bodin et la littérature géographique* (Caen: Paradigme, 1993); P. J. Marshall and Glyndwr Williams, *The Great Map of Mankind: Perceptions of New Worlds in the Age of the Enlightenment* (Cambridge: Harvard University, 1982); Jeremy Black, *Maps and Politics* (London: Reaktion Books, 1997).

2. Rémi Brague, *Aristote et la question du monde* (Paris: PUF, 1988); Brague, *La Sagesse du monde: Histoire de l'expérience humaine de L'univers* (Paris: Fayard, 1999).

3. "Henan Puyang Xi shui po yizhi fajue jianbao 河南濮阳西水坡遺址發掘簡報," *Wenwu* 1988 (3), pp. 1–6, drawing on p. 4, photo on plate #1; "1988 nian Henan Puyang Xi shui po yizhi fajue jianbao," *Kaogu* 1989 (12), pp. 1057–1066, drawing on p. 1060; "Anhui Han shan Lingjia tan xin shiqi shidai mudi fajue jianbao 安徽含山凌家灘新石器時代墓地發掘簡報," *Wenwu* 1989 (4), pp. 1–9, 30; Chen Jiujin 陳久金 and Zhang Jingguo 張敬國, "Han shan chutu yu pian tuxing shi kao 含山出土玉片圖形試考," *Wenwu* 1989 (4), pp. 14–17, drawing on p. 15, photo on plate #1.

4. Hu Houxuan 胡厚宣, "Jiaguwen sifang fengming kaozheng 甲骨文四方風名考證," in *Jiaguxue Shang shi luncong chu ji* 甲骨學商史論叢初集 (Taipei: Datong, 1972), pp. 369–381; Yan Yiping 嚴一萍, "Buci si fang feng xin yi 卜辭四方風新義," in *Jiagu wenzi yanjiu* 甲骨文字研究 (Taipei: Yiwen, 1976), pp. 173–185; Akatsuka Kiyoshi 赤塚忠, "Chūgoku kodai ni okeru kaze no shinkō to gogyō setsu 中國古代における風の信仰と五行説," in *Nishō-gakusha Daigaku ronshū* 二松學社大學論集 (Tokyo: Nishō-gakusha Daigaku, 1977), pp. 52–91; Keightley, *The Ancestral Landscape*, ch. 5–6;

Wang Aihe, *Cosmology and Political Culture in Early China* (Cambridge: Cambridge University, 2000), ch. 2.

5. Sarah Allan, *The Shape of the Turtle: Myth, Art, and Cosmos in Early China* (Albany: State University of New York, 1991), ch. 4. Some scholars deny that this cosmic model is based on tortoise plastrons used in divination, and argue that it was patterned on sacred architecture, but they concur that the model is well attested in Shang writing and burial practices. See Chen Mengjia 陳夢家, *Yinxu buci zongshu* 殷墟卜辭綜述 (Beijing: Science Press, 1956), p. 481; Gao Quxun 高去尋, "Yindai da mu de mu shi ji qi hanyi de tuice 殷代大墓的木室及其含義的推測," *Zhongyang Yanjiuyuan Lishi Yuyan Yanjiusuo jikan* 39 (1969), pp. 175–188; Chang Kwang-chih 張光直, "Shuo Yindai de ya xing 說殷代的亞形," in *Qingzhu Gao Quxun Xiansheng bashi sui lun wen ji* 慶祝高去尋先生八十歲論文集 (Taipei: Zhengzhong, 1990), pp. 25–34; Hwang Ming-chorng, "Ming-Tang: Cosmology, Political Order and Monuments in Early China" (Ph.D. dissertation, Harvard University, 1996), ch. 3.

6. Hwang, "Ming-tang," p. 126 note 29. The Harvard-Yenching concordance to the *Shi jing* lists twenty-eight examples. See *Harvard-Yenching Institute Sinological Index Series: Supplement No. 9, A Concordance to Shih Ching* (reprint ed., San Francisco: Chinese Materials Center, 1974), pp. 69–70. The *Shang shu zhu zi suo yin* 尚書逐子索引 (Hong Kong: Commercial, 1995) lists thirty-one occurrences, and there are also cases of related phrases such as *si hai* (四海).

7. Wang Jianmin et al., "Zeng Hou Yi mu chutu de ershiba xiu qing long bai hu tuxiang 曾侯乙墓出土的二十八宿青龍白虎圖象," *Wenwu* 1979 (7), pp. 40–45; Hubeisheng Bowuguan 湖北省博物館, *Zeng Hou Yi mu* 曾侯乙墓 (Beijing: Wenwu, 1989), p. 356.

8. Wang Aihe, *Cosmology and Political Culture*, ch. 3–5.

9. Lewis, *Writing and Authority*, pp. 200–201, 261–262, 278–284.

10. Robin D. S. Yates, "Body, Space, Time, and Bureaucracy: Boundary Creation and Control Mechanisms in Early China," in *Boundaries in China*, ed. John Hay (London: Reaktion Books, 1994), pp. 56–80; Yates, "Cosmos, Central Authority, and Communities in the Early Chinese Empire," in *Empires*, ed. Susan E. Alcock et al. (Cambridge: Cambridge University, 2001), pp. 351–368.

11. John S. Major, "The Five Phases, Magic Squares, and Schematic Cosmography," in *Explorations in Early Chinese Cosmology*, ed. Henry Rosemont, Jr., JAAR Thematic Studies 50/2 (Chico: Scholars Press, 1984), pp. 133–166; Schuyler Cammann, "The Evolution of Magic Squares in China," *Journal of the American Oriental Society* 80 (1960), pp. 116–124; Cammann, "The Magic Square of Three in Old Chinese Philosophy and Religion," *History of Religions* 1 (1961), pp. 37–80; Cammann, "Old Chinese Magic Squares," *Sinologica* 7 (1963), pp. 14–53; John B. Henderson, *The Development and Decline of Chinese Cosmology* (New York: Columbia University, 1984), ch. 2. Divinatory charts such as the "Nine Palaces" chart, the *Xing-de* chart, and the chart for deciding the burial of the afterbirth—all from Mawangdui—as well as the *Tai yi* diviner's board from the Fuyang tomb all take the form of a grid.

12. *Mengzi zheng yi* IIIA "Teng Wen Gong shang," pp. 205–213. The most precise sketch of the system is on p. 213. The discussion of demarcating fields is on pp. 205–206.

13. Lsewis, *Writing and Authority*, pp. 298–302.

14. Lewis, *Sanctioned Violence*, pp. 63–64.

15. The *Mencius* argues that while the "countryside (*ye* 野)" contributes one-ninth of its production as agricultural work on the lord's field, those in the "city/capital (*guo* 國)" pay a tax (*fu* 賦) of one-tenth of their income. See *Mengzi zheng yi* IIIA, "Teng Wen Gong shang," p. 207.

16. Koga, *Kan Chōanjō to senpaku kenkyōteiri seido*, pp. 92–108.

17. *Mengzi zheng yi* VB "Wan Zhang xia," p. 424; *Zhuangzi ji shi*, ch. 24 "Xu Wugui," p. 361; *Guo yu* 6 "Qi yu," p. 226; *Yi li zhu shu*, ch. 7, "Shi xiang jian 士相見," p. 14a; *Zhan guo ce*, ch. 27, "Han er," pp. 994, 996; *Han Feizi ji shi*, ch. 2, "Ba jian 八姦," p. 152; *Guanzi jiao zheng*, ch. 8, "Xiao kuang 小匡," p. 121; *Shang Jun shu zhu yi*, ch. 9, "Cuo fa 錯法," p. 226; *Shi ji* 25, p. 1243; 30, p. 1418 (2); 77, p. 2381; 86, pp. 2522, 2523; 129, p. 3272. Some commentators say that the phrase indicates that markets developed around, or required, wells. However, there is no textual evidence for this, nor are wells more essential to markets than many other items that are never linked with the graph for market. The rows of stalls forming a grid, however, are often mentioned in texts and depicted in art. See chapter three, notes 115 and 116.

18. *Mao shi zhengyi*, ch. 20.3, #303, "Xuan niao 玄鳥," p. 15a; ch. 20.4, #304, "Chang fa 長發," pp. 4b, 7a. These both appear in the "Shang song 商頌" section of the *Shi jing*, usually dated to the Spring-and-Autumn period. The nine sections of the realm in these poems are called either the "Nine Possessions (*jiu you* 九有)" or the "Nine Enclosures (*jiu wei* 九圍)". The second poem describes the "Nine Possessions" occupied by the Shang founder, King Tang, as "clear-cut" or "regular" (*jie* 截), which suggests that the idea of a nine-part state tended toward the schematic or geometric from its beginnings. *Mengzi zheng yi* IA "Liang Hui Wang shang," p. 54.

19. Shi Nianhai 史念海, *He shan ji* 河山集 (Beijing: Sanlian, 1981), pp. 391–434.

20. *Shi ji* 74, p. 2344. See also *Shi ji* 26, p. 1259: states that with his interest in the cycle of the Five Powers and in historical waxing and waning, Zou Yan was the only philosopher to pursue an interest in calendrics in the Warring States; 28, pp. 1368–1369: states that Qin Shihuang adopted Zou Yan's theories, and that the masters of esoteric arts from the northeast based their proposals on distorted versions of these theories; 34, p. 1558; 44, p. 1847; 76, p. 2370: Zou Yan is portrayed as a rival of Gongsun Long. The commentary quotes Liu Xiang's *Bie lu* 別錄 for an extended critique attributed to Zou Yan of philosophical disputation about language.

21. The nine provinces of China are also discussed in the *Lü shi chun qiu*, *Zhou li*, and the early Han *Huainanzi*. See *Lü shi chun qiu jiao shi*, ch. 13, "You shi 有始," pp. 657, 658; *Zhou li zhu shu*, ch. 33, "Zhi fang shi 職方氏," pp. 10a–14b. *Huainanzi*, ch. 4, "Di xing," p. 55 also lists the names of *jiu zhou*, but these appear to be "nine [lesser] continents" from Zou Yan's model, and not the nine provinces of the "Yu gong."

22. Major, "The Five Phases, Magic Squares, and Schematic Cosmography," pp. 146–152.

23. Marc Kalinowski, "Mawangdui boshu Xingde shitan"; Kalinowski, "Astrologie calendaire et calcul de position dans la Chine ancienne: Les mutations de l'hémérologie sexagésimale entre le IVe et le IIe siècle avant notre ère"; Kalinowski, "The *Xingde* 刑德 Text from Mawangdui"; Kalinowski, "La transmission du dispositif des Neuf Palais

sous les Six-Dynasties," in *Tantric and Taoist Studies in Honour of R. A. Stein*, ed. Michel Strickmann (Brussels: Institut Belge des Hautes Études Chinoises, 1985), vol. 3, pp. 773–811.

24. Chen Pan 陳槃, "Lun zaoqi chan wei ji qi yu Zou Yan shu shuo zhi guanxi 論早期讖緯及其與鄒衍書説之關係," *Lishi Yuyan Yanjiusuo jikan* 20 (1948), pp. 159–187; Yasui Kōzan 安居香山 and Nakamura Shōhachi 中村璋八, *Isho no kisoteki kenkyū* 緯書の基礎的研究 (Kyoto: Kokusho Kankō, 1978), pp. 201–240.

25. Major, *Heaven and Earth in Early Han Thought*, ch. 2, 4.

26. Only Major's sections seven and seventeen derive from the "Yu gong." See pp. 143–144.

27. *Huainanzi*, ch. 4, "Di xing," p. 55.

28. *Huainanzi*, ch. 4, "Di xing," p. 56; Major, *Heaven and Earth*, p. 148. Wang Chong argued that the *Huainanzi* mentioned only the "nine provinces" of the "Yu gong," but given the evidence from nomenclature and dimensions, this is surely wrong. As Yasui Kōzan has pointed out, Wang Chong's writings on this subject are quite muddled. See Yasui, *Kisoteki kenkyū*, pp. 219–229.

29. *Lun heng ji jie*, ch. 11, "Tan tian 談天," pp. 217, 219; ch. 24, "Nan sui 難歳," p. 493; *He tu kuo di xiang* 河圖括地象 in *Gu wei shu* 古微書, ch. 32, p. 3a, in *Wei shu ji cheng* 緯書集成 (Shanghai: Guji, 1994), p. 352; *He tu kuo di xiang*, in *Taiping yu lan*, ch. 157, p. 1a.

30. Mitarai Masaru 御手洗勝, "Chiriteki sekai kan no hensen—Sū En no dai kyū shū setsu ni tsuite 地理的世界觀の變遷―鄒衍の大九州説に就いて," *Tōyō no bunka to shakai* 6 (1957), pp. 1–24.

31. *Shi ji* 74, pp. 2344, 2345.

32. See Lewis, *Writing and Authority*, pp. 341–346.

33. *Yan tie lun* 53 "Lun Zou 論鄒," pp. 109–110.

34. *Lun Heng ji jie*, ch. 11, "Tan tian," pp. 217–218. The same chapter also notes the difficulty of reconciling the logical celestial midpoints, the North Pole and the equator, with placing China's continent in the southeast corner.

35. Elsewhere Wang Chong recognizes the existence of the model of a world of eighty-one continents. See *Lun heng ji jie*, ch. 24, "Nan sui," p. 494. While in this second passage Wang Chong states that Zou Yan's theory is "probably false" he accepts it as possibly true in order to argue against the popular idea that the movements of Sui made certain days inauspicious. This is yet another case in which Wang Chong dismisses a proposition as absurd in one place and then accepts it elsewhere for the sake of attacking a hypothetical opponent. On Sui see Kalinowski, "Les traités de Shui-hudi et l'hémérologie Chinoise," *T'oung Pao* 72 (1986), pp. 216–219; Harper, "Warring States Natural Philosophy and Occult Thought," p. 856.

36. Wang Chong's most eminent predecessor as a critic of the apocrypha was Huan Tan. See *Hou Han shu* 28a, pp. 959–960. For Wang Chong's arguments against the apocrypha and the technical traditions, see, *Lun heng ji jie*, ch. 3, "Qi guai," p. 73; ch. 4, "Shu xu 書虛," p. 91; ch. 23, "Si hui," p. 466; ch. 24, "Ji ri 譏日," p. 480; "Bian sui 辨祟," pp. 487 (2), 491 (2); "Nan sui," pp. 492 (2), 496, 498; ch. 26, "Shi zhi," p. 519; ch. 29 "An shu 案書," p. 568.

37. *Lun heng ji jie*, ch. 19, "Xuan Han 宣漢," p. 391; "Hui guo 恢國," p. 392.

38. *Lun heng ji jie*, ch. 19, "Hui guo," pp. 394–395; ch. 20, "Xu song 須頌," pp. 404–405.

39. *Huainanzi*, ch. 1, "Yuan dao," p. 1; ch. 2, "Chu zhen," p. 19; ch. 3, "Tian wen," p. 35; ch. 4, "Di xing," p. 55; ch. 7, "Jing shen," p. 99; ch. 8, "Ben jing," p. 113; ch. 10, "Miu cheng 繆稱," p. 153; ch. 14, "Quan yan," p. 235; ch. 20, "Tai zu," p. 347. On Daoists' grounding texts in the origins of the cosmos, see Lewis, *Writing and Authority*, pp. 123–129.

40. *Huainanzi*, ch. 21, "Yao lüe," pp. 376–377.

41. For fragments see *Wei shu ji cheng*, pp. 125–126, 351–354, 1063, 1104–1105, 1520–1522, 1567–1576, 2112–2113; *Taiping yu lan*, ch. 157, p. 1a. Chen Pan argued that many of the themes of the apocryphal literature may have been derived from the *Huainanzi* or from shared sources. See Chen Pan, "Lun zaoqi chenwei ji qi yu Zou Yan shu shuo zhi guanxi," pp. 163–164.

42. *Shi ji* 26, p. 1259; 28, p. 1368; 74, p. 2344.

43. Chen Pan, "Lun zaoqi chenwei ji qi yu Zou Yan shu shuo zhi guanxi." On this article, see Yasui, *Isho no seiritsu to sono tenkai*, pp. 268–273. On possible relations between *fang shi* and the apocryphal literature, see Yasui, *Isho no seiritsu to sono tenkai*, pp. 57–85, 278–283, 319–329, 331–332, 502; Yasui and Nakamura, *Isho no kisoteki kenkyū*, ch. 2. The early Eastern Han critic of the apocryphal literature, Huan Tan, linked them to the *fang shi*. See *Hou Han shu* 28a, p. 960. Sima Qian stated that the *fang shi* were men who had adopted Zou Yan's models without fully understanding them. See *Shi ji* 28, pp. 1368–1369.

44. *Han shu* 36, pp. 1928–1929.

45. Rémi Mathieu, "*Mu t'ien tzu chuan* 穆天子傳," in *Early Chinese Texts: A Bibliographical Guide*, ed. Michael Loewe (Berkeley: Society for the Study of Early China, 1993), p. 342; Mathieu, *Le Mu Tianzi Zhuan: Traduction annotée, Étude critique* (Paris: Collège de France, Institut des Hautes Études Chinoises, 1978).

46. Deborah Lynn Porter, *From Deluge to Discourse: Myth, History, and the Generation of Chinese Fiction* (Albany: State University of New York, 1996), ch. 2, esp. p. 27; pp. 61–65, 73–75, 77, 79–84, 89–90, 97–98, 119–123, 130–131, 137–138, 144–147.

47. Porter, *From Deluge to Discourse*, pp. 137–138; Mathieu, *Le Mu Tianzi Zhuan*, p. 173. On the mythology of Yu and the flood, see my companion volume *Flood Myths in Early China*.

48. *Shang shu zheng yi*, ch. 6, p. 21b. On the limited role of Kunlun in the "Yu gong" see Gu Jiegang 顧頡剛, "'Yu gong' zhong de Kunlun 禹貢中的昆侖," *Lishi dili* 1 (1981), pp. 3–8. For a summary of theories about the origins of the name "Kunlun," see Ling Chunsheng 凌純聲, "Kunlun qiu yu Xiwangmu 昆侖丘與西王母," *Zhongyang Yanjiuyuan Minzu Yanjiusuo jikan* 22 (1966), pp. 215–255.

49. *Mu Tianzi zhuan xi zheng jiangshu* 穆天子傳西征講疏, annotated by Gu Shi 顧實 (Shanghai: Shangwu, 1934. Reprint ed., Taipei: Shangwu, 1976), pp. 29–33, 61–63, 68, 72, 77, 81, 83, 89, 96. On the "Suspended Garden" see *Chu ci bu zhu*, ch. 1, "Li sao," pp. 21a–b; ch. 3, "Tian wen," p. 7a: here the "Suspended Garden" is linked to Kunlun; *Huainanzi*, ch. 4, "Di xing," pp. 56, 57.

50. *Jin ben zhu shu ji nian shu zheng* 今本竹書紀年疏證, annotated by Wang Guowei 王國維, in *Gu ben zhu shu ji nian ji zheng* 古本竹書紀年輯證, annotated by Fang Shiming 方詩銘 and Wang Xiuling 王修齡 (Shanghai: Shanghai Gu Ji, 1981),

pp. 198, 246. See also *Da Dai li ji jie gu*, ch. 11, "Shao jian 少間," p. 216; Edward L. Shaughnessy, "On the Authenticity of the *Bamboo Annals*," *Harvard Journal of Asiatic Studies* 46 (1986), pp. 149–180; David S. Nivison, "The Dates of the Zhou Conquest of the Shang," *Harvard Journal of Asiatic Studies* 43 (1983), pp. 481–580. A good summation of the theory that "Xiwangmu" originated as a foreign name appears in Mathieu, *Le Mu Tianzi Zhuan*, pp. 43 note 108; 44 note 109; 180–185.

51. Porter, *From Deluge to Discourse*, pp. 18–23, 91–104, 134–137.

52. *Mu Tianzi zhuan xi zheng jiangshu*, pp. 144, 163.

53. Porter, *From Deluge to Discourse*, p. 136; Donald Harper, "The Sexual Arts of Ancient China as Described in a Manuscript of the Second Century B.C.," *Harvard Journal of Asiatic Studies* 47.2 (1987), p. 550.

54. Some scholars argue that these poems are later interpolations, but Marcel Granet has shown that the rhymes are archaic. See *Danses et légendes de la Chine ancienne* (reprint edition, Paris: Presses Universitaires de France, 1994), p. 587, note 2.

55. *Mu Tianzi zhuan*, Si bu bei yao edition, ch. 6. Some scholars think this was a separate text that was found in the same tomb and mistakenly appended to the *Mu Tianzi zhuan*. See *Jin shu* 51, p. 1433.

56. Wolfgang Bauer, *China and the Search for Happiness: Recurring Themes in Four Thousand Years of Chinese Cultural History* (New York: Seabury Press, 1976), part 4, ch. 1, pp. 205–212.

57. *Wen xuan*, ch. 6, "Wei du fu," p. 117.

58. Liang Qichao 梁啓超, *Yin bing shi quan ji* 飲冰室全集 (Taipei: Zonghe, 1975) "Sanshi zi shu 三十自述," pp. 462, 463.

59. For dated but useful presentations in Western languages, see William Edward Soothill, *The Hall of Light* (New York: Philosophical Library, 1952); Henri Maspero, "Le Ming-T'ang et la crise religieuse chinoise avant les Han," in *Mélanges chinois et bouddhiques* (1948–1951), pp. 1–71; Granet, *La pensée chinoise*, pp. 90–97, 149–152, 210–229. For a classic Chinese account, see Wang Guowei 王國維, "Ming tang miao qin tong kao 明堂廟寢通考," in *Guan tang ji lin* 觀堂集林 (reprint edition, Beijing: Zhonghua, 1959 [1921]), pp. 123–144. For a more recent discussion see Wu, *Monumentality*, pp. 176–187. On debates during the Han dynasty, see Fujikawa Masakazu 藤川正數, *Kandai ni okeru reigaku no kenkyū* 漢代における禮學の研究 (Tokyo: Kazama Shobō, 1968), pp. 237–270.

60. On the role of charts see Florian C. Reiter, "Some Remarks on the Chinese Word T'u 'Chart, Plan, Design'," *Oriens* 32 (1990), pp. 308–327; Michael Lackner, "Argumentation par diagrammes: une architecture à base de mots. Le *Ximing* (L'Inscription occidentale) depuis Zhang Zai jusqu'au *Yanjitu*," *Extrême-Orient Extrême-Occident* 14 (1992), pp. 131–168; Lackner, "Die Verplanung des Denkens am Beispiel der *tu*," in *Lebenswelt und Weltanschauung in frühzeitlichen China*, ed. H. Schmidt-Glintzer (Stuttgart: Franz Steiner Verlag, 1990), pp. 134–156; Alain Arrault, "Les diagrammes de Shao Yong (1012–1077). Qui les a vus?" *Études chinoises* 19:1–2 (Printemps-Automne 2000), pp. 67–114.

61. Shandong Sheng Bowuguan 山東省博物館, "Linzi Langjiazhuang yi hao Dong Zhou xun ren mu 臨淄郎家庄一號東周殉人墓," *Kaogu xuebao* 1977 (1), pp. 73–103; fig. 14 on p. 82; plate 18. A photograph of the lid appears in Wang Shixiang 王世襄, *Zhongguo gudai qi qi* 中國古代漆器 (Beijing: Wenwu, 1987), plate #3. For discussions

see Cao Chunping 曹春平, "Ming tang fawei 明堂發微," *Jianzhu xuebao* 9 (1994), pp. 65–84; Hwang Ming-chorng, "Ming-tang," pp. 61–64.

62. Noel Barnard, "The Ch'u Silk Manuscript and Other Archaeological Documents of Ancient China," in *Early Chinese Art and Its Possible Influence in the Pacific Basin*, ed. Noel Barnard (New York: Intercultural Art Press, 1972), vol. 1, *Ch'u and the Silk Manuscript*, pp. 77–101; Barnard, *The Ch'u Silk Manuscript* (Canberra: Australian National University, 1973); Li Ling, *Changsha Zidanku Zhanguo Chu bo shu yanjiu* 長沙子彈庫戰國楚帛書研究 (Beijing: Zhonghua, 1985); Li Ling, "Chu bo shu de zai renshi 楚帛書的再認識," *Zhongguo wenhua* 10 (1994), pp. 42–62; Li Ling, *Zhongguo fang shu kao*, pp. 178–196; Rao Tsung-yi [Zongyi], "Some Aspects of the Calendar, Astrology, and Religious Concepts of the Ch'u People as Revealed in the Ch'u Silk Manuscript," in *Early Chinese Art and Its Possible Influence*, pp. 113–122; Rao Zongyi 饒宗頤 and Zeng Xiantong 曾憲通, *Chu bo shu* 楚帛書 (Hong Kong: Zhonghua, 1985); Hayashi Minao, "The Twelve Gods of the Chan-kuo Period Silk Manuscript Excavated at Ch'ang-sha," in *Early Chinese Art and Its Possible Influence*, pp. 123–186.

63. Hunan Sheng Bowuguan, "Changsha Zidanku Zhanguo mu guo mu 長沙子彈庫戰國木槨墓," *Wenwu* 1974 (2), pp. 36–40.

64. Li Xueqin 李學勤, "Zhanguo ti ming gaishu, part 2 戰國題名概述 (下)," *Wenwu* 1959 (9), pp. 58–61; Rao and Zeng, *Chu bo shu*, pp. 101–120.

65. Chen Mengjia 陳夢家, "Zhanguo Chu bo shu kao 戰國楚帛書考," *Kaogu xuebao* 1984 (2), pp. 137–158; Cao Jinyan 曹錦炎, "Chu bo shu 'Yue ling' pian kaoshi 楚帛書月令篇考試," *Jiang Han kaogu* 1985 (1), pp. 63–67.

66. Li Ling, *Changsha Zidanku Zhanguo Chu bo shu yanjiu*, pp. 64–75; Li Ling, *Zhongguo fang shu kao*, pp. 192–194; He Linyi 何琳儀, "Changsha bo shu tongshi 長沙帛書通釋," *Jiang Han kaogu* 1986 (2), pp. 77–82; Rao Zongyi and Zeng Xiantong, *Chu bo shu*, pp. 4–35; Li Xueqin, "Chu bo shu zhong de gushi yu yuzhouguan 楚帛書中的故事與宇宙觀," in *Chu shi luncong* 楚史論叢, no. 1 (Wuhan: Hubei Renmin, 1982), pp. 145–154. For an English translation see *Defining Chu*, ed. Constance A. Cook and John S. Major, pp. 173–176.

67. Li Ling, *Zhongguo fang shu kao*, pp. 191–192; He Linyi, "Changsha bo shu tongshi," *Jiang Han kaogu* (1986:1), pp. 51–57; Rao Zongyi, "Chu bo shu tian xiang zai yi 楚帛書天象再議," *Zhongguo wenhua* 3 (1991), pp. 66–73; Li Xueqin, "Lun Chu bo shu zhong de tian xiang 論楚帛書中的天象," *Hunan kaogu jikan* 1 (1982), pp. 68–72.

68. Guo Moruo 郭沫若, Wen Yiduo 聞一多, and Xu Weiyu 許維遹, ed., *Guanzi jijiao* 管子集校 (Beijing: Kexue, 1956), vol. 1, plate facing p. 140, and p. 141. On "Xuan gong," see *Guanzi jijiao*, pp. 104–105; W. Allyn Rickett, *Guanzi: Political, Economic, and Philosophical Essays from Early China*, vol. 1 (Princeton: Princeton University, 1985), pp. 148–169 (the reconstruction by Wang and Guo is reproduced on p. 151); Li Ling, *Zhongguo fang shu kao*, pp. 135–137; Li Ling, "*Guanzi* sanshi shijie yu ershisi jieqi 管子三十時節與二十四節氣," *Guanzi jikan* 1988 (2), pp. 18–24; Miura Yoshiaki 三浦吉明, "*Kanshi* Yōkan hen ni tsuite—sanjūsekki o chūshin ni 管子幼官篇について—三十節氣を中心に," *Nihon Chūgoku Gakkai hō* 42 (1990), pp. 32–46.

69. Li Ling, *Changsha Zidanku Zhanguo Chu bo shu yanjiu*, pp. 41–42; Li Ling, *Zhongguo fang shu kao*, p. 137; Wang Meng'ou 王夢鷗, "Gu ming tang tu kao 古明堂圖考," *Kong Meng xuebao* 11 (1966), pp. 221–229; Wang Meng'ou, *Zou Yan yi*

shuo kao 鄒衍遺説考 (Taipei: Shangwu, 1966), p. 96; Hwang Ming-Chorng, "Ming-tang," pp. 90–91, 729.

70. *Mozi jian gu*, ch. 5, "Fei gong 非攻," p. 92; *Zhuangzi ji shi*, ch. 6, "Da zong shi," p. 113. For the *Lü shi chun qiu* linking the "Dark Hall" to the "Bright Hall", see *Lü shi chun qiu jiao shi*, ch.10, "Meng dong ji 孟冬紀," p. 515; ch. 11, "Zhong dong ji 仲冬紀," p. 567; ch. 12, "Ji dong ji 季冬紀," p. 615. For the uses of "Bright Hall" see ch. 4, "Meng xia ji," p. 185; ch. 5, "Zhong xia ji," p. 241; ch. 6, "Ji xia ji," p. 311.

71. Rickett, *Guanzi*, vol. 1, pp. 152–158, 166–169.

72. In what follows, as in all the discussion of the Bright Hall, I have relied heavily on the valuable research presented by Hwang Ming-chorng in "Ming-tang," ch. 2.

73. *Shang shu zheng yi*, ch. 14 "Kang gao," pp. 1b–2a. On this passage see Qu Wanli 屈萬里, *Shang shu ji shi* 尚書集釋 (Taipei: Lianjing, 1983), pp. 145–146.

74. Shaughnessy, "On the Authenticity of the *Bamboo Annals*," pp. 159–160.

75. *Li ji zhu shu*, ch. 31, "Ming tang wei," pp. 2a–4a; *Yi Zhou shu hui jiao ji zhu*, pp. 759–765. The last two sentences appear here in the *Yi Zhou shu* chapter. On names of the gods of the four directions in this text in later religious Daoism, see Kalinowski, "La transmission du dispositif des Neufs Palais," p. 805 note 96; Anna Seidel, *La divin-isation de Lao-tseu dans le taoïsme des Han* (Paris: École Française d'Extrême-Orient, 1969), pp. 56–57.

76. Two quotations attributed to the "Ming tang" chapter of the *Yi Zhou shu* describe it as a large square building in the middle of a square platform, with four buildings of three rooms each placed around the central building. See *Sui shu* 隋書 (Beijing: Zhonghua, 1973) 68, pp. 1590–1591; *Taiping yu lan*, ch. 533, pp. 1a–b. These may be later commentary taken as original text.

77. For an account of these temples and their uses, see Wu, *Monumentality*, pp. 77–88.

78. *Li ji zhu shu*, ch. 31, "Mingtang wei," ch. 31, p. 10b.

79. *Li ji zhu shu*, ch. 39, "Yue ji," p. 14a; ch. 48, "Ji yi," p. 11b.

80. *Huainanzi*, ch. 11, "Qi su," p. 183; *Han shu* 25a, p. 1193. See also *Huainanzi*, ch. 14 "Quan yan," p. 249: "When the lord of a state of ten thousand chariots dies, they bury his body in the vast fields, but sacrifice to his spirit in the Bright Hall. This is because the spirit is nobler than the body."

81. See, for example, *Li ji zhu shu*, ch. 26, "Jiao te sheng," pp. 12a–b; ch. 43, "Za ji xia 雜記下," p. 13b; ch. 38, "Yue ji," p. 16a; ch. 47, "Ji yi," pp. 6a, 7b–8a.

82. *Mengzi zheng yi* IB "Liang Hui Wang xia," pp. 77–78; *Xunzi ji jie*, ch. 11, "Qiang guo," pp. 201–202; *Zuo zhuan zhu*, Wen year 2, p. 520.

83. *Huainanzi*, ch. 9, "Zhu shu," pp. 127–128, 149.

84. *Huainanzi*, ch. 20, "Tai zu 泰族," p. 351.

85. On the Warring States date for the "Kao gong ji" see Chen Zhi 陳植 in Zheng Liangshu 鄭良樹, ed., *Xu wei shu tong kao* 續偽書通考 (Taipei: Xuesheng, 1984), pp. 501–502.

86. *Zhou li zhu shu*, ch. 41 "Jiang ren," pp. 24b–27a. Here the Xia equivalent of the Bright Hall was the "Generational Chamber," also imagined as an ancestral temple. For a modern attempt to turn the "Kao gong ji" description into a model, largely

based on later Han commentators, see Tanaka Tan 田中淡, "Sen Shin kyūshitsu kenchiku josetsu 先秦宮室建築序説," in *Chūgoku kenchiku shi no kenkyū* 中國建築史 の研究 (Tokyo: Kōbundō, 1988), pp. 1–91, esp. pp. 10–13.

87. *Lü shi chun qiu jiao shi*, ch. 15, "Shen da 慎大," p. 845; ch. 19, "Shang de 上德," p. 1256; ch. 20, "Zhao lei 召類," p. 1361; *Huainanzi*, ch. 8, "Ben jing," pp. 122–123; ch. 9, "Zhu shu," p. 128; *Da Dai li ji jie gu*, ch. 8, "Ming tang," pp. 149, 152; Cai Yong 蔡邕, "Mingtang yue ling lun 明堂月令論," in Yan Kejun, *Quan Shanggu Sandai Qin Han Sanguo Liuchao wen*, vol. 1, "Quan Hou Han wen," ch. 80, p. 6a.

88. *Da Dai li ji jie gu*, ch. 8, pp. 149–152.

89. Wen Yiduo 聞一多, "Qi shi er 七十二," in *Shen hua yu shi* 神話與詩, in *Wen Yiduo quan ji* 全集, vol. 1 (1948; reprint edition, Beijing: Sanlian, 1982), pp. 207–220.

90. Kalinowski, "La transmission du dispositif des Neufs Palais sous les Six-Dynasties," pp. 779–780.

91. *Bo hu tong de lun*, ch. 1, p. 59b: "The Bright Hall is round on top and square at the bottom. Each room has eight windows and four doors. It is the palace in which policies are set forth. It is to the *yang* side of the capital. Being round on top imitates Heaven, and square on the bottom imitates earth. The eight windows are an image of the eight winds [and by association 'directions'], and the four doors copy the four seasons. The nine chambers imitate the nine continents. The twelve seats [or 'statues'] imitate the twelve months. The thirty-six total doors imitate the thirty-six types of rain, and the seventy-two total windows imitate the seventy-two winds."

92. Joseph Needham, Lu Gwei-djen, John Combridge, and John S. Major, *The Hall of Heavenly Records: Korean Astronomical Instruments and Clocks, 1380–1780* (Cambridge: Cambridge University, 1986), pp. 4–6; Major, *Heaven and Earth in Early Han Thought*, pp. 69–70; Sun Xiaochun and Jacob Kistemaker, *The Chinese Sky During the Han: Constellating Stars and Society* (Leiden: Brill, 1997), pp. 22–23, 119–135.

93. *Taiping yu lan*, ch. 533, p. 2b; *Sui shu* 49, p. 1304.

94. *Shi ji* 27, pp. 1289, 1295–1296, 1299, 1304, 1309. This places the Purple Palace in the center as the palace of the Grand Unity, the Heavenly Market in the east (but not the eastern palace), Taiwei as the celestial southern palace, Wuhuang (the celestial chariot store) as the western palace, and Yingshi in the north as the ancestral temple. The celestial equivalent of the Hall of Light is the constellation that forms the eastern palace. *Huainanzi*, ch. 3, "Tian wen," pp. 36–37 elaborates the "nine-field" system, but the "five-palace" system is also used on p. 39. However, the selected asterisms or astral regions do not overlap with those in the *Mingtang yin yang*, except for the Purple Palace in the center.

95. *Shi ji* 28, p. 1401. The idea that the Hall of Light had no walls but only a roof on pillars also figures in the contemporary *Huainanzi*, ch. 9 "Zhu shu," p. 128. The thatched roof, along with other "primitive" features and the absence of ornament, are cited in the aforementioned *Da Dai li ji*, the *Huainanzi* passage cited in the preceding sentence; the *Lü shi chun qiu jiao shi*, ch. 20, "Zhao lei," p. 1361; *Huainanzi*, ch. 8, "Ben jing," pp. 122–123; Cai Yong, "Mingtang yue ling lun," in Yan Kejun, *Quan Shanggu Sandai Qin Han Sanguo Liuchao wen*, vol. 1, "Quan Hou Han wen," ch. 80, p. 6a.

96. Lewis, "The *Feng* and *Shan* Sacrifices of Emperor Wu," pp. 50–80.

97. See Wu, *Monumentality*, pp. 184–187.

98. *Han shu* 99a, pp. 4069, 4080–4081.

99. Gu Jiegang 顧頡剛, "Wu de zhong shi shuo xia de zhengzhi he lishi 五德終始說下的政治和歷史," in *Gu shi bian* 古史辨 (reprint ed., Hong Kong: Taiping, 1962), vol. 5, pp. 404–617. On a political lineage constituted in ritual, see Lewis, "The *Feng* and *Shan* Sacrifices of Emperor Wu," pp. 71–76.

100. *Bo hu tong de lun*, ch. 1, pp. 59a–b.

101. Liu Zhiping 劉致平, "Xi'an xibei jiao gudai jianzhu yizhi kancha chu ji 西安西北郊古代建築遺址勘察初記," *Wenwu cankao ziliao* 1957 (3), pp. 5–12; Qi Yingtao 祁英濤, "Xi'an de ji chu Han dai jianzhu yizhi 西安的幾處漢代建築遺址," *Wenwu cankao ziliao* 1957 (5), pp. 57–58; Luo Zhongru 雒忠如, "Xi'an xi jiao faxian Han dai jianzhu yizhi 西安西郊發現漢代建築遺址," *Kaogu tongxun* 1957 (6), pp. 26–30; Tang Jinyu 唐金裕, "Xi'an xi jiao Han dai jianzhu yizhi fajue baogao 西安西郊漢代建築遺址發掘報告," *Kaogu xuebao* 1959 (2), pp. 45–54; Xu Daolin 許道麟 and Liu Zhiping, "Guanyu Xi'an xi jiao faxian de Han dai jianzhu yizhi shi Mingtang huo Piyong de taolun 關於西安西郊發現的漢代建築遺址是明堂或辟雍的討論," *Kaogu* 1959 (4), pp. 193–196; "Han Chang'an cheng nan jiao li zhi jianzhu yizhiqun fajue jianbao 漢長安城南郊禮制建築遺址群發掘簡報," *Kaogu* 1960 (7), pp. 36–39; Huang Zhanyue 黃展岳, "Han Chang'an cheng nan jiao li zhi jianzhu de weizhi ji qi you guan wenti 漢長安城南郊禮制建築的位置及其有關問題," *Kaogu* 1960 (9), pp. 53–58; Wang Shiren 王世仁, "Han Chang'an cheng nan jiao li zhi jianzhu yuanzhuang de tuice 漢長安城南郊禮制建築原狀的推測," *Kaogu* 1963 (9), pp. 501–515; Wang Shiren, "Mingtang xingzhi chu tan 明堂形制初探," *Zhongguo wenhua yanjiu jikan* 中國文化研究集刊 4 (1987), pp. 1–71; Yang Hongxun 楊鴻勛, "Cong yizhi kan Xi Han Chang'an Mingtang Piyong xingzhi 從遺址看西漢長安明堂辟雍形制," in *Jianzhu kaoguxue lunwen ji* 建築考古學論文集 (Beijing: Wenwu, 1987), pp. 169–200; Steinhardt, *Chinese Imperial City Planning*, pp. 70–77; Wu, *Monumentality*, pp.176–187; Hwang Ming-chorng, "Ming-tang," pp. 27–31.

102. Yan, *Quan Hou Han wen*, ch. 80, pp. 5b–8a.

103. *Quan Hou Han wen*, ch. 80, p. 6a.

104. One passage quotes the "Yue ling ji (月令記)": "The Bright Hall is the means to make clear all of Heaven and Earth, and to unite all things. Above it communicates with Heaven, and below there are twelve palaces, so it can model the sun and stars. Water rings it on four sides. This indicates that the king's actions copy Heaven and Earth, and his virtuous power extends to the four seas." See p. 7a.

105. *Shang shu zheng yi*, ch. 6, "Yu gong," pp. 30a–32b; *Han shu* 28a, p. 1537. The *Zhou li* expanded this model to nine zones. See *Zhou li zhu shu*, ch. 33, "Zhi fang shi," pp. 15a–b; ch. 37, "Da xing ren," pp. 18b–20b. On the five-zone version, see Yü Ying-shih, "Han Foreign Relations," in *The Cambridge History of China, Volume 1: The Ch'in and Han Empires*, pp. 379–381.

106. See the memorial by a group of Qin ministers in *Shi ji* 6, p. 236. On the historical bases of the three-zone model, see Gu Jiegang, *Shi lin za shi* 史林雜識 (Beijing: Zhonghua, 1963), pp. 1–19. For the use of the multizone model in Han political discourse, see *Han shu* 63, p. 2759; 99b, pp. 4136–4137.

107. *Yi Zhou shu hui jiao ji zhu*, ch. 7, "Wang hui," pp. 863–866. The "Kang gao" lists terms—*hou* 侯, *dian* 甸, *nan* 男, *cai* 采, *wei* 衛—that elsewhere are the names of zones, so the Han commentator perceives a five-zone model. See *Shang shu zheng yi*, ch. 14, "Kang gao," pp. 1b–2a.

108. *Yi Zhou shu hui jiao ji zhu*, ch. 7, "Wang hui," pp. 876–968.

109. *Yi Zhou shu hui jiao ji zhu*, ch. 7, "Wang hui," pp. 969–982.

110. *Zhou li zhu shu*, ch. 33, "Zhi fang shi," pp. 9a–18b; ch. 37, "Da xing ren," pp. 9b–22b.

111. Komai Kazuchiku 駒井和愛, "Kikumon oyobi rokuhakuzu 規矩文および 六博圖," in *Chūgoku kokyō no kenkyū* 中國古鏡の研究 (Tokyo: Iwanami, 1953), pp. 123–219; *Moriya Kōzō shūshū hōkaku kiku shishin kyō zuroku* 守屋孝藏蒐集方格規矩四 神鏡圖錄 (Kyōto: Kyōto Kokuritsu Hakubutsukan, 1969); Umehara Sueji 梅原末治, *Kan Sangoku Rikuchō kinen kyō zusetsu* 漢三國六朝紀年鏡圖説 (Kyoto: Kyōto Teikoku Daigaku, 1943); Umehara, *Kan Sangoku Rikuchō kinen kyō shūroku* 集錄 (Tokyo: Oka Shoin, 1947); Umehara, "The Late Mr. Moriya's Collection of Ancient Chinese Mirrors," *Artibus Asiae* 18 (1955), pp. 238–256; Hayashi Minao 林巳奈夫, "Kan kyō no zugara ni, san ni tsuite 漢鏡の圖柄二，三について," *Tōhō gakuhō* 44 (1973), pp. 1–66; Kung Xiangxing 孔祥星 and Liu Yiman 劉一曼, *Zusetsu Chūgoku kodai dōkyō shi* 圖説中國古代銅鏡史, tr. Takakura Hiroaki 高倉洋彰, Tazaki Hiroyuki 田崎博之, and Watanabe Yoshirō 渡邊芳郎 (Tokyo: Chūgoku Shoten, 1991); Bernhard Karlgren, "Early Chinese Mirror Inscriptions," *Bulletin of the Museum of Far Eastern Antiquities* 6 (1934), pp. 9–79; A. G. Bulling, "The Decoration of Some Mirrors of the Chou and Han Periods," *Artibus Asiae* 18.1 (1955), pp. 20–43; Bulling, *The Decoration of Mirrors of the Han Period, Artibus Asiae*, suppl. XX (Ascona, 1960); Loewe, *Ways to Paradise*, pp. 60–85.

On the diviner's boards and related patterns, including the TLV mirror, as a world model, see Li Ling, *Zhongguo fang shu kao*, ch. 2, "Shi yu Zhongguo gudai de yuzhou moshi 式與中國古代的宇宙模式," pp. 89–176. For discussions of the relation of such objects as sundials, game boards, divination boards, and apotropaic coins to the decor of the TLV mirrors see Lao Gan 勞榦, "Liubo ji bo ju zhi yanbian 六博及博局之演變," *Lishi Yuyan Yanjiusuo jikan* 35 (1964), pp. 15–30; Li Jianmin 李建民, "Han dai ju xi de qiyuan yu yanbian 漢代局戲的起源與演變," *Dalu zazhi* 1988 (3), pp. 1–20; 1988 (4), pp. 27–47; Liu Fu 劉復, "Xi Han shidai de rigui 西漢時代的日晷," *Guoxue jikan* 3:4 (1932), pp. 573–610; Yang Lien-sheng, "A Note on the So-Called TLV Mirrors and the Game *Liu-po*," *Harvard Journal of Asiatic Studies* 9 (1947), pp. 202–206; Yang, "An Additional Note on the Ancient Game *Liu-po*," *Harvard Journal of Asiatic Studies* 15 (1952), pp. 124–139.

112. W. D. Yetts, *The Cull Chinese Bronzes* (London: Courtauld Institute, 1939), pp. 116–120, 151, 155; Joseph Needham, *Science and Civilisation in China*, vol. 3, *Mathematics and the Sciences of the Heavens and Earth* (Cambridge: Cambridge University, 1970), pp. 302–309, and figs. 126, 128–129, 132.

113. Schuyler Cammann, "The 'TLV' Pattern on Cosmic Mirrors of the Han Dynasty," *Journal of the American Oriental Society* 68 (1948), pp. 159–167; Bulling "The Decoration of Some Mirrors of the Chou and Han Periods."

114. Harper, "Warring States Natural Philosophy and Occult Thought," pp. 836–839; Kalinowski, "Astronomie calendaire et calcul de position," pp. 87–89; Kalinowski, "The *Xingde* Texts from Mawangdui," pp. 135–145. For the references to cords

and hooks, both in astronomy and construction, see *Huainanzi*, ch.1, "Yuan dao," p. 16; ch. 3, "Tian wen," pp. 37, 39; ch. 11, "Qi su," pp. 179, 185.

115. Hayashi, "Kan kyō no zugara ni, san ni tsuite," pp. 1–66, esp. pp. 10–11.

116. Loewe, *Ways to Paradise*, pp. 75–85; Sidney M. Kaplan, "On the Origin of the TLV Mirror," *Revue des Arts Asiatiques* 11 (1937), pp. 21–24.

117. *Shi ji* 127, p. 3218. See also *Zhou li zhu shu*, ch. 26, "Da shi 大史," p. 15a. In his commentary on the line "The Grand Astrologer held in his arms the seasons of Heaven and shared a chariot with the Grand Musician," the Eastern Han commentator Zheng Zhong, writing in the middle of the first century A.D., stated: "When one sent out a large army, the Grand Astrologer was in charge of holding the diviner's board in order to know the seasons of Heaven and fix good and bad fortune. Astrologers were in charge of knowing the way of Heaven."

118. *Shi ji* 128, p. 3229; *Han shu* 99c, p. 4190.

119. Judy Chungwa Ho, "The Twelve Calendrical Animals in Tang Tombs," in *Ancient Mortuary Traditions in China*, ed. George Kuwayama (Los Angeles: Far Eastern Art Council and Los Angeles County Museum of Art, 1991), pp. 66–68.

120. *Jiangling Yutaishan Chu mu* 江陵雨台山楚墓 (Beijing: Wenwu, 1984), pp. 103–104; "Hebei sheng Pingshan xian Zhanguo shiqi Zhongshan guo muzang fajue jianbao 河北省平山縣戰國時期中山國墓葬發掘簡報," *Wenwu* 1979 (1), p. 13, figs. 32, 33; *Yunmeng Shuihudi Qin mu* 云夢睡虎地秦墓 (Beijing: Wenwu, 1981), pp. 55–56; "Hubei Jiangling Fenghuangshan Xi Han mu fajue jianbao 湖北江陵鳳凰山西漢墓發掘簡報," *Wenwu* 1974 (6), pp. 50–51; "Changsha Mawangdui er, san hao Han mu fajue jianbao 長沙馬王堆二三號漢墓發掘簡報," *Wenwu* 1974 (7), pp. 45–46; Xiong Chuanxin 熊傳新, "Tan Mawangdui san hao Han mu chutu de lubo 談馬王堆三號漢墓出土的陸博," *Wenwu* 1979 (4), pp. 35–39; Fu Juyou and Chen Songchang, *Mawangdui Han mu wenwu*, p. 76; Fu Juyou, "Lun Qin Han shiqi de boju boxi jian ji bowenjing 論秦漢時期的博局，博戲，兼及博紋鏡," *Kaogu xuebao* 1986 (1), pp. 25–26. For a Han tomb tile that clearly depicts a *liu bo* board as a classic TLV pattern, see Wang Baoxiang 王襃祥, "Henan Xinye chutu de Han dai huaxiangzhuan 河南新野出土的漢代畫像磚," *Kaogu* 1964 (2), p. 91, fig. 1:5. The major Warring States anecdotes involving *liu bo* are discussed in Yang Lien-sheng, "An Additional Note on the Ancient Game Liu-po," p. 138.

121. Yin Difei 殷滌非, "Xi Han Ruyin Hou de zhanpan he tianwen yiqi 西漢汝陰侯的占盤和天文儀器," *Kaogu* 1978 (5), pp. 338–343, fig. on p. 340; "Fuyang Shuanggudui Xi Han Ruyin Hou mu fajue jianbao 阜陽雙古堆西漢汝陰侯墓發掘簡報," *Wenwu* 1978 (8), pp. 12–19, fig. 3, ill. on p. 25.

122. Li Ling, *Zhongguo fang shu kao*, pp. 90–99; Wang Zhenduo 王振鐸, "Sinan, zhinan zhen, yu luojing pan 司南，指南針，與羅經盤," *Zhongguo kaogu xuebao* 3 (1948), pp. 119–259; Yan Dunjie 嚴敦傑, "Ba liuren shipan 跋六任式盤," *Wenwu cankao ziliao* 1958 (7), pp. 20–26; Yan Dunjie, "Guanyu Xi Han chuqi de shipan he zhanpan 關於西漢初期的式盤和占盤," *Kaogu* 1978 (5), pp. 334–337; Yan Dunjie, "Shipan zongshu 式盤總述," *Kaogu xuebao* 1985 (4), pp. 445–464; Chen Mengjia 陳夢家, "Han jian nianlibiao shu 漢簡年歷表敘," *Kaogu xuebao* 1965 (2), pp. 103–147; Luo Fuyi 羅福頤, "Han shipan xiao kao 漢式盤小考," *Gu wenzi yanjiu* 11 (1985), pp. 252–264; Lian Shaoming 連劭名, "Shipan zhong de si men yu ba gua 式盤中的四門與八卦," *Wenwu* 1987 (9), pp. 33–36; Li Xueqin 李學勤, "Zai lun bo shu shier shen 再論帛書十二神," in *Jianbo yi ji yu xueshu shi* 簡帛佚籍與學術史 (Taipei: Shibao

Wenhua, 1994), pp. 58–70; Needham, *Science and Civilisation in China*, vol. 4:1, *Physics and Physical Technology: Physics* (Cambridge: Cambridge University, 1962), pp. 261–269; Donald Harper, "The Han Cosmic Board," *Early China* 4 (1978–1979), pp. 1–10; Christopher Cullen, "Some Further Points on the *Shih*," *Early China* 6 (1980–1981), pp. 31–46; Harper, "The Han Cosmic Board: A Response to Christopher Cullen," *Early China* 6 (1980–1981), pp. 47–56; Marc Kalinowski, "Les instruments astro-calendériques des Han et la méthode *liu ren*," *Bulletin de l'École Française d'Extrême-Orient* 72 (1983), pp. 309–419; Harper, "Warring States Natural Philosophy and Occult Thought," pp. 833–843; Stephen Field, "Cosmos, Cosmograph, and the Inquiring Poet: New Answers to the 'Heaven Questions,'" *Early China* 17 (1992), pp. 83–110.

123. K. E. Brashier, "Longevity Like Metal and Stone: The Role of the Mirror in Han Burials," *T'oung Pao* 81 (1995), pp. 202–214; Kalinowski, "The *Xingde* Texts from Mawangdui," p. 143 note 44.

124. *Shandong Han huaxiang shi xuanji* 山東漢畫像石選集 (Qi Lu Shu She, 1982), fig. 143.

125. Thus, Zhou Zheng insists that the TLV pattern came from the *liu bo* board, as indicated by an inscription describing the making of a mirror which states, "they carved into it the *liu bo* board to drive off the inauspicious." See Zhou Zheng 周錚, "'Guijujing yinggai wei bojujing 規矩鏡應改為博局鏡," *Kaogu* 1987 (12), pp. 1116–1118. Li Ling, however, argues that the *liu bo* board was patterned on the diviner's board, and that the TLV mirror—which he calls a *bo* board mirror—was patterned on the *liu bo* board. See *Zhongguo fang shu kao*, pp. 172–174. Sun Ji, in contrast, argues that both the TLV mirror decor and the *liu bo* board were derived from something else. See Sun Ji 孫機, *Han dai wenhua ziliao tushuo* 漢代文化資料圖說 (Beijing: Wenwu, 1991), pp. 270–273.

126. In addition to these features, the creation of these small images encompassing the world could be considered as an early form of the Chinese fascination with the miniature. See Rolf A. Stein, *Le monde en petit*, pp. 57–118.

127. Lewis, *Writing and Authority*, pp. 278–284.

128. Lewis, *Writing and Authority*, pp. 262–272.

129. *Han shu* 99c, p. 4190. See also *Shi ji* 128, p. 3229: "Wei Ping then set down the diviner's board and arose. He gazed up at the sky to examine the light from the moon, observe where the Dipper was pointing, and fix the direction of the sun. He was assisted by the carpenter's square and compass, backed up by the balances. When the four cords were fixed, the eight trigrams faced one another [as cast into the decor of the board]. He looked for good and bad fortune, and the beetle appeared first." The beetle mentioned here would be one of the animals that ringed the circular disk.

130. This procedure is described in *Taichan shu* (胎產書) from Mawangdui. See *Mawangdui Han mu bo shu* 馬王堆漢墓帛書), vol. 4, ed. Guojia Wenwuju Gu Wenxian Yanjiushi (Beijing: Wenwu, 1985), p. 134; Harper, *Early Chinese Medical Literature*, pp. 374–377.

131. Li Ling, *Zhongguo fang shu kao*, pp. 146–154.

132. There are three texts from Mawangdui that the editors have grouped under the title of *Xingde*. The most studied is the so-called text B. This is transcribed in Fu Juyou and Chen Songchang, *Mawangdui Han mu wenwu*, pp. 132–143 and examined in detail in Marc Kalinowski, "Mawangdui boshu *Xingde* shitan," 1 (1995), pp. 82–110; Kalinowski, "The *Xingde* Texts from Mawangdui."

133. Li Ling, *Zhongguo fang shu kao*, pp. 129–146.

134. Lewis, *Writing and Authority*, ch. 2–4, 7.

135. Harper, "Warring States Natural Philosophy and Occult Thought," pp. 831–832. See also Li Ling, *Zhongguo fang shu kao*, pp. 150–165.

136. Cammann, "The 'TLV' Pattern on Cosmic Mirrors of the Han Dynasty," pp. 159–167; Hwang, "Ming-tang," pp. 91–118, esp. pp. 94–98.

137. Loewe, *Ways to Paradise*, pp. 68, 70, 79, 83, 165, 166, 170–172, 174 note 25, 210–211; Komai, *Chūgoku kokyō no kenkyū*, p. 96; Hayashi, "Kan kyō no zugara ni, san ni tsuite," p. 15.

138. Umehara, *Kan Sangoku Rikuchō kinen kyō shūroku*, pp. 4–5. Michael Loewe uses a circular argument to suggest that the mirror is a forgery, but all other leading scholars accept it as genuine.

139. *Moriya Kōzō shūshū hōkaku kiku shishinkyō zuroku*, #JA 162 is the fullest version. Shorter ones appear in Chen Peifen 陳佩芬, *Shanghai Bowuguan cang qingtongqi* 上海博物館藏青銅器 (Shanghai: Shanghai Shuhua, 1987), #39, #40; Tomioka Kenzō 富岡謙藏, *Kokyō no kenkyū* 古鏡の研究 (Kyoto: Tomioka Masutarō, 1919), plate 41, #1, #2. Loewe, *Ways to Paradise*, p. 202 cites *Shodō zenshū* 書道全集 (Tokyo: Heibonsha, 1958), vol. 2, p. 172, plate 33.

140. Wang Shilun 王士倫, *Zhejiang chutu tongjing* 浙江出土銅鏡 (Beijing: Wenwu, 1987), #20.

141. Chen Peifen, *Shanghai Bowuguan cang qingtongqi*, #41. Loewe notes another inscription on the submission of barbarians from the time of Wang Mang. See *Ways to Paradise*, pp. 165, 174 note 25.

142. The idea that building a ritual structure could induce the submission of alien peoples figures in two poems in the *Shi jing*: See *Mao shi zhengyi*, ch. 16.2, #237, pp. 20a–22a; ch. 20.1, # 299, p. 17a.

143. *Huainanzi*, ch. 2, "Chu zhen," p. 112. The rhyming final characters are 方 *piwang, ("square"); 堂 *d'âng, ("hall"), and 光 *kwâng, ("brilliant").

144. Bulling, *The Decoration of Mirrors of the Han Period*, plates 15, 16. For inscriptions that liken mirrors to the sun and the moon, and speak of illumination, see Karlgren, "Early Chinese Mirror Inscriptions," pp. 9–79.

145. Umehara Sueji, *Kan izen no kokyō no kenkyū* 漢以前の古鏡の研究 (Kyoto: Tōhō Bunka Gakuin Kyōto Kenkyūsho, 1935), plate 23, #1; Hayashi Minao, "In—Shunjū zenki kinbun no shoshiki to jōyō goku no jidai hensen 殷—春秋前期金文の書式と常用語句の時代變遷," *Tōhō gakuhō* 55 (1983), supplementary leaf, fig. 8. On "four cosmic trees" in early China and the Bright Hall, see Hwang, "Ming-tang," ch. 5.

146. Yang, "An Additional Note on the Ancient Game Liu-po," p. 138; Lao, "Liubo ji boju zhi yanbian," p. 22.

147. *Shi ji* 3, p. 104; *Zhanguo ce*, ch. 5, "Qin san 秦三," p. 197; *Han Feizi ji shi*, ch. 11, "Wai chu shuo zuo shang 外儲說左上," p. 644. The "youth" in this story is another of the violent youths discussed in chapter three. On the *cong* 叢 discussed in the final story as a shrine to the earth god (or goddess), see Wen Yiduo, "Gaotang shennü chuanshuo zhi fenxi 高唐神女傳說之分析," in *Shenhua yu shi*, in *Wen Yiduo quan ji*, vol. 1, pp. 81–116.

148. *Fengsu tong yi jiao shi*, pp. 54, 55–56. Ying Shao ridicules these stories, noting that the forty-seven-year-old emperor could not have had an allotted span of eighteen years. The important point, however, is the existence of the stories. The tradition that Mt. Tai knew the length of people's lifespans appears in the third-century A.D. text, the *Bo wu zhi*. See *Bo wu zhi jiao zheng* 博物志校證 (Beijing: Zhonghua, 1980), ch. 1, "Di 地," p. 10.

149. Finsterbusch, *Verzeichnis und Motivindex der Han-Darstellungen*, figs. 49, 118, 143, 148, 260a, 1001. Other examples are listed in Loewe, *Ways to Paradise*, p. 145 note 40.

150. Hayashi, "Kankyō no zugara," pp. 24–65; Loewe, *Ways to Paradise*, pp. 60, 70, 72, 83.

151. *Shi ji* 127, p. 3218, where the *liu bo* board and the diviner's board are two methods of divination.

152. "Jiangling Wangjiatai 15 hao Qin mu 江陵王家台15號秦墓," *Wenwu* 1995 (1), pp. 37–43; Li Ling, *Zhongguo fangshu xu kao*, pp. 312–313.

153. *Xi jing za ji* 西京雜記, in *Han Wei Liuchao biji xiaoshuo daguan* 漢魏六朝筆記小說大觀 (Shanghai: Shanghai gu ji, 1999), p. 107. The nine characters on the Yinwan chart are *fang* 方, *lian* 廉, *jie* 楬, *dao* 道, *zhang* 張, *qu* 曲, *qu* 詘, *chang* 長, and *gao* 高. The four characters 方, 道, 張, and 高 appear in the formula from the *Xi jing za ji*. The character 楬 appears in the formula with the hand radical as 揭. The character 詘 appears with the corpse radical as 屈. The character 廉 is apparently replaced by its sometime synonym *pan* 畔, since both characters can mean "side." The characters 長 and 曲, which are both phonetically and semantically related to other characters on the list (張 and 詘), do not appear in the formula, which instead features *xuan* 玄 and *jiu* 究. However, the four-line formula in the *Xi jing za ji* uses nine characters, exactly the number of columns in the Yinwan chart.

154. "Jiangsu Donghai xian Yinwan Han mu qun fajue jianbao 江蘇東海縣尹灣漢墓群發掘簡報," *Wenwu* 1996 (8), plate 2 (between pp. 16–17); "Yinwan Han mu jiandu shiwen xuan 尹灣漢墓簡牘釋文選," *Wenwu* 1996 (8), pp. 30–31. For discussions of the manner of using the chart for divination, see Li Xueqin, "Bo ju zhan' yu guiju wen 博局占與規矩文," *Wenwu* 1997 (1), pp. 49–51; Liu Hongshi 劉洪石, "Donghai Yinwan Han mu shushulei jiandu shidu 東海尹灣漢墓術數類簡牘試讀," *Dongnan wenhua* 1997 (4), pp. 67–73; Liu Lexian 劉樂賢, "Yinwan Han mu chutu shushu wenxian chutan 尹灣漢墓出土數術文獻初探," in *Yinwan Han mu jiandu zonglun* 尹灣漢墓簡牘綜論 (Beijing: Kexue, 1999), pp. 177–182; Zeng Lanying 曾藍瑩, "Yinwan Han mu 'Bo ju zhan' mu du shijie 尹灣漢墓博局占木牘試解," *Wenwu* 1999 (8), pp. 62–65; Li Jiemin 李解民, "'Yinwan Han mu Bo ju zhan mu du shijie' ding bu 尹灣漢墓博局占木牘試解訂補," *Wenwu* 2000 (1), pp. 73–75.

155. Xue Xiaotong 薛孝通, "Bo pu 博譜," quoted in *Taiping yu lan*, ch. 754, p. 4a.

156. Loewe, *Ways to Paradise*, p. 36. For a color plate, see Fu and Chen, *Mawangdui Han mu wenwu*, p. 19; *Changsha Mawangdui Yi hao Han mu* 長沙馬王堆一號漢墓 (Beijing: Wenwu, 1973), p. 40.

157. Hwang Ming-chorng, "Ming-tang," pp. 105–106.

158. *Chu ci bu zhu*, ch. 9, "Zhao hun," p. 4a. This poem itself is a verbal chart, moving through the four directions in turn, up to Heaven, and down to the underworld before returning to the world of men.

159. Yuan Ke 袁珂, *Shan hai jing jiao zhu* 山海經校注 (Shanghai: Guji, 1980), pp. 47, 294, 298.

160. "Hebei sheng Pingshan xian Zhanguo shiqi Zhongshan guo muzang fajue jianbao," *Wenwu* 1979 (1), p. 26. On the identification as *liu bo* boards, see Kominami Ichirō 小南一郎, "Rokuhaku no uchūron 六博の宇宙論," *Gekkan hyakka* (1987: 7–8); Hayashi, *Kandai no kamigami*, p. 22; Li Xueqin, "Lun Hanshan Lingjiatan yu gui, yu ban 論含山凌家灘玉龜，玉版," *Zhongguo wenhua* 4 (1992), pp. 144–149; Li Xueqin, "A Neolithic Jade Plaque and Ancient Chinese Cosmology," *National Palace Museum Bulletin* 27:5–6 (1993), pp. 1–8.

161. *Huainanzi*, ch. 4, "Dixing," p. 58.

162. On mirrors in the coffin, see *Han shu* 68, pp. 2948–2949; Brashier, "Longevity Like Metal and Stone," pp. 203, 207–210, 213, 222, 226–27. On the banner, see Loewe, *Ways to Paradise*, p. 30.

163. The secondary literature on the *Shan hai jing* consists largely of brief articles on aspects of the work. Many try to identify modern equivalents of the places named, a futile task given the mythical core of the text. Among the few book-length treatments are Matsuda Minoru 松田稔, *Sangaikyō no kisoteki kenkyū* 山海經の基礎的研究 (Tokyo: Rikkan Shoin, 1995); Xu Xianzhi 徐顯之, *Shan hai jing tan yuan* 山海經探原 (Wuhan: Wuhan Chubanshe, 1991); Yun Ruxin 惲茹辛, ed., *Shan hai jing yanjiu lunji* 山海經研究論集 (Hong Kong: Zhongshan Tushu, 1974). There is also a dissertation: Suh Kyung Ho, "A Study of 'Shan-hai-ching': Ancient Worldviews Under Transformation" (Ph.D. diss., Harvard University, 1993). Dealing with spatial organization there is a valuable article: Véra V. Dorofeeva-Lichtmann, "Conception of Terrestrial Organization in the *Shan Hai Jing*," *Bulletin de l'École Française d'Extrême Orient* 82 (1995), pp. 57–110. There is also a translation: Rémi Mathieu, tr., *Étude sur la mythologie et l'ethnologie de la Chine ancienne: Traduction annotée du Shanhai jing*, 2. vols. (Paris: Collège de France, Institut des Hautes Études Chinoises, 1983). On the text, editions, and major studies, see the article by Riccardo Fracasso in *Early Chinese Texts: A Bibliographical Guide*, pp. 357–367.

164. The shortest is only a dozen characters. The longest is more than four hundred, but this is often regarded as a later interpolation from the *Shui jing zhu*. See Ogawa Takuchi 小川琢治, "Shan hai jing kao 山海經考," in *Xian Qin jing ji kao* 先秦經籍考 (reprint ed., Shanghai: Shanghai Wenyi, 1990), part 3, pp. 13–14.

165. *Shi ji* 123, p. 3178; *Han shu* 30, pp. 1774–1775. The explanation of the subcategory "Methods of Forms" is: "To show on a large scale the topography of the Nine Provinces, and thereby establish a proper form for city walls and houses. [They deal with] the degrees and numbers of the bone structure [i.e., physiognomy] of men and domestic animals, as well as the shapes of vessels, in order to distinguish noble from base and auspicious from inauspicious in their 'tone/energy'." See Chen Pan 陳槃, "Zhanguo Qin Han jian fangshi kaolun 戰國秦漢間方士考論," *Lishi Yuyan Yanjiusuo jikan* 17 (1948), pp. 32–33; Ngo Van Xuyet, *Magie et politique dans la Chine ancienne* (Paris: Presses Universitaires de France, 1976), pp. 151–152.

166. Bi Yuan 畢沅, *Shan hai jing xin jiao zheng* 山海經新校正 (1781, rep. ed., Taipei: Xin Xing, 1962); Wu Chengzhi 吳承志, *Shan hai jing dili jin shi* 山海經地理今釋, in *Qiu shu zhai congshu* 求恕齋叢書 (Liu Chenggan 劉承幹, 1922); Wei Tingsheng 衛挺生 and Xu Shengmo 徐聖謨, *Shan hai jing dili tu kao* 山海經地理圖考 (Taipei: Huagang, 1974); Fu Yongfa, *Shenzhou de faxian: Shan hai jing de dili kao*

神州的發現：山海經的地理考 (Kunming:Yunnan Renmin, 1992); Section F of Riccardo Fracasso, "The Shanhaijing: A bibliography by subject," *Cina* 23 (1991), pp. 81–104. Mathieu's translation also seeks modern equivalents.

167. Dorofeeva-Lichtmann, "Terrestrial Organization," pp. 61–66; Unno Kazutaka 海野一隆, "Kodai Chūgokujin no chiriteki sekaikan 古代中國人の地理的世界觀," *Tōhō shūkyo* 43 (1973), pp. 35–51.

168. Lewis, *Writing and Authority*, ch. 7.

169. Matsuda, *Sangaikyō no kisoteki kenkyū*, part 1, ch. 1; part 3, ch. 3–4; Suh, "A Study of 'Shan-hai-ching'," ch. 5–8. Matsuda divides the book into two sections, while Suh distinguishes three by separating the "Great Wilderness" section from the "Classic of Seas." See also Gu Jiegang, "Wu zang shan jing shi tan 五臧山經試探," *Shixue luncong* 1 (1934); Hou Renzhi 侯仁之, "Hai wai si jing, Hai nei si jing, yu Da huang si jing Hai nei jing bijiao 海外四經，海內四經，與大荒四經海內經比較," *Yu gong* 7 (1937), pp. 319–326.

170. Lestrignant, "Fortunes de la singularité à la Renaissance: le genre de l'Isolario'," in *Écrire le monde à la Renaissance*, pp. 17–48.

171. Dorofeeva-Lichtmann, "Conception of Terrestrial Organization," pp. 58, 60, 86.

172. *Shan hai jing jiao zhu*, p. 477. Another reference to the text as the work of Yu and his followers appears at the end of the *Shan jing*. Here Yu states he has passed through 5,370 mountains, gives the dimensions of the world, describes products of mountains and their importance, and repeats a formula on the centrality of the *feng* and *shan* sacrifices. See *Shan hai jing jiao zhu*, pp. 179–180. The work itself ends with the announcement: "The emperor then commanded Yu to apply soil in order to fix the Nine Provinces." See *Shan hai jing jiao zhu*, p. 472.

173. Lewis, *Writing and Authority*, pp. 35–42, 54–63, 308–325.

174. Keightley, "The Late Shang State," pp. 548–558; Keightley, *The Ancestral Landscape*, ch. 5, 7.

175. Ogura Yoshihiko 小倉芳彥, *Chūgoku kodai seiji shisō kenkyū* 中國古代政治思想研究 (Tokyo: Aoki, 1970), pp. 62–73; Lewis, *Sanctioned Violence*, pp. 182, 187–194; *Writing and Authority*, pp. 41–42; Bilsky, *The State Religion of Ancient China*, vol. 2, pp. 248–250.

176. Jiang Shaoyuan 江紹源, *Zhongguo gudai lüxing zhi yanjiu* 中國古代旅行之研究 (Shanghai: Shangwu, 1935); Lewis, *Sanctioned Violence*, pp. 23, 182, 187–194.

177. Kaizuka Shigeki 貝塚茂樹, "Kamigami no tanjō 神神の誕生," in *Kaizuka Shigeki chosaku shū* 著作集, vol. 5 (Tokyo: Chūō Kōron, 1978), p. 16. See also the discussion in chapter four.

178. Matsuda, *Sangaikyō no kisoteki kenkyū*, section 3, chapter 5; Itō Seiji 伊藤清司, "Yamagawa no kamigami—*Sangaikyō* no kenkyū 山川の神神—山海經の研究," *Shigaku* 41:1 (1969), pp. 31–61; 42:2 (1969), pp. 29–78; 42:4 (1969), pp. 73–106.

179. Matsuda, *Sangaikyō no kisoteki kenkyū*, pp. 159–165, 175. Matsuda points out that in this regard the work has links to the *Shi jing* and the *Chu ci*, while remaining distinct from the ritual texts.

180. Matsuda, *Sangaikyō no kisoteki kenkyū* devotes chapters to each of these. On animals see section 2, ch. 1. On plants see section 2, ch. 2. On minerals see section

2, chapter 3. On spirits see section 3, chapter 1. On God-on-High see section 1, ch. 3.

181. On hybrid creatures in the *Shan hai jing*, see Riccardo Fracasso, "Teratoscopy or Divination by Monsters, Being a Study on the *Wu-tsang Shan-ching*," *Hanxue yanjiu* 1:2 (December 1983), pp. 669–677. An appendix on pp. 681–90 has assembled the appearances of strange creatures from the five chapters of the *Shan jing*; Michael Loewe, "Man and Beast: The Hybrid in Early Chinese Art and Literature," *Numen* 25:2 (1978), pp. 97–117.

182. He Guanzhou 何觀州, "Shanhaijing zai kexue shang zhi pipan ji zuozhe zhi shidai kao 山海經在科學上之批判及作者之時代考," *Yanjing xuebao* 7 (1930), pp. 1363–1375.

183. Itō Seiji, "Kodai Chūgoku no minkan iryō—*Sangaikyō* no kenkyū 古代中國 の民間醫療—山海經の研究," *Shigaku* 42:4 (1969), pp. 41–62; 43:3 (1970), pp. 17–33; 43:4 (1971), pp. 39–87; John W. Schiffeler, "Chinese Folk Medicine: a Study of the Shan-hai ching," *Asian Folklore Studies* 39:2 (1980), pp. 41–83.

184. *Shan hai jing jiao zhu*, pp. 3, 5–6; Matsuda, *Sangaikyō no kisoteki kenkyū*, pp. 196–201.

185. *Shan hai jing jiao zhu*, pp. 36, 115.

186. *Shan hai jing jiao zhu*, pp. 18, 28, 30, 41, 130–31, 142 (2), 143, 144 (2), 147.

187. *Shan hai jing jiao zhu*, p. 41. Page 141 tells of a type of stone that can also be eaten.

188. *Shan hai jing jiao zhu*, p. 30.

189. For names only, see *Shan hai jing jiao zhu*, pp. 45 (2), 51, 54, 56, 124, 135, 144, 159. For their appearance, see pp. 45, 47, 50, 55, 61, 125, 128, 151–152, 153 (2), 176 (2). For their sounds, see pp. 47, 55, 61, 125.

190. *Shan hai jing jiao zhu*, p. 159.

191. *Shan hai jing jiao zhu*, pp. 45, 47, 50, 52, 56, 125, 128, 159. For the reference to a spirit as an omen, see p. 165. For the reference to an animal in God-on-High's government, see p. 47.

192. *Shan hai jing jiao zhu*, pp. 8, 15, 19, 32, 38, 58, 66, 79, 84, 99, 105, 110, 113, 116, 124, 128, 132, 135, 141, 150, 156, 160, 163, 174.

193. J.-P. Vernant, "Le mythe prométhéen chez Hésiod," in *Mythe et société en Grèce ancienne* (Paris: François Maspero, 1981), pp. 177–194; Charles Segal, *Tragedy and Civilization: An Interpretation of Sophocles* (Cambridge: Harvard University, 1981), pp. 34–41.

194. The only spirits with no reference to human forms are *Shan hai jing jiao zhu*, pp. 8, 15, 160.

195. Dorofeeva-Lichtmann, "Conception of Terrestrial Organization in the *Shan hai jing*," pp. 86–87.

196. *Shan hai jing jiao zhu*, pp. 29, 38, 45, 47, 125, 141, 142, 167, 169. There is also a tree named the "god's Room [*di wu* 帝屋]." See p. 148.

197. *Shan hai jing jiao zhu*, pp. 42–43. There is also a mountain named Guzhong 鼓鍾 that thus combines the name of the son of the god with the name of the mountain. See p. 142. This mountain is identified as the site of "God-on-High's Tower (*di tai* 帝臺)," also mentioned on pp. 141, 167.

198. *Shan hai jing jiao zhu*, pp. 92, 142, 176, 170. A fragment of the *Guang yi ji* in the *Tai ping yu lan* explains that this last was a daughter of the Red God who lived in the tree and studied the methods of immortality. The Red God set the tree ablaze and she ascended to Heaven as an immortal.

199. On the identity of the Fiery and Red Gods, see Lewis, *Sanctioned Violence*, pp. 175–176, 179–181.

200. Edward H. Schafer, *The Divine Woman: Dragon Ladies and Rain Maidens in T'ang Literature* (Berkeley: University of California, 1973).

201. Yuan Weichun, *Qin Han bei shu*, pp. 103, 253, 511. The mountain spirit's "hidden assistance" with its direct links to Heaven and Earth echoes the "Shuo gua" in the *Yi jing*, which tells how the sage received "hidden assistance from the spirits and initiated the use of yarrow stalks." *Zhou yi zheng yi*, ch. 9, "Shuo gua," p. 1b.

202. *Shang shu zhu shu*, ch. 6, "Yu gong," p. 28b; *Huainanzi*, ch. 4, "Di xing," p. 55; *Lü shi chun qiu jiao shi*, ch. 13, "You shi," pp. 657, 658. I amend *zhou* 州 to *shan* 山 in the "Yu gong" because (1) otherwise there would be a duplication of the phrase "Nine Provinces," (2) the commentary indicates the character *shan*, and (3) it is followed immediately by *kan* 刊 and *lü* 旅. The first is the verb used in the chapter to describe Yu's treatment of the mountains and the second is the standard name for mountain sacrifices. The *Shi ji* also indicates a reference to "Nine Mountains" in the version of the text that existed in the time of Sima Qian. See *Shi ji* 2, p. 67.

203. Yuan, *Qin Han bei shu*, pp. 103–104, 253–254, 511–513. For the account in the geography monograph, see *Han shu* 28a, pp. 1545, 1566.

204. See *Shang shu zhu shu*, ch. 6, "Yu gong," p. 22a (2).

205. *Li ji zhu shu*, ch. 32, "Sang fu xiao ji 喪服小記," pp. 7b–8a; ch. 34, "Da zhuan," pp. 7b, 10a–b.

206. On mountain chains and kin ties, see Brashier, "Baishi Mountain," pp. 176–181.

207. Dorofeeva-Lichtmann, "Territorial Organization," pp. 71–84, 96–101, produces more than a dozen charts without settling on a single one. See also Suh, "A Study of the 'Shan-hai-ching'," pp. 302–309.

208. See R. Fracasso, "Shan hai ching," p. 358.

209. Dorofeeva-Lichtmann argues that "Inside the Seas" and "Outside the Seas" form a center-periphery pair divided on the horizontal dimension, while "Mountains" and "Vast Wilds" form a center-periphery pair divided on the vertical dimension. She argues that since the character translated "wilds"—*huang* 荒—has the signific for "grass," it refers to "grasslands," which are opposed to mountains. See pp. 82–84. This is forced. Moreover, far from emphasizing the lowness of the "wilds," the section refers to mountains far more frequently than the two "Seas" sections. Suh argues that the same regions are treated from different perspectives or viewpoints, with the later chapters emphasizing the extent of the physical world, and above all a clear division between inner and outer. See "A Study of the Shan-hai-ching," pp. 101–103, 306–307. My own exposition is based on this argument.

210. Lewis, *Writing and Authority*, ch. 7–8.

211. *Shan hai jing jiao zhu*, p. 184. The first half of this passage also appears with minor variations in *Huainanzi*, ch. 4, "Di xing," p. 55. It is attributed to Yu in the

Liezi. See *Liezi ji shi* 列子集釋, annotated by Yang Bojun 楊伯峻 (Beijing: Zhonghua, 1979), ch. 5, "Tang wen 湯問," p. 162. Since the preceding chapter of the *Shan hai jing* ends with a speech attributed to Yu about the mountains that he has traversed, Bi Yuan has suggested that this was originally a single speech split into two by later editors, perhaps Liu Xiang.

212. *Shan hai jing jiao zhu*, pp. 206, 227, 248, 265. The gods are Zhurong in the south, Rushou in the west, Yujiang in the north, and Goumang in the east. On two of these deities, see Riegel, "Kou-mang and Ju-shou," pp. 55–83.

213. *Shan hai jing jiao zhu*, pp. 188, 260, 340, 344, 346, 348, 354, 356, 357, 358, 391, 394, 396, 400, 402, 404, 406, 409, 413.

214. Matsuda, *Sangaikyō no kisoteki kenkyū*, pp. 7–19.

215. *Shan hai jing jiao zhu*, pp. 185, 187.

216. *Huainanzi*, ch. 4, "Di xing," pp. 62–64.

217. *Shan hai jing jiao zhu*, pp. 267, 269, 283, 293, 309, 311, 315, 321 (3), 322, 324, 327, 330, 331 (2).

218. *Shan hai jing jiao zhu*, p. 478.

219. Probably the most comprehensive attempt to explain monstrous appearances in terms of misunderstood folkways is the notes to Rémi Mathieu's translation. For the ethnological approach, see Sun Zuoyun 孫作雲, "Shuo yuren: yuren tu yuren shenhua ji fei sian sixiang zhi tuteng zhuyi de kaocha 說羽人：羽人圖羽人神話及飛仙思想之圖騰主義的攷察," *Guoli Shenyang Bowuyuan Choubei Weiyuanhui huikan* 1 (1947), pp. 29–74; Xu Xianzhi, *Shan hai jing tanyuan*, pp. 1–4.

220. Edith Hall, *Inventing the Barbarian: Greek Self-Definition through Tragedy* (Oxford: Oxford University, 1989); Romm, *The Edges of the Earth in Ancient Greek Thought*; Hartog, *Le miroir d'Hérodote: Essai sur la représentation de l'autre*; Hartog, *Mémoire d'Ulysse: Récits sur la frontière en Grèce ancienne*.

221. *Mozi jian gu*, ch. 6, "Jie zang xia 節葬下," pp. 115–116; ch. 13, "Lu wen," p. 285; *Mengzi zhengyi* IIIA "Teng Wen gong shang," pp. 230–233: China is identified with sages, in contrast to southern language and culture; *Xunzi ji jie*, ch. 5, "Wang zhi," p. 107; ch. 14, "Yue lun," p. 253: "barbarian customs" are paired with "heterodox music" as that which negates "refined" culture; *Lü shi chun qiu jiao shi*, ch. 14, "Yi shang 義賞," p. 779: non-Chinese peoples are the image of a state where villainy and chaos have become human nature.

222. *Han shu* 49, p. 2284. See also p. 2281: "Now the topography and the skills of the Xiongnu are completely different from those of China"; pp. 2282–2283: "Now those Hu, Yiju, and other barbarians who have surrendered and come over to us as dependent states number in the thousands. Their diet and skills are the same as those of the Xiongnu."

223. *Shi ji* 43, pp. 1808, 1809 note 2; *Xin xu shu zheng*, p. 310; *Huainanzi*, ch. 11 "Qi su," pp. 174 (2); *Li ji zhu shu*, ch. 12, "Wang zhi," p. 26b; *Liezi ji shi*, ch. 5, p. 165.

224. *Han shu* 48, p. 2240; *Jiazi xin shu jiao shi*, ch. 3.11, "Wei bu xin 威不信," pp. 417–418; ch. 4.1, "Xiongnu 匈奴," pp. 421–423; ch. 7.2, "Er bi 耳痺," p. 834; ch. 9.3, "Xiu zheng yu shang 脩政語上," pp. 1044–1045. Without pejorative intent, the *Huainanzi* also treats the non-Chinese as the opposite of the sages and diametrically

opposed to Chinese customs. See *Huainanzi*, ch. 9, "Zhu shu," p. 131; ch. 11, "Qi su," pp. 174, 175. It also establishes a direct progression from neighboring barbarians to the bizarre peoples at the edges of the earth: "Therefore when you enter a state you follow its customs, and when you enter a house you observe its tabooed names. If you do not violate prohibitions when entering or go against practices when advancing, then even if you go to the states of the Yi [eastern barbarians], the Di [northern barbarians], or the naked people, connecting your chariot tracks to beyond the most distant regions, you will never be in desperate straits." See ch. 11, "Qi su," p. 175.

225. *Shan hai jing jiao zhu*, pp. 343, 344, 347, 371–72.

226. *Shan hai jing jiao zhu*, pp. 225, 347. The state of the "big people" is mentioned in both the "Outside the Seas" and the "Vast Waste." The former cites the great size of the inhabitants, while the latter mentions only their distinctive marketplace and hall. See pp. 252, 341. The "Beyond the Seas" section describes "the people who do not die" as being black and immortal, while the "Vast Waste" section gives their surname and describes their diet. See pp. 196, 370. "Beyond the Seas" states that the "hairy people" have hair all over their bodies, while the "Vast Waste" gives their surname, describes their diet and the animals they train, and traces their genealogy back to Yu. See pp. 264, 424.

227. *Jiazi xin shu jiao shi*, ch. 5.2, "Bao fu," p. 626; *Han shu* 48, p. 2252: "The formation of customs and accumulation of habits depends entirely on those around you. When the northern barbarians and the southern barbarians are born they produce the same sounds, and there is no difference in their desires. But when they have grown up and formed customs, even passing through a series of translators they cannot communicate, and even if it meant their deaths they would not act like each other. Teaching and habits make them like this." See also *Huainanzi*, ch.11, "Qi su," p. 172; *Lun heng ji jie*, ch. 25, "Jie chu," pp. 506–507.

228. *Shan hai jing jiao zhu*, pp. 202 (2), 244, 273 (2), 291, 364, 380, 419, 445.

229. *Shan hai jing jiao zhu*, pp. 338, 344, 346, 350, 351, 367, 368, 371, 377, 378, 381, 388, 392, 395, 402, 410, 413, 415, 423, 424, 434, 435, 436 (3), 438, 442, 453, 462, 465 (2), 466, 468 (2), 469, 471.

230. *Chu ci bu zhu*, ch. 1, pp. 2b–3a. The fact that divinities have tombs is not surprising, as the Yellow Emperor also had a tomb in the Han despite having ascended to Heaven as an immortal.

231. *Shan hai jing jiao zhu*, pp. 355: "There are multi-colored birds who whirl around while facing one another. The god Jun descended and befriended them. He sent down two altars, which these multi-colored birds supervise"; 359: "In the northeast corner of the Vast Waste there is a mountain called Xiongli. The Responding Dragon resides at its southern extremity. He killed Chi You and Kuafu, but could not ascend again. Therefore he sends down many droughts. If during a drought one makes an image of the Responding Dragon, one gets a great rain"; 392: "The god Jun sired Hou Ji. [Hou] Ji descended into the world with the hundred grains"; 407: "There is a red dog called 'Heaven's Dog'. Wherever he descends there is war"; 414: "Beyond the southwestern sea, south of the Vermilion River, and west of the Flowing Sands there is a man with earrings made from two blue-green snakes who rides on two dragons. He is called Qi of the Xia [the son of Yu]. He made three offerings to Heaven, obtained the "Nine Changes" and the "Nine Songs" [now included in the *Chu ci*] and came back down with them"; 430: "The Yellow God than sent down a

celestial woman named Ba. The rain stopped, and he killed Chi You. Ba could not ascend again"; 466: "The god Jun presented to Yi a vermilion bow with white-feathered arrows in order that he could give comfort to the states down below. Yi from this time began to take pity on [the people] and eliminate all the hazards in the territory below." Moreover, three different passages in the final section tell of places where beings can go up to Heaven and back down again. See pp. 415, 444, 448. On their towers, and that of the God-on-High, see pp. 141, 167, 233 (2), 313 (4), 380, 399, 428, 430.

232. *Shan hai jing jiao zhu*, pp. 198, 372. Zuochi figures little in other texts. Granet constructs a model in which Yi kills destructive beings associated with each of the directions, and Zuochi is associated with the south. See Granet, *Danses et légendes*, pp. 378–381. Another passage indicates that, at least in the *Shan hai jing*, Yi acted as the agent of the god Jun. See p. 466 quoted in the previous note.

233. *Shan hai jing jiao zhu*, p. 214.

234. *Shan hai jing jiao zhu*, pp. 218, 253 (2), 307, 311: these last two refer to a corpse described as a rebel whose name consists of two characters [*er fu* 貳負] that can both mean "treason," 314—this corpse is described as an executed criminal, 319: this corpse has been torn to pieces, 351, 355, 375, 400, 411: this figure, like Xingtian, is a beheaded rebel who clutches a lance and shield, 435, 462: this corpse is a criminal with bound hands, wearing a cangue, and carrying a lance.

235. Lewis, *Sanctioned Violence*, ch. 5. In his commentary on the *Shan hai jing*, Yuan Ke interprets all the tales of combat in the text as folk memories of battles between early, tribal peoples.

236. *Shan hai jing jiao zhu*, pp. 359, 361, 427, 442, 430, 448. In one account the killing of Chi You is paired with the killing of Kuafu, a rebel who pursued the sun. See p. 238.

237. Anthony Pagden, *The Fall of Natural Man: The American Indian and the Origins of Comparative Ethnology* (Cambridge: Cambridge University, 1982); Antonello Gerbi, *The Dispute of the New World: The History of a Polemic, 1750–1900*, tr. Jeremy Moyle (Pittsburgh: University of Pittsburgh, 1973); Gerbi, *Nature in the New World: From Christopher Columbus to Gonzalo Fernández de Oviedo*, tr. Moyle (Pittsburgh: University of Pittsburgh, 1985).

238. Johannes Fabian, *Time and the Other: How Anthropology Makes Its Object* (New York: Columbia University, 1983).

239. Lewis, *Sanctioned Violence*, pp. 180, 191–192, 307, note 53.

240. *Shi ji* 7, p. 338.

241. *Xunzi ji jie*, ch. 3, "Fei xiang," pp. 46–48; *Huainanzi*, ch. 19, "Xiu wu," p. 337; *Lun heng ji jie*, ch. 2, "Gu xiang," pp. 52–53.

242. Lewis, *Sanctioned Violence*, pp. 155–157, 165–174; Lewis, *Writing and Authority*, pp. 109–129, 197–198.

243. *Shan hai jing jiao zhu*, pp. 465, 466, 468 (2), 469.

244. *Mengzi zheng yi* IA, "Liang Hui Wang shang," p. 54; IIIB, "Teng Wen Gong xia," p. 271: here the commanding of the barbarians follows immediately after Yu's controlling the flood and is linked directly to the expulsion of the animals; *Mozi jian gu*, ch. 5, "Fei gong zhong 非攻中," p. 86; "Fei gong xia," pp. 94, 95; *Li ji zhu shu*,

ch. 52, "Zhong yong 中庸," pp. 20b (2), 21b; *Lü shi chun qiu jiao shi*, ch. 2, "Gong ming 功名," p. 110; ch. 17, "Zhi du 知度," p. 1092; ch. 19, "Wei yu 為欲," pp. 1293–1294; *Guanzi jiao zheng*, ch. 5, "Ba guan 八觀," p. 73; ch. 8, "Xiao kuang," p. 126; ch. 11, "Xiao cheng 小稱," p. 181; ch. 23, "Qing zhong jia 輕重甲," p. 395; *Huainanzi*, ch. 11, "Qi su," p. 173; *Jiazi xin shu jiao shi*, ch. 3.11 "Wei bu xin," p. 417; ch. 9.3 "Xiu zheng yu shang," p. 1033: the Yellow God travels to the extremities of the earth before assuming rulership, pp. 1044–1045. The idea also figured in the stone inscriptions of Qin Shihuang. See *Shi ji* 6, p. 243 (2): the emperor visits distant lands where none failed to submit and "illuminates inner and outer," p. 245: his authority reaches wherever the sun shines and wherever human tracks reach, so that diverse customs are all corrected, p. 250: he shakes "the four extremities," p. 262: he unites "the entire universe."

245. *Shi ji* 117, pp. 3044, 3047, 3049, 3051 (4), 3065, 3067, 3071; *Han shu* 22, pp. 1052, 1054, 1056, 1060–1061, 1067, 1069. On these poems and their relation to earlier temple hymns, see Martin Kern, *Die Hymnen der chinesischen Staatsopfer: Literatur und Ritual in der politischen Repräsentation von der Han-zeit bis zu ende den Sechs Dynastien* (Stuttgart: Franz Steiner Verlag, 1997), pp. 174–303.

CONCLUSION

1. *Li ji zhu shu*, ch. 21, "Li yun," pp. 3a–4b. On the Han interpretation, see Ogata Isamu 尾形勇, *Chūgoku kodai no ie to kokka* 中國古代の家と國家 (Tokyo: Iwanami, 1979), pp. 241–279.

2. Ogata, *Chūgoku kodai no ie to kokka*.

3. Lewis, *Writing and Authority*, pp. 358–362.

WORKS CITED

PRIMARY SOURCES

Baopuzi nei pian jiao shi 抱朴子內篇校釋. Written by Ge Hong 葛洪. Annotated by Wang Ming 王明. Beijing: Zhonghua, 1980.

Baoshan Chu jian 包山楚簡. Beijing: Wenwu, 1991.

Bo hu tong de lun 白虎通德論. In *Han Wei cong shu* 漢魏叢書. Vol. 1. Taipei: Xinxing, 1977.

Bo wu jing yi yi 駁五經異義. Written by Xu Shen 許慎 and Zheng Xuan 鄭玄. In *Hou zhi bu zu zhai congshu* 後知不足齋叢書. N.p.: Chang Shubao, 1884.

Bo wu zhi jiao zheng 博物志校證. Compiled by Zhang Hua 張華. Annotated by Fan Ning 范寧. Beijing: Zhonghua, 1980.

Cai, Yong 蔡邕. *Cai Zhonglang wen ji* 蔡中郎文集. Si bu cong kan ed.

Chu ci bu zhu 楚辭補注. Annotated by Hong Xingzu 洪興祖. Si bu cong kan ed.

Chun qiu fan lu yi zheng 春秋繁露義證. Annotated by Su Yu 蘇輿. Beijing: Zhonghua, 1992.

Da Dai li ji jie gu 大戴禮記解詁. Annotated by Wang Pinzhen 王聘珍. Reprint ed. Beijing: Zhonghua, 1964.

Di wang shi ji ji cun 帝王世紀輯存. Compiled by Xu Zongyuan 徐宗元. Beijing: Zhonghua, 1964.

Dong guan Han ji jiao zhu 東觀漢記校注. Compiled by Liu Zhen 劉珍 et al. Annotated by Wu Shuping 吳樹平. Zhongzhou: Zhongzhou gu ji, 1987.

Du duan 獨斷. Written by Cai Yong. In *Han Wei cong shu*. Vol. 1. Taipei: Xinxing, 1977.

Er ya zhu shu 爾雅注疏. In *Shisan jing zhu shu* 十三經注疏. Vol. 8. Taipei: Yiwen, 1976.

Feng su tong yi jiao shi 風俗通義校釋. Written by Ying Shao 應劭. Annotated by Wu Shuping 吳樹平. Tianjin: Renmin, 1980.

Guanzi jijiao 管子集校. Ed. Guo Moruo 郭沫若, Wen Yiduo 聞一多, and Xu Weiyu 許維遹. Beijing: Kexue, 1956.

Guanzi jiao zheng 管子郊正. Annotated by Dai Wang 戴望. In *Xin bian zhu zi ji cheng* 新編諸子集成. Vol. 5. Taipei: Shijie, 1974.

[*Chun qiu*] *Gongyang zhuan zhu shu* 春秋公羊傳注疏. In *Shisan jing zhu shu*. Vol. 7. Taipei: Yiwen, 1976.

[*Chun qiu*] *Guliang zhuan zhu shu* 春秋穀梁傳注疏. In *Shisan jing zhu shu*. Vol. 7. Taipei: Yiwen, 1976.

Guodian Chu mu zhu jian 郭店楚墓竹簡. Beijing: Wenwu, 1998.

Guo yu 國語. Shanghai: Guji, 1978.

Han Feizi ji shi 韓非子集釋. Annotated by Chen Qiyou 陳奇猷. Shanghai: Renmin, 1974.

Han ji 漢紀. Written by Xun Yue 荀悦. Taipei: Shangwu, 1971.

Han shi wai zhuan ji shi 韓氏外傳集釋. Annotated by Xu Weiyu 許維遹. Beijing: Zhonghua, 1980.

Han shu 漢書. Compiled by Ban Gu 班固. Beijing: Zhonghua, 1962.

He tu kuo di xiang 河圖括地象. In *Gu wei shu* 古微書. In *Wei shu ji cheng* 緯書集成. Shanghai: Guji, 1994.

Hou Han shu 後漢書. Compiled by Fan Ye 范曄. Beijing: Zhonghua, 1965.

Hou Han shu ji jie 集解. Annotated by Wang Xianqian 王先謙. Taipei: Yiwen, 1956.

Houma meng shu 侯馬盟書. Ed. Shanxisheng Wenwu Gongzuo Weiyuanhui 山西省文物工作委員會. Shanghai: Wenwu, 1976.

Huainanzi 淮南子. Annotated by Gao You 高誘. In *Xin bian zhuzi ji cheng*. Vol. 7. Taipei: Shijie, 1974.

Huainanzi ji shi 集釋. Annotated by Wang Niansun 王念孫. Beijing: Zhonghua, 1998.

Huang Di nei jing ling shu jiao zhu yu yi 黃帝內徑靈樞校注語譯. Annotated by Guo Aichun 郭靄春. Tianjin: Tianjin kexue jishu, 1989.

Huang Di nei jing su wen ji zhu 黃帝內徑素問集注. Annotated by Zhang Yin'an 張隱菴. Shanghai: Shanghai kexue jishu, 1959.

Huayang guo zhi jiao zhu 華陽國志校注. Compiled by Chang Qu 常璩. Annotated by Liu Lin 劉琳. Taipei: Xin wen feng, 1988.

Ji gu lu 集古錄. Compiled by Ouyang Xiu 歐陽修. In *Shi ke shi liao cong shu* 石刻史料叢書. Vol. 77. Taipei: Yiwen, 1966.

Jiao Shi Yi lin 焦氏易林. Si bu cong kan edition.

Jiazi xin shu jiao shi 賈子新書校釋. Annotated by Qi Yuzhang 祁玉章. Taipei: Qi Yuzhang, 1974.

Jin shu 晉書. Beijing: Zhonghua, 1974.

Jing fa 經法. Beijing: Wenwu, 1976.

Juyan xin jian: Jiaqu hou guan 居延新簡：甲渠侯官. Beijing: Zhonghua, 1994.

Laozi dao de jing zhu 老子道德經注. Annotated by Wang Bi 王弼. In *Xin bian zhuzi ji cheng*. Vol. 3. Taipei: Shijie, 1974.

Li Bo ji jiaozhu 李白集校注. Shanghai: Gu ji, 1980.

Li He shi ji 李賀詩集. Beijing: Renmin Wenxue, 1984.

Li ji zhu shu 禮記注疏. In *Shi san jing zhu shu.* Vol. 5. Taipei: Yiwen, 1976.

Li shi 隸釋. Compiled by Hong Gua 洪适. In *Shike shiliao congshu.* Vol. 1–3. Taipei: Yiwen, 1966.

Liang Han jin shi ji 兩漢金石記. In *Shike shiliao congshu.* Vol. 4–5. Taipei: Yiwen, 1966.

Liang Jiang Wentong wenji 梁江文通文集. Si bu cong kan ed.

[*Gu*] *Lie nü zhuan* 古列女傳. Si bu cong kan ed.

Lie xian zhuan 列仙傳. In *Zheng tong Dao zang* 正統道藏. Vol. 8. Reprint ed. Taipei: Yiwen, 1976.

Liezi ji shi 列子集釋. Annotated by Yang Bojun 楊伯峻. Beijing: Zhonghua, 1979.

Lun heng ji jie 論衡集解. Written by Wang Chong 王充. Annotated by Liu Pansui 劉盼遂. Beijing: Gu ji, 1957.

Lun yu zheng yi 論語正義. Annotated by Liu Baonan 劉寶楠 and Liu Gongmian 劉恭冕. In *Xin bian zhu zi ji cheng.* Vol. 1. Taipei: Shijie, 1974.

Luoyang qielan ji jiao zhu 洛陽伽藍記校注. Written by Yang Xuanzhi 楊衒之. Annotated by Fan Xiangyong 范祥雍. Shanghai: Guji, 1958.

Lü shi chun qiu jiao shi 呂氏春秋校釋. Annotated by Chen Qiyou 陳奇猷. Shanghai: Xuelin, 1984.

Mao shi zheng yi 毛詩正義. In *Shi san jing zhu shu.* Vol. 2. Taipei: Yiwen, 1976.

Mawangdui Han mu bo shu 馬王堆漢墓帛書. Vol. 4. Beijing: Wenwu, 1985.

Mengzi zheng yi 孟子正義. Annotated by Jiao Xun 焦循. In *Xin bian zhuzi ji cheng.* Vol. 1. Taipei: Shijie, 1974.

Mozi jian gu 墨子間詁. Annotated by Sun Yirang 孫詒讓. In *Xin bian zhuzi ji cheng.* Vol. 6. Taipei: Shijie, 1974.

Mu Tianzi zhuan xi zheng jiangshu 穆天子傳西征講疏. Annotated by Gu Shi 顧實. Shanghai: Shangwu, 1934. Reprint ed. Taipei: Shangwu, 1976.

Qian fu lun jian 潛夫論箋. Written by Wang Fu 王符. Annotated by Wang Jipei 汪繼培. Beijing: Zhonghua, 1979.

Qin Han bei shu 秦漢碑述. Ed. Yuan Weichun 袁維春. Beijing: Gongyi meishu, 1990.

Quan shanggu sandai Qin Han Sanguo Liuchao wen 全上古三代秦漢三國六朝文. Ed. Yan Kejun 嚴可均. Beijing: Zhonghua, 1965.

[*Jiao zheng*] *San fu huang tu* 校正三輔黃圖. Annotated by Zhang Zongxiang 張宗祥. Shanghai: Gudian, 1958.

Sanfu jue lu 三輔決錄. In *Guanzhong cong shu* 關中叢書. Compiled by Song Liankui 宋聯奎. 1934. Reprint ed. Taipei: Yiwen, 1970.

San guo zhi 三國志. Compiled by Chen Shou 陳壽. Beijing: Zhonghua, 1959.

Shan hai jing jiao zhu 山海經校注. Annotated by Yuan Ke 袁珂. Shanghai: Guji, 1980.

Shan hai jing xin jiao zheng 山海經新校正. Annotated by Bi Yuan 畢沅. 1781. Reprint ed. Taipei: Xinxing, 1962.

Shang Jun shu zhu yi 商君書注譯. Annotated by Gao Heng 高亨. Beijing: Zhonghua, 1974.

Shang shu da zhuan ji jiao 尚書大傳輯校. Annotated by Chen Shouqi 陳壽祺. In *Huang Qing jing jie xu bian* 皇清經解續編. N.p.: Nanqing Shuyuan, 1888.

Shang shu ji shi 尚書集釋. Annotated by Qu Wanli 屈萬里. Taipei: Lianjing, 1983.

Shang shu zheng yi 尚書正義. In *Shi san jing zhu shu*. Vol. 1. Taipei: Yiwen, 1974.

Shen xian zhuan 神仙傳. Compiled by Ge Hong 葛洪. Abridged version in *Yun ji qi qian* 雲笈七籤. In *Zheng tong Dao zang*. Vol. 36–38. Reprint ed. Taipei: Yiwen, 1976.

Shi ji 史記. Written by Sima Qian 司馬遷. Beijing: Zhonghua, 1959.

Shi ming shu zheng bu 釋名疏證補. Written by Liu Xi 劉熙. Annotated by Wang Xianqian 王先謙. Reprint ed. Shanghai: Guji, 1984.

Shi yi ji 拾遺記. Compiled by Wang Jia 王嘉. Annotated by Qi Zhiping 齊治平. Beijing: Zhonghua, 1981.

Shizi 尸子. Si bu bei yao ed.

Shu yi ji 述異記. Compiled by Ren Fang 任昉. In *Bai zi quan shu* 百子全書. Hangzhou: Zhejiang guji, 1998.

Shuihudi Qin mu zhu jian 睡虎地秦慕竹簡. Beijing: Wenwu, 1978.

Shui jing zhu 水經注. Compiled by Li Daoyuan 李道元. Shanghai: Shijie, 1936.

Shuo wen jie zi zhu 説文解字注. Compiled by Xu Shen 許慎. Annotated by Duan Yucai 段玉裁. Taipei: Yiwen, 1974.

Shuo yuan 説苑. In *Han Wei cong shu*. Vol. 1. Taipei: Xinxing, 1977.

Si min yue ling ji shi 四民月令輯釋. Written by Cui Shi 崔寔. Annotated by Miao Qiyu 繆啓愉 and Wan Guoding 萬國鼎. Beijing: Nongye, 1981.

Sima fa zhi jie 司馬法直解. In *Ming ben wu jing qi shu zhi jie* 明本武經七書直解. Vol. 1. Taipei: Shi di jiaoyu, 1972.

Song shu 宋書. Compiled by Shen Yue 沈約. Beijing: Zhonghua, 1974.

Sou shen ji 搜神記. Compiled by Gan Bao 干寶. Annotated by Wang Shaoying 汪紹楹. Beijing: Zhonghua, 1979.

Sui shu 隋書. Beijing: Zhonghua, 1973.

[*Shi yi jia zhu*] *Sunzi* 十一家注孫子. Shanghai: Guji, 1978.

Taiping huan yu ji 太平寰宇記. N.p.: Hongxing Shan fang, 1803.

Taiping yu lan 太平御覽. Taipei: Shangwu, 1935.

Wen xuan 文選. Hong Kong: Shangwu, 1936.

Wenzi yao quan 文子要詮. Annotated by Li Dingsheng 李定生 and Xu Huijun 徐慧君. Shanghai: Fudan Daxue, 1988.

Wu Yue chun qiu 吳越春秋. Si bu bei yao ed.

Wuzi zhi jie 吳子直解. In *Ming ben wu jing qi shu*. Vol. 1. Taipei: Shi di jiaoyu, 1972.

Xi jing za ji 西京雜記. In *Han Wei Liuchao biji xiaoshuo daguan* 漢魏六朝筆記小説大觀. Shanghai: Shanghai gu ji, 1999.

Xian Qin Han Wei Jin Nanbeichao shi 先秦漢魏晉南北朝詩. Compiled by Lu Qinli 逯欽立. 3 vols. Beijing: Zhonghua, 1983.

Xin xu shu zheng 新序疏證. Compiled by Liu Xiang 劉向. Annotated by Zhao Shanyi 趙善詒. Shanghai: Huadong Shifan Daxue, 1989.

Xin yu 新語. Written by Lu Jia 陸賈. In *Xin bian zhu zi ji cheng*. Vol. 2. Taipei: Shijie, 1974.

Xunzi ji jie 荀子集解. Annotated by Wang Xianqian 王先謙. In *Xin bian zhuzi ji cheng*. Vol. 2. Taipei: Shijie, 1974.

Yan shi jia xun hui zhu 顏氏家訓彙注. Written by Yan Zhitui 顏之推. Annotated by Zhou Fagao 周法高. Taipei: Zhongyang Yanjiuyuan Lishi Yuyan Yanjiusuo, 1960.

Yan tie lun 鹽鐵論. Shanghai: Renmin, 1974.

Yanzi chun qiu ji shi 晏子春秋集釋. Annotated by Wu Zeyu 吳則虞. Beijing: Zhonghua, 1962.

Yi li zhu shu 儀禮注疏. In *Shi san jing zhu shu*. Vol. 4. Taipei: Yiwen, 1974.

Yi wen lei ju 藝文類聚. Taipei: Wenguang, 1974.

Yi yuan 異苑. Compiled by Liu Jingshu 劉敬叔. In *Han Wei Liuchao biji xiaoshuo daguan*. Shanghai: Shanghai gu ji, 1999.

Yi Zhou shu hui jiao ji zhu 逸周書彙校集注. Annotated by Huang Huaixin 黃懷信, Zhang Maorong 張懋鎔, and Tian Xudong 田旭東. Shanghai: Shanghai gu ji, 1995.

You yang za zu 酉陽雜俎. Compiled by Duan Chengshi 段成式. Beijing: Zhonghua, 1981.

Yue jue shu 越絕書. Shanghai: Shangwu, 1956.

Yue jue shu jiao zhu gao ben 越絕書校注稿本. Taipei: Shijie, 1967.

Yunmeng Longgang Qin jian 云夢龍崗秦簡. Ed. Liu Xinfang 劉信芳 and Liang Zhu 梁柱. Beijing: Kexue, 1997.

Yunmeng Shuihudi Qin mu zhujian 雲蒙睡虎地秦墓竹簡. Beijing: Wenwu, 1981.

Zhangjiashan Han mu zhujian 張家山漢墓竹簡. Beijing: Wenwu, 2001.

Zhanguo ce 戰國策. Shanghai: Gu ji, 1978.

Zhou li zhu shu 周禮注疏. In *Shisan jing zhu shu*. Vol. 3. Taipei: Yiwen, 1974.

Zhou yi zheng yi 周易正義. In *Shi san jing zhu shu* 十三經注疏. Vol. 1. Taipei: Yiwen, 1976.

[*Gu ben*] *zhu shu ji nian ji zheng* 古本竹書紀年輯證. Annotated by Fang Shiming 方詩銘 and Wang Xiuling 王修齡. Shanghai: Shanghai gu ji, 1981.

Zhuangzi ji shi 莊子集釋. Annotated by Guo Qingfan 郭慶藩. In *Xin bian zhuzi ji cheng*. Vol. 3. Taipei: Shijie, 1974.

Zi zhi tong jian 資治通鑑. Written by Sima Guang 司馬光. 4 vols. Beijing: Zhonghua, 1956.

[*Chun qiu*] *Zuo zhuan zhu* 春秋左傳注. Annotated by Yang Bojun 楊伯峻. Beijing: Zhonghua, 1983.

SECONDARY WORKS IN CHINESE AND JAPANESE

Akatuska, Kiyoshi 赤塚忠. "Chūgoku kodai ni okeru kaze no shinkō to gogyō setsu 中國古代における風の信仰と五行説." In *Nishō-gakusha Daigaku ronshū* 二松學社大學論集. Tokyo: Nishō-gakusha Daigaku, 1977, pp. 52–91.

——. *Chūgoku kodai no shūkyō to bunka: In ōchō no saishi* 中國古代の宗教と文化：殷王朝の祭祀. Tokyo: Kadokawa, 1977.

——. "Dōka shisō no gensho no keitai 道家思想の原初の形態." *Tōkyō Daigaku Bungakubu kenkyū hōkoku: Tetsugaku ronbunshū.* Tokyo: Tokyo Daigaku, 1968.

An, Jinhuai 安金槐, et al. "Mi xian Dahuting Han dai huaxiangshi mu he bihua mu 密縣打虎亭漢代畫像石墓和壁畫墓," *Wenwu* (1972:10), pp. 849–862.

"Anhui Han shan Lingjia tan xin shiqi shidai mudi fajue jianbao 安徽含山凌家灘新石器時代墓地發掘簡報." *Wenwu* (1989:4), pp. 1–9, 30.

Baoshan Chu mu 包山楚墓. 2 vols. Beijing: Wenwu, 1991.

Cai, Biming 蔡璧名. *Shenti yu ziran—yi "Huangdi nei jing suwen" wei zhongxin lun gudai sixiang chuantong zhong de shenti guan* 身體與自然—以黃帝內經素問為中心論古代思想傳統中的身體觀. Taipei: Guoli Taiwan Daxue, 1997.

Cao, Chunping 曹春平. "Ming tang fawei 明堂發微." *Jianzhu xuebao* 9 (1994), pp. 65–84.

Cao, Jinyan 曹錦炎. "Chu bo shu 'Yue ling' pian kaoshi 楚帛書月令篇考試." *Jiang Han kaogu* (1985:1), pp. 63–67.

Cao, Xuequn 曹學群. "Mawangdui Han mu Sangfutu jian lun 馬王堆漢墓喪服圖簡論." *Hunan kaogu jikan* 6 (1994), pp. 226–229, 225.

Chang, Wenzhai 暢文齋. "Houma diqu gu cheng zhi de xin faxian 侯馬地區古城址的新發現." *Wenwu* (1958:12), pp. 32–33.

"Changsha Mawangdui er, san hao Han mu fajue jianbao 長沙馬王堆二三號漢墓發掘簡報." *Wenwu* 1974 (7), pp. 39–48, 63.

Changsha Mawangdui yi hao Han mu 長沙馬王堆一號漢墓. Beijing: Wenwu, 1973.

"Changsha Zidanku Zhanguo mu guo mu 長沙子彈庫戰國木槨墓." *Wenwu* (1974:2), pp. 36–40.

Chen, Huan 陳歡. *Daojia jin shi lüe* 道家金石略. Beijing: Wenwu, 1988.

Chen, Jiujin 陳久金 and Zhang, Jingguo 張敬國. "Han shan chutu yu pian tuxing shi kao 含山出土玉片圖形試考." *Wenwu* (1989:4), pp. 14–17.

Chen, Mengjia 陳夢家. "Han jian nianlibiao shu 漢簡年歷表敘." *Kaogu xuebao* (1965:2), pp. 103–147.

——. *Yinxu buci zongshu* 殷墟卜辭綜述. Beijing: Science Press, 1956.

——. "Zhanguo Chu bo shu kao 戰國楚帛書考." *Kaogu xuebao* (1984:2), pp. 137–158.

Chen, Pan 陳槃. "Lun zaoqi chen wei ji qi yu Zou Yan shu shuo zhi guanxi 論早期讖緯及其與鄒衍書說之關係." *Lishi Yuyan Yanjiusuo jikan* 20 (1948), pp. 159–187.

——. "Zhanguo Qin Han jian fangshi kaolun 戰國秦漢間方士考論." *Lishi Yuyan Yanjiusuo jikan* 17 (1948), pp. 7–57.

Chen, Peifen 陳佩芬. *Shanghai Bowuguan cang qingtongqi* 上海博物館藏青銅器. Shanghai: Shanghai Shuhua, 1987.

Chen, Ping 陳平. "Yizheng Xupu 'Xian ling quan shu' xu kao 儀征胥浦 "先令券書" 續考." *Kaogu* (1992:2), pp. 84–92, 83.

——. "Zai tan Xupu 'Xian ling quan shu' zhong de jige wenti 再談胥浦 "先令券書" 中的幾個問題." *Wenwu* (1992:9), pp. 62–65.

Chen, Ping and Wang, Qinjin 王勤金. "Yizheng Xupu 101 hao Xi Han mu 'xian ling quan shu' chu kao 儀征胥浦101號西漢墓 "先令券書" 初考." *Wenwu* (1987:1), pp. 20–25, 36.

Chen, Quanfang 陳全方. *Zhouyuan yu Zhou wenhua* 周原與周文化. Shanghai: Renmin, 1988.

Chen, Shan 陳山. *Zhongguo wuxia shi* 中國武俠史. Shanghai: Sanlian, 1992.

Chen, Songchang 陳松長. "Boshu *Xingde* bing pian shitan 帛書刑德丙篇試探." *Jianbo yanjiu* 3 (1998), pp. 242–247.

——. "Boshu *Xingde* lüe shuo 帛書刑德略説." *Jianbo yanjiu* 1 (1993), pp. 96–107.

——. "Boshu *Xingde* yi ben shiwen jiaodu 帛書刑德乙本釋文校讀." In *Hunansheng Bowuguan sishi zhounian jinian lunwen ji* 湖南省博物館四十週年紀念論文集. Changsha: Hunan jiaoyu, 1996.

——. "Mawangdui boshu *Xingde* jia yi pian de bijiao yanjiu 馬王堆帛書刑德甲乙篇的比較研究." *Wenwu* (2000:3), pp. 75–84.

Chen, Yinglüe 陳英略. *Gui guzi douzhi mijue* 鬼谷子鬥智秘訣. Taipei: Xin Dongli Zazhi, 1972.

——. *Gui guzi shen ji bingfa* 鬼谷子神機兵法. Taipei: Xin Dongli Zazhi, 1972.

Cui, Chen 崔陳. "Yibin diqu chutu Han dai huaxiang shi guan 宜賓地區出土漢代畫像石棺." *Kaogu yu wen wu* (1991:1), pp. 34–40.

Ding, Shan 丁山. *Jiaguwen suojian shizu ji qi zhidu* 甲骨文所見氏族及其制度. Beijing: Kexue, 1956.

Du Zhengsheng 杜正勝. *Bian hu qi min: chuantong zhengzhi shehui jiegou zhi xingcheng* 編戶齊民：傳統政治社會結構之形成. Taipei: Lianjing, 1989.

——. "Bian hu qi min de chuxian ji qi lishi yiyi: bianhu qimin de yanjiu zhi yi 編戶齊民的出現及其歷史義意：編戶齊民的研究之一." *Zhongyang Yanjiuyuan Lishi Yuyan Yanjiushuo jikan* 54:3 (1983), pp. 77–111.

——. "Xingti, jingqi yu hunpo—Zhongguo chuantong dui 'ren' renshi de xingcheng 形體，精氣與魂魄—中國傳統對・人・認識的形成." *Xin shixue* 2:3 (1991), pp. 1–65.

——. *Zhou dai chengbang* 周代城邦. Taipei: Lianjing, 1979.

——. "Zhou li shenfen de xiangzheng 周禮身分的象徵." In *Zhongyang Yanjiuyuan di er jie guoji Han xue huiyi lunwenji* 中央研究院第二屆國際漢學會議論文集 (Taipei: Zhongyang Yanjiuyuan, 1989).

Feng, Chengji 馮承基. "Fu Wuji suo ji Dong Han hukou shuzi zhi jiantao 伏無忌所記東漢戶口數字之檢討." *Dalu zazhi* 27.2 (1963), pp. 9–15.

Feng, Youlan 馮友蘭. *Zhongguo zhexue shi bu* 中國哲學史補. Shanghai: Shangwu, 1936.

Fu Juyou 傅舉有. "Lun Qin Han shiqi de boju boxi jian ji bowenjing 論秦漢時期的博局，博戲，兼及博紋鏡." *Kaogu xuebao* (1986:1), pp. 21–42.

Fu, Juyou and Chen, Songchang. *Mawangdui Han mu wenwu* 馬王堆漢墓文物. Changsha: Hunan, 1992.

Fu, Xinian 傅熹年. "Zhanguo Zhongshan wang Cuo mu chutu de zhaoyu tu ji qi lingyuan guizhi de yanjiu 戰國中山王響墓出土的兆域圖及其陵園規制的研究." *Kaogu xuebao* (1980:1), pp. 97–119.

Fu, Yongfa. *Shenzhou de faxian: Shan hai jing de dili kao* 神州的發現：山海經的地理考. Kunming: Yunnan Renmin, 1992.

Fujikawa, Masakazu 藤川正數. *Kandai ni okeru reigaku no kenkyū* 漢代における禮學の研究. Tokyo: Kazama shobō, 1968.

"Fuyang Shuanggudui Xi Han Ruyin Hou mu fajue jianbao 阜陽雙古堆西漢汝陰侯墓發掘簡報." *Wenwu* (1978:8), pp. 12–19.

Gao, Cheng 高承. *Shi wu ji yuan* 事物紀原. Taipei: Zhonghua, 1989.

Gao, Dalun 高大倫. *Zhangjiashan Han jian "Yin shu" yanjiu* 張家山漢簡 "引書" 研究. Chengdu: Ba Shu, 1995.

Gao, Min 高敏. *Yunmeng Qin jian chutan* 雲夢秦簡初探. Henan: Renmin, 1979.

Gao, Quxun 高去尋. "Yindai da mu de mu shi ji qi hanyi de tuice 殷代大墓的木室及其含義的推測." *Zhongyang Yanjiuyuan Lishi Yuyan Yanjiusuo jikan* 39 (1969), pp. 175–188.

Gao, Wen 高文. *Han bei ji shi* 漢碑集釋. Kaifeng: Henan Daxue, 1985.

Gao, Wen and Gao, Chengying 高成英. "Han hua guibao—Sichuan xin chutu de ba ge huaxiang shi guan 漢畫瑰寶—四川新出土的八個畫像石棺." *Wen wu tian di* (1988:3), pp. 47–49.

Gu, Donggao 顧東高. *Chun qiu da shi biao*, 春秋大事表. In *Huang Qing jing jie xu bian*, *ce* 67–133. Nanqing Shuyuan, 1888.

Gu, Jiegang 顧頡剛. *Shi lin za shi* 史林雜識. Beijing: Zhonghua, 1963.

——. "Wu de zhong shi shuo xia de zhengzhi he lishi 五德終始說下的政治和歷史." In *Gu shi bian* 古史辨. Vol. 5. Reprint ed. Hong Kong: Taiping, 1962.

———. "'Yu gong' zhong de Kunlun 禹貢中的昆侖." *Lishi dili* 1 (1981), pp. 3–8.

——. "Zhongguo yingxi lüe shi ji qi xianzhuang 中國影戲略史及其現狀." *Wen shi* 19 (1983), pp. 109–136.

Guo, Moruo 郭沫若. "Chutu wenwu er san shi: Fusang mu yu Guanghan gong 出土文物二三事：扶桑木與与廣寒宮." *Wenwu* (1972:3), pp. 7–10.

——. "Luoyang Han mu bihua shitan 洛陽漢墓壁畫試探." *Kaogu xuebao* (1964:2), pp. 1–7.

——. *Shi pipan shu* 十批判書. Beijing: Kexue chubanshe, 1956.

"Han Chang'an cheng nan jiao li zhi jianzhu yizhiqun fajue jianbao 漢長安城南郊禮制建築遺址群發掘簡報." *Kaogu* (1960:7), pp. 36–39.

Han, Wei 韓偉. "Lüe lun Shaanxi Chunqiu Zhanguo Qin mu 略論陝西春秋戰國秦墓." *Kaogu yu wenwu* (1981:1), pp. 83–93.

Hattori, Katsuhiko 服部克彥. *Kodai Chūgoku no gun ken to sono shūhen* 古代中國の郡縣とその周邊. Kyoto: Mineruba [Minerva], 1969.

Hayashi, Minao 林巳奈夫. *Chūgoku kodai no seikatsu shi* 中國古代の生活史. Tokyo: Yoshikawa Kōbunkan, 1992

——. "In—Shunjū zenki kinbun no shoshiki to jōyō goku no jidai hensen 殷—春秋前期金文の書式と常用語句の時代變遷." *Tōhō gakuhō* 55 (1983), pp. 1–101.

——. *Ishi ni kizamareta sekai* 石に刻まれた世界. Tokyo: Tōhō shoten, 1992.

——. "Kan kyō no zugara ni, san ni tsuite 漢鏡の圖柄二，三について." *Tōhō gakuhō* 44 (1973), pp. 1–66.

——. *Kandai no bunbutsu* 漢代の文物. Kyoto: Kyoto Daigaku Jinbun Kagaku Kenkyushō, 1977.

——. *Kan dai no kamigami* 漢代の神神. Kyoto: Nozokawa, 1989.

He, Changqun 賀昌群. *Lun liang Han tudi zhanyou xingtai de fazhan* 論兩漢土地佔有形態的發展. Shanghai: Renmin, 1956.

He, Guanzhou 何觀州. "Shanhaijing zai kexue shang zhi pipan ji zuozhe zhi shidai kao 山海經在科學上之批判及作者之時代考." *Yanjing xuebao* 7 (1930), pp. 1363–1375.

He, Linyi 何琳儀. "Changsha bo shu tongshi 長沙帛書通釋." *Jiang Han kaogu* (1986:1), pp. 51–57; (1986:2), pp. 77–82.

He, Zhiguo 何志國. "Woguo zuizao de renti jingmai qidiao 我國最早的人體經脈漆雕." *Zhongguo wenwu bao* 15 (1994), p. 4.

——. "Xi Han renti jingmai qidiao kao 西漢人體經脈漆雕考." *Daziran tansuo* (1995:3), pp. 16–20.

He, Ziquan 何茲全. "Zhou dai tudi zhidu he ta de yanbian 周代土地制度和它的演變." *Lishi yanjiu* (1964:3), pp. 145–162.

"Hebei Ding xian Beizhuang Han mu fajue baogao 河北定縣北庄漢墓發掘報告." *Kaogu xuebao* (1964:2), pp. 127–133.

"Hebei sheng Pingshan xian Zhanguo shiqi Zhongshan guo muzang fajue jianbao 河北省平山縣戰國時期中山國墓葬發掘簡報." *Wenwu* (1979:1), pp. 1–31.

"Hechuan Dong Han huaxiang shi mu 合川東漢畫象石墓." *Wenwu* (1977:2), pp. 63–69.

"Helin'ge'er faxian yi zuo zhongyao de Dong Han mu bihua mu 和林格爾發現一坐重要的東漢壁畫墓." *Wenwu* (1974:1), pp. 8–23.

Helin'geer [Holingor] Han mu bihua 和林格爾漢墓壁畫. Beijing: Wenwu, 1987.

"Henan Puyang Xi shui po yizhi fajue jianbao 河南濮陽西水坡遺址發掘簡報." *Wenwu* (1988:3), pp. 1–6.

Hiranaka, Reiji 平中苓次. *Chūgoku kodai no densei to zeihō* 中國古代の田制と税法. Kyoto: Tōyōshi Kenkyūkai, 1967.

Hong, Yi 弘一. "Jiangling Fenghuangshan 10 hao Han mu jiandu chu tan 江陵鳳凰山十號漢墓簡牘初談." *Wenwu* (1974:6), pp. 78–84.

Hori, Toshikazu 崛敏一. "Chūgoku kodai no ie to ko 中國古代の家と戶." *Chūgoku kankei ronsetsu shiryō* 31:3 (1989), pp. 306–331.

Hou, Renzhi 侯仁之. "Hai wai si jing, Hai nei si jing, yu Da huang si jing Hai nei jing bijiao 海外四經，海內四經，與大荒四經海內經比較." *Yu gong* 7 (1937), pp. 319–326.

Hu, Houxuan 胡厚宣. "Jiaguwen sifang fengming kaozheng 甲骨文四方風名考證." In *Jiaguxue Shang shi luncong chu ji* 甲骨學商史論業初集. Taipei: Datong, 1972.

Hu, Shi 胡適. "Shuo ru 說儒." In *Hu Shi lun xue jin zhu* 胡適論學今注. Vol. 1. Shanghai: Shangwu, 1935.

Huang, Jinshan 黃金山. "Lun Handai jiating de ziran goucheng yu dengji goucheng 論漢代家庭的自然構成與等級構成." *Zhongguo shi yanjiu* (1987:4), pp. 81–89.

Huang, Shengzhang 黃盛璋. "Jiangling Fenghuangshan Han mu jiandu ji qi zai lishi dili yanjiu shang de jiazhi 江陵鳳凰山漢墓簡牘及其在歷史地理研究上的價值." In *Lishi dili yu kaogu luncong* 歷史地理與考古論叢. Ji'nan: Qilu, 1982.

——. "Yunmeng Qin mu liang feng jia shu zhong you guan lishi dili de wenti 雲蒙秦墓兩封家書中有關歷史地理的問題." *Wenwu* (1980:8), pp. 74–77.

Huang, Zhanyue 黃展岳. "Han Chang'an cheng nan jiao li zhi jianzhu de weizhi ji qi you guan wenti 漢長安城南郊禮制建築的位置及其有關問題." *Kaogu* (1960:9), pp. 53–58.

"Hubei Jiangling Fenghuangshan Xi Han mu fajue jianbao 湖北江陵鳳凰山西漢墓發掘簡報." *Wenwu* (1974:6), pp. 41–61.

"Hubei Yunmeng Shuihudi 11 zuo Qin mu fajue jianbao 湖北雲蒙睡虎地十一座秦墓發掘簡報." *Wenwu* (1976:9), pp. 51–61.

Ikeda, On 池田溫. "Chūgoku rekidai boken ryakkō 中國歷代墓券略考." *Tōyō bunka kenkyūsho kiyō* 86:6 (1981), pp. 193–278.

Ikeda, Suetoshi 池田末利. *Chūgoku kodai shūkyō shi kenkyū* 中國古代宗教史研究. Tokyo: Tōkai Daigaku, 1983.

Ikeda, Tomohisa 池田知久. *Maōtai Kan bo hakusho gogyōhen kenkyū* 馬王堆漢墓帛書五行篇研究. Tokyo: Kyūko shoin, 1993.

Inaba, Ichiro 稻葉一郎. "Kandai no kazoku keitai to keizai hendō 漢代の家族形態と經濟變動." *Tōyōshi kenkyū* 43.1 (1984), pp. 88–117.

Ishida, Hidema 石田秀實. "Kaze no byōinron to chūgoku dentō igaku shisō no keisei 風の病因論と中國傳統醫學思想の形成." *Shisō* 799 (1991), pp. 105–124.

Itō, Michiharu 伊藤道治. *Chūgoku kodai kokka no shihai kōzō* 中國古代國家の支配構造. Tokyo: Chuō kōron, 1987.

——. *Chūgoku kodai ōchō no keisei* 中國古代王朝の形成. Tokyo: Sōbunsha, 1975.

Itō, Seiji 伊藤清司. "Kodai Chūgoku no minkan iryō—*Sangaikyō* no kenkyū 古代中國の民間醫療—出海經の研究." *Shigaku* 42:4 (1969), pp. 41–62; 43:3 (1970), pp. 17–33; 43:4 (1971), pp. 39–87.

——. "Yamagawa no kamigami—*Sangaikyō* no kenkyū 山川の神神—山海經の研究." *Shigaku* 41:1 (1969), pp. 31–61; 42:2 (1969), pp. 29–78; 42:4 (1969), pp. 73–106.

Jiang, Shaoyuan 江紹源. *Zhongguo gudai lüxing zhi yanjiu* 中國古代旅行之研究. Shanghai: Shangwu, 1935.

Jiang, Yihua 姜義華 et al. *Kongzi—Zhou Qin Han Jin wenxian ji* 孔子—周秦漢晉文獻集. Shanghai: Fudan Daxue, 1990.

Jiang, Yuxiang 江玉祥. "Zhongguo yingxi tanyuan 中國影戲探源." *Minjian wenxue luntan* 2 (1988), pp. 85–92.

"Jiangling Wangjiatai 15 hao Qin mu 江陵王家台15號秦墓." *Wenwu* (1995:1), pp. 37–43.

Jiangling Yutaishan Chu mu 江陵雨台山楚墓. Beijing: Wenwu, 1984.

"Jiangsu Donghai xian Yinwan Han mu qun fajue jianbao 江蘇東海縣尹灣漢墓群發掘簡報." *Wen wu* (1996:8), pp. 4–25.

"Jiangsu Yizheng Xupu 101 hao Xi Han mu 江蘇儀征胥浦101號西漢墓." *Wenwu* (1987:1), pp. 1–16.

"Jiyuan Sijiangou san zuo Han mu de fajue 濟源泗澗溝三坐漢墓的發掘." *Wenwu* (1973:2), pp. 46–53.

Kageyama, Tsuyoshi 影山剛. *Chūgoku kodai no shōkōgyō to sembaisei* 中國古代の商工業と專賣制. Tokyo: Tōkyō Daigaku, 1984.

Kaizuka, Shigeki 貝塚茂樹. *Kaizuka Shigeki chosaku shū* 貝塚茂樹著作集. Vols. 1, 2, and 5. Tokyo: Chuō Kōron, 1978.

Kimura, Masao 木村正雄. *Chūgoku kodai teikoku no keisei* 中國古代帝國の形成. Tokyo: Fumeito, 1979.

Koga, Noboru 古賀登. *Kan Chōanjō to sempaku, kenkyōteiri seido* 漢長安城と阡陌縣鄉亭里制度. Tokyo: Yūsankaku, 1980.

———. "Kan Chōanjō no kensetsu puran: Sempaku kenkyō seido to no kankei o chūshin to shite 漢長安城の建設ぷらん：阡陌縣鄉制度との關係を中心として." *Tōyō shi kenkyū* 31:2 (September 1972), pp. 28–60.

Komai, Kazuchiku 駒井和愛. "Kikumon oyobi rokuhakuzu 規矩文および六博圖." In *Chūgoku kokyō no kenkyū* 中國古鏡の研究. Tokyo: Iwanami, 1953.

Kominami, Ichirō 小南一郎. "Rokuhaku no uchūron 六博の宇宙論. "*Gekkan hyakka* (1987:7–8).

Kung, Xiangxing 孔祥星 and Liu, Yiman 劉一曼. *Zusetsu Chūgoku kodai dōkyō shi* 圖説中國古代銅鏡史. Tr. Takakura Hiroaki 高倉洋彰, Tazaki Hiroyuki 田崎博之, and Watanabe Yoshirō 渡邊芳郎. Tokyo: Chūgoku shoten, 1991.

Lai, Ming-chiu [Li Mingjian] 黎明劍. "Han dai difang guanliao jiegou: Jun gong cao zhi zhizhang yu Yinwan Han mu jiandu zhi guanxi 漢代地方官僚結構：郡功曹之職掌與尹灣漢墓簡牘之關係." *Zhongguo Wenhua Yanjiusuo xue bao* 8 (1999), pp. 35–72.

———. "Han dai Donghai jun de hao zu da xing: yi 'Donghai jun xia xia zhang li ming ji' ji 'Zeng qian ming ji' wei zhong xin 漢代東海郡的豪族大姓：以 "東海郡下轄長吏名籍" 及 "贈錢名籍" 為中心." *Zhongguo Wenhua Yanjiusuo xue bao* 9 (2000), pp. 47–96.

———. "Qin dai shi wu lianzuo zhidu zhi yuan yuan wenti 秦代什伍連坐制度之淵源問題." *Dalu zazhi* 79:4 (1989), pp. 27–44.

———. "Xi Han zhongqi zhi 'San lao' yu haoqiang 西漢中期之三老與豪彊." *Xin shi xue* 8:2 (1997), pp. 59–91.

Lao, Gan 勞榦. *Juyan Han jian kaoshi* 居延漢簡考釋. Taipei: Zhongyang Yanjiuyuan Lishi Yuyan Yanjiusuo zhuankan 40, 1960.

———. "Liang Han huji yu dili zhi guanxi 兩漢戶籍與地理之關係." *Zhongyang Yanjiu Yuan Lishi Yuyan Yanjiusuo jikan* 5:2 (1935), pp. 179–214.

———. "Liang Han jun guo mianji zhi guji ji koushu zengjian zhi tuice 兩漢郡國面積之估計及口數增減之推測." *Zhongyang Yanjiu Yuan Lishi Yuyan Yanjiusuo jikan* 5:2 (1935), pp. 215–240.

———. "Liubo ji bo ju zhi yanbian 六博及博局之演變. *Lishi Yuyan Yanjiusuo jikan* 35 (1964), pp. 15–30.

———. "Lun Han dai de nei chao yu wai chao 論漢代的內朝與外朝." *Lishi Yuyan Yanjiusuo jikan* 13 (1948), pp. 227–267.

———. "Lun Han dai de youxia 論漢代的游俠." In *Lao Gan xueshu lunwen ji* 勞榦學術論文集. Vol. 2. Taipei: Yiwen, 1976.

Li, Chenguang 李陳廣. "Han hua Fu Xi Nü Gua de xingxiang tezheng ji qi yiyi 汉画伏羲女娲的形象特征及其意义." *Zhongyuan wen wu* (1992:1), pp. 33–37.

Li, Fuhua 李复華 and Guo, Ziyou 郭子游. "Pi Xian chutu Dong Han huaxiang shi guan tuxiang lüe shuo 郫縣出土東漢畫象石棺圖象略説." *Wen wu* (1975:8), pp. 60–67.

Li, Jiahao 李家浩. "Qin Yin yu ban mingwen yanjiu 秦駰玉版銘文研究." *Beijing Daxue Zhongguo guwenxian yanjiu zhongxin jikan* 2 (2001), pp. 99–128.

Li, Jianmin 李建民. *Fangshu, yixue, lishi* 方術，醫學，歷史. Taipei: Nantian, 2000.

——. "Han dai ju xi de qiyuan yu yanbian 漢代局戲的起源與演變." *Dalu zazhi* (1988:3), pp. 1–20; (1988:4), pp. 27–47.

——. *Sisheng zhi yu: Zhou Qin Han maixue zhi yuanliu* 死生之域：周秦漢脈學之源流. Taipei: Zhongyang Yanjiuyuan, 2000.

Li, Jiemin 李解民. "'Donghai jun xia xia zhangli ming ji' yanjiu 東海郡下轄長吏名藉研究." In *Yinwan Han mu jian du zong lun* 尹灣漢墓簡牘綜論. Beijing: Kexue, 1999.

——. "'Yinwan Han mu Bo ju zhan mu du shijie' ding bu 尹灣漢墓博局占木牘試解訂補." *Wenwu* (2000:1), pp. 73–75.

Li, Junming 李均明 and Ho, Shuangquan 何雙全. Ed. *San jian jiandu ho ji* 散見簡牘合集. Beijing: Wenwu, 1990.

Li, Ling 李零. *Changsha Zidanku Zhanguo Chu bo shu yanjiu* 長沙子彈庫戰國楚帛書研究. Beijing: Zhonghua, 1985.

——. "Chu bo shu de zai renshi 楚帛書的再認識." *Zhongguo wenhua* 10 (1994), pp. 42–62.

——. "Du ji zhong chutu faxian de xuanze lei gu shu 讀幾種出土發現的選擇類古書." *Jianbo yanjiu* 3 (1998), pp. 96–104.

——. "*Guanzi* sanshi shijie yu ershisi jieqi 管子三十時節與二十四節氣." *Guanzi jikan* (1988:2), pp. 18–24.

——. "Qin Yin dao bing yu ban de yanjiu 秦駰禱病玉版的研究." *Guoxue yanjiu* 6 (1991), pp. 525–548.

——. *Zhongguo fangshu kao* 中國方術考. Revised and expanded ed. Beijing: Dongfang, 2000.

——. *Zhongguo fangshu xu kao* 續考. Beijing: Dongfang, 2000.

——. "Zhongguo gudai jumin zuzhi de liang da leixing ji qi butong laiyuan 中國古代居民組織的兩大類型及其不同來源." *Wen shi* 28 (March 1987), pp. 59–78.

Li, Song 李淞. *Lun Han dai yishu zhong de Xi Wang Mu tuxiang* 論漢代藝術中的西王母圖像. Hunan: Hunan jiaoyu, 2000.

Li, Xueqin 李學勤. "'Bo ju zhan' yu guiju wen 博局占與規矩文." *Wenwu* (1997:1), pp. 49–51.

——. "Chu bo shu zhong de gushi yu yuzhouguan 楚帛書中的故事與宇宙觀." In *Chu shi luncong* 楚史論叢. No. 1. Wuhan: Hubei Renmin, 1982.

——. "Fangmatan jian zhong de zhiguai gushi 放馬灘簡中的志怪故事." *Wenwu* (1990:4), pp. 43–47.

——. "Lun Chu bo shu zhong de tian xiang 論楚帛書中的天象." *Hunan kaogu jikan* 1 (1982), pp. 68–72.

——. "Lun Hanshan Lingjiatan yu gui, yu ban 論含山凌家灘玉龜，玉版." *Zhongguo wenhua* 4 (1992), pp. 144–149.

——. "Mawangdui boshu *Xingde* zhong de junli 馬王堆帛書刑德中的軍吏." *Jianbo yanjiu* 2 (1996), pp. 156–159.

——. "Qin yu du suoyin 秦玉牘索隱." *Gu gong bowuyuan yuan kan* (2000:2), pp. 41–45.

——. "Shuihudi Qin jian de *gen shan tu* 睡虎地秦簡的艮山圖." *Wenwu tiandi* (1991:4), pp. 30–32.

——. "Shuihudi Qin jian 'Ri shu' yu Chu Qin shehui 睡虎地秦簡日書與楚秦社會." *Jiang Han kaogu* (1985:4), pp. 60–64.

——. "Zai lun bo shu shier shen 再論帛書十二神." In *Jianbo yi ji yu xueshu shi* 簡帛佚籍與學術史. Taipei: Shibao Wenhua, 1994.

——. "Zhanguo ti ming gaishu, part 2 戰國題名概述（下）." *Wenwu* (1959:9), pp. 58–61.

Li, Yuzheng 李域錚, Zhao, Minsheng 趙敏生, and Lei, Bing 雷冰. *Xi'an beilin shufa yishu* 西安碑林書法藝術. Xi'an: Shaanxi Renmin, 1983.

Li, Zhaohe 李昭和. "Qingchuan xian chutu mu du wenzi jian kao 青川縣出土木牘文字簡考." *Wenwu* (1982:1), pp. 24–27.

Lian, Shaoming 連邵名. "Qin Huiwen Wang daoci Hua Shan yu jian wen yanjiu 秦惠文王禱辭華山玉簡文研究." *Zhongguo Lishi Bowuguan guan kan* (2001:1), pp. 49–57.

——. "Qin Huiwen Wang daoci Hua Shan yu jian wen yanjiu buzheng 補正." *Zhongguo Lishi Bowuguan guan kan* (2001:2), pp. 52–54.

——. "Shipan zhong de si men yu ba gua 式盤中的四門與八卦." *Wenwu* (1987:9), pp. 33–36.

Liang, Fangzhong 梁方仲. *Zhongguo lidai hukou tiandi tianfu tongji* 中國歷代戶口田地天賦統計. Shanghai: Renmin, 1980.

Liang, Qichao 梁啓超. *Yin bing shi quan ji* 飲冰室全集. Taipei: Zonghe, 1975.

Ling, Chunsheng 凌純聲. "Kunlun qiu yu Xiwangmu 昆侖丘與西王母." *Zhongyang Yanjiuyuan Minzu Yanjiusuo jikan* 22 (1966), pp. 215–255.

"Linzi Langjiazhuang yi hao Dong Zhou xun ren mu 臨淄郎家庄一號東周殉人墓." *Kaogu xuebao* (1977:1), pp. 73–103.

Liu, Dunyuan 劉敦願. "Chunqiu shiqi Qi guo gu cheng de fuyuan yu chengshi buju 春秋時期齊國故城的復原與城市佈局." *Lishi dili* (1981:1), pp. 148–159.

——. "Han huaxiangshi shang de yinshi nannü—Pingyin Meng Zhuang Han mu shizhu jisi gewu tusiang fenxi 漢畫像石上的飲食男女—平陰孟莊漢墓石柱祭祀歌舞圖像分析." *Gu Gong wenwu yuekan* 141 (December 1994), pp. 122–135.

Liu, Fu 劉復. "Xi Han shidai de rigui 西漢時代的日晷." *Guoxue jikan* 3:4 (1932), pp. 573–610.

Liu, Hongshi 劉洪石. "Donghai Yinwan Han mu shushulei jiandu shidu 東海尹灣漢墓術數類簡牘試讀." *Dongnan wenhua* (1997:4), pp. 67–73.

Liu, Lexian 劉樂賢. "Mawangdui Han mu xingzhan shu chutan 馬王堆漢墓星占書初探." *Huaxue* 1 (1995), pp. 111–121.

——. "Yinwan Han mu chutu shushu wenxian chutan 尹灣漢墓出土數術文獻初探." In *Yinwan Han mu jiandu zonglun* 尹灣漢墓簡牘綜論. Beijing: Kexue, 1999.

Liu, Qingzhu 劉慶柱 and Li, Yufang 李毓芳. *Xi Han shiyi ling* 西漢十一陵. Xi'an: Shaanxi renmin, 1987.

Liu, Xiaolu 劉曉路. *Zhongguo bo hua* 中國帛畫. Beijing: Zhongguo shudian, 1994.

Liu, Xingang 劉昕崗. "Guodian Chu jian 'Xing zi ming chu' pian jianshi 郭店楚簡 "性自命出" 篇箋釋." In *Guodian Chu jian Guoji Xueshu Yantaohui: lunwen ji* 郭店楚簡國際學術研討會：論文集. Wuhan: Hubei renmin, 2000.

Liu, Yunyong 劉運勇. *Xi Han Chang'an* 西漢長安. Beijing: Zhonghua, 1982.

Liu, Zenggui 劉增貴. "Menhu yu Zhongguo gudai shehui 門戶與中國古代社會." *Lishi Yuyan Yanjiusuo jikan* 68:4 (1997), pp. 817–897.

Liu, Zhiping 劉致平. "Xi'an xibei jiao gudai jianzhu yizhi kancha chu ji 西安西北郊古代建築遺址勘察初記." *Wenwu cankao ziliao* (1957:3), pp. 5–12.

Luo, Fuyi 羅福頤. "Han shipan xiao kao 漢式盤小考." *Gu wenzi yanjiu* 11 (1985), pp. 252–264.

Luo, Zhewen 羅哲文. "Helin'ge'er Han mu bihua zhong suo jian de yixie gu jianzhu 和林格爾漢墓壁畫中所見的一些古建築." *Wenwu* (1974:1), pp. 31–37.

Luo, Zhongru 雒忠如. "Xi'an xi jiao faxian Han dai jianzhu yizhi 西安西郊發現漢代建築遺址." *Kaogu tongxun* (1957:6), pp. 26–30.

Luoyang Shaogou Han mu 洛陽燒溝漢墓. Beijing: Kexue, 1959.

"Luoyang Xi Han Bu Qianqiu bihua mu fajue jianbao 洛陽西漢卜千秋壁畫墓發掘簡報." *Wenwu* (1977:6), pp. 1–12.

Ma, Changyi 馬昌儀. *Zhongguo linghun xinyang* 中國靈魂信仰. Taipei: Hanzhong, 1996.

Ma, Jixing 馬繼興. *Mawangdui gu yi shu kaoshi* 馬王堆古醫書考釋. Changsha: Hunan kexue jishu, 1992.

Ma, Xianxing 馬先醒. *Han jian yu Han dai chengshi* 漢簡與漢代城市. Taipei: Jiandu she, 1976.

Ma, Xin 馬新. "Handai xiao nong jiating lüe lun 漢代小農家庭略論." *Wen shi zhe* (1986:4), pp. 14–18.

Ma, Xin and Qi, Tao 齊濤. "Lüe lun Zhongguo gudai de jiachan jicheng zhidu 略論中國古代的家產繼承制度." *Renmin zazhi* (1987:5), pp. 101–104, 110.

Makino, Tatsumi 牧野巽. *Makino Tatsumi Chosaku shū.* Vols. 1, 7. *Chūgoku kazoku kenkyū* 著作集：中國家族研究. Tokyo: Ochanomizu, 1980.

Mancheng Han mu 滿城漢墓. Beijing: Wenwu, 1978.

Mancheng Han mu fajue baogao 發掘報告. Beijing: Wenwu, 1980.

Masabuchi, Tatsuo 增淵龍夫. *Chūgoku kodai no shakai to kokka* 中國古代の社會と國家. Tokyo: Kōbundō, 1962.

——. "Shunjū Sengoku jidai no shakai to kokka 春秋戰國時代の社會と國家." In *Iwanami kōza sekai rekishi*, vol. 4. Tokyo: Iwanami, 1970.

Matsuda, Minoru 松田稔. *Sangaikyō no kisoteki kenkyū* 山海經の基礎的研究. Tokyo: Rikkan Shoin, 1995.

Matsumoto, Yoshimi 松本善海. *Chūgoku sonraku seido no shiteki kenkyū* 中國村落制度の史的研究. Tokyo: Iwanami Shoten, 1977.

Mitarai, Masaru 御手洗勝. "Chiriteki sekai kan no hensen—Sū En no dai kyū shū setsu ni tsuite 地理的世界觀の變遷—鄒衍の大九州説に就いて." *Tōyō no bunka to shakai* 6 (1957), pp. 1–24.

Miura, Yoshiaki 三浦吉明. "*Kanshi* Yōkan hen ni tsuite—sanjūsekki o chūshin ni 管子幼官篇について—三十節氣を中心に." *Nihon Chūgoku Gakkai hō* 42 (1990), pp. 32–46.

Miyazaki, Ichisada. "Chūgoku jōdai no toshi kokka to sono bōchi 中國上代の都市國家とその墓地." In *Ajia shi ronkō*. Vol. 2. Tokyo: Asahi Shimbun, 1978.

——. "Chūgoku ni okeru shuraku keitai no hensen ni tsuite 中國における聚落形體の變遷について." In *Ajia shi ronkō*. Vol. 2. Tokyo: Asahi Shimbun, 1978.

——. "Chūgoku jōdai wa hōkensei ka toshi kokka ka 中國上代は封建制か都市國家か." In *Ajia shi kenkyū*. Vol. 3. Kyoto: Dōshōsha, 1957.

——. "Sengoku jidai no toshi 戰國時代の都市." In *Ajia shi ronkō*. Vol. 2. Tokyo: Asahi Shimbun, 1978.

——. "Yūkyo ni tsuite 游俠について." In *Ajia shi kenkyū*. Vol. 1. Kyoto: Dōshōsha, 1957.

Morino, Shigeo 森野繁夫. *Rikuchō shi no kenkyū: shūdan bungaku to kojin bungaku* 六朝詩の研究：集團文學と個人文學. Tokyo: Daiichi gakushū, 1976.

Moriya Kōzō shūshū hōkaku kiku shishin kyō zuroku 守屋考藏蒐集方格規矩四神鏡圖錄 Kyōto: Kyōto Kokuritsu Hakubutsukan, 1969.

Moriya, Mitsuo 守屋美都雄. *Chūgoku kodai no kazoku to kokka* 中國古代の家族と國家. Kyoto: Tōyōshi Kenkyūkai, 1968.

——. "Furō 父老." *Tōyōshi kenkyū* 14 (1955), pp. 43–60.

Nagahiro, Toshio 長廣敏雄. *Kandai gazō no kenkyū* 漢代畫像の研究. *Chūō kōron no bijutsu*, 1965.

Niida, Noboru 仁井田陞. *Chūgoku no hō to shakai to rekishi* 中國の法と社會と歷史. Tokyo: Iwanami shoten, 1967.

Nishijima, Sadao 西島定生. *Chūgoku kodai no shakai to keizai* 中國古代の社會と經濟. Tokyo: Tōkyō Daigaku, 1981.

——. *Chūgoku kodai teikoku no keisei to kōzō—nijūtō shakusei no kenkyū* 中國古代帝國の形成と構造—二十等爵制の研究. Tokyo: Tōkyō Daigaku, 1961.

Nishikawa, Motoharu 西川素治. "Kandai no igenjō—Kōso Gicho Shoho 101 gō Zenkan shutsudo 'Senrei kensho' ni tusite 漢代の遺言書—江蘇儀征胥浦一零一號前漢出土先令券書について." In *Chūgoku kodai no hō to shakai* 中國古代の法と社會. Ed. Hori Toshikazu 崛敏一. Tokyo: Kyūko shoin, 1988.

Ōba, Osamu 大庭脩. "Kan no shokufu 漢の嗇夫." In *Shin kan hōseishi no kenkyū* 秦漢法制史の研究. Tokyo: Sōbunsha, 1982.

Obi, Kōichi 小尾郊一. *Chūgoku bungaku ni okeru shizen to shizenkan* 中國文學における自然と自然觀. Tokyo: Iwanami, 1963.

Ochi, Shigeaki 越智重明. "Kan jidai no ie o megutte 漢時代の家おめぐって." *Shigaku zasshi* 86.6 (1977), pp. 1–36.

——. "Kan jidai no ko to ie 漢時代の戶と家." *Shigaku zasshi* 78.8 (1969), pp. 1–44.

——. "Kyūzoku to sanzoku 九族と三族." *Kurume Daigaku hikaku bunka kenkyūsho kiyō* 13 (1993), pp. 1–61.

Ogata, Isamu 尾形勇. *Chūgokyu kodai no ie to kokka* 中國古代の家と國家. Tokyo: Iwanami, 1979.

Ōgata, Osamu 大形徹 . "Hihatsu kō: hakkei to reikon no kanren ni tsuite 被髪考：髪型と靈魂の關連について." *Tōhō shūkyō* 86 (Nov. 1995), pp. 2–14.

Ogawa, Takuchi 小川琢治. "*Shan hai jing* kao 山海經考." In *Xian Qin jing ji kao* 先秦經籍考. Reprint ed. Shanghai: Shanghai Wenyi, 1990.

Ogura, Yoshihiko 小倉芳彦 . *Chūgoku kodai seiji shisō kenkyū* 中國古代政治思想研究. Tokyo: Aoki, 1970.

Okazaki, Fumio 岡崎文夫 . *Gi Kin Nambokuchō tsū shi* 魏晉南北朝通史. Tokyo: Heibonsha, 1989.

Pu, Muzhou (Mu-chou Poo) 蒲慕州 . "Lun Zhongguo gudai muzang xing zhi 論中國古代墓葬形制." *Guoli Taiwan Daxue wen shi zhe xuebao* 37 (1989), pp. 235–279.

——. *Muzang yu shengsi: Zhongguo gudai zongjiao zhi xingsi* 墓葬與生死：中國古代宗教之省思. Taipei: Lianjing, 1993.

Qian, Jianfu 錢劍夫. *Qin Han fu yi zhidu kao lüe* 秦漢賦役制度考略. Hubei: Renmin, 1988.

Qiao, Muqing 喬木青 . "Zu xing lianzuo fa de chubu tantao 族形連坐法的初步探討." *Falü shi luncong* (1981:1), pp. 68–85.

"Qin du Xianyang de yi hao gongdian jianzhu jianbao 秦都咸陽的一號宮殿建築簡報." *Wenwu* (1976:11), pp. 12–24.

Qin Shihuang ling bing ma yong keng yi hao keng fajue baogao 秦始皇陵兵馬佣坑一號坑發掘報告. Beijing: Wenwu, 1988.

"Qin Shihuang ling dong ce di er hao bing ma yong keng zuantan jianbao 秦始皇陵東側第二號兵馬佣坑鑽探簡報." *Wenwu* (1978:5), pp. 1–19.

"Qin Shihuang ling dong ce di san hao bing ma yong keng qingli jianbao 秦始皇陵東側第三號兵馬佣坑清理簡報." *Wenwu* (1979:12), pp. 1–12.

"Qin Shihuang ling er hao tong chema qingli jianbao 秦始皇陵二號銅車馬清理簡報." *Wenwu* (1983:7), pp. 1–16.

"Qin Shihuang ling majiu keng zuantan jianbao 秦始皇陵馬厩坑鑽探簡報." *Kaogu yu wenwu* (1980:4), pp. 31–41.

Qin Shihuang ling tong chema fajue baogao 秦始皇陵銅車馬發掘報告. Beijing: Wenwu, 1998.

Qin Shihuang ling tong chema xiufu baogao 秦始皇陵銅車馬修复報告. Beijing: Wenwu, 1998.

"Qin Shihuang ling xi ce Zhaobeihucun Qin xingtu mu 秦始皇陵西側趙背戶村秦刑徒墓 " *Wenwu* (1982:3), pp. 1–11.

"Qin Shihuang ling yuan peizang zuantan qingli jianbao 秦始皇陵園陪葬鑽探清理簡報." *Kaogu yu wenwu* (1982:1), pp. 25–29.

Qin yong xue yanjiu 秦佣學研究. Xi'an: Shaanxi renmin jiaoyu, 1996.

"Qingchuan xian chutu Qin geng xiu tian lü mu du 青川縣出土秦更修田律木牘." *Wenwu* (1982:1), pp. 1–21.

Qiu, Xigui 裘錫圭. "Hubei Jiangling Fenghuangshan 10 hao Han mu chutu jiandu kaoshi 湖北江陵鳳凰山十號漢墓出土簡牘考釋." *Wenwu* (1987:7), pp. 49–62.

Qu, Yingjie 曲英傑. *Xian Qin ducheng fuyuan yanjiu* 先秦都城復原研究. Harbin: Heilongjiang renmin, 1991.

"Qufu Jiulongshan Han mu fajue jianbao 曲阜九龍山漢墓發掘簡報." *Wenwu* (1975:5), pp. 39–41.

Qun, Li 群力. "Linzi Qi gu cheng kantan jiyao 臨淄齊故城勘探紀要." *Wenwu* (1972:5), pp. 45–54.

Rao, Zongyi 饒宗頤. "Chu bo shu tian xiang zai yi 楚帛書天象再議." *Zhongguo wenhua* 3 (1991), pp. 66–73.

———. "Mawangdui *Xingde* yi ben jiugongtu zhu shen shi, jianlun chutu wenxian zhong de Zhuanxu yu Sheti 馬王堆刑德乙本九宮圖諸神釋，兼論出土文獻中的顓頊與葉提." *Jiang Han kaogu* (1993:1), pp. 84–87.

Rao, Zongyi and Zeng, Xiantong 曾憲通. *Chu bo shu* 楚帛書. Hong Kong: Zhonghua, 1985.

———. *Yunmeng Qin jian ri shu yanjiu* 雲蒙秦簡日書研究. Hong Kong: Zhongwen Daxue, 1982.

Ri, Zhi 日知. "Chengbang shi zong lun 城邦史總論." In *Gu dai chengbang shi yanjiu* 古代城邦史研究. Ed. Ri Zhi. Beijing: Renmin, 1989.

Rui, Yifu 芮逸夫. "Jiu zu zhi yu *Er ya* 'Shi qin' 九族制與爾雅釋親." In *Zhongguo minzu ji qi wenhua lungao* 中國民族及其文化論稿. 3 vols. Taipei: Yiwen, 1972.

Sakade, Yoshinobu 坂出祥伸. "Kaze no kannen to kaze uranai 風の觀念と風占い." In *Chūgoku kodai no senpō: Gijutsu to jujutsu no shūhen* 中國古代の占法：技術と咒術の週邊. Tokyo: Kenbun shuppan, 1991.

Satake, Yasuhiko 佐竹靖彦. "Shin koku no kazoku to Shō Yō no bun'i rei 秦國の家族と商鞅の分異令." *Shirin* 63 (1980), pp. 1–29.

Satō, Taketoshi 佐藤武敏. *Chūgoku kodai kinu orimono shi kenkyū* 中國古代絹織務史研究. 2 vols. Fūkan shobō, 1978.

"Shandong Cangshan Yuanjia yuan nian huaxiangshi mu 山東蒼山元嘉元年畫像石墓." *Kaogu* (1975:2), pp. 124–125.

Shandong Han huaxiang shi xuanji 山東漢畫像石選集. Qi Lu shu she, 1982.

"Shandong Linzi Qi gu cheng shijue jianbao 山東臨淄齊故城試掘簡報." *Kaogu* (1961:6), pp. 289–297.

"Shandong Zao zhuang huaxiang shi diaocha ji 山東棗庄畫像石調查記." *Kaogu yu wen wu* (1983:3), pp. 24–30, 23.

Shao, Junpu 劭君樸. "Shi jia 釋家." *Zhongyang Yanjiuyuan Lishi Yuyan Yanjiusuo jikan* 5:2 (1935), pp. 279–282.

Shen, Jiaben 沈家本. *Lidai xingfa kao* 歷代刑法攷. 4 vols. Beijing: Zhonghua, 1985.

Shi, Lei 石磊. "*Yi li* 'Sangfu' pian suo biaoxian de qinshu jiegou 儀禮喪服篇所表現的親屬結構." *Minzuxue Yanjiusuo jikan* 53 (1982), pp. 24–26.

Shi, Nianhai 史念海. *He shan ji* 河山集. Beijing: Sanlian, 1981.

Shi, Zhicun 施蟄存. *Shui jing zhu bei lu* 水經注碑錄. Tianjin: Tianjin guji, 1987.

Shirakawa, Shizuka 白川靜. "In no ōzoku to seiji no keitai 殷の王族と政治の形態." *Kodaigaku* 3 (1954), pp. 19–44.

——. "Yin no kiso shakai 殷の基礎社會 " In *Ritsumeikan sōritsu gojū shūnen kinen ronbun shū Bungaku hen* 立命館創立五十週年紀年論文集文學篇. Kyoto: Ritsumeikan, 1958.

——. "Indai yūzoku kō, sono ni, Jaku 殷代雄族考，其二，雀." *Kōkotsu kinbungaku ronsō* 6 (1957), pp. 1–62.

Shodō zenshū 書道全集. Tokyo: Heibonsha, 1958.

"Sichuan Changning 'qi ge dong' Dong Han jinian huaxiang ya mu 四川長宁七個洞東漢紀年畫像崖墓." *Kaogu yu wen wu* (1985:5), pp. 43–55, 34.

"Sichuan Jianyang xian Guitou shan Dong Han yamu 四川建陽縣鬼頭山東漢崖墓." *Wenwu* (1991:3), pp. 20–25.

"Sichuan Pi xian Dong Han zhuan mu de shi guan huaxiang 四川郫縣東漢磚墓的石棺畫象." *Kaogu* (1979:6), pp. 495–503.

Sōfukawa, Hiroshi 曾布川寬. "Konronzan to shōsenzu 崑崙山と昇仙圖." *Tōhō gakuhō* 51 (1979), pp. 87–102.

Sun, Ji 孫機. *Han dai wenhua ziliao tushuo* 漢代文化資料圖説. Beijing: Wenwu, 1991.

Sun, Zuoyun 孫作雲. "Shuo yuren: yuren tu yuren shenhua ji fei xian sixiang zhi tuteng zhuyi de kaocha 説羽人：羽人圖羽人神話及飛仙思想之圖騰主義的攷察." *Guoli Shenyang Bowuyuan Choubei Weiyuanhui huikan* 1 (1947), pp. 29–74.

Tanaka, Tan 田中淡. *Chūgoku kenchiku shi no kenkyū* 中國建築史の研究. Tokyo: Kōbundō, 1995.

Tang, Jinyu 唐金裕. "Xi'an xi jiao Han dai jianzhu yizhi fajue baogao 西安西郊漢代建築遺址發掘報告." *Kaogu xuebao* (1959:2), pp. 45–54.

Tang, Zhangru 唐長孺. "Nanchao han ren de xingqi 南朝寒人的興起." In *Wei Jin Nanbeichao shi luncong xu bian* 魏晉南北朝史論叢續編. Beijing: San lian, 1959.

Tao, Xisheng 陶希聖. *Bianshi yu youxia* 辨士與游俠. Shanghai: Shangwu, 1933.

Tomioka, Kenzō 富岡謙藏. *Kokyō no kenkyū.* 古鏡の研究 Kyoto: Tomioka Masutarō, 1919.

Tong, Shuye 童書業. *Chun qiu shi* 春秋史. Shanghai: Kaiming, 1946.

——. *Chun qiu Zuo zhuan yanjiu* 春秋左傳研究. Shanghai: Renmin, 1980.

Umehara Sueji 梅原末治. *Kan izen no kokyō no kenkyū* 漢以前の古鏡の研究. Kyoto: Tōhō Bunka Gakuin Kyōto Kenkyūsho, 1935.

——. *Kan Sangoku Rikuchō kinen kyō zusetsu* 漢三國六朝紀年鏡圖説. Kyoto: Kyōto Teikoku Daigaku, 1943.

——. *Kan Sangoku Rikuchō kinen kyō shūroku* 集錄. Tokyo: Oka shoin, 1947.

Unno, Kazutaka 海野一隆. "Kodai Chūgokujin no chiriteki sekaikan 古代中國人の地理的世界觀." *Tōhō shūkyo* 43 (1973), pp. 35–51.

Utsunomiya, Kiyoyoshi 宇都宮清吉. *Chūgoku kodai chūsei shi kenkyū* 中國古代中世史研究. Tokyo: Sōbunsha, 1977.

——. *Kandai shakai keizai shi kenkyū* 漢代社會經濟史研究. Tokyo: Kōbundō, 1955.

Wang, Baoxiang 王褒祥. "Henan Xinye chutu de Han dai huaxiangzhuan 河南新野出土的漢代畫像磚." *Kaogu* (1964:2), pp. 90–93.

Wang, Guoliang 王國良. *Xu Qi xie ji yanjiu* 續齊諧記研究. Taipei: Wen shi zhe, 1987.

Wang, Guowei 王國維. "Ming tang miao qin tong kao 明堂廟寢通考." In *Guan tang ji lin* 觀堂集林. 1921. Reprint ed. Beijing: Zhonghua, 1959.

Wang, Hui 王輝. "Qin zeng sun yin gao Hua Shan da shan ming shen wen kaoshi 秦曾孫駰告華山大山明神文考釋." *Kaogu xue bao* (2001:2), pp. 143–158.

Wang, Jianmin 王健民 et al. "Zeng Hou Yi mu chutu de ershiba xiu qing long bai hu tuxiang 曾侯乙墓出土的二十八宿青龍白虎圖象." *Wenwu* (1979:7), pp. 40–45.

Wang, Liqi 王利器. *Xiao chuan shuzhai wen shi lun ji* 曉傳書齋文史論集. Hong Kong: Zhongwen Daxue, 1989.

Wang, Meng'ou 王夢鷗. "Gu ming tang tu kao 古明堂圖考." *Kong Meng xuebao* 11 (1966), pp. 221–229.

——. *Zou Yan yi shuo kao* 鄒衍遺說考. Taipei: Shangwu, 1966.

Wang, Shilun 王士倫. *Zhejiang chutu tongjing* 浙江出土銅鏡. Beijing: Wenwu, 1987.

Wang, Shiren 王世仁. "Han Chang'an cheng nan jiao li zhi jianzhu yuanzhuang de tuice 漢長安城南郊禮制建築原狀的推測." *Kaogu* (1963:9), pp. 501–515.

——. "Mingtang xingzhi chu tan 明堂形制初探." *Zhongguo wenhua yanjiu jikan* 4 (1987), pp. 1–71.

Wang, Shixiang 王世襄. *Zhongguo gudai qi qi* 中國古代漆器. Beijing: Wenwu, 1987.

Wang, Xueli 王學理. *Qin Shihuang ling yanjiu* 秦始皇陵研究. Shanghai: Shanghai Renmin, 1994.

——. *Xianyang di du ji* 咸陽帝都記. Xi'an: San Qin, 1999.

Wang, Zhenduo 王振鐸. "Sinan, zhinan zhen, yu luojing pan 司南，指南針，與羅經盤." *Zhongguo kaogu xuebao* 3 (1948), pp. 119–259.

Wang Zhongshu 王仲殊. "Chūgoku kodai tojōsei gairon 中國古代都城制概論." In *Nara Heian no miyako to Chōan* 奈良平安の都と長安. Ed. Nishijima Sadao. Tokyo: Shōgakukan, 1983.

——. "Han Chang'an cheng kaogu gongzuo de chu bu shouhuo 漢長安城考古工作的初步收獲." *Kaogu* (1957:5), pp. 102–110.

——. "Han Chang'an cheng kaogu gongzuo shouhuo xu ji 漢長安城考古工作收獲續記," *Kaogu* (1958:4), pp. 23–32.

Wangdu er hao Han mu 望都二號漢墓. Beijing: Wenwu, 1959.

Wangdu Han mu bihua 望都漢墓壁畫. Beijing: Chinese Classic Art, 1955.

Wei, Tingsheng 衛挺生 and Xu, Shengmo 徐聖謨. *Shan hai jing dili tu kao* 山海經地理圖考. Taipei: Huagang, 1974.

Wen, Yiduo 聞一多. "Qi shi er 七十二." In *Shen hua yu shi* 神話與詩. In *Wen Yiduo quan ji* 全集. Vol. 1. 1948. Reprint ed. Beijing: Sanlian, 1982.

——. *Zhuangzi yanjiu* 莊子研究. Rep. ed. Shanghai: Fudan Daxue, 1986.

Wen, You 聞宥. *Sichuan Handai huaxiang xuan ji* 四川漢代畫象選集. Shanghai: Qunlian, 1955.

Wu, Chengzhi 吳承志. *Shan hai jing dili jin shi* 山海經地理今釋. In *Qiu shu zhai congshu* 求恕齋叢書. Liu Chenggan 劉承幹, 1922.

Wu, Ge 無戈. *Qin Shihuang ling yu bing ma yong* 秦始皇陵與兵馬佣. Xi'an: Shaanxi Renmin, 1982.

Wu, Jiulong 吳九龍. *Yinqueshan Han jian shi wen* 銀雀山漢簡釋文. Beijing: Wenwu, 1988.

Wu, Rongzeng 吳榮曾. "Helin'ge'er Han mu bihua zhong fanying de Dong Han shehui shenghuo 和林格爾漢墓壁畫中反映的東漢社會生活." *Wenwu* (1974:1), pp. 24–30.

"Xi'an shi faxian yi pi Han dai tongqi he tong yu ren 西安市發現一批漢代銅器和銅羽人," *Wenwu* (1966:4), pp. 7–8.

Xie, Duanju 謝端琚. "Shilun wo guo zaoqi tudongmu 試論我國早期土洞墓." *Kaogu* (1987:12), pp. 1097–1104.

Xie, Li 謝荔 and Xu, Lihong 徐利紅. "Sichuan Hejiang xian Dong Han zhuan shi mu qingli jian bao 四川合江縣東漢磚室墓清理簡報." *Wen wu* (1992:4), pp. 45–48.

Xin shixue 10:4 (December 1999). Special issue on "The History of the Body."

Xing, Yitian 邢義田. "Han dai de Fulao Dan yu ju zu li ju—'Han Shiyan li Fulao Dan mai tian yueshu shi quan duji 漢代的父老僤與聚族里居—漢侍延里父老僤買田約束石券讀記." *Hanxue yanjiu* 1:2 (December 1983), pp. 355–377.

Xiong, Chuanxin 熊傳新. "Tan Mawangdui san hao Han mu chutu de lubo 談馬王堆三號漢墓出土的陸博." *Wenwu* (1979:4), pp. 35–39.

Xu, Daolin 許道麟 and Liu, Zhiping. "Guanyu Xi'an xi jiao faxian de Han dai jianzhu yizhi shi Mingtang huo Piyong de taolun 關於西安西郊發現的漢代建築遺址是明堂或辟雍的討論." *Kaogu* (1959:4), pp. 193–196.

Xu, Fuguan 徐復觀. *Liang Han sixiang shi* 兩漢思想史. Vol. 3. Taipei: Xuesheng, 1979.

Xu, Xianzhi 徐顯之. *Shan hai jing tan yuan* 山海經探原. Wuhan: Wuhan chubanshe, 1991.

Xu, Zhuoyun [Hsü Cho-yün] 許倬雲. *Qiu gu pian* 求古篇. Taipei: Lianjing, 1982.

Yamada, Keiji 山田慶兒. "Kyūkyū happū setsu to Shōshi ha no tachiba 九宮八風説と少師派の立場." *Tōhō gakuhō* 52 (1980), pp. 199–242.

Yan, Dunjie 嚴敦傑. "Ba liuren shipan 跋六任式盤." *Wenwu cankao ziliao* (1958:7), pp. 20–26.

——. "Guanyu Xi Han chuqi de shipan he zhanpan 關於西漢初期的式盤和占盤." *Kaogu* (1978:5), pp. 334–337.

——. "Shipan zongshu 式盤總述." *Kaogu xuebao* (1985:4), pp. 445–464.

Yan, Gengwang 嚴耕望. *Zhongguo difang xingzheng zhidu shi*, vol. 1, *Qin Han difang xingzheng zhidu* 中國地方行政制度史：秦漢地方行政制度. Taipei: Zhongyang Yanjiuyuan Lishi Yuyan Yanjiusuo zhuankan 45, 1974.

Yan, Yiping 嚴一萍. "Buci si fang feng xin yi 卜辭四方風新義." In *Jiagu wenzi yanjiu* 甲骨文字研究. Taipei: Yiwen, 1976.

Yang, Hongxun 楊鴻勛. "Cong yizhi kan Xi Han Chang'an Mingtang Piyong xingzhi 從遺址看西漢長安明堂辟雍形制." In *Jianzhu kaoguxue lunwen ji* 建築考古學論文集. Beijing: Wenwu, 1987.

——. "Zhanguo Zhongshan wangling ji zhaoyu tu yanjiu 戰國中山王陵及兆域圖研究." *Kaogu xuebao* (1980:1), pp. 119–137.

——. "Zhongguo zaoqi jianzhu de fazhan 中國早期建築的發展. In *Jianzhu lishi yu lilun* 建築歷史與理論 Vol. 1. Jiangsu: Jiangsu Renmin, 1981, pp. 112–135.

Yang, Kuan 楊寬. *Gu shi xin tan* 古史新探. Beijing: Zhonghua, 1965.

——. *Zhan guo shi* 戰國史. 2nd ed. rev. Shanghai: Renmin, 1980.

Yang, Shuda 楊樹達. *Han dai hunsang li su kao* 漢代婚喪禮俗考. Shanghai: Shangwu, 1933.

Yasui, Kōzan 安居香山. *Isho no seiritsu to sono tenkai* 緯書の成立とその展開. Tokyo: Kokusho kankō, 1981.

Yasui, Kōzan and Nakamura, Shōhachi 中村璋八. *Isho no kisoteki kenkyū* 緯書の基礎的研究. Kyoto: Kokusho kankō, 1978.

Ye, Xiaojun 葉曉軍. *Zhongguo ducheng fazhan shi* 中國都城發展史. Xi'an: Shaanxi renmin, 1988.

Yin, Difei 殷滌非. "Xi Han Ruyin Hou de zhanpan he tianwen yiqi 西漢汝陰侯的占盤和天文儀器." *Kaogu* (1978:5), pp. 338–343.

Yin, Ruzhang 殷汝章. "Shandong Anqiu Moushan Shuiku faxian daxing shike Han mu 山東安邱牟山水庫發現大型石刻漢墓." *Wenwu* (1960:5), pp. 55–59.

Ying, Yongshen 應永深. "Lun Chunqiu shidai Lu guo he Jin guo de shehui tedian jian ji rujia he fajia chansheng de lishi beijing 論春秋時代魯國和晉國的社會特點兼及儒家和法家產生的歷史背景." *Lishi yanjiu* (1964:1), pp. 151–168.

"Yinqueshan zhu shu 'Shou fa', 'Shou ling', deng shisan pian 銀雀山竹書 "守法"，"守令" 等十三篇." *Wenwu* (1985:4), pp. 27–38.

"Yinwan Han mu jiandu shiwen xuan 尹灣漢墓簡牘釋文選." *Wen wu* (1996:8), pp. 26–31.

Yoshinaga, Shinjirō 吉永慎二郎. "Mō Ka no fudōshin no shisōshi teki yimi 孟軻の不動心の思想史的意味." *Nippon Chūgoku Gakkai hō* 37 (1985), pp. 32–46.

Yoshinami, Takeshi 好並隆司. *Shin Kan teikoku shi kenkyū* 秦漢帝國史研究. Tokyo: Mirai, 1978.

Yu, Haoliang 于豪亮. "Shi Qingchuan Qin mu mu du 釋青川秦墓木牘." *Wenwu* (1982:1), pp. 22–24.

Yu, Weichao 俞偉超. *Xian Qin Liang Han kaoguxue lunji* 先秦兩漢考古學論集. Beijing: Wenwu, 1985.

Yuan, Weichun 袁維春. *Qin Han bei shu* 秦漢碑述. Beijing: Gongyi meishu, 1990.

Yuan, Zhongyi 袁仲一. *Qin Shihuang bing ma yong* 秦始皇兵馬俑. Beijing: Wenwu, 1983.

——. *Qin Shihuang ling bing ma yong yanjiu* 秦始皇陵兵馬俑研究. Beijing: Wenwu, 1990.

Yun, Ruxin 惲茹辛. Ed. *Shan hai jing yanjiu lunji* 山海經研究論集. Hong Kong: Zhongshan tushu, 1974.

Yunmeng Shuihudi Qin mu 云夢睡虎地秦墓. Beijing: Wenwu, 1981.

Zeng Hou Yi mu 曾侯乙墓. 2 vols. Beijing: Wenwu, 1989.

Zeng Hou Yi mu wenwu yishu 文物藝術. Wuhan: Hubei meishu, 1992.

Zeng, Lanying 曾藍瑩. "Yinwan Han mu 'Bo ju zhan' mu du shijie 尹灣漢墓博局占木牘試解." *Wenwu* (1999:8), pp. 62–65.

Zeng, Xiantong 曾憲通, Yang, Zesheng 楊澤生, and Xiao, Yi 肖毅. "Qin yin yu ban chutan 秦駰玉版初探." *Kaogu yu wenwu* (2001:1), pp. 49–53.

Zeng, Zhaoyu 曾昭燏, Jiang, Baogeng 蔣寶庚, and Li, Zhongyi 黎忠義. *Yinan gu huaxiangshi mu fajue baogao* 沂南古畫像石墓發掘報告. Beijing: Wenhuabu Wenwu Guanliju, 1956.

Zhang, Guangzhi [Chang Kwang-chih] 張光直. "Shuo Yindai de ya xing 説殷代的亞形." In *Qingzhu Gao Quxun Xiansheng bashi sui lun wen ji* 慶祝高去尋先生八十歲論文集. Taipei: Zhengzhong, 1990.

Zhang, Longhai 張龍海 and Zhu, Yude 朱玉德. "Linzi Qi gu cheng de paishui xitong 臨淄齊故城的排水系統." *Kaogu* (1988:9), pp. 784–787.

Zhao, Dianzeng 趙殿增. "'Tianmen' kao—jianlun Sichuan Han huaxiang zhuan de zuhe yu zhuti 天門考—兼論四川漢畫像磚的組合與主題." *Sichuan wenwu* (1990:6), pp. 3–11.

Zhao, Liying 趙立瀛. "Lun Tang Chang'an de guihua sixiang ji qi lishi pingjia 論唐長安的規劃思想及其歷史評價." *Jianzhushi* 29 (June 1988), pp. 41–50.

Zheng, Liangshu 鄭良樹. Ed. *Xu wei shu tong kao* 續偽書通考. Taipei: Xuesheng, 1984.

Zhou, Dao 周到 and Li, Jinghua 李京華. "Tanghe Zhenzhichang Han huaxiangshi mu de fajue 唐河針織廠漢畫像石墓的發掘," *Wenwu* (1973:6), pp. 26–27, 33–36.

Zhou, Fengwu 周鳳五. "Qin Huiwen Wang daoci Hua Shan yu ban xin tan 秦惠文王禱辭華山玉版新探." *Lishi yuyan yanjiusuo jikan* 72:1 (2001), pp. 217–231.

Zhou, Shirong 周世榮. "Luetan Mawangdui chutu de boshu zhujian 略談馬王堆出土的帛書竹簡." In *Mawangdui yishu yanjiu zhuankan* 馬王堆醫書研究專刊 2 (1981).

Zhou, Zheng 周錚. "'Guijujing yinggai wei bojujing 規矩鏡應改為博局鏡." *Kaogu* (1987:12), pp. 1116–1118.

SECONDARY WORKS IN EUROPEAN LANGUAGES

Akhundov, Murad D. *Conceptions of Space and Time*. Tr. Charles Rougle. Cambridge: MIT, 1986.

Allan, Sarah. *The Shape of the Turtle: Myth, Art, and Cosmos in Early China*. Albany: State University of New York, 1991.

Ames, Roger. "The Focus-Field Self in Classical Confucianism." In *Self as Person in Asian Theory and Practice*. Ed. Roger T. Ames with Wimal Dissanayake and Thomas P. Kasulis. Albany: State University of New York, 1994.

——. "The Local and Focal in Realizing a Daoist World." In *Daoism and Ecology: Ways within a Cosmic Landscape*. Ed. N. J. Girardot, James Miller, and Liu Xiaogan. Cambridge: Harvard University, 2001.

——. "The Meaning of Body in Classical Chinese Philosophy." In *Self as Body in Asian Theory and Practice*. Ed. Thomas P. Kasulis, Wimal Dissanayake, and Roger T. Ames. Albany: State University of New York, 1993.

Arrault, Alain. "Les diagrammes de Shao Yong (1012–1077). Qui les a vus?" *Études chinoises* 19:1–2 (Printemps-Automne 2000), pp. 67–114.

Austin, M. M. and Vidal-Naquet, Pierre. *Economic and Social History of Ancient Greece.* Tr. and rev. M. M. Austin. Berkeley: University of California, 1977.

Aymard, Andre. "Hiérarchie du travail et autarcie individuelle dans la Grèce archaïque." *Revue d'histoire de la philosophie et d'histoire générale de la civilisation* 2 (1943), pp. 124–46.

Bagley, Robert. Ed. *Ancient Sichuan: Treasures from a Lost Civilization.* Seattle: Seattle Art Museum, 2001.

Barber, Elizabeth Wayland. *Women's Work: The First 20,000 Years: Women, Cloth, and Society in Early Times.* New York: W. W. Norton, 1994.

———. *Prehistoric Textiles.* Princeton: Princeton University, 1991.

Barnard, Noel. *The Ch'u Silk Manuscript.* Canberra: Australian National University, 1973.

———. "The Ch'u Silk Manuscript and Other Archaeological Documents of Ancient China." In *Early Chinese Art and Its Possible Influence in the Pacific Basin.* Vol. 1. *Ch'u and the Silk Manuscript,* Ed. Noel Barnard. New York: Intercultural Art Press, 1972.

Baron, Hans. *The Crisis of the Early Italian Renaissance.* Princeton: Princeton University, 1955.

Bauer, Wolfgang. *China and the Search for Happiness: Recurring Themes in Four Thousand Years of Chinese Cultural History.* New York: Seabury Press, 1976.

Berkowitz, Alan J. *Patterns of Disengagement: The Practice and Portrayal of Reclusion in Early Medieval China.* Stanford: Stanford University, 2000.

Berthier, Brigitte. *La Dame-du-bord-de-l'eau.* Nanterre: Société d'Ethnologie, 1988.

Bielenstein, Hans. "The Census of China during the Period 2–742 A.D." *Bulletin of the Museum of Far Eastern Antiquities* 19 (1946), pp. 125–163.

———. "Lo-yang in Later Han Times." *Bulletin of the Museum of Far Eastern Antiquities* 48 (1976), pp. 1–142.

Bilsky, Lester. *The State Religion of Ancient China.* Taipei: The Chinese Association for Folklore, 1975.

Black, Jeremy. *Maps and Politics.* London: Reaktion Books, 1997.

Bodde, Derk. *Festivals in Classical China: New Year and Other Annual Observances During the Han Dynasty.* Princeton: Princeton University, 1975.

Booth, William James. *Households: On the Moral Architecture of the Economy.* Ithaca: Cornell University, 1993.

Bourdieu, Pierre. *Ce que parler veut dire: l'économie des échanges linguistiques.* Paris: Fayard, 1982.

———. *La distinction: critique social du jugement.* Paris: Minuit, 1979.

———. *Méditations pascaliennes.* Paris: Seuil, 1997.

Boyd, Andrew. *Chinese Architecture and Town Planning: 1500 B.C.–A.D. 1911.* Chicago: University of Chicago, 1962.

Brague, Rémi. *Aristote et la question du monde.* Paris: PUF, 1988.

——. *La Sagesse du monde: Histoire de l'expérience humaine de L'univers*. Paris: Fayard, 1999.

Brashier, K. E. "Evoking the Ancestor: The Stele Hymn of the Eastern Han Dynasty." Ph.D. dissertation. Cambridge University, 1997.

——. "Han Thanatology and the Division of 'Souls'." *Early China* 21 (1996), pp. 125–158.

——. "Longevity Like Metal and Stone: The Role of the Mirror in Han Burials." *T'oung Pao* 81 (1995), pp. 201–229.

——. "The Spirit Lord of Baishi Mountain: Feeding the Deities or Heeding the Yinyang." *Early China* 26–27 (2001–2002), pp. 159–231.

Bray, Francesca. *Technology and Gender: Fabrics of Power in Late Imperial China*. Berkeley: University of California, 1997.

Brownell, Susan. *Training the Body for China: Sport in the Moral Order of the People's Republic*. Chicago: University of Chicago, 1995.

Bujard, Marianne. "Célébration et Promotion des Cultes Locaux: Six Stèles des Han Orientaux." *Bulletin de l'École Française d'Extrême-Orient* 87 (2000), pp. 247–266.

——. *Le sacrifice au ciel dans la Chine ancienne: théorie et pratique sous les Han occidentaux*. Paris: Ecole Française d'Extrême-Orient, 2000.

Bulling, A. G. *The Decoration of Mirrors of the Han Period*. Artibus Asiae. Suppl. XX. Ascona, 1960.

——. "The Decoration of Some Mirrors of the Chou and Han Periods." *Artibus Asiae* 18.1 (1955), pp. 20–43.

Cammann, Schuyler. *China's Dragon Robes*. New York: Ronald Press, 1952.

——. "The Evolution of Magic Squares in China." *Journal of the American Oriental Society* 80 (1960), pp. 116–124.

——. "The Magic Square of Three in Old Chinese Philosophy and Religion." *History of Religions* 1 (1961), pp. 37–80.

——. "Old Chinese Magic Squares." *Sinologica* 7 (1963), pp. 14–53.

——. "The 'TLV' Pattern on Cosmic Mirrors of the Han Dynasty." *Journal of the American Oriental Society* 68 (1948), pp. 159–167.

Casey, Edward S. *Getting Back into Place: Toward a Renewed Understanding of the Place-World*. Bloomington: Indiana University, 1993.

——. *The Fate of Place: A Philosophical History*. Berkeley: University of California, 1997.

Chan, Alan K. L. "A Matter of Taste: *Qi* (Vital Energy) and the Tending of the Heart (*Xin*) in *Mencius* 2A2." In *Mencius: Contexts and Interpretations*. Ed. Alan K. L. Chan. Honolulu: University of Hawai'i, 2002.

Chang, Kwang-chih. *The Archaeology of Ancient China*. 4th edition. Revised and enlarged. New Haven: Yale University, 1986.

——. *Shang Civilization*. New Haven: Yale University, 1980.

Chard, Robert. "The Imperial Household Cults." In *State and Court Ritual in China*. Ed. Joseph P. McDermott. Cambridge: Cambridge University, 1999.

Ch'ü, T'ung-tsu. *Han Social Structure*. Seattle: University of Washington, 1972.

Cohen, Alvin P. "Avenging Ghosts and Moral Judgment in Ancient Chinese Historiography: Three Examples from *Shi-chi*." In *Legend, Lore, and Religions in China: Essays in Honor of Wolfram Eberhard on His Seventieth Birthday*. Ed. Sarah Allan and Alvin P. Cohen. San Francisco: Chinese Materials Center, 1979.

——. "The Avenging Ghost: Moral Judgment in Chinese Historical Texts." Ph.D. dissertation. University of California at Berkeley, 1971.

Crowe, Norman. *Nature and the Idea of a Man-made World: An Investigation into the Evolutionary Roots of Form and Order in the Built Environment*. Cambridge: MIT, 1995.

Cullen, Christopher. "Some Further Points on the *Shih*." *Early China* 6 (1980–81), pp. 31–46.

Defoort, Carine. *The Pheasant Cap Master: A Rhetorical Reading*. Albany: State University of New York, 1997.

Denton, Kirk A. *The Problematic of Self in Modern Chinese Literature: Hu Feng and Lu Ling*. Stanford: Stanford University, 1998.

Despeux, Catherine. "Le corps, champ spatio-temporel, souche d'identité." *L'Homme* 137 (January–March 1996), pp. 87–118.

——. *Taoisme et corps humain*. Paris: Guy Tredaniel, 1994.

Dickinson, R. E. *The City Region in Western Europe*. London: Routledge, 1967.

——. *The Regions of Germany*. London: Kegan Paul, Trench, Trubner & Co., 1945.

Diény, Jean-Pierre. *Aux origines de la poésie classique en Chine: étude de la poésie lyrique à l'époque des Han*. Leiden: E. J. Brill, 1968.

Dorofeeva-Lichtmann, Véra V. "Conception of Terrestrial Organization in the *Shan Hai Jing*." *Bulletin de l'École Française d'Extrême Orient* 82 (1995), pp. 57–110.

——. "Mapping a "Spiritual" Landscape: Representations of Terrestrial Space in the *Shanhaijing*," in *Political Frontiers, Ethnic Boundaries, and Human Geographies in Chinese History*. Ed. Nicola Di Cosmo and Don J. Wyatt. London: Rutledge/Curzon, 2003.

——. "Text as a Device for Mapping a Sacred Space: A Case of the Wu Zang Shan Jing ('Five Treasuries: The Itineraries of Mountains')." *Göttinger Beiträge zur Asienforschung* 2–3 (2003). Ed. Tatyana Gardner and Daniela Moritz,. Special Double Issue. "Creating and Representing Sacred Spaces," pp. 147–210.

Duara, Prasenjit. *Sovereignty and Authenticity: Manchukuo and the East Asian Modern*. Oxford: Rowman & Littlefield, 2003.

Duby, Georges. *Rural Economy and Country Life in the Medieval West*. Tr. Cynthia Postan. London: Edward Arnold, 1968.

Dull, Jack L. "Marriage and Divorce in Han China: A Glimpse at 'Pre-Confucian' Society." In *Chinese Family Law and Social Change in Historical and Comparative Perspective*. Ed. David C. Buxbaum. Seattle: University of Washington, 1978.

Durkheim, Emile. *The Division of Labor in Society*. Tr. George Simpson. New York: The Free Press, 1933.

Early Chinese Texts: A Bibliographical Guide. Ed. Michael Loewe. Berkeley: Society for the Study of Early China, 1993.

Eberhard, Wolfram. *Social Mobility in Traditional China*. Leiden: E. J. Brill, 1962.

Ebrey, Patricia Buckley. "Later Han Stone Inscriptions." *Harvard Journal of Asiatic Studies* 40:2 (1980), pp. 325–53.

——. "The Early Stages in the Development of Descent Group Organization." In *Kinship Organization in Late Imperial China: 1000–1940*. Ed. Patricia Buckley Ebrey and James L. Watson. Berkeley: University of California, 1986.

——. "The Economic and Social History of the Later Han." In *The Cambridge History of China, Vol. 1: The Ch'in and Han Empires*. Ed. Denis Twitchett and Michael Loewe. Cambridge: Cambridge University, 1986.

——. *The Inner Quarters*. Berkeley: University of California, 1994.

Ehrenberg, Victor. *The Greek State*. New York: W. W. Norton, paperback edition, 1960.

Elisseeff, Danielle and Vadime. *New Discoveries in China*. Seacaucus, New Jersey: Chartwell, 1983.

Elvin, Mark. *The Pattern of the Chinese Past*. London: Eyre Methuen, 1973.

Eno, Robert. *The Confucian Creation of Heaven*. Albany: State University of New York, 1990.

Erickson, Susan N. "Money Trees of the Eastern Han Dynasty." *Bulletin of the Museum of Far Eastern Antiquities* 11 (1994), pp. 1–116.

van Ess, Hans. "The Old Text/New Text Controversy: Has the 20th Century got it Wrong?" *T'oung Pao* 80 (1994), pp. 146–70.

Fabian, Johannes. *Time and the Other: How Anthropology Makes its Object*. New York: Columbia University, 1983.

von Falkenhausen, Lothar. "Grabkult und Ahnenkult im Staat Qin: Der religiöse Hintergrund der Terrakotta-Armee." In *Jenseits der Grossen Mauer: Der Erste Kaiser von China und seine Terrakotta-Armee*. Ed. Lothar von Ledderose and Adele Schlombs. Munich: Bertelsmann Lexikon Verlag, 1990.

——. "Issues in Western Zhou Studies: A Review Article." *Early China* 18 (1993), pp. 145–171.

——. "Review of Wu Hung, *Monumentality in Early Chinese Art and Architecture*." *Early China* 21 (1996), pp. 183–199.

——. "Sources of Taoism: Reflections on Archaeological Indicators of Religious Change in Eastern Zhou China." *Taoist Resources* 5.2 (1994), pp. 1–12.

——. "The Waning of the Bronze Age: Material Culture and Social Developments, 770–481 B.C." In *The Cambridge History of Ancient China*. Ed Michael Loewe and Edward L. Shaughnessy. Cambridge: Cambridge University, 1999.

Faure, Bernard. *The Rhetoric of Immediacy: A Cultural Critique of Chan/Zen Buddhism*. Princeton: Princeton University, 1991.

Feher, Michael and Naddaff, Ramona and Tazi, Nadia, eds. *Fragments for a History of the Human Body*, 3 vols. New York: Zone, 1989.

Feng, Han-yi. *The Chinese Kinship System*. Cambridge: Harvard University, 1967.

Field, Stephen. "Cosmos, Cosmograph, and the Inquiring Poet: New Answers to the 'Heaven Questions.'" *Early China* 17 (1992), pp. 83–110.

Finley, Moses. *The Ancient Economy*. Berkeley: University of California, 1973.

——. *The World of Odysseus*. London: Penguin, 1979.

Finsterbusch, Käte. *Verzeichnis und Motivindex der Han-Darstellungen*. 2 vols. Wiesbaden: Otto Harrasowitz, 1971.

Fox, Robin. "Kinship, Family, and Descent." In *Kinship and Marriage: An Anthropological Perspective*. Harmondsworth: Penguin, 1967.

Fracasso, Riccardo. "The Shanhaijing: a Bibliography by Subject." *Cina* 23 (1991), pp. 81–104.

———. "Teratoscopy or Divination by Monsters, Being a Study on the *Wu-tsang Shanching*." *Hanxue yanjiu* 1:2 (December 1983), pp. 657–700.

Geaney, Jane. *On the Epistemology of the Senses in Early Chinese Thought*. Honolulu: University of Hawai'i, 2002.

Gerbi, Antonello. *The Dispute of the New World: The History of a Polemic, 1750–1900*. Tr. Jeremy Moyle. Pittsburgh: University of Pittsburgh, 1973.

———. *Nature in the New World: From Christopher Columbus to Gonzalo Fernández de Oviedo*. Tr. Jeremy Moyle. Pittsburgh: University of Pittsburgh, 1985.

Gernet, Jacques. "Note sur les villes chinoises au moment de l'apogée islamique." In *The Islamic City*. Ed. A. H. Hourani and S. M. Stern. Oxford: Bruno Cassirer, 1970.

Gernet, Louis. *Droit et institutions en Grèce antique*. Paperback ed. Paris: Flammarion, 1982.

Giddens, Anthony. "Time, Space, and Regionalisation." In *Social Relations and Spatial Structures*. Ed. Derek Gregory and John Urry. London: MacMillan, 1985.

Goody, Jack. *The Development of the Family and Marriage in Europe*. Cambridge: Cambridge University, 1983.

———. *The Oriental, the Ancient and the Primitive: Systems of Marriage and the Family in the Pre-Industrial Societies of Eurasia*. Cambridge: Cambridge University, 1990.

Goody, Jack and Thirsk, Joan, and Thompson, E. P. Eds. *Family and Inheritance: Rural Society in Western Europe 1200–1800*. Cambridge: Cambridge University, 1976.

Graham, A. C. *Disputers of the Tao*. LaSalle: Open Court, 1989.

———. *Later Mohist Logic, Ethics and Science*. Hong Kong: Chinese University of Hong Kong, 1978.

———. "A Neglected Pre-Han Philosophical Text: *Ho Kuan-tzu*." *Bulletin of the School of Oriental and African Studies* 52.3 (1989), pp. 497–532.

———. "The Origins of the Legend of Lao Dan." In *Studies in Chinese Philosophical Literature*. Singapore: Institute of East Asian Philosophies, 1986.

Graham, A. C. and Sivin, Nathan. "A Systematic Approach to the Mohist Optics." In *Chinese Science*. Ed. Shigeru Nakayama and N. Sivin. Cambridge: MIT, 1973.

Granet, Marcel. *La Civilisation chinoise*. Paris: Renaissance du Livre, 1929.

———. *Danses et légendes de la Chine ancienne*. Rep. ed. Paris: Presses Universitaires de France, 1994.

———. *La pensée chinoise*. 1934. Reprint ed. Paris: Albin Michel, 1968.

Graziani, Romain. "De la régence du monde à la souveraineté intérieure: Une étude des quatre chapitres de 'L'art de l'esprit' du *Guanzi*". Ph. D. dissertation. Université Paris VII, 2001.

Hall, David and Ames, Roger. *Thinking From the Han: Self, Truth, and Transcendence in Chinese and Western Culture*. Albany: State University of New York, 1998.

———. *Thinking Through Confucius*. Albany: State University of New York, 1987.

Hall, Edith. *Inventing the Barbarian: Greek Self-Definition through Tragedy.* Oxford: Oxford University, 1989.

Hallpike, Christopher R. "Social Hair." *Man* (N.S.) 4 (1969), pp. 256–64.

Hardy, Grant. *Worlds of Bronze and Bamboo: Sima Qian's Conquest of History.* New York: Columbia University, 1999.

Harper, Donald. *Early Chinese Medical Literature.* London: Kegan Paul, 1998.

——. "The Han Cosmic Board." *Early China* 4 (1978–79), pp. 1–10.

——. "The Han Cosmic Board: A Response to Christopher Cullen." *Early China* 6 (1980–81), pp. 47–56.

——. "Iatromancy, Diagnosis, and Prognosis in Early Chinese Medicine." In *Innovation in Chinese Medicine.* Ed. Elizabeth Hsu. Cambridge: Cambridge University, 2001.

——. "Resurrection in Warring States Popular Religion." *Taoist Resources* 5:2 (December 1994), pp. 13–28.

——. "The Sexual Arts of Ancient China as Described in a Manuscript of the Second Century B.C." *Harvard Journal of Asiatic Studies* 47.2 (1987), pp. 539–593.

——. "Warring States Natural Philosophy and Occult Thought." In *The Cambridge History of Ancient China.* Ed. Michael Loewe and Edward L. Shaughnessy. Cambridge: Cambridge University, 1999.

——. "The *Wu Shih Erh Ping Fang*: Translation and Prolegomena." Ph.D. dissertation. University of California at Berkeley, 1982.

Harris, Christopher. *The Family.* London: George Allen and Unwin, 1969.

——. *Kinship.* Milton Keynes: Open University, 1990.

Hartog, François. *Mémoire d'Ulysse: Récits sur la frontière en Grèce ancienne.* Paris: Gallimard, 1996.

——. *Le miroir d'Hérodote: Essai sur la représentation de l'autre.* Paris: Gallimard, 1980.

Hay, John. "The Body Invisible in Chinese Art." In *Body, Subject & Power in China.* Ed. Angela Zito and Tani E. Barlow. Chicago: University of Chicago, 1994.

——. "The Human Body as Microcosmic Source for Macrocosmic Values in Calligraphy." In *Theories of the Arts in China.* Ed. Susan Bush and Christian Murck. Princeton: Princeton University, 1983.

Hayashi, Minao. "The Twelve Gods of the Chan-kuo Period Silk Manuscript Excavated at Ch'ang-sha." In *Early Chinese Art and Its Possible Influence in the Pacific Basin.* Vol. 1. *Ch'u and the Silk Manuscript,* Ed. Noel Barnard. New York: Intercultural Art Press, 1972.

He, Zhiguo and Lo, Vivienne. "The Channels: A Preliminary Examination of a Lacquered Figurine from the Western Han Period." *Early China* 21 (1996), pp. 81–123.

Henderson, John B. *The Development and Decline of Chinese Cosmology.* New York: Columbia University, 1984.

Hershatter, Gail and Honig, Emily and Lipman, Jonathan N., and Strauss, Randall eds. *Remapping China: Fissures in Historical Terrain.* Stanford: Stanford University, 1996.

Hillier, Bill. *Space is the Machine.* Cambridge: Cambridge University, 1996.

Hillier, Bill and Hanson, Julienne. *The Social Logic of Space.* Cambridge: Cambridge University, 1984.

Hiltebeitel, Alf and Miller, Barbara D., eds. *Hair: Its Power and Meaning in Asian Cultures* Albany: State University of New York, 1998.

Hinsch, Bret. "Women, Kinship, and Property as Seen in a Han Dynasty Will." *T'oung Pao* 84 (1998), pp. 1–21.

Hirsch, Eric and O'Hanlon, Michael, eds., *The Anthropology of Landscape: Perspectives on Place and Space.* Cambridge: Cambridge University, 1995.

Ho, Judy Chungwa. "The Twelve Calendrical Animals in Tang Tombs." In *Ancient Mortuary Traditions in China.* Ed. George Kuwayama. Los Angeles: Far Eastern Art Council and Los Angeles County Museum of Art, 1991.

Holenstein, Elmar. "The Zero-Point of Orientation: The Placement of the I in Perceived Space." In *The Body: Classic and Contemporary Readings.* Ed. Donn Welton. Oxford: Blackwell, 1999.

Holzman, Donald. "The Cold Food Festival in Early Medieval China." *Harvard Journal of Asiatic Studies* 46:1 (1986), pp. 51–79.

Hotaling, Stephen. "The City Walls of Han Ch'ang-an." *T'oung Pao* 64 (1978), pp. 1–36.

Hsu, Cho-yun. *Han Agriculture: The Formation of Early Chinese Agrarian Economy.* Seattle: University of Washington, 1980.

———. "The Spring and Autumn Period." In *The Cambridge History of Ancient China.* Ed. Michael Loewe and Edward L. Shaughnessy. Cambridge: Cambridge University, 1999.

Hsu, Cho-yun and Linduff, Katheryn. *Western Zhou Civilization.* New Haven: Yale University, 1988.

Huang, Philip C. C. *The Peasant Economy and Social Change in North China.* Stanford: Stanford University, 1985.

Hughes, E. R. *Two Chinese Poets: Vignettes of Han Life and Thought.* Princeton: Princeton University, 1960.

Hulsewe, A. F. P. *Remnants of Ch'in Law.* Leiden: E. J. Brill, 1985.

Husserl, Edmund. "Material Things in Their Relation to the Body" and "The Constitution of Psychic Reality Through the Body." In *The Body: Classic and Contemporary Readings.* Ed. Donn Welton. Oxford: Blackwell, 1999.

Hwang, Ming-chorng. "Ming-Tang: Cosmology, Political Order and Monuments in Early China." Ph.D. dissertation. Harvard University, 1996.

James, Jean. *A Guide to the Tomb and Shrine Art of the Han Dynasty.* Lewiston, NY: Edwin Mellen, 1996.

Jansen, Thomas. *Heimische Offentlichkeit in frühmitteralterliche China: Debatten im Salon des Prinzen Xiao Ziliang.* Rombach: Freiburg in Breisgau, 2000.

Jensen, Lionel M. "Wise Man of the Wilds: Fatherlessness, Fertility, and the Mythic Exemplar, Kongzi." *Early China* 20 (1995), pp. 407–437.

Jones, A. H. M. *The Later Roman Empire, 284–602: A Social, Economic and Administrative Survey.* Norman: University of Oklahoma, 1964.

Kalinowski, Marc. "Astrologie calendaire et calcul de position dans la Chine ancienne: Les mutations de l'hémérologie sexagésimale entre le IVe et le IIe siècle avant notre ère." *Extrême-Orient, Extrême-Occident* 18 (1996), pp. 81–101.

——. "Les instruments astro-calendériques des Han et la méthode *liu ren*." *Bulletin de l'École Française d'Extrême-Orient* 72 (1983), pp. 309–419.

——. "Mawangdui boshu Xingde shitan 馬王堆帛書刑德試探." *Huaxue* 1 (1995), pp. 82–110.

——. "Mythe, cosmogénèse et théogonie dans la Chine ancienne." *L'Homme* 137 (Jan.–March 1996), pp. 41–60.

——. "Les traités de Shuihudi et l'hémérologie Chinoise," *T'oung Pao* 72 (1986), pp. 175–228.

——. "La transmission du dispositif des Neuf Palais sous les Six-Dynasties." In *Tantric and Taoist Studies in Honour of R. A. Stein*. Vol. 3. Ed. Michel Strickmann. Brussels: Institut Belge des Hautes Études Chinoises, 1985.

——. "The *Xingde* Text from Mawangdui." *Early China* 23–24 (1998–1999), pp. 125–202.

Kaltenmark, Max. *Le Lie-sien Tchouan*. Beijing: Université de Paris, Publications du Centre d'études sinologiques de Pékin, 1953.

Kant, Immanuel. "Concerning the Ultimate Ground of the Differentiation of Regions in Space." In *Theoretical Philosophy, 1755–1770*. Tr. D. Walford and R. Meerbote. Cambridge: Cambridge University, 1992.

Kaplan, Sidney M. "On the Origin of the TLV Mirror." *Revue des Arts Asiatiques* 11 (1937), pp. 21–24.

Karlgren, Bernhard. "Early Chinese Mirror Inscriptions." *Bulletin of the Museum of Far Eastern Antiquities* 6 (1934), pp. 9–79.

Kasulis, Thomas P. and Ames, Roger T. and Dissanayake, Wimal, eds. *Self as Body in Asian Theory and Practice*. Albany: State University of New York, 1993.

Keightley, David. "Akatsuka Kiyoshi and the Culture of Early China: A Study in Historical Method." *Harvard Journal of Asiatic Studies* 42.1 (1982), pp. 267–320.

——. *The Ancestral Landscape: Time, Space, and Community in Late Shang China*. Berkeley: Institute of East Asian Studies, University of California at Berkeley, 2000.

——. "The Late Shang State: When, Where, and What?" In *The Origins of Chinese Civilization*. Ed. David Keightley. Berkeley: University of California, 1983.

Kern, Martin. *Die Hymnen der chinesischen Staatsopfer: Literatur und Ritual in der politischen Repräsentation von der Han-zeit bis zu ende den Sechs Dynastien*. Stuttgart: Franz Steiner Verlag, 1997.

——. *The Stele Inscriptions of Ch'in Shih-huang: Text and Ritual in Early Chinese Imperial Representation*. New Haven: American Oriental Society, 2000.

Kiang, Heng Chye. *Cities of Aristocrats and Bureaucrats: The Development of Medieval Chinese Cityscapes*. Honolulu: University of Hawai'i, 1999.

Kinney, Anne Behnke. *The Art of the Han Essay: Wang Fu's Ch'ien-fu Lun*. Tempe: Center for Asian Studies, Arizona State University, 1990.

——. *Representations of Childhood and Youth in Early China*. Stanford: Stanford University, 2004.

——. "Dyed Silk: Han Notions of the Moral Development of Children." In *Chinese Views of Childhood*. Ed. Anne Behnke Kinney. Honolulu: University of Hawai'i, 1995.

Kipnis, Andrew B. *Producing Guanxi: Sentiment, Self, and Subculture in a North China Village*. Durham: Duke University, 1997.

Knapp, Ronald G. *China's Old Dwellings*. Honolulu: University of Hawai'i, 2001.

——. *China's Traditional Rural Architecture: A Cultural Geography of the Common House*. Honolulu: University of Hawai'i, 1986.

——. *China's Vernacular Architecture: House Form and Culture*. Honolulu: University of Hawai'i, 1989.

Knechtges, David. "The Emperor and Literature: Emperor Wu of the Han." In *Imperial Rulership and Cultural Change in Traditional China*. Ed. Frederick Brandauer and Chun-chieh Huang. Seattle: University of Washington, 1994.

Knoblock, John. *Xunzi: A Translation and Study of the Complete Works*. 3 vols. Stanford: Stanford University, 1988.

Ko, Dorothy. "Pursuing Talent and Virtue: Education and Women's Culture in Seventeenth- and Eighteenth-Century China." *Late Imperial China* 13:1 (June 1992), pp. 9–39.

Korsmeyer, Carolyn. *Making Sense of Taste: Food and Philosophy*. Ithaca: Cornell University, 1999.

Kroll, Paul W. "On 'Far Roaming'." *Journal of the American Oriental Society* 116:4 (October–December 1996), pp. 653–659.

Kuriyama, Shigehisa. *The Expressiveness of the Body and the Divergence of Greek and Chinese Medicine*. New York: Zone, 1999.

——. "The Imagination of Winds and the Development of the Chinese Conception of the Body." In *Body, Subject & Power in China*. Ed. Angela Zito and Tani E. Barlow. Chicago: University of Chicago, 1994.

Lackner, Michael. "Argumentation par diagrammes: une architecture à base de mots. Le *Ximing* (L'Inscription occidentale) depuis Zhang Zai jusqu'au *Yanjitu*." *Extrême-Orient Extrême-Occident* 14 (1992), pp. 131–168.

——. "Die Verplanung des Denkens am Beispiel der *tu*." In *Lebenswelt und Weltanschauung in frühzeitlichen China*. Ed. H. Schmidt-Glintzer. Stuttgart: Franz Steiner Verlag, 1990.

Lai, Guolong. "The Diagram of the Mourning System from Mawangdui: Numerology, Kinship, and Women in Early China." Paper presented at "From Image to Action." Collège de France. Paris, France. September 3–5, 2001.

Lai, Ming-chiu. "Familial Morphology in Han China: 206 B.C.–A.D. 220." Ph. D. dissertation. University of Toronto, 1995.

Lakoff, George. *Women, Fire, and Dangerous Things: What Categories Reveal about the Mind*. Chicago: University of Chicago, 1987.

Lakoff, George and Johnson, Mark. *The Metaphors We Live By*. Chicago: University of Chicago, 1980.

——. *Philosophy in the Flesh: The Embodied Mind and Its Challenge to Western Thought*. New York: Basic Books, 1999.

Lang, Olga. *Chinese Family and Society*. New Haven: Yale University, 1946.

Laslett, Peter. "Introduction: The History of the Family." In *Household and Family in Past Time*. Ed. Peter Laslett. Cambridge: Cambridge University, 1972.

Leach, E. R. "Magical Hair." *Journal of the Royal Anthropological Institute* 88 (1958), pp. 147–64.

Lefebvre, Henri. *La production de l'espace*. Paris: Editions anthropos, 1974.

The Leibniz-Clarke Correspondence. Ed. H. G. Alexander. Manchester: Manchester University, 1956.

Lestrignant, Frank. *L'atelier du cosmographe ou l'image du monde à la Renaissance*. Paris: Albin Michel, 1991.

——. *Écrire le monde à la Renaissance: Quinze études sur Rabelais, Postel, Bodin et la littérature géographique*. Caen: Paradigme, 1993.

Lewis, Mark Edward. "The City-State in Spring-and-Autumn China." In *A Comparative Study of Thirty City-State Cultures*. Ed. Mogens Herman Hansen. Copenhagen: C. A. Reitzels Forlag, 2000.

——. "The *Feng* and *Shan* Sacrifices of Emperor Wu of the Han." In *State and Court Ritual in China*. Ed. Joseph P. McDermott. Cambridge: Cambridge University, 1999.

——. "The Han Abolition of Universal Military Service," in *Warfare in Chinese History*. Ed. Hans van de Ven. Leiden: E. J. Brill, 2000.

——. *Sanctioned Violence in Early China*. Albany: State University of New York, 1990.

——. "Warring States Political History." In *The Cambridge History of Ancient China*. Ed. Michael Loewe and Edward L. Shaughnessy. Cambridge: Cambridge University, 1999.

——. *Writing and Authority in Early China*. Albany: State University of New York, 1999.

Li, Bozhong. *Agricultural Development in Jiangnan, 1620–1850*. London: Macmillan, 1998.

Li, Ling. "Formulaic Structure of Chu Divinatory Bamboo Slips." *Early China* 15 (1990), pp. 71–86.

Li, Xueqin. "A Neolithic Jade Plaque and Ancient Chinese Cosmology." *National Palace Museum Bulletin* 27:5–6 (1993), pp. 1–8.

Lim, Lucy. Ed. *Stories from China's Past: Han Dynasty Pictorial Reliefs and Archaeological Objects from Sichuan Province, People's Republic of China*. San Francisco: Chinese Culture Foundation, 1987.

Little, Stephen with Eichman, Shawn. *Taoism and the Arts of China*. Chicago: Art Institute of Chicago, 2000.

Liu, James J. Y. *The Chinese Knight Errant*. London: Routledge & Kegan Paul, 1967.

Loewe, Michael. *Chinese Ideas of Life and Death: Faith, Myth and Reason in the Han Period*. London: George Allen & Unwin, 1982.

——. "Man and Beast: the Hybrid in Early Chinese Art and Literature." *Numen* 25:2 (1978), pp. 97–117.

——. *Records of Han Administration*. 2 vols. Cambridge: Cambridge University, 1967.

——. *Ways to Paradise: The Chinese Quest for Immortality*. London: Allen & Unwin, 1979.

Lowenthal, D. and Bowden, M. J. Eds. *Geographies of the Mind: Essays in Honor of Historical Geosophy*. Oxford: Oxford University, 1976.

McClelland, J. S. *The Crowd and the Mob.* London: Unwin Hyman, 1989.

McGlew, J. F. *Tyranny and Political Culture in Ancient Greece.* Ithaca: Cornell University, 1993.

Major, John. "The Five Phases, Magic Squares, and Schematic Cosmography." In *Explorations in Early Chinese Cosmology.* Ed. Henry Rosemont, Jr., JAAR Thematic Studies 50/2 (Chico, Calif.: Scholars Press, 1984), pp. 133–166.

———. *Heaven and Earth in Early Han Thought: Chapters Three, Four, and Five of the Huainanzi.* Albany: State University of New York, 1993.

———. "The Meaning of *Hsing-te* [*Xingde*]." In *Chinese Ideas about Nature and Society.* Ed. Charles Le-Blance and Susan Blader. Hong Kong: Hong Kong University, 1987.

Malkin, Irad. *The Returns of Odysseus: Colonization and Ethnicity.* Berkeley: University of California, 1998.

Marshall, P. J. and Williams, Glyndwr. *The Great Map of Mankind: Perceptions of New Worlds in the Age of the Enlightenment.* Cambridge, Mass.: Harvard University, 1982.

Martin, François. "Le cas Zichan: Entre légistes et confucianistes." In *En suivant la Voie Royale: Mélanges en hommage à Léon Vandermeersch.* Ed. J. Gernet and M. Kalinowski. Paris: École Française d'Extrême-Orient, 1997.

Martines, Lauro. *Power and Imagination: City-States in Renaissance Italy.* New York: Random House, 1979.

Maspero, Henri. *China in Antiquity.* Tr. Frank A. Kierman, Jr. Amherst: University of Massachusetts, 1978.

———. "Le Ming-T'ang et la crise religieuse chinoise avant les Han." In *Mélanges chinois et bouddhiques* (1948–1951), pp. 1–71.

Mathieu, Rémi. Tr. *Étude sur la mythologie et l'ethnologie de la Chine ancienne: Traduction annotée du Shanhai jing.* 2. vols. Paris: Collège de France, Institut des Hautes Études Chinoises, 1983.

———. *Le Mu Tianzi Zhuan: Traduction annotée, Étude critique.* Paris: Collège de France, Institut des Hautes Études Chinoises, 1978.

Mauss, Marcel. "Les techniques du corps." In *Sociologie et anthropologie.* Paris: Presses Universitaires de France, 1950.

Moscovici, Serge. *L'âge des foules.* Paris: Fayard, 1981.

Mote, F. W. "The City in Traditional China." In *Traditional China.* Ed. J. T. C. Liu and Tu Wei-ming. New York: Prentice-Hall, 1970.

———. "A Millenium of Chinese Urban History: Form, Time, and Space Concepts in Soochow." *Rice University Studies* 59:4 (Fall 1973), pp. 35–65.

———. "The Transformation of Nanking, 1350–1400." In *The City in Late Imperial China.* Ed. G. William Skinner. Stanford: Stanford University, 1977.

Mueggler, Erik. *The Age of Wild Ghosts: Memory, Violence, and Place in Southwest China.* Berkeley: University of California, 2001.

Mukerji, Chandra. *Territorial Ambitions and the Gardens of Versailles.* Cambridge: Cambridge University, 1997.

Murdock, Peter. *Social Structure.* New York: Macmillan, 1960.

Murphey, Rhoads. "The City as a Center of Change: Western Europe and China." *Annals of the Association of American Geographers* 44:4 (December 1954), pp. 349–362.

——. "The City as a Mirror of Society: China, Tradition, and Transformation." In *The City in Cultural Context*. Ed. John A. Agnew, John Mercer, and David E. Sopher. Boston: Allen & Unwin, 1984.

Needham, Joseph. *Science and Civilisation in China*, vol. 3, *Mathematics and the Sciences of the Heavens and Earth*. Cambridge: Cambridge University, 1970.

——. *Science and Civilisation in China*, vol. 4:1, *Physics and Physical Technology: Physics*. Cambridge: Cambridge University, 1962.

——. *Science and Civilisation in China*, vol. 4:III, *Civil Engineering and Nautics*. Cambridge: Cambridge University, 1971.

Needham, Joseph and Lu, Gwei-djen, and Combridge, John, and Major, John S. *The Hall of Heavenly Records: Korean Astronomical Instruments and Clocks, 1380–1780*. Cambridge: Cambridge University, 1986.

Nerlich, G. *The Shape of Space*. Cambridge: Cambridge University, 1976.

Ngo, Van Xuyet. *Magie et politique dans la Chine ancienne*. Paris: Presses Universitaires de France, 1976.

Nicolet, Claude. *Space, Geography, and Politics in the Early Roman Empire*. Ann Arbor: University of Michigan, 1991.

Nishijima, Sadao. "The Economic and Social History of Former Han." In *The Cambridge History of China*: Vol. 1, *The Ch'in and Han Empires*. Ed. Michael Loewe. Cambridge: Cambridge University, 1986.

Nivison, David S. "The Dates of the Zhou Conquest of the Shang." *Harvard Journal of Asiatic Studies* 43 (1983), pp. 481–580.

Nylan, Michael. "The Chin Wen/Ku Wen Controversy in Han Times." *T'oung Pao* 80 (1994), pp. 83–144.

——. "The Ku Wen Documents in Han Times." *T'oung Pao* 81 (1995), pp. 25–50.

Obeyesekere, Gananath. *Medusa's Hair: An Essay on Personal Symbols and Religious Experience*. Chicago: University of Chicago, 1981.

Owen, Stephen. *Remembrances: The Experience of the Past in Classical Literature.* Cambridge: Harvard University, 1986.

Pagden, Anthony. *The Fall of Natural Man: The American Indian and the Origins of Comparative Ethnology*. Cambridge: Cambridge University, 1982.

Pasternak, Burton. "On the Causes and Demographic Consequences of Uxorilocal Marriage in China." In *Family and Population in East Asian History*. Ed. Susan B. Hanley and Arthur P. Wolf. Stanford: Stanford University, 1985.

Peters, Heather. "Towns and Trade: Cultural Diversity in Chu Daily Life." In *Defining Chu: Image and Reality in Ancient China*. Ed. Constance A. Cook and John S. Major. Honolulu: University of Hawai'i, 1999.

Plato: The Collected Dialogues. Princeton: Princeton University, Bollingen, 1961.

Pommier, Édouard. "Versailles, l'image du souverain." In *Les lieux de mémoire*. Vol. 1. Ed. Pierre Nora. Paperback ed. Paris: Gallimard, 1997.

Poo, Mu-chou [Pu Muzhou]. "Ideas Concerning Death and Burial in Pre-Han China." *Asia Major*, 3rd series, 3:2 (1990), pp. 25–62.

——. *In Search of Personal Welfare: A View of Ancient Chinese Religion*. Albany: State University of New York, 1998.

Porkert, Manfred. *Die chinesische Medizin*. Dusseldorf, 1982.

——. *The Theoretical Foundations of Chinese Medicine*. Cambridge: MIT, 1974.

Porter, Deborah Lynn. *From Deluge to Discourse: Myth, History, and the Generation of Chinese Fiction*. Albany: State University of New York, 1996.

Powers, Martin J. *Art and Political Expression in Early China*. New Haven: Yale University, 1991.

Pred, Allan. "The Social Becomes the Spatial, the Spatial Becomes the Social." *Social Relations and Spatial Structures*. Ed. Derek Gregory and John Urry. London: MacMillan, 1985.

Puett, Michael J. *To Become a God: Cosmology, Sacrifice, and Self-Divination in China*. Cambridge: Harvard University, 2002.

Qian, Nanxiu. *Spirit and Self in Medieval China: The Shih-shuo hsin-yü and Its Legacy*. Honolulu: University of Hawai'i, 2001.

Radcliffe-Brown, A. R. *The Social Anthropology of Radcliffe-Brown*. Harmondsworth: Penguin, 1977.

Rao Tsung-yi [Zongyi]. "Some Aspects of the Calendar, Astrology, and Religious Concepts of the Ch'u People as Revealed in the Ch'u Silk Manuscript." In *Early Chinese Art and Its Possible Influence in the Pacific Basin*. Vol. 1. *Ch'u and the Silk Manuscript*. Ed. Noel Barnard. New York: Intercultural Art Press, 1972.

Rawson, Jessica. Ed. *Mysteries of Ancient China: New Discoveries from the Early Dynasties*. London: British Museum Press, 1996.

——. "Western Zhou Archaeology." In *The Cambridge History of Ancient China*. Ed. Michael Loewe and Edward L. Shaughnessy. Cambridge: Cambridge University, 1999.

Ray, Christopher. *Time, Space and Philosophy*. London: Routledge, 1991.

Reichenbach, H. *The Philosophy of Space and Time*. New York: Dover, 1957.

Reiter, Florian C. "Some Remarks on the Chinese Word *T'u* 'Chart, Plan, Design'." *Oriens* 32 (1990), pp. 308–27.

Rickett, W. Allyn. *Guanzi: Political, Economic, and Philosophical Essays from Early China, A Study and Translation*. Vol. 1–2. Princeton: Princeton University, 1985, 1998.

Riegel, Jeffrey K. "Kou-mang and Ju-shou." *Cahiers d'Extrême-Asie: Special Issue, Taoist Studies II* 5(1989–1990), pp. 55–83.

Romm, James S. *The Edges of the Earth in Ancient Thought*. Princeton: Princeton University, 1992.

Roth, Harold. *Original Tao: Inward Training and the Foundations of Taoist Mysticism*. New York: Columbia University, 1999.

Russell, Josiah Cox. *Medieval Regions and their Cities*. Bloomington: Indiana University, 1972.

Sabatier, Gérard. *Versailles ou la figure du roi*. Paris: Albin Michel, 1999.

Sage, Steven F. *Ancient Sichuan and the Unification of China*. Albany: State University of New York, 1992.

Schaberg, David. "Confucius as Body and Text: On the Generation of Knowledge in Warring States and Han Anecdotal Literature." Paper presented at "Text and Ritual in Early China." Princeton University. October 20–22, 2000.

——. "Travel, Geography, and the Imperial Imagination in Fifth-Century Athens and Han China." *Comparative Literature* 55.2 (1999), pp. 152–191.

Schafer, Edward H. *The Divine Woman: Dragon Ladies and Rain Maidens in T'ang Literature*. Berkeley: University of California, 1973.

Scheid, John and Svenbro, Jesper. *Le métier de Zeus: Mythe du tissage et du tissu dans le monde gréco-romaine*. Paris: Editions La Découverte, 1994.

Schiffeler, John W. "Chinese Folk Medicine: a Study of the *Shan-hai ching*." *Asian Folklore Studies* 39:2 (1980), pp. 41–83.

Schipper, Kristofer. "Le culte de l'immortel Tang Gongfang." In *Cultes populaires et sociétés asiatiques*. Ed. Alain Forest, Yoshiaki Ishizawa, and Léon Vandermeersch. Paris: L'Harmattan, 1991.

——. "Une stèle taoiste des Han orientaux récemment découverte." In *En suivant la voie royale: Mélanges en hommage à Léon Vandermeersch*. Ed. Jacques Gernet and Marc Kalinowski. Paris: Ecole Française d'Extrême Orient, 1997.

Scott, James. *The Moral Economy of the Peasant*. New Haven: Yale University, 1976.

Scully, Stephen. *Homer and the Sacred City*. Ithaca: Cornell University, 1990.

Segal, Charles. *Tragedy and Civilization: An Interpretation of Sophocles*. Cambridge: Harvard University, 1981.

Segalen, Martine. *Historical Anthropology of the Family*. Tr. J. C. Whitehouse and Sarah Matthews. Cambridge: Cambridge University, 1986.

Seidel, Anna. *La divinisation de Lao-tseu dans le taoïsme des Han*. Paris: École Française d'Extrême-Orient, 1969.

——. "*Post-Mortem* Immortality, or: The Taoist Resurrection of the Body." In *Gilgul: Essays on Transformation, Revolution and Permanence in the History of Religions*. Ed. Sh. Shaked, et al. Leiden: E. J. Brill, 1987.

——. "Tokens of Immortality in Han Graves." *Numen* 29 (1982), pp. 79–122.

——. "Traces of Han Religion in Funeral Texts Found in Tombs." In *Dōkyō to shūkyō bunka* 道教と宗教文化. Ed. Akizuki Kan'ei 秋月觀暎. Tokyo: Hirakawa, 1987.

Sennett, Richard. *The Conscience of the Eye: The Design and Social Life of Cities*. New York: Alfred A. Knopf, 1991.

Serres, Michel. *Les cinq sens: Philosophie des corps mêlés*. Paris: Grasset, 1985.

——. *Les origines de la géométrie*. Paris: Flammarion, 1993.

——. *Rome: le livre des fondations*. Paris: Bernard Grasset, 1983.

——. *Le système de Leibniz et ses modèles mathématiques*. Paris: Presses Universitaires de France, 1968.

Shapiro, Judith. *Mao's War Against Nature*. Cambridge: Cambridge University, 2001.

Shaughnessy, Edward L. "On the Authenticity of the *Bamboo Annals*." *Harvard Journal of Asiatic Studies* 46 (1986), pp. 149–180.

Sivin, Nathan. *Traditional Medicine in Contemporary China*. Ann Arbor: Center for Chinese Studies, University of Michigan, 1987.

Skinner, G. William. "Cities and the Hierarchy of Local Systems." In *The City in Late Imperial China*. Ed. G. William Skinner. Stanford: Stanford University, 1977.

———. "Marketing and Social Structures in Rural China." 3 parts. *Journal of Asian Studies* 24.1 (1964), pp. 3–44; 24.2 (1964), pp. 195–228; 24.3 (1965), pp. 363–99.

———. "Regional Urbanization in Nineteenth-Century China." In *The City in Late Imperial China*. Ed. G. William Skinner. Stanford: Stanford University, 1977.

Slicker van Bath, B. H. *The Agrarian History of Western Europe, A.D. 500–1850*. London: Edward Arnold, 1963.

Soothill, William Edward. *The Hall of Light*. New York: Philosophical Library, 1952.

Sorabji, Richard. *Matter, Space and Motion: Theories in Antiquity and their Sequel*. London: Duckworth, 1988.

Spiro, Audrey. *Contemplating the Ancients: Aesthetic and Social Issues in Early Chinese Portraiture*. Berkeley: University of California, 1990.

Stein, Rolf. *Le monde en petit: Jardins en miniature et habitations dans la pensée religieuse d'Extrême-Orient*. Paris: Flammarion, 1987.

Steinhardt, Nancy S. *Chinese Imperial City Planning*. Honolulu: University of Hawai'i, 1990.

Sterckx, Roel. *The Animal and the Daemon in Early China*. Albany: State University of New York, 2002.

———. "Le Pouvoir du Sens: Sagesse et Perception Sensorielle en Chine Ancienne." In *Cahiers d'Institut Marcel Granet* 1. Paris: Presses Universitaires de France, 2003.

Stewart, Susan. *Poetry and the Fate of the Senses*. Chicago: University of Chicago, 2002.

Suh, Kyung Ho. "A Study of 'Shan-hai-ching': Ancient Worldviews Under Transformation." Ph.D. dissertation. Harvard University, 1993.

Sukhu, Gopal. "Monkeys, Shamans, Emperors, and Poets: The *Chuci* and Images of Chu during the Han Dynasty." In *Defining Chu: Image and Reality in Ancient China*. Ed. Constance A. Cook and John S. Major. Honolulu: University of Hawai'i, 1999.

Sun, Xiaochun and Kistemaker, Jacob. *The Chinese Sky During the Han: Constellating Stars and Society*. Leiden: E. J. Brill, 1997.

Thorp, Robert L. "The Mortuary Art and Architecture of Early Imperial China. Ph.D. dissertation. University of Kansas, 1980.

———. "Mountain Tombs and Jade Burial Suits: Preparations for Eternity in the Western Han." In *Ancient Mortuary Traditions of China: Papers on the Chinese Ceramic Funerary Sculptures*. Ed. George Kuwayama. Los Angeles: Los Angeles County Museum of Art, 1991.

———. "Origins of Chinese Architectural Style: The Earliest Plans and Building Types." *Archives of Asian Art* 36 (1983), pp. 22–39.

———. "The Sui Xian Tomb: Re-thinking the Fifth Century." *Artibus Asiae* 43:5 (1981), pp. 67–92.

Thote, Alain. "The Double Coffin of Leiguden Tomb No. 1: Iconographic Sources and Related Problems." In *New Perspectives on Chu Culture During the Eastern Zhou Period*. Ed. Thomas Lawton. Washington, DC: Arthur M. Sackler Gallery, 1991.

———. "Une tombe princière du Ve siècle avant notre ère." *Comptes rendus de l'Académie des Inscriptions et Belles-lettres* (Avril–Juin 1986), pp. 393–413.

———. "I Zhou orientali." In *La Cina*. Ed. Michèle Pirazzoli-t'Serstevens. Turin: UTET; Storia Universale dell'Arte, Vol. 1. 1996.

Tu, Wei-ming. "Embodying the Universe." In *Self as Body in Asian Theory and Practice.* Ed. Thomas P. Kasulis, Wimal Dissanayake, and Roger T. Ames. Albany: State University of New York, 1993.

Twitchett, Denis. "The T'ang Market System," *Asia Major* 12:2 (1966), pp. 202–248.

Umehara, Sueji. "The Late Mr. Moriya's Collection of Ancient Chinese Mirrors." *Artibus Asiae* 18 (1955), pp. 238–256.

Unschuld, Paul. *Medicine in China: A History of Ideas.* Berkeley: University of California, 1985.

———. "Der Wind als Ursache des krankseins." *T'oung Pao* 68 (1982), pp. 91–131.

Vernant, J.-P. "Le mythe prométhéen chez Hésiod." In *Mythe et société en Grèce ancienne.* Paris: François Maspero, 1981.

Vervoorn, Aat. *Men of the Cliffs and Caves: The Development of the Chinese Eremitic Tradition at the End of the Han Dynasty.* Hong Kong: The Chinese University, 1990.

Vilatte, Sylvie. *Espace et Temps: La cité aristotélicienne de la Politique.* Paris: Les Belles Lettres, 1995.

Vlachos, Georges C. *Les sociétés politiques homériques.* Paris: Presses Universitaires de France, 1974.

Wakefield, David. *Fenjia: Household Division and Inheritance in Qing and Republican China.* Honolulu: University of Hawai'i, 1998.

Wakeman, Jr., Frederic. "Mao's Remains." In *Death Ritual in Late Imperial and Modern China.* Ed. James L. Watson and Evelyn S. Rawski. Berkeley: University of California, 1988.

Waldenfels, Bernhard. *Das leibliche Selbst: Vorlesungen zur Phänomenologies des Leibes.* Frankfurt am Main: Suhrkamp Verlag, 2000.

Wang, Aihe. *Cosmology and Political Culture in Early China.* Cambridge: Cambridge University, 2000.

Wang, Yü-chüan. "An Outline of the Central Government of the Former Han Dynasty." *Harvard Journal of Asiatic Studies* 12 (1949), pp. 134–187.

Wang, Zhongshu. *Han Civilization.* Tr. K. C. Chang and collaborators. New Haven: Yale University, 1982.

Watson, James L. "Of Flesh and Bones: the Management of Death Pollution in Cantonese Society." In *Death and the Regeneration of Life.* Ed. Maurice Bloch and Jonathan Parry. Cambridge: Cambridge University, 1982.

Weber, Charles D. *Chinese Pictorial Bronze Vessels of the Late Zhou Period.* Ascona: Artibus Asiae, 1968.

Welskopf, Elisabeth. *Probleme der Musse im alten Hellas.* Berlin: Rütten & Loening, 1962.

Welton, Donn, ed. *The Body: Classic and Contemporary Readings.* Oxford: Blackwell, 1999.

Wheatley, Paul. *The Pivot of the Four Quarters.* Edinburgh: Aldine, 1971.

Whyte, Martin K. "Death in the People's Republic of China." In *Death Ritual in Late Imperial and Modern China.* Ed. James L. Watson and Evelyn S. Rawski. Berkeley: University of California, 1988.

Wickert-Micknat, Gisela. *Unfreiheit im Zeitalter der homerischen Epen.* Wiesbaden: Franz Steiner Verlag, 1983.

Wilk, Richard R. *Household Ecology: Economic Change and Domestic Life among the Kekchi Maya in Belize.* Tucson: University of Arizona, 1991.

Wilk, Richard and Netting, Robert. "Changing Forms and Functions." In *Household: Comparative and Historical Studies of the Domestic Group.* Ed. Robert Netting, Richard Wilk, and Eric Arnould. Berkeley: University of California, 1984.

Will, Edouard. *Le monde grecque et l'orient.* Paris: Presses Universitaires de France, 1974.

Wolf, Margery. *Woman and the Family in Rural Taiwan.* Stanford: Stanford University, 1972.

Wright, Arthur F. "The Cosmology of the Chinese City." In *The City in Later Imperial China.* Ed. G. William Skinner. Stanford: Stanford University, 1977.

Wu, Hung. "Art and Architecture of the Warring States Period." In *The Cambridge History of Ancient China.* Ed. Michael Loewe and Edward L. Shaughnessy. Cambridge: Cambridge University, 1999.

———. "Art in Ritual Context: Rethinking Mawangdui." *Early China* 17 (1992), pp. 111–144.

———. "Beyond the 'Great Boundary': Funerary Narrative in the Cangshan Tomb." *Boundaries in China.* Ed. John Hay. London: Reaktion Books, 1994.

———. "Mapping Early Taoist Art: The Visual Culture of Wudoumi Dao." In *Taoism and the Arts of China.* Ed. Stephen Little. Chicago: The Art Institute of Chicago, 2000.

———. *Monumentality in Early Chinese Art and Architecture.* Stanford: Stanford University, 1995.

———. "Private Love and Public Duty: Images of Children in Early Chinese Art." In *Chinese Views of Childhood.* Ed. Anne Behnke Kinney. Honolulu: University of Hawai'i, 1995.

———. *The Wu Liang Shrine: The Ideology of Early Chinese Pictorial Art.* Stanford: Stanford University, 1989.

Wu, Kuang-ming. *On Chinese Body Thinking: A Cultural Hermeneutic.* Leiden: E. J. Brill, 1997.

Xiong, Victor Cunrui. *Sui-Tang Chang'an: A Study in the Urban History of Medieval China.* Ann Arbor: Center for Chinese Studies, University of Michigan, 2000.

Xu, Yinong. *The Chinese City in Space and Time: The Development of Urban Form in Suzhou.* Honolulu: University of Hawai'i, 2000.

Yamaguchi, Ichiro. *Ki als leibhaftige Vernunft: Beitrag zur interkulturellen Phänomenologie der Leiblichkeit.* Munich: Wilhelm Fink, 1997.

Yan, Yunxiang. *The Flow of Gifts: Reciprocity and Social Networks in a Chinese Village.* Stanford: Stanford University, 1996.

Yang Lien-sheng. "An Additional Note on the Ancient Game *Liu-po.*" *Harvard Journal of Asiatic Studies* 15 (1952), pp. 124–139.

———. "A Note on the So-Called TLV Mirrors and the Game *Liu-po.*" *Harvard Journal of Asiatic Studies* 9 (1947), pp. 202–206.

Yang, Mayfair Mei-hui. *Gifts, Favors, and Banquets.* Ithaca: Cornell University, 1994.

Yates, Robin D. S. "Body, Space, Time and Bureaucracy: Boundary Creation and Control Mechanisms in Early China." In *Boundaries in China*. Ed. John Hay. London: Reaktion Books, 1994.

——. "The City-State in Ancient China." In *The Archaeology of City-States: Cross-Cultural Approaches*. Ed. Deborah L. Nichols and Thomas H. Charlton. Washington, DC: Smithsonian Institution, 1997.

——. "Cosmos, Central Authority, and Communities in the Early Chinese Empire." In *Empires*. Ed. Susan E. Alcock et al. Cambridge: Cambridge University, 2000.

——. "Purity and Pollution in Early China." In *Integrated Studies of Chinese Archaeology and Historiography*, Symposium Series of the Institute of History and Philology, Academia Sinica 4 (July 1997), pp. 479–536.

——. "The Yin-Yang Texts from Yinqueshan: an Introduction and Partial Reconstruction with Notes on their Significance in Relation to Huang-Lao Taoism." *Early China* 19 (1994), pp. 75–144.

Yetts, W. D. *The Cull Chinese Bronzes*. London: Courtauld Institute, 1939.

Yü, Ying-shih. "Han Foreign Relations." In *The Cambridge History of China, Volume 1: The Ch'in and Han Empires*. Ed. Michael Loewe. Cambridge: Cambridge University, 1986.

——. "'O Soul, Come Back!': A Study in the Changing Conceptions of the Soul and Afterlife in Pre-Buddhist China." *Harvard Journal of Asiatic Studies* 47:2 (1987), pp. 363–395.

Zito, Angela. *Of Body and Brush: Grand Sacrifice as Text/Performance in Eighteenth-Century China*. Chicago: University of Chicago, 1997.

——. "Silk and Skin: Significant Boundaries," in *Body, Subject & Power in China*. Ed. Angela Zito and Tani E. Barlow. Chicago: University of Chicago, 1994.

Zito, Angela and Barlow, Tani E., eds., *Body, Subject & Power in China*. Chicago: University of Chicago, 1994.

Zumthor, Paul. *La Mesure du monde: représentation de l'espace au Moyen Âge*. Paris: Seuil, 1993.

INDEX